The Political Economy of the European Social Model

This book seeks to analyse the development of the European Union (EU), which was founded upon the principle of the free movement of capital, goods, services and people in 1957. Its central thesis is that, from a practical and theoretical point of view, such a basis is fundamentally at odds with the creation of an interventionist regime that the construction of a Social Europe would require.

The authors argue convincingly that – economically: the EU does not currently possess the budget or the economic tools to pursue such a strategy; politically: close to none of the institutions of the EU have backed such a policy; practically: conservative and neo-liberal forces (among member states and the institutions of the EU) have repeatedly thwarted any moves in this direction. In reality, the single internal market, Economic and Monetary Union, enlargement, the Lisbon Agenda and European Constitution projects all prioritize supply-side measures and expanding the scope of the market rather than the boosting of demand and other economic intervention. Consequently, constructing a Social Europe in the face of this would appear problematic. Hence, in both theory and practice, the idea that there can be a Social Europe vis-à-vis neoliberalization is a contradiction in terms.

This controversial book will be an educating and refreshing read for advanced students and academics involved with European politics, the European Union, European economics and economic institutions.

Philip B. Whyman is Professor of Economics at the University of Central Lancashire, UK.

Mark Baimbridge is Senior Lecturer in Economics at the University of Bradford, UK.

Andrew Mullen is Senior Lecturer in Politics at Northumbria University, UK.

Routledge studies in the European economy

The Political Economy of the European Social Model

Philip B. Whyman, Mark Baimbridge and Andrew Mullen

Routledge
Taylor & Francis Group

LONDON AND NEW YORK

First published 2012
by Routledge
2 Park Square, Milton Park, Abingdon, Oxfordshire OX14 4RN

Simultaneously published in the USA and Canada
by Routledge
711 Third Avenue, New York, NY 10017

First issued in paperback 2014

Routledge is an imprint of the Taylor and Francis Group, an informa business

British Library Cataloguing in Publication Data
A catalogue record for this book is available from the British Library

Library of Congress Cataloging in Publication Data
Whyman, Philip.
The political economy of the European social model / Philip B. Whyman,
Mark J. Baimbridge, and Andrew Mullen.
   p. cm.
   1. European Union countries–Social policy. 2. European Union
   countries–Economic policy. I. Baimbridge, Mark. II. Mullen, Andrew.
   III. Title.
   HN373.5.W49 2012
   305.80094–dc23   2011051051

ISBN 978-0-415-47629-4 (hbk)
ISBN 978-1-138-80835-5 (pbk)
ISBN 978-0-203-11330-1 (ebk)

Typeset in Times New Roman
by Wearset Ltd, Boldon, Tyne and Wear

Contents

Illustrations

Preface

There are many people to think for their input into making of this book possible. Most obviously, we must thank our commissioning editor at Routledge, Terry Clague, for his immediate support for this project and Simon Holt (editorial assistant – Economics). Second, we would like to thank our colleagues at the universities of Central Lancashire, Bradford and Northumbria for their comradeship and general support for our research on European economic integration. Finally, we owe a deep sense of gratitude to our families and partners for their forbearance during the preparation of this book. It is to them that this book is dedicated: PW: Barbara, Boyd and Claire; MB: Mary, Ken, Beibei and Douglas.

Any remaining errors and omissions we gladly attribute to each other.

Heaton Norris, Haworth and Gateshead
December 2011

European integration timeline

From its beginnings, half a century ago, in the immediate aftermath of the Second World War, through the expansion of the 1970s and 1980s and the great debate surrounding the Maastricht Treaty, here we highlight some of the key events which have shaped the development of the EU towards closer integration.

1948   The Organization for European Economic Co-operation (OEEC) is set up in Paris in April 1948, co-ordinating the distribution of the Marshall Plan financial aid which will amount to $12.5 billion from 1948 to 1951. The OEEC consists of one representative from each of the 17 Western European countries which join the organization. In May 1948 in The Hague, the Congress of Europe (a meeting of delegates from 16 European countries) agree to form the Council of Europe with the aim of establishing closer economic and social ties.

1951   The European Coal and Steel Community (ECSC) is established by the signing of the Treaty of Paris in April 1951. Along with France and West Germany, Italy, Belgium, Luxembourg and the Netherlands also choose to join the organization. Members of the ECSC pledge to remove all import duties and quota restrictions on the trade of coal, iron ore, and steel between the member states.

1952   The European Defence Community (EDC) Treaty is signed by France, West Germany, Italy, Belgium, Holland and Luxembourg in May 1952. It includes the provision for the formation of a parallel European Political Community. However both initiatives are destined to founder since the French National Assembly never ratifies the EDC Treaty, finally rejecting it in August 1954.

1955   The process of further European integration is given fresh impetus by a conference of ECSC foreign ministers at Messina, Italy, in June 1955. The meeting agrees to develop the community by encouraging free trade between member states through the removal of tariffs and quotas. Agreement is also reached to form an Atomic Energy Community to encourage co-operation in the nuclear energy industry.

1958   The two Treaties of Rome are signed, establishing the European Economic Community (EEC) and the European Atomic Energy Community

(Euratom). As well as stipulating the eventual removal of customs duties on trade between member countries (over a period of 12 years) the EEC Treaty sets out allow the free movement of workers, capital and services across borders and to harmonize policies on agriculture and transport.

1960   At the Stockholm Convention in January 1960 Austria, Britain, Denmark, Norway, Portugal, Sweden and Switzerland form the European Free Trade Association (EFTA). The objective of EFTA is to promote free trade but without the formal structures of the EEC.

1961   The United Kingdom applies to join the EEC.

1963   British application for EEC membership fails.

1967   The United Kingdom submits second application to join EEC.

1968   Customs union completed and Common Agricultural Policy enacted.

1972   In October, following the recommendations of the Werner Report, the EEC launches its first attempt at harmonizing exchange rates. The mechanism adopted is the so called 'snake in the tunnel' whereby participating governments are required to confine the fluctuations of their currencies within a range of ±1 per cent against each other. The value of the group of currencies (the snake) is also to be maintained within a range of ±2.25 per cent against the US dollar (the tunnel). Countries requiring assistance to keep their currencies within the required band may receive help only in the form of loans.

1973   Denmark, Ireland and the United Kingdom join the EEC.

1975   A UK referendum supports staying in EEC.

1978   At a summit in Bremen in July, the French and West German governments announce their intention to create the European Monetary System (EMS). At the centre of the EMS is the European currency unit (ecu). The value of the ecu is to be derived from a weighted basket of all participating currencies with the greatest weighting against the West German mark.

1981   Greece joins the European Community (EC).

1986   Portugal and Spain join the EC.

1990   The United Kingdom joins the EMS.

1992   At a summit of the European Council in Maastricht, Holland, the Treaty on the European Union (TEU), also known as the Maastricht Treaty, is signed. Originally intended to include a declaration of an intention to move towards a federal union, at Britain's insistence this aspect is played down. Subsequent to the signing of the Maastricht Treaty, the EC is referred to as the European Union (EU).
The United Kingdom leaves the EMS.

1993   The Single European Market takes effect. Trade tariffs are scrapped, but duty-free shopping remains until 1999.

1994   Stage 2 of EMU is initiated on 1 January with the establishment of the European Monetary Institute (EMI) to oversee the co-ordination of the monetary policies of the individual national central banks. The EMI will also work towards the introduction of stage 3 by organizing the creation of the European Central Bank (ECB).

1995   Austria, Finland and Sweden join the EU, bringing membership to 15.
The Schengen agreement comes into force and scraps border controls.
The United Kingdom and Ireland stay out of the agreement.

1997   Heads of government draft a new agreement in Amsterdam which
updates the Maastricht Treaty and prepares the EU for its eastward
expansion. Qualified majority voting (QMV) is introduced into new
areas, reducing individual countries' powers to veto new measures.

1998   At the beginning of May, at a summit of EU officials and heads of state
in Brussels, the announcement is made as to which countries will participate in the launch of the euro the following January. In June the
ECB is established in Frankfurt, Germany. The ECB together with the
national central banks of the 15 EU member states form the European
System of Central Banks (ESCB) which will be responsible for setting
monetary policy for the euro countries and managing those countries'
foreign reserves.
The EU opens accession negotiations with Hungary, Poland, Estonia,
the Czech Republic, Slovenia and Cyprus.

1999   Romania, Slovakia, Latvia, Lithuania, Bulgaria and Malta are invited to
begin accession negotiations.
The euro is adopted by 11 countries as their official currency (although
national currency notes and coins remain in circulation), but Sweden,
Denmark and the United Kingdom stay out.

2000   The Nice summit agrees to limit the size of the commission and increase
the president's powers. QMV is introduced in new areas, but members
keep their vetoes on social security and tax. A timetable for taking
forward accession negotiations is endorsed.

2001   The Laeken European Council establishes the Convention on the Future
of Europe.

2002   Euro notes and coins are introduced in 12 EU countries.
The European Commission announces that ten countries are on course
to meet the criteria for accession to the EU in 2004.

2003   The United Kingdom has been a member of the EU for 30 years.

2004   EU enlargement to 25 member states with addition of Slovakia, Latvia,
Lithuania, Malta, Hungary, Poland, Estonia, the Czech Republic, Slovenia and Cyprus.

2005   EU Constitution ratification ended by referendum defeats in France and
the Netherlands.
The UK holds EU presidency, but fails to make progress on new
2007–2013 budget.
Accession negotiations are opened with Turkey and Croatia.

2006   Slovenia's entry into the euro on 1 January 2007 is confirmed.
Accession negotiations with Turkey are suspended.

2007   EU enlargement to 27 member states with the addition of Bulgaria and
Romania.

2008   Slovenia becomes the first of the recent enlargement members to hold
        the presidency of the council of the EU.
        Treaty of Lisbon ratification ended by referendum defeat in Ireland.
2009   Final year of the Barroso Commission.
        Seventh series of elections to the European Parliament.
        Second Irish referendum approves the Treaty of Lisbon.
        Herman Van Rompuy is appointed first permanent president of the EU
        council.
2010   Spain takes over the rotating presidency of the council of the EU, the
        first under the Lisbon Treaty and the new 'trio presidency system'.
        The European Parliament approves the Barroso II Commission.
        EU leaders adopt Europe 2020 targets.
        Heads of state within the euro area agree to deeper fiscal consolidation,
        stronger economic coordination and budgetary surveillance to defend
        the euro.
2011   Estonia adopts the euro as its currency, becoming the seventeenth
        member of the euro area.
        Three new European financial supervisory authorities begin operating:
        the European Banking Authority, the European Insurance and Occupa-
        tional Pensions Authority and the European Securities and Markets
        Authority.
        The European Council agrees that the accession negotiations with
        Croatia should be concluded by the end of June 2011, paving the way
        for the country to become the twenty-eighth EU member in 2013.
        The EU seeks to resolve the eurozone crisis centred on Greece through
        establishing the European Financial Stability Facility (EFSF) to become
        the European Stability Mechanism from 2013.
2012   Croatia vote 'yes' by 66 to 33 per cent in its accession referendum and
        so will become the twenty-eighth EU member on 1 July 2013.
        The European Council proposed a new treaty on stability, coordination
        and governance in the economic and monetary union, which is agreed
        by all EU countries with the exception of the Czech Republic and the
        UK.

Abbreviations

AC	Accession country
AES	Alternative economic strategy
APEC	Asia Pacific Economic Cooperation
ASEAN	Association of Southeast Asian Nations
BCC	British Chambers of Commerce
BWS	Bretton Woods system
CAP	Common Agricultural Policy
CBI	Confederation of British Industry
CC	Candidate country
CEEC	Central and Eastern European country
CFR	Council on Foreign Relations
CFSP	Common Foreign and Security Policy
CIA	Central Intelligence Agency
CPE	Critical political economy
CWO	Cold War Order
DWSR	Dollar–Wall Street Regime
EC	European Community
ECB	European Central Bank
ECJ	European Court of Justice
ECOFIN	Economic and Financial Affairs Council
ECSC	European Coal and Steel Community
ecu	European currency unit
EDC	European Defence Community
EEC	European Economic Community
EEP	European employment pact
EES	European Employment Strategy
EFSF	European Financial Stability Facility
EFTA	European Free Trade Association
EFTS	European Federal Transfer Scheme
EIB	European Investment Bank
EIF	European Investment Fund
EMI	European Monetary Institute
EMS	European Monetary System

EMU	Economic and Monetary Union
EPC	European Political Co-operation
EPU	European Political Union
ERM	Exchange Rate Mechanism
ERP	European Recovery Program
ERT	European Round Table of Industrialists
ESF	European Social Forum
ESM	European Social Model
ETUC	European Trade Union Confederation
EU	European Union
EWC	European works council
FDI	Foreign direct investment
FSB	Federation of Small Businesses
GATT	General Agreement on Tariffs and Trade
GDP	Gross domestic product
GRP	Gross regional product
HICP	Harmonized Index of Consumer Prices
IGC	Intergovernmental conference
IMF	International Monetary Fund
IoD	Institute of Directors
IS-LM	Investment–saving/liquidity preference–money supply
JHA	Justice and Home Affairs
KWNS	Keynesian welfare national state
MCC	Maastricht Convergence Criteria
MEP	Member of the European Parliament
MTEPC	Medium-term Economic Policy Committee
NAFTA	North American Free Trade Agreement
NAIRU	Non-accelerating inflation rate of unemployment
NATO	North Atlantic Treaty Organization
NEC	National Executive Committee
NMD	National Missile Defense
NMS	New member states
NSC	National Security Council
NRU	Natural rate of unemployment
NMW	National minimum wage
NWO	New World Order
OCA	Optimum Currency Area
OECD	Organization for Economic Co-operation and Development
OEEC	Organization for European Economic Co-operation
OMC	Open Method of Coordination
PAC	Potential accession country
PCC	Potential candidate country
PCF	*Parti Communiste Français*
PCG	*Programme Commun du Gouvernement*
PS	*Parti Socialiste*

QMV	Qualified majority voting
R&D	Research and development
SAP	Structural adjustment programme
SEA	Single European Act
SGP	Stability and Growth Pact
SIM	Single internal market
SM	Single market
SPD	*Sozialdemokratische Partei Deutschland*
SWPR	Schumpeterian workfare post-national regime
TEU	Treaty on the European Union
TNC	Transnational corporation
TUC	Trades Union Congress
UNCTAD	United Nations Conference on Trade and Development
UNICE	Union of Industrial and Employers' Confederations of Europe
WTO	World Trade Organization

1   The European Social Model

Introduction

One distinctive feature of the model of regional integration advanced by the European Union (EU) concerns the creation of a social dimension (*espace social européen*) or European Social Model (ESM). This is a relatively new phenomenon, having been grafted onto a predominately economic or trade-orientated focus for economic integration. Nevertheless, it is one which has had increasing resonance amongst certain parts of the European citizenry as economic integration has deepened, as it is perceived as a means of counter-balancing the less desirable consequences likely to arise from the unfettered operation of free market forces (Bean *et al.*, 1998). In this way, the ESM sets the EU apart from other contemporary examples of regional economic integration (Vaughan-Whitehead, 2003: 23).

In general discussion, the concept of a 'Social Europe' is typically counter-poised against the neo-liberal, free market 'Anglo-Saxon' model. Not surprisingly, therefore, it has proven particularly popular amongst social democratic and trade union constituencies. Indeed, it represents a significant reason why these groupings remain amongst the most enthusiastic advocates of deeper European integration (Strange, 1997; Edmonds, 2000: 194; Whyman, 2002, 2007). Nevertheless, there remains a deep ambivalence concerning the precise meaning of the ESM, its importance and how (or indeed, whether) it complements other aspects of policies intended to promote a broadening and deepening of European integration. It is these aspects of the subject matter that this book is intended to evaluate.

Foremost an economic union?

The EU was founded as an economic organization, focused upon promoting integration through trade, and facilitated through the progressive removal of trade barriers between EU member states, whilst maintaining barriers against the rest of the world. As such, the employment and social aspects remained underdeveloped. The Treaty of Rome did include a Title on Social Policy, within Article 117 (later to become Article 136), which committed the organization to 'promote improved working conditions and standards of living of workers', however this statement of intent was not accompanied by a consideration of measures to deliver these objectives (EU, 1957). Indeed, the early years of the organization made little impact upon the social and employment spheres, outside the impact arising from economic integration, except in so far as the free movement of labour has an impact upon employment opportunities for European workers and the subsidies extended to rural employment through the Common Agricultural Policy (CAP).

This began to change in the mid-1970s, with the development of the first Social Action Programme, although this aspect remained marginalized until the Delors presidency of the European Commission, when a Charter of Fundamental Social Rights of Workers was established, in 1989, and which advocated the creation of a minimum set of social rights for EU citizens. Yet even this remained a non-binding, political declaration, signed by 11 of the then 12 EU member states (the United Kingdom being the exception) until its evolution into a social protocol annexed to the Treaty on European Union (TEU or Maastricht Treaty) in 1992. Once again, opposition from the UK Conservative administration and their consequent opt-out from the provisions prevented the protocol from being included in the main body of the treaty itself. Nevertheless, it was cited in the preamble and Article 2 of the TEU committed the EU

> To promote economic and social progress and a high level of employment and to achieve balanced and sustainable development, in particular through the creation of an area without internal frontiers, through the strengthening of economic and social cohesion and through the establishment of economic and monetary union, ultimately including a single currency in accordance with the provisions of this Treaty.
>
> (EU Commission, 1992)

This, in turn, resulted in the adoption of a wave of directives relating to employment and social policy, including, amongst others, measures to regulate collective redundancies, maternity rights and working time. Moreover, this area was further strengthened by incorporating the protocol into the main body of the subsequent Amsterdam Treaty, where the resulting Article 11 provided the EU Commission new competences in the areas of industrial relations and combating social exclusion (Adnett, 2001).

ESM: a contested ideal

Despite its centrality as a feature of debate relating to the future development of the 'new Europe', it is perhaps surprising that the ESM remains poorly defined – including by the EU itself, possibly as a deliberate attempt to obfuscate the political differences between conservative and social democratic groupings likely to surface if greater clarity was forthcoming (Vaughan-Whitehead, 2003: 3). One of the few attempts, arising from the Nice summit in 2000, suggested that the

ESM derived from a "common core of values" relating to the provision of a high degree of social protection, the recognition of the importance of dialogue between social partners and the necessity to promote social cohesion as essential elements within the process of European integration (EU, 2000: 4). It is therefore intended to be more than the sum of the approximately 70 directives or legislative tools that seek to influence European social policy, principally in the fields of labour law, equal opportunities within the workplace, occupational health and safety and the free movement of labour.

Despite these attempts, the concept of the ESM remains both unclear and contested territory. For its advocates, the ESM has been viewed as a means to 'construct a progressive counterweight to an increasingly pervasive global market ideology' (Kenner, 2000; Watson, 2006: 146). Indeed, it may be argued that it was conceived at least partly as a result of popular dissatisfaction with the shift in economic stance towards a neo-liberal Europe (Mathers, 2007: 49–84). For its most consistent advocates, organized labour, the ESM offers a means of evading declining national influence, establishing bargaining rights in transnational corporations (TNCs) whilst helping to evade the economic logic arising from Economic and Monetary Union (EMU), that wage restraint and reductions in social provision are the most obvious ways to slow cost increases and maintain international competitiveness within a single currency zone (Crouch, 2002: 297; Whyman, 2002, 2008). When combined with a neo-liberal advocacy of deregulation, the absence of an ESM is likely to result in pressure towards a competitive diminution of employment conditions and welfare provision across the European single market (SM).

The evidence is, however, more problematic, as it would appear that the drift of policy has been in the opposite direction, with the creation of a more 'unsocial Europe' (Gray, 2004; Mathers, 2007: 2). The removal of barriers to financial flows and increasing integration of European capital markets has led to an increasing dominance of capital market over bank credit financing, resulting in a shift in corporate control and governance across much of the European economic space. This creates a further potential rift with the ESM ideal, as labour market strategy, intended to protect workers from at least certain market vagaries, would conflict more clearly with this new focus upon market-driven corporate strategy, whilst conceptions of employee participation in corporate decision-making and/ or economic democracy, would appear less likely to be accommodated (Watson, 2006). Moreover, the economic architecture surrounding EMU would appear to encourage the consideration of wages and social protection as costs rather than benefits, likely to undermine the competitiveness of a participating nation unable to restore competitive advantage through devaluation and/or changes in monetary policy due to the single currency.

The result is tension over both the definition of what the ESM should be, alongside what Bieler (2006) has termed a "struggle" for a Social Europe – where progressive forces within the European economy press for greater state involvement in economic policy, promoting employment and developing the ESM to the benefit of citizens and workers, against the neo-liberal logic of the single internal market (SIM) and EMU. Thus, Mathers (2007) highlights the consistent critique of neo-liberal solutions to Europe's economic difficulties, and details the various marches and pressure inflicted by a combination of new social movements and organized labour.

Yet, the fact remains that this has failed in its primary mission, namely to arrest the permeation of neo-liberal economics and develop a truly alternative conception of a Social Europe. Indeed, it might be argued that organized labour and progressive political forces remain divided as how to advance a preferred conception of ESM without damaging the goal of deeper European integration, to which they remain committed. Hence, when opposition to neo-liberal permeation led to national labour movements supporting a 'no' vote in Dutch and French referendums on the Constitutional Treaty, in 2005, the European Trade Union Confederation (ETUC) announced its disappointment in the result and insisted that the proposed constitution was not, after all, neo-liberal in intent, and therefore trade unionists should support, not oppose, its implementation (Mathers, 2007: 191). Thus, whilst many progressive political forces might wish to utilize the larger European space to extend the ESM such that progressive priorities supersede market determination, there is an equal if not greater argument in favour of the need for national systems to be defended against neo-liberal economic imperatives emanating from the EU (Watson, 2006: 146).

One possible definition (amongst many)

For the purposes of this book, a maximal (or strong) definition of ESM is employed, where it is considered to be a multi-faceted approach encompassing elements of economic, social and labour market policy, including:

1   Competitive market economy, but where social institutions mediate between state and market
2   Promoting social solidarity, primarily through initiatives designed to reduce inequality and protect worker–citizen rights
3   Combining the desirability of universality (through social protocols) with the realisation of the subsidiarity principle through encouraging social partners to complement state activity

Traditionally, the ESM has been associated with the prioritization of full employment, often through Euro-Keynesianism, as advocated by the Tindemans (1976) report prepared for the EU Commission, although this emphasis has markedly lessened amongst leading figures in the EU Commission in recent times (Coates, 1999; Notermans, 2000). This, in turn, is supported by a quasi-corporatist interest in the co-ordination of wage formation – the latter has the ability to promote a stable labour market at internationally competitive aggregate wage rates, whilst preventing high quality producers being undercut by 'sweatshop' employers. It has been suggested that the impact of the globalization of production and international freedom of movement of capital have combined to weaken the ability of national governments to pursue progressive policies, and therefore full employment policies may be more successfully re-created on a larger geographical basis. Thus, in the eurozone, trade and capital flows will be of lesser proportionate significance, and hence counter-cyclical macroeconomic policy will have fewer leakages and will be proportionately more vigorous (Coates, 1999; Notermans, 2000).

The social policy element of the ESM is viewed as favouring the extension of universal, comprehensive welfare state provision to cover all EU citizens, and thereby creating a minimum safety net for European citizens across the entire SIM. Social policy aims are considered to include a reduction in the degree of inequality within and between European member states, in order to promote conceptions of equity and social cohesion. Social policy has been, moreover, associated with the decommodification of labour and knowledge; in the process, encouraging investment in human capital (Esping-Andersen, 1990; Teague, 1997). Furthermore, decommodification arguably empowers employees and enables the development of work relationships based upon trust and loyalty, rather than the market nexus; a difference increasingly important in the dynamic knowledge-based sectors of the economy.

In contrast to neo-liberal theorists, this conception of social protection advances the proposition that a trade-off between social equity and economic efficiency is not inevitable, and, rather, the former can enhance efficiency through reducing poverty, thereby reducing constraints upon participation in economic activity (de Neubourg and Casonguay, 2006: 180). Indeed, in the long term, there does appear to be some evidence that reductions in inequality may have a positive impact upon economic growth developments (Wilkinson and Pickett, 2009). Of course, social expenditure must be financed, and this may lead to higher costs for employees or firms, but the net impact upon productivity depends upon how policy design enhances incentives to invest in human capital and the extent to which training opportunities are available (de Neubourg and Casonguay, 2006: 201–2). Hence, generous social security systems do not *necessarily* result in lower labour market participation rates and higher unemployment if this is supplemented by active labour market measures (de Groot *et al.*, 2006: 175).

The ESM is, furthermore, considered to embrace an employment aspect, whereby European citizen rights and wellbeing is promoted through the enhancement of social partnership between employers and employees – typically, though not exclusively, through trade unions. The emphasis upon the inclusion of workers and their unions in the working of the economy is intended to facilitate 'voice' rather than 'exit', and in turn, facilitating co-operation in adapting to change, superior morale resulting in enhanced productivity and lower employee turnover, and finally the prevention of low skill, low investment competitive alternatives stimulates productive investment and innovation (Streeck, 1992: 5; Hutton, 1994; Coates, 1999: 654–5). The introduction of European works councils (EWCs), in large TNCs operating within the EU economies, demonstrates an interest in facilitating consultation and enhancing micro-level flexible adaptation. Furthermore, universal employee protection whilst at work forms a core element of the ESM (Strange, 1997).

The broadening of collective bargaining across member states rather than remaining a predominantly national preserve – so-called euro-bargaining – reinforces social partnership as a component of wider integration objectives. However, although advocated by the ETUC, European employer organizations remain hostile to this development. Nevertheless, a large body of the literature has indicated that co-ordinated wage formation produces a superior macroeconomic flexibility in real wages and hence industrial adjustment to external shocks to the economy (Bruno and Sachs, 1985; Calmfors and Driffill, 1988; Rowthorn and Glyn, 1990).

The ESM is, as thus conceived, a variant of the post-war German *social market*, which has combined a successful, competitive market economy with generous welfare provision, labour protection and an exceptional vocational training system that produced skilled workers of sufficient quantity and quality, thereby rectifying the corporate tendency to under-invest in skill formation (Glasman, 1997: 136; Teague, 1997). Yet, the precise nature of the social dimension remains the focus of political struggle, as diverse opinions seek to realize their preferred interpretation of the concept.

A coherent model?

The discussion of the ESM, thus far, suggests that it is a well considered, internally consistent entity, fully realized in practice across the internal market created by the EU(15) member states, and largely on the way to fulfilment in those new member states (NMS) joining following one of the enlargement phases. However, this is far from the case. There is considerable divergence between the social and employment policies pursued by individual member states, with the Scandinavian and UK Anglo-Saxon models representing two extremes, whilst many of the NMS appear to be pursuing quite a different employment and social policy, in order to maintain economic competitiveness amidst lower productivity rates.

The current form of social dimension being constructed across the EU is, arguably, a *minimalist* (or weak) version of a fully-fledged system of social protection of the kind idealized in discussion of the ESM (Keller and Sorries, 1997: 93; Whyman, 2001, 2007). This is why critics of the current position describe it as having 'retarded [the] advancement of European-level political rights', alongside the 'almost complete absence of a European system of industrial citizenship' indicating that there is little reason to anticipate these initiatives will prove particularly successful (Streeck, 1992: 218–19). Consequently, it is a moot point whether the subsidiarity principle informs and reinforces the considerable fragmentation in this area of policy, or is actually an *ex post facto* attempt to recognize and provide a narrative to justify the divergence in social and employment matters across the EU member states. The contrast between current and ideal type of ESM is illustrated in Table 1.1.

The fact that the ESM is an idealized form of reality does not, however, imply that the concept of creating a 'Social Europe' may be dismissed completely. The minimalist version of the ESM that has been created amongst EU nations has still provided notable benefits for workers and citizens in less regulated economies (such as the United Kingdom), whilst other initiatives (i.e. the EWC Directive) have the potential to develop into a more significant form over time. Moreover, the idealized version of the ESM can be utilized by social democrats, trade unionists and other progressives, to argue the case for further advances to be pursued in this area (Bieler, 2006). Consequently, it is of great significance to ascertain how, first, the ESM may impact upon the EU's NMS and, second, how their accession may influence the future development of the social dimension.

Is the Lisbon Agenda compatible with the ESM?

In the Lisbon Summit, in March 2000, EU member state governments committed themselves toward ensuring that the EU became 'the most competitive and dynamic knowledge-based economy in the world by 2010, capable of sustainable economic growth, with more and better jobs and greater social cohesion'

Table 1.1 Comparison of social market and current EU 'social dimension'

	EU social dimension	*European social market*
Welfare State		
Type	Minimalist	Comprehensive
Coverage	Safety net	Universal
Replacement Ratio	Low	High
Association with labour market	Re-commodification	De-commodification
Response to globalisation	Competitive – improve labour market skills	Protective – social citizenship requires non-market income source to make effective choices
Industrial Relations		
Collective bargaining recognition	Patchy	High/comprehensive
Corporatist	Diverse – some member states deregulated wage formation, whilst others rely upon social contracts to secure budget cuts	Established – facilitates superior inflation: employment trade-off
Euro-level IR	Minimum – EWC, consultation only	Developed – framework bargaining between federal-level social partners
Labour regulation	Minimum – complements single market; over-regulation impedes competitiveness	Fundamental – basis of social accord, combining industrial adjustment with employee protection

(cited in Mundschenk *et al.*, 2006: 3). The Lisbon Strategy was the mechanism intended to achieve this goal. However, this was largely a symbolic expression of intent, being based upon neither academic research nor considered policy appraisal, and therefore it fell to later work to try and place flesh upon the bones outlined. The Sapir Report (2004) was the first significant contribution to this endeavour.

The Lisbon Agenda, therefore, seeks to pursue a dynamic economic strategy, enhancing productivity and international competitiveness, whilst simultaneously seeking to protect and, indeed, enhance social equity through the development of the ESM. It sought to close the persistent GDP gap with the United States, through enhancing productivity per hour, even though lower employment rates and shorter working hours would actually appear to account for a greater element of this differential (Sapir *et al.*, 2004: 27–50; Dierx and Ilzkovitz, 2006: 17). The aims are, undoubtedly, laudable. However, the means, expressed through the Sapir Report (and more generally, under the auspices of what has come to be known as the 'Brussels–Frankfurt Consensus'), and the development of the ESM, would appear to be fundamentally conflicted.

Structural reforms have sought to enhance allocative efficiency through the creation of better functioning markets. In the labour market, this has focused upon flexible working arrangements, active labour market policies and reform of wage setting institutions to decentralize or individualize wage formation, in order to better reflect productivity rates (Dreger, 2006). Similarly, product market reforms focused upon enhancing competition, removing remaining barriers to inter-union trade, furthering financial market integration, encouraging productive investment and innovation (Dierx and Ilzkovitz, 2006).

Thus the Lisbon Treaty which was signed by EU member states on 13 December 2007 and entered into force on 1 December 2009 represents the current zenith of EU treaty making and places into context the present position of whether a Social Europe is attainable in any meaningful sense, as we argue in this book.

The 'Brussels–Frankfurt Consensus' and the Sapir Report

The 'Brussels–Frankfurt Consensus', as described in the Sapir Report, provides the focus for a new and quite different approach to the slow rates of growth and lagging productivity which have characterized many parts of the European economy for several decades (Sapir *et al.*, 2004). The 'Brussels–Frankfurt Consensus' focuses upon the importance of economic stability, and claims that this is to be achieved via price stability and fiscal discipline (Issing *et al.*, 2001). The hypothesized relationship is therefore seen to follow that price stability is the central focus of economic policy, as it is predicted to result in higher economic growth over the medium term and lower rates of cyclical instability. Constrained (or 'sound') public finances are therefore necessitated to dampen demand, in pursuit of this causal relationship, and in turn, is expected to lead to lower budget deficits and public debt, thereby facilitating a lower long-term interest rate and reducing the possibility of crowding out productive private sector investment (Sapir *et al.*, 2004: 51).

This 'consensus' is based upon a shared understanding of macroeconomic forces, such that: (a) The economy has a tendency to fluctuate around an objective conception of a NAIRU (non-accelerating inflation rate of unemployment), meaning that, when unemployment is below this rate, inflation will occur, whereas when above the rate, it will decline; (b) The level of economic activity, and the level of economic growth, are both determined by the interaction of supply (not demand) factors (Sapir *et al.*, 2004: 5). This is an example of a pre-Keynesian or neo-liberal, New Keynesian synthesis version of economic policy, in which supply-side interventions dominate considerations of aggregate demand (Arestis and Sawyer, 2001: 2, 2006: 57–8). Whilst noting the availability of contrary evidence in the literature, however, the Sapir Report largely accepts this analysis. So, for example, it suggests that the ECB should take greater note of potential deflationary aspects of its policy, without challenging the fact that its sole objective is price stability – defined at an inflation rate of approximately 2 per cent per annum (Sapir *et al.*, 2004: 166). This is not a step towards greater symmetry, as the report suggests, but simply a restatement of the existing asymmetric approach. Similarly, whilst conceding that newer member states might be allowed an element of greater flexibility in their fiscal policy rules, and suggesting the establishment of a 'rainy day' fund, funded through retained surpluses during boom years to help to stabilize EMU through less buoyant periods, the report nevertheless sticks firmly to the importance of the excessive deficit procedure element of the Stability and Growth Pact (SGP), which is the primary means of constraining fiscal policy and undermining its ability to pursue an aggressive counter-cyclical strategy.

The resulting policy stance is therefore to maintain a neutral fiscal policy and rely primarily upon monetary policy, through the medium of the interest rate policy instrument, to smooth demand shocks and thereby enable supply-side factors to determine development in the real economy. There is, therefore, no need for democratic control over fiscal or monetary policy, as these are supportive to the primary drivers of economic growth, and therefore these instruments can be subcontracted to technocratic specialists in the ECB and/or be constrained by the operation of the SGP.

'Brussels–Frankfurt Consensus' economics

The two foundations of the 'Brussels–Frankfurt Consensus', namely the belief in a NAIRU and the supremacy of supply-side economics, are both controversial and subject to significant criticism within the literature.

Supply-side determined equilibrium rate of unemployment

The acceptance of a *supply-side determined equilibrium rate of unemployment* is common to two economic schools of thought. In the first, the monetarist natural rate of unemployment (NRU) derives from the adaptive expectations-augmented, vertical long run Phillips Curve, first developed by Friedman (1968) and Phelps (1968). Its rationale relies upon the neo-classical view of the labour market, where individuals seek to optimize their satisfaction by determining how much time they allocate to work and leisure at the prevailing real wage rate. In this model, workers recognize (whether through adaptive or rational expectations) whether changes in nominal wages convert into real wage effects, and therefore government attempts to boost economic activity and reduce unemployment below the supply-determined long run equilibrium rate, will be ultimately self-defeating.

A more recent variant of this general approach is the NAIRU, it is defined as that level of unemployment, determined by the interaction between market forces of demand and supply within the labour market, which maintains a steady rate of inflation. There are orthodox and imperfect competition variants of this theory, yet both hold that if unemployment is pushed below the NAIRU rate, it will result in rising inflation, and consequently the NAIRU, which is determined in the labour market in the same way as the NRU theory, essentially determines the long run level of economic activity.[1] Depending on the particular variant of the theory, policies which may shift the NAIRU may include increasing the supply of labour through lowering reservation wages via reducing marginal taxation, tightening the generosity and duration of social security transfer payments, changes in union bargaining power, state incomes policies, variations in taxation and external shocks to the economy. Thus, it is the labour market, and not the time path of aggregate demand, that determines the equilibrium position to which the economy would converge. This is, therefore, highly significant for the development of an ESM, since labour market issues form a core element of the initiative.

The NAIRU has become a widely accepted theoretical tool, not necessarily because it accurately describes objective reality, but because it is considered to be a *useful* aid to policymaking even though it can only really be estimated after the fact (Eller and Gordon, 2002). There is, however, a large literature which highlights the uncertainty and unreliability surrounding NAIRU estimates (Setterfield *et al.*, 1992; Staiger *et al.*, 1997; Sawyer, 2003). Estimates of the NAIRU have rather large statistical error terms and the estimated NAIRU tends to track the actual unemployment rate, although subject to a small but significant time lag. All of which raise the difficulty in basing economic policy decisions upon a theoretical proposition which may not be a strong attractor for the actual level of unemployment (Galbraith, 1997: 102; Arestis and Sawyer, 2004: 33).

Indeed, one of the originators of the concept of NAIRU, Modigliani (cited in Mitchell and Muysken, 2006: 6), recently criticized the 'objectionable use of the so-called NAIRU approach', based upon 'an obsessive fear of inflation', to neglect the reduction of unemployment as a policy objective and hence overly constrain economic activity. Indeed, Modigliani is quoted as stating, in no uncertain terms, that unemployment arises 'primarily due to *lack of aggregate demand*', which is in clear contrast to how the Brussels–Frankfurt Consensus appears to have designed its macroeconomic stance.

Supply-side economics

The second element of the 'Brussels–Frankfurt Consensus' derives from the first, namely that if government policy can have little or no sustainable impact upon real economic variables, with the exception of measures intended to alter the supply side of the labour market, then macroeconomic policy should be constrained to prevent negative consequences. Thus, the traditional Keynesian-social democratic utilization of discretionary fiscal policy to influence the level of aggregate demand in the economy, to pursue full employment objectives, is considered to be self-defeating, as it will only impact upon inflation levels. Part of this critique rests upon the concept of crowding out, whereby government spending displaces more productive private investment because of how this is financed. Thus, this may result from disincentive effects caused by taxation, inflationary effects of printing money, and/or rising interest rates caused by an increase in the demand for money, assuming, of course, a neo-classical model of the money markets (Friedman, 1962: 81; Neville, 2000: 159).[2] However, fiscal activism is further criticized on the grounds that time lags inherent within the policy determination and implementation process may be sufficiently long that fiscal policy leads to the mistiming of fiscal boosts and reductions, thereby exacerbating business cycles rather than counteracting their fluctuations (Friedman, 1962: 38; Hemming *et al.*, 2002a).

In the place of discretionary fiscal policy, a combination of pre-commitment to fiscal rules, combined with transparency of operations, has been adopted as the modus operandi for policy makers, as this is intended to promote the credibility of economic policymakers with economic actors (Lucas, 1976; Barro and Gordon, 1983). The intention is to solve what is known as the time inconsistency problem, whereby economic actors are suspicious that government may try to fool them into changing their behaviour through an inflationary expansion of demand, and therefore they may only respond hesitantly, after a time lag, to real expansions in demand (Kydland and Prescott, 1977). Convincing economic actors that government will not use fiscal policy to inflate the economy is supposed to increase responses to real changes in economic variables. Moreover, it is suggested that the policy reduces risk premiums added to internationally determined interest rates by the financial markets, as investors feel less threatened by unexpected inflation undermining asset value, hence securing lower interest rates consequent to a given level of inflation and growth in a nation-state. This should in turn encourage investment and productivity growth, and hence economic growth rates (Baker, 2000: 230). Fiscal policy should, therefore, be largely passive in nature and be left to automatic stabilizers, operating alongside budgets balanced over the business cycle (Arestis and Sawyer, 2004: 119).

One variant of this approach has been termed constrained discretion, as the intention is to circumscribe the freedom of fiscal authorities to act according to their short-term assessment of optimal policy options in order to keep to their pre-commitment to their budgetary rules, and as a result, the cost of operating economic policy declines because international financiers are willing to reduce risk premiums placed upon interest rates due to the lowered perceived risk of unwise, inflationary fiscal and monetary policy (Blanchard, 1984). To the extent that economic actors grow to trust the government to keep to its fiscal rules. This approach provides for a moderate, time limited opportunity to engage in expansionary discretionary policy, as long as this does not detract from meeting the long-term fiscal rules. In essence, it is based upon the strategy of pleasing the markets, and once achieved they will give the government the benefit of the doubt if it engages in short-term expansionary policy because of the belief that it will reverse this quickly and keep to its long-term fiscal rules. In essence, lower interest rates are said to 'crowd in' private activity (Elmendorf *et al.*, 2002). Note, however, that this new approach depends upon the existence of crowding out for the crowding in effect to work, and this, as previously stated, is hotly disputed by Keynesian theorists.

Demand matters

There are, however, a number of fundamental weaknesses with reliance upon supply-side determined equilibrium rates of unemployment, such as the natural rate and NAIRU approaches. A Keynesian critique reiterates Keynes' observation that workers are concerned with *relative* wages in addition to real wages, and yet they can only negotiate for nominal wages, thus undermining the concept of a classical labour supply curve (and hence an aggregate labour market) upon which orthodox variants of equilibrium theories are based. Instead, the post-Keynesian theory of employment arises out of Keynes' discussion of 'the principle of effective demand' in the *General Theory*, when he argued that the demand for labour is derived from the equilibrium rate where the aggregate supply function and aggregate demand intersect, at the point where entrepreneurs expectations of future profits will be realized, an effective demand point determined in the product markets (Keynes, 1936). Thus, for post-Keynesians, no aggregate demand for labour schedule exists whereby the real wage is capable of determining employment level (Davidson, 1983 and 1998; Galbraith, 1997: 95). Employment is determined in the product market by the aggregate demand for output. Thus, 'mass unemployment is a macroeconomic phenomenon and can never be a real wage problem' (Mitchell, 1998: 2).

Second, contrary to the assumptions made by the 'Brussels–Frankfurt Consensus', there is little evidence to suggest that wage inflexibility and rigidities associated with labour market institutions have acted as significant factors in the increase in European unemployment (Madsen, 1998; Baker *et al.*, 2002b; Ball, 1999; OECD, 1999b; Blanchard and Wolfers, 2000). Instead, a more plausible explanation envisages demand shocks leading to lower rates of capital accumulation; an initial impact which was magnified due to the existence of hysteresis (Rowthorn, 1995). Indeed, this conclusion would appear to be confirmed by the experience of those European nations (i.e. Ireland, Netherlands, Portugal and the United Kingdom) that managed to significantly reduce high levels of unemployment, which suffered during recession periods in the early 1980s and 1990s, due to expansionary monetary policy pursued during subsequent periods of recovery (Ball, 1994, 1999).

Regional variations in levels of unemployment would seem to fit poorly with explanations based upon factors such as the NAIRU, labour market institutions, regulations and unemployment benefits, as these typically apply throughout the entire economy, whereas regional variations in industrial structure, productive capacity and aggregate demand may offer a more plausible rationale (Arestis and Sawyer, 2004: 93). Furthermore, there is a large and growing literature that claims that productive capacity has a large, statistically significant impact upon employment (Bean, 1989, 1994; Rowthorn, 1995, 1999; Arestis and Mariscal, 1997: 191; Miaouli, 2001: 23; Alexiou and Pitelis, 2003: 628; Baddeley, 2003: 214). Indeed, in one study, Stockhammer (2004a) contrasted the NAIRU explanation of unemployment with the Keynesian alternative, and found capital accumulation to be a far better explanatory for changes in unemployment than labour market factors.

A considerable body of evidence, therefore, indicates that aggregate demand does in fact have an impact upon the real economy principally because it influences, and in turn is influenced by, the rate of investment, which alters the stock of capital and thereby affects productive capacity. A larger capital stock will permit a higher level of aggregate demand – and hence higher output and employment – without resulting in an increase in inflation. Depressed economic conditions result in the deterioration and premature scrapping of productive capital, whilst the accompanying dismissal or underemployment of a firm's workforce damages a firm's intangible capital through eroding corporate learning resources, customary working practices and industrial relations. An economic recovery will not immediately rectify this deterioration in economic performance, and thus demand shocks can have a significant impact upon the real economy that are still being experienced several years after the initial event. Major recessions cause a downward shift in the growth path of productivity and hence potential productive capacity, with stable growth paths resuming in the aftermath of the recession, but only from the low point that capacity scrapping first caused (Arestis and Mariscal, 2000: 487). As a result, the important finding is that the utilization of Keynesian measures to prevent the disruption to economic development caused by economic recessions can have a significant impact upon investment rates, industrial capacity, output and productivity. As Rowthorn (1995: 38) states, 'the problem of unemployment is ultimately one of investment'.

The fact that sufficient productive capacity can shift the NAIRU to full employment does not mean that this will necessarily occur, and indeed the existence of high rates of unemployment, together with low levels of capacity, will dissuade investors to finance the construction of such an extension in future capacity. This would leave the economy stuck in deflation, as the necessary increase in aggregate demand, required to raise expectations sufficiently to facilitate an expansion in investment, would, according to the NAIRU theory, result in inflation.

The recognition of the importance of aggregate demand upon employment and inflation does not, however, marginalize other factors that have been found to influence macroeconomic variables. Ownership and corporate governance have been found to influence the investment climate and, therefore, productive capacity and employment. Stockhammer (2004b: 19–24), for example, identified globalization leading to liberalized financial markets as resulting in a shift in many countries from a bank-based to a market-based financial system, which, in turn, led to increased instability and asset price speculation (Minsky, 1985; Shleifer and Summers, 1990; Skott, 1995). Furthermore, 'financialization' may have caused a shift in corporate governance, empowering shareholders relative to managerial interests, and consequently prioritizing profitability at the expense of a decrease in investment and hence productive capacity (Stockhammer, 2004c).

One further source of theoretical challenge to a supply-side determined equilibrium rate of unemployment relates to the hysteresis hypothesis. First developed by Phelps in 1972, this approach suggests that the equilibrium rate of unemployment is *path-dependent*, in that it depends upon the actual history or path of unemployment. Unemployment persistence can be considered to influence future unemployment rates because the skills held by an unemployed individual may deteriorate over time, as can their work discipline, confidence and hence employability in the eyes of the employer. The longer an individual remains unemployed, the more their search efforts may decline, together with their expectation that they may succeed in securing a new job.

The literature relating to hysteresis is split between those who hold a 'weak' and a 'strong' version of the theory. The former typically adopt the New Keynesian assumption that aggregate demand policies have no impact upon long-term equilibrium unemployment (Layard *et al.*, 1991). Consequently, hysteresis may have a marginal impact upon unemployment rates during the short term, but in the medium and longer term the supply-determined equilibrium rate of unemployment will hold. However, those theorists who advocate a 'strong' version of hysteresis believe that it is sufficiently powerful that actual unemployment largely determines equilibrium unemployment, and therefore governments can shift the NAIRU by affecting actual unemployment (Blanchard and Summers, 1988; Ball, 1994).

In the latter case, an increase in *actual* unemployment can, in the medium term, cause the *equilibrium* rate of unemployment to similarly rise, whereas a reduction in unemployment in the short term may cause a reduction in the equilibrium rate of unemployment. Empirical evidence tends to support this position, as Arestis and Mariscal (1998: 202) identified hysteresis effects in addition to worker militancy and the level of capital stock, as significant determinants of the level of unemployment. The 'strong' version of hysteresis, therefore justifies policy activism to reduce unemployment beneath the prevailing equilibrium rate, because by doing so it will enable that equilibrium rate to decline itself in the future.

Hysteresis thereby implies that any equilibrium rate is only a temporary phenomenon, since current unemployment remains a significant factor determining future rates. This is tantamount to rejecting the concept of an equilibrium rate at all, and replacing the concept with a *disequilibrium* analysis so favoured by the famous Stockholm School of economics.[3] If an equilibrium rate of unemployment can be altered by every shift in government policy, together with demand and supply shocks to the economy, and is influenced considerably by the actual unemployment rate pertaining at any one moment, it is scarcely of any practical use. It will not provide a fundamental barrier to lowering actual unemployment in the longer term because actual unemployment can be reduced by demand stimulation and, through hysteresis, can itself cause the original equilibrium rate to be reduced. Hence, the practical result is that government might as well operate as though disequilibrium is the natural state of affairs, because even if the economy is ultimately converging to a long-term equilibrium position, it does so slowly. Thus, short-term policy changes can shift the long-term equilibrium so that it is likely to have shifted position long before actual unemployment could ever have converged with the original equilibrium position.

Lisbon – a dead end?

The Lisbon process has provided the ESM with a problem which may prove difficult (if not impossible) to solve. On the one hand, the EU is committed to developing a more participatory, citizen-friendly form of social and economic governance, involving employees in decision-making within the workplace and creating a form of economics centred upon maintaining a high level of employment. However, at the same time, the EU is committed to an economic agenda seeking to raise productivity through market determination in the social and labour market spheres. One vision of the future takes as its basis a quasi-Keynesian, negotiated economy model, whereas the other has supply-side, neo-liberal foundations. To prevent cognitive dissonance, the EU needs to either demonstrate how it can square this particular circle, or else decide which approach it wishes to pursue.

Structure of the book

The book is divided into four principal parts which essentially adhere to the chorological development of ideas relating to the ESM from the immediate post-war era of the rebuilding of Europe to the aftermath of the 2008 credit crunch financial crisis/recession.

The first part of the book *From liberal to neo-liberal Europe* contains four chapters which provide the historical backdrop to the overall narrative commencing with the first of these chapters: *Liberal Europe during the Cold War Order (1947–1982): from the European Recovery Program to the socialist challenge*. This chapter presents a brief overview of the European integration process during the Cold War Order (CWO) from 1947 until 1982 through advancing six main arguments. First, that the nature and trajectory of the European project during the CWO resulted, in part, from the contest between anti- and pro-European forces and conservative, liberal and socialist forces within EEC/EC (European Economic Community/European Community) member states, and between intergovernmental and supranationalist forces and conservative, liberal and socialist forces at the EEC/EC level and beyond. Second, that the liberal and supranationalist forces were, generally speaking, the dominant ones in this struggle. Third, and following from the second argument, that the European project evolved as a *liberal entity* during this period, whereby the founding treaties of the EEC ensured the pre-eminence of market liberalism and thus negative, rather than positive, integration. Consequently, the EEC/EC prioritized economic liberalization rather than social policy and, in so doing, precluded the creation of a common, Europe-wide social model and/or a unified EEC/EC-level welfare state. Finally, that the European project influenced the development of Western Europe's welfare states in a structural rather than direct sense.

Chapter 3, *The political economy of Western Europe's social models in the Cold War Order: inevitable and convergent welfare states?*, explores the development of Western Europe's social models in the context of the CWO, drawing upon the critical political economy (CPE) tradition, which utilizes a comprehensive set of analytical and conceptual tools to identify a diverse range of explanatory factors which orthodox approaches tend to ignore. Hence, it situates the development of Western Europe's welfare states within a specific 'historical structure': the CWO. By attending to the nature of the *capitalist* system during this epoch, the *historical* specificities of this era and the *global* configuration of social forces during this period, it seeks to chart a new course for the study of these formations through identifying the dominant actors and structures, often neglected by the existing literature, which both shaped and constrained these formations during the CWO. In particular, the chapter advances four main arguments. First, that the nature and trajectory of Western Europe's welfare states were the product of the struggle between social forces at the national, European *and* global levels during the CWO. Second, that the deployment of US power in Western Europe was decisive in determining the outcome of this struggle. Third, that Western Europe's welfare states were *shaped by*, and, equally importantly, *constrained by*, the structure of the World Order during this period. Fourth, that the nature and trajectory of the European project, as an integral part of the World Order, precluded the creation of a common, Europe-wide social model and/or a unified EEC/EC-level welfare state.

Chapter 4, *Neo-liberal Europe in the New World Order (1985–2007): From the single market to the European Constitution*, presents an overview of the European integration process during the New World Order (NWO) from 1985 until 2007. The chapter advances six main arguments. First, that the nature and trajectory of the European project during the NWO was shaped by the struggle between competing social forces in Europe and beyond. Second, that the hegemony of liberal and supranationalist forces was repeatedly challenged during the NWO by advocates of an alternative World Order and by the rising tide of Euro-scepticism. Third, that in the face of such opposition the European project evolved as a *neo-liberal* entity during this period. Fourth, that EC/EU reification of market liberalism, bias towards negative integration, choice of social regulation and preference for competition and economic liberalization was consolidated, if not accelerated, by a series of treaties in the 1980s, 1990s and 2000s. Fifth, that although the EC/EU became more active in terms of social policy, its efforts were directed at both 'reforming' the supply-side of Europe's economies and 'modernizing' Western Europe's welfare states rather than creating a unified EC/EU-level welfare state. Consequently, the European project influenced the development of Western Europe's welfare states in an increasingly direct as well as structural sense. Sixth, that the ESM concept and the Social Europe discourse emerged in the early 1990s as a result of one of the periodic crises faced by the EC/EU – namely the problematic passage of the Maastricht Treaty – and that these constructions represented an attempt to neutralize opposition to the neo-liberal trajectory of the EC/EU and to incorporate progressive social forces.

The final chapter in this opening part is: *The political economy of Western Europe's social models in the New World Order: retrenching welfare states and the emergence of Social Europe?*. This chapter explores the retrenchment of Western Europe's social models and the emergence of the ESM concept and the Social Europe discourse in the context of the NWO. The chapter draws upon the CPE tradition, which utilizes a comprehensive set of analytical and conceptual tools to identify a diverse range of explanatory factors which orthodox approaches tend to ignore. Put simply, it situates the retrenchment of Western Europe's welfare states and the emergence of the ESM concept and the Social Europe discourse within a specific 'historical structure': the NWO. By attending to the nature of the capitalist system during this epoch, the historical specificities of this era and the global configuration of social forces during this period, it seeks to chart a new course for the study of these formations and ideas. The chapter does not advance a CPE-inspired conceptual and/or theoretical exposition of the retrenchment of Western Europe's welfare states and the emergence of the ESM concept and the Social Europe discourse, within the context of European integration and the NWO, as such work has been initiated elsewhere. Instead, it seeks to identify the dominant actors and structures, often neglected by the existing literature, which both shaped and constrained these formations and ideas during the NWO. Specifically, the chapter advances four main arguments. First, that the nature and trajectory of Western Europe's welfare states, the ESM concept and the Social Europe discourse were the product of the struggle between social forces at the national, European *and* global levels in the NWO. Second, that the continued deployment of US power in Europe influenced this struggle. Third, that Western Europe's welfare states, the ESM concept and the Social Europe discourse were *shaped by*, and, equally importantly, *constrained by*, the structure of the World Order in this period. Fourth, that the retrenchment of Western Europe's welfare states and the failure to create a unified EU-level welfare state in their place has fatally undermined the ESM concept and the dream, held by many social democratic and socialist political parties, trade unions and other progressive social forces, of constructing a Social Europe.

The second part of the book, *Alternative social models to neo-liberal Europe*, focuses on both national and pan-nation radical alternatives. Hence, Chapter 6, *Progressive Social Forces and the Transformation of the World Order: Radical National Alternatives*, discusses how, in the midst of the transformation of the World Order from the CWO to the NWO, progressive social forces in Britain and France sought to fashion radical and national alternatives to neo-liberalism. The previous four chapters assessed the impact of competing social forces and the transformation of the World Order on Western Europe's welfare states, the ESM concept and the Social Europe discourse, focusing in particular on the role of *hegemonic* social forces in shaping and constraining these formations and ideas. This chapter, by contrast, evaluates the attempts of *counter-hegemonic* social forces – more specifically social democratic and socialist political parties, trade unions and other progressive social forces – to develop an *enhanced* social model on a *national* basis. That is to say, rather than merely defending the social democratic consensus which underpinned the CWO, with its particular balance of power between capital and labour, from the 1970s the left in Britain and in France sought to radically shift power and wealth from capital to labour and to deepen and widen the welfare state as part of a transition to socialism. Thus, the chapter advances three main arguments. First, that the social democratic consensus underpinning the CWO – more specifically its economic, ideological and institutional arrangements – was relatively conducive to the construction of an enhanced social model on a national basis. Second, that although the British and French experiments ended in failure, there was nothing inevitable about this; these attempts at reflation encountered a range of problems, many of which were anticipated, but they were not intrinsically flawed. Third, that these experiments provide some valuable lessons for contemporary progressive social forces that are seeking to defend Europe's social models against globalization and neo-liberalism.

In contrast, Chapter 7, *Progressive social forces and the transformation of the World Order: Euro-Keynesian and radical European alternatives* discusses how, in the midst of the transformation of the World Order from the CWO to the NWO, progressive social forces sought to fashion Euro-Keynesian or radical European alternatives to neo-liberalism. Following the previous chapter, which focused upon national experiments, this chapter reviews the proposals put forward by counter-hegemonic social forces to develop a *Europe-wide social model* or an *enhanced* social model on a *European* basis. Hence, the chapter advances five main arguments. First, that any attempt to redirect the European project towards positive integration had to overcome the EC/EU reification of market liberalism, bias towards negative integration, choice of social regulation and preference for competition and economic liberalization. Such a transformation required the reform of the EC/EU treaties by all member states. Second, and following from the first argument, that the unanimity needed to revise the EC/EU treaties required the simultaneous election of left-wing governments in all member states. This problem was compounded by the existence of different electoral cycles in each country. Third, that in the absence of such a transformation, the ideological and material resources for constructing an enhanced social model on a European basis were lacking; in short, there was no European polity and the EC/EU budget was too small. Fourth, that when the opportunity to initiate such a transformation arose, in the 1990s when most member states were governed by the left, social democratic governments were successfully outflanked by a right-wing alliance that sought to defend the neo-liberal trajectory of the EU. Fifth, that because of the aforementioned hurdles, the chances of progressive social forces successfully constructing an enhanced social model on a European basis *using the present-day EU as a vehicle* are poor.

Part III of the book, *The neoliberalization of EU policy*, addresses the contemporary situation in relation to economic policy, fiscal federalism, the operation of the ESM and labour market flexibility. Hence, Chapter 8, *Operation of economic policy*, explores how a crucial idea introduced by Keynes into the corpus of economic thought is that the level of output and employment under market capitalism depends upon interaction between total spending and the economy's capacity to produce. Decisions to produce are made primarily by private profit-making firms; production, the source of employment, takes place only if companies anticipate a market in which goods and services can be sold at a profit. If demand is insufficient, productive capacity will stand idle and people will be without jobs. There is no automatic mechanism, which guarantees that output and spending decisions always coincide. Imbalances between aggregate demand and aggregate supply require active government policy to change either its own or private expenditure through budgetary or monetary instruments. The neoclassical assumption of an automatic tendency towards market clearing is replaced by the necessity for active government intervention in the economy to secure simultaneous internal and external balance in the economy. Thus the chapter highlights the incompatibility between the monetarist model, upon which EMU is constructed and the possibility of creating an alternative economic strategy (AES) grounded in Post-Keynesian tradition. Despite the inability of theorists to develop a universal Post-Keynesian theoretical model, due in large part to the complexity and dynamic nature of modern economies, it is nevertheless possible to identify a number of important themes that denote the essence of Post-Keynesian/traditional democratic-socialist thought.

Chapter 9, *Fiscal federalism: a missed opportunity or an emerging consensus?*, examines this notion, whereby the pace of European integration accelerated considerably during the past decade, stimulated by the agreement to form the SM and enhanced by the process of forming an EMU amongst EU member states. However, whilst the nature of this community of nations significantly changed over this period, many aspects of the EU financial and administrative apparatus failed to evolve to meet these challenges. Whilst detailed consideration has been given to whether individual member states will meet the Maastricht Convergence Criteria (MCC) for membership of the EMU, the inadequacies of the EU's budgetary arrangements have received far less attention. Nevertheless, the advent of EMU would necessitate a fundamental review of fiscal policy within the EU. The present crisis talks, arising from the Greek fiscal crisis and destabilization of the eurozone, have meant tentative moves in this general direction, but a final consensus on these issues remains elusive and further work would appear necessary. Hence, this chapter seeks to complement and extend the existing literature which discusses the evolution of fiscal policy within the context of EMU, and examines the potential for fiscal federalism to negate certain design flaws within EMU economic architecture, whilst providing a degree of stabilization for a diverse eurozone economy.

Chapter 10, *European social policy: constructing a European Social Model and defending the European model of society?* provides an overview of the development of European social policy during the CWO and NWO periods and, in so doing, it challenges the claim put forward that European social policy aimed to construct an ESM so as to defend the European model of society. The chapter advances four main arguments. First, that the European social policy agenda was consistently subjugated to the economic imperatives of competitiveness and economic liberalization and was not valued in its own right. Second, that the reification of market liberalism, the bias towards negative integration, the choice of social regulation and the EEC/EC/EU-level preferences for competition and economic liberalization – conspired to preclude the creation of a common, Europe-wide social model and/or a unified EEC/EC/EU-level welfare state. Third, that during the CWO the EEC/EC influenced the nature and trajectory of Western Europe welfare states in a structural rather than direct sense. Fourth, that in the NWO the EC/EU aimed to influence the development of these entities in a direct as well as structural sense. Consequently, the chapter is divided into three main sections. The first section explores Europe's preference for soft rather than hard law in terms of European social policy development. The second section assesses the development of European social policy during the CWO. The third section evaluates the development of European social policy in the NWO.

Chapter 11, *Social partnership and labour market flexibility* is the final chapter in this section; one of the central tenets of the ESM involves the creation of social partnership between employer and employee representatives in order to develop positive-sum solutions to issues pertaining to industrial relations. Social partnership between peak level actors is, additionally, intended to develop a wider legitimacy for the EU's decision-making process, and tailor directives to meet the requirements of those most closely affected by work-related relations. However, this model of inclusivity is contrasted against another stated aim advanced by the EU in the years since the production of the Lisbon Treaty, namely the promotion of a more flexible labour market. It is, therefore, this potential contradiction that this chapter examines.

The fourth part of the book completes the chorological progression of our analysis of the ESM by addressing the question of *What future for a Social Europe?* through three chapters relating to enlargement and the possibility of developing nation-based options. The section begins with Chapter 12 *Neoliberalization and enlargement: incompatible goals?*; a significant transformation has taken place in Europe since the late 1980s when the EU was still emerging from its internal difficulties of Eurosclerosis and the 'iron curtain' was firmly in place across the continent. However, with the EU pursuing the single internal market programme and monetary union, the collapse of Communism triggered both an economic and political transformation that swept across Central and Eastern European countries (CEECs) and ultimately led to the clamour for EU membership. Consequently, together with the four potential candidate countries (PCCs), EU membership is likely to extend towards 40 member states by the mid-2020s. Hence, the trajectory is clear in terms of the most recent and likely future enlargements encompassing countries with characteristics significantly more divergent than previous accessions as they are now extending beyond established western European mixed economies. Consequently, the key issue becomes whether this central tenet to European integration of 'widening' is compatible with that of 'deepening' in relation to EMU, which encapsulates the quintessence of EU neoliberalization. Hence, the initial part of the chapter reviews the major challenges raised by accession in terms the main economic conditions of the Copenhagen and MCC criteria, followed by the route towards membership and macroeconomic policy reforms, which are necessary to meet the Copenhagen Criteria and to endorse the aim of EMU. Second, the chapter reviews the current position of the accession countries (ACs) that are outside the eurozone, together with the candidate countries (CCs) and potential accession countries (PACs), against the stipulated convergence criteria for EMU membership. Finally, the major part of the chapter examines the potential problems and prospects for the recent enlargement countries in achieving eurozone membership. These relate to the initially over-optimistic timetable envisaged, the necessity of addressing structural weaknesses, the frequently problematic definition of fiscal measures, conformity to ERM II, the interaction between inflation and exchange rates, together with adherence to the notions of Optimum Currency Area (OCA) criteria. Hence this chapter seeks to explore whether enlargement possesses a heightened dilemma for the EU in terms of whether the push to broaden its membership is wholly compatible with its current neo-liberal philosophy.

Chapter 13, *Social Europe and enlargement: threat or opportunity?*, continues this general theme in relation to how the enlargement process has created a larger and more diverse European SM, and this has potentially far-reaching consequences, not only for individual member states (both established and newer entrants), but also for the sustainable development of a Social Europe as a whole. For example, has enlargement effectively ended the conception of creating a single, homogenous European labour market, complete with identical labour regulation and social protection, or will the NMS rapidly converge towards this norm? If not, then are existing differences in social provision and labour protection an example of unacceptable 'social dumping', whereby states seek to gain a cost advantage within a SM by beggar-thy-neighbour competition for the lowest value placed on workers and citizens, or is it a natural reflection of states at different levels of economic development needing to maintain international competitiveness through a lower wage economy? These are fundamental questions which need to be satisfactorily answered before the future development of the ESM can be accurately predicted.

In contrast, to the previous two chapters focusing upon the potential clash between the EU's neoliberalization and enlargement, Chapter 14 *National economic policy alternatives* is concerned with the potential for such alternatives, whereby participation in further EU integration will place an additional straightjacket upon sovereign macroeconomic policy and increase the difficulty of pursuing those policies optimal to its own national interest. For example, the model for the EMU seeks to impose a particular institutional framework that restricts the flexibility of action of individual countries in order to enable economic policy to be determined, or at least co-ordinated, from the centre. In contrast, greater autonomy for individual nation-states, under the principle of subsidiarity, might provide a more stable economic environment in which to pursue further co-operation between countries. However, largely due to the political desire to tie members more closely together, the EU is seeking to progressively replace economic autonomy for a nation-state by the requirement to co-ordinate its economic strategy with the EU norm, or else be subject to sanctions levied by the EU Commission. Hence, to illustrate the broad range of different policies that could be enacted, this chapter outlines a number of broad alternative economic strategies that could be pursued, once a nation is freed from the restrictive grip of the ECB and the requirements of the TEU, let alone any future developments. Additionally, it discusses the development of complementary industrial strategy and exchange rate policy. The former can only prove effective if supplemented by fiscal and monetary policies that target growth and reject deflation. For example, inflation is not a disease in itself, but the symptom of an economy that cannot produce enough to satisfy domestic demand. The solution is to boost demand and channel it to domestic industry, improving profits, stimulating production and hence productivity, and providing the incentive to invest; thereby cutting unit costs and inflation through a considered policy of economic expansion. It can be achieved, free from EU constraints, through control of the exchange rate and the accompanying interest rate changes. Such a policy makes it profitable to produce domestically, by utilizing the price mechanism to boost exports, encourage import substitution and lure British industry back into sectors it has abandoned. A tax on imports would provide crucial support. An effective exchange rate policy is critical to the successful implementation of the outlined options for macroeconomic policy. The intention is to demonstrate, not only that national economic management is still feasible, but also that it is preferable to transferring the main levers of macroeconomic policy into the hands of the EU, which is incapable of using them consistently in the best interests of all member states simultaneously.

Finally, the book concludes with Chapter 15, *From rescue and stimulus to the age of austerity: the European response to the great recession and the prospects for Social Europe*, which locates the issue of the ESM within the context of the recent 2008 credit crunch recession through reviewing the responses of the EU and its member states. The chapter advances four main arguments. First, that the response of the EU and its member states during the first phase of the economic crisis – the coordinated and Keynesian rescue and stimulus packages – was a temporary one to rescue capitalism; it did not signal a fundamental shift in the nature and trajectory of the EU or its member states. Second, that the response during the second phase of the economic crisis – the adoption of austerity measures – consolidated the neo-liberal nature and trajectory of the EU and accelerated the transformation of Europe's social models towards the market liberal form. Third, that the medium-term plans devised by the EU in the wake of the economic crisis – to expand its power over member states' economic policy-making – amounted to a power grab. Fourth, and following from the second and third arguments, that the prospects for Social Europe in the so-called age of austerity are grim. While progressive social forces such as the far left and the greens favour the construction of radical alternatives to the EU, and while social democratic parties favour the reform of the EU, the balance of power lies with the international financial nexus, and capital more generally, which demand the dismantling of social protection systems.

Part I

From liberal to neo-liberal Europe

2 Liberal Europe during the Cold War Order (1947–1982)

From the European Recovery Program to the socialist challenge

Introduction

This chapter presents a brief chronological overview of the European integration process during the CWO – more specifically from 1947 until 1982. The chapter advances six main arguments. First, that the nature and trajectory of the European project during the CWO resulted, in part, from the contest between anti- and pro-European forces and conservative, liberal and socialist forces within EEC/EC member states, and between and intergovernmental and supranationalist forces and conservative, liberal and socialist forces at the EEC/EC level and beyond. Second, that the liberal and supranationalist forces were, generally speaking, the dominant ones in this struggle. Third, and following from the second argument, that the European project evolved as a *liberal entity* during this period. Fourth, that the founding treaties of the EEC ensured the pre-eminence of market liberalism and thus negative, rather than positive, integration. Fifth, and following from the fourth argument, that the EEC/EC prioritized economic liberalization rather than social policy and, in so doing, precluded the creation of a common, Europe-wide social model and/or a unified EEC/EC-level welfare state. Sixth, and following from the fifth argument about the limited nature of social policy action at the EEC/EC level, that the European project influenced the development of Western Europe's welfare states in a structural rather than direct sense.

The chapter is divided into eight main sections. The first section reviews some of the early ideas and practical attempts at European integration, while the sections that follow survey the main phases of the European integration process during the CWO. These include the laying of Europe's foundations (1952–1957), the intergovernmental challenge (1959–1966), completion, deepening and enlargement (1969–1979) and the socialist challenge (1981–1982).

Pre-war European integration

The idea and practice of European integration predates the present-day EU. Ideas include Friedrich List's customs union (dating from 1841), Leon Trotsky's United Socialist States of Europe (1915), Friedrich Naumann's European confederation (1917), Richard Coudenhove-Kalergi's Pan-European Union (1923) and Aristide Briand's European federal union (1929). Practical attempts include the creation of a European common market through a network of tariff-reducing treaties between 1860 and 1892, the Latin Monetary Union of 1865–1925 and the Scandinavian monetary union of 1873–1924. The critical point is that most of these ideas and practical attempts were *intergovernmental* in nature. By contrast, the present-day EU is based on four sources of inspiration that are *supranational* in character. First, the 1919 plan devised by the then French minister, Louis Loucheur, to integrate the coal and steel industries of France and Germany under a supranational higher authority. Second, the 1931 design of the then British civil servant, Arthur Salter, for a United States of Europe with a secretariat, council of ministers, assembly and court. Third, the 1941 federalist Ventotene Manifesto produced by the Italian socialists, Ernesto Rossi and Altiero Spinelli, and fourth, the 1942 Nazi scheme for some form of economic community in Europe.

Liberal Europe

During the CWO, the countries of Western Europe evolved as *liberal* entities. That is to say, as a result of the 'regime change' which followed the Great Depression and the protectionist interregnum of the 1930s (Forsyth and Noter-mans, 1997; Gillingham, 2003), the countries of Western Europe rejoined the liberal road they had embarked upon in the late eighteenth century (Henderson, 1998) and proceeded to *embed* (Polanyi, 1957) the liberal economic and political order which characterized the CWO (Ruggie, 1982). Economically, these entities embraced modern rather than classical liberal ideas and they sought a partic-ular mix of market and state with an emphasis on the former. Politically, these entities were dominated by conservative, liberal and social democratic parties which favoured Keynesianism and the welfare state. The European project also developed as a liberal entity. Economically, it was committed to an open trading system. Politically, the institutional and treaty architecture that was created reflected and reinforced this preference.

The first attempt to launch Europe: the European Recovery Program (1948)

One of the principal architects of the European project in the 1940s and 1950s was the then director of the French planning commission, Jean Monnet, who, by working behind the scenes, put some of these ideas into practice. Monnet's pre-ferred strategy for European integration, which later became known as the Monnet method or Community method, was based upon two principles: safe-guarding the political autonomy of the supranational European Commission and encouraging the process of 'spill-over'.[1] Following two failed attempts to insti-tutionalize the Monnet method in 1948 and 1949, the European project was launched on the third attempt in 1951.

Western Europe's response to the European Recovery Program (ERP), or Marshall Plan, was the formation of the Committee for European Economic Co-operation by 16 countries in July 1947. Chaired by the then British civil servant, Oliver Franks, with Monnet as vice-chair, the Committee for European Economic Co-operation requested $19 billion in aid from the United States. To administer the aid, the Organization for European Economic Co-operation (OEEC) was established in April 1948 with Paul-Henri Spaak, the then Belgian prime minister, as director. In the debate over the structure of the OEEC, the French advocated the fashioning of a supranational executive with a permanent secretariat. Britain and several other member states opposed this, however, leaving the OEEC controlled by the intergovernmental Council of Ministers. The first attempt to institutionalize the Monnet method had failed.

The second attempt: the Council of Europe (1949)

The Congress of Europe, held in May 1948, recommended the organization of a Council of Europe to devise a strategy for the integration of Western Europe. Its Message to Europeans advocated 'a united Europe, throughout whose area the free movement of persons, ideas and goods is restored' (cited in Bainbridge, 2002: 84). Division between supporters of intergovernmentalism and supranationalism, however, was settled decisively in favour of the former; the Council of Europe was set up on an intergovernmental basis in May 1949. The second attempt to institutionalize the Monnet method had failed.

The third attempt: the European Coal and Steel Community (1951)

Reflecting upon his failures, Monnet (1978: 273–4) lamented that neither the OEEC nor the Council of Europe could 'ever give concrete expression to European unity' and that a 'start would have to be made by doing something more practical and more ambitious'. Opposition to the International Ruhr Authority, and the concomitant pressure on the French to devise an alternative solution to the 'German problem' (i.e. rearmament) presented Monnet with the ideal opportunity. Monnet prepared a memorandum for the then French foreign minister, Robert Schuman, recommending the integration of the French and German coal and steel industries under supranational control. Schuman adopted the idea, seeing it as a potential lock on Germany's war machine and as a means of reconstructing the French economy.

The Schuman Plan of May 1950 proposed that the 'Franco-German production of coal and steel be placed under a common High Authority, within the framework of an organization open to the participation of the other countries of Europe'. Such an arrangement would 'provide for the setting up of common foundations for economic development, as a first step in the federation of Europe' (cited in Booker and North, 2003: 50). The French made the acceptance in principle of a High Authority a condition of participating in the negotiations, which was unacceptable to the British. Nevertheless, Belgium, France, Italy, Luxembourg, the Netherlands and West Germany – hereafter known as the Six – signed the Paris Treaty in April 1951 establishing the European Coal and Steel Community (ECSC) with its High Authority, Council of Ministers, Common Assembly and Court of Justice. As the first High Authority president, Monnet told delegates at the inaugural session of the Common Assembly that they were taking part in 'the first government of Europe' (ibid.: 57).

Phase 1 of European integration: the laying of Europe's foundations (1952–1957)

During the first phase of the European integration process, the constitutional, institutional and policy foundations upon which Europe was built were established and these decisively shaped the nature and trajectory of the European project. In response to the demands for German rearmament and working closely with the then French prime minister, René Pleven, Monnet advocated a European Defence Community (EDC) to complement the ECSC. The negotiations that followed the publication of the Pleven Plan in October 1950 culminated in the Six signing the EDC Treaty in May 1952. During these negotiations, Spaak recommended forming a European Political Community to incorporate the ECSC and EDC. The proposal was accepted and the subsequent draft treaty pledged to establish 'a European Community of a supranational character' (cited in Bainbridge, 2002: 259). The Six formally adopted the draft treaty in March 1953. The following year, however, the French National Assembly voted against the EDC and European Political Community proposals on the basis that they threatened national sovereignty. Monnet revised his tactics and prepared another memorandum for Spaak, this time advocating the integration of Western Europe's energy and transport sectors.

The Six, plus Britain, gathered at the Messina Conference in June 1955 to discuss the Spaak proposal and the Dutch plan for a West European Common Market. Conference delegates agreed to establish a committee, with Spaak as chair, to consider these proposals in more detail. The subsequent Spaak Committee report, published in May 1956, recommended the creation of a West European Common Market, co-operation in the areas of energy, telecommunications and transport, plus an ECSC-type institutional structure. There were significant divisions within the Six about these proposals, and British opposition to the whole enterprise. Concerted lobbying by Monnet, however, plus several interventions by the United States, enabled Spaak to outmanoeuvre the British. The Spaak Committee report formed the basis of the protracted intergovernmental negotiations that culminated in the March 1957 Treaties of Rome which established the European Atomic Energy Community and the EEC. The Six ratified the Treaties of Rome in their national assemblies, while in the preamble to the treaties, member states pledged to 'lay the foundations of an ever-closer union among the peoples of Europe' (ibid.: 84). The Treaties of Rome created the European Commission, Council of Ministers and European Court of Justice (ECJ), plus an assembly composed of delegates from national parliaments.

Importantly, the Treaties of Rome explicitly committed member states to the free movement of persons, goods, services and capital – the so-called four freedoms – and thus determined the *nature* of the European integration process by privileging a particular socio-economic model: market liberalism. For Moravcsik (1998), the 'liberal framework document' that was the EEC Treaty was liberal in the sense that it aimed to create a customs union, prioritized competition and forbade any state intervention which distorted investment and trade. More specifically, of the 248 clauses in the EEC Treaty, 112 were concerned with institutions and administrative and financial rules. Of the remaining clauses, 73 were concerned with the four freedoms: 29 related to the free movement of goods, 26 related to the free movement of persons, capital and services, and 18 related to the elimination of distortion to competition. By contrast, only 55 clauses were concerned with state intervention: 14 related to common economic policies, 12 related to social policy, 11 related to transport, ten related to agriculture, six related to overseas territories and two related to the European Investment Bank (EIB) (Lewis, 1971). Put simply, and as Gillingham (2003: 61) noted, 'policies for market freedom ... predominated over those for planning and control'.

The Treaties of Rome also shaped the *trajectory* of the European integration process. Focusing upon international economic integration, Tinbergen (1954) contrasted *negative* and *positive* integration. Negative integration involved the dismantling of barriers: an internal market abolished tariff and non-tariff barriers to trade, a customs union rejected member states' right to impose independent external tariffs, a common market negated the power of member states to impose limits on the movement of capital and labour, and monetary union denied member states the right to independent exchange rate and monetary policies. Positive integration, on the other hand, could result in new institutions for centralized and coordinated policy-making. Focusing upon the European dimension and drawing upon the work of Hayek (1948) and Pelkmans (1980), Gillingham (2003: xiii) argued that the liberal bias in the founding treaties encouraged negative integration, which 'takes place either through markets or institutions created to make markets operate properly', rather than positive integration, 'the organization of Europe by means of bureaucracy or regulation in order to compensate for market failure'. With the exception of the CAP and in the absence of a significant federal budget,[2] EEC/EC attempts at positive integration – in the areas of industrial policy, regional policy and social policy – were relatively underdeveloped. Indeed, as Holland (1993: 14) noted,

> The difference between them is not just a matter of political will. It reflects something fundamental about the political dynamics of negative and positive integration. However hard in itself, it is easier to agree to remove barriers to capital or labour flows or trade than to devise and agree an agenda for economic and social cohesion.

Comparing the progress made in terms of economic liberalization (i.e. negative integration) with the relative lack of social policy action (i.e. positive integration) at the EEC/EC level during the CWO illustrates the point. Driven by the imperatives of the General Agreement on Tariffs and Trade (GATT), the competition policy established by the EEC Treaty and the judicial activism of the ECJ,[3] economic liberalization progressed through two main stages. The first stage, starting in 1958, involved the elimination of customs duties and quantitative restrictions and was completed in 1968 with the introduction of the common external tariff. The second stage, between 1973 and 1986, witnessed successive EC enlargements and thus the expansion of the Common Market. By contrast, European social policy was relatively underdeveloped. Although the EEC Treaty included a section on social policy which contained an explicit commitment to social policy harmonization, and although the Council of Ministers agreed a Social Action Programme in January 1974, 'no clear consensus existed about the need for social intervention, the form it might take and the instruments that might be used for delivery' (Hantrais, 2007: 237). Furthermore, given that European social policy was subjugated to the competitiveness and economic liberalization agenda, action was limited to encouraging co-operation in matters relating to the labour market and labour mobility, establishing the principle of equal pay and operationalizing the European Social Fund. The priority accorded to the removal of barriers to competition, however, meant that the EEC/EC did not see fit to 'interfere with redistributive benefits' which remained 'a matter for individual states' (Collins, 1975: 9).

Majone (1993: 156) identified the *objective* of the negative integration trend in terms of social policy:

> Measures proposed ... in the social field must be compatible with the 'economic constitution' of the Community, that is, with the principles of a liberal economic order. This requirement creates an ideological climate quite unlike that which made possible the development of the welfare state in the member states.... The economic liberalism that pervades the Founding Treaty and its subsequent revisions gives priority to the allocation function of public policy over distributional objectives. Hence the best rationale for social initiatives at Community level is one which stresses the efficiency-improving aspects of the proposed measures.

Social regulation – which aimed to change the behaviour of companies, governments and other social actors, to construct and maintain new markets, and to develop regulatory frameworks (i.e. consumer protection, environmental standards, health and safety, etc.) to guide those markets – rather than traditional social policy thus became the preferred method of countering the power of the market at the EEC/EC level (Majone, 1996).

Sbragia (2000: 223–4) identified the *means* by which the negative integration trend was sustained:

> Governance within the European Union ... takes place within an institutionalized policy framework which structurally privileges certain policy content

or at least policy norms [and competition and the liberalization of the market, rather than its restriction, are the privileged positions]. The fact that the Union is based on treaties – which are about policy choices – rather than a constitution is fundamental to understanding why the Union can steer in areas where national governments find it difficult.... [The treaty approach] allows the executives of national governments to privilege [competition and] economic liberalization in Brussels as opposed to their own national capitals (where networks of all types may view such norms as antithetical to their own interests).

These structural forces – the reification of market liberalism, the bias towards negative integration, the choice of social regulation and the EEC/EC-level preference for competition and economic liberalization – conspired to preclude the creation of a common, Europe-wide social model and/or a unified EEC/EC-level welfare state. Furthermore, although the EEC/EC did not *directly* attempt to determine the *nature* of Western Europe's welfare states via its social policy, these structural forces *indirectly* influenced the *trajectory* of these formations in the sense that, over time, they both shaped and constrained their development.

Phase 2: the intergovernmental challenge (1959–1966)

During the second phase of the European integration process, intergovernmental forces led by Britain and France challenged the nature and trajectory of the EEC. The first intergovernmental initiative led to the creation of the European Free Trade Association (EFTA). Britain had proposed a free trade area for industrial products at the 1955 Messina Conference, as both a response and an alternative to the supranational ambitions of the Six. Austria, Britain, Denmark, Norway, Portugal, Sweden and Switzerland – hereafter known as the Seven – ratified the Stockholm Convention establishing the EFTA in November 1959.

The second intergovernmental initiative followed the election of Charles de Gaulle as French president in December 1958. De Gaulle favoured shifting the balance of power within the EEC in an intergovernmental direction. The November 1961 plan produced by the then French minister, Christian Fouchet, advocated the formation of a union of states which would co-exist with the EEC and which would be independent of the United States. Many of its recommendations, however, were deemed unacceptable to other member states and the plan, rejected outright by the United States, was abandoned.

The third intergovernmental initiative involved the forging of closer links between France and Germany. In an attempt to both corral Germany and steer the European project, de Gaulle signed the Treaty of Friendship and Reconciliation in January 1963. The treaty established biannual Franco-German summits and joint ministerial councils, effectively institutionalizing the Franco-German axis widely considered to be the motor of European integration. The Versailles Declaration, which attempted to reinvigorate the partnership, was signed in June 2003.

The fourth intergovernmental initiative resulted in the formation of the Medium-term Economic Policy Committee (MTEPC) in April 1964. The Council of Ministers agreed to develop a common medium-term economic policy for the EEC and tasked the MTEPC with producing economic prospect studies and a common medium-term economic programme. In macroeconomic and practical terms, as Holland (1993: 15) noted,

> the committee achieved significant results when its members discovered that several of their economies had planned to export more to each other than others planned to import from them. In this regard, it became a forum for reconciling and balancing macroeconomic targets.

Importantly, the MTEPC was set up as an ad hoc panel composed of national representatives rather than an integral part of the European Commission, and as Holland (1980: 37) complained, it consequently 'became a mere talking shop for macroeconomic forecasting and for making statements of good intention in structural and regional policy'. It possessed significant potential however: 'If the MTEPC had been sustained as a powerhouse of both European Commission and national officials, it could in practice – thirty years ago – have become a de facto committee for cohesion.'

The fifth intergovernmental initiative resulted in the national veto within the EEC policy-making process. A further attempt by de Gaulle to curtail the supranational elements of the EEC led to the 'empty chair' crisis of July 1965 when France withdrew its representatives from the Council of Ministers and the Committee of Permanent Representatives over the planned introduction of majority voting. It was resolved by the Luxembourg Compromise of January 1966 which created a national veto within the Council of Ministers.

Phase 3: 'completion, deepening and enlargement' (1969–1979)

During the third phase of the European integration process, and following the intergovernmental challenge of the previous decade, liberal and supranationalist forces revived the European project. At the Hague Summit in December 1969, the then French president, Georges Pompidou, called for the 'completion, deepening and enlargement' of the EC. In terms of *completion*, in April 1970 member states agreed to finance the CAP by providing the EC with its 'own resources' (i.e. agricultural levies, customs duties and value added tax), while sanctioning some limited budgetary powers for the European Assembly.

In terms of *deepening*, in October 1970 member states adopted the recommendation of the Davignon Report to institute a system of European Political Co-operation (EPC), proceeding on an intergovernmental basis through biannual meetings of EC foreign ministers. The idea of coordinating decision-making was extended to other policy areas. The Hague Summit declared that EMU should be the long-term objective of the EC and a working group was established to consider its implementation.

The Werner Plan of October 1970 set out a seven-stage process for EMU based upon economic convergence and institutional reform. It stated that

> Economic and monetary union cannot be created without the establishment or adaptation of a number of Community agencies to which the powers now held by the national authorities will have to be transferred. These shifts of responsibility represent a process of fundamental political importance entailing the progressive development of political co-operation.
>
> (European Commission, 1970a: 9)

The report promised, however, that EMU would not lead to 'a new autarchic bloc within the international economy' (ibid.: 11) – a key US concern. The first step towards EMU was the creation of an exchange rate management system. Initial attempts to establish such a system were undermined by the instability caused by the 1973–1974 oil crises and the objective of EMU was postponed. The plan was revived in July 1978, however, when a new system of monetary coordination, the European Monetary System (EMS) with its Exchange Rate Mechanism (ERM), was agreed.

Building upon the success of the first, Pompidou convened another summit in October 1972 to consider the future direction of the EC. The Paris Summit pledged to transform the European Assembly of national delegates into a directly elected European Parliament by 1979. It also decided to hold regular summits of the heads of state and government, plus the European Commission president, henceforth known as European Councils.

In terms of *enlargement*, Pompidou agreed to the lifting of the French veto on British entry, opening the way for the first enlargement of the EC. The French referendum on the principle of enlargement in April 1972 produced a 61 per cent vote in favour. Referendums were subsequently held in three of the four applicant states, with the British preferring parliamentary ratification. The Irish referendum on entry in May produced an 83 per cent 'Yes' vote, the Norwegian referendum in September delivered a 53.5 per cent 'No' vote, while the Danish referendum in October resulted in a 63.5 per cent 'Yes' vote. Britain, Denmark and Ireland joined the EC in January 1973.

This period also witnessed the publication of two important reports. The Tindemans Report of January 1976 set out the steps deemed necessary to achieve a more integrated EC: the extension of EC competence, the introduction of the concept of subsidiarity[4] and the toleration of differential rates of integration. The MacDougall Report of April 1977 studied the health of member states' public finances and considered how an expanded EC budget could be utilized to ameliorate regional inequalities, through intra-EC redistribution.

Phase 4: the socialist challenge (1981–1982)

During the fourth phase of the European integration process, socialist forces, once again led by Britain and France, challenged the nature and trajectory of the EC. Exchange rate instability, global recession and declining international competitiveness all contributed to a state of malaise in West European politics in the 1970s. This contributed to the election of François Mitterrand as French president in May 1981 and the formation of the Socialist government in June. While in opposition, the French left had reasoned that, to facilitate a policy of reflation, it would have to consider devaluation and protectionist measures which were at odds with both the Treaties of Rome and ERM membership. In power, however, Mitterrand and the Socialist government pursued a *franc fort* policy of shadowing the deutschmark within the ERM. Their room for manoeuvre was thus severely curtailed and by March 1983 the so-called Mitterrand experiment had collapsed. Faced with the choice of pursuing its programme or maintaining its European policy, the French left opted for the latter (Halimi *et al.*, 1994).

From a broader perspective, the full implementation of the French left's programme and other socialist plans, such as the British left's radical strategy, may have precipitated conflict with the EC. One of the possible outcomes may have been the renegotiation of member states' terms of membership and a new intergovernmental direction for the European project. Indeed, this was anticipated by the Out of Crisis Project established in 1981, coordinated by the then Labour Member of Parliament, Stuart Holland, and sponsored by key members of the French government and many of Western Europe's left-wing economists, politicians and trade unionists.

Greenland, as part of Denmark, joined the EC in January 1973. Three years later, however, the country was granted home rule. A referendum in February 1982 produced a 74.9 per cent vote against continued membership and in July 1986 Greenland became the first country to leave the EC, thereby setting a precedent for any country to withdraw in the future.

Conclusion

European integration during the CWO was a dynamic and fractious, rather than linear and unproblematic, process which was shaped by a multitude of competing social forces in Europe, the United States and elsewhere. For most of this period, the EEC/EC was dominated by forces committed to economic liberalism and political supranationalism. It faced a number of challenges and internal crises however – notably the intergovernmental challenge in the 1960s and the socialist challenge in the 1980s. Nevertheless, the EEC/EC made significant progress towards its stated goal of 'ever-closer union'. Although member states surrendered much of their sovereignty, the EEC/EC did not develop into a US-type federation however. Kleinman (2002: 216) described the situation as one of 'incomplete federalism'. In common with the countries of Western Europe, the European project developed as a liberal (i.e. modern rather than classical liberal) entity during the CWO in the sense that it reflected and reinforced a particular mix of market and state. Much of the effort of the EEC/EC, however, was directed towards market-building rather than state-building.

While the EEC/EC was actively concerned with reshaping the economic sphere so as to integrate and liberalize the economies of Western Europe, its approach to the social sphere was somewhat different. Although the 1957 Treaties of Rome contained some fundamental social objectives and although the Council of Ministers agreed a Social Action Programme in 1974, European social policy was relatively underdeveloped when compared to European economic policy. EEC/EC reification of market liberalism, bias towards negative integration, choice of social regulation and preference for competition and economic liberalization – manifest in the founding treaties which determined the nature and trajectory of the European project – conspired to preclude the creation of a common, Europe-wide social model and/or a unified EEC/EC-level welfare state. Nevertheless, over time these structural forces shaped and constrained the development of Western Europe's welfare states.

3 The political economy of Western Europe's social models in the Cold War Order

Inevitable and convergent welfare states?

Introduction

This chapter explores the development of Western Europe's social models (i.e. welfare states) in the context of the CWO. The chapter draws upon the CPE tradition, which utilizes a comprehensive set of analytical and conceptual tools to identify a diverse range of explanatory factors which orthodox approaches tend to ignore. Put simply, it situates the development of Western Europe's welfare states within a specific 'historical structure' (Cox, 1996): the CWO. By attending to the nature of the *capitalist* system during this epoch, the *historical* specificities of this era and the *global* configuration of social forces during this period, it seeks to chart a new course for the study of these formations. The chapter does not advance a CPE-inspired conceptual and/or theoretical exposition of the development of Western Europe's welfare states within the context of European integration and the CWO, nor does it offer a comparative account of welfare state development in Western Europe, and nor does it endeavour to explore particular cases, as such work has been initiated elsewhere.[1] Instead, it seeks to identify the dominant actors and structures, often neglected by the existing literature, which both shaped and constrained these formations during the CWO.

The chapter advances four main arguments. First, that the nature and trajectory of Western Europe's welfare states were the product of the struggle between social forces at the national, European *and* global levels during the CWO. Second, that the deployment of US power in Western Europe was decisive in determining the outcome of this struggle. Third, that Western Europe's welfare states were *shaped by*, and, equally importantly, *constrained by*, the structure of the World Order during this period. Fourth, that the nature and trajectory of the European project, as an integral part of the World Order, precluded the creation of a common, Europe-wide social model and/or a unified EEC/EC-level welfare state.

The chapter is divided into five main sections. The first section discusses the different types of social models that developed in Western Europe during the CWO. The second section reviews the two main debates about the welfare state during this period: the inevitability of welfare state development and the existence of welfare state convergence towards high levels of social expenditure. In an attempt to enrich the existing literature, the third section assesses the potential contribution of the CPE tradition to understanding and explaining Western Europe's social models, while the fourth section seeks to show how the particular configuration of social forces during the CWO influenced the development of Western Europe's welfare states; utilizing declassified state planning documents and long-neglected studies, it discusses the broader historical and political context within which these formations developed. Having discussed the weaknesses of the existing literature, highlighted the potential contribution of the CPE tradition and identified the key events and processes that engender the CWO, the fifth section contributes to the aforementioned debates by investigating the impact of the structure of the World Order, and the role of the United States in constructing and maintaining this World Order, on Western Europe's welfare states. In short, this chapter presents a political economy of Western Europe's welfare states during the CWO.

West European Social Model(s)?

The debate about whether or not there is a single and distinctive ESM or whether in fact there are many different social models in Western Europe is, essentially, a debate about the existence and form of particular state–society complexes (ibid.), or put another way, varieties of capitalism (Albert, 1993; Hall and Soskice, 2001; Rhodes, 2005; *Comparative Social Research*, 2007; Hancké, 2008; Macartney, 2011). The dominant view in much of the existing literature is that it is *not* possible to identify a single and distinctive ESM; rather, there are a number of different West European Social Models in existence.

Utilizing three criteria, namely the extension of citizenship, the introduction of social insurance and the growth of social expenditure, Pierson (1991) argued that the welfare state emerged in the 1880s and expanded considerably in the post-1945 period (see Tables 3.1, 3.2, 3.3 and 3.4).

Titmuss (1974) distinguished between three main forms of welfare state: residual, industrial-achievement-performance and institutional-redistributive models. Esping-Andersen (1985, 1990, 1999) categorized three main regimes in advanced capitalist democracies: conservative, liberal and social democratic models. Therborn (1987) defined four main types: full employment-oriented, market-oriented, soft-compensatory and strong-interventionist models. Albert (1993) juxtaposed Atlantic (i.e. Anglo-American) capitalism and Rhenish (i.e. German) capitalism. Building upon these, plus the formulations of other scholars (Abrahamson, 1992; Bislev, 1992; Castles and Mitchell, 1993; Leibfried, 1993; Ebbinghaus, 1999; Ferrera and Rhodes, 2000), it is possible to construct a typology of social models.

Kleinman (2002) and Jessop (2003) identified four ideal-typical formations in Western Europe. The *conservative-corporatist* model, exemplified by France and West Germany, was based upon contributory social insurance schemes with little emphasis on redistribution. The *market liberal* model, exemplified by Britain and Ireland, was predicated on minimal, means-tested welfare benefits and the promotion of market forms of welfare such as private insurance and occupational pensions. The *Mediterranean* model, exemplified by Greece, Italy, Portugal and Spain, was characterized as fragmentary, if not rudimentary, with a small group of highly protected workers (i.e. insiders) benefiting from the relatively underdeveloped welfare state and a larger group of under-protected individuals (i.e. outsiders) excluded from it. The *social democratic* model, exemplified by Denmark, Finland, Norway and Sweden, had a preference for decommodification, solidarity and universalism and was underpinned by full employment. Importantly, variations existed because each country had a specific history, place in the global economy and form of state (Milward, 1994; Jessop, 2003; Korpi, 2003), plus different levels of public support for the welfare state (Svallfors, 1997; Svallfors and Taylor-Gooby, 1999; Gelissen, 2000; Kananen *et al.*, 2006; Giger, 2011) – or 'embedded preferences' (Brooks and Manza, 2007: 7) – all of which reflected a particular balance of social forces.

Western Europe's welfare states: inevitable and convergent?

There were two main debates about welfare states in advanced capitalist democracies during the CWO: one concerned the inevitability of welfare state development and the second questioned the existence of welfare state convergence towards high levels of social expenditure. These debates were synthesized into what Montanari (2001) termed the *old convergence* hypothesis:

Table 3.1 The extension of citizenship

Country	Universal male suffrage	Universal suffrage
Austria	1907	1919
Australia	1902*	1902*
Belgium	1894	1948
Canada	1920	1920
Denmark	1849*	1918
Finland	1907	1907
France	1848	1945
Germany	1871	1919
Ireland	1918	1923
Italy	1913	1946
Netherlands	1918	1922
New Zealand	1879*	1893*
Norway	1900	1915
Sweden	1909	1921
Switzerland	1848	1971
United Kingdom	1918	1928
United States	1860*	1920

Source: adapted from Pierson (1991: 110).

Note
* = With significant restrictions.

Table 3.2 The introduction of social insurance

Country	Industrial accident	Health	Pension	Unemployment	Family allowance
Austria	1887	1888	1927	1920	1921
Australia	1902	1945	1909	1945	1941
Belgium	1903	1894	1900	1920	1930
Canada	1930	1971	1927	1940	1944
Denmark	1898	1892	1891	1907	1952
Finland	1895	1963	1937	1917	1948
France	1898	1898	1895	1905	1932
Germany	1871	1883	1889	1927	1954
Ireland	1897	1911	1908	1911	1944
Italy	1898	1886	1898	1919	1936
Netherlands	1901	1929	1913	1916	1940
New Zealand	1900	1938	1898	1938	1926
Norway	1894	1909	1936	1906	1946
Sweden	1901	1891	1913	1934	1947
Switzerland	1881	1911	1946	1924	1952
United Kingdom	1897	1911	1908	1911	1945
United States	1930	–	1935	1935	–

Source: adapted from Pierson (1991: 108).

Table 3.3 The growth of social expenditure

Country	Social expenditure ≥3 per cent of gross domestic product (GDP)	Social expenditure ≥5 per cent of GDP
Austria	1926	1932
Australia	1922	1932
Belgium	1923	1933
Canada	1921	1931
Denmark	1908	1918
Finland	1926	1947
France	1921	1931
Germany	1900	1915
Ireland	1905	1920
Italy	1923	1940
Netherlands	1920	1934
New Zealand	1911	1920
Norway	1917	1926
Sweden	1905	1921
Switzerland	1900	1920
United Kingdom	1905	1920
United States	1920	1931

Source: adapted from Pierson (1991: 111).

Table 3.4 The growth of social expenditure, 1960–1975 (as a percentage of GDP)

Country	1960	1975
Canada	11.2	20.1
France	14.4	26.3
Italy	13.7	20.6
Japan	7.6	13.7
United Kingdom	12.4	19.6
United States	9.9	18.7
West Germany	17.1	27.8
Average	12.3	21.9

Source: adapted from Organization for Economic Cooperation and Development (1988: 10).

Firstly, that some measure such as social expenditure as a proportion of GDP captured the essence of a welfare state and that the relevant data were adequately consistent across countries. Secondly, that the prime or even sole cause of this was the level of economic development. Thirdly, and often implied rather than stated, that over time international levels of development will converge, leading to (and indeed logically entailing) convergent welfare states.

(Kleinman, 2002: 11)

The inevitability debate

Several theories were advanced to explain the development of the welfare state and each of these, to a greater or lesser extent, viewed welfare state expansion as inevitable. *Functional or structural* theories – such as the democracy thesis and nation-state building thesis (de Tocqueville, 2003 [1851]; Mill, 2005 [1859]; Polanyi, 1944; Marshall, 1950; Tufte, 1978), the logic of industrialism thesis (Pryor, 1969; Wilensky, 1975, 2002; Flora and Alber, 1981; Flora and Heidenheimer, 1981; Iversen and Cusack, 2000; Lindert, 2004a, 2004b) and the (Marxist) logic of capitalism thesis (O'Connor, 1973; Ginsberg, 1979; Gough, 1979; Offe, 1984; Lash and Urry, 1987) – looked to capitalism, democratization, modernization and/or economic growth to account for the emergence of the welfare state in the nineteenth century and its growth in the twentieth century. These theories sought to explain why all advanced capitalist countries adopted some kind of social security system. Accordingly, they were interested in explaining the general pattern of welfare state development rather than any differentiation. The *power resources* approach by contrast – exemplified by Moore (1966), Stephens (1979), Korpi (1983), Esping-Andersen (1985), Hicks (1999), Huber and Stephens (2001), and Korpi and Palme (2003) – sought to explain the differences within this trend and viewed welfare state development as the outcome of, and an arena for, conflict between classes, political parties and socio-economic groups. *Institutional or state-centric* models – such as those proposed by Skocpol and Amenta (1986), and Obinger *et al.* (2005) – stressed the importance of institutions, particularly the state, in shaping welfare regimes.

Several scholars challenged the notion that welfare state development was inevitable, which logically entailed uniformity across the industrialized world. Comparative studies by Titmuss (1974), Mishra (1977, 1990), Castles (1982), Esping-Andersen (1985, 1990, 1999), Flora (1986), Therborn (1987), Baldwin (1991), Abrahamson (1992), Bislev (1992), Ginsberg (1992), Castles and Mitchell (1993), Leibfried (1993), Ebbinghaus (1999), Ferrera and Rhodes (2000), Kleinman (2002) and Jessop (2003) highlighted the persistence of welfare state diversity, while Flora and Alber (1981) pointed out that, although there was indeed some diffusion of the welfare state model across the world, its exact form varied from place to place. Similarly, Mann (1996) conducted a comparative study of citizenship and welfare states across several countries and found that the extension of citizenship rights at the social level occurred in authoritarian–conservative regimes just as often as progressive–liberal democratic ones. In other words, social rights were sometimes granted before political rights. Mann concluded, therefore, that the development of the welfare state was not inevitable but was in fact contingent on a variety of factors.

The convergence debate

Wilensky (1975, 2002) found that social expenditure across advanced capitalist democracies had increased since the 1950s as part of a general trend towards *convergence*, while Lindert (2004a, 2004b) pointed to a similar pattern which had started in the eighteenth century. O'Connor (1988), on the other hand, questioned whether welfare state expansion entailed convergence towards high levels of social expenditure; presenting empirical data on social expenditure and social transfers in 17 countries between 1960 and 1980, O'Connor found minimal evidence of convergence. Furthermore, Tomka (2003) found evidence of *divergence* in some areas of social expenditure from the 1970s.

Surveying the existing literature and the empirical data, Kleinman (2002: 12) noted that 'most evidence to date suggests that economic integration, whether in federal states or through increased trade between independent nations, leads to some convergence in GDP and in living standards'. At the same time, however, he noted that 'there is considerable evidence that economic growth and increased economic integration are quite compatible with increased inequalities across individuals, households and geographical areas'. In short, although social expenditure generally increased over time, this did not necessarily mean that there was convergence in the levels of expenditure between countries or convergence within these countries in terms of its distribution (i.e. greater equality).

Although the existing literature generated a great deal of insight into the development of the welfare state, it suffered from a number of limitations. First, following the retreat from grand theory, and Marxism in particular, from the 1970s, it often neglected to situate the development of Western Europe's welfare states within the broader context of the capitalist system. Second, it often failed

to consider how the particular historical period of the CWO influenced these formations. Third, its focus upon the state and its tendency to describe, categorize
and compare national welfare regimes often precluded any assessment of the
role played by social forces beyond the state – such as civil society, elite power
groups, employers' associations, financial capital, trade unions, TNCs, etc. – in
the development of these formations. Fourth, it often omitted to evaluate the
impact of the US design for the post-war order, the Grand Area plan, on these
formations. In short, much of the existing literature generally neglected the political economy of Western Europe's welfare states and the specific historical
context within which they developed.

CPE

In the 1970s, following many decades of neglect, there was a renewed interest in
CPE as scholars attempted to overcome the limitations of orthodox theories of
European integration and international relations (Gill and Law, 1988; Hettne,
1995; Pistor, 1995; van Apeldoorn *et al.*, 2003; Burchill *et al.*, 2009; Weiner and
Diez, 2009). These deficiencies included state-centrism and the associated
assumption that states pursued the 'national interest' rather than particularistic
interests, the marginalization of economics, and the failure to locate European
integration and international relations within the broader context of the capitalist
system.

The CPE tradition, which can be traced back to the work of Marx (1977
[1859]) and Polanyi (1944), amongst others, includes dependency theory
(Gunder Frank, 1967; Cardoso, 1971), structural Marxism (Althusser, 1969,
1970; Poulantzas, 1973, 1975, 1978), the market-state model developed by
Strange (1970, 1988), the regulation school (Aglietta, 1976; Boyer, 1989; Jessop,
1990; Lipietz, 1992), Open Marxism (Holloway and Piciotto, 1978, 1980;
Bonefeld,1992, 1995; Burnham, 1994, 1995; Holloway, 1995), the world-
systems approach (Wallerstein, 1979; Hopkins and Wallerstein, 1996), the
Amsterdam school (van der Pijl, 1984, 1998; Holman, 1992; van Apeldoorn,
1998, 2000, 2001 2002; Overbeek, 1990, 2000, 2003), the York school (Cox,
1987, 1996; Bieler and Morton, 2001; Gill, 2001) and the class analysis of
Carchedi (2001).

Although there is great deal of debate within the CPE tradition, it arguably
provides a comprehensive and diachronic conceptual–theoretical framework for
understanding and explaining the social world. The utilization of analytical and
conceptual tools such as class, hegemony, ideology, social forces, state–society
complexes and world orders, for example, help to identify important explanatory
factors – such as the structural power of capitalism, the realities of class conflict,
the contingent and dialectical nature of social change, the role of social forces
beyond the state, the impact of world orders, etc. – which orthodox theories tend
to overlook. Moreover, the insights provided by the CPE tradition can also help
to overcome the aforementioned weaknesses of the existing literature on Western
Europe's welfare states.

Social forces in the CWO

Drawing upon the CPE tradition, more specifically the neo-Gramscian work of Cox (1987, 1996), the CWO can be conceptualized as a particular constellation of ideological, institutional and material forces, a 'historical structure', which shaped both collective and individual action. Importantly, this configuration of social forces was underpinned by a specific set of production relations and these social forces can be analysed at the global, European and national levels.

Social forces at the global level

With much of Asia and Europe in ruins, the United States emerged from the Second World War in a stronger position – economically, militarily and politically – than its allies and the Axis powers. Such a position enabled the United States to displace Britain as global hegemon and to implement its Grand Area plan; a 'world settlement' that would 'enable us to impose our own terms, amounting perhaps to a *Pax Americana*' (cited in Shoup and Minter, 1980: 164). The blueprint for post-war US hegemony was devised by state planners during the Second World War. The Council on Foreign Relations (CFR) – with the active support of the then US president, Franklin Roosevelt, the State Department and numerous CFR members in the Roosevelt Administration – conducted an extensive series of studies between 1939 and 1945, as part of the War and Peace Studies Project, into possible post-war world orders (Shoup and Minter, 1977). These reports recommended that the western hemisphere, centred upon the United States, should unite with another bloc as such an alliance would provide new sources of export markets and raw materials, thus obviating the need to radically reconstruct the US economy. In the early stages of its planning, the Grand Area was conceived as a non-German bloc including the western hemisphere, the Far East and the British Empire. With the Allied victory imminent, however, the concept was revised and extended into a global vision centred upon Germany, Japan and the United States. In the new conception, Western Europe and Japan were to be consumers of US goods and services. The South was to serve the needs of these industrial centres: Africa was to aid the reconstruction of Western Europe, Southeast Asia was to assist Western Europe and Japan, and the Americas and Middle East were to supply the United States.

The implementation of the Grand Area plan on a global level was achieved in three main ways. First, the United States displaced Britain as a 'great power' to a subordinate role by covert, diplomatic and economic means. Second, the United States led the process of constructing new international institutions, such as the GATT, the International Monetary Fund (IMF), the World Bank and the United Nations. These were designed to ensure 'the proper functioning of the world economy', while making the exercise of US power 'international in character so as to avoid conventional forms of imperialism' (CFR, 1941, 1942a). Third, the United States covertly and overtly intervened in over 70 countries that threatened the Grand Area plan (Chomsky and Zinn, 1972; Agee and Wolf,

1978, 1979; Barnes, 1981, 1982; Chomsky, 1985, 1992, 1994; Klare and Korn-bluh, 1988; Cumings, 1988, 2010; Kolko, 1988; George, 1991; McClintock, 1992; O' Brien, 1995; Blum, 2000, 2003).

The primary objectives of post-war US foreign policy, which underpinned the Grand Area plan, were access to strategic resources and the development and maintenance of an 'open door' policy in international investment and trade. In terms of access, state planners argued that it was

> Important to maintain in friendly hands areas which contain or protect sources of metals, oil and other national resources, which contain strategic objectives, or areas strategically located, which contain a substantial indus-trial potential, which possess manpower and organized military forces in important quantities.
>
> (Special Ad hoc Committee, 1947)

In terms of the 'open door' policy, state planners declared that the United States was opposed to 'barriers or onerous restrictions imposed by governments on the investment and withdrawal of foreign capital' (State Department, 1948b). Furthermore,

> American enterprises in other countries should be assured the same right of access to raw materials and markets and to the labour supply of the host country on the same terms as business enterprises operated therein by its citizens or by citizens of third countries.
>
> (State Department, 1949)

The United States insisted upon an 'open door' policy on the basis that US-based corporations could, in any competition, exploit their size and utilize a variety of economic mechanisms to outmatch their rivals and thus dominate foreign markets (Leffler, 1992).

The principal threats to US foreign policy objectives during the CWO were eco-nomic nationalism (i.e. independent economic and political development) and ultra-nationalism (i.e. de-linking from the international capitalist economy). The State Department, for example, referring specifically to Latin America, lamented that the 'philosophy of the New Nationalism … embraces policies designed to bring about a broader distribution of wealth and to raise the standard of living of the masses' (cited in Green, 1971: 175–6). The general problem was that

> Nationalist regimes are responsive to popular pressure for immediate improvements in the low living standards of the masses. This tendency con-flicts with the need to protect *our resources* and provide a climate conducive to private investment and, in the case of foreign capital, to repatriate a rea-sonable return.
>
> (National Security Council (NSC), 1954, emphasis added)

In short, such tendencies interfere with the unspoken 'Fifth Freedom' of the United States: the 'freedom to rob and to exploit' (Chomsky, 1985: 47). Furthermore, economic nationalism and ultra-nationalism were perceived as contagious, in the sense that successful experiments threatened to set an example to other countries – the so-called 'domino effect' (*Pentagon Papers*, 1971; Dower, 1972).

Critically, declassified state planning documents are replete with examples that clearly indicate that economic nationalism, rather than communism, was the main concern of the corporate and political elite in the United States and elsewhere. The State Department, for example, did not see 'communist activities as the root of the difficulties of Western Europe. [Rather] it believes that the present crisis results in large part from the disruptive effects of the war on the economic, political and social structure of Europe' (State Department, 1947). Reports on Africa, Asia, Latin America and the Middle East came to similar conclusions (Curtis, 1995). Likewise, a study of the political economy of US foreign policy in the early 1950s, sponsored by the National Planning Association and the Woodrow Wilson Foundation, observed that the primary threat to the capitalist system was the economic transformation of communist societies 'in ways which reduce their willingness and ability to complement the industrial economies of the West' (Elliott, 1955: 42).

One of the solutions to the problem of economic nationalism, recommended by Kennan and supported by successive US administrations, was the creation of 'national security states' (Chomsky and Herman, 1979; Hogan, 1998):

> Harsh government measures of repression [should cause the United States no qualms as long as the] results are on balance favourable to our purposes. In general, it is better to have a strong regime in power than a liberal government if it is indulgent and relaxed and penetrated by Communists.
>
> (Cited in LaFaber, 1984: 107)

Other solutions included covert and military operations, diplomacy and economic warfare. The pretext for such action was the fear of communism – real, imagined and/or manufactured – which could be used to justify domestic repression and foreign policy intervention against economically nationalist and ultra-nationalist regimes and social forces.

Social forces at the European level

At the European level, the CWO witnessed the division of Europe between the two superpowers, with Western Europe firmly within the US sphere of influence. The Soviet Union was initially supportive of European integration and some form of Europe-wide recovery programme. In a meeting in December 1941 with the then British foreign secretary, Anthony Eden, the then Soviet leader, Joseph Stalin, announced his support for an alliance of democratic states in Western Europe with a military force at its disposal. Stalin added that he had 'no objection if certain [unnamed] European states wished to federate' (Cabinet Office, 1941). The prospect of the US domination of Western Europe, however, denounced at the Paris Conference in June 1947, precipitated a major policy reversal. Communist parties in Western Europe henceforth adopted a position of opposition to the ERP and European integration. With the exception of the French, Italian and Spanish parties, which later adopted the more independent trajectory of Eurocommunism – seeking to transform the EEC/EC from within – most communist parties sustained their opposition throughout the Cold War. The United States, on the other hand, consistently supported the European project.

The implementation of the US Grand Area plan in Western Europe was achieved in three main ways. One way was through initiatives and programmes such as the ERP, Truman Doctrine aid, the formation of the North Atlantic Treaty Organization (NATO) and the stationing of US military forces in Western Europe. The Second World War and the Cold War division of Europe severely disrupted the trading systems between Britain and its colonies, Western Europe and its Eastern European hinterland, and the United States. This situation, compounded by the fact that the United States uniquely benefited from the war and was increasingly self-sufficient, precipitated a shortage of dollars in Western Europe known as the 'dollar gap'. In Western Europe, it threatened to lead to the

> deterioration of the European economy [which] would force European countries to resort to trade by government monopoly – not only for economic but for political ends. The United States would almost inevitably have to follow suit. The resulting system of state controls, at first relating to foreign trade, would soon have to be extended into the domestic economy to an extent that would endanger the survival of the American system of free enterprise.
>
> (Cited in Leffler, 1992: 162)

Furthermore, Acheson feared that a West European collapse 'would be a boon to Soviet expansion and disastrous for American interests' (cited in Newton, 1984: 394), while the 'dollar gap' might lead to 'Soviet domination of the potential power of Eurasia, whether achieved by armed aggression or by political and subversive means, which would be strategically and politically unacceptable to the United States' (NSC, 1948b). In the United States, the then under-secretary of state for economic affairs, Will Clayton, feared that 'the fully extended American war economy would suffer from overcapacity in peacetime unless export markets worth at least $14 billion a year could be secured' (Newton, 1984: 394).

The solution to the 'dollar gap' was the ERP, which granted $13 billion in aid to 17 West European countries between 1947 and 1951 (Hogan, 1987). The ERP was not a noble act of charity, however, but a means of securing several US objectives. First, the ERP boosted the fortunes of US-based corporations by increasing their exports to Western Europe; recipient countries were required to use the aid to purchase goods and services from US-based corporations. Second, the ERP prevented Western Europe from 'going communist'; as van de Pijl (1984: 149) noted, the ERP was directed 'against the national, self-contained reconstruction programmes pursued by most Western European states in the immediate post-war period. These programmes, in which local communist parties participated, were judged unsuited for maintaining capitalist rule in the long run'. Indeed, the then deputy administrator of the Economic Co-operation Administration, established to oversee the ERP, Paul Hoffman, told the US Senate Foreign Relations Committee in February 1950 that 'Europe would have been communistic if it had not been for the Marshall Plan' (cited in van der Pijl, 1984: 149). Third, the ERP reoriented Western Europe's economies by deterring economic nationalism and protectionism in favour of trade liberalization, thus providing the foundations for European integration. Fourth, the ERP promoted the development of an integrated West European bloc. Hoffman, in his appearance before the Senate Foreign Relations Committee, stated that

> we know that there is no possibility of Europe becoming the kind of economy that will make it a great factor of strength in the Atlantic community unless we break down the barriers between those 17 political subdivisions with which we are working ... so that you can have a single market, or something close to it, in which you can have large-scale manufacturing because you have a large market in which to sell.
>
> (Ibid.)

Hoffman also expressed US support for the European Payments Union:

> This Union is, in its initial stages, simply a clearing house for Europe's many currencies; however carried, as I believe it will be in time, to its logical conclusion, it will mean a central bank, with one currency, for all of Europe.
>
> (Ibid.: 653)

The implementation of the ERP, however, was far from straightforward; the US Congress was reluctant to fund the programme and it encountered widespread opposition in Western Europe. The NSC established the Central Intelligence Agency (CIA) in September 1947 to counter such hostility and to contribute to the wider project of US psychological warfare (McClintock, 1992; Simpson, 1994). The first major CIA assignment was to assist the ERP through economic, political and psychological operations, and, where necessary, paramilitary activity (Carew, 1987; Pisani, 1992).

The second way in which the United States implemented the Grand Area plan in Western Europe was by supporting the European project more generally. Lundestad (1998) identified five motivations to explain such support: promoting the US economic and political model, constructing an economically efficient Western Europe, reducing the US burden of global governance, opposing the Soviet Union and containing Germany. Two additional motivations can be identified: overcoming the 'dollar gap' and thwarting West European socialism.

The United States cultivated the European project in three main ways. First, the United States provided overt diplomatic support for European integration from the 1950s onwards (ibid.). Second, the United States organized pro-European covert operations; Aldrich (2001) claimed that, between 1949 and 1960, the United States channelled approximately $4 million into supporting federalist activities, while Peters (1996) revealed that the European Movement was one of the principal recipients, receiving substantial contributions from both government funds and private sources. Such operations were complemented by the secret funding of right-wing social democrats across Western Europe (Coleman, 1989; Stoner Saunders, 2000) and 'Operation Stay Behind': a network of extra-state armies set up under NATO command ostensibly to defend Western Europe from the Soviet Union – in reality to prevent the left from gaining power (Norton-Taylor, 1990; *Open Eye*, 1991; Ganser, 2005).

The third way in which the United States supported the European project was via the Bilderberg Group (Eringer, 1980; Thompson, 1980; Pilger, 2003; Estulin, 2009; Jeffers, 2009; Richardson *et al.*, 2011), which first met in May 1954 in response to the rising tide of anti-Americanism across Western Europe. In an interview on Belgian radio in June 2010, the former Belgian foreign minister and secretary general of NATO, Willy Claes, admitted that the Bilderberg Group had been created by NATO members in order to counter the Soviet Union and communism more generally (Zonnewind, 2010). With a membership composed of West European and North American elites – such as academics, bankers, industrialists, politicians and trade unionists – its aims were to provide a private forum for discussion and to ensure that the decisions that resulted from these deliberations were executed. Indeed, Claes revealed that each participant at the Bilderberg Group conference was 'given a report' and that they were expected 'to use this report in setting their policies in the environments in which they affect' (ibid.). As Skelton (2010) noted, 'this is revealing of the Bilderberg dynamic: the flowing of policy out from Bilderberg and into the world, from power towards political implementation'. In terms of the European project, the Bilderberg Group conference in May 1954 agreed to support the formation of a European free market and to establish committees in various West European countries 'to direct publicity in its favour' (Bilderberg, 1956). Furthermore, the then US under-secretary of state for political affairs, George McGhee, confirmed that 'the Treaties of Rome, which brought the Common Market into being, was nurtured at these meetings' (cited in Thompson, 1980: 170).

US support for the European project, however, was not unqualified; as Chomsky argued,

> The primary concern of the US, when it took over as global manager in the 1940s, was to ensure that Europe would follow the 'right course'. It favoured European integration because of the enormous advantages that it provides to US-based corporate power. On the other hand, it has always been wary of the threat that Europe might adopt an independent course, undermining US global domination – not by military force but in other ways.[2]

In short, the United States was opposed to the development of an independent Western Europe acting as a third force in the World Order. Indeed, the CFR issued a warning in September 1942 that a 'united Europe might develop as an autarkic entity with a nationalist economic policy characterized by a high tariff' (CFR, 1942b). Similarly, the State Department warned in June 1951 that 'Western Europe might emerge as a separate entity of great potential power not allied to us in a dependable fashion' (State Department, 1951). Such fears prompted the United States to encourage Britain to lead the European integration process, viewing its ally as a 'Trojan horse' for US interests in Europe. Britain 'should be applying its talents and resources to the leadership of Western Europe' because 'it would provide the balance in Europe that might tend to check the dangerous tendencies which French nationalism is already producing' (State Department, 1966).

As a consequence of their colonial possessions and imperial histories, the economies of many West European countries were highly internationalized in the eighteenth, nineteenth and early twentieth centuries. In other words, while some fractions of capital (e.g. national capital) produced for the home market, other fractions (e.g. European capital and global capital) were involved in European and/or global investment, production and trade (Bieler and Morton, 2001; Macartney, 2011). Following the protectionist interregnum of the 1930s and the destruction of the Second World War, the reconstruction of Western European economies in the late 1940s and early 1950s, facilitated by the ERP, proceeded along mainly national lines (Milward, 1984). The exceptions were Britain with its Commonwealth preference system and sterling area, and France with its French Union/French Community. The ERP, however, also encouraged the integration of Western European economies (see Table 3.5).

Importantly, the dual processes of national economic reconstruction and Western European economic integration, Milward argued, were reinforcing rather than mutually exclusive – hence his thesis that the European project rescued the nation-state (Milward, 1994). The formation of the EEC in 1957 reinforced the process of economic integration (see Table 3.6).

If these national and European processes constitute two of the dynamics within Western European economies, it is important to attend to the third: the

Table 3.5 Intra-Western European foreign trade as a percentage of national income, 1938–1951

Country	1938	1947	1951
Belgium	19.2	17.3	23.6
Denmark	21.7	11.5	22.5
France	4.3	2.5	5.3
Netherlands	14.5	12.8	28.3
Norway	14.9	15.0	18.8
Switzerland	10.5	11.2	14.1
United Kingdom	4.3	2.5	5.3

Sources: adapted from OEEC *Statistical Bulletin of Foreign Trade*; OEEC *International Financial Statistics*.

Atlantic dimension. Van der Pijl (1984: 40) noted that portfolio investment (i.e. assets, bonds and shares) in the United States in the late nineteenth century 'was largely financed by foreign funds, mainly from Britain, Germany and the Netherlands'. Following the ERP and formation of the EEC, however, US portfolio investment in Europe began to increase, from '$1.8 billion in 1957 to $5.4 billion in 1964', while US productive investment (i.e. manufacturing) in Western Europe increased from $2.1 billion in 1957 to $6.5 billion in 1964 and $12.2 billion in 1969 (ibid.). In terms of West European investment,

> a comparable movement towards the internationalization of productive capital to the US became visible only from 1968 onwards. It took until 1973 before Western European productive investment in the US reached the level of the hitherto predominant European direct investment in American bank, insurance and oil ventures.
>
> (Ibid.: 237)

In other words, national economic development in Western Europe occurred within the wider context of Atlantic as well as European economic integration.

Social forces at the national level

At the national level, the CWO was characterized by state-led industrialization and modernization. Although by no means uniform, given the different histories

Table 3.6 The regional structure of EC-12 trade, 1958–1990 (as percentage of total EC-12 trade)

Year	EC-12	EFTA	Total
Exports			
1958	37.2	12.2	49.4
1965	49.6	13.0	62.6
1970	53.4	11.7	65.1
1975	52.4	10.6	63.0
1980	56.1	11.2	67.3
1985	55.2	10.0	65.2
1990	61.2	10.4	71.6
Imports			
1958	35.2	9.3	44.5
1965	44.9	9.0	53.9
1970	50.3	8.7	59.0
1975	49.5	7.9	57.4
1980	49.3	8.6	57.9
1985	53.4	9.4	62.8
1990	59.0	9.6	68.6

Source: Eurostat.

of each country, Milward (1994: 27) argued that it was possible to 'characterize the Western European state of 1945–1973 in terms of a common model' which possessed a number of key features. First, public expenditure on agricultural incomes in an attempt to forestall rural support for authoritarianism, hence the CAP. Second, the incorporation of labour into the policy-making process, plus rhetorical commitments to full employment, in a conscious bid for political stability (Maier, 1987). Third, the expansion and extension of welfare policies – encompassing education, health, housing and social security – in order to boost economic growth and ensure the political allegiance of the masses. Fourth, the use of Keynesian macroeconomic policy tools – such as 'defence' expenditure or military Keynesianism (Kidron, 1970; Melman, 1970; Chomsky, 1994; Turgeon, 1996), fiscal policy, interest rate policy, government intervention in industry to modernize manufacturing and the associated 'neo-mercantilist effort of the post-war state to shift the patterns of comparative advantage in its own favour in selected manufacturing sectors' (Milward, 1994: 37), plus public expenditure (e.g. investment in research and development (R&D), and government procurement of goods and services) – which aimed to deliver high rates of economic growth. Similarly, Jessop (2003: 31) claimed that 'the ideal-typical post-war welfare regime in advanced capitalist economies' during this period was Keynesian, welfare-oriented, national and statist – a model he termed the 'Keynesian welfare national state' (KWNS).

The relative success of the 'common model' or KWNS model, engendering what has been called the 'golden age' of social democracy (Milward, 1994; Mills, 1998; Eichengreen and Iversen, 1999; Eichengreen 2007), bolstered the fortunes of productive capital and national productive capital in particular. Financial capital, meanwhile, was effectively constrained by the Bretton Woods system (BWS) of politically controlled capital markets and fixed exchange rates.

The United States and Europe

There was a darker side to this, in many ways progressive, era which the existing literature completely ignored; the third way in which the United States implemented the Grand Area plan in Europe was through a series of covert operations which targeted countries in which there was an actual or perceived threat of economic nationalism and/or ultra-nationalism. Hundreds of thousands of people were killed, tortured or harmed as a result of these interventions.

The United States and its allies attempted to destabilize Eastern Europe and the Soviet Union during the 1940s and 1950s (Dorril, 2000); inspired by the 1918 assault on Russia by Britain, France, Japan and the United States following the Russian Revolution, for example, plans were drawn up for the invasion of the Soviet Union. 'Operation Unthinkable', conceived in 1945, called for 'hundreds of thousands of British and American troops, supported by 100,000 rearmed German soldiers, to unleash a surprise attack' (Aldrich, 2001: 58).

The United States and its allies conspired to partition Germany into East and West in 1945 (Eisenberg, 1998). Meanwhile, by late 1945 the labour movement had begun to revive. Works councils ... and trade unions surfaced across the country [and] labour activists appeared determined to smash the power of the financial and industrial magnates and to institute some form of socialization and workers' participation in management.

(Eisenberg, 1983: 283–4)

The United States feared that

the radical character of this incipient German labour movement would jeopardize their plans for the restoration of capitalism. They also worried that left-wing labour organizations would eventually come under Soviet control, upsetting the 'balance of power' that policy-makers deemed vital to the peace.

(Ibid.: 284)

In short, the United States was opposed to the development of 'a unified, centralized, politicized labour movement committed to a far-reaching programme of social change' (ibid.: 300). Its response was to turn to

sympathetic right-wing socialists ... while using their control of ... food and other supplies to overcome the opposition of rank and file workers. It was finally necessary to 'wall off' the Western zone by partition, to veto the major trade union constitutions, to forcefully terminate social experiments, and to veto state legislation and co-determination efforts.

(Chomsky, 1992: 341)

These actions were part of a concerted campaign in which

the US government enlisted the assistance of anti-communist US trade unionists in a multifaceted effort to determine the leadership, programme and structure of German working class organizations. Initially focused only on the US zone, the campaign eventually encompassed all of Germany.

(Eisenberg, 1983: 284)

The United States also rejected a 1952 Soviet proposal for the reunification and neutralization of Germany. The plan contained 'no conditions on economic policies' and offered 'guarantees for basic freedoms including freedom of speech, press, religious persuasion, political conviction and assembly, plus freedom of activity for democratic parties and organizations' (ibid.). Critically, 'neither the text of the proposal, nor even the fact of its arrival, were disclosed by Washington until after the Western reply [rejecting it] had been sent' (Warburg, 1953: 188). US thinking was that such a plan might lead to a 'free, neutral, democratic and demilitarized Germany' which might be 'subverted into the Soviet orbit' (ibid.).

In France the United States pressured the main political parties to form a coalition government that excluded the communists; 'it was made clear and explicit that [Marshall Plan] aid was contingent on preventing an open political competition in which the left and labour might dominate' (Chomsky, 1992: 343). Communist ministers were duly expelled from the government in May 1947. Furthermore, 'the post-war destitution was exploited to undermine the French labour movement, along with direct violence. Desperately needed food supplies were withheld to coerce obedience, and gangsters were organized to provide goon squads and strike-breakers' (ibid.).

In Greece

> hundreds of thousands were killed, tortured, imprisoned or expelled in the course of a 'counter-insurgency' operation in 1947, organized and directed by the US, which restored traditional elites to power, including Nazi collaborators, and suppressed the peasant and worker-based Communist-led forces that had fought the Nazis.
>
> (Ibid.: 335)

The United States later supported the 'national security state' that was the 'regime of the colonels' (1967–1974). The United States also supported the fascist regimes in Portugal, until 1974, and in Spain, until 1978, to counter the economically nationalist threat posed by the left.

In Italy the United States used a 'combination of violence, manipulation of aid and other threats', plus a huge propaganda campaign, to determine 'the outcome of the critical 1948 general election' (ibid.: 344). Plans for a military invasion were also drawn up 'in the event that the Communists obtain domination of the Italian government by legal means' (NSC, 1948a). Covert intervention by the United States and its allies continued until the 1970s; declassified Foreign Office documents, for example, show that the United States, Britain and other NATO allies considered backing a right-wing coup in order to prevent the Italian Communist Party from coming to power in 1976 (Kington, 2008).

In the 1980s, during the so-called 'Second Cold War' (Halliday, 1983), the United States exploited Yugoslavia's indebtedness and, operating through the IMF, launched an economic war against the federation in an attempt to dismantle its 'market socialism' and reintegrate it into the global economy. This operation was part of a broader strategy against the Soviet bloc; the Ronald Reagan Administration issued several National Security Decision Directives in 1982 and 1983 which recommended a '"quiet revolution" to overthrow Communist governments and parties' while 'reintegrating the countries of Eastern Europe into the EC' (cited in Gervasi, 1992: 42; see also van der Pijl, 2006: 234).

Western Europe's welfare states in the CWO

In abstract terms and drawing upon the CPE tradition, van der Pijl (1984: xiv) argued that the CWO was marked by the hegemony of corporate liberalism:

> the liberal internationalist bourgeoisie associated with the development of an Atlantic circuit of financial capital at the turn of the [twentieth] century

[was challenged by] the bourgeoisie protecting industry in a national (or, at most, regional) context ... [thus] the state monopoly tendency [representing productive capital] was counter-posed in most West European nations to the liberal internationalist fraction.... The synthetic ruling class strategy which transcended and subsumed this antimony was corporate liberalism [which] denotes the synthesis between the original laissez-faire liberalism of the liberal internationalist fraction ... and the state intervention elicited by the requirements of large-scale industry and organized labour, which in the period between the [First and Second World Wars] accompanied various forms of class conciliation generally referred to as corporatism.

Mirroring the neo-Gramscian concept of an historical structure (Cox, 1996), with its hegemonic congruence of social forces, Ruggie (1982) described the post-1945 system as one of embedded liberalism, while Jessop (2003) labelled it Atlantic Fordism. Whichever term is used, Gill and Law (1988: 79–80) argued that, during this period, there was a ' "fusion" of interests, power and "legitimate social purpose" in the major capitalist states'. Furthermore,

This system gained widening degrees of acceptance, and came to embrace more and more countries, as the post-war period developed. In addition, as a result of the establishment of certain international institutions ... and the corresponding international regimes for money and trade ... the system was ... premised on the internationalization of authority in a non-state form. The class aspect of this settlement was that the material interests of both capital and labour appeared to be in some sort of balance, with the hegemonic ideology of the mixed economy legitimizing the new post-war Keynesian welfare states. The strategic framework for this was the US worldwide system of alliances, rationalized by a Cold War ideology and the US policy of the global containment of communism. The major political parties in the post-war Western consensus – the conservative, liberal and social democratic parties – all subscribed to the anti-communism which this strategic posture entailed. The settlement [thus] reflected a particular conjuncture and balance between ideological, institutional and material forces in post-war capitalism.

(Ibid.)

In more concrete terms, the post-1945 social democratic consensus witnessed labour movements 'settle for a situation in which they would regulate and tax capitalism but not challenge it in any fundamental way', while capital 'had to concede legitimacy to forms of government intervention that they had denounced as Bolshevism in the not-too-distant past' (Harrington, 1989: 105). Such a settlement was beneficial to both capital and labour. For the latter, the development of the welfare state helped to ameliorate the inequality and poverty associated with capitalism (Tanzi and Schuknecht, 2000; Moller *et al.*, 2003; Brady, 2005). For the former, and contrary to the arguments put forward by the right – that public expenditure is inherently unproductive (Hayek, 1944; Friedman, 1962) and serves only the 'crowd out' the more efficient private sector (Bacon and Eltis, 1976) – the evidence over a 200-year period demonstrated that the welfare state contributed to high and sustained economic growth (Middleton, 1996; Tanzi and Schuknecht, 2000; Lindert, 2004a, 2004b; Lightfoot, 2010) and thus boosted the profits of capital.

The historical structure of the CWO represented a specific configuration of social forces. Within this configuration, four sets of social forces were particularly important in terms of influencing the development of Western Europe's welfare states: the forces of capital, the forces of labour, the EEC/EC and the United States. The forces of capital – whether national, European and/or global capital – supported, to varying degrees, the development of Western Europe's welfare states. In Britain, for example, the Conservative and Liberal parties – representing different fractions of capital – campaigned in favour of universal education, high if not full employment, health reforms, more homes and a national insurance-based welfare system during the 1945 general election (Morgan, 1985), while the British Employers' Confederation acquiesced in the formation of the National Health Service and the welfare state by the 1945–1951 Labour government (Rogow and Shore, 1955; Middlemas, 1979, 1986; Turner, 1984; Cox, 1988; Sneddon, 1999).

Western Europe's welfare states were beneficial to capital in four interrelated ways. First, the creation of consumer demand for goods and services in Western Europe, and in Japan and the United States, helped to consolidate the revival of the capitalist system in the wake of the Great Depression and the Second World War. Second, the increasing demand for goods and services in Western Europe – as a result of rising levels of employment, increased social expenditure (i.e. welfare benefits) and higher wages – boosted the sales and profitability of national capital within Western European countries, Western Europe-wide capital and Western Europe-based global capital. The increase in government revenues as a result of higher levels of economic activity allowed the state to expand its welfare provision. This, in turn, boosted the purchasing power of the masses, producing even greater demand and additional government revenues in a virtuous cycle. Third, the increasing demand for goods and services in Western Europe assisted the main fractions of capital in the United States. The implementation of the ERP – followed by the creation of the Western European Common Market and the tariff-reducing efforts of GATT – opened up new markets for the export-oriented sector of the US economy which faced an over-production problem in the 1940s. Furthermore, the construction of the circuit of capital envisaged by the Grand Area plan, which involved securing capital's access to markets and raw materials, served the interests of US-based global capital and global capital based elsewhere. Fourth, increased social expenditure by the state, together with high if not full employment, improved the living standards of the masses and helped to prevent the spread of revolutionary ideas; in short, Western Europe's welfare states helped to counter the power of those social forces that threatened the capitalist system.

The forces of labour – composed of social democratic and socialist political parties, trade unions and other progressive social forces – had a major impact on the development of Western Europe's welfare states. As Stephens (1979), Korpi (1983), Esping-Andersen (1990) and Scarbrough (2000) empirically demonstrated, the relative strength of left-wing parties and trade unions was positively correlated with welfare state expansion.

The EEC, following its creation in 1957, played an increasingly significant role in the development of Western Europe's welfare states, in three main ways. First, the EEC/EC actively pursued the integration and liberalization of Western Europe's economies and thus transformed the foundations upon which Western Europe's welfare states were constructed. Put simply, while Western Europe's welfare states were national in orientation and were sustained by extensive state intervention, Western Europe's economies were increasingly subjected to EEC/EC treaties which aimed to curtail such intervention in favour of market forces. Second, although European social policy was relatively underdeveloped when compared to European economic policy – there was no attempt to create a single and distinctive ESM and no attempt to rescale welfare provision from the national to the EEC/EC level for example – the EEC/EC did issue a number of social policy regulations and directives. Although member state compliance varied, and although the way in which these measures were implemented differed, the attempts to establish social policy harmonization across the EEC/EC inevitably influenced the nature of Western Europe's welfare states – if only in a limited sense. Third, EEC/EC reification of market liberalism, bias towards negative integration, choice of social regulation and preference for competition and economic liberalization inevitably influenced the trajectory of Western Europe's welfare states in the sense that, over time, these structural forces both shaped and constrained their development.

The United States played a pivotal role in the development of Western Europe's welfare states, in four main ways. First, the United States encouraged the export of Fordism and Taylorism, which were key components of the social democratic consensus that provided the ideological and material 'space' within which Western Europe's welfare states could develop. Second, the pump-priming effects of US-sponsored programmes such as the ERP, together with the military Keynesianism associated with NATO and the stationing of US military forces in Western Europe, helped to increase consumer demand and government revenues in Western Europe. Third, US encouragement of European economic integration and trade liberalization increased economic activity within Western Europe, which further stimulated consumer demand and government revenues. Fourth, the construction and maintenance of the Grand Area plan encouraged international trade which, again, boosted consumer demand and government revenues. It also enabled private businesses and states in the North to access the raw materials which they needed and it created new markets for West European-based global capital, alongside US-based global capital. It is worth reiterating at this point that much of the existing literature on Western Europe's welfare states focused upon the national and/or European context of welfare state development and often neglected to consider the critical global dimension – more specifically the impact of the World Order and the role of the United States in constructing and sustaining this World Order.

Drawing upon the insights provided by the CPE tradition and locating Western European welfare state development within the broader economic and political context of the CWO, it is possible to argue that Western Europe's welfare states were *shaped* by the structure of the World Order. During the CWO, these formations were national in orientation and were constructed within an overarching framework of Atlantic Fordism/corporate liberalism/embedded liberalism.

It is possible to identify six *endogenous* factors which influenced Western European welfare state development. First, the particular pre-welfare state configuration of social forces upon which the social democratic consensus was grafted influenced, in a path-dependency sense (North, 1990), the type of welfare model that developed; in short, Western Europe's welfare states had different starting points and they developed in different ways. Second, the nature of the settlement between capital and labour in each country, and the extent to which the social democratic consensus was embedded, influenced the type of welfare model that developed. Third the elevation of productive capital over financial capital, within the BWS framework of politically controlled capital markets and fixed exchange rates, facilitated the construction of a national economy which could sustain the welfare state. Fourth, the scope, or limits upon, state intervention influenced the type of welfare model that developed. Fifth, the relatively high rates of economic growth, in the context of an expanding world economy, helped to generate the resources for welfare state development. Sixth, the commitment to high levels of employment, if not full employment, also helped to generate the necessary resources.

It is possible to identify five *exogenous* factors which influenced Western European welfare state development. First, the pivotal function of the state in the BWS helped to legitimize and embed its role; state intervention was, after all, critical to welfare state development. Second, the ERP and other US-sponsored programmes provided the short-term finance that, in turn, kick-started the economic growth which enabled Western Europe's welfare states to continue to expand. Third, the relative lack of European social policy action, particularly its failure to construct a unified EEC/EC-level welfare state, enabled member states to develop their own welfare models. Fourth, the Grand Area plan, which was underpinned by the 'open door' policy, allowed Western European countries to access the markets and the resources that they desired (i.e. the ability to import raw materials and the ability to export to foreign markets). Fifth, NATO, or more specifically the accompanying US military aid and stationing of US military forces in Western Europe, boosted economic growth and provided a security guarantee against Soviet communism and Western European socialism. These endogenous and exogenous factors, and the social forces that they engendered, conspired to produce a dominant trend (i.e. the hegemonic 'common model' or KWNS model) even if there were significant variations within this general pattern (i.e. particular social models).

It is also possible to argue that Western Europe's welfare states were *constrained by* the structure of the World Order. During the CWO, any attempt to construct a social model, whether at the national or European level, which was radical in nature, going beyond the parameters laid down by the social democratic consensus, was dealt with, usually covertly, by the hegemonic United States and its allies within the capitalist system. These included cases of economic nationalism and ultra-nationalism, which constituted challenges to the US 'open door' policy and capital's access to markets and resources more generally. They included independent development, which undermined US hegemony while serving as a potential example to other nations. They included neutrality, which endangered the US sphere of influence and the capitalist system more generally. They included over-extending the role of the state, which 'crowded out' the private sector and profit-making opportunities. They included creating an independent social democratic or socialist 'third force' between the two superpowers, which imperilled the Cold War division of the globe, and they included workers' control of industry, which confronted the prerogatives of managers and owners and opened the way to a socialized economy. Such threats were pre-empted, manifest in the ERP and the EEC/EC reification of market liberalism, bias towards negative integration, choice of social regulation and preference for competition and economic liberalization. They were guarded against, hence NATO's 'Operation Stay Behind' and the US support for the 'national security states' in Greece, Portugal and Spain, and/or they were thwarted – witness the covert US-led interventions in France, Greece and West Germany in the 1940s and 1950s and in Italy until the 1970s.

The two main elements of the *old convergence* hypothesis were therefore flawed. First, the development of Western Europe's welfare states was not inevitable. Instead, their creation and growth reflected a specific configuration of social forces during a particular time period. The welfare state was established to meet both the demands of capital, for new markets and profit-making opportunities, and of labour, for improved living standards. The welfare state also benefited capital and, it should be noted, the right-wing of the labour movement, in that it satisfied at least some of the demands of workers and thus weakened the appeal of radical ideas such as anarcho-syndicalism, communism and socialism which enjoyed widespread support across Western Europe during the nineteenth and twentieth centuries. Second, the expansion of Western Europe's welfare states did not necessarily entail convergence towards a particular regime. Instead, the development of these formations was contingent, mediated and varied. In short, Western Europe's social models were the products of the struggle between social forces at the national, European *and* global levels.

Conclusion

Following the end of the Second World War, hegemonic social forces in Western Europe and the United States constructed a World Order which determined the type of capitalism that developed on both sides of the Atlantic and which influenced the nature and trajectory of Western Europe's welfare states and the European project. Furthermore, the forging of the transatlantic alliance ensured that these entities were firmly anchored within the capitalist system as managed by the United States – hence Lundestad's (1998) thesis of 'empire' by integration.

The dominant economic and political model in Western Europe during the CWO was Keynesian, national, statist and welfare-oriented – although its exact form varied from country to country. Consequently, Western Europe's welfare states were constructed on a national rather than European basis, giving rise to a range of social models. The EEC/EC, on the other hand, developed as an economic rather than social entity, thus precluding the emergence of a single and distinctive ESM and/or a unified EEC/EC-level welfare state. Attending to the struggle between social forces at the national, European and global levels reveals that Western Europe's welfare states were both shaped by, and constrained by, the structure of the World Order during this period – a point generally missed by the existing literature.

Although the CWO boosted the fortunes of national capital, the dual processes of West European and Atlantic economic integration, plus the fact that many of Western Europe's economies were already highly internationalized, reinforced those social forces that sought to transcend the state and the national economy, thus paving the way for the transformation of the World Order. This, in turn, precipitated the restructuring of Western Europe's welfare states from the 1970s and the emergence of the ESM concept and the Social Europe discourse in the early 1990s.

4 Neo-liberal Europe in the New World Order (1985–2007)

From the single market to the European Constitution

Introduction

This chapter presents a brief chronological overview of the European integration process during the NWO[1] – more specifically from 1985 until 2007. The chapter advances six main arguments. First, that the nature and trajectory of the European project during the NWO was shaped by the struggle between competing social forces in Europe and beyond. Second, that the hegemony of liberal and supranationalist forces was repeatedly challenged during the NWO by advocates of an alternative World Order and by the rising tide of Euroscepticism. Third, that in the face of such opposition the European project evolved as a *neo-liberal* entity during this period. Fourth, that EC/EU reification of market liberalism, bias towards negative integration, choice of social regulation and preference for competition and economic liberalization was consolidated, if not accelerated, by a series of treaties in the 1980s, 1990s and 2000s. Fifth, that although the EC/EU became more active in terms of social policy, its efforts were directed at both 'reforming' the supply-side of Europe's economies and 'modernizing' Western Europe's welfare states rather than creating a unified EC/EU-level welfare state. Consequently, the European project influenced the development of Western Europe's welfare states in an increasingly direct as well as structural sense. Sixth, that the ESM concept and the Social Europe discourse emerged in the early 1990s as a result of one of the periodic crises faced by the EC/EU – namely the problematic passage of the Maastricht Treaty – and that these constructions represented an attempt to neutralize opposition to the neo-liberal trajectory of the EC/EU and to incorporate progressive social forces.

The chapter is divided into four main sections. The first section discusses the transformation of the EC/EU from the mid-1980s, while the following sections survey the main phases of the European integration process during the NWO. These include the creation of the SM (1985–1987), EMU (1990–1999) and the battle over Lisbon (2000–2007).

Neo-liberal Europe

During the NWO, the countries of Europe, both East and West, and the European project evolved as *neo-liberal* entities. That is to say, as a result of the 'regime change' which followed the so-called 'crisis of Keynesianism' in the 1970s (Forsyth and Notermans, 1997; Gillingham, 2003), the countries of Europe and the European project continued on the liberal road but, from 1985, they sought to *dis-embed* (Holman, 2004) the mixed economy system in favour of the market:

> Where the former [regime change] resulted in a shift from warfare state to welfare state, the latter [regime change] shifted the balance of power between public and private power, reduced market-correcting intervention-ism, unleashed competition between governments as well as producers, and created a long-term tidal pull toward an open economy that could not easily be reversed.
>
> (Gillingham, 2003: 98)

Phase 5: the creation of the SM (1985–1987)

Following the socialist challenge of the early 1980s, liberal and supranationalist forces once again revived the European project; building upon the Messina Con-ference and Hague Summit, the third attempt to reinvigorate the EC was argua-bly the most determined and enduring. Following the four main phases of the European integration process during the CWO, the fifth phase witnessed the cre-ation of the SM and at this point the EC took a decidedly neo-liberal turn. That is to say, in agreeing to participate in the SM project, and subsequent EC/EU ini-tiatives, member states voluntarily surrendered control over a range of macr-oeconomic policy tools, facilitated the restructuring of their economies, colluded in the expansion of corporate power and subjected themselves to additional structural constraints.

This period witnessed the rapid growth of lobbying at the EC level as the cor-porate sector in particular promoted its liberalization objectives and sought to prevent any attempt to re-regulate at the EC level. With 10,000 professional lob-byists, 500 corporate lobby groups and 200 TNCs based in Brussels, with privi-leged access to European Commission working groups and with little or no oversight or scrutiny of their activities, the corporate sector was able to able to pursue its agenda relatively unencumbered (Balanyá *et al.*, 2000; Gillingham, 2003; Alter-EU, 2008, 2010).

Jacques Delors and the 'Russian doll' strategy

The French federalist and social democrat, Jacques Delors, was appointed Euro-pean Commission president in January 1985 and in his initial speech to the Euro-pean Parliament he proclaimed his support for a 'European Union' underpinned by a 'big market' and a 'European social space' with 'new regulatory frame-works' (cited in Ross, 1995: 30). To achieve these objectives, Delors adopted the so-called 'Russian doll'[2] strategy which – echoing the Monnet approach – entailed 'episodes of strategic action to seize upon openings in the political opportunity structure, resource accumulation through success, and reinvestment of these resources in new actions to capitalize on new opportunities' (ibid.: 39). Such a staged strategy, it was hoped, would transform the focus of the European project from mere market-building to state-building. Indeed, Delors' promise of a shift from a *liberal Europe*, based upon on negative integration, to the upward harmonization of social standards and the creation of a *European social space*, predicated on positive integration, was sufficient to secure the cautious support of many progressive social forces and it was during this period that the objective of constructing an albeit undefined Social Europe entered the mainstream discourse. The question of the sequencing of the stages, however, was critical and for Delors the market came first: 'market-building through "1992" was essential in liberalizing Europe's economic space' as it provided 'the resources to shift to more state-building (Ross, 1995: 240). Somewhat predictably, the strategy was a failure:

> If market-building succeeded but state-building faltered, Europe could end up an even less 'organized space' than it had been prior to the Delors presidency, more a liberal free trade zone than the socio-political community with regulatory integrity that Delors desired. The contradiction in this strategic staging was that there was a much greater likelihood that the first, market-building, stages of the Delors strategy would work out than the second, state-building, plans. This, in fact, was close to what happened. Delors' greatest ambition, to use the dynamics of European integration to shore up ... the European model of society was thus frustrated.
>
> (Ibid.)

Gillingham (2003) recounted how the first 'Russian doll', the 1987 Single European Act (SEA), was followed by the 1988 Delors I package (i.e. the expansion of the EC budget), the 1989 Social Charter, the 1991 Maastricht Treaty and the 1992 Delors II package (i.e. the further expansion of the EC budget).

The SEA

The European Council in June 1985 adopted the European Commission White Paper, entitled 'Completing the Internal Market', which contained a detailed programme and a timetable for the creation of a single European market by 1992. The White Paper, produced by the then British-appointed European commissioner, Arthur Cockfield, contained over 300 legislative measures deemed necessary to implement this programme. Having established a common market via the abolition of tariff-based trade barriers between member states, the SM project aimed to accelerate the rate of progress towards the realization of the four freedoms by creating an internal market – an area without frontiers in which the free movement of persons, goods, services and capital would be assured – by eliminating over 300 non-tariff trade barriers. Three categories of barrier were identified: fiscal (e.g. excise and value added taxes), physical (e.g. border controls) and technical (e.g. capital controls and different product standards). Their removal required the reform of customs procedures, the harmonization or coordination of industrial regulations and standards, the liberalization of investment and trade, the abolition of discriminatory taxation, and the elimination of preferential public procurement and state aid (Blanchard, 1995). The European Council also discussed the recommendations of the reports produced by the Dooge Committee and the Institutional Affairs Committee. These called for a new institutional settlement and EC treaty to underpin the SM project. Several member states favoured convening an intergovernmental conference (IGC) to consider treaty revisions and institutional reform, while others did not. For the first time, the European Council resolved the matter by voting; Britain, Denmark and Greece were defeated and an IGC was held in September 1985 to revise the Treaties of Rome.

The stated objectives of the resulting draft SEA, agreed in December 1985, were to complete the SM project by the end of 1992, to increase economic and social cohesion, to forge a common scientific and technology policy, to further progress the EMS, to develop a European social dimension and to coordinate action on the environment. The SEA officially recognized the European Council, amended the Treaties of Rome and formalized EPC. The main changes to the Treaties of Rome included extending the use of qualified majority voting (QMV) in the Council of Ministers, to make it more difficult to block SM-related legislation, and introducing a new co-operation procedure to strengthen the role of the European Parliament in the legislative process. The ratification process for the SEA was straightforward. The Danish referendum in February 1986 produced a 56.2 per cent 'Yes' vote and the Irish referendum in May 1987 delivered a 69.9 per cent 'Yes' vote. The other ten member states ratified the SEA in their national assemblies and it came into force in July 1987.

In terms of achieving the stated objectives of the SEA, it is instructive to compare the progress made in terms of economic liberalization with the relative lack of social policy action at the EC level prior to 1989. The adoption of SM-related regulations and directives (i.e. those concerned with competition and economic liberalization) was determined and successful. By contrast, before the 1989 Social Charter and partly reflecting British opposition to the development of a European social dimension, the EC merely focused upon the harmonization of health and safety legislation and on encouraging dialogue between employers and trade unions as 'social partners'.

The economic impact of the SM project, judged in terms of the transformation of the European economy, was unquestionable. Jacquemin and Sapir (1991) and Jacquemin and Wright (1993) observed increased competition within the European market and higher levels of corporate restructuring – such as cross-border co-operative agreements, mergers and acquisitions, etc. – while Eichengreen (2007: 346) noted that 'a more integrated European market led to the rationalization and consolidation of industries previously fragmented along national lines' and this, in turn, 'made it attractive for extra-European producers to seek a foothold in the European market'. The impact of the SM project in terms of winners and losers, however, was disputed. In terms of the *benefits*, Emerson (1989) argued that the SM project encouraged the exploitation of comparative advantage, increased competition, improved efficiency, stimulated innovation and facilitated economies of scale, and was thus economically and socially positive. Indeed, the European Commission estimated that the 'static' (i.e. one-off) gains from the completion of the SM project would amount to between 4.3 and 6.4 per cent of European gross domestic product (GDP) (Cecchini *et al.*, 1988), while Baldwin (1992) argued that the 'dynamic' (i.e. catalysing) gains from greater capital accumulation could be as high as 15.4 per cent of GDP. In reality, a summary of the Single Market Review Series, a set of 38 independent studies published by the European Commission in 1996, concluded that the SM project had increased European GDP by 1.1 per cent over the previous six years, had generated between 300,000 and 900,000 jobs and had reduced inflation by 1.1 per cent (European Commission, 1996). In terms of the *costs*, Smith and Wanke (1993), Collier (1994) and Mills (1998) pointed to the lower growth rates, increasing regional disparities and higher unemployment rates within Europe during this period, while Cheshire (1999: 850), summarizing the findings of several studies on the spatial impact of the SM project, concluded that

> The great, almost overwhelming majority of them identify European integration in general, and the SM in particular, as differently benefiting 'core' or central regions of Europe compared to peripheral ones ... the greatest potential gains are concentrated in the core of Europe.

The 1980s witnessed two further expansions of the EC: Greece became a member in January 1981, followed by Portugal and Spain in January 1986. During this period, the EC made significant progress towards its stated goal of the free movement of persons. The Schengen Agreement, signed in June 1985, committed Belgium, France, Germany, Luxembourg and the Netherlands to the abolition of border controls. Following the ratification of the intergovernmental Schengen Convention in June 1990, the pledge was implemented in March 1995 when the borderless Schengen Area was created. The 1997 Amsterdam Treaty incorporated these arrangements and, over time, the Schengen Area expanded to encompass 22 member states, plus Iceland, Norway and Switzerland. The principle of the free movement of persons was challenged in May 2011, however, when, in the wake of so-called 'Arab spring' and the uprisings in North Africa and the Middle East, 15 countries voted to curtail passport-free travel in an attempt to stem the immigration from these troubled regions.

Phase 6: EMU (1990–1999)

The sixth phase of the European integration process witnessed the EC/EU embark upon another round of deepening and enlargement which culminated in the launch of the European single currency.

The Maastricht Treaty

The European Council accepted the three-stage plan for EMU set out in the Delors Report of June 1989 and agreed to hold an IGC. Responding to widespread unease about the prospect of German reunification, Delors called for European Political Union (EPU) to assuage these concerns. The 1990–1991 IGCs on EMU and EPU elicited major disagreements, both within and between member states and EC institutions. The Luxembourg-sponsored treaty model attempted to overcome these divisions by proposing that, rather than adopting a unitary institutional structure in which all policy areas would come under a single treaty, the EC should become a 'temple with pillars'. Three 'pillars' would encompass the policy areas of the EC, termed the 'temple'. The first supranational pillar would revise the Treaties of Rome to include EMU, while the second and third pillars, namely the Common Foreign and Security Policy (CFSP) and Justice and Home Affairs (JHA) policy, would proceed on an intergovernmental basis.

The draft Maastricht Treaty, agreed in December 1991, officially renamed the EC which, together with the CFSP and JHA pillars, constituted the EU. The treaty set out the stages of EMU. Britain and Denmark negotiated opt-outs from Stage 3 of EMU, the introduction of the European single currency, while Sweden, which constitutionally required a referendum before it could replace its currency, could not participate in EMU. The treaty detailed the new co-decision procedure which augmented the powers of the European Parliament, granted the ECJ the power to fine member states, defined the principle of subsidiarity,[3] created citizenship of the EU and extended EU competence into several new policy areas. To enhance economic policy coordination, the treaty tasked the European Commission with producing annual and referential Broad Economic Policy Guidelines. Having been endorsed by the European Council, these were implemented by member states and were evaluated on the basis of peer review. The treaty also specified the statute of the European Central Bank (ECB), the so-called MCC[4] and associated excessive deficit procedure, and the protocol establishing the Cohesion Fund.

It was originally envisaged that the treaty would include a social chapter. Britain refused to accept it, however, leaving the other 11 member states to adopt a separate Agreement on Social Policy which was not legally binding; the annexed protocol contained 47 supply-side-oriented proposals covering the freedom of movement of workers, collective bargaining, equality, health and safety, training, etc. As Hantrais (2007: 12–13) noted,

> Although, together, the Community charter of 1989, the action programmes and the Agreement on Social Policy in the Maastricht Treaty provided a clearer statement of thinking on social policy at the EU level than was present in the EEC Treaty ... they did not signal a strong commitment to social affairs as an objective in its own right, or on a par with economic union. Nor did they put in place the administrative structures needed for producing a common European social policy.

To enhance social policy coordination, and to ensure that it complemented economic policy coordination, the Agreement on Social Policy officially recognized federations of private companies, public enterprises and trade unions as corporatist 'social partners' that could, through the social dialogue process, devise Europe-wide collective agreements and have them ratified by the European Council and transposed at the national level.

Stage 1 of EMU began in July 1990 and involved EMS entry, the abolition of capital and exchange controls, and adherence to the MCC. Stage 2 began in January 1994 and saw the creation of the European Monetary Institute (EMI) and a network of central banks that were independent of governments. Stage 2 also included the agreement that, by the end of 1996, the European Council would decide by QMV whether aspirant countries had satisfied the MCC and so could proceed to Stage 3. This stage began in January 1999 with the inauguration of the ECB, tasked with the sole objective of achieving price stability, and the launch of the European single currency – known as the euro. In an effort to satisfy the MCC, several member states engaged in creative accounting to improve their short-term fiscal position. Through such measures, all member states, bar Greece, met the criteria and the euro was launched as planned as a virtual currency in January 1999.

In contrast to the SEA, the ratification process for the Maastricht Treaty was problematic. The Irish referendum in June 1992 produced a 69 per cent Yes vote. The Danish referendum that same month delivered a 50.7 per cent No vote, while the French referendum in September resulted in a 51.05 per cent Yes vote. Intriguingly the then British prime minister, John Major, implied that the French referendum may have been rigged: 'French predictions of the result were relayed to us hours before the count was over – which raised eyebrows on this side of the Channel. How could they know?' (Major, 1999: 338). Whether or not this is true, the narrow victory of the pro-EU forces in France led many to question the legitimacy of EMU. Following the negotiation of an opt-out from Stage 3 of EMU, the second Danish referendum in May 1993 generated a 56.7 per cent Yes vote. The other nine member states ratified the treaty in their national assemblies and it came into force in November 1993.

The Copenhagen Criteria

The European Council adopted what became known as the Copenhagen Criteria, for countries that aspired to join the EU, in June 1993:

> Membership requires that the candidate country has achieved stability of institutions guaranteeing democracy, the rule of law, human rights and respect for and protection of minorities, the existence of a functioning market economy as well as the capacity to cope with competitive pressure and market forces within the Union. Membership presupposes the candidate's ability to take on the obligations of membership including adherence to the aims of political, economic and monetary union.
>
> (European Council, 1993: 1)

In Western Europe, the Austrian referendum on joining the EU in June 1994 produced a 66.6 per cent Yes vote, the Finnish referendum in October delivered a 52.9 per cent Yes vote, the Swedish referendum in November resulted in a 52.3 per cent Yes vote, while the Norwegian referendum that same month saw 52.8 per cent voting No to entry for the second time. The fourth enlargement of the EU occurred in January 1995 when Austria, Finland and Sweden joined. In Eastern Europe, the adoption of the *acquis communautaire*[5] – together with IMF and World Bank-sponsored reforms – consolidated the neo-liberal project across Eastern Europe which, as a result of the associated liberalization and privatization, experienced significant increases in inequality, unemployment and other social problems as they integrated into the global economy and as they prepared to join the EU.

The ESM

The European Commission, acknowledging the difficulties of the Maastricht Treaty ratification process, launched a raft of new economic and social initiatives in an attempt to counter the unpopularity of the EU in the wake of the SEA and the Maastricht Treaty. The 'Growth, Competitiveness, Employment' White Paper, adopted in December 1993, established the target of creating 15 million new jobs by 2000, while the 'European Social Policy' White Paper, adopted in December 1994, attempted to define the ESM:

> there are a number of shared values which form the basis of the European Social Model. These include democracy and individual rights, free collective bargaining, the market economy, equality of opportunity for all and social welfare and solidarity. These values … are held together by the conviction that economic and social progress must go hand in hand. Competitiveness and solidarity have both to be taken into account in building a successful Europe for the future.
>
> (European Commission, 1994: 2)

Crucially, however, these documents prioritized international competitiveness and supply-side reforms, rather than Euro-Keynesianism and demand management, as the key to the aspirations of the EU. Nonetheless, it was during this period that the ESM concept entered the mainstream discourse.

The Essen strategy

The European Council in Essen in December 1994 sanctioned the coordination of national employment policies. Known as the Essen strategy, this involved the creation of a multilateral employment policy monitoring procedure and the production of common employment guidelines. The European Council specifically agreed to promote new sources of jobs, to improve the access of women, young people and the long-term unemployed to the labour market, and to increase training opportunities for all. Laudable as these were, however, the European Council also emphasized the need to reduce non-wage labour costs if Europe was to solve its unemployment problems and compete globally. It also recommended that, 'above all, structural deficits must decline in order to prevent a further increase in the rate of debt' (European Council, 1994: 9).

The Amsterdam Treaty

The 1996–1997 IGC was convened as a requirement of the Maastricht Treaty to address unfinished business. The resulting draft Amsterdam Treaty, agreed in June 1997, simplified the co-decision procedure, capped the number of Members of the European Parliament (MEPs) at 700, strengthened the powers of the European Commission president and introduced suspension as a sanction against member states. The treaty incorporated the CFSP into the Treaties of Rome, transferred the provision for the free movement of persons from the JHA pillar into the supranational first pillar and introduced new rules on flexibility known as 'differentiated integration' or 'variable geometry'. The treaty also included a supply-side-orientated employment chapter and a social chapter. Building upon the common employment guidelines and reporting procedures agreed by the European Council in December 1994, plus the Confidence Pact on Employment produced by the European Commission in June 1996, the employment chapter stated that the EU should develop a coordinated strategy for employment, promote skilled, trained and adaptable workforces, and ensure that labour markets were responsive to economic change. Britain's adoption of the Social Charter in May 1997 enabled what was previously an annexed protocol to be formally incorporated as a social chapter. The treaty failed to address the system of QMV, however, which was postponed to a future IGC. The ratification process for the Amsterdam Treaty was straightforward. The Irish referendum in May 1998 produced a 61.74 per cent Yes vote and the Danish referendum that same month delivered a 55.1 per cent Yes vote. The other 13 member states ratified the treaty in their national assemblies and it came into force in May 1999.

The SGP

The austerity associated with the deflationary MCC exacerbated the already high unemployment rates across Western Europe, prompting several member states to introduce extensive privatization programmes, in addition to welfare state retrenchment, in an attempt to reduce their budget deficits and public debt levels. Such measures provoked a series of mass demonstrations and strikes. Despite the promotion of alternatives by Our Europe, the think tank established by Delors, the then French prime minister, Lionel Jospin, and the then German finance minister, Oskar Lafontaine, the primary response of the June 1997 European Council was to formulate the SGP,[6] the main objective of which was to safeguard member states' commitment to the MCC. Under the terms of the SGP, member states were required to produce Stability and Convergence Programmes for the European Commission and European Council. The summit also established the ERM2 to coordinate eurozone and non-euro currencies.

The European Employment Strategy and European employment pact

Critics berated the EU for adopting orthodox measures such as the SGP and for ignoring the unemployment problem in Europe. In an attempt to address these concerns, the European Council organized the jobs summit in Luxembourg in November 1997 which endorsed the supply-side-oriented European Employment Strategy (EES). Building upon the Essen strategy and the Amsterdam Treaty employment chapter themes of adaptability, employability, entrepreneurship and equal opportunities, the EES enabled the European Commission to issue Employment Policy Guidelines to member states, subject to the approval of the European Council via QMV. Member states developed and implemented their National Action Plans, evaluated them on the basis of peer review and then published the results in the Joint Employment Report which was approved by the European Commission and European Council. The coordination of employment policies was known as the Luxembourg process.

The European Council in Cardiff in June 1998 agreed that budgetary discipline (i.e. 'sound' public finances) and structural reforms (i.e. supply-side measures to improve competitiveness) were essential for Europe's growth, jobs and prosperity. The achievement of economic reforms was known as the Cardiff process. The European Council in December 1998 called for the creation of a European employment pact (EEP). The European Council in Cologne in June 1999 decided to coordinate budgetary, fiscal and monetary policy with wage developments in an attempt to achieve non-inflationary growth. The establishment of a macroeconomic dialogue process was known as the Cologne process. The European Council also endorsed the EEP. Underpinned by the three pillars of the Luxembourg process, the Cardiff process and the Cologne process, the EEP aimed to deliver non-inflationary and job-creating growth. The EEP emphasized the need to improve Europe's competitiveness, to increase investment in infrastructure and R&D so as to deliver added value, to match labour supply and demand via employability, entrepreneurialism, lifelong learning, etc. and to ensure that Europe's financial and trading systems remained open. The EEP also stressed the need to achieve price stability, to respect the SGP, to exercise wage restraint, to reform the welfare state and to lower the burden on workers by reviewing social security and taxation systems.

Foreign and military policy I

The 1990s and early 2000s witnessed the development of EU foreign policy and military policy. Foreign policy-wise, the EU signed a trade agreement with the 19-member European Economic Area in January 1994, signed a free trade agreement with the *Mercado Común del Sur* (Mercosur) in December 1995, signed the Cotonuo Agreement with 77 African, Caribbean and Pacific countries in June

2000 and pursued its neo-liberal agenda through the World Trade Organization (WTO) (Mahnkopf, 2008). Military policy-wise, the EU pledged in November 2000 to create a Rapid Reaction Force to facilitate military operations independent of NATO.

Phase 7: the battle over Lisbon (2000–2007)

The seventh phase of European integration was even more turbulent than the sixth. While neo-liberalism was being consolidated within member states and at the EU level, social forces across Europe increasingly questioned and challenged the nature and trajectory of the European project and put forward alternatives.

Eurozone divergence

The advent of the euro was expected to lead to economic convergence across the EU. In the decade following its launch, however, differences in economic performance within the eurozone persisted or worsened. Indeed, surveying the macroeconomic indicators pertaining to debt levels, economic competitiveness, economic growth rates, inflation rates, interest rates and unemployment levels suggested a trend of divergence rather than convergence. In terms of economic competitiveness, the European commissioner for economic and financial affairs, Olli Rehn (2011), delivered a presentation at the European Commission-sponsored conference on European economic governance in January 2011 in which he expressed alarm about macroeconomic imbalances and the divergent trend within the eurozone since the creation of the euro (see Figure 4.1).

In terms of economic growth rates and inflation rates, Ernst and Young (2010) found evidence of enduring differences, if not divergence, within the eurozone (see Table 4.1).

Table 4.1 Divergence within the eurozone

	1999–2003	*2004–2008*
Growth and incomes		
Standard deviation of GDP* growth rates	1.9	1.9
Growth rate gap (max–min)	7.2	7.2
Highest GDP per capita (eurozone=100)	228.1	244.5
Lowest GDP per capital (eurozone=100)	23.6	23.7
Inflation and prices		
Standard deviation of inflation rates	2.1	0.9
Inflation rate gap (max–min)	8.1	3.7
Highest price level (eurozone=100)	114.9	116.7
Lowest price level (eurozone=100)	42.6	56.1

Source: adapted from Ernst and Young (2010).

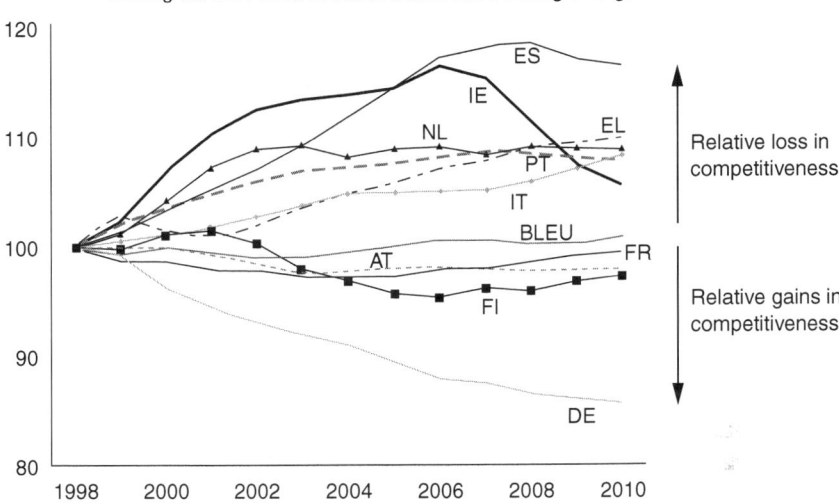

Trends during the past decade in price and cost competitiveness
among the euro area member states show strong divergences

Figure 4.1 Eurozone macroeconomic imbalances, 1998–2010 (source: presentation by
Commissioner Olli Rehn, 12 January 2011).

In terms of interest rates, the Euroland Interest Rate Convergence Index
developed by Chantrey Vellacott (2001) revealed that, with perfect convergence
set at zero, the index for the euro-11 in January 1999 was 62. One year later,
however, it was 111. The House of Lords EU Select Committee (2000) also presented evidence of interest rate divergence (see Table 4.2).

These divergent trends were compounded by and reflected in the decline of the
value of the euro vis-à-vis the US dollar and the pound sterling. These falls, which
undermined the expectation that the euro would rival the dollar as a reserve
currency, prompted the ECB to intervene in the currency markets in June 1999,

Table 4.2 Comparison of the ECB interest rate with the notional 'appropriate rate' in
member states

	Notional rate (ECB rate adjusted for the cost of living) in August 2000	*Difference from the ECB rate in August 2000 of 4.5%*
Austria	5.49	+0.99
Belgium	5.29	+0.79
France	3.77	−0.73
Germany	3.37	−1.13
Italy	4.42	−0.08
Netherlands	6.22	+1.72
Spain	6.84	+2.34

Source: House of Lords EU Select Committee (2000).

September 2000 and November 2000 – and again in March 2011. Nevertheless, a 2001 survey of eurozone citizens found that 52 per cent of those polled were 'dissatisfied about the euro replacing their national currency' (Travis, 2001).

The Nice Treaty

The primary focus of the 2000 IGC, culminating in the draft Nice Treaty agreed in February 2001, was the need to reform decision-making within the EU. The treaty re-weighted the voting system of the Council of Ministers to employ a double majority system, fixed the number of MEPs in the European Parliament, set the number of European commissioners to one per member state and extended QMV to 27 new policy areas. The treaty also provided for enhanced co-operation and thus the development of a 'two-speed' EU. The European Commission, in alliance with several member states, aimed to incorporate the Charter of Fundamental Rights into the treaty. British opposition, however, led to its voluntary adoption outside of the treaty framework. Consequently, it was not legally binding. As with the Maastricht Treaty, the ratification process for the Nice Treaty was problematic. The first Irish referendum in June 2001 produced a 53.9 per cent No vote. Following the negotiation of safeguards on neutrality, however, the second Irish referendum in October 2002 delivered a 62.89 per cent Yes vote. The other 14 member states ratified the treaty in their national assemblies and it came into force in February 2003.

The Lisbon Strategy

The European Council ratified the Lisbon Strategy, which established the strategic aim for the EU to become 'the most competitive and dynamic knowledge-based economy in the world' (European Council, 2000: 1), in March 2000. To achieve this aim, the European Council agreed three specific objectives: to increase the average EU growth rate to 3 per cent, to increase the average proportion of GDP spent on R&D to 3 per cent, and to increase the employment rate to 70 per cent by 2010. The Lisbon Strategy, which advocated supply-side measures to 'modernize' the ESM, contained a number of policy recommendations. Economically, it emphasized the importance of active employment policies pertaining to education, entrepreneurialism, innovation, research and training. It specifically called for the full implementation of the SM, particularly in services, the creation of a single financial market, fiscal consolidation and 'sound' public finances, and greater coordination of macroeconomic policies. Socially, it supported active and dynamic welfare states which prioritized good quality health provision, gender equality and social inclusion. Furthermore, it recommended that, given Europe's aging populations, Europe's welfare states should be sustainable in the longer-term and needed to ensure that 'work pays'.

In terms of implementing the Lisbon Strategy, it is instructive to compare how the EU relied upon voluntary mechanisms to deliver its social objectives but used legislation to achieve its economic liberalization objectives. The

European Council in March 2000 decided to formalize the *discretionary* Open Method of Coordination (OMC) – which was based upon benchmarking and the issuance of guidelines, the use of indicators and the sharing of best practice – and to apply it to the EES/EEP, pension reform and social inclusion initiatives. Importantly, the OMC was an intergovernmental mechanism based upon voluntary co-operation rather than sanctions for non-compliance. By contrast, to advance the liberalization of the service sector, the European Commission issued a *legally-binding* directive in January 2004. The original Directive on Services in the Internal Market contained two provisions – the country of original principle and the posting of workers principle – which were condemned by progressive social forces on the grounds that the directive would encourage competitive deregulation and social dumping. The ECJ rulings in the *Viking* and *Laval* cases, for example, were particularly concerning; Bercusson (2007) and Davies (2008) argued that, by subordinating the right to strike to the free movement of capital – more specifically the freedom of establishment and the freedom to provide services – these judgments posed a serious problem to trade unions and other progressive social forces attempting to defend the ESM. Such controversy and the opposition it elicited from the European Parliament to revise the legislation in February 2006 by removing the country of origin principle. The objective of the liberalization of the service sector, however, was maintained.

Although the European Council reaffirmed its commitment to the aim and objectives of the Lisbon Strategy in March 2004, several reports were published, such as the Sapir Report in July 2003, which warned about the state of EU competitiveness vis-à-vis Asia and North America. These prompted the creation of a high-level expert group, chaired by the former Dutch prime minister, Wim Kok, as part of the mid-term review of the Lisbon Strategy. The Kok Report of November 2004 concluded that progress had been limited due to an overloaded agenda, poor coordination and conflicting priorities. The Lisbon Strategy was thus re-launched in March 2005 with the sole objectives of growth and job creation. The European Council agreed that, nationally, member states should develop and implement National Reform Programmes and that the European Commission should evaluate these and publish Annual Progress Reports. Several eurozone members subsequently introduced measures designed to reform their health and pension systems, plus their labour markets. At the EU level, the European Council decided that the European Commission should produce Integrated Guidelines for Growth and Jobs, which brought together the Broad Economic Policy Guidelines and the Employment Policy Guidelines and which contained both microeconomic and macroeconomic policy recommendations. The European Council also decided that the initiatives pursued by the European Commission would form the basis of the Community Lisbon Programme.

The launch of the euro

The technically successful launch of the euro as an actual currency occurred in January 2001. The launch was preceded by a €80 million propaganda campaign to 'sell the euro to EU citizens' (Miller, 2001). Additionally, substantial change-over costs were borne by each member state. It was widely expected that the introduction of the euro would reduce prices. The 2002 UBS Warburg study, however, estimated that 'the first month of the changeover cost eurozone citizens approximately €3 billion in higher prices' (Islam and Keegan, 2002). A European Commission survey in March 2002 found that 67 per cent of citizens felt that retailers had rounded up prices upon conversion to the euro (Barber and Guerrera, 2002), while a second survey in June revealed that 69 per cent of people 'believed that prices had increased' (Dombey, 2002). Consequently, in a 2002 Forsa Institute survey, '61 per cent of Germans wanted to replace the euro with the deutschmark' (No Campaign, 2002). Concerns about the cost of euro adoption and the stability of the European single currency contributed to the 53.1 per cent No vote in the Danish referendum on euro entry in September 2000, while the Swedish referendum on euro entry in September 2003 produced a 55.9 per cent No vote. Greece adopted the euro in January 2002, followed by Slovenia in 2007, Cyprus and Malta in 2008, Slovakia in 2009 and Estonia in 2011 – taking the total membership of the eurozone to 17.

Permanent austerity

To comply with the MCC/SGP, Britain instituted its 'golden rules'[7] for public finances, Germany imposed a stability pact upon its *Länder* and local authorities, Portugal introduced an austerity package to reduce public spending and Spain enacted a zero deficit law. Nevertheless, from 2001 the European Commission reprimanded Britain, France, Germany, Ireland, Italy, the Netherlands and Portugal for breaching the SGP. The European Commission reformed the SGP in September 2002 by extending the deadline for budgets to be balanced, while demanding reductions in structural deficits by 0.5 per cent per year. In November 2003, however, the Economic and Financial Affairs Council (ECOFIN) suspended the SGP sanctions mechanism, designed to enforce fiscal discipline, against France and Germany. This prompted the European Commission to take these countries to the ECJ for failing to uphold treaty obligations. Germany subsequently revised its constitution in June 2009 to include a balanced budget law which will prohibit the federal government from running a deficit of more than 0.35 per cent of GDP from 2016 and the *Länder* from running any deficits from 2020. Similarly, the then French president, Nicolas Sarkozy, announced in May 2010 that France would amend its constitution so that, from 2012, all new governments would have to devise a strategy for reducing the structural deficit and set a date for returning the budget to balance.

The convention on the future of Europe

The Laeken Declaration of December 2001 proposed 'a simpler Union, one that is stronger in the pursuit of its essential objectives and more definitely present in the world' (cited in Bainbridge, 2002: 345). The European Council duly established a Convention on the Future of Europe to prepare a constitution for the EU. At its inauguration in February 2002, parallels were draw with the 1787 Philadelphia Convention that produced the US Constitution. The 105-member convention, chaired by the former French president, Giscard D'Estaing, produced a draft EU constitutional treaty in February 2003 and an IGC began. Disagreements over the voting system within the Council of Ministers, the mutual defence clause, economic, defence and foreign policy, the size of the European Commission, Britain's EU budget rebate and the status of God in the draft treaty proved insurmountable, however, and the 2003 ICG was a failure.

The European Social Forum

The inaugural meeting of the biennial European Social Forum (ESF) took place in November 2002. Modelled on the World Social Forum, the ESF brought together left-wing political and trade union activists and representatives from non-governmental organizations and social forces which were opposed to globalization and imperialism and who were committed to the campaign for global justice. The ESF adopted the Charter for 'Another Europe' in January 2008. Rejecting a centralizing and neo-liberal EU, the charter called for a union of peoples freely associating through democratic assemblies at the local, regional, national and European levels. It also supported fiscal harmonization, common ownership, anti-discrimination measures, the extension of economic and social rights, and the dissolution of NATO.

Enlargement

The European Council in December 2002 agreed that the countries of Eastern Europe had met the Copenhagen Criteria, thus paving the way for the fifth enlargement of the EU. Following a series of referendums in nine countries (see Table 4.3), with Cyprus preferring parliamentary ratification, ten countries joined the EU in May 2004.

Table 4.3 EU enlargement referendum results, 2003

Country	Date of referendum	Result (%)
Malta	8 March 2003	53.60
Slovenia	23 March 2003	89.61
Hungary	12 April 2003	83.76
Lithuania	10–11 May 2003	89.95
Slovakia	16–17 May 2003	92.46
Poland	7–8 June 2003	77.45
Czech Republic	13–14 June	77.33
Estonia	14 September 2003	66.83
Latvia	20 September 2003	67.00

Two additional countries, Bulgaria and Romania, joined in January 2007 as part of the fifth enlargement – taking the total membership of the EU to 27.

The European Constitution

The failure of the 2003 IGC resulted in a further round of negotiations and the European Constitution was drafted in June 2004. It granted the EU a legal identify, reformed EU decision-making, created the new posts of EU foreign minister and president, and extended QMV to 43 new policy areas. As with the Maastricht and Nice treaties, the ratification process was problematic. The European Parliament endorsed the European Constitution by 500 votes to 137 in January 2005, while the Spanish referendum in February produced a 76.7 per cent Yes vote. The French referendum in May, however, delivered a 54.68 per cent No vote and the Dutch referendum in June resulted in a 61.5 per cent No vote. Although the Luxembourg referendum in July generated a 56.52 per cent Yes vote, planned referendums in Britain, the Czech Republic, Denmark, Ireland, Poland and Portugal were postponed. Despite the fact that 16 member states – namely Austria, Belgium, Bulgaria, Cyprus, Estonia, Finland, Germany, Greece, Hungary, Italy, Latvia, Lithuania, Malta, Romania, Slovakia and Slovenia – had ratified the European Constitution in their national assemblies, the requirement of unanimity meant that it fell; the European Council subsequently announced a 'period of reflection', which, one year later, was extended into 2007.

In a speech to the European Parliament in January 2007, the then German chancellor, Angela Merkel, announced that she would use the German presidency of the EU to revive the European Constitution, arguing that 'we must give Europe a soul' and warning that 'failure would be a historic failure' (quoted in Traynor, 2007). That same month, the 18 countries that had ratified the European Constitution met in Madrid and agreed to re-launch it. Their strategy was predicated on repackaging the European Constitution as a mere amending/reforming treaty, avoiding any mention of a constitution, removing the trappings of statehood (i.e. anthem, flag, motto, etc.) and relegating the Charter of Fundamental Rights to an annex. These changes, it was hoped, would allow member states to avoid having to hold referendums and would thus enable the European Constitution to be ratified.

The Berlin Declaration

The Berlin Declaration, which marked the fiftieth anniversary of the signing of the Treaties of Rome, was signed in March 2007 by the presidents of the European Commission, European Council and European Parliament. It stated that 'we, the citizens of the European Union, have united for the better', resulting in peace and prosperity, plus the strengthening of democracy, equality, individual rights and the rule of law. It celebrated the SM, EMU and EU enlargement projects, praised the ESM, pledged to tackle global warming, racism and terrorism, highlighted the need for a common energy policy and for the EU to remain open to future enlargement, insisted that, globally, the EU had a progressive role to play and concluded that 'we are united in our aim of placing the European Union on a renewed common basis before the European Parliament elections in 2009. For we know, Europe is our common future' (European Council, 2007). Merkel used the fiftieth-anniversary celebrations to lay out the 'road map' to a new treaty.

The Lisbon Treaty

The European Council agreed to hold another IGC to finalize a new treaty and the draft EU Reform Treaty, the so-called Lisbon Treaty, was concluded in October 2007. In terms of institutional changes, the Lisbon Treaty created the posts of President of the European Council and High Representative of the Union for foreign affairs and security policy. It revised the double majority voting system, eliminated the automatic right of member states to appoint a European commissioner, expanded the power of the European Parliament by extending the co-decision procedure to 40 new policy areas, granted the EU a legal personality that enabled it to sign treaties, formalized an exit clause that facilitated withdrawal from the EU and agreed to the formation of an EU diplomatic service. Critically, it was also a 'self-amending treaty' with so-called *passarelle* (i.e. bridging clauses) which allowed the EU to increase its power *without* the need for a new treaty agreed by all member states.

Policy-wise, the Lisbon Treaty abolished the national veto in over 60 policy areas such as energy, immigration, social security and transport, introduced new EU powers in the legal domain – such as the harmonization of civil and criminal law, the ability to rule on criminal law, the enforcement of mutual recognition of legal judgments and the establishment of a European public prosecutor with the power to initiate prosecutions – and enhanced the role of Europol. It included a commitment that the EU would develop a common defence policy, a 'structured co-operation' group (i.e. an inner core of member states committed to EU military integration), a mutual defence commitment and a terrorism solidarity clause. The Charter on Fundamental Rights, which included the rights to health care and welfare benefits and the right to take industrial action, was included as a separate protocol – although Article 6 of the Lisbon Treaty gave the document a legally binding status. Many British politicians, who were eager to avoid having to hold a referendum, argued that the European Constitution and the Lisbon Treaty were not the same. Analysis by Open Europe, however, found that only ten out of the 250 proposals in the Lisbon Treaty were different from those in the European Constitution. 'In other words, 90 per cent of the text is the same' (Open Europe, 2007: 4).

As with the Maastricht and Nice treaties, and the European Constitution, the ratification process was problematic. Although the European Parliament endorsed the Lisbon Treaty by 525 votes to 115 in February 2008, the Irish referendum in June produced a 53.4 per cent No vote. Moreover, although by that point 21 out of the 27 member states had already ratified the Lisbon Treaty – the exceptions being the Czech Republic, Finland, Germany, Ireland, Poland and Sweden – the need for unanimity meant that the process was effectively stalled. A leaked document produced by an EU official in September 2008 accurately forecast that Ireland would be pressurized into holding a second referendum so that ratification could proceed:

> a guarantee will be provided in advance of the second vote that Ireland will not lose its EU Commissioner. In addition, there will be 'declarations' or protocols making clear that Ireland's right to set its own policy on abortion, neutrality and taxation will not be affected by Lisbon.
>
> (Open Europe, 2008)

Having secured such guarantees, the second Irish referendum in October 2009 produced a 67 per cent Yes vote. Nevertheless, the Czech Republic further delayed the ratification process by insisting upon an exemption from the Charter of Fundamental Rights. Having obtained the opt-out, already granted to Britain and Poland, the presidents of the Czech Republic and Poland subsequently ratified the Lisbon Treaty and it came into force on 1 December 2009.

Foreign and military policy II

The mid- to late 2000s witnessed the further development of EU foreign policy and military policy. Foreign policy-wise, the EU established the Euro-Mediterranean Partnership in November 2005 which aimed to create a 40-member free trade area by 2010. The EU concluded a number of association agreements – as part of the European Neighbourhood Policy and the Stabilization and Association Process – with countries in the Balkans, the Caucasus region, Eastern Europe, the Mediterranean region and the Middle East. The EU offered these countries access to its market for their agricultural and/or industrial goods in return for economic and political reforms (Mayhew, 1998; Swain and Swain, 2009). Similarly, the EU negotiated several Economic Partnership Agreements with African, Caribbean and Pacific countries, which were criticized for encouraging de-industrialization, creating unfair trading rules and granting EU-based corporations greater control over the economies of participant countries (Action Aid, 2004; Knottnerus and Estaban, 2007; Oxfam, 2008).

Military policy-wise, the EU adopted the common policy on weapons of mass destruction and the common security doctrine in December 2003. The European Security Strategy pledged to

> be more active in pursuing our strategic objectives. This applies to the full spectrum of instruments ... including political, diplomatic, military and civilian, trade and development activities. Active policies are needed to counter the new dynamic threats [and] we need to develop a strategic culture that fosters early, rapid, and when necessary, robust intervention.
>
> (European Council, 2003: 12)

Although the EU is commonly seen as a practitioner of 'soft' power (Nye, 1990, 2004) – which involves the use of attraction and co-optation in terms of culture, institutions and policies – rather than 'hard' (i.e. military) power, the EU undertook military and/or police missions in Aceh (Indonesia), Afghanistan, Albania, Bosnia-Herzegovina, Chad, the Central African Republic, the Democratic Republic of the Congo, Georgia, Guinea-Bissau, Iraq, Kosovo, Macedonia, Moldova, the Palestinian Territories, the Sudan and Ukraine in the 1990s and 2000s. Such operations led Slijper (2005) to warn against the emergence of an EU military-industrial complex.

The European Commission launched the Raw Materials Initiative in November 2008 which addressed Europe's dependence on the import of strategically important raw materials, including high-technology metals such as cobalt, rare earths and titanium, seen as critical for Europe's industrial competitiveness (European Commission, 2008a, 2010c, 2011b – also see Curtis, 2010). The European Commission recommended 'policy actions to improve access to primary resources' (European Commission, 2010c: 4) and the resulting EU strategy aimed to ensure 'a level playing field in access to resources in third countries' by pursuing 'raw materials diplomacy' (European Commission, 2011b: 11). Although not explicitly mentioned, military intervention could be deployed in the future. Indeed, the EU established an independent military planning unit within NATO in December 2003 and created the European Defence Agency in July 2004.

Conclusion

European integration during the NWO, as during the CWO, was a dynamic and fractious, rather than linear and unproblematic, process which was shaped by a multitude of competing social forces in Europe, the United States and elsewhere. Although the EC/EU continued to be dominated by liberal and supranationalist forces, it faced a number of challenges and internal crises. These included the problematic ratification of the Maastricht, Nice, European Constitution and Lisbon treaties, the rejection of the euro by Denmark and Sweden, economic divergence within the eurozone, the ESF campaign for 'Another Europe', and the rising tide of Euroscepticism across Europe – reflected in Eurobarometer polls, the falling turnout in European Parliament elections and the electoral success of Eurosceptic parties (Taylor, 2007). Nevertheless, the EC/EU continued to make significant progress towards its stated goal of 'ever-closer union' during this period.

The European project developed as a neo-liberal entity during the NWO in the sense that it aimed to shift the balance of power from the state to the market at both the EC/EU level and the member state level. EC/EU reification of market liberalism, bias towards negative integration, choice of social regulation and preference for competition and economic liberalization was codified in the SEA, Maastricht, Amsterdam, Nice, European Constitution and Lisbon treaties and was manifest in the SM, EMU, EU enlargement and Lisbon Strategy projects.

The neo-liberal trajectory was reflected in member states' voluntary surrender of control over a range of macroeconomic policy tools such as capital, exchange, export and import controls, interest rates and state aid, plus border controls, and, in the case of accession states, their incorporation of the *acquis communautaire*. The neo-liberal trajectory was reflected in the restructuring of member states' and accession states' economies as previously sheltered, if not protected, sectors of the economy were opened up to competition. This set in train centrifugal forces which exacerbated existing economic divergence and social inequalities. The neo-liberal trajectory was reflected in the growth of corporate power as the EU policy-making process was effectively captured by corporate interests with progressive social forces effectively neutered through their participation in so-called 'social partnership' arrangements. Furthermore, the neo-liberal trajectory was essentially locked in. As a result of the SM, EMU, enlargement and Lisbon Strategy projects, the MCC/SGP requirements to limit budget deficits and public debt levels and pursue 'sound' (i.e. balanced) public finances, the need to implement supply-side-oriented EU macroeconomic and employment policy guidelines, the obligation to produce Stability and Convergence Programmes and National Reform Programmes, and the demands to reform labour market, pension and social security systems so as to ensure the long-term 'sustainability' of welfare states, member states faced an ever-widening array of structural constraints on their room for manoeuvre.

Although the EC/EU became more active in terms of social policy during the NWO, manifest in the increasing number of regulations, directives and recommendations that were issued, the 1957 EEC Treaty objective of harmonizing social policy was replaced by the 1989 Social Charter priorities of respecting national differences in social systems and maintaining the competitiveness of Europe's economies. Consequently, as during the CWO, there was no attempt to create a unified EC/EU-level welfare state. Instead, European social policy aimed to bolster the economic liberalization process by both 'reforming' the supply side of Europe's economies and 'modernizing' Western Europe's welfare states. Utilizing a range of approaches – from legally-binding regulations and directives to recommendations and the voluntary OMC – the EC/EU aimed to influence the development of Western Europe's welfare states in a direct as well as structural sense. More specifically, the EC/EU aimed to steer Western Europe's welfare states towards the market liberal model in terms of objectives (i.e. improved competitiveness, labour market flexibility, increased means testing, lower social expenditure, reduced welfare benefits to ensure 'work pays', etc.) if not outcomes (eroded entitlements, increased inequality and poverty, more means testing, etc.) – though these will surely follow if they have not materialized already. The ESM project and Social Europe discourse were forged by social forces within member states – such as social democratic and socialist political parties, trade unions and other progressive forces – and social forces at the EC/EU level – particularly the European Commission under Delors – as a defensive means of safeguarding the integration process during the problematic Maastricht Treaty ratification process. It was recognized that if the European project was not to be derailed, following its neo-liberal turn in the mid-1980s, then the ongoing support of progressive social forces would need to be secured. The EC/EU treaties and the SM, EMU, enlargement and Lisbon Strategy projects would, therefore, have to be balanced with, at the very least, the rhetoric of defending the ESM and constructing a Social Europe, if not some concrete social advances.

5 The political economy of Western Europe's social models in the New World Order

Retrenching welfare states and the emergence of Social Europe?

Introduction

This chapter explores the retrenchment of Western Europe's social models (i.e. welfare states) and the emergence of the ESM concept and the Social Europe discourse in the context of the NWO. The chapter draws upon the CPE tradition, which utilizes a comprehensive set of analytical and conceptual tools to identify a diverse range of explanatory factors which orthodox approaches tend to ignore. Put simply, it situates the retrenchment of Western Europe's welfare states and the emergence of the ESM concept and the Social Europe discourse within a specific 'historical structure' (Cox, 1996): the NWO. By attending to the nature of the *capitalist* system during this epoch, the *historical* specificities of this era and the *global* configuration of social forces during this period, it seeks to chart a new course for the study of these formations and ideas. The chapter does not advance a CPE-inspired conceptual and/or theoretical exposition of the retrenchment of Western Europe's welfare states and the emergence of the ESM concept and the Social Europe discourse, within the context of European integration and the NWO, as such work has been initiated elsewhere.[1] Instead, it seeks to identify the dominant actors and structures, often neglected by the existing literature, which both shaped and constrained these formations and ideas during the NWO.

The chapter advances four main arguments. First, that the nature and trajectory of Western Europe's welfare states, the ESM concept and the Social Europe discourse were the product of the struggle between social forces at the national, European *and* global levels in the NWO. Second, that the continued deployment of US power in Europe influenced this struggle. Third, that Western Europe's welfare states, the ESM concept and the Social Europe discourse were *shaped by*, and, equally importantly, *constrained by*, the structure of the World Order in this period. Fourth, that the retrenchment of Western Europe's welfare states and the failure to create a unified EU-level welfare state in their place has fatally undermined the ESM concept and the dream, held by many social democratic and socialist political parties, trade unions and other progressive social forces, of constructing a Social Europe.

The chapter is divided into four main sections. The first section reviews the three main debates about the welfare state, the ESM concept and the Social

Europe discourse during this period: the impact of globalization and EU enlargement, the existence of welfare state convergence towards retrenchment, and the
emergence of a single and distinctive ESM. In an attempt to enrich the existing
literature, the second, third and fourth sections look at the broader economic and
political context within which these formations and ideas have developed. More
specifically, the second section focuses upon the transformation of the World
Order from the 1960s, which laid the foundations for the NWO. The third
section, which utilizes official and leaked state planning documents and long-
neglected studies, seeks to show how the struggle between social forces in the
NWO influenced the nature and trajectory of Western Europe's welfare states,
the ESM concept and the Social Europe discourse. Having discussed the weaknesses of the existing literature and having identified the key events and processes that engendered the NWO, the fourth section – which draws upon the
CPE tradition summarized in Chapter 3 – contributes to the aforementioned
debates by investigating the impact of the structure of the World Order on
Western Europe's welfare states, the ESM concept and the Social Europe
discourse. In short, this chapter presents a political economy of these formations
and ideas during the NWO.

Western Europe's welfare states: retrenching or building anew?

There were three main debates about the welfare state, the ESM concept and the
Social Europe discourse in the NWO: one was concerned with the impact of globalization and EU enlargement, the second considered the existence of welfare
state convergence towards retrenchment, and the third focused upon the claimed
emergence of a single and distinctive ESM. The first two debates were synthesized into what Montanari (2001) described as the *new convergence* hypothesis:

> the belief that everywhere the welfare state is being reduced or 'retrenched'
> in the face of the growing power of markets, the desire of politicians to
> reduce state expenditure and public borrowing, and the unwillingness of cit-
> izens to fund welfare expenditure through either taxes or contributions.
>
> (Kleinman, 2002: 12)

The globalization and EU enlargement debate

Therborn and Roebroek (1986), Esping-Andersen (1996), Zysman (1996), Weiss
(1998), Stephens *et al.* (1999), Hirst and Thompson (2000a), van Kersbergen
(2000), Kuhnle (2000), Ross (2000a), Kitschelt (2001), Green-Pedersen and
Haverland (2002), Palier (2002), Navarro *et al.* (2004) and Starke (2006)
defended the *resilience thesis* which emphasized the resilience of the welfare
state in the face of globalization. Cameron (1978), Katzenstein (1985), Rodrik
(1997, 1998), Burgoon (2001) and Swank (2002) found a positive relationship
between the capital mobility and trade openness associated with globalization

and social expenditure levels, while Gough (1999) and Castles (2004) argued that the relationship was contingent but not necessarily negative. Greve (1996), Stephens *et al.* (1999), Garrett (2000), Scharpf (2000), Cornelisse and Goudswaard (2002), Kleinman (2002), Bouget (2003), Castles (2004), Pestieau (2006), Adelantado and Calderón Cuevas (2006), Alsasua *et al.* (2007), Begg *et al.* (2007), Brooks and Manza (2007), Starke *et al.* (2008), Van Vliet (2010) and Draxler and Van Vliet (2010) presented empirical data suggesting continuity, if not increases, in social expenditure across the EU from 1980 (see Table 5.1).

Strange (1988), Esping-Andersen (1996), Greider (1997), Martin and Schumann (1997), Giddens (1998), Gray (1998), Mishra (1990, 1998) and Gilbert (2002), on the other hand, supported the *globalization thesis* and its contention that globalization had precipitated the retrenchment of the welfare state. Globalization, it was claimed, had ushered in an era of 'competitive austerity' (Albo, 1994; Mishra, 1998) or 'permanent austerity' (Pierson, 2001; Ferrera, 2008), while for Giddens (1998) it necessitated the construction of a 'third way' between neo-liberalism and social democracy.

Esping-Andersen (1996), Giddens (1999), Svallfors and Taylor-Gooby (1999), Bonoli *et al.* (2000), Ferrera and Rhodes (2000), Sykes *et al.* (2001), Ferrera (2005, 2008) and Kleinman (2002) identified a number of endogenous and exogenous factors to explain the reform, if not retrenchment, of the welfare state. The former included demographic shifts, such as aging populations and the associated decline in the size of the labour force, changing family and gender

Table 5.1 Social protection expenditure in EU member states as a percentage of GDP, 1980–1997

Country	1980	1990	1997
Austria	30.1	32.5	30.3
Belgium	28.0	26.7	28.5
Denmark	28.7	29.7	31.4
Finland	n/a	25.5	29.9
France	25,4	27.7	30.8
Germany	28.8*	25.4	29.9
Greece	9.7	23.2	23.6
Ireland	20.6	19.1	17.5
Italy	19.4	24.1	25.9
Luxembourg	26.5	22.6	24.8
Netherlands	30.1	32.5	30.3
Portugal	12.8	15.6	22.5
Spain	18.1	19.9	21.4
Sweden	n/a	33.1	33.7
United Kingdom	21.5	23.2	26.8
EU-15	24.3**	25.4	28.2

Source: Eurostat.

Notes
* = West Germany (1980); ** = EU-12 (1980); n/a = not available.

relations, the assumption that politicians and the public would not tolerate high taxes to finance the welfare state, and high unemployment across Europe, while the latter included increased economic competition, the disciplinary power of financial markets, and the constraining effects of the MCC and SGP.

Focusing upon the impact of exogenous factors, Kapstein (1994), Strange (1996) and Garrett and Mitchell (2001) found a negative correlation between the capital mobility and trade openness associated with globalization and social expenditure levels. Focusing upon the impact of both endogenous and exogenous factors, Clayton and Pontusson (1998), Micklewright and Stewart (1999), Korpi (2003), Korpi and Palme (2003), Montanari *et al.* (2008), Nelson (2008) and Caminada *et al.* (2010) presented empirical data suggesting that social expenditure levels across the EU relative to social need had slowed, that differences between member states in terms of social expenditure had increased, that welfare entitlements had been eroded, and that inequality and poverty levels had increased since 1980.

Critiquing the empirical basis of the resilience thesis, more specifically its reliance on aggregate social expenditure levels, Korpi (2003) argued that the end of the commitment to full employment and the associated 'right to work' in the NWO was, in itself, indicative of welfare state retrenchment. Likewise, Ryner (2009: 51) insisted that, rather than concentrating upon social expenditure levels, as much of the existing literature did, it was preferable to focus upon effective entitlements and the 'extent to which they correspond to the norms of distributive justice and legitimacy that is contained in the social citizenship accords'. Accordingly, Ryner contended that, given Western Europe's aging population, rise of single parent households and increase in the female labour force (with associated childcare costs, etc.),

> the stability of social expenditure levels may actually be an indicator of significant welfare state retrenchment. [This is because] from the point of view of social citizenship norms, it makes more sense to focus on the interrelationships of welfare state programmes and what they provide in terms of entitlement. Given the increased demand for, and claims on, these programmes despite fixed resources, we can expect that there has been significant retrenchment.
>
> (Ibid.)

The collection edited by Mullally and O'Brien (2006) insisted that the ESM was failing economically and socially, and that to succeed in the era of globalization, Western Europe's welfare states needed to adopt the market liberal model. Panić (2007), on the other hand, compared the three main models of capitalism – corporatist, market liberal and social democratic – in terms of their economic and social performance and concluded that the social democratic model outperformed 'its corporatist alternative … and even more so the liberal model' (ibid.: 166).

Several scholars considered the impact of *EU enlargement* on Europe's welfare states, both East and West, to ascertain whether the East was converging towards the West in a 'race to the top', or whether the West was converging towards the East in a 'race to the bottom'. The collected volume edited by Ingham and Ingham (2002), the special issue of *West European Politics* (2002), the special issue of *Global Social Policy* (2003), Sinn (2003) and Manning (2004) concluded that it was too early to fully assess the impact because of the lack of comprehensive and comparative data. Nevertheless, Glyn (1992), Kregel *et al.* (1992), UNICEF (1993), Gorzelak *et al.* (1994), Parker (1994), the World Bank (1994), the International Labour Organization (1995a), Chossudovsky (1997), Andor and Summers (1998), Feffer (1999), Gowan (1999a), the collection edited by Klein and Pomer (2001), Baker (2005) and Klein (2008) documented the huge economic and social costs borne by the masses during the 'shock therapy' of the 1990s in Eastern Europe, which the EU enlargement process reinforced.

The retrenchment debate

The debate about welfare state retrenchment progressed in three main directions, generating economic, institutional and political theories. One group of scholars developed a set of *economic* theories to account for welfare state resilience or retrenchment and these centred upon the arguments for and against the globalization and resilience theses discussed above. George and Taylor-Gooby (1996), Taylor-Gooby (1999, 2001, 2004), Bonoli *et al.* (2000), Palier and Sykes (2001), Armingeon and Bonoli (2006) and Begg *et al.* (2007), however, rejected such a polarized discourse and suggested that globalization came in different guises and had different effects in different West European countries. These scholars pointed to the existence of different institutional arrangements underpinning the welfare state and, drawing upon the notion of path-dependency (North, 1990), argued that such diversity helped to explain why Western Europe's welfare states had not converged during the post-war period and, similarly, why the retrenchment trend was differentiated.

A second group of scholars advanced a number of *institutional* theories to account for welfare state resilience or retrenchment. Goodin and LeGrand (1987), Taylor-Gooby (1988) and Korpi and Palme (2003) stressed the differential involvement of the middle classes in social security systems and their role as powerful interest groups resistant to change. Esping-Andersen (1996), Pierson (1996), Palier (2000), Rothstein (2000) and Swank (2001) emphasized the impact of policy feedback effects, which could be negative or positive depending upon whose interests were affected by the policy change, the magnitude of the costs and benefits associated with the change, and the extent to which interest groups attempted to influence the government to minimize the cost or maximize the benefits. Coughlin (1980), Svallfors (1997), Svallfors and Taylor-Gooby (1999), Gelissen (2000), Scarbrough (2000), Kananen *et al.* (2006), Brooks and Manza (2007) and Giger (2011) pointed to the variations in public opinion on welfare cuts and social expenditure. Garrett (1998), Levy (1999), Ross (2000a), Huber and Stephens (2001), Kitschelt (2001), Green-Pedersen (2002), Kittel and

Obinger (2003), Korpi and Palme (2003), Allen and Scruggs (2004), Ferrera (2005), Rueda (2005) and Trampusch (2006) prioritized the impact of political party competition, and the role of other actors such as the EU and trade unions, on the welfare state.

Similarly, Pierson (1998), Crepaz and Birchfield (2000), Bonoli (2001), Huber and Stephens (2001), Swank (2001) and Obinger *et al.* (2005) highlighted the influence of constitutional arrangements and electoral systems. They specifically utilized the notion of veto points, where a large number of veto players can inhibit retrenchment and vice versa.

While there was a consensus that globalization had transformed the balance of power that underpinned the post-war welfare state, the trajectory of Western Europe's welfare states was disputed. The *new politics of the welfare state approach*, advanced by Pierson (1994a, 1996, 1998, 2001) and supported by Hemerijck (2002), Rhodes (2002) and others, argued that Western Europe's welfare states were being reformed so as to take account of the new economic and political context: permanent austerity. Pierson put forward two significant arguments in this regard. First, Pierson conceded that the welfare state was changing but insisted that this was due to domestic factors rather than globalization:

> the slower economic growth and related problems associated with rising service employment, the tremendous expansion of governmental commitments, the fiscal demands stemming from population aging in countries with mature social programmes, and the restructuring of the households would, by themselves, have generated much of the current turmoil around the welfare state. Had economic openness remained constant over the past quarter-century, governments would nonetheless face increasing inflexibility and intense fiscal pressure, including tendencies towards deficit spending and demands for programme cutbacks and policy reform.
>
> (Pierson 2001: 83)

Second, Pierson suggested that the political logic of retrenchment was fundamentally different to that of welfare state expansion in the early post-war period; in short, the expansion of social security schemes over time had created two policy feedback effects – the popular entrenchment of the welfare state and the creation of powerful interest groups – which made retrenchment difficult. In other words, the welfare state had entered a phase of maturity and inevitable reform but, contrary to the globalization thesis, it was not facing an existential crisis.

Scarbrough (2000: 226) critiqued the core of the Pierson thesis: 'that there are such discontinuities – of politics and policy environments – between welfare expansion and welfare retrenchment that one cannot contribute to an explanation of the other'. Instead, Scarbrough argued that the political institutions and social forces that had influenced the post-war expansion of the welfare state – the strength of left-wing political parties and trade unions and the particular traditions of state governance – were the same political institutions and social forces which, in the era of globalization, were 'far from spent' and were thus 'obstacles to radical reform' (ibid.).

Building upon Pierson's work, Hemerijck (2002) and Rhodes (2002) advanced three main arguments. First, while Hemerijck and Rhodes acknowledged that, as a result of the MCC, there had been some adverse deflationary effects on employment rates, some increase in inequality and some important changes in terms of welfare entitlement, they contended that these were necessary changes that placed Western Europe's welfare states on a more secure and sustainable basis. In this sense, the ESM was 'undergoing a rational "self-transformation"' and EMU had been 'good for the welfare state' (Ryner, 2009: 50).

Second, Hemerijck and Rhodes claimed that the fear of social dumping – where economic competition from less developed welfare states in Southern (and now also Eastern) Europe would compel the Northern European welfare states to 'retrench in a race to the bottom' (ibid.) – was misplaced as some welfare states had actually expanded during this period. Likewise, Erickson and Kuruvilla (1994), Adnett (1995), Alber and Standing (2000), Deacon (2000), Guillén and Matsaganis (2000), Hall *et al.* (2007) and Rüdiger (2007) found little or no empirical evidence to substantiate the social dumping hypothesis. The Trade Union Advisory Committee (of the OECD) (2004), Kirkegaard (2005) and Galgóczi *et al.* (2007), on the other hand, found that international outsourcing and off-shoring had resulted in significant job losses across the EU. Similarly, Begg *et al.* (2007) found evidence that outsourcing had led to significant wage losses for some unskilled workers.

Third, Hemerijck and Rhodes – in common with the International Labour Organization (1995b), Rhodes (1996, 1997) and Fajertag and Pochet (1997) – noted that the 1990s saw the proliferation of social pacts between capital, labour and the state after a decade of corporatist decline in the 1980s. Indeed, they argued that the SGP had increased the need and scope of corporatist collective agreements and industrial relations. Pointing to the alleged success of the Dutch model in particular, Rhodes (1998) suggested a new term for these arrangements: competitive corporatism. Similarly, Visser and Hemerijck (1997) and Hirst and Thompson (2000b) pointed to the 'Dutch miracle' as an example of how welfare states could adapt, reform and prosper in an era of globalization; the Netherlands allegedly represented a successful case of enhancing international competitiveness while maintaining social cohesion (Svallfors and Taylor-Gooby, 1999).

Several scholars critiqued the claims of the *new politics of the welfare state* approach and offered support to the basic tenet of the *new convergence* hypothesis: retrenchment. Rejecting the notions of path-dependency and the maintenance of the status quo, Bonoli and Palier (1998), Palier and Sykes (2001) and Starke (2008) found evidence of path-shifting welfare reforms in Britain and France. Likewise, the studies by Cave and Himmelstrup (1995), Torfing (1999), Cox (2001) and Sykes *et al.* (2001) found evidence of significant welfare reform in France, Ireland, the Netherlands and the countries of Eastern and Southern Europe.

A third group of scholars put forward *political* theories to account for welfare state resilience or retrenchment. Ross (2000b), Cox (2001), Hay and Rosamond (2002), Schmidt (2000, 2002, 2005) and Slothuus (2007) explored the discursive dimension of welfare state retrenchment; that is to say, the construction of the austerity agenda and the framing of retrenchment as a necessary policy response.

Working within the CPE tradition, Abrahamson (1991) predicted that the neo-liberalism associated with the SM project – more specifically the lack of minimum income schemes in member states, the erosion of citizen and workers' rights, and the lack social policy action at the EU level – would worsen poverty levels and would lead to the 'Americanization' of Western Europe's welfare states. Similarly, Holman (1992, 1996), Overbeek (1993), Gill (1998, 2001), the two special issues of the *International Journal of Political Economy* (1998a, 1998b), Bieler (2000), the collection edited by Bieler and Morton (2001), van Apeldoorn (2002), the collection edited by Cafruny and Ryner (2003), the collection edited by Overbeek (2003), the collection edited by van Apeldoorn *et al.* (2009), Preece (2009) and the collection edited by Nousios *et al.* (2011) critiqued the neo-liberal basis of the SM, EMU, Lisbon Strategy, EU enlargement and European Constitution/Lisbon Treaty projects and argued that the consequent reconfiguration of social forces had weakened Western Europe's welfare states.

Boyer (1995) observed that the link between economic growth and social wage increases during the 'golden age' of the 1950s and 1960s was broken in the 1970s. Thereafter wages were simply defined as a market variable rather than an integral part of the social democratic settlement, thus eroding the basis upon which Western Europe's welfare states were founded.

Teague (1998) and Ryner and Schulten (2003) questioned the progressive credentials of the social pacts of the 1990s, arguing that they

> fundamentally change the nature of the 'social compromise' which becomes increasingly asymmetrical and unfavourable to labour: trade unions are asked to provide certain effective guarantees in exchange for the rather vague, and by no means ensured, hope that this will induce increased employment.
>
> (Ibid.: 189)

Meanwhile, Western Europe continues to suffer from persistently high levels of unemployment (Michie and Grieve Smith, 1994; Mills, 1998).

Several scholars challenged the notion that the so-called 'Dutch miracle' represented a successful model to be emulated. Delsen (2002) observed that income and wealth inequality rose significantly in the Netherlands from the 1980s. Becker (2003, 2005) revealed that the Dutch economy was not the claimed 'jobs machine'. Instead, the 'miracle years' of negotiated labour market flexibility and wage restraint had induced a shift from relatively secure, full-time jobs to more precarious, flexible and part-time working. Becker found that these part-time jobs were in the more sheltered service sector of the economy rather than the more exposed sectors. Furthermore, Becker found that, despite the concerted attempts to reduce labour costs, etc., the performance of the export sector actually worsened during the 1990s and early 2000s. Keman (2003) pointed to a major retrenchment of the welfare state during this period, while van Apeldoorn (2009) argued that these developments, together with the austerity measures, marketization and privatization associated with EMU, contributed to the No result of the 2005 referendum on the European Constitution.

The ESM debate

If Western Europe's welfare states were indeed changing, then the critical question became: were they converging towards one social model – downwards to the market liberal model, upwards to the social democratic model or towards a hybrid ESM, etc. – or, in a path-dependency sense, did they continue to diverge by travelling along their own particular lines of development thus ensuring the persistence of different, albeit reformed, social models? This fundamental question formed the basis of the third debate, which focused upon the emergence of a single and distinctive ESM.

Following Hay *et al.* (1999) and pointing to the normative and rhetorical nature of the term, Jepsen and Serrano Pascual (2005, 2006) argued that the ESM concept was underpinned by a number of assumptions, most of which had not been empirically verified. Indeed, they highlighted the polysemous nature of the ESM and identified a number of different ways in which the concept was understood and discussed. Building upon the work of Hay *et al.* (1999) and Jepsen and Serrano Pascual (2006), it was possible to identify four, by no means mutually exclusive, approaches to the study of the ESM.

One group of scholars treated the ESM as a model that incorporated common features, such as *shared institutions and values*. For Vaughan-Whitehead (2003), the ESM was underpinned by principles such as anti-discrimination, equal opportunities, full employment, public services, regional cohesion, social dialogue, social inclusion, transnational social policies and tools, fair wages, workers' participation and workers' rights. More recently, Philine ter Haar and Copeland (2010) defined the ESM as a mixture of hard law (i.e. collective agreement and EU directives), soft law (i.e. Action Programmes, the EES, the OMC, European Commission and European Council recommendations) and underlying norms and values.

Scharpf (2002), Foster and Scott (2003), and Sakellaropoulos and Berghman (2004) focused upon the economic aspects of the ESM – more specifically the reality of regulated, mixed economies across Western Europe. The collection edited by Martin and Ross (2004) investigated the impact of EMU on the ESM. Grahl and Teague (1997), Ferrera *et al.* (2000a, 2000b, 2001), Ferrera (2003), Foster and Scott (2003) and Hyman (2005) focused upon the industrial relations dimension – more specifically the 'social partnership' arrangements that underpinned the ESM, while Grahl and Teague (1997), Ferrera and Rhodes (2000), Ferrera *et al.* (2000a, 2000b, 2001), Scharpf

(2002), Ferrera (2003), Sakellaropoulos and Berghman (2004), Blanpain *et al.* (2006), Follesdal *et al.* (2007), Lauk (2009) and McCormick (2010) focused upon the social components – more specifically the extensive social services and comprehensive welfare systems across Western Europe, plus the common objectives of equality, social justice and solidarity.

From a comparative perspective, several scholars distinguished the ESM from the US model of capitalism and pointed to the superiority of the former. Cox (1996), Vobruba (2001), Kupchan (2002), Habermas and Derrida (2003), Haseler (2004), Reid (2004), Adnett and Hardy (2005), Judt (2005), Leonard (2005), Pontusson (2005), Giddens *et al.* (2006), Giddens (2007), McCormick (2007) and Hill (2010) argued that Social Europe represented a necessary and viable response to the forces of globalization and/or an actual or potential counter-hegemonic project within the US-dominated NWO – thus implying the existence of an identifiable ESM. DuBoff (1989), Mishel *et al.* (1999), Sapir (2005), the OECD (2006) and Wilkinson and Pickett (2009) compared the performance of advanced capitalist countries across a range of economic performance indicators and quality of life variables and found that European countries, particularly those with social democratic welfare states, consistently outperformed the United States. Alber (2006, 2010) challenged this view, however, and noted that, in terms of longitudinal data, variation within the EU was bigger than the gap between Western Europe and the United States.

A second group of scholars treated the ESM as an *ideal-typical* model, in the Weberian sense, which combined economic efficiency with social justice. Ebbinghaus (1999) categorized four groups of welfare state in Western Europe, which together formed the 'European social landscape', and he argued that the unity of these, in combination with such diversity, was the hallmark of the EU. More recently, Hantrais (2007) described the moves towards a consolidated ESM, from the objective of social policy harmonization in the 1950s, 1960s and 1970s through to coherence, social cohesion and convergence in the 1980s and co-operation, coordination and dialogue from the 1990s.

A third group of scholars conceived the ESM as a *European project*. In other words, the ESM was seen as a work-in-progress and an emerging transnational phenomenon. Palme (2001), O'Hagan (2002), O'Connor (2005), Jepsen and Serrano Pascual (2006), Heidenreich and Zeitlin (2009), and Kröger (2009) pointed to the cognitive-discursive function of the ESM and argued that it was changing the way in which general publics, politicians and policy-makers thought and talked about European integration (also see Walters and Henrik Haahr, 2005; Rhinard, 2010).

Marginson and Sisson (2002) claimed that the ESM was helping to bring about a multi-level system of industrial relations in Europe. Kersbergen (2000), Sapir (2005), Hopkin and Wincott (2006), Annesley (2007), Stråth (2007), Aiginger (2008), Swedenborg (2008) and Madsen (2008) saw the ESM as a means of modernizing Western Europe's welfare states. Kuhnle (2000), Kvist and Saari (2007) and Philine ter Haar and Copeland (2010) highlighted the role of the ESM in encouraging the Europeanization of social policy, while Leibfried and Pierson

(1995a), Adnett (2001), de la Porte and Pochet (2002), Martin (2004), Adnett and Hardy (2005), Falkner et al. (2005), Jørgensen and Madsen (2007), Barnier (2008), Blanpain and Dickens (2008), Hendrickx (2008), Rogowski (2008), Heidenreich and Zeitlin (2009) and Schmidt (2009) emphasized the role of the ESM – specifically EWCs, the EES, the OMC, the notion of flexicurity,[2] etc. – in bringing about policy transfer and policy convergence within the EU.

A fourth group of scholars, many of whom drew upon the CPE tradition, denied the existence of the ESM and/or argued that such a formation was unlikely to develop or was under threat. In short, the ESM was seen as an *impossible dream*. Grahl and Teague (1989, 1997) and Vaughan-Whitehead (2003) argued that globalization and EU enlargement had undermined the ESM. Michie and Grieve Smith (1994), Mills (1998), Teague (1994, 1998) and Huffschmid (2005) insisted that the SM and EMU projects had locked the EU into a low growth-high unemployment trajectory, while Frangakis *et al.* (2009) and Preece (2009) stated that EU- and member state-sponsored liberalization and privatization were embedding neo-liberalism in Europe.

Leibfried (1993) pointed out that the EU was founded upon a negative conception of integration, namely the removal of barriers to the free market, rather than a positive conception and that the EU treaties were consequently constraining social policy action at the EU level. Similarly, Scharpf (1997, 1999, 2002) pointed to the asymmetry between economic and political integration in the EU. One of the outcomes of this state of affairs was that, in social policy terms, the EU had proved incapable of effective action:

> National welfare states are legally and economically constrained by European rules of economic integration, liberalization and competition law, whereas efforts to adopt European social policies are politically impeded by the diversity of national welfare states, differing not only in levels of economic development and hence in their ability to pay for social transfers and services but, even more significantly, in their normative aspirations and institutional structures.
>
> (Scharpf, 2002: 645)

Kuhnle (1999) and Jessop (2003) pointed out that there was no EU-level welfare state. The former, for example, explained that

> There exists as of today no European social law on the basis of which individual citizens can claim benefits from Brussels; no direct taxation or social contributions to the EU which can finance social welfare; and there hardly exists any welfare bureaucracy in the EU.
>
> (Kuhnle, 1999: 6)

Ziltener (2000) and Neergaard *et al.* (2008) critiqued specific initiatives such as the Social Charter, the EES, the notion of flexicurity and the Services Directive and argued that these would not deliver a Social Europe. Sciarra (2001, 2002), Bercusson (2007), Collins (2008), Davies (2008) and Schmid (2010) focused upon the legal dimension, more specifically the rulings of the ECJ in favour of economic rather than social rights, and questioned whether these judgments were undermining the ESM. Turning the pro-European argument that the EU constitutes the only viable response of Europe's nation-states to globalization on its head, Streeck (2001) contended that European integration had reinforced, rather than helped to contain, international competition, while Hyman (2005) argued that trade unions' conceptions of a Social Europe were defensive and rhetorical rather than proactive and that the institutionalization of trade unions at the EU level precluded the development of a distinctive agenda.

Kleinman (2002: 58) condemned the ESM as a myth and pointed to its broader significance:

> In an analogous way to the national myths that create and sustain both nationalism and nations, the idea of a 'European Social Model' should be considered perhaps as a founding myth which helps create (not defend) the concept and reality of 'Europeanism' and a politically integrated Europe.

Similarly, Hermann and Hofbauer (2007: 126) emphasized the shifting nature of the ESM:

> While initially invented in order to distinguish Europe from the US and to emphasize the social dimension of the integration process, the ESM is now expected to enhance Europe's competitiveness in a globalized world.
>
> Accordingly, the role of the ESM has shifted from symbolizing an alternative to unregulated capitalism to legitimizing a predominantly neo-liberal integration process, to demanding far-reaching restrictions and reforms of national welfare states under the pretence of modernization.

Although the existing literature generated a great deal of insight into welfare state retrenchment in Western Europe and the status of the ESM concept and the Social Europe discourse, it suffered from a number of limitations. First, following the retreat from grand theory, and Marxism in particular, from the 1970s, it often neglected to situate welfare state retrenchment and the ESM concept and the Social Europe discourse within the broader context of the contemporary capitalist system. Second, it often failed to consider how the particular historical period of the NWO influenced these formations and ideas. Third, its focus upon the state and the role of national actors at the EU level often precluded any assessment of the role played by social forces beyond the state – such as civil society, elite power groups, employers' associations, financial capital, trade unions, TNCs, etc. – in the development of these formations and ideas. Fourth, it often omitted to evaluate the continued influence exerted by the United States on these formations and ideas. In short, much of the existing literature continued to generally neglect the political economy of Western Europe's welfare states, the ESM concept and the Social Europe discourse and the specific historical context within which these formations and ideas developed.

The transformation of the World Order

International co-operation, manifest in the BWS, contributed to a sustained period of economic expansion and stability in the world economy in the 1950s and 1960s. The post-war Keynesian period witnessed higher economic growth compared to the pre-1945 and post-1980 periods (see Tables 5.2 and 5.3).

Furthermore, the rate of unemployment and the level of inequality were lower during the Keynesian period compared to the pre-1945 and post-1980 periods (Skidelsky, 2009) and this epoch experienced fewer banking crises and was more financially stable (World Bank, 2001; Skidelsky, 2009; Wolf, 2009).

The falling rate of profit in the North from the mid-1960s – as a result of 'intensified, horizontal inter-capitalist competition' (Brenner, 1998: 8) – produced an economic crisis which undermined the post-war social democratic consensus. The situation was compounded by the 1971 suspension of the BWS unilaterally by the United States, the 1973–1974 oil price hikes, the 1974 call by the South for a New International Economic Order (South Commission, 1990),

Table 5.2 Average growth rates in the pre-Keynesian and Keynesian periods

Country	1913–1950 (%) pre-Keynesian	1950–1959 (%) Keynesian	1960–1969 (%) Keynesian
Britain	1.7	2.7	2.8
France	0.7	4.6	5.8
Italy	1.3	5.8	5.7
Japan	1.8	9.5	10.5
United States	2.9	3.2	4.3
West Germany	1.2	7.8	4.8

Source: adapted from Newton (2004: 56).

Table 5.3 The Keynesian and neo-liberal periods compared

	'Golden age' 1951–1973 (%) (Keynesian)	'Washington consensus' post-1980 (%) (neo-liberal)
Average global growth	4.8	3.2
Average growth in France	4.0	1.6
Average growth in Germany	4.9	1.8
Average growth in Japan	8.0	2.0
Average growth in United Kingdom	2.5	2.1
Average growth in United States	2.2	1.9
Average global inflation	3.9	3.2
Unemployment rate in France	1.2	9.5
Unemployment rate in Germany	3.1	7.5
Unemployment rate in United Kingdom	1.6	7.4
Unemployment rate in United States	4.8	6.1

Source: adapted from Skidelsky (2009: 118–26).

the 1975 US defeat in Vietnam, economic 'stagflation', and a general 'crisis of democracy' in Europe and North America (Crozier *et al.*, 1973).

The response of capital, which required new opportunities for investment in order to restore its profitability, was to reshape the World Order and to shift from a generally *defensive* to a largely *offensive* strategy. The planning for such a transformation was conducted by the CFR and the Trilateral Commission[3] in the midst of the crisis-ridden 1970s. As the CFR president, Bayless Manning, explained in 1974,

> The last systematic, overall examination of the international system – its structure, key relationships, rules, processes and institutions – took place during the Second World War and in the early years of the Cold War. Since then there have been some adjustments but no thoroughgoing attempts to re-examine the pattern as a whole. Much has happened since the late 1940s and early 1950s, and many new demands have been put on the international system: scientific and economic developments have eroded the traditional insulators of time and space and given rise to new interdependencies, population has soared, power has shifted, new states have proliferated, and the number and importance of non-state actors in international affairs have increased. The time is ripe for an attempt to analyze the characteristics of the kind of international system that would be suited to deal with the conditions and problems of the upcoming decade. Systematic intellectual effort is required to identify the changes in policies, institutions and attitudes that such an international system would imply and to suggest ways to bring about those changes. The Council's 1980s Project will undertake that effort.
>
> (Cited in Shoup and Minter, 1977: 255)

The 1980s Project established a number of working groups in order to develop 'strategies for modifying the behaviour of all the relevant actors in the international community – individuals, governments, agencies within governments, elite groups, industrial firms, interest groups, mass societies, and other groups and organizations at the sub-national and transnational levels' (ibid.: 256). The 'necessary' changes in policy were encapsulated in a background paper prepared for the US Federal Reserve prior to the G-7 Summit in June 1976:

> Governments [in industrial states] strongly committed themselves to ameliorate social inequities at home and abroad and to achieve an ever rising standard of living. However socially commendable, these commitments proved to be too ambitious in economic terms – both in what they attempted to achieve and in the expectations they raised among the public. Thus, the major task for the next several years is both economic and political – *not only to regain acceptable levels of output but also to set realistic goals that are accepted by the public at large.* Growth rates that will restore the industrial economies to high employment levels with sufficient price stability to

be sustainable are clearly achievable, but they presuppose a reordering of priorities and a shift in resource allocation towards private investment.

(Cited in Harmon, 1997: 231, emphasis in original)

The 1980s Project was complemented by the work of the Trilateral Commission which came to similar conclusions (Bergsten, 1973; Brzezinski, 1974; Camps, 1974). These initiatives reaffirmed the basic principles of the post-war Grand Area plan but recommended a number of reforms: that the international system should be managed by Europe, Japan and North America (termed Trilateral leadership), that Eastern Europe, the Soviet Union and the South should be integrated with the Trilateral regions, that such a global economy should be based on free trade, that the South should continue to supply raw materials to the industrialized North, and that, in return, the South should benefit from a 'World Order bargain' [which] would involve trading access ... to capital, markets and technology' (Trilateral Commission, 1974). As with the earlier War and Peace Studies Project, many of these ideas were translated into practical politics.

Capital's strategy, the neo-liberal counter-revolution, was a three-stage one. The first stage featured the promotion of neo-liberal ideas by a network of right-wing think tanks. These included the Institute for Economic Affairs (established in 1955), the Centre for Policy Studies (1974), the Freedom Association (1975) and the Adam Smith Institute (1976) in Britain, and the American Enterprise Institute (1943) and the Heritage Foundation (1973) in the United States (Cockett, 1995; Desai, 1994; Miller and Dinan, 2008). The second stage saw the capture of the British Conservative Party, the US Republican Party and international institutions such as the IMF and World Bank, by neo-liberal forces, while the third stage involved the forced implementation of neo-liberal ideas during a series of economic and political crises – described by Klein (2008) as the 'shock doctrine'. The objective of the strategy was the liberation of capital from restrictive controls exercised by nation-states and other regulatory bodies and it was overwhelmingly successful.

The transformation of the World Order was profound in a number of ways. First, corporations became more powerful and wealthy in the NWO, often matching if not exceeding the power and wealth of many nation-states, as a direct result of the process of globalization and the associated neo-liberal counter-revolution. In 1960, worldwide sales by foreign affiliates of TNCs were smaller than world exports, but in 2000 they amounted to 247 per cent of world exports. By 2000, the total assets of foreign affiliates of TNCs stood at $21 trillion, while sales by foreign affiliates totalled £15.7 trillion[4] (United Nations on Trade and Development (UNCTAD), 1998, 2000, 2001). Consequently, corporations increasingly dominated the economies of many countries, in both the North and the South.

Second, corporations became more adept at securing their commercial interests and pursuing their policy agenda vis-à-vis politicians, regulators and general publics. Through their financing of political parties (Ferguson, 1995; Challen, 1998; Ewing, 2007; Liptak, 2010), lobbying efforts (Balanyá *et al.*, 2000; Monbiot, 2000; Corporate Europe Observatory, 2005; McRea, 2005; Alter-EU, 2010;

Weissman and Donohue, 2009), colonization of the media (Herman and Chomsky, 1988; Franklin, 1994; Herman and McChesney, 1997; McChesney, 1999; McChesney *et al.*, 1998; Bagdikian, 2004), utilization of propaganda (Fones-Wolf, 1994; Hughes, 1994; Carey, 1995; Davis, 2002; Sussman, 2005; Beder, 2006a, 2006b; Edwards and Cromwell, 2006, 2009; Dinan and Miller, 2007; Miller and Dinan, 2008), manipulation of the 'revolving door' between business and politics (Project on Government Oversight, 2004) and privileged access to the policy-making process (Alter-EU, 2008), corporations exerted considerable influence over the political process at the national, regional and global levels. Indeed one commentator in the *Financial Times* in 1992 speculated that a ' "de facto world government" was taking shape, in the form of the GATT, G7, IMF, World Bank and other structures designed to serve the interests of banks, investment firms and TNCs in a "new imperial age" ' (cited in Chomsky, 1994: 178).

Third, in geographical terms and building upon the formal empire systems of earlier centuries, there was a clear core-periphery system in operation. There were 78,000 TNCs in existence in 2006 and 58,000 of these were based in the North – principally the 'triad' of Europe, Japan and North America (UNCTAD, 2007). Furthermore, foreign direct investment by TNCs, plus cross-border mergers and acquisitions, were increasingly concentrated within the core economies thus reinforcing the interpenetration of the 'triad' economies.

Fourth, following the liberalization of capital, exchange, export and import controls from the 1970s, the volume of financial and productive capital flowing around the global economy increased markedly. In terms of financial capital, the liberalization of national financial markets in the 1970s and 1980s led to the development of an integrated global financial market (Strange, 1988; Helleiner, 1994; Macartney, 2011). Such processes contributed to the collapse of the BWS, driven by the so-called 'Dollar–Wall Street Regime' (DWSR) (Gowan, 1999a: 4). Based upon dollar hegemony and the 'increasingly US-centred international financial markets', the DWSR 'operated both as an instrument of economic statecraft and power politics' to give the US government 'far more influence over the international financial and monetary relations of the world than it had enjoyed under the Bretton Woods rules' (ibid.: 4, 24). In short, the DWSR facilitated 'the penetration of economies by foreign capital in order to incorporate them into the domestic capital circuit of the US' (Bieling and Jäger, 2009: 87). Importantly, the EU and its member states played a significant role in this transformation (Becht and da Silva, 2007; Ryner, 2007; Macartney, 2011). This reflected both the penetration of Europe's economies by US capital (Panitch and Gindin, 2005; Ryner, 2007) and the choices made by the EU as it moved towards an increasingly 'finance-dominated regime of accumulation' (Bieling and Jäger, 2009: 88 – also see Bieling, 2003, 2006; Macartney, 2011).

In terms of the nature of such capital flows, Eatwell (1993) reported that

in 1971, just before the collapse of the BWS, about 90 per cent of all foreign exchange transactions were for the finance of trade and long-term investment, and only about 10 per cent were speculative. Today those percentages are reversed, with well over 90 per cent of all transactions being speculative. Daily speculative flows now regularly exceed the combined foreign exchange reserves of all the G-7 governments.

The global daily turnover of foreign exchange and currency-based derivatives expanded from $880 billion in 1989 to $3.2 trillion in 2007 (Bank for International Settlements, 2007). In addition, in 2006 the daily trading in equities and government bonds was $450 billion and $1,500 billion respectively (GoForex, 2007; SIMFA, 2007), while the daily turnover of derivatives in 2007 was $4.2 trillion (Bank for International Settlements, 2007). Not surprisingly, the top 50 financial TNCs possessed $32.5 trillion in assets in 2003 (UNCTAD, 2005) and their commanding position was confirmed by Standard Chartered and Oxford Analytica in a 2007 report (see Table 5.4).

In terms of productive capital, UNCTAD (1992: 5) concluded that 'the growth of cross-national production networks of goods and services of some 35,000 TNCs and their more than 150,000 foreign affiliates is beginning to give rise to a transnational production system, organized and managed by TNCs'. Regarding the nature of such a system,

> [TNCs] organize the production process internationally: by placing their affiliates world-wide under common governance systems, they interweave production activities located in different countries, create an international intra-firm division of labour and, in the process, internalize a range of international transactions that would otherwise have taken place in the market.
>
> (UNCTAD, 1994: 9)

In other words, a significant amount of global 'trade' in goods and services was actually intra-firm, that is, within TNCs; consequently TNCs effectively operated as islands of central planning in a sea of market relationships (Coase, 1937). Such corporate concentration, whether in financial and/or productive terms, was facilitated, indeed accelerated, by trade deals such as the GATT (ratified in 1948), the SM project (1987) and NAFTA (1994), plus the myriad of bilateral and regional arrangements concluded over the last two decades.

Table 5.4 Ownership of financial assets by type of institution, 2007

Type of institution	Value of financial assets (e.g. bank deposits, bonds and stocks) ($)
Hedge funds	1.0–1.5 trillion
Institutional investors (including financial TNCs)	53 trillion
Private equity funds	700 billion–1.1 trillion
States: official currency reserves	5.6 trillion
States: sovereign wealth funds	2.2 trillion

Source: adapted from Wolf (2007).

Fourth, as a direct result of such liberalization much of this capital took refuge in 'offshore' tax havens as corporations and wealthy individuals sought to reduce their liabilities via tax avoidance, tax evasion and transfer pricing (Baker, 2005; Mallet and Dinmore, 2011; Shaxson, 2011). Centred upon about 60 'secrecy jurisdictions' – such as the City of London, Britain's Crown Dependencies and Overseas Territories, Ireland, the Netherlands, Switzerland and the United States – this system was vast:

> More than half of world trade passes, at least on paper, through tax havens. Over half of all banking assets and a third of foreign direct investment by TNCs are routed offshore. Some 85 per cent of international banking and bond issuance takes place in the so-called Euromarket, a stateless offshore zone.
>
> (Shaxson, 2011: 8)

The Tax Justice Network (2005), for example, estimated that wealthy individuals hold about $11.5 trillion worth of wealth offshore and that nation-states lost around $250 billion in taxes every year as a result. Furthermore, as Reich (2011) noted, corporations and wealthy individuals now *lend* to governments, via the financial markets and at a profit, rather than contribute towards the cost of government through taxation. Their influence, if not veto power, over government policy has therefore increased.

Fifth, the corporate sector became more integrated and organized over time. Fenema (1982), Useem (1984), Mattera (1992), Robinson and Harris (2000), Sklair (2000), Carroll and Fennema (2002), Beder (2006a, 2006b) and Carroll (2007, 2010) presented empirical evidence of an emerging network of interlocking corporate directorates. Operating through these networks, together with elite planning organizations such as the Bilderberg Group, the European Round Table of Industrialists (ERT), the Trilateral Commission, the World Economic Forum, and others, the corporate sector pursued its commercial interests and its policy agenda in a systematic way on a national, regional and global level (van Apeldoorn, 2000, 2002; Carroll and Carson, 2003; Beder, 2006a, 2006b; Carroll, 2010).

Sixth, and somewhat paradoxically, some nation-states became more not less economically powerful as a result of the process of globalization. The foreign exchange reserves of many nation-states in Asia, Latin America, the Middle East and elsewhere expanded significantly during the 1990s and 2000s. The resulting imbalances within the global economy produced tensions between deficit nation-states (e.g. the United States) and surplus nation-states (e.g. China and Germany) and led the former British prime minister, Gordon Brown, to complain at the G-20 Summit in Pittsburgh in September 2009 that there were $7 trillion of global foreign exchange reserves which were 'not necessarily being used in a constructive way' (quoted in Desai, 2009 – also see Brown, 2010). Furthermore, these reserves were frequently invested – via state-owned corporations, sovereign wealth funds, etc. – in foreign assets which exacerbated such tensions

(Yi-Chong and Bahgat, 2011); between 1999 and 2004, for example, global cross-border investment of this type increased by around 175 per cent (Truman, 2007).

Social forces in the NWO

Drawing upon the CPE tradition, more specifically the neo-Gramscian work of Cox (1987, 1996), the NWO can be conceptualized as a particular constellation of ideological, institutional and material forces, a 'historical structure', which shaped both collective and individual action. Importantly, this configuration of social forces was underpinned by a specific set of production relations and these social forces can be analysed at the global, European and national levels.

Social forces at the global level

Where Fukuyama (1989) claimed that the NWO signalled the 'end of history' and the victory of the liberal democratic model, Chomsky (1994) argued that the basic contours of the World Order remained intact even if some of the modalities of population control had altered. Following the end of the Cold War, the United States was left as the world's sole superpower. To maintain this position, the United States needed to defend the global circuit of capital, and its access to markets and raw materials, which the implementation of the Grand Area plan had brought about. The existence of such objectives was clearly set out in official and leaked state planning documents.

The primary objectives of US foreign policy, access to strategic resources and the maintenance of the 'open door' policy, endured in the NWO. In terms of access, the Southern Command of the US military warned that 'future supplies of oil from Latin America are at risk because of the spread of resource nationalism' (Webb-Vidal, 2006) – oil nationalism being one manifestation of economic nationalism. In terms of the 'open door' policy, the 1995 National Security Strategy prioritized the need 'to press for open and equal US access to foreign markets' (White House, 1995: 7).

In terms of maintaining US hegemony, the 1990 National Security Strategy, which contained a revealing passage about the rhetorical function of the 'Kremlin conspiracy', stated that:

> In the new era, we foresee that our military power will remain an essential underpinning of the global balance, but less prominently and in different ways. We see that the more likely demands for the use of our military forces may not involve the Soviet Union and may be in the Third World, where new capabilities and approaches may be required.... The growing technological sophistication of Third World conflicts will place serious demands on our forces [and may] continue to threaten US interests. [For such reasons, we need to be more able to] project power into areas where we have no permanent presence.... The Middle East is a vivid example ... of a region in

which, even as East–West tensions diminish, American strategic concerns remain. Threats to our interests – including the security of Israel and moderate Arab states as well as the free flow of oil – come from a variety of sources. In the 1980s, our military engagements – in Lebanon in 1983–84, Libya in 1986 and the Persian Gulf in 1987–88 – were in response to *threats that could not be laid at the Kremlin's door*. The necessity to defend our interests will continue.

(White House, 1990: 13, 15, 26, emphasis added)

The draft Defense Planning Guidance for fiscal years 1994–1999, leaked to the *New York Times* (Tyler, 1992; Gellman, 1992) in 1992, proclaimed that

Our first objective is to prevent the re-emergence of a new rival, either on the territory of the former Soviet Union or elsewhere, which poses a threat on the order of that posed formerly by the Soviet Union. This ... requires that we endeavour to prevent any hostile power from dominating a region whose resources would, under consolidated control, be sufficient to generate global power. These regions include Western Europe, East Asia, the territory of the former Soviet Union and Southwest Asia. [To achieve this] the US must show the leadership necessary to establish and protect a new order that holds the promise of convincing potential competitors that they need not aspire to a greater role or pursue a more aggressive posture to protect their legitimate interests. [Furthermore] we must account sufficiently for the interests of the advanced industrial nations to discourage them from challenging our leadership or seeking to overturn the established political and economic order [and] we must maintain the mechanisms for deterring potential competitors from even aspiring to a larger regional or global role.

(Cited in Tyler, 1992)

In addition, the document specified the main US goals in Europe:

[It] is of fundamental importance to preserve NATO as the primary instrument of Western defense and security as well as the channel for US influence and participation in European security affairs. While the US supports the goal of European integration, we must seek to prevent the emergence of European-only security arrangements which would undermine NATO.... The most promising avenues for anchoring the East-Central Europeans into the West and for stabilizing their democratic institutions are their participation in Western political and economic organizations. [This requires] East-Central European membership in the (European Community) at the earliest opportunity and expanded NATO liaison.

(Ibid.)

The 2000 Department of Defense document, *Joint Vision 2020*, set out the means that the United States would employ to maintain its hegemony:

The strategic concepts of decisive force, power projection, overseas presence, and strategic agility will continue to govern our efforts to fulfil those responsibilities and meet the challenges of the future.... The label full spectrum dominance implies that US forces are able to conduct prompt, sustained, and synchronized operations with combinations of forces tailored to specific situations and with access to and freedom to operate in all domains – space, sea, land, air, and information. Additionally, given the global nature of our obligations, the United States must maintain its overseas presence forces and the ability to rapidly project power worldwide in order to achieve full spectrum dominance.

(Department of Defense, 2000: 1, 8)

Likewise, the 2006 Department of Defense document, the *Quadrennial Defense Review*, announced that 'long-duration, complex operations involving the US military, other government agencies and international partners will be waged simultaneously in multiple countries around the world, relying on a combination of direct (visible) and indirect (clandestine) approaches' (Department of Defense, 2006: 23).

Despite such state planning, with its associated hubris, US hegemony was repeatedly challenged in the NWO. Contenders included the EU, particularly the 'old Europe' of France and Germany, the emerging powers of China and India, the resurgent Russia, and economic nationalism in Latin America and the Middle East. In an attempt to counter these threats, the United States consolidated its power via the DWSR, re-launched NATO by expanding its membership and extending its reach, maintained 700 military bases in 130 countries and militarized space through its National Missile Defense (NMD) project. Furthermore, the United States conducted a number of covert operations, such as the attempted coup in Venezuela in April 2002 (Golinger, 2006) and the secret funding of several 'colour revolutions' in the Middle East and the former Soviet bloc (Chaulia, 2005; William Engdhal, 2009), in pursuit of its economic and strategic objectives. The United States also militarily intervened in Panama (in 1989), Iraq (1991), Somalia (1993), the former Yugoslavia (1999), Afghanistan (2001) and Iraq (2003) – under the pretexts of the 'war of drugs', 'humanitarian intervention' and, more recently, the 'war on terror'.

Social forces at the European level

At the European level, the NWO precipitated a major foreign policy reversal on the part of the former Soviet Union, as Russia sought to re-establish its economic and political links with Western Europe, including the EU. It signed a Partnership and Co-operation Agreement with the EU in December 1997 and agreed a joint policy in May 1999 to 'bring Russian economic, political and social institutions into a "common European space"' (Walker, 1999). Likewise, the Russian government established the United Europe committee in May 2001 to 'embark on the long haul towards what it hopes will result in full integration with, if not membership of, the EU' (Traynor and Pilkington, 2001). Buoyed by expanding natural gas and oil revenues, however, an increasingly assertive Russia reappraised its strategy; the then president, Vladimir Putin, stated in March 2007 that Russia had 'no intention of either joining the EU or establishing any form of institutional association with it' (cited in Borger, 2007). Meanwhile, Russia clashed with Europe and the United States over Chechnya, Georgia and Kosovo, energy security, Iran, the Anglo-American war on Iraq, the NMD project, NATO enlargement, WTO membership and the structure of the World Order.

The NWO also witnessed an important shift in US foreign policy. The postwar objective of supporting European integration as a bulwark against European socialism and Soviet communism was replaced by the objective of undermining Europe as a rival economic, military and political bloc. Despite the proliferation of conflict between the EU and the United States over a whole range of issues – including the euro–dollar exchange rate, subsidies and tariffs, genetically modified products, the International Criminal Court, the Kyoto Protocol, the Anglo-American war on Iraq, relations with Russia and the structure of the World Order – the consolidation of US power over Europe, through the operation of the DWSR and the expansion of a revitalized NATO, effectively locked in the EU. Consequently, 'the possibilities for a European challenge are sharply circumscribed by its subordinate participation within a US-led neo-liberal transnational financial order and its related inability to develop an autonomous regional security structure' (Cafruny, 2009: 65).

Following the re-launch of the European project in the mid-1980s, the internationalization and regionalization of Europe's economies continued apace. Indeed, by 2005 trade between member states represented, for the EU(25) as a whole, two-thirds of all EU trade (see Table 5.5).

Similarly, the economies of Europe and the United States became increasingly interdependent with, in 2008, \$2.1 trillion of foreign direct investment in each other's economies. These economies accounted for almost half of the global economy and one or the other of them was the biggest investment and trade partner for every other economy in the world (European Commission, 2010d). Furthermore, the desire to re-embed the transatlantic alliance following its rupture over the 2003 Iraq war was reflected in the objective to establish a transatlantic SM; the EU and the United States agreed in April 2008 to establish an economic council to oversee the Transatlantic Economic Partnership project.

The political trajectory of the EU, however, was contested; a number of rival projects emerged, 'each of which must be seen as linked to specific transnational political and social forces, and as constituting contending responses on the part of these forces to the crisis of European capitalism within the context of global capitalist restructuring' (van Apeldoorn, 2001: 74). There were three main projects. First, the neo-liberal project which sought to expand the market and shrink the state, viewing 'Europe as an advanced free trade zone within a free trading world' (ibid.). Second, the neo-mercantilist project which favoured the development of 'European champions' that could, through an active industrial policy, investment in technology and greater economies of scale, effectively compete with Japanese and US corporations within the context of globalization and thus restore Europe's international competitiveness; 'a strong European home market was expected to serve as both a stepping-stone to conquer the world market as well as a protective shield against outside competition' (ibid.: 75). Third, the social democratic project associated with the European Commission under Delors, the trade union movement and other progressive social forces, which strove to 'protect the "European model of society", and its traditions of the mixed economy and high levels of social protection, against the potentially destructive forces of globalization and neo-liberalism' (ibid.: 76).

One of the main drivers behind the re-launch of Europe in the mid-1980s and a key player in the struggle between the aforementioned rival projects was the ERT, a corporate network established in 1983 by the chief executives of several EU-based corporations in order to transcend the more traditional lobbying efforts of the Union of Industrial and Employers' Confederations of Europe (Gardner, 1991; Green Cowles, 1995; van Apeldoorn, 2000, 2001, 2002; Balanyá *et al.*, 2000; Nollert and Fielder, 2000). The ERT was initially populated by

Table 5.5 Exports to EU member states as a percentage of each country's total exports, 2005

Country	Percentage
Austria	69.3
Belgium	76.4
Cyprus	71.7
Czech Republic	84.2
Denmark	70.5
Estonia	77.9
Finland	56.0
France	62.6
Germany	63.4
Greece	52.9
Hungary	76.3
Ireland	63.4
Italy	58.6
Latvia	76.4
Lithuania	65.3
Luxembourg	89.4
Malta	51.6
Netherlands	79.2
Poland	77.2
Portugal	79.8
Spain	71.8
Slovakia	85.4
Slovenia	66.4
Sweden	58.4
United Kingdom	56.9

Source: Eurostat.

representatives of European capital who favoured the neo-mercantilist project. From 1988, however, the composition of the ERT changed and representatives of global capital, who supported the neo-liberal project, began to dominate (van Apeldoorn, 2001). Furthermore, the linkages among members of the ERT had deepened over time; Nollert and Fielder (2000) found that financial inter-connections (i.e. mergers and acquisitions, plus joint ventures and strategic alliances) and management inter-connections (i.e. interlocking directorates) had increased between 1984 and 1994. It was thus possible to conceive of the ERT as a transnational corporate formation. Importantly, the ERT played a critical role in the neo-liberal turn of the EU in the mid-1980s; Balanyá *et al.* (2000) and Lucas and Hines (2000) found a positive correlation between the recommendations of reports produced by the ERT and the policies and treaties adopted by the EU. Equally importantly, these developments were supported by the United States; in the NWO

> The US has been pressing the EU to integrate the Eastern European countries and Turkey in the expectation that they will serve as, in effect, US agents blocking the threat that a prosperous and powerful Europe will follow an independent path. Sometimes the expectations are expressed with astonishing vulgarity, as in an article in the *Washington Post* cheering the prospect that the accession of these countries will erode Europe's welfare states, undermine labour, and generally drive Europe towards the US model.[5]

Social forces at the national level

At the national level, the NWO accelerated the restructuring of the state in response to the perceived crisis of the 'common model' or KWNS model and Atlantic Fordism/corporate liberalism/embedded liberalism more generally. In the core capitalist countries of Britain and the United States, a new form of capitalism, termed 'hyper-liberalism', emerged (Cox, 1996). Predicated on a return to nineteenth-century economic liberalism and the abandonment of Keynesian policies, 'hyper-liberalism' sought to transform the state by 'rolling back' its progressive functions (i.e. social services), extending its repressive apparatus (i.e. intelligence agencies and the military) and expanding corporate welfare (i.e. public subsidy for private profit through military Keynesianism and other measures), while re-organizing the labour force (i.e. 'flexible' labour markets). Implemented by the British Conservative Party and the US Republican Party, neo-liberals attempted to export this model globally through the IMF, World Bank, WTO and other international financial institutions.

Just as the 'common model' or KWNS model had a differentiated impact across the globe during the CWO, in terms of whether or not it was embedded, so the restructuring of this model in the NWO varied from place to place. Nevertheless, several scholars have pointed to the emergence of a new model. Reflecting the increased importance of competition in the era of globalization, Cerny (1990) highlighted the evolution of what he termed the 'competition state', with its prioritization of economic competitiveness, while Jessop (2003: 38–9) described the new ideal-typical formation as the Schumpeterian workfare post-national regime (SWPR). Such a regime was Schumpeterian in the sense that the role of the state vis-à-vis private capital was to 'promote permanent innovation and flexibility in relatively open economies by intervening on the supply side and to strengthen as far as possible [its] structural and/or systemic competitiveness'. It constituted a workfare regime insofar as it 'subordinates social policy to the demands of labour market flexibility and employability and to the demands of structural or systemic competitiveness' and it was post-national because policy-making functions were transferred 'upwards, downwards or sideways' to new international organizations and forums – such as the EU. Furthermore, these 'general tendencies can be identified and grounded in the logic of contemporary capitalism' even if they did not 'justify a simple "one-size-fits-all" account of welfare restructuring' (ibid.).

The Unites States and Europe

As with the CWO, there was a darker side to the NWO which the existing literature completely ignored. While the re-integration of China into the global economy after 1979 and the demise of the Soviet bloc between 1989 and 1991 vanquished the spectre of ultra-nationalism – leading Lloyd (1994) to claim that the NWO heralded 'the death not of communism but of economic nationalism' – and while capital may have withdrawn support for the social democratic consensus in favour of neo-liberalism, the reality is that economic nationalism remained a threat in the NWO. Consequently, the United States – acting at the behest of financial capital and TNCs – continued to intervene in Europe to defend its interests against economic nationalism and hundreds of thousands of people were killed, tortured or harmed as a result.

The then general secretary of the Soviet Communist Party, Mikhail Gorbachev, launched his policies of glasnost (i.e. openness) and perestroika (i.e. restructuring) in 1986 in an attempt to reform the Soviet Union. Under Gorbachev,

> the press had been freed, Russia's parliament, local councils, president and vice-president had been elected, and the constitutional court was independent. [Economically] Gorbachev [favoured] moving towards ... a free market with an extensive safety net, with key industries under public control – a process he predicted would take 10 to 15 years to complete.
>
> (Klein, 2008: 219)

In short, Gorbachev aimed to lead the Soviet Union towards the Scandinavian social democratic model. The public supported such a policy; polls conducted in 1992, for example, found that 67 per cent of Russians supported the transformation of state-run enterprises into workers' co-operatives, while 79 per cent believed that maintaining full employment should be a key government objective

(Mau, 1994). Gorbachev also promoted the 'One Europe' plan which envisaged a pan-European economic, political and security system encompassing Western Europe, a unified Germany outside of NATO, Eastern Europe and the Soviet Union. Such a system would have enabled Eastern Europe to also shift towards social democracy. France and Germany supported the plan between 1989 and 1991, while the United States was implacably opposed (Gowan, 1999a, 1999b, 1999c) because

> The big loser from One Europe would be the United States, since it would lose political hegemony over Western Europe and would lose control of a new and potentially very dynamic capital accumulation process harmonizing the West European economy and the Russian economy.
>
> (Gowan, 1999c: 94)

Having initially supported Gorbachev and his reforms, the United States and its allies, including France and Germany, turned against him at the G-7 Summit in July 1991. They rejected Gorbachev's plea for financial assistance to facilitate the transformation and thus deliberately precipitated a crisis because, as the neo-liberal economist, Friedman (1962: ix), observed, 'only a crisis – actual or perceived – produces real change'. The United States and its allies called for the Soviet Union to implement 'shock therapy' – a message reinforced by the IMF, the World Bank and other international financial institutions (Gowan, 1999a, 1999b; Klein, 2008). The United States subsequently threw its weight behind Boris Yeltsin and supported his 1993 coup against parliament, his dissolution of the Constitutional Court and his imposition of neo-liberalism in the form of an IMF-sponsored structural adjustment programme (SAP) (Chossudovsky, 1997; Reddaway and Glinski, 2001; Klein, 2008).

Opposition to Soviet rule in Poland led to the formation of the Solidarity trade union in September 1980. Backed by the United States as part of its so-called 'crusade for democracy' (Lowenthal, 1991; Chomsky, 1997), the Solidarity movement was elected in June 1989. Some sections of the movement favoured transforming the state-run factories and farms into workers' co-operatives, thus forming the basis of a socialized economy, while others urged the adoption of the Scandinavian social democratic model. Faced with $40 billion of debt, food shortages, high inflation and a dysfunctional economy, however, the new government required external financial assistance to transform the country. The United States offered only $119 million and insisted that Poland had to honour the debts of the previous regime. The government was thus forced to adopt an IMF-sponsored SAP in August 1990 (Andor and Summers, 1998; Chomsky, 1994; Gowan, 1999a, 1999b; Klein, 2008).

Having supported the neutrality and territorial integrity of Yugoslavia throughout the Cold War period, the United States and its allies actively dismembered the federation in the NWO. Economically, Yugoslav indebtedness to Western creditors and US insistence that such debts be honoured forced the federation to adopt IMF-sponsored SAPs in 1980, 1983, 1988 and

1990. The socialized economy was dismantled and was colonized instead by financial capital and TNCs (Chossudovsky, 1997). Politically, the United States and its allies, particularly Germany, encouraged secessionist tendencies and thus precipitated the 1992–1995 civil war in which hundreds of thousands of people were killed (Woodward, 1995). Croatia and Slovenia subsequently emerged as independent states – later joining the EU, the eurozone and NATO – while Bosnia remained a NATO protectorate (Petras and Vieux, 1996). Under the direction of the Office of the High Representative and the US Agency for International Development, the Bosnian 'reconstruction package' witnessed the extensive privatization of the Bosnian economy (Donais, 2002) – facilitating Western access to its oil resources (Chossudovsky, 1997).

The former Yugoslavia was also the terrain upon which Europe and the United States struggled to determine the nature and trajectory of the NWO. While France and Germany unsuccessfully sought to resolve the Yugoslav crisis and thus demonstrate the efficacy of an independent Europe, the United States successfully exploited the situation and utilized NATO to reassert its hegemony. This was reinforced by the 1999 NATO-led war against Serbia in which thousands were killed. This assault extinguished the economic nationalist threat posed by the Serbian Socialist Party and led to the creation of Kosovo as an EU–UN protectorate. As in Bosnia, much of the Kosovan economy was privatized (Mulaj, 2005). Importantly, the US deputy secretary of state under the Bill Clinton Administration, Strobe Talbott, admitted that 'it was Yugoslavia's resistance to the broader trends of political and economic reform – not the plight of Kosovar Albanians – that best explains NATO's war' (cited in Norris, 2005: xxii–xxiii – also see Chomsky, 1999; Gowan, 2000; Hammond and Herman, 2000; Johnstone, 2002; Cafruny, 2003; Bricmont, 2007; and Herman and Peterson, 2007).

US policy towards other countries in the region followed a similar pattern. The indebtedness and economic dislocation of Eastern European countries in the wake of the collapse of the Soviet bloc was exploited by the United States which, operating through the IMF and World Bank, insisted that these countries undergo 'shock therapy'-style reforms regardless of domestic opposition (Gowan, 1999a).

Western Europe's welfare states in the NWO

In abstract terms and drawing upon the CPE tradition, the NWO witnessed the displacement of Atlantic Fordism/corporate liberalism/embedded liberalism by neo-liberalism or embedded neo-liberalism (Van Apeldoorn, 1998) which is

> neo-liberal inasmuch as it emphasizes the primacy of global market forces and the freedom of transnational capital. Yet, as a result of such processes, markets become increasingly *disconnected* from their post-war national social institutions. Embedded neo-liberalism is thus 'embedded' to the

extent that it recognizes the limits to laissez-faire, and thus to the dis-embedding process, and accepts that certain compromises need to be made.

(Van Apeldoorn, 2001: 82, emphasis in original)

Economically, the construction of the NWO accelerated the internationalization of finance and production, augmenting the already considerable power of TNCs and precipitating the restructuring of production from Fordism to post-Fordism, that is to say, from mass production utilizing economies of scale to 'just-in-time' flexible production. This new regime of accumulation and mode of regulation – which involved the restructuring of the global economy and the creation of a World Order in which labour was subordinate – was termed the neo-liberal consensus.

Politically, the post-1970s period witnessed the internationalization of the social structure – specifically the emergence of a transnational capitalist class (Fennema, 1982; Robinson and Harris, 2000; Sklair, 2001; Carroll and Fennema, 2002; Carroll and Carson, 2003; Beder, 2006a, 2006b; Carroll, 2007, 2010) – and the internationalization of the state whereupon it became a 'transmission belt from the global to the national economy'; an 'agency for adjusting national economic practices and policies to the perceived exigencies of the global economy' (Cox, 1996: 302). The internationalization of the state, in turn, precipitated the transformation of the Westphalian state system. Consequently, two new levels of political authority developed within the structure of the World Order, above and below existing nation-states at the macro- and micro-regional levels (ibid.: 308). Gill (2001: 47) referred to this process as one of 'new constitutionalism':

New constitutionalism is an international governance framework. It seeks to separate economic policies from broad political accountability in order to make governments more responsive to the disciplines of market forces, and correspondingly less responsive to popular-democratic forces and processes. New constitutionalism is the politico-legal dimension of the wider discourse of disciplinary neo-liberalism. Central objectives in this discourse are security of property rights and investor freedoms, and market discipline on the state and on labour, to secure 'credibility' in the eyes of private investors (in both the global currency and capital markets).

In more concrete terms, the consequences of the shift from the CWO to the NWO, from the social democratic consensus to the neo-liberal consensus, were predictable. Labour's share of global GDP, relative to capital, fell markedly from 1980, particularly in Europe and Japan (IMF, 2007), while inequality and poverty worsened almost everywhere (Chomsky, 1994; Culpeper, 2002).

The historical structure of the NWO represented a specific configuration of social forces. Within this configuration, four sets of social forces were particularly important in terms of influencing the retrenchment of Western Europe's welfare states and the emergence of the ESM concept and the Social Europe discourse: the forces of capital, the forces of labour, the EU and the United States.

The forces of capital – whether national, European and/or global capital – supported, to varying degrees, the retrenchment of Western Europe's welfare states. Such retrenchment was beneficial to capital because, through liberalization, outsourcing, privatization and public–private partnerships (i.e. transferring the production and distribution of goods and services from the state to the private sector), the profit-making opportunities of the private sector were boosted considerably (Balanyá *et al.*, 2000; Barratt Brown, 2001; Latham, 2001; Monbiot, 2000; Whitfield, 2001, 2010; Pollock, 2004; Harvey, 2007; Klein, 2008; Frangakis *et al.*, 2009).

By contrast, the forces of capital offered only conditional and tentative support for the ESM. The Europe-wide federation of national corporate federations, Business-Europe, provided a rhetorical defence of the ESM but argued that it needed to be 'modernized'. In a speech to the ETUC Congress in May 2007, the then president of Business-Europe, Antoine Seillière, spelt out what this entailed:

> if we want to be able to keep our social model, it urgently needs to be adapted. Our major challenges for the twenty-first century remain: globalization, technological change, an aging population.... They will be met only if the EU itself is capable of steering a clear course towards modernization and reform. Our view is that our societies do not suffer from a deficit in social legislation or insufficient public expenditure but from a low appetite to adapt to change. Introducing the necessary reforms can only be achieved in member states themselves.
>
> (Seillière, 2007: 2)

The 'necessary reforms' included higher employment levels, increased productivity, more sustainable health, pension and welfare systems, and flexicurity. Seillière also reported that Business-Europe had issued a declaration in December 2006 to mark the fiftieth anniversary of the EU which contained six suggested priorities: to implement the Lisbon Strategy, complete the internal market, reform EU governance, resist national protectionism, promote further EU enlargement and adapt national pension system and labour markets. Furthermore, Business-Europe and other employer organizations, such as the ERT, vigorously pursued this 'modernization' agenda; analysis by Corporate Europe Observatory (2011) found a positive correlation between the recommendations of reports produced by Business-Europe and the ERT and the neo-liberal measures adopted by the EU. Similarly, in Britain the corporate sector opposed the New Labour government's ratification of the Social Chapter in 1997, rejected the Charter of Fundamental Rights in 2000 and publicized its concerns about the imposition of EU legislation (Confederation of British Industry, 2000, 2006; House of Lords EU Select Committee, 2007), while the Institute of Directors (IoD) claimed that the imposition of the ESM cost the British economy about 1 per cent of GDP every year (Leach, 2000).

During the CWO, much of the left in Europe was sceptical about, if not hostile towards, European integration (Castellina, 1988; Sassoon, 1996; Dunphy,

2004; Mullen, 2007). In the NWO, by contrast, and despite some reservations about whether or not the existing EU could be reformed from within to deliver a desirable social model, the forces of labour generally supported the objective of some form of Social Europe, with its implicit ESM, as an alternative to the neo-liberal EU and as a potential counterweight to the forces of globalization (Geyer, 1993; Bieler and Torjenson, 2001; Bieler, 2003, 2005, 2006, 2009; Ryner and Schulten, 2003; Strange, 2006; Strange and Worth, 2007; Taylor, 2007; Dimitra-kopoulos, 2010). Meanwhile, the forces of labour generally opposed the retrenchment of Western Europe's welfare states. There were exceptions however. In terms of the MCC-induced austerity of the 1990s, Levy (1999) and Ross (2000a) critiqued Castles' (1998) notion that parties did not matter under conditions of austerity by arguing that, in cases such as Britain and Italy, there was more extensive retrenchment under the left than the right. Likewise, under the guise of the 'third way' (Giddens, 1998; Blair and Schröder, 1999; Hale *et al.*, 2004), social democratic parties, when in government, often prioritized welfare state 'reform' (i.e. retrenchment).

The EU rhetorically supported the ESM and the objective of a Social Europe but its actions, economic and social policy-wise, were directed at both 'reform-ing' the supply side of Europe's economies and 'modernizing' Western Europe's welfare states rather than creating a unified EU-level welfare state. EU reifica-tion of market liberalism, bias towards negative integration, choice of social reg-ulation and preference for competition and economic liberalization influenced the *trajectory* of the European project and Western Europe's welfare states. By participating in neo-liberal initiatives such as the SM, EMU, EU enlargement and Lisbon Strategy projects, member states voluntarily surrendered control over a range of macroeconomic policy tools, facilitated the restructuring of their economies, colluded in the expansion of corporate power and subjected them-selves to additional structural constraints. Furthermore, the EU increasingly directed its attention to the *nature* of Western Europe's welfare states. The MCC/SGP requirements to limit budget deficits and public debt levels and pursue 'sound' (i.e. balanced) public finances, the need to implement supply-side-oriented EU macroeconomic and employment policy guidelines, the obliga-tion to produce Stability and Convergence Programmes and National Reform Programmes, and the demands to reform labour market, pension and social secu-rity systems so as to ensure long-term 'sustainability' represented attempts by the EU to steer Western Europe's welfare states towards the SWPR (i.e. the market liberal model). Consequently, the EU encouraged the retrenchment of Western Europe's welfare states in both a structural and direct sense.

Although the United States rhetorically supported the process of European integration during the NWO (Lundestad, 1998), its policy actions continued to reflect its economic and strategic interests. US policy in the 1990s and 2000s was underpinned by three main objectives. First, the United States sought to reintegrate Eastern Europe's economies into the global economy and thus expand the Grand Area. Second, the United States sabotaged any moves towards social democracy and insisted that these countries adopt 'shock therapy'-style reforms instead. A further benefit of such a transformation was that, when these countries joined the EU and NATO, they tipped the balance of power in Europe as a whole in favour of neo-liberalism. Third, the United States strove to deter any moves towards an independent EU by derailing the Gorbachev 'One Europe' plan and by intervening in the former Yugoslavia via NATO.

Under President Bill Clinton, the United States rhetorically supported the ESM. At the international 'third way' conference in Italy in November 1999, however, Clinton echoed the concerns of Western Europe's social democratic leaders and called for the 'modernization' of the welfare state model to take account of rapid changes in economic and social trends as a result of globalization. The United States also supported the retrenchment of Western Europe's welfare states, in two main ways. First, it supported the neo-liberal SM, EMU and EU enlargement projects, and second and operating through the DWSR, it demanded market-friendly policies in Western and Eastern Europe.

Drawing upon the CPE perspectives and locating Western European welfare state development and the emergence of the ESM concept and Social Europe discourse within the broader economic and political context of the NWO, it is possible to argue that these formations and ideas were *shaped* by the structure of the World Order. In the NWO, Western Europe's welfare states remained largely national in orientation but, as a result of the neo-liberal consensus, they retrenched towards the SWPR model.

Building upon the work of Kleinman (2002), it is possible to identify six *endogenous* factors which contributed to the retrenchment of Western Europe's welfare states. First, the particular CWO configuration of social forces upon which the neo-liberal consensus was grafted influenced, in a path-dependency sense (North, 1990), the extent of retrenchment. Put another way, although the general direction of travel was towards the SWPR model, different levels of support for, and opposition to, neo-liberalism resulted in different rates of retrenchment – hence the persistence of welfare state diversity. Second, changes in public opinion, more specifically the falling level of electoral support for the public expenditure and taxation levels necessary to sustain the welfare state, facilitated retrenchment. Third, changes in elite opinion, more specifically the embrace of neo-liberalism and thus welfare state 'reform', by many of Western Europe's political parties encouraged retrenchment. Fourth, demographic changes (i.e. aging populations), and the associated argument about the falling worker-to-pensioner ratios, were deployed to justify retrenchment. Fifth, the slower rate of economic growth in Western Europe from the 1970s reputedly made it difficult to generate the resources necessary to sustain the welfare state. Sixth, the changes in Western Europe's labour markets, more specifically rising unemployment, also made it difficult to generate the necessary resources.

It is possible to identify two *exogenous* factors which contributed to the retrenchment of Western Europe's welfare states. First, the process of Europeanization as the EU increasingly influenced the nature and trajectory of Western Europe's welfare states via its economic and social policy (i.e. macroeconomic and employment guidelines, Stability and Convergence Programmes, National

Reform Programmes, reform of labour market, pension and social security systems, etc.). Second, the process of globalization whereby the increased mobility and power of capital, and the associated increase in the levels of competition in the global economy, served to erode the nation-state's ability and willingness to sustain the KWNS model. Commenting upon the ERM crisis and the austerity programmes pursued by Italy and Sweden in the 1990s, for example, the IMF noted that 'these experiences show how the international financial markets can serve to "discipline" governments (either by raising default premiums or by forcing adjustments in exchange rates), encouraging the adoption of appropriate [i.e. neo-liberal] policies' (1997: 66). These endogenous and exogenous factors, and the social forces that they engendered, conspired to produce a dominant trend towards the SWPR model even if variations within this general pattern persisted (i.e. welfare state diversity).

It is also possible to argue that Western Europe's welfare states were *constrained by* the structure of the World Order. In the NWO, any attempt to resist the neo-liberal consensus was dealt with, overtly and covertly, by the hegemonic United States and its allies within the capitalist system. These included cases of economic nationalism, such as in the former Yugoslavia, the attempts to defend the social democratic consensus and the KWNS model in Western Europe, and the aspirations to transition from communism to social democracy as in Eastern Europe. Such threats were pre-empted, manifest in EU treaty obligations, ECJ rulings, the MCC/SGP requirements, the risk of capital flight and capital strikes, and the veto power of financial markets and rating agencies, etc. They were guarded against, hence the continued presence and expansion of NATO in Europe, and/or they were thwarted – witness the EU–US military interventions in the Balkans during the 1990s and 2000s.

In the NWO, the ESM concept and Social Europe discourse emerged as a result of bottom-up pressures and top-down concessions. Activists within social democratic and socialist parties, trade unions and other progressive social forces across Europe promoted the ESM and a Social Europe as an alternative to the neo-liberal EU. The elite response, at the member state and EU level, was to rhetorically embrace such ideas in an attempt to co-opt these forces and thus sustain the neo-liberal project. These constructions therefore constituted a particular compromise at a specific historical juncture (i.e. the problematic passage of the Maastricht Treaty and its aftermath – namely rising Euroscepticism).

The two main elements of the *new convergence* hypothesis were therefore confirmed. First, the evidence pointed to the retrenchment of Western Europe's welfare states and their convergence towards the SWPR model. There was a slowdown if not decline in social expenditure relative to social need, the policy objectives of full employment and the 'right to work' which sustained the welfare state were abandoned, there was a concerted erosion of welfare entitlement across a range of social policy areas, and there was a general embrace of neo-liberalism – with its pro-market, anti-welfare state agenda – and the SWPR model across much of the political spectrum. Second, exogenous factors, particularly the processes of Europeanization and globalization, effectively locked in such retrenchment.

Conclusion

From the 1960s, hegemonic social forces in Western Europe and the United States precipitated the transformation of the World Order and this shift, from the liberal CWO to the neo-liberal NWO, influenced the nature and trajectory of Western Europe's welfare states and the European project. Importantly, the transatlantic alliance endured during this transition and these entities remained firmly anchored within a global capitalist system, managed by the United States for the benefit of the corporate elite which was increasingly transnational.

In the NWO, Western Europe's welfare states remained largely national in orientation – hence the persistence of welfare state diversity and the absence of a unified EU-level welfare state – but, as a result of the neo-liberal consensus, they retrenched towards a model which was Schumpeterian, workfare-oriented and post-national in nature. In short, Western Europe's welfare states were moving towards the market liberal model, at least in terms of objectives if not outcomes, albeit at different speeds. Importantly, the EU played a significant role in this transformation via its economic and social policy. The ESM concept and Social Europe discourse, on the other hand, emerged at a particular historical juncture and represented, in large part, a defensive elite response to one of the periodic crises faced by the EU. Attending to the struggle between social forces at the national, European and global levels reveals that Western Europe's welfare states, the ESM concept and the Social Europe discourse were both shaped by, and constrained by, the structure of the World Order during this period.

Just as the CWO contained the seeds of its own destruction, the NWO unleashed forces which ultimately led to the 2008 economic crisis and the Great Recession that followed. The response of the EU and its member states to this crisis, Keynesianism and then neo-liberalism, brought to the fore, once again, the debate about the nature and trajectory of the European project.

Part II

Alternative social models to neo-liberal Europe

6 Progressive social forces and the transformation of the World Order
Radical national alternatives

Introduction

This chapter discusses how, in the midst of the transformation of the World Order from the CWO to the NWO, progressive social forces in Britain and France sought to fashion radical and national alternatives to neo-liberalism. The previous four chapters assessed the impact of competing social forces and the transformation of the World Order on Western Europe's welfare states, the ESM concept and the Social Europe discourse, focusing in particular on the role of *hegemonic* social forces in shaping and constraining these formations and ideas. This chapter, by contrast, evaluates the attempts of *counter-hegemonic* social forces – more specifically social democratic and socialist political parties, trade unions and other progressive social forces (i.e. the left) – to develop an *enhanced* social model on a *national* basis. That is to say, rather than merely defending the social democratic consensus which underpinned the CWO, with its particular balance of power between capital and labour, from the 1970s the left in Britain and in France sought to radically shift power and wealth from capital to labour and to deepen and widen the welfare state as part of a transition to socialism.

The chapter advances three main arguments. First, that the social democratic consensus underpinning the CWO – more specifically its economic, ideological and institutional arrangements – was relatively conducive to the construction of an enhanced social model on a national basis. Second, that although the British and French experiments ended in failure, there was nothing inevitable about this; these attempts at reflation encountered a range of problems, many of which were anticipated, but they were not intrinsically flawed. Third, that these experiments provide some valuable lessons for contemporary progressive social forces that are seeking to defend Europe's social models against globalization and neo-liberalism.

The chapter is divided into four main sections. The first section explores the nature of the economic crisis during the 1970s, which precipitated the transformation of the World Order, and notes the very different solutions to the economic crisis that were advanced. The second section provides an overview of the development of the British left's AES during the 1970s and 1980s and evaluates why successive Labour governments failed to implement such a programme. The third section provides an overview of the development of the French left's

Programme Commun du Gouvernement (PCG) during the 1970s and reviews the results of the Mitterrand experiment during the early 1980s. The fourth section looks at some of the broader lessons that can be drawn from these experiments, for social democracy and progressive social forces more generally.

The crisis and rival solutions

Brenner (1998) critiqued the near-consensus about the *cause* of the economic crisis during the 1970s – which precipitated the transformation of the World Order – and lamented that 'Marxists and radicals have joined liberals and conservatives in explaining the long downturn as a "supply-side" crisis, resulting from a squeeze on profits, reflecting pressure on capital from labour' (ibid.: 13). In other words, the declining rate of productivity growth from the 1960s did not result in a corresponding and necessary fall in wages because of trade unions and the welfare state; the 'wage squeeze thesis' posited that 'political interference' had prevented 'the market mechanism from bringing about the necessary economic adjustment' (ibid.: 12). Furthermore, Brenner observed that, for many economists on the left and the right,

> labour's institutionally based power perpetuated [the long downturn] by standing in the way of the proper functioning of the labour market. Either unions succeeded, by directly preventing the growing masses of non-union or unemployed 'outsiders' from affecting the wage bargain; or, the level of welfare state support allowed the unemployed to refrain from entering the labour market at an insufficiently reduced wage; or a combination of both.
>
> (Ibid.: 140)

Put simply, the near-consensus was that labour had caused the economic crisis and, by its actions, had prolonged the recession. Brenner rejected these arguments as conceptually and empirically false and insisted that the system-wide economic downturn from the 1960s had been caused by the unplanned, uncoordinated and competitive nature of capitalist production, and by investors' short-termism, rather than wage pressure by workers.

In terms of the *solution* to the economic crisis, the response of the right was to experiment with monetarism and to pursue deregulation, liberalization, privatization and welfare state retrenchment so as to restore profitability – hence neo-liberalism. The answer for some sections of the left was to abandon Keynesianism and to embrace the supply-side reform agenda, hence the emergence of the 'third way'. The solution for other sections of the left, however, was to confront the unplanned, uncoordinated and competitive nature of capitalism – hence the British and French experiments.

The British left and the AES

The AES, of which there were several versions, emerged in response to the alleged failures of the 1964–1970 Labour governments (Coates, 1979; Dorey,

2006; O'Hara and Parr, 2006) and the need to overcome the perceived 'crisis of Keynesianism' (i.e. 'stagflation') (Pilling, 1987; Skidelsky, 2009) in the 1970s. Utilizing a combination of capital controls, exchange controls, import controls, nationalization, planning agreements, price controls, industrial democracy and increased public expenditure, the AES aimed to reflate the British economy, and thus solve the problems of inequality, poverty and unemployment, in a way which avoided balance of payment problems and sabotage by the international financial markets (London Conference of Socialist Economists, 1980; Aaronovitch, 1981; Callaghan, 2000). Building upon the work of individuals such as Michael Barratt Brown, Tony Benn, Ken Coates, John Eaton, Geoff Hodgson and Stuart Holland and organizations such as the Cambridge Political Economy Group, the Communist Party, the Conference of Socialist Economists, the Institute for Workers' Control and the Labour Coordinating Committee, plus the trade union movement, the AES was adopted by the Labour Party in 1973 and it remained official party policy until 1983.

Concern about the slow rate of economic growth, the 'stop–go' oscillation of macroeconomic policy and the need to modernize British industry (Tomlinson, 2009), plus the results of successful experiments elsewhere (Holland, 1978), stimulated cross-party interest in economic planning during the 1960s. Indeed, the Conservative government established the corporatist and tripartite National Economic Development Council in March 1962, while the Labour government created the Department for Economic Affairs and the Ministry of Technology in December 1964 and launched its National Plan in September 1965.

The Labour government, elected in October 1964 with Harold Wilson as prime minister, inherited an £800 million balance of payments deficit largely caused by the 'dash for growth' by the previous Conservative government. Newton and Porter (1988: 151) argued that the ensuing economic crisis was compounded by government inaction:

> The key to the success of the National Plan was high economic growth and it was up to the government to create the conditions which would allow this to happen. At no stage ... did Labour commit itself to the necessary degree of economic expansion. [Indeed] Labour presided over the most prolonged period of deflation since the war. By 1970 hardly any of the projections set out in the National Plan had been achieved because the harsh economic regime had discouraged rather than stimulated investment.

Put simply, the Labour government proved unwilling and/or unable to resist the pressure from the Bank of England, the Treasury, some European governments, the US government, the City of London and the international financial markets (i.e. the international financial nexus) to implement orthodox measures (i.e. public spending cuts and tax increases) so as to defend the value of, and the confidence in, the pound sterling. Paradoxically, however, these efforts were ultimately unsuccessful and this period – 'a long process of humiliation by which Labour gradually lost control over the British economy and was forced into increasingly deflationary measures to satisfy foreign creditors' (ibid.: 153) – culminated in the 1967 devaluation of the currency.

Back in opposition from 1970 and determined to avoid a repeat performance, sections of the British left formulated the AES (Hatfield, 1978; Seyd, 1987; Wickham-Jones, 1996). The aim of *Labour's Programme 1973*, adopted by the Labour Conference in October 1973, was that the next Labour government would 'bring about a fundamental and irreversible shift in the balance of power and wealth in favour of working people and their families' (Labour Party, 1973: 7). The programmatic policy document contained three main objectives: to maintain full employment, to control inflation and to increase the standard of living – in a personal, social and environmental sense – for everyone. Acknowledging the problems that arose during the 1960s (i.e. the external constraints that were encountered), the document pledged that a future Labour government would not 'distort the domestic economy in order to maintain an unrealistic exchange rate', that although devaluation was not 'a cure for all ills ... our exports must not be allowed to become uncompetitive', that capital and exchange controls were vital 'to protect the economy against the international currency sharks', and that protective measures against any country 'undercutting its competitors by subsidizing its exports or undervaluing its currency' (ibid.: 16) would be considered. Acknowledging the changing nature of capitalism (i.e. the increasingly monopolistic and transnational mode of production, distribution and exchange), the document stated that 'we cannot ... afford to rely on indirect measures to control the economy – whether these are fiscal or monetary measures, or generalized hand-outs and tax concessions; instead, we must act *directly* at the level of the giant firm itself' (ibid.: 13). In other words, conventional Keynesian macroeconomic management, as practiced during the 1950s and 1960s, was no longer sufficient and a more radical approach was needed.

The *Labour Programme 1973* contained a list of specific measures deemed necessary if Labour's aim and objectives were to be fulfilled. First, that a new state holding company was required to extend public ownership. A future labour government would establish a National Enterprise Board which would initially acquire 25 of Britain's top manufacturing companies operating in different sectors of the economy. Industries such aircraft, energy, finance, pharmaceuticals and shipbuilding were identified as prime candidates for nationalization. Second, that a comprehensive planning agreement system was required to enable the state to direct, if not control, the economy. A future Labour government would seek planning agreements with all of the major public enterprises and around 100 of the largest manufacturing companies. Agreement would be sought over industrial relations, investment, prices, profits, etc. but it warned that a future Labour government would not hesitate to issue directives, remove directors and/or nationalize companies where it saw the need. Third, that a new industry act was required to provide the state with the powers that it would need. In addition to nationalization and the introduction of planning agreements, a future Labour government would prevent the takeover of British companies by foreign companies and would apply its powers to TNCs. Fourth, that an extension of democracy to the economy was required, so as to act as a check on corporate power. A future Labour government would strengthen collective bargaining and employment protection and would encourage the formation of joint control committees, composed of managers and workers' representatives, to run British industry. Fifth, that a concerted redistribution of wealth was required to deal with Britain's inequality and poverty. A future Labour government would introduce a wealth tax, combat tax avoidance and evasion, recalibrate income tax rates to ensure that they are progressive, and reform corporation tax and indirect taxes. Sixth, that a future Labour government would renegotiate the terms of Britain's membership of the EC so as to ensure that there would be no barriers to the implementation of its programme. A future Labour government would ensure 'the retention by Parliament of those powers over the British economy needed to pursue effective fiscal, industrial and regional policies. Equally we need an agreement on capital movements which protects our balance of payments and full employment policies' (ibid.: 41). It also ruled out British participation in EMU.

Labour's Programme 1973 formed the basis of the manifestos put forward during the February and October 1974 general elections. Furthermore, the document's aim and objectives formed the basis of the 1976 and 1982 programmatic policy documents and the 1983 general election manifesto. There were three important additions however. First, Labour's National Executive Committee (NEC) agreed to sanction import and price controls in 1975. The purpose of the former was not to reduce imports but 'to plan the growth of imports to match foreign exchange earnings and to determine their composition in accordance with social priorities' (London Conference of Socialist Economists, 1979: 79), while the latter would help to control inflation and combat profiteering. Second, Labour's NEC demanded the nationalization of the banking and insurance sector in 1976. Britain's financial institutions, Callaghan (2000: 116–17) reported

> were seen as almost useless because their preference was for investment in bonds, futures and property rather than the long-term commitment to manufacturing which the country needed. They also represented a cartelized concentration of power. Since they played a crucial role in government financing, it was understood that their behaviour helped to determine the rate of interest and the exchange rate. They could mobilize short-term finance or 'hot money' into or out of the country and help turn balance of payments deficits into financial crisis. As the principal holders of shares they were able to exercise a baleful influence in favour of short-term shareholder value.

Third, the 1980 Labour Conference insisted that the next Labour government should withdraw from the EC. The principal reason put forward was that the Treaties of Rome would be utilized to obstruct any attempt to plan the economy. Importantly, as Callaghan (2000: 115) acknowledged:

At this stage in Britain's relationship with the EC … the costs of withdrawal were not great. In 1974 one estimate calculated the balance of payments effect of withdrawal as a net loss of £280 million or one-and-a-half percent of Britain's total export earnings.

As in 1964, the economic circumstances that the Labour government inherited upon taking office in 1974 were not propitious: the balance of payments deficit was £383 million, inflation was running at nearly 20 per cent and unemployment was approaching one million. Indeed, according to the head of the US NSC, the economic crisis in Britain was considered by the then US government 'as the greatest single threat to the stability of the Western world' (cited in Fay and Young, 1978: 5). Like the 1964–1970 Labour governments, the 1974–1979 Labour governments also failed to fully implement Labour's programme (Artis and Cobham, 1991; Callaghan *et al.*, 2003; Plant *et al.*, 2004; Seldon and Hickson, 2004). This was due to both internal and external factors.

Internally, the economic crisis provided the Labour leadership – often with the support of the leaders of the big trade unions and the Trades Union Congress (TUC) – with the excuse it needed to repudiate the more radical aspects of Labour's programme. The first set of commitments to be abandoned included the pledges to extend nationalization and to introduce planning agreements. Wilson had expressed his opposition to these measures at the 1973 Labour Conference and, as prime minister, issued a White Paper in August 1974, entitled 'The Regeneration of British Industry', which rejected both. As Holland (2004: 296–7) explained, Wilson believed that

> the National Enterprise Board should only take a shareholding in companies with the consent of their management … and that unlike their French counterparts, planning agreement should be voluntary rather than bargained in return for public grants or purchasing. This was a worst case scenario. It would mean that instead of reinforcing and promoting industrial success, as in the original statement of the case for new public enterprise and planning agreements, the companies most likely to agree to either would be those that were in difficulty.

Examples such as this led McKenzie (1955) and Minkin (1980) to argue that Labour's policy-making process, with the Labour Conference acting as the sovereign body, was a 'managed process' that involved the 'manipulation of procedures' and the 'mobilization of bias' (ibid.: 320) in favour of the Labour leadership. Moreover, Benn (1981) identified five ways in which the Labour leadership effectively exercised control over policy-making. First, by vetoing policy with which it did not agree (e.g. nationalization and planning agreements); the refrain, 'back me or sack me' was a popular one with Labour leaders. Second, by covertly sabotaging policy; Benn revealed that Wilson 'drafted letters addressed to himself for the City to send back to give him a chance to repudiate National Executive Committee policy' (ibid.: 184). Third, by appointing special advisors to devise policy alternatives; Benn recalled how one such advisor boasted that, as a result of his efforts, 'the main areas of economic policy, fiscal and monetary, were conducted without the ministers involved' (ibid.). Fourth, using the system of patronage to promote allies and to sideline opponents; Benn argued that the Labour leadership used its power of appointment to control both the Cabinet/Shadow Cabinet and the Parliamentary Labour Party. Fifth, dominating the drafting of election manifestos; Benn claimed that the then prime minister, James Callaghan, effectively dominated the drafting of the 1979 manifesto to the exclusion of the Cabinet and the NEC.

The second set of commitments to be abandoned included the pledges to renegotiate the terms of Britain's membership of the EC and, if a satisfactory outcome was not obtained, to campaign for withdrawal. The 1972 Labour Conference agreed a statement listing the six issues upon which a future Labour government would renegotiate: Britain's EC Budget contributions, the CAP, the protection of Commonwealth interests, powers over fiscal, industrial and regional policy, and value added tax. As Wilson's then private secretary, Michael Palliser, admitted, however, 'the whole object of the [renegotiation] exercise was to keep Britain in, and get something that could be presented to the British as politically adequate' (cited in Young, 1998: 281). Indeed, as Newton and Porter (1988: 174) concluded, the renegotiations managed to secure

> some minor concessions on EC regional policy, on the level of the contribution to the Community budget and on imports of dairy produce from New Zealand. Of these only the third had a meaning. The first proved to be of very modest benefit and the second, in the light of later events, to be practically worthless. Nothing substantial had changed and none of Britain's negotiators had seriously intended otherwise.

Nevertheless, Wilson argued that 'we have substantially achieved our objectives' and that the EC 'has changed de facto and *de jure*' (Benn, 1990: 345–6). The Cabinet voted to accept the revised terms by 16 to 7 and the Labour right (i.e. the social democrats), joined by a handful of trade unions, subsequently campaigned alongside the Conservative Party, the corporate sector and most of the media in favour of a Yes vote in the 1975 Referendum on continued EC membership – and won (Butler and Kitzinger, 1996; Baimbridge *et al.*, 2006; Baimbridge, 2007; Mullen, 2007). Thereafter, the Labour government pursued a policy of reforming the EC – specifically advocating derogations from EC law to safeguard its industrial strategy, opposition to direct elections, EMU and value added tax, and the renegotiation of the CAP – which was unsuccessful.

The third set of commitments to be abandoned were the other key tenets of Labour's industrial strategy. As noted, Callaghan wrested control of the drafting of the 1979 general election manifesto from the NEC. While the 1979 European elections manifesto, produced by the NEC, reemphasized the case for the AES, the 1979 general election manifesto was much more corporatist and modest and stressed that 'the government's industrial strategy is about how to create more wealth and more jobs through a constructive national partnership with unions and management' (Labour Party, 1979: 1). Labour's research officer, Geoff Bish (1979: 179), later complained that 'not only did [the draft manifesto] ignore entire chapters of party policy, it overturned and ignored many of the agreements which had been laboriously hammered out in the NEC–Cabinet working group'.

Externally, the economic crisis induced by the international financial nexus provided the forces of capital and their political allies with the required opportunities to sabotage the more radical aspects of Labour's programme – just as it had done in the 1960s. The international financial nexus worked in concert with sections of the 'permanent state' (i.e. the civil service), the 'secret state' (i.e. the intelligence agencies), the media, the military and the monarchy. The first example of sabotage was the destabilization campaign waged by the intelligence agencies in Britain, the United States and elsewhere against the Labour government between 1974 and 1976. During this period, there were calls for military intervention against strikes, the military and the police organized joint exercises at Heathrow Airport without ministerial authorization, there were media rumours of an imminent military coup and the replacement of the Labour government with a 'government of national unity', several 'private armies' were reportedly formed in the event of a 'communist takeover' in Britain, and there were several media smears against Wilson in particular and Labour more generally, including allegations that there was a 'communist cell' operating in Downing Street and that up to 30 Labour Members of Parliament were secretly communists. Meanwhile, the Labour Party headquarters was bugged (Ramsay, 1986; Ramsay and Dorril, 1986; Foot, 1989). This campaign was part of a series of psychological warfare operations against social democratic governments elsewhere (Leigh, 1988).

The second example of sabotage was the attempt by the Bank of England and the Treasury to 'bounce'[1] the Labour government into adopting a statutory incomes policy, so as to control inflation, with criminal sanctions for noncompliance (Ramsay, 1998). The Cabinet and the prime minister favoured a voluntary incomes policy and Wilson instructed the Treasury to devise such a scheme. As the then head of the Downing Street Policy Unit, Bernard Donoughue (1987: 66), later revealed, however, 'the Treasury ignored the Prime Minister's instructions' and worked covertly with the Bank of England to achieve its objective by exploiting a sterling crisis in June 1975. On Monday 30 June, the governor of the Bank of England reported that sterling was collapsing and he urged the prime minister to support the chancellor, Dennis Healey, and his preference for a statutory incomes policy. Intriguingly, 'no attempt had been made by the Bank of England to keep the pound above the crucial $2.20 level. No money had been spent to bolster the rate … it was a veritable cornucopia of coincidence' (ibid.: 59).

The third example of sabotage was the issuance of false figures regarding the projected public sector borrowing requirement by the Treasury in February 1976. While the borrowing figure was actually 46 per cent of GDP in 1976, the Treasury released an estimate suggesting it could be as high as 60 per cent. As Ramsay (1998: 41) noted,

Only the terminally naïve could believe this was a mistake. There had been no previous estimates of the public sector even remotely approaching 60 per cent. The figure must have looked absurd inside the Treasury. This, surely, was just another example of psychological warfare. The Treasury rigged the figures to make life difficult for the government. By this stage, an approach to the IMF was being discussed.

The fourth example of sabotage was the engineered IMF crisis in December 1976. The Labour government's attempt to reduce inflation through its voluntary incomes policy, while maintaining the parity of the pound sterling, was repeatedly tested during 1975 and 1976. The downward pressure on the currency was such that Callaghan, as prime minister, approached the IMF for a loan in September (Burk and Cairncross, 1992; Ludlam, 1992; Harmon, 1997; Hickson, 2005). Intriguingly, Donoughue recounted how

> In the middle of the crisis I was privately summoned to the United States Embassy for a secret meeting with a very senior official there who said, 'You should be aware of something, which is that parts of the Treasury are in very deep cahoots with parts of the US Treasury and with certain others in Germany who are of a very right-wing inclination and they are absolutely committed to getting the IMF here and if it brings about the break-up of this government, they will be very, very happy'. He actually showed me a copy of the secret communication between London and Washington which seemed to confirm this view.
>
> (Donoughue in Institute of Contemporary British History, 1989: 43)

Similarly, Haines (1977: 58) reported that one government official complained that

> One of the problems is the axis between your [US] Treasury and our Treasury. They seem to be agreed that the Labour Manifesto is a manual for suicide ... they are in constant touch with our people saying, 'Don't bale these bastards out'.

The international financial nexus pursued a well-established strategy, as Donoughue (1987: 95–6) explained:

> We were not being paranoid in 1976 in our suspicion that the IMF was capable of launching economic 'remedies' which would destroy governments (especially governments of the left). A year later, in November 1977, the IMF mission to Portugal (including a senior member of the 1976 mission to Britain) refused to grant a credit tranche to the socialist minority government led by Mario Soares because he would not make immediate savage economies, which would certainly have brought down his administration.... An internal IMF briefing, which we saw among diplomatic papers in

Downing Street at that time, stated quite brutally that the IMF policy was to create a foreign exchange crisis over the next two months. The IMF staff explicitly asked the Western governments of the United States, Germany, Japan and Britain to withhold economic and financial aid in order to create a foreign exchange crisis which would bring the Soares Government to its knees and so force it to accept the harsh IMF prescription.

During the course of the IMF negotiations in the autumn of 1976, there was considerable resistance within the Cabinet to seeking such a loan and even more resistance to the conditions attached to it: substantial public expenditure cuts. The Cabinet held its final debate in December. Benn (1989: 665) presented his paper, a version of the AES, and he presciently warned his Cabinet colleagues that

> nothing would be more fatal to Labour's electoral chances than the party going to the country having laid off employees in manufacturing industries and in the public service sector on the grounds that the bankers wanted unemployment to restore confidence.

Peter Shore tabled his paper, which advocated short-term import controls until North Sea oil revenues began to flow. Anthony Crosland put forward his paper, which recommended the maintenance of the existing policy of wage control, while Healey (i.e. the chancellor) attacked all three proposals and argued that there was no alternative to a conditional IMF loan.

The Cabinet met the following day for the 'moment of decision' and Crosland withdrew his proposal and supported the chancellor and prime minister. A majority of his colleagues did the same. The Cabinet requested a $3.9 billion loan from the IMF and in return agreed to implement £1 billion of public expenditure cuts in 1977–1978, £1.5 billion of cuts in 1978–1979 and a £500 million sale of state-owned British Petroleum shares. The general situation, which culminated in this decision, prompted Callaghan to declare at the 1976 Labour Conference that Keynesianism was redundant:

> We used to think that you could spend your way out of a recession and increase employment by cutting taxes and boosting government spending. I tell you in all candour that that option no longer exists, and in so far as it ever did exist, it only worked on each occasion since the war by injecting a bigger dose of inflation into the economy, followed by a higher level of unemployment as the next step.
>
> (Labour Party, 1976: 188)

Despite such defeatism, and in an attempt to extract some concessions from the IMF during the negotiations, Callaghan issued veiled threats about Britain's ability to maintain its NATO obligations in an era of austerity. In response, and in a final attempt to 'bounce' the Labour government into making the cuts it had originally proposed, the IMF Letter of Intent contained some important small print. Having been stonewalled by the Treasury, Donoughue (1987: 99) eventually found the document amongst the prime minister's box of papers and 'it seemed to me very important to scrutinize the small print on this document in case some nasty and unnecessarily harsh conditions had been slipped in at the last moment'. The suspicion was justified; Donoughue found that

> The terms were extremely tough, much tougher than had been agreed with the Prime Minister as far as detailed monetary targets were concerned. The imposition of tight ceilings on both the Public Sector Borrowing Requirement and on Domestic Credit Expansion ... seemed to rule out any possibility of reflation before the next election and even made it likely that we would be forced to trigger off a fresh round of deflationary cuts in order to meet these targets.
>
> (Ibid.: 100)

In the event, public expenditure fell short of expectations in 1976–1977 and some of the cuts were deemed unnecessary. Furthermore, the balance of payments deficit had been eliminated by 1977, economic growth had returned, and inflation and unemployment were falling. Echoing earlier concerns about Treasury machinations, however, even Healey (1990: 402) was moved to complain that

> I cannot forgive [the Treasury], or those politicians who preceded me as Chancellor, for misleading the Government, the country and the world for so many years about the true state of public spending in Britain. Indeed, I suspect that Treasury officials were content to overstate public spending in order to put pressure on governments which are reluctant to cut it.

Nonetheless, the IMF crisis had the desired effects: the Labour government abandoned its programme and pursued austerity instead. These actions – particularly the Labour government's attempt to impose wage restraint, in effect, a wage cut – precipitated the collapse of the voluntary incomes policy, which underpinned the Social Contract, and the radicalization of the trade union movement. The result was the so-called 'winter of discontent' (Hay, 2010), which contributed to Labour losing the 1979 general election.

Back in opposition from 1979, and mindful of the failure to implement both the AES and Labour's European policy, the Labour left (i.e. the socialists) and their trade union allies reemphasized Labour's commitment to the AES and introduced a number of constitutional reforms in an attempt to ensure that a future Labour government would implement the policy agreed by the Labour Conference and NEC. These included the mandatory reselection of MPs in between general elections, NEC control over the manifesto and the formation of an electoral college to elect the Labour leader. These changes, plus the commitment to the AES and the adoption of radical policies such as withdrawal from the EC and NATO and unilateral disarmament, prompted sections of the Labour right to defect and form the Social Democratic Party in March 1981. Benn later claimed that this was a 'British Establishment- and US-backed political party, whose aims were to split the vote and thus prevent the election of a radical Labour government'.[2]

The AES encountered a range of problems which were institutional, economic and political in nature. *Institutionally*, the Labour Party was divided about the AES. While socialists within the party advocated a radical break with the post-war consensus, social democrats favoured the maintenance of the status quo. Such fissures were exploited by external forces as part of a classic divide-and-rule strategy to neutralize the AES and to contain the Labour Party as a progressive social force. This was manifest in the repeated failure of the Labour leadership – supported by the 'permanent state', the 'secret state', the corporate sector, much of the media and the international financial nexus – to implement the radical programme democratically endorsed by the party membership and affiliated trade unions. In short, the Labour leadership colluded in the sabotage of Labour's programme. Furthermore, the attempts in the early 1980s to tackle the party's 'democratic deficit' were too timid and came too late. The wider British left was also divided about the AES: some sections of the revolutionary left and trade union movement favoured the AES, while other sections opposed it. Again, such differences were exploited to prevent the emergence of a united front.

Economically, the situations faced by the Labour governments in 1964 and 1974 made it difficult to implement a radical programme. Put simply, solving immediate and short-term problems, such as currency and trade deficit crises, took priority over implementing the medium- and long-term vision. These problems were compounded by the structural weakness of the British economy and the transformation of the global economy. The British economy was in decline in the 1960s and 1970s – manifest in rising inflation and unemployment and falling investment, productivity and profits (Newton and Porter, 1988; Eatwell, 1989; Gamble, 1994; Grant, 2002) – and this denied the Labour governments the resources that they needed. The British economy was increasingly dominated by financial capital and TNCs and economic policy was formulated to serve their interests (Moran, 1981; Ingham, 1984; Newton and Porter, 1988; Green, 1992; Grant, 1993; Ramsay, 1998). Meanwhile, the British economy was progressively integrated with that of continental Europe and North America which reinforced the power of financial capital and TNCs (van der Pijl, 1984, 1998). In short, the external constraints faced by the sponsors of the AES were considerable.

Politically, the supporters of the AES underestimated the determination of the 'permanent state' and the 'secret state' – acting at the behest of national, European and global capital – to resist any attempt to transform Britain and its role in the World Order. The AES represented an enhanced social model in the sense that it aimed to expand the process of decommodification and the socialization of the economy. If successfully implemented, it would have transformed the British economy and society more generally. The AES also constituted an economically nationalist threat to the Grand Area plan and its prioritization of open markets. If successfully implemented, it would have set an example to other countries. During the 1976 IMF crisis, for example, the US State Department recognized the challenge posed by the AES and viewed the situation as

> a choice between Britain remaining in the liberal financial system of the West as opposed to a radical change of course, because we were concerned about Tony Benn precipitating a policy decision by Britain to turn its back on the IMF. I think if that had happened, the whole system would have begun to come apart. God knows what Italy would have done; and France might have taken a radical change in the same direction. It would not only have had consequences for the economic recovery, it would have had great political consequences.
>
> (William Rodgers quoted in Fay and Young, 1978: 30)

Supporters of the AES also underestimated the role of the media. Its hostility towards the left (Butler and Kavanagh, 1974, 1975, 1980, 1984; Glasgow University Media Group, 1976, 1980, 1982; Hollingsworth, 1986; Freedman, 2003; Thomas, 2005; Wring, 2005; Tunney, 2007; Price, 2010), plus its ability to influence the policy agenda and to shape public opinion (Mullen, forthcoming), made the task of securing an electoral mandate for Labour's programme and public support for the AES much more difficult.

The French left, the common programme for government and the Mitterrand experiment

The PCG was signed by the leaders of the *Parti Communiste Français* (PCF) and the *Parti Socialiste* (PS) in June 1972. Following the disappointment associated with previous attempts at co-operation – the Popular Front government of 1934–1936 and the Provisional government of 1944–1947 – and in the aftermath of the protests and strikes of May 1968, the PCF and PS agreed a common programme, rather than just an electoral alliance, in the hope of exploiting the upsurge of radicalism in France.

The PCG contained three main sets of objectives: to extend democracy to the economy, to boost public expenditure and to develop international relations that were conducive to its implementation. The document included a number of pledges. First, that a future left government would democratize the workplace in the private and public sectors by introducing committees composed of consumers and workers to run French industry. Second, that a future left government would expand the public sector by nationalizing the banking and insurance sector and national enterprises operating in strategically important sectors of the economy, such as aerospace, armaments, chemicals, computers and electronics, natural resources, nuclear energy, pharmaceuticals, space, etc. Third, that a future left government would boost public expenditure so as to bring about improvements in education, housing and social provision. It also promised better working conditions, including an increase in the minimum wage. Fourth, that a future left government would support the process of European integration as long as this did not threaten the necessary freedom of action that the left required.

Although there were tensions within and between the members of this alliance of convenience, and ongoing conflict over its contents (Brown, 1979; Bell and Shaw, 1983), the PCG possessed significant electoral appeal. Indeed, in the presidential election in May 1974, the then leader of the PS and the common candidate for the left, Mitterrand, came close to victory by obtaining 49.19 per cent of the vote. The left also performed well in the 1977 municipal elections and the 1978 national assembly elections. Mitterrand, who promised a 'rupture with capitalism' (Harrington, 1986: 118), finally achieved victory in the presidential election in May 1981, obtaining 52 per cent of the vote, on the basis of the PCG-inspired *Projet Socialiste* document, adopted in January 1980, and the 110 propositions that formed his manifesto. Furthermore, the PS achieved an overall majority in the national assembly elections in June 1981 and a Socialist government, with several PCF members, was formed. The results of the radical phase of the Mitterrand presidency during 1981 and 1982 – the Mitterrand experiment – were mixed.

Some aspects of the Mitterrand experiment were relatively successful. In anticipation of a new five-year plan in 1984, the Socialist government adopted an interim plan in December 1981. The plan aimed to create 400,000 new jobs in two years, to introduce a 35-hour working week by 1985, to build 500,000 new homes in 1982, to increase the minimum wage, to increase the average purchasing power of wages by 2 per cent per annum, to increase family allowances by 50 per cent and to increase expenditure on R&D. These reflationary measures, it was hoped, would boost the economic growth rate to 3 per cent. Many of the plan's objectives were fully, or at least partially, fulfilled. The Socialist government created 88,000 additional jobs in the public sector during 1981 and 1982 and reduced working hours, restricted overtime, increased annual paid holiday and lowered the retirement age (Halimi *et al.*, 1994). The expectation of reduced hours for the same pay, however, was dashed as 'work sharing' arrangements led to reduced hours for less pay (Hahnel, 2005). The Socialist government increased the minimum wage: in 1981–1982, the wages of the lowest paid rose by 29 per cent, while wages across the economy as a whole rose by 16 per cent. Given inflation, this translated into a 3.5 per cent increase in real purchasing power (Harrington, 1986). The Socialist government increased social benefits by 6.2 per cent in real terms (ibid.), while family allowance and housing benefits increased by 50 per cent (Hall, 1987). In total, these redistributionist measures were worth around 2 per cent of GDP (ibid.).

There were other notable successes during the Mitterrand experiment. First, the Social government pursued an incomes policy (i.e. the minimum wage, plus credit controls, wage indexation, etc.) which was relatively successful at controlling inflation. Second, the Socialist government introduced significant political reforms, including the decentralization of government (Bell and Shaw, 1983). Third, the Socialist government established planning agreements with the nationalized enterprises and the regions to direct, if not control, the French economy (Ozenda and Strauss-Kahn, 1985). Fourth, the Socialist government spent over 70 billion francs on capital investment, via the nationalized enterprises, and loaned almost 87 billion francs to private companies to help modernize the French economy. These helped to transform the French economy and society more generally.

The macroeconomic indicators pertaining to the Mitterrand experiment suggest that the Socialist government managed to deliver some improvement in the performance of the French economy (Machin and Wright, 1985; Hall, 1987). The economic growth rate was 0.3 per cent in 1981, 1.6 per cent in 1982 and 0.7 per cent in 1983. Inflation rose in 1981 and fell slowly in 1982 and 1983. Unemployment rose from 7.5 per cent in 1981 to 8.2 per cent in 1982 and 8.4 per cent in 1983 (Halimi *et al.*, 1994), while the budget deficit increased from 1.8 per cent of GDP in 1981 to 2.6 per cent in 1982 and 3.3 per cent in 1983 (Machin and Wright, 1985). Although these results were modest, the figures compared favourably with other EC member states (Hall, 1987).

Other aspects of the Mitterrand experiment were less successful. Although the Socialist government nationalized 11 industrial conglomerates, 36 private banks and two finance companies, it encountered a number of problems. First, some members of the Socialist government – the minister for planning, Michel Rocard and Delors as finance minister – favoured acquiring a *controlling* stake in these enterprises, while Mitterrand and others called for *total* public ownership. In the event, Mitterrand prevailed. The 150 billion franc cost of nationalization and the fact that some of these enterprises had a poor performance record, however, meant that these entities were subsequently 'starved of cash in order to finance their own acquisition' (Harrington, 1986: 137).

Second, and paradoxically, these enterprises were run in a capitalist manner. The Socialist government instructed the managers of these enterprises to 'seek, first of all, economic efficiency through a constant bettering of productivity'. It insisted that the 'normal criteria of the management of industrial enterprises will apply' and that these actions should 'guarantee that the profitability of the invested capital will be normal' (ibid.: 135–6). Another Socialist government member put it even more bluntly:

> My job is to get surplus value.... To be 'left' is to have a certain idea of the allocation of the national wealth. This has nothing to do with the techniques that must be put into motion to produce that wealth.
>
> (Ibid.)

As Hahnel (2005: 120–1) warned however

> if nationalized enterprises are managed no differently than private enterprises, the only thing that will change is who employees and taxpayers will resent. Instead of resenting greedy capitalists they will resent the socialist government, the socialist ministers and their new socialist bosses.

Third, the nationalized enterprises were expected to play a 'locomotive role', in the sense that they would facilitate further changes such as the extension of democracy to the economy. The legislation enacted by the Socialist government, however, granted workers the right to be consulted on workplace issues but not the right to make decisions. Furthermore, such participation was no more successful in the public sector than it was in the private sector (ibid.).

The least successful aspect of the Mitterrand experiment was the response of the Socialist government to the external constraints that it encountered. These were entirely predictable – having thwarted the British left in the 1960s and 1970s – and, indeed, had been anticipated: 'Before it took office [the PS] had assessed the pitfalls of a policy of reflation. And to avoid them, it had, either implicitly or explicitly, accepted the need to consider currency devaluation and trade protection' (Halimi *et al.*, 1994: 101). In terms of devaluation, the *Projet Socialiste* document stated that

> At the European level, the PS cannot agree to the existing EMS which entails the alignment of weaker currencies with the deutschmark and, therefore, short of a new emergency exit from the system [like that of 1976 when the franc was devalued by 30 per cent] requires a toughened policy of austerity.
>
> (PS, 1980: 181)

In terms of trade protection, the document warned that

> A strong growth rate will not be possible without an external imbalance and an increased economic dependence, unless French industry is able to handle by itself the burst in demand that will result from the rise in purchasing power. This involves the indispensable re-conquest of the domestic market.... The French understand that the balance of trade will be a key to the success of the left. A failure in that area would lead us either to call into question the *Projet Socialiste* or to run into depreciation and debt.... Free market logic depends on the deceleration of economic activity to slow down the growth of imports. It is the worst possible solution. A country that makes the effort to stimulate its economy must avail itself of the necessity to curb an unlimited swelling of imports.... Its responsibility can be met by domestic production without risking inflation.
>
> (Ibid.: 190, 222, 224)

Concerning imports, the document pledged to 'stop the increase and then to reverse the share of GDP attributable to foreign trade' (ibid.: 180). Indeed, Proposition 20 of the Mitterrand manifesto promised to reduce it to below 20 per cent by 1990. Concerning the domestic market, the document said it was 'urgent to reduce the abusive penetration of our market by products coming from our major industrial competitors ... by investing in the sectors to make them competitive' (ibid.: 189). To aid the re-conquest of the domestic market, Proposition 15 of the

Mitterrand manifesto recommended extensive industrial activism. Concerning the balance of payments, the document promised to consider selective protectionism: 'the free flow of trade is a means that can be justified insofar as it contributes to growth and to better jobs, but not when its effects are ... inflation, deflation and unemployment' (ibid.: 223–4). Critically, in government the 'Socialists ran into precisely the problems which they themselves had anticipated' (Halimi *et al.*, 1994: 101). The Socialist government's response, however, was disappointing; it failed to devalue the franc in a meaningful and timely manner and it refused to countenance protectionist measures.

The Mitterrand experiment was conducted in an unfavourable economic environment. There was a global recession during the early 1980s which coincided with a sustained increase in the value of the US dollar and rising interest rates around the world. The Socialist government confronted three main problems as a result. First, the balance of payments deficit increased from $4.7 billion in 1981 to $12.1 billion in 1982. Reflation and the associated increase in consumer spending contributed to a rise in the volume of imports:

> The Socialist stimulus created new jobs in Japan, the United States and West Germany as much as, or more than, in France. The industrial plant was simply not capable of taking advantage of the burst of prosperity that took place in the second half of 1981 and early 1982.
>
> (Harrington, 1986: 133)

Meanwhile, the global recession reduced the demand for exports. France, it was said, 'could not afford to run a relatively large internal (government) deficit and an external (balance of trade) deficit at the same time' (ibid.: 117). Second, the currency was increasingly overvalued relative to the US dollar, the West German deutschmark and other currencies and this encouraged speculation against the franc. Third, the country experienced significant capital flight during this period, as much as $5 billion in one week during May 1981, and its currency reserves shrank rapidly.

The initial response of the Socialist government to these problems was to resist devaluation and to increase interest rates in an attempt to defend the parity of the franc within the ERM. Speculation against the franc, which had begun before the Socialists came to power, intensified as a result. These measures failed, however, and in October 1981 the franc was devalued by 3.0 per cent within the ERM and the deutschmark was revalued by 5.5 per cent. Nevertheless, speculation continued and the Socialist government convinced itself that a series of temporary deflationary measures were required to reduce the budget and trade deficits, restore the level of foreign exchange reserves and appease foreign creditors (Hall, 1987). The Social government introduced a raft of austerity measures in June 1982, including a four-month price and wage freeze, a budget deficit limit of 3 per cent and public expenditure cuts of 20 billion francs. Furthermore, the currency was devalued for a second time: the franc was devalued by 5.75 per cent and the deutschmark was revalued by 4.25 per cent. These measures were also unsuccessful and speculation persisted.

In an echo of the 1976 Labour government split over the IMF loan and public expenditure cuts, the Socialist government in March 1983 was divided over how to cope with the external constraints. The then minister of industry, Jean-Pierre Chevènement, and other left-wing ministers demanded an end to austerity and the resumption of reflation. Furthermore, some of Mitterrand's advisors recommended an exit from the ERM, to enable a more radical devaluation and the introduction of import controls, while the PCF called for withdrawal from the EC. Delors, took the opposite view and insisted that deflation and continued ERM membership were essential. Delors prevailed and the Socialist government introduced another round of austerity measures. Public expenditure was cut by another 24 billion francs in 1983 and taxes increased by 40 billion francs. In addition, the currency was devalued for a third time: the franc was devalued by 2.5 per cent and the deutschmark was revalued by 5.5 per cent. The programme upon which the Socialists were elected was abandoned and the Mitterrand experiment came to an end.

Like the British left's AES, the PCG and the Mitterrand experiment encountered a range of problems which were institutional, economic and political in nature. *Institutionally*, the French left was divided about the PCG and about which policies to pursue in government. The social democrats within the PS, centred upon Delors and Rocard, were sceptical about power-sharing with the PCF, cautious about nationalization, hostile towards protectionism, and firmly in favour of the German 'social market' model and the EC. The socialists within the PS, by contrast, associated with Chevènement and the *Centre d'Études de Recherche et d'Éducation Socialiste*,[3] supported a governing alliance with the PCF, backed economic planning, nationalization, protectionism and workers' control, and were opposed to supranational European integration. The PCF, as a reformist Eurocommunist party, advocated left union but was concerned about the rising popularity of the PS from 1978. It called for a break with capitalism and withdrawal from the EC but was dubious about workers' control. The tensions, which came to the fore when the left was in power, were exploited by the right, the corporate sector and sections of the media (Dixon and Perraud, 1982), plus the international financial nexus, in their bid to neutralize the French left. They were resolved in 1983 when the Socialist government abandoned its radical programme.

Economically, despite some early success in terms of redistribution, plus an above average macroeconomic performance, the Socialist government faced a worsening balance of payments situation, massive capital flight and an ongoing currency crisis. The failure of the Socialist government to resolve these problems *without* sacrificing its reflationary programme, and the failure to implement the British left's AES, were cited as evidence that national and radical strategies – whether 'Keynesianism in one country' or 'socialism in one country' – were redundant (Hall, 1986; Clift, 2005). Halimi *et al.* (1994) and Lombard (1995) challenged this conventional view, on three counts. First, regarding the balance of payments situation,

> The sharp rise in the value of the dollar multiplied the cost of French imports (especially imports) without helping French exports to the US much

(a limited amount in a very competitive market). Thus the domestic contribution to the 1982 trade deficit amounted to 27 billion francs, whereas international factors (a soaring dollar and rising interest rates) represented 57 billion francs.

(Halimi *et al.*, 1994: 108)

In short, it could be argued that the *timing* of the reflation by the Socialist government was problematic, but not the reflationary programme per se.

Second, capital flight and the investment strike by the corporate sector were creating difficulties for the Socialist government in *addition* to the global recession and the costly defence of the franc:

Between the first quarter of 1981 and the second quarter of 1982, 81 per cent of the deterioration in the balance of payments was due to the capital, not the current, account, and private investment fell sharply from 1981 to 1983.

(Ibid.: 109)

Put simply, the critical question becomes one of *how* a government responds to such a situation, not *whether* such a situation will arise, because, 'in reality, such a response' by the forces of capital 'to any radical government is likely to be hard to avoid' (ibid.).

Third, although devaluation was not a panacea for France's economic problems during this period, the Socialist government delayed taking such action, thus rendering devaluation a defensive rather than offensive policy. It devalued in three stages rather than one, thus dissipating the impact of the change. It did so in a timid way, thus providing little stimulus to exports. It did so with the support of Germany, France's main trading partner, thus doing little to fundamentally alter the relationship, and it did so while maintaining its membership of the ERM, thus committing itself to the continued defence of the franc within the fixed exchange rate system. There was an alternative however:

A withdrawal from the EMS was likely to succeed immediately after 10 May 1981. It would have entailed a sharp drop in the franc. But then, the French government would have acquired the latitude to choose the parity it wanted between the franc and the deutschmark. It would availed itself of the necessary margin, as proven by the successful devaluations of 1958 [17 per cent] and 1969 [12.5 per cent], without which French devaluations are almost always ineffective.

(Ibid.: 106)

In other words, the Socialist government could have implemented its devaluation policy much more effectively.

Politically, the PCG and the Mitterrand experiment, like the AES, held the promise of an enhanced social model which, if successfully implemented, would have transformed the French economy and society more generally. The PCG and the Mitterrand experiment, like the AES, also constituted economically nationalist threats to the Grand Area plan and its prioritization of open markets. If successfully implemented, the French left's reflationary programme would have set an example to other countries. As such, it was no surprise that it encountered resistance from the corporate sector, much of the media and the international financial nexus. What was disappointing, if not surprising given the social democratic influence within the PS, was that the French left had anticipated the external constraints that it encountered but, instead of pursuing the necessary remedial action, it capitulated.

> The reasons for the failure of the Mitterrand experiment are quite straightforward. Once the political decision had been taken to put the ERM (and, by extension, the alliance and integration with West Germany) above all other policy goals, the U-turn of March 1983 was unavoidable. The commitment to the narrow band of the ERM meant that no independent fiscal and monetary policy could conceivably be followed.... The devaluations ... were too little, too late.... The international recession of the time meant that the room for manoeuvre was much reduced. Sharp devaluations (and probably some form of protection of the kind advocated by Chevènement) were necessary. But in addition, the recession meant that ... the reflation was in fact much too timid. Far from being the reckless 'dash for growth' that is often portrayed, the expansion was too weak to offset the contractionary influences from outside.
>
> (Ibid.: 109)

In short, the French left failed to implement its reflationary programme, despite anticipating the problems that it encountered, and it did so to preserve its European policy.

Lessons to be drawn

The broader lessons to be drawn from the British and French experiments depend upon how social democracy is perceived. Wickham-Jones (1996) identified three main theories of social democracy – the revisionist model, the labour movement model and the structural constraints model – and noted that each one had a specific set of objectives, a particular economic theory, a recommended set of policy tools and a favoured electoral strategy. In terms of objectives, the *revisionist* model – promoted by Crosland (1956) – held that social democracy should be concerned with distribution (i.e. equality and social justice) rather than production (i.e. market versus state). In terms of economic theory, it postulated that capitalism had been transformed by the Keynesian revolution in economic thought and practice, that the state possessed the ability to manage the economy successfully, that full employment had shifted power from the capitalists to the managers and workers, and that the latter could co-operate to achieve shared objectives. In terms of policy tools, it suggested that indirect interventions in the economy, more specifically the setting of public expenditure and taxation levels, were sufficient to achieve economic growth and full employment. 'Keynesian economics allowed for the extraction of a surplus from the economy, taken through taxation, which could be reallocated through the welfare programmes at the centre of social democratic objectives' (Wickham-Jones, 1996: 19). Consequently, economic planning, public ownership and workers' control were considered unnecessary if not harmful. In terms of electoral strategy, it emphasized the importance of responding to the growth of the middle class in contemporary society and the need to appeal to the 'moderate' voter.

In terms of objectives, the *labour movement* model – advanced by Stephens (1979), Korpi (1983) and Esping-Anderson (1985) – held that social democracy should be concerned with both distribution and production. In terms of economic theory, it held that the power of the state to secure social democratic objectives was conditional upon the relative power resources of the labour movement in a society characterized by class conflict, that private control over the means of production remained a matter for concern, and that the structural reform of the economy was both necessary and possible. As Meidner (1993: 218) argued, 'experience has taught us that the free market forces guarantee neither full employment nor equality; to give the highest priority to these goals means challenging the principles of the capitalist system'. In terms of policy tools, it argued that indirect interventions in the economy were insufficient and that radical measures such as nationalization and workers' control would be required to deliver full employment. In terms of electoral strategy, it advanced the optimistic view that social democrats could be elected on the basis of a radical programme and that their success in office would produce a virtuous cycle promoting further achievements. Over time, social democracy would shift in a radical direction away from conventional Keynesianism towards socialism.

In terms of objectives, the *structural constraints* model – conceived by Przeworski (1985) – held that social democracy would be characterized by moderate Keynesianism as it strove to deliver capitalist efficiency and guarantee private property. In terms of economic theory, it noted that social democratic governments, indeed all governments, required material wealth and economic growth to deliver their programmes and that the investment decisions of private capitalists were critical for wealth creation. Consequently,

> The very capacity of social democrats to regulate the economy depends upon the profitability of the private sector and the willingness of capitalists to co-operate. This is the structural barrier which cannot be broken: the limit of any policy is that investment and thus profits must be protected in the long run.
>
> (Przeworski, 1985: 42)

There was thus very little that was distinctive about social democracy because capitalism imposed major constraints upon the freedom of action of *all* governments. In terms of policy tools, it asserted that any policies which damaged or deterred profitability, whether nationalization or redistribution, should be avoided. In terms of electoral strategy, it pessimistically noted that, to secure electoral victory and to maintain a coalition of popular support, social democrats would have to dilute their class focus and would have to appeal to an electorate that purportedly supported, and benefited from, capitalism.

A revisionist assessment of the British and French experiments would high-light the misplaced prioritization of production over distribution, the eschewal of class compromise and the emphasis on direct rather than indirect intervention in the economy. Revisionists would argue that policy mistakes such as these guaranteed the failure of these experiments. Similarly, a structural constraints assessment would castigate the Labour Party and the PS for confronting capital and would urge them to work within the parameters of the capitalist system. Only by improving the profitability of British and French capitalists and their market share within the global economy, they would argue, could social democratic governments hope to generate the necessary resources for redistribution and social investment. A labour movement assessment, by contrast, would focus upon the failure of the left in Britain and France to fully realize their power resources in opposition and in government. It would welcome their analyses and preparations for government and it would acknowledge that a radical programme would face significant obstacles. It would criticize the British and French labour movements, however, for their timidity and for abandoning their programmes in the face of anticipated external constraints. Their surrender was fatal to the electoral prospects and self-confidence of the left in Britain, France and elsewhere.

In an attempt to transcend this impasse and inject some logic into the debate, Hahnel (2005: 122–3) argued that progressive social forces had three options when in government. First, 'don't stimulate the economy in the first place because you are not willing to stand the inevitable heat'. Second, 'stimulate, but back off as soon as new international investment boycotts your economy, domestic wealth takes flight, financial markets drive interest rates on government debt through the ceiling and your currency drops'. Third,

> stimulate, but be prepared to face the heat international capital markets will bring with strong measures restricting imports and capital flight, by substituting government investment for declines in international and private investment, and by telling creditors you will default unless they agree to rollovers and concessions. Option three *is* the economic equivalent in the neo-liberal era of not only playing hardball with international creditors, but going to financial war if need be.

Option one, which equates to the structural constraints model, arguably negates the purpose, if not existence, of social democratic parties and other progressive social forces. What is the point of such movements, and aspiring to government, if capitalists are too powerful and capitalism is beyond reform? Option one is not cost-free either:

greater international economic integration means that the impact of successful national intervention is paradoxically greater than before. Conversely, a
resigned abdication from active industrial and macroeconomic policy which
allows a loss of competitive advantage, whether by one European country or
by Europe as a whole, will have disastrous effects, magnified by global
markets into a far faster loss of domestic and world markets, employment
and production.

(Halimi *et al.*, 1994: 115)

In short, inaction was not a viable course of action for the left in Britain and
France.

Option two, which equates to the revisionist model, was the approach adopted
in Britain by the Labour leadership in the 1960s and 1970s and in France by
Mitterrand and the social democrats after 1983. Not only does option two not
work – the Labour Party lost the election in 1979 and was out of power for 18
years and 'within less than two years of their election the French Socialists were
engaged in administering a regime of "rigour", otherwise known as capitalist
austerity' (Harrington, 1989: 19–20) – but it

almost always leads to even worse austerity measures than option one
because regaining credibility with global financial markets is usually more
difficult than not losing it in the first place. Option two also creates more
political damage because voters understandably hold the reformers responsible for the pain caused by the austerity programme reformers preside over.
[Moreover] option one inevitably undermines support from the social
sectors that bring governments to power in the first place.

(Hahnel, 2005: 123)

Although the British and French experiments were initially promising, option
three, which equates to the labour movement model, was not fully implemented by the left anywhere in Western Europe in the post-1945 period. Paradoxically, however, the social democratic consensus underpinning the CWO
was relatively conducive to the construction of an enhanced social model on a
national basis, in three main ways. First, because the economies of Western
Europe were organized on a largely national basis, and because the BWS
enabled the political control of capital markets and exchange rates, it was theoretically and practically possible for the left to direct, if not control, the
economy. Second, the left had significant electoral and popular appeal in
several Western European countries – hence the US interventions in France,
Greece, Italy, Portugal and elsewhere during the CWO. Third, the institutionalization of state intervention (i.e. Keynesianism) provided the left with many
of the policy tools that it required. In short, the economic, ideological and
institutional arrangements during this period could have been more effectively
exploited by the left. Political will, public support and timing, however, were
critical.

In terms of political will, Hahnel (2005: 124) argued that, although social democracy delivered a more equal society and the welfare state, 'the problem with social democratic reforms was not that they were too successful, but that they were not successful enough'. More specifically,

> the problem was that they ceased to keep fighting for further reforms when their initial reforms fell short of achieving democracy and economic justice because they agreed to accept a system of competition and greed [i.e. capitalism] even though the system obstructed the democracy and economic justice they had pledged to fight for.
>
> (Ibid.: 125)

In terms of public support, the electoral popularity and/or success of the left in Britain in 1945, 1964 and 1974, in France in 1947, 1968, the late 1970s and early 1980s, in Italy in 1948 and thereafter, in Portugal and Spain from the late 1970s, in Sweden throughout the post-war period, in West Germany from 1969 until 1982, and elsewhere, provided the opportunities it needed to construct an enhanced social model. In terms of timing, the period of high economic growth during the 1950s and 1960s was arguably more favourable to the implementation of radical left programmes than the recessionary 'stagflation' of the 1970s and 1980s. Moreover, the British and French attempts at reflation, and the labour movement approach more generally, were not intrinsically flawed as any left-wing project which aspired to develop a particular state–society complex within the capitalist system, which itself was marked by contradictions, would engender contradictions and would encounter a range of problems.

The British and French experiments arguably provide some valuable lessons for contemporary progressive social forces that are seeking to defend Europe's social models against globalization and neo-liberalism. First, if reflation was necessary during the CWO to tackle the problems of inequality, poverty and unemployment, it is needed all the more in the contemporary period to counter the deflationary pressures exerted by the increasingly powerful international financial nexus. Second, the British and French cases highlight the need to both anticipate the external constraints and to implement remedial actions. Third, the British and French cases illustrate the need for a united left, in opposition and in government, and for a leadership that is accountable to the party membership, the wider left and the general public rather than the corporate and political elite. Fourth, the British and French experiments were ultimately dashed because social democrats chose to prioritize the EC over the implementation of their radical programmes.

Conclusion

The British and French experiments in reflation were conducted by counter-hegemonic social forces during the 1970s and 1980s when the economic, ideological and institutional arrangements underpinning the CWO (i.e. the social democratic consensus) were relatively conducive to the construction of an enhanced social model on a national basis. These attempts to provide an alternative to both conventional Keynesianism and neo-liberalism ultimately failed because of a combination of internal factors (e.g. sabotage by the party leadership and lack of left unity) and external factors (e.g. currency and trade deficit crises and worldwide recession) which conspired to prevent the implementation of the AES and the PCG. These experiments were not inherently flawed, however, and the problems they encountered, many of which were anticipated, could have been ameliorated or averted if the radical programmes had been fully implemented. These experiments provide some valuable lessons for contemporary progressive social forces that are seeking to defend Europe's social models against globalization and neo-liberalism. Rather than demonstrating the futility of a national and radical strategy, these experiments suggest that, to counter the international financial nexus and its deflationary bias, the left must utilize the state to refashion the economy to ensure that it meets the needs of labour rather than capital. To turn a right-wing concept on its head, the left has no alternative but to confront the power of capital and it has no alternative but to use the state to do so.

7 Progressive social forces and the transformation of the World Order

Euro-Keynesian and radical European alternatives

Introduction

This chapter discusses how, in the midst of the transformation of the World Order from the CWO to the NWO, progressive social forces sought to fashion Euro-Keynesian (i.e. Keynesianism but practiced on an EC/EU-level rather than a national basis) or radical European alternatives to neo-liberalism. Following the previous chapter, which focused upon national experiments, this chapter reviews the proposals put forward by counter-hegemonic social forces to develop a *Europe-wide social model* (i.e. Euro-Keynesianism) or an *enhanced* social model on a *European* basis (i.e. radical alternatives).

The chapter advances five main arguments. First, that any attempt to redirect the European project towards positive integration had to overcome the EC/EU reification of market liberalism, bias towards negative integration, choice of social regulation and preference for competition and economic liberalization. Such a transformation required the reform of the EC/EU treaties by all member states. Second, and following from the first argument, that the unanimity needed to revise the EC/EU treaties required the simultaneous election of left-wing governments in all member states. This problem was compounded by the existence of different electoral cycles in each country. Third, that in the absence of such a transformation, the ideological and material resources for constructing an enhanced social model on a European basis were lacking; in short, there was no European polity and the EC/EU budget was too small. Fourth, that when the opportunity to initiate such a transformation arose, in the 1990s when most member states were governed by the left, social democratic governments were successfully outflanked by a right-wing alliance that sought to defend the neo-liberal trajectory of the EU. Fifth, that because of the aforementioned hurdles, the chances of progressive social forces successfully constructing an enhanced social model on a European basis *using the present-day EU as a vehicle* are poor.

The chapter is divided into seven main sections. The first section details the EC budget proposals put forward in the 1970s to fund a Euro-Keynesian regime. The second section describes the intergovernmental and radical Out of Crisis Project, launched during the early 1980s, which aimed to reflate and restructure Europe's economies, and to redistribute within them, using policy tools such as economic democracy, economic planning, public enterprises and public spending. The third section outlines the Euro-Keynesian plan produced by the Centre for European Policy Studies Macroeconomic Group during the early 1980s which aimed to reflate Europe's economies. The fourth section evaluates the Euro-Keynesian potential of the European Commission under Delors in the late 1980s and early 1990s. The fifth section considers the Economic and Social Cohesion report, produced in the early 1990s, which recommended using the Delors II package to develop a Social Europe. The sixth section assesses the Euro-Keynesian ideas developed by the Our Europe think tank. The seventh section explores the Euro-Keynesian proposals developed by Jospin and Lafontaine during the late 1990s.

European Community budget proposals

Following the publication of the Werner Plan in October 1970, a plethora of independent working groups formed to consider the practicalities of realizing the objective of EMU. Some of these working groups recommended a significant increase in the size and scope of the EC budget to underpin EMU and to counter some of the problems associated with economic integration: growing disparities between member states, regions and social groups.

The European Commission proposal

The European Commission published a report in April 1973, entitled 'Attainment of the Economic and Monetary Union' (European Commission, 1973b), which, in addition to economic policy coordination, called for the development of EC industrial policy, regional policy, social policy and structural policy, the EC regulation of European capital markets, tax harmonization across member states, and an expanded and flexible EC budget. In terms of social policy, it advocated the creation of a substantial EC unemployment fund to 'transfer income to redress the balance between areas where structural unemployment is high and those where it is low' and argued that 'this would provide solid proof of Community solidarity' (ibid.: 14). It noted that 'the Community must be given the institutional means to cope with increased tasks and responsibilities' (ibid.: 17) and it forecast that the EC budget would expand to around 1 per cent of EC GDP by 1976.

The Federal Trust Study Group

The Federal Trust Study Group was established in 1973 and was composed mainly of British civil servants. The Federal Trust Study Group published its report, entitled 'The Administrative Implications of Economic and Monetary Union' (Wallace, 1973), in the *Journal of Common Market Studies*. The report complained that insufficient progress was being made towards EMU and it specifically lamented that 'there was little room in [the founding treaties'] provisions for any positive conception of budgetary policy as an economic instrument, or of a Community budget sufficiently large to be a significant factor in the European economy' (ibid.: 414). One Federal Trust Study Group member estimated that, to have such an impact, a budget of 10 per cent of EC GDP would be required. Another member reasoned that 'a Community with, in effect, a common currency is best organized on a federal system, like that in the US, with a central government wielding substantial economic control' (ibid.: 422). The report noted, however, that this was 'a conclusion which the Werner Committee hinted at, but were unable for political reasons to develop' (ibid.).

The report argued that EMU would necessitate an EC central bank, an EC Treasury and a significant EC budget with

> a degree of control over national budgetary policies sufficiently great to limit effectively the possibility of national governments being able to pursue distinctive policies in the distribution of income and of taxation and in the allocation of resources between the private and the public sectors.
>
> (Ibid.: 422–3)

It further argued that

> The massive scale of resource transfers between different regions of the Community required under conditions of a common currency, and the political desirability of disguising their scale by drawing contributions from Community taxation rather than from direct levies on national budgets, will also strengthen the argument for a substantial Community budget.... This will, of course, require a considerable administrative machine even if execution of Community policies is decentralized to national governments.
>
> (Ibid.: 423)

In terms of policy content, it stated that

> We are considering a Community which would need to develop a set of clear central policies on prices, on the desirable growth and distribution of incomes, on the control of inflation and the level of employment, on the distribution of social benefits and of incentives to industry: that is to say, a Community which will have to decide many of the central questions of national politics in contemporary Western Europe.... It is inconceivable that this can operate without the creation of a European government politically responsible to an elected parliament. Thus Economic and Monetary Union cannot be achieved without the establishment of a federal government within the European Community.
>
> (Ibid.)

The report warned, however, that 'the continuing evolution of economic interdependence' – more specifically capital and labour mobility and increased trade – was 'making it increasingly difficult for national governments to operate as if they were managing separate economies' (ibid.: 438) and it concluded that

> Unless some means are developed for regaining the control over the Community economy as a whole which will by [1980] have been lost at national level, European economies will be open to sharp and politically unacceptable disequilibria; and the degree of coordination which will be needed to ensure the relatively smooth functioning of the European economy will be such as to require considerable centralization.
>
> (Ibid.)

In short, the Federal Trust Study Group called for the creation of a Euro-Keynesian and federal Europe.

The economists' panel led by Cairncross

A panel of five economists, led by the former advisor to the British government in the early 1960s, Alec Cairncross, published *Economic Policy for the European Community: The Way Forward* in 1974. To prepare for EMU, the economists argued, the EC budget should expand to permit 'a steady enlargement of its tasks' and they reasoned that

> If progress is to be made towards fiscal integration, the composition and direction of public spending needs to be analyzed in terms of distortions of competition, the contribution to growth and equality, the regional allocation of resources, and the relief of inflationary pressures.
>
> (Cairncross *et al.*, 1974: 60)

They presciently highlighted the dangers of tax competition and competitive deflation and warned that, without a larger EC budget,

> governments will continue to compete with each other in granting fiscal concessions in order to attract investment in industrial development. They will also continue to sacrifice public investment which generally contributes more to social amenities and the quality of life than does industrial competitiveness.... Harmonization in the proper sense is ... needed to forestall the unwanted consequences of competition left to itself.
>
> (Ibid.)

To guard against this eventuality, they suggested a 'move towards a distribution of power within the EC which limits the authority of ... national governments' (ibid.: xv). Furthermore, they called for the development of EC-level public services, funded by an enlarged EC budget, and proposed a new tax on the increase in land values in Europe to help finance such a system. They suggested delaying EMU to prevent the free flow of capital from destroying the efficacy of national economic policy and they argued that fiscal policy should be utilized to redistribute wealth within and between member states, that a larger EC budget should be used to overcome disparities in incomes and public services and to halt migration from poor to rich regions, that a common industrial policy should be developed and that the growth of EC-based 'mega-corporations' should be encouraged to assist with technological development. Like the Federal Trust Study Group, the economists supported the creation of a Euro-Keynesian and federal Europe.

The MacDougall Report

The European Commission sponsored a committee of seven economists in 1974 to produce a report on the role of public finance in European integration. Chaired by the then chief economic advisor to the Confederation of British Industry (CBI), Donald MacDougall, the committee's work was published in April 1977. Having studied the role of public finance in both unitary states and federations – focusing in particular on its redistributive effects, its counter-cyclical potential and its contribution to long-term economic growth – the report aimed to draw some lessons that could be applied at the EC level.

The 'Report of the Study Group on the Role of Public Finance in European Integration' (European Commission, 1977) envisaged the construction of a European federation in three steps. The first step, the pre-federal integration phase, would see public expenditure at the EC level increase to between 2.0 and 2.5 per cent of EC GDP. The second step would see the emergence of a federation with a small EC-level public sector which would entail public expenditure rising to between 5 and 7 per cent. The third step would see the development of a federation with a large EC-level public sector and public expenditure would approach between 20 and 25 per cent.

The report identified the potential benefits of an EC-level public sector: greater economies of scale, economic convergence and reduced inequalities within the EC. It also sketched out how the role of the EC might change as its budget expanded, what the macroeconomic role of the budget may be and how the budget could be financed. In terms of the role of the EC, in the pre-federal integration phase the budget would continue to fund the CAP and may be used to subsidize other industrial sectors where EC intervention was established or plausible (e.g. fisheries, steel, etc.). It suggested that 'much larger sums of parallel loan financing, borrowed by the Community on capital markets or under Community guarantee, might be appropriate in some cases' (ibid.: 15). It forecast that EC expenditure on employment, regional and structural policies, including a possible EC unemployment fund, would grow considerably during this phase. In terms of macroeconomics, it argued that the budget would be too small to help stabilize cyclical and short-term fluctuations in the European economy, and in terms of financing, it advised that such a budget could be underpinned by EC 'own resources' and additional value added tax revenues. During the small federation phase, education, health, social security and welfare provision would remain at the member state level but the equalization of public service provision between member states could be achieved via financial transfers. Furthermore, federal aid may be granted to particular industries and regions to augment national efforts. During the large federation phase, most social and welfare expenditure would be administered by the federal government, and federal taxes, boosted by new EC borrowing powers, would predominate. Furthermore, the equalization, redistributive and stabilization functions of the EC would be considerable.

These ambitious proposals to significantly increase the EC budget to fund a Euro-Keynesian regime – more specifically to develop interventionist EC policies, to facilitate intra-European redistribution and to construct an EC-level public sector (i.e. positive integration) – were sidelined. The economic crisis during the 1970s (i.e. 'stagflation') and the dominant policy response in key member states (i.e. neo-liberalism) ensured that the reification of market liberalism, the bias towards negative integration, the choice of social regulation and the EC-level preference for competition and economic liberalization prevailed. In short, Euro-Keynesianism was anathema to the dominant social forces in Europe at that time. Indeed, it remains so; the proposed 2011 EU budget totalled only 1.11 per cent of EU GDP, thus falling well short of even the pre-federal integration scenario set out in the MacDougall Report.

The Out of Crisis Project

The Out of Crisis Project or Project for European Recovery was established in 1981, published its report in 1983 and was composed of left-wing economists, members of the French, Greek, Italian, Portuguese, Spanish and Swedish socialist parties, plus members of the British Labour Party, and trade unionists. Arguing that the global economy was gripped by a 'slump syndrome' – with spiralling debt, falling incomes and output, contracting trade, and rising inequality, inflation and unemployment – and that the welfare state was under attack from public expenditure cuts, the project aimed to develop an alternative to both conventional Keynesianism and monetarism.

The *Out of Crisis* report (Holland, 1983) identified 'beggar my neighbour' deflation, the collapse of demand and domination by TNCs as the principal threats to Europe's economies in the 1980s. In terms of 'beggar my neighbour' deflation and demand, the report noted that 'several countries reduce domestic demand to restrain imports and preserve or secure a balance in their payments [and] reduced demand lowers the rate of growth of exports between the countries concerned' (ibid.: 19). This scenario typically gave rise to a vicious circle as balance of payments problems precipitated a currency crisis and a 'loss of confidence'. Governments responded by cutting public expenditure and thus demand, so as to achieve a balanced budget and trade account, and by raising interest rates to strengthen the currency. Consequently, bankruptcies and unemployment rose, economic growth declined, government revenue fell and the increased need for government borrowing induced a 'fiscal crisis for the state' (ibid.: 20). Governments then had to approach the financial markets to borrow and the price exacted was even more deflation. In terms of TNCs, the report suggested that their increasing size and power presented governments with a range of problems, including outflows of foreign direct investment, offsetting of exchange rate changes, oligopoly, relocation of production, transfer pricing, etc.

Arguing that Keynes' most important contribution 'was to give a coherent rationale for state intervention in demand' (ibid.: 44), the report insisted that the strategies of reflation, restructuring and redistribution provided the solution to Europe's economic and social crisis. In terms of *reflation*, the report set out three 'better my neighbour' reflationary scenarios. The first scenario, namely unilateral reflation, was attempted in France by Mitterrand and the Socialist government in 1981–1982. The report observed that such an approach 'benefits other countries on a major scale but can impose debilitating costs on the country directly concerned' (see Table 7.1).

More specifically,

> For each 1 per cent gain to its own production and income a West European country could typically lose about half a per cent of GDP on its balance of payments. To put the matter another way, for every 100,000 jobs created by unilateral ... reflation, the country's trade balance might deteriorate by some $5 billion. No European country could go very far in creating jobs and raising income if this were the cost.
>
> (Ibid.: 59)

The second scenario, namely cumulative reflation, involves action by a limited number of governments who may be joined, in time, by groups of others as the 'better my neighbour' benefits take effect. 'Through this kind of process, the rate

Table 7.1 Effects of a $1billion reflation in a single European country ($ million)

	Reflating economy	Rest of Europe	Rest of world	Total world
Direct stimulus	1,000	–	–	1,000
Indirect effects	500	350	375	1,225
Rise in domestic spending	1,500	350	375	2,225
Less rise in imports	−600	−430	−270	−1,300
Rise in domestic income	950	650	625	2,225
Government budget	−450	230	160	−60
Balance of payments (current account)	−550	300	250	0
Employment (thousands)	15	10	15	40

Source: adapted from Holland (1983: 193).

Note
Illustrative calculation based on estimate values of import propensities, export market shares, domestic multipliers and fiscal drag for Western Europe, the rest of the world and a typical individual European country.

of job creation might reach 1.5–2 million a year by the end of decade' and could increase employment in Europe by nine million by 1991 (see Table 7.2).

The third scenario, namely general reflation, 'implies that major expansion programmes are begun immediately by most of the developed economies' (ibid.: 61). The report identified a range of policy measures that could be deployed as part of these reflationary scenarios: devaluation, economic planning, incomes policy, nationalization, public enterprise (e.g. co-operative enterprises, local enterprise agencies, state holding companies, etc.) and selective trade protection (i.e. import controls). The report contended, however, that 'we simply cannot spend our way out of the crisis' (ibid.: 61) and that reflation, under whichever scenario, would not of itself tackle the problems of inequality, poverty and unemployment. Restructuring and redistribution were also necessary.

In terms of *restructuring*, the report rejected the capitalist logic of improving competitiveness and ensuring short-term profits by cutting investment, jobs and production capacity. Instead, the report advocated long-term and sustainable social investment:

> In practice this means intervening in the market in such a way as to stem deindustrialization resulting from the crisis of small and medium enterprise under private ownership, and to promote production and employment in the

Table 7.2 Cumulative reflation: illustrative projection (addition to output and employment)

Countries	1983–1985	1985–1987	1987–1989	1989–1991	Cumulative
Group 1:					
Output (%)	3	4	5	6	19
Employment (thousands)	350	550	725	925	2,550
Group 2:					
Output (%)	(0.3)	4	5	6	16
Employment (thousands)	(65)	975	1,300	1,650	3,990
Group 3:					
Output (%)	(0.4)	(1.5)	5	6	13
Employment (thousands)	(50)	(250)	800	1,025	2,125
Group 4:					
Output (%)	(0.3)	(1.1)	(2.5)	6	10
Employment (thousands)	(175)	(700)	(1,750)	4,500	7,125
Total Western Europe:					
Output (%)	1	3	5	6	16
employment (thousands)	465	1,775	2,825	3,600	8,665

Source: adapted from Holland (1983: 193).

Notes
Group 1 – France, Greece and Spain; Group 2 – Austria, Britain, Denmark, Italy, Norway, Portugal and Sweden; Group 3 – Belgium, Finland, Germany, Ireland, the Netherlands and Switzerland; Group 4 – United States and others.
Figures in brackets show the 'better my neighbour' effect through raised exports for country groups before they have joined the cumulative reflation.

small firm sector, with a redistribution of resources towards those small and medium enterprises which can achieve a transformation of their mode of ownership and control towards co-operative and social enterprise.

(Ibid.: 77)

The report specifically recommended using public credit and finance agencies, public procurement and regional policy to assist with credit and finance, product development and sales promotion. Furthermore, to avoid a large and growing European trade deficit with the rest of the world as a result of Europe-wide reflation – more specifically the increase in the imports of manufactures, oil and raw materials – the report favoured the adoption of energy conservation measures, export promotion and the use of selective import controls so that 'European governments could attempt to swing the balance of market shares in their favour' (ibid.: 84).

In terms of *redistribution*, the report supported the reallocation of incomes and wealth by equalizing personal incomes, extending public services which are free at the point of use (i.e. decommodification), lowering the retirement age and reducing working hours. The report claimed that such a strategy 'amounts to a new model of socialized development and it is on such a basis that we can move from a welfare state in crisis to conditions for a welfare society' (ibid.: 90).

The report conceded that any programme of reflation, restructuring and redistribution would generate significant opposition and would encounter at least four major problems. First, the report recognized that the deployment of import controls could damage the development prospects of other countries – particularly those in the South. The report countered, however, that

> The case for limited protection must be seen in the context of the increase in overall trade on the 'better my neighbour' basis which would accompany a major European reflation. European countries could accept a long-run net reduction in their *share* of world industrial markets necessary to provide space for industrialization elsewhere [but] the *pace* of these developments ought to be controlled by reference to the rate of economic growth in the world as a whole.
>
> (Ibid.: 183)

On this point, the report made reference to, and common cause with, the Brandt Commission (1980, 1983) reports on North–South relations and the Socialist International Committee on Economic Policy (1985) report – each of which called for a fundamental redistribution and restructuring of power on a global scale.

Second, the report lamented that 'the multinational trend in world trade has profoundly qualified the effectiveness of devaluation as an instrument of trade adjustment' (ibid.: 34). The empirical evidence suggested that TNCs were unwilling to reduce their prices in the country that had devalued because to do so would undercut the price of their competing products in other countries. 'In this way the "own competitor" effect has transformed the alleged price competitiveness gains and potential export-led growth available from devaluation' (ibid.). The report qualified such pessimism however: 'this is not to say that devaluation no longer has a role to play in offsetting the decline in export competitiveness of individual countries' (ibid.).

Third, the report was ambivalent about the role of the EC in any programme of reflation, restructuring and redistribution. The report noted that Europe was split into two main blocs, the EC and the EFTA, and that the left in most member states was divided about continued membership with some sections committed to federalism, other sections to reform of the EC and other sections to withdrawal. The report hinted at the obstructive nature of the Treaties of Rome and the structural constraints imposed by EC membership (i.e. the four freedoms) but it neglected to acknowledge the European dimension of the failed 'Mitterrand experiment'. Instead, the report blithely asserted that EC and EFTA member states could participate in the intergovernmental European Recovery Project; indeed 'the project aims to create a political initiative that transcends the existing organizational structure within Europe' (ibid.: 164).

Fourth, the report warned that the international financial nexus and the capital markets in particular would strongly resist a programme of reflation, restructuring and redistribution and would likely engineer a crisis to compel a change of policy. The corporate sector more generally would also oppose such a radical programme because, although it would boost their sales and profits, 'it may jeopardize managerial authority by putting workers in a better position to press any pay claims or demands for improved working conditions' (ibid.: 63). More fundamentally, the resulting full employment would transform the nature of the settlement between capital and labour because, as Kalecki (1943: 325) pointed out,

> The maintenance of full employment would give new impetus to the opposition of business leaders. Indeed, under a regime of permanent full employment, the 'sack' would cease to play its role as a disciplinary measure. The social position of the boss would be undermined and the self-assurance and class consciousness of the working class would grow.... It is true that profits would be higher under a regime of full employment ... but 'discipline in the factories' and 'political stability' are more appreciated than profits by business leaders. Their class instinct tells them that lasting full employment is unsound from their point of view, and that unemployment is an integral part of the 'normal' capitalist system.

To counter the power of the international financial nexus, the report recommended capital controls and the public ownership of banking and credit and insurance institutions.

> The government should be able to prevent domestic funds being used for speculation against its own policies. It seems an elementary precaution that

pension funds and savings built up in one country should be prevented from leaving the country if this would jeopardize the government's economic policies.

(Ibid.: 66)

The report also recommended exchange controls to facilitate the isolation of the financial system in any one country, and thus state control, a significant increase in official IMF lending and the abolition of IMF loan 'conditionality' to enable countries to borrow without recourse to private capital, and joint action at the European level. In terms of the latter, the report specifically called for the reform of the EMS, to include both EC and non-EC members and to 'provide for mutual support operations to assist individual currencies which come under financial pressure' (ibid.: 165).

Six changes to the EMS were suggested. First, it should focus upon constraining the stronger currencies rather than the weaker ones via a 'divergence indicator'. Second, it should amass considerable intervention finance and these monies should be governed by European rather than national criteria. Third, it should counter the hegemony of the dollar by encouraging European countries to co-operate and focus upon internal monetary policy rather than the needs of the United States. Fourth, it should recognize that inflation rate convergence within Europe was implausible, if not impossible, and it should therefore allow its members to periodically adjust their exchange rates in a managed rather than crisis-driven manner. Fifth, it should be underpinned by a composite European currency, backed by sufficient intervention funds, which would 'shift the focus of international finance away from volatile national currencies while ... providing a stable basis to the system' (ibid.: 166). Sixth, it should provide credit support to those governments that were willing to undertake radical programmes. These changes would be 'a major step towards reform of the international monetary system; not least it would reduce the dependence of Europe and the international community on the vagaries of the dollar' (ibid.: 167).

The implementation of the Out of Crisis Project was predicated on a shift to the left across Europe, which did not happen. Although it formed the basis of the joint manifesto of the Confederation of the Socialist Parties of the European Communities for the 1984 European election, the direction of travel in many European countries during the 1980s was to the right. Although comprehensive, coherent and practical, the project relied upon the simultaneous election of left-wing governments in several European countries and their unwavering commitment to radical programmes which, in the post-Mitterrand experiment era, were known to engender significant costs and risks vis-à-vis the international financial nexus. Furthermore, the report evaded two important questions concerning the European dimension. First, how would the EC respond to member states' radical programmes if they involved capital, import and exchange controls, economic planning, nationalization, etc. which were contrary to the EC treaties? Second, if the response was negative and the EC attempted to obstruct such radical programmes how could member states circumvent this? The logical answer would be for member states to withdraw from the EC in anticipation of such obstruction and thereby neutralize the threat. Although the *Out of Crisis* report ignored these questions, because the left was divided about EC membership, any EC member state that intended to pursue a radical programme along these lines would need to formulate an answer to question two. Otherwise it would risk repeating the mistakes of the French left in the early 1980s.

The Centre for European Policy Studies plan

A group of economists associated with the Centre for European Policy Studies Macroeconomic group were sponsored by the European Commission in 1982 to investigate the macroeconomic prospects and policies of the EC. *Restoring Europe's Prosperity* was published in 1986 and many of these economists went on to serve as senior EC policy-makers.

The economists condemned the high levels of unemployment across Europe, criticized the unwarranted fiscal conservatism of member states and lamented the associated 'beggar my neighbour' approach. They rejected the right-wing arguments that the high level of real wages in Europe were to blame for high levels of unemployment, and that real wages should therefore be reduced, and argued instead for 'an expansion of aggregate demand accompanied by incomes policies that render more favourable the trade-off between recovery and disinflation' (Blanchard *et al.*, 1986: 2). They specifically called for coordinated fiscal expansion – centred upon Britain and Germany on the basis that these countries had the necessary fiscal room for manoeuvre – and claimed that such an approach would reduce 'the costs in terms of budget deficits and external imbalances' (ibid.).

They rejected work sharing arrangements as a solution to mass unemployment and recommended instead the introduction of a temporary investment subsidy to expand aggregate supply – and thus increase accumulated capital, raise productivity and reduce unit labour costs – as well as aggregate demand. They also recommended the provision of subsidies or tax credits to increase employment levels. To finance these measures they sanctioned rising budget deficits, and to maintain the effective exchange rate of the European currency unit (ecu) they favoured an 'accommodating' monetary policy. The economists conceded that the experience of Mitterrand and the Socialist government in France in 1981–1982 illustrated the problems associated with fiscal expansion, namely exchange rate pressures and external trade deficits, but insisted that 'these risks do not attach to a coordinated EC-wide expansion' because 'in a coordinated expansion increased imports are matched by increased export revenues due to partner country expansion' (ibid.: 23).

Like the Out of Crisis Project, the Centre for European Policy Studies plan was intergovernmental in nature although it did envisage that the EC would play a coordinating, as opposed to an active (i.e. budgetary), role. In contrast to the Out of Crisis Project, however, the plan focused upon reforming the supply side of the economy rather than boosting demand per se, and it was an 'explicitly temporary' form of reflation, 'to get the economies moving again' (ibid.: 37), rather than one that aspired to the fundamental reform of the economy. Compared to the Out of Crisis Project, the plan – with its preoccupation with supply-side economics – was somewhat more in tune with the politics of the time. Nevertheless, there was no support for such a plan in Britain or Germany.

Jacques Delors and Euro-Keynesianism

Under the Delors' presidency, from 1985 until 1994, the policy activism, power, scope and size of the European Commission expanded and the EC/EU budget increased. As in the 1970s, many progressive social forces hoped that the European Commission would pursue a Euro-Keynesian strategy to realize Delors' dream of creating a European social space with new regulatory frameworks. Several opportunities to do so arose during this period, including the Delors I package, the Social Charter, the Delors Report on EMU, the relaunch of EC industrial policy, the IGCs on EMU and EPU, the Delors II package and the 'Growth, Competitiveness and Employment' White Paper.

The Delors I package

The signing of the SEA in December 1985 and its commitment to economic and social cohesion necessitated the renewal of the EC budget. The Delors I package, presented by the European Commission in February 1987 and agreed by the European Council in February 1988, involved a five-year pledge to significantly enlarge the EC budget, which totalled 1.2 per cent of EC GDP by 1992. The package added a fourth source of revenue to EC 'own resources' based on per capita GDP, capped CAP expenditure, extended the British rebate and boosted the EC Structural Funds – more specifically the European Regional Development Fund and the European Social Fund. These were henceforth administered by the European Commission which, together with the EIB which provided loans, distributed monies in a coordinated manner to aid the less developed regions of the EC, to assist with the restructuring of regions in industrial decline, to help with rural development and to combat long-term and youth unemployment. Ross (1995: 40) described the package as 'the most under-discussed major event in Europe's post-1985 renewal' and argued that the reformed structural funds, which amounted to 25 per cent of EC expenditure by 1992, 'brought the first really substantial European-level commitment to planned redistribution among member states' (ibid.: 41). Given that the EC budget at this point was still well short of the pre-federal integration scenario set out in the MacDougall Report, however, such a bold claim is difficult to substantiate.

The Social Charter

In a series of speeches delivered in 1988, Delors elaborated on his vision of a European social space. At the ETUC conference in May, Delors stated that the adoption of the SEA was 'not a question of ... simply creating a free-trade zone, but rather an organized space endowed with common rules to ensure economic and social cohesion and equality of opportunity' (cited in Ross, 1995: 43). At the European Parliament in July, Delors predicted that 'in ten years, 80 per cent of economic legislation, perhaps even tax and social, will come from the EC' (cited in Grant, 1994: 88) and he suggested that, for the sake of efficiency, some form of European government should be created. At the British TUC in September, Delors boasted that the European Commission would, as a result of the Delors I package, spend £40 billion between then and 1992 on EC social objectives. Delors invited the trade union movement to abandon its scepticism, if not hostility, towards the EC and promised, in return, that the European Commission would establish, as an integral part of the SM project, a minimum level of workers' rights, a European Company Statute and the right to lifelong education and training. Despite such promises, the resulting supply-side-oriented Social Charter, agreed in May 1989, was not legally binding – prompting Pierson (1996: 26) to characterize it as 'a saga of high aspirations and modest results ... cheap talk'. Furthermore, the subsequent Action Programme to operationalize the Social Charter, launched in January 1993, contained non-binding recommendations and made no attempt to enforce social policy harmonization.

The Delors Report on EMU

The Delors Report on EMU, agreed in June 1989, argued that the 'removal of market barriers' as part of the SM project would require a 'strengthening of regional and structural policies' to help 'prevent the emergence or aggravation of regional and sectoral imbalances' (European Commission, 1989: 10–12). The report stated that EMU necessitated greater policy coordination, 'not only in the monetary field but also in areas of national economic management affecting aggregate demand, prices and costs of production' (ibid.: 10). Highlighting in particular the importance of fiscal policy, the report recommended that these policies should prioritize 'price stability, balanced growth, converging standards of living, high employment and external equilibrium' (ibid.: 13). Acknowledging that EMU would 'remove the exchange rate as an instrument of adjustment from the member states' set of economic tools', the report suggested that 'economic imbalances among member countries would have to be corrected by policies affecting the structure of their economies and costs of production if major regional disparities in output and employment were to be avoided' (ibid.: 12). The report cautioned, however, that EMU 'should be based on the same market-oriented economic principles that underlie the economic order of its member states', that there should be 'a large degree of freedom for market behaviour and private economic initiative' and that 'public intervention' should be limited to 'the provision of certain social services and public goods' (ibid.: 16–17).

The report signalled that, while 'voluntary co-operation' between member states was preferable, there may be a need to develop 'more binding procedures' (ibid.: 11) in three main areas. First, EMU would need to be complemented by an EC competition policy to ensure that 'the use of government subsidies to assist particular industries' was 'strictly circumscribed' (ibid.: 18). Second, regional and structural policies would need to be strengthened but the principal objective of such policies 'should not be to subsidize incomes and simply offset inequalities in the standards of living'. Instead, they should 'help to equalize production conditions through investment programmes in areas such as communications, education, physical infrastructure and transportation so that large-scale movements of labour do not become the major adjustment factor'. Nevertheless, 'wage flexibility and labour mobility are necessary to eliminate differences in competitiveness' (ibid.: 18–19). Third, in terms of macroeconomic policy

> Many developments ... would continue to be determined by factors and decisions operating at the national or local level. This would include not only wage negotiations and other economic decisions in the fields of production, savings and investment, but also the action of public authorities in the economic and social spheres. Apart from the system of binding rules governing the size and financing of national budget deficits, decisions on the main components of public policy in such areas as internal and external security, justice, social security, education and hence on the level and composition of government spending, as well as many revenue measures, would remain the preserve of member states even at the final stage of EMU. Moreover, the fact that the centrally managed Community budget is likely to remain a very small part of the total public sector spending and that much of this budget will not be available for cyclical adjustments will mean that the task of setting a Community-wide fiscal policy stance will have to be performed through the coordination of national budgetary policies.
>
> (Ibid.: 19–20)

The report warned, however, that monetary policy alone would not be sufficient to preserve 'internal balance' and that wage increases would need to be linked to improvements in productivity, that national budget deficits would have to be constrained, that central banks should resist direct credit financing and that member states should be prevented from borrowing in non-EC currencies. Essentially, there was very little in Delors' plan for EMU to assuage or regale the advocates of Euro-Keynesianism.

Industrial policy

The European Commission published its 'Industrial Policy in an Open and Competitive Environment' document in November 1990. The aim of the new policy, given the SM and EMU projects, was to 'facilitate the process of internationalization by strengthening the ability of European industry to compete both on its own market and globally'; in short, to 'prepare European industry for stronger competition' (European Commission, 1990: 5). The document endorsed a horizontal EC approach to industrial policy, based upon supporting R&D and training to benefit the whole economy, to replace the previous vertical approach of channelling aid to particular sectors. The EC and member state objectives of 'picking winners' and creating 'national champions' were abandoned and the new policy prioritized the needs of corporations; 'firms were the key actors who made the final decisions: there could be no question of substituting public action for firm decisions in old-fashioned *dirigiste* ways' (Ross, 1995: 116).

The document stated that, henceforth, the role of the EC was to create a favourable business environment and to avoid 'unnecessary' regulation, to prevent member states from adopting 'defensive' (i.e. protectionist) industrial policies, to facilitate rather than retard the necessary structural adjustment to economic change on the part of member states and to deliver a stable macroeconomic environment. It stated that the EC also aimed to boost educational attainment, to promote economic and social cohesion, to achieve a high level of environmental protection, and to ensure open markets both within the EC and externally. The European Commission reserved the right to take direct action where it saw fit however:

> the experience of the 1970s and 1980s has shown that sectoral policies of an interventionist type are not an effective instrument to promote structural adaptation [but] especially grave problems of adjustment have been tackled at the Community level in the past, for instance in shipbuilding, steel and textiles. Equally, the Community has had to pay special attention, and will continue to do so in future, to areas that can play a key role for the development of the European industry and of the European economy as a whole, such as aeronautics, information technology, the maritime industry and telecommunications.
>
> (Ibid.: 19)

Delors' ultimate objective was to create a European technology community and the EC subsequently spent a considerable amount of money on both horizontal and vertical programmes. The results, however, were mixed. The efforts of the European Commission to develop a Europe-wide high-definition television industry (i.e. vertical action) produced very little, while the internal auditors of the European Commission found that the European Program for Research and Development in Information (i.e. horizontal action) was ineffective. Although industrial policy was included as a chapter in the Maastricht Treaty, Delors later admitted to being

> 'greatly disappointed' with what he has achieved on industrial policy in his time as president. He says he never wanted a *dirigiste* policy, with the European Commission picking winners. 'I'm asking that firms co-operate together and that Community policies support them – either through a research and development effort or through training people to adapt to new methods of work'.
>
> (Quoted in Grant, 1994: 156)

Moreover, unlike the Out of Crisis Project, the industrial policy developed by the European Commission was aimed at the supply side and sought to reshape the labour force to meet the needs of corporations in a globalizing European economy.

The IGCs

In October 1990, in anticipation of the IGCs on EMU and EPU which produced the Maastricht Treaty, the European Commission published its 'opinion' on political union. The document suggested that European Commission powers over the free movement of persons, infrastructure networks and social affairs should be strengthened and that policy areas such as the environment, R&D and taxation should be subjected to QMV so as to improve decision-making.

During the IGCs, launched in December 1990, the European Commission submitted its own draft treaties on EMU and EPU. In terms of EMU, the draft treaty recommended that, to ensure economic policy coordination, three new instruments and/or procedures should be established. Two of these, multi-annual economic policy guidelines and multilateral surveillance of economic policies, were subsequently adopted. The third proposal, however, was not accepted; the European Commission favoured the creation of a conditional 'financial support mechanism', with special EC grants and loans, to assist member states facing major economic difficulties and/or where economic convergence required additional EC action.

In terms of EPU, the draft treaty was much more ambitious than the earlier 'opinion' document that it built upon. Additional ideas in the draft treaty included a new legislative system whereby, instead of directives, the European Council and European Parliament would agree the general principles of 'laws' which the European Commission would then expand upon. The draft treaty also provided for the European Commission to replace member states in international organizations such as the IMF, for it to acquire tax-raising powers and for it to be granted the right to initiate foreign policy. Furthermore, the European Commission, together with several member states, opposed the Luxembourg treaty model (i.e. the 'temple with pillars') and favoured a unitary structure instead. Unfortunately for the European Commission, 'few governments took the draft seriously, which left Delors on the sidelines of the IGC' (Grant, 1994: 188).

The then Spanish minister for Europe complained that the principal concern of the European Commission during the IGCs 'seems to have been to give itself more power' and that while 'its role should be to search for common ground ... it has behaved like a thirteenth member instead' (quoted in Grant, 1994: 189). The relative weakness of the European Commission during these negotiations, and the rejection of many of its ideas, meant that the radical potential was lost. In short, progressive social forces were denied the opportunity to exploit a federal structure and EC tax-raising powers to construct a Euro-Keynesian regime.

The Delors II package

The signing of the Maastricht Treaty in December 1991, with its ambitious institutional and policy agenda, necessitated the renewal of the EU budget. The Delors II package, presented by the European Commission in February 1992 and agreed by the European Council in December, involved financial support for the new Cohesion Fund – in effect an 'efficiency-based, long-run strategy' to bring about 'catch-up growth' (Pelkmans, 2006: 5) – which totalled 11 billion ecu over five years. The package also included 3.5 billion ecu for external action (i.e. foreign aid and foreign policy) and 3.5 billion ecu to promote a favourable environment for competitiveness (i.e. industrial policy), plus an additional four billion ecu for the CAP. Although the EU budget increased from 1.20 to 1.37 per cent of EU GDP between 1992 and 1997, it still fell well short of the pre-federal integration scenario set out in the MacDougall Report.

The 'Growth, Competitiveness, Employment' White Paper

In an effort to tackle Europe's unemployment problem, the European Commission published its 'Growth, Competitiveness, Employment' White Paper in December 1993. The White Paper argued that there was 'no miracle cure'. Protectionism would be 'suicidal' for an open trading bloc such as the EU, a 'dash for growth' via government expenditure would result in inflation and external imbalance, reduced working hours and work sharing would lead to a loss of production, while a drastic cut in wages for the sake of competition would be politically untenable, socially unacceptable and self-defeating – as it would depress domestic demand which contributes to growth and employment.

The strategy favoured by the European Commission would be applied in two stages. During the first stage, the White Paper suggested that member states could recover from recession by reducing their budget deficits, restructuring their public spending in favour of long-term investment in infrastructure, tackling inflation, lowering their interest rates and moderating their costs – including wage demands. At the European level, the European Commission recommended a target of 15 million new jobs by 2000, the acceptance of globalization as unavoidable and a commitment to the judicious management of interdependence. During the second stage, the White Paper forecast that member states could return to a path of strong and healthy growth by forging a public–private partnership to establish information superhighways (i.e. broadband networks), supporting small and medium sized enterprises on account of their employment-creating potential, further developing the trans-European infrastructure networks and fostering greater inter-company co-operation, as part of the EU R&D policy, by focusing in particular on the biotechnology, eco-technology and information technology industries. The White Paper envisaged that expenditure on such projects would range from 150 billion to 550 billion ecu.

Acknowledging that national welfare regimes were under pressure, the White Paper called for the development of a 'new model of European society' underpinned by a 'less passive and more active solidarity' (European Commission, 1993: 15). Active solidarity was understood in four different ways. First, solidarity between those who had jobs and those who did not; the White Paper proposed a decentralized and negotiated 'European social pact' where 'new gains in productivity would essentially be applied to forward-looking investments and to the creation of jobs' (ibid.). The White Paper also sanctioned greater labour market flexibility inside corporations and across the economy as a whole, increased labour mobility, reduced unemployment benefits, cuts in income tax for low earners to ensure that 'work pays', less restrictive employment contracts, and a lower wage bill through reductions in social insurance contributions by employers and workers. Second, solidarity between the generations; the White Paper stressed the need to address the demographic problem (i.e. aging populations) by reforming national social security systems. Third, solidarity between the regions; the White Paper emphasized the continued importance of EU cohesion and structural policies. Fourth, solidarity in the fight against social exclusion; the White Paper highlighted the role of preventive and remedial action to assist the estimated 40 million people in Europe living below the poverty line.

To finance the programme set out in the White Paper, the European Commission recommended that the European Investment Fund (EIF) – which, in December 1992, the European Council had agreed in principle to create – should be allowed to raise the necessary monies on the international financial markets by issuing EU bonds. The added benefit of such a scheme would be that such borrowing, in effect EU debt, would not be subject to the borrowing limits imposed on member states (i.e. the MCC). When the EIF became operational in March 1994, however, its remit and size were limited. The EIF could only issue EU single project (i.e. specific) bonds rather than EU (i.e. macroeconomic) bonds, and a borrowing limit of eight billion ecu was imposed which was insufficient given the scale of the programme. Progressive social forces within the European Parliament campaigned for increased borrowing rights, passing favourable Resolutions in December 1994 and July 1995, and the idea was supported by the French PS and other European socialist parties. It was opposed, however, by the European Commission president, Jacques Santer, who was appointed in January 1995, and by several member states. Indeed, the then British prime minister, Major, and German chancellor, Helmut Kohl, voted against the principle of EU bonds at the European Council in June 1996. When the proposal was tabled again at the European Council one year later, Tony Blair, the then British prime minister, also objected, later revealing that he 'had been briefed to argue against any new European financial instruments' (Holland, 1997). The practical effect of these manoeuvres was that the European Commission was deprived of the financial mechanism it needed to deliver its job creation target and to implement its industrial policy proposals. Consequently, the Euro-Keynesian potential of Delors' White Paper was severely circumscribed.

From a progressive perspective, the Delors' presidency of the European Commission undoubtedly produced some tangible benefits. Delors oversaw a significant expansion of the EU budget and increased EU expenditure on cohesion and structural funds and industrial policy. Delors also supervised the introduction of the Social Charter. While these may have been welcomed, they hardly amounted to a fully-fledged European social space with new regulatory frameworks. Furthermore, progressives' hope that Delors would deliver a Euro-Keynesian regime was dashed. The EU budget remained relatively small and was thus unable to perform any significant counter-cyclical, redistribution or reflation functions. Economic intervention, by the EU and member states, was limited. There was little progress towards a fiscal union and no substantial EU borrowing instruments (i.e. EU bonds) were created. There was no development of an EU-wide public sector or an EU-level welfare state and EU social policy was not legally binding. Despite the Euro-Keynesian potential provided by numerous EU budget, policy and treaty revisions during Delors' presidency, the European Commission failed to deliver. Instead, by focusing upon competitiveness and supply-side reforms, the European Commission reinforced the neoliberal trajectory of the EU. This contradictory mix of orthodox and progressive action was recognized by Dahrendorf (1981: 79) when he concluded that 'Delors' prescriptions are an astonishing mixture of Keynes and Friedman – of demand- and supply-side economics, or as he himself puts it, a "judicious blend of different instruments"'.

The Economic and Social Cohesion report

A group of economists led by Holland, then an academic, were sponsored by the European Commission in 1991 to investigate how the EU objective of economic and social cohesion could be realized. *The European Imperative: Economic and Social Cohesion in the 1990s* was published in 1993 and, following the Out of Crisis Project, it set out the case for a revised ERP that would operate until 1997.

The *European Imperative* report (Holland, 1993) identified two main sets of problems for progressive social forces. The first set related to the structural transformation of the global economy, more specifically the emergence of TNCs and the associated concentration of economic and political power, which demanded that progressive social forces reconsider their national strategies. The report argued that reflation by individual EU member states would make it difficult for these countries to achieve the MCC and that the 'financial markets would be more likely under such conditions to destabilize the currencies of those countries' (ibid.: 46). Furthermore, the report claimed that the policy tool of devaluation was redundant:

> The efficacy of devaluation as an instrument of export promotion was eroded years ago. The reasons are fundamental to justification of the European project. The conventional case for devaluation lies on the assumption of international trade between different firms in different national economies…. The case is profoundly qualified when investment, production and pricing is undertaken in different markets by multinational companies.

Essentially multinational companies have no interest in following through devaluation of a national currency by charging lower prices on another market in which they are already producing and selling. To do so would be to compete against themselves. Likewise multinationals have no interest in undertaking net investment in the country of the devalued currency in such a way as to under-employ capacity in the other countries in which they already produce. To do so would be to invest against themselves.

(Ibid.: 33–4)

The solutions, the report suggested, were that progressive social forces should support the EU, and projects such as EMU, and should work within the framework of the EU treaties to achieve their objectives. Where the Out of Crisis Project was ambivalent about EU membership, by the early 1990s Holland and many other left-wing economists and politicians could no longer see any viable alternative. Indeed, the shift in thinking was evident as early as 1984 when Holland and several others penned articles calling for an Alternative European Strategy (Kinnock, 1984; Holland, 1985; Morrell, 1985, 1988; Coates, 1986).

The second set of problems concerned the unbalanced way in which EMU was proceeding. More specifically, the report held that the Maastricht Treaty was being interpreted in a way that rendered EMU deflationary:

The interim EMS regime has obliged national governments to exercise caution in fiscal and monetary decisions in order to keep market-determined exchange rates within the agreed bands. This regime has unavoidably subordinated other policy aims to the imperatives of price stability and balance of payments adjustment. For most member states the consequence of fiscal and monetary interactions during the second half of the 1980s has been high real interest rates and pressure on public finances.

(Holland, 1993: 32)

The report agreed with the Resolution passed by the European Parliament (1992) that 'the Maastricht Treaty fails to provide any economic policy authority to counterbalance the monetary authority of the European central bank' (Holland, 1993: 21). Critically, the terms of reference for the ECB, the report pointed out, were far wider than price stability. Article 105 of the Maastricht Treaty stipulated that

Without prejudice to the objectives of price stability, the European System of Central Banks shall support the general economic policies in the Community with a view to contributing to the achievement of the objectives of the Community as laid down in Article 2.

Article 2 specified that

The Community shall have as its task, by establishing a common market and an economic and monetary union and by implementing the common policies or activities referred to in Articles 3 and 3a, to promote throughout the Community a harmonious and balanced development of economic activities, sustainable and non-inflationary growth respecting the environment, a high degree of convergence of economic performance, a high level of employment and of social protection, the raising of the standard of living and quality of life, and economic and social cohesion and solidarity among member states.

The report asserted that

> These articles are well drafted. They not only cover monetary union but also set an agenda for economic and social cohesion. The problem is that many people simply do not see how this is compatible with the budgetary conditions for financial convergence [i.e. MCC]. They are concerned that monetary policy will determine the rest of macroeconomic policy and that Europe will be run by an unaccountable committee of governors of central banks.
>
> (Ibid.: 21)

The report presciently warned that

> In the absence of corrective action, there will inevitably be a growing imbalance in the relative positions of the poorer and richer regions in the Community. As these resource-scarce regions are not evenly distributed across the member states, there is a pressing need for a more effective mechanism for resource distribution between the member states.... Without a resource transfer of this kind, the income gap between the poor and the rich member states will inevitably widen and intra-Community relations become severely strained.
>
> (Ibid.: 35)

The solutions were to ensure that the ECB fulfilled all of its responsibilities, and not just price stability, and to devise a substantial resource transfer mechanism. In terms of the former, the report recommended reinforcing the power of the Economic Policy Committee, which had superseded the MTEPC, to act as a formal or de facto committee for cohesion. In terms of the latter, the report favoured an increase in the EU budget and the use of new financial instruments to deliver economic and social cohesion. The 'Community option', as the report described it, would see the EU, on its own budget and that of member states, undertake an ERP. It was thus quite different to the intergovernmental Out of Crisis Project.

The report specifically advocated five key measures. First, the EU budget should be expanded and two scenarios were identified. In the lower scenario, the budget would build upon the Delors II package and would increase by 0.19 per cent of EU GDP by 1997 and 0.44 per cent by 2002. In the more preferable higher scenario, the budget would increase by just over 1 per cent by 2002, in a phased manner, with a 0.44 per cent increase by 1997 and an additional 0.60 per cent by 2002. Second, a 'European investment fund should be created, equivalent at Community level to a common national debt instrument' (ibid.: 46), and its funding should rise by 0.5 per cent of EU GDP for four years to a maximum level of 2 per cent. Member states and regions should be able to draw upon the fund for cohesion expenditure and it should be administered by the European Commission rather than the ECB. The costs of servicing such debt, which should be financed as part of the EU budget, would be relatively low and, by 1997, would amount to perhaps only 0.02 per cent of EU GDP. The size of the fund, on the other hand, might be as much as 140 billion ecu by 1997. Third, the power of the EIB should be extended to allow it to borrow from the private sector and to enable it to provide credit to Eastern European countries and the South. Fourth, member states should receive a rebate on their contributions to the EU budget. This would enable member states to sustain their social expenditure, which was vital for cohesion, and to reduce their budget deficits and thereby achieve the MCC and limit speculative attacks against their currencies. Fifth, the working hours of those employed by bigger corporations and those within the public sector should be reduced, via the social dialogue procedure, by 2.5 per cent by 1997 and by 3.5 per cent by 2002. These 'transitional arrangements' would stimulate the European economy and should facilitate a 'phased reduction of national interest rates' and a 'reduction of national value added tax rates' (ibid.: 48). The combined effect under the lower scenario would be 4.5 million new jobs by 2002. Under the higher scenario, by contrast, over 11 million new jobs would be created.

Some of the report's suggestions were adopted by the EU. The European Council agreed to revise the remit of the EIB, later including its statute in the Maastricht Treaty, and it also sanctioned the creation of the EIF. While Holland (2004: 182) maintained that 'the potential to avoid deflationary pressures by a social investment-led recovery programme financed by the bank is vast', the funding made available by the EIB and the EIF was only a fraction of what the report envisaged. Most of the report's suggestions, however, were rejected. A political counterbalance to the ECB was deemed unacceptable. There was no expansion of the EU budget along the lines set out in the report. No EU bonds were issued. With the exception of Britain, no member state received rebates and there was no EU-wide reduction in working hours. In short, no substantial resource transfer mechanism was established. Unemployment across Europe remained high and the growing imbalance that the report warned about worsened over time. Nevertheless, the report's agenda was subsequently promoted by members and allies of the Socialist Group in the European Parliament (Coates and Barratt Brown, 1993; Cripps and Ward, 1993; Coates and Holland, 1995; Coates *et al.*, 1998), by the Our Europe think tank, and by Jospin and Lafontaine.

The *Our Europe* think tank

Having published a book in 1992, entitled *Our Europe*, and following the end of his tenure at the European Commission, Delors established the Our Europe or *Notre*

Europe think tank in October 1996. Funded mainly by the European Commission, and enjoying the patronage of several former and serving European commissioners, the think tank had three main objectives. First, it sought to create a European Political Community or 'federation of nation-states' which was committed to the Community method of European integration. Second, it strove to maintain Europe's social market economy by promoting economic and social cohesion, the completion of the internal market and macroeconomic coordination. Third, it supported a global role for the EU underpinned by a 'soft power' approach (Our Europe, 1996).

The work of the think tank focused upon four key themes – 'visions of Europe', 'European democracy in action', 'co-operation, competition, solidarity' and 'Europe and world governance' – and it published hundreds of policy briefs, policy statements, seminar reports and studies on these areas. The first study, entitled 'Lack of Economic Growth and Unemployment: The Costs of Non-co-operation', was published on the eve of the European Council in June 1997 – which agreed the SGP – and it argued that the high unemployment across Europe was due to member states' abandonment of expansionary policies because of the MCC, rather than labour market rigidities, and that the EU should focus upon demand as well as the supply side (Muet, 1997). In terms of the social dimension, the think tank broadly endorsed the EU approach to economic and social cohesion (Arnaud, 1998; Jouen, 2001), the EES (Palpant, 2006), the reform of the ESM (Arnaud, 1997; Jouen and Palpant, 2005a, 2005b; Bomba, 2006; Rubio, 2009) and the OMC (Collignon *et al.*, 2005). However, while the first study emphasized the importance of demand management, and while the think tank's EU budget proposals (Le Cacheux, 2005, 2007) and institutional and treaty reform suggestions (Arnaud, 2001; Sidjanski, 2001) were radical, there were no calls for the creation of a Euro-Keynesian regime.

Lionel Jospin, Oskar Lafontaine and Euro-Keynesianism

Jospin was the prime minister of the Socialist government elected in France in June 1997. Following the neo-liberal U-turn in March 1983, which signalled the end of the Mitterrand experiment, the PS pursued a policy of 'competitive disinflation' (Fitoussi *et al.*, 1993; Lordon, 1998) – composed of three key elements: the maintenance of the *franc fort* policy within the ERM, the exercise of wage restraint through de-indexation and the reduction of the budget deficit. For capital, the policy was successful in a short-term sense: competitiveness and profitability were restored and inflation fell significantly. For labour, however, the economic and social consequences were predictable. Income and wealth inequality widened and unemployment rose from 7.4 per cent in May 1981 to 10.3 per cent in December 1992 and 12.6 per cent in June 1997 (Blanchard and Muet, 1993; Halimi *et al.*, 1994; Fitoussi *et al.*, 1993; Lordon, 1998; Clift, 2005). Indeed, Blanchard and Muet (1993) argued that such an approach was doomed as even a 30 per cent competitiveness gain – impossible within the ERM and unacceptable to France's trading partners – would only have reduced the unemployment rate by 3 per cent.

The poor performance prompted a rethink of PS strategy and the development of an alternative, neo-Keynesian approach (Clift, 2005). The 1991 *Projet Social-iste* document stated that 'socialism ... is developing at the heart of a globalized capitalism which today restricts our vision but not our will to act' (PS, 1992: 18), while the 1993 PS Conference observed of the 1983 U-turn that

> this choice did not instigate an authentic economic policy debate concerning the use of the available room to manoeuvre ... as a result we were too ready to believe that the economy was not a matter of politics but rather of techni-cal management.
>
> (PS, 1992: 18)

The PS thus acknowledged the structural constraints of globalization but refused to accept that social democratic parties such as the PS had no agency. Instead, the PS endorsed 'activism at both the national and supranational levels – both European and global' (Clift, 2005: 150).

At the *national* level, the neo-Keynesian mode of thinking was reflected in the policies pursued by the PS in government. Although reflation was not coun-tenanced, the Socialist government boosted the incomes and purchasing power of low and non-earners via redistribution. More specifically, universal healthcare insurance was introduced, the eligibility criteria of the minimum income guaran-tee was expanded, the minimum wage was increased, and social security benefit reforms and tax cuts were targeted at low income groups. The Socialist govern-ment established state-sponsored employment-creation schemes which particu-larly targeted the young, introduced the 35-hour week, reduced non-wage employer costs and subsidized low earners. The Socialist government also sought to rebalance the relationship between the market and the state by vigor-ously pursuing a privatization programme, leading some commentators to point to the '"paradox" of the "leftist" Jospin government privatizing more than its right-wing predecessors' (ibid.: 176).

At the *European* level, the neo-Keynesian mode of thinking was manifest in the Euro-Keynesian strategy of the PS:

> PS macroeconomic policy, while eschewing myopic concentration on infla-tion rates, involves commitments to deficit reduction, price stability and sound public finances. These commitments reflect changed economic reali-ties in the global economy but, in seeking to reconcile them with other social democratic objectives, including full employment and redistribution, the PS also justify them in terms of the 'long game' the Socialists are playing in seeking to create a Euro-Keynesian economic space as a context for national policy activism. The Socialists saw accepting neo-liberalism in 1983 as a necessary means to achieve European integration and thence, eventually, to recover Keynesian economic sovereignty This 'long game' involves more ambitious, Keynesian-inspired aspirations to cement the part-nership of '*l'Europe sociale*' to 'monetarist' EMU through coordinated

fiscal activism at the European level to deliver full employment and redistribute wealth.

(Ibid.: 155)

The PS implicitly accepted the neo-liberal EMU as the price to be paid for the opportunity to construct a Euro-Keynesian regime.

At the *global* level, the neo-Keynesian mode of thinking influenced the ideas put forward by Jospin in his failed 1995 presidential campaign. Jospin specifically called for the re-regulation of the international financial system with stricter supervision of hedge funds and offshore tax havens and the introduction of a Tobin tax[1] on global financial transactions. Together with the reform of the IMF and World Bank, a 'new BWS' would help social democratic governments bring globalization under control (Jospin, 2002).

Returning to the European dimension, the PS recognized the Euro-Keynesian potential of Delors' 1993 White Paper and sought to 'introduce jobs and growth-oriented elements into the EMU architecture' (Clift, 2005: 154). The 1996 PS Conference pledged to create a Social Europe on the foundations of EMU, while the PS manifesto for the 1997 national assembly elections made clear that French support for the single currency was conditional. First, the single currency should encompass as many countries as possible, including Italy and Spain. Second, Europe should be political and social and should encourage job creation and social cohesion rather than austerity. Third, a European economic government should be established to counterbalance the ECB. Fourth, the single currency should not be overvalued vis-à-vis the US dollar and the Japanese yen.

At the European Council in June 1997, Jospin proposed a solidarity and growth pact as an alternative to the German stability pact tabled at the European Council in December 1996. Jospin's proposals were supported by Delors who, echoing the first Our Europe report (Muet, 1997), urged European leaders to abandon their fixation with budgetary and monetary policy and to set minimum income levels for each country and to coordinate taxation levels as part of a growth pact. 'What about a policy on education, incomes, jobs and research? The dogma that has dominated governments has meant several points of output lost' (quoted in Steele, 1997). Indeed, Delors described the MCC targets as 'blackmail' when not 'combined with job-creation goals' and he announced that 'if I had had responsibility at Dublin [the December 1996 European Council] I would not have signed the stability pact' (ibid.). Jospin's proposals included the establishment of an EU growth fund to underpin Europe's technology sectors, the expansion of the EIF to fund job creation programmes and EU-wide regulation to protect workers. Furthermore, Jospin and the then finance minister, Dominique Strauss-Kahn, 'threatened not to endorse the stability pact' (Ladrech, 1998: 7) unless it met French demands. As a result of opposition from Blair and Kohl, however, plus pressure from the then French president, Jacques Chirac, Jospin and Strauss-Kahn backed down and signed the renamed but still neo-liberal SGP. Resolutions were added which 'urged' member states to pursue policies in favour of employment and growth but such interventionism was not legally binding.

At the jobs summit organized by the European Council in November 1997, Jospin once again tabled an alternative package of measures. Jospin called for a binding commitment to create 12 million new jobs in Europe in five years, for the EU-level regulation of employment policy, for mandatory European Commission approval of industrial closures and redundancies, and for additional spending commitments at the EU level. Although there was some progress in terms of employment policy coordination, the resulting EES and EEP were concerned with international competitiveness and supply-side reforms rather than the Jospin agenda. As Clift (2005: 183) concluded, 'Jospin's more ambitious and maximalist plans foundered in the face of an unenthusiastic response from European partners'.

The election of the *Sozialdemokratische Partei Deutschland* (SPD)–Green Party alliance in Germany in October 1998, with Gerhard Schröder as chancellor and Lafontaine as finance minister, boosted the Delors–Jospin–Strauss-Kahn axis and the prospects for Euro-Keynesianism (Dyson, 1999). Indeed, at this point 13 out of the 15 member states were governed by social democratic parties, including the critical Franco-German motor of European integration, with only Britain under Blair and Spain governed by conservatives.

Lafontaine and Strauss-Kahn drafted a joint policy paper in October 1998, entitled, 'A Policy of Growth in Europe to Fight against Unemployment', which was distributed at the informal meeting of heads of state and government that month. The policy paper called for a target of at least 3 per cent annual average growth for the EU as a whole, for the ECB to pursue low interest rates, for an increase in public infrastructure investment, for the merging of ECOFIN and the European council of employment ministers to create an embryonic European economic government, and for a new global system of managed exchange rates – setting targets for the value of the dollar, euro and yen. Lafontaine's challenge to the international financial nexus, including the ECB, was forthright:

> The international financial markets don't need deregulation, but more regulation. Politics and the international order have to regain their rightful place after the declaration of war from the neo-liberals. [At the EU and international levels he urged] exchange rate stabilization, interest rate policy geared to stability and growth, budgets geared to jobs, fair taxation policies, common technology policies, an international social charter, policies against the global threat to the environment and sustained strengthening of demand.
>
> (Quoted in Traynor and Walker, 1998)

Sensing a 'window of opportunity', Jospin tabled his ideas for EU-level action on employment and growth. These included the coordination of economic policies, the setting of minimum social standards across the EU and the tackling of unfair tax competition.

To fund such a programme, the then European commissioner for the internal market, Mario Monti, argued that long-term infrastructure investment projects, which benefit the EU as a whole, should not count against national budget accounts and national debt. Instead, public investment should be funded by public debt monitored at the EU level. Jospin believed that the EU should be allowed to raise 'development loans' on the private capital markets to fund high-technology and public infrastructure projects – including those associated with enlargement to Eastern Europe. The then Italian prime minister, Romano Prodi, suggested that the residual non-euro foreign exchange reserves held by member states' central banks after their contributions to the ECB reserve – which were no longer needed to finance trade – could be sold to provide the collateral for EU bonds issued by the EIF. The idea was quashed, however, on the basis that the sale of dollars on such a scale would depress its value and make euro-denominated exports more expensive. Instead, Jospin recommended that the estimated $100 billion of reserves could be used to underpin euro-denominated EU bonds.

Lafontaine, Strauss-Kahn and other left-wing finance ministers challenged the orthodoxy of the ECB in November 1998 by demanding that it should be democratically accountable and transparent in its decision-making. The Euro-Keynesian challenge was effectively thwarted at the European Council in December, however, by Blair and Chirac. Although the European Council called for an EEP, greater regulation of the international financial system and an end to harmful tax competition, and although it increased the borrowing limit of the EIB to 1 billion ecu, the more radical measures proposed by Jospin and Lafontaine were vetoed. On the eve of the launch of the euro, and anxious not to 'spook' the international financial markets, Europe's social democrats, presented with an opportunity to transform the nature and trajectory of the European project, opted for the status quo instead.

Despite such setbacks, the campaign for Euro-Keynesian continued into 1999. Launching his country's presidency of the EU in January, Schröder reiterated Jospin's plea for EU-level action on employment and growth. At the European Council in December 1998, member states had pledged to

> jointly monitor nominal and real wage developments with reference to the broad economic policy guidelines and member states' structural policies in labour, product and services markets, as well as of cost and price trends, particularly insofar as they affect the chances of achieving non-inflationary growth and job creation.
>
> (Cited in Walker, 1999)

Schröder indicated that the German presidency would consider this a 'charter to pursue a prices and incomes strategy for Europe that would deepen economic convergence through more policy coordination' (ibid.).

Lafontaine, meanwhile, announced his support for a Tobin tax and continued to berate the ECB for not lowering interest rates and for not intervening on the foreign exchange markets to reduce the value of the euro – and thus boost Europe's exports. Lafontaine (2000: 135, 138) was well aware of predictably hostile response of the international financial nexus:

In a whole series of speeches and discussions I constantly emphasized that the key to bringing worldwide financial speculation under control lay in the regulation of short-term movements of capital.... The criticism to which my ideas were subjected lacked all sense of balance and objectivity.... The greatest wrath that the disciples of neo-liberalism showered on my head, however, was when I challenged a taboo by daring to recommend that the European national banks should reduce their interest rates.

Following the 'angry revolt' (*Financial Times*, 1999) by 'the European Central Bank and German businesses threatening to relocate abroad' (Atkins, 1999), the pressure proved too much and Lafontaine was forced to resign in March 1999. The departure of 'the most dangerous man in Europe', as the *Sun* dubbed him, elicited 'euphoria' in 'jubilant' financial markets, editorial offices and newsrooms (Andrews, 1999a, 1999b). Lafontaine felt vindicated by subsequent events however: in June 1999 the ECB confirmed that it had intervened in the foreign exchange markets to stabilize exchange rates, while in December it reduced interest rates to 3 per cent.

Without the countervailing influence of Lafontaine, Schröder shifted to the right. Schröder published 'Europe: The Third Way' with Blair in June 1999 which set out a 'new supply-side agenda for the left' (Blair and Schröder, 1999: 5). Lafontaine (2000: 122) later complained that 'it had been prepared by Bodo Hombach [a fellow cabinet minister] at Schröder's behest behind my back'. The SPD–Green coalition government instituted the 'biggest tax reforms in fifty years' (Gillingham, 2003: 394) in December 1999: the top tax rate was reduced from 51 to 42 per cent, the corporate tax rate was reduced from 40 to 25 per cent and the capital gains tax on acquiring stakes in other companies was abolished. The government continued the privatization programme of previous administrations (Schröter, 2004) and, in March 2003, the government launched its 'Agenda 2010' reforms of the labour market and welfare state. Inequality, poverty and unemployment subsequently increased significantly (Bosch, 2009; OECD, 2011).

Conclusion

During the CWO and NWO, counter-hegemonic social forces devised a number of European-level alternatives to the liberal/neo-liberal EEC/EC/EU. These included plans to construct a Europe-wide social model, underpinned by Euro-Keynesianism, and the intergovernmental and radical Out of Crisis Project which, if successfully implemented, would have produced an enhanced social model on a European basis. Some elements of these alternatives were adopted – the EC/EU budget was expanded, new institutions such as the EIF were created and greater policy coordination was pursued – but none of these alternatives was fully enacted. In short, pro-European progressive social forces lacked the necessary power resources to realize their ideas.

Those proposals which sought to transform the liberal/neo-liberal EEC/EC/ EU into a Euro-Keynesian regime – the European Commission, Federal Trust,

Cairncross-led panel of economists and MacDougall committee in the 1970s, the Centre for European Policy Studies in the 1980s, and the Holland-led group of economists, plus Jospin and Lafontaine, in the 1990s – failed to generate enough support to dislodge the dominant market liberal model and the bias towards negative integration. To succeed, pro-European progressive social forces needed to restructure the institutional and policy bases of the European project and this required fundamental treaty revision. This, in turn, required the unanimous support of member states.

If national radical programmes were likely to confront two major barriers – domestic antipathy and attempted sabotage by the international financial nexus – then pro-European progressive social forces were likely to face four major obstacles. First, they would need to build a coalition of support for Euro-Keynesianism within each member state in the face of a concerted campaign of opposition by the forces of capital and their allies in the media and political elite. Second, they would need to coordinate the simultaneous election of such coalitions – a difficult prospect given the different electoral cycles in each country. Third, they would need to achieve unanimity, and thus avoid national vetoes, if they were to successfully revise the EEC/EC/EU treaties. Fourth, in common with national radical programmes, they would have to overcome the wrecking efforts of the international financial nexus. As history has demonstrated, the chances of clearing these four hurdles successfully were slight. Indeed, even when the situation seemed propitious, such as in the late 1990s when most member states were governed by social democratic parties, the Euro-Keynesian ambitions of the majority were thwarted by the vetoes of a minority alliance composed of Britain, Germany and Spain.

Once enmeshed in the European project, and constrained by its market liberal orientation and negative integration bias, individual countries would find it difficult to resist the pressures to conform. Furthermore, individual countries or groups of countries would find it nigh impossible to reform the European project from within because of this quadruple lock. Indeed, thwarting West European socialism in this manner was one of the main reasons why capitalist forces in Europe and the United States supported the European project during the CWO and NWO and why they continue to do so. In short, any attempt to construct a Euro-Keynesian regime would have to overcome these four problems.

The Out of Crisis Project, which sought to build a new ESM *outside* of the structures of the EC, would have encountered a similar set of problems. First, it would need to build a coalition of support within several countries – particularly those with larger economies which could 'drive' the reflation process. Second, it would need to coordinate the simultaneous election of such coalitions. Third, given that most West European countries were members of the EC in the early 1980s, it would need to overcome the probable resistance of the EC itself to such a radical programme. Such opposition would have resulted in expulsion and/or a decision to withdraw from the EC, with all the attendant economic and political dislocation. Fourth, the combined reflationary programmes of individual countries would have been targeted by the international financial nexus. In short, an intergovernmental European strategy would not have escaped the quadruple lock.

Many on the left hoped that the European Commission under Delors in the late 1980s and early 1990s would provide a useful ally in the struggle to transform the nature and trajectory of the European project. Although there were some significant social advances, the Delors presidency was a failure in terms of constructing a Euro-Keynesian regime. Furthermore, the Euro-Keynesian rhetoric at that particular historical juncture – more specifically the ESM concept and the Social Europe discourse – helped to secure the support of many progressive social forces was thus critical for the continuation of the neo-liberal project in Europe.

The brief flirtation with Keynesianism by the EU and its member states in 2008–2009 aside, the current state of play is such that the chances of progressive social forces successfully constructing an enhanced social model on a European basis using the present-day EU as a vehicle are poor. The EU budget is too small, there is no European polity to support such a project and the EU and its member states – more specifically Europe's political elites – have been captured by neo-liberal forces.

Part III
The neoliberalization of EU policy

8 Operation of economic policy

Introduction

This chapter explores how a crucial idea introduced by Keynes (1936) into the corpus of economic thought is that the level of output and employment under market capitalism depends upon interaction between total spending and the economy's capacity to produce. Decisions to produce are made primarily by private profit-making firms; production, the source of employment, takes place only if companies anticipate a market in which goods and services can be sold at a profit. If demand is insufficient, productive capacity will stand idle and people will be without jobs. There is no automatic mechanism, which guarantees that output and spending decisions always coincide. Imbalances between aggregate demand and aggregate supply require active government policy to change either its own or private expenditure through budgetary or monetary instruments. The neoclassical assumption of an automatic tendency towards market clearing is replaced by the necessity for active government intervention in the economy to secure simultaneous internal and external balance in the economy.

Such a Keynesian framework is explicitly receded by the monetarist ideology of the TEU. A clear example of its approach is its reliance upon monetary tests of convergence rather than examining real variables of output growth and rates of unemployment. Its convergence criteria include restrictions upon discretionary fiscal policy through the implementation of maximum permitted budget deficits backed by the possibility of levying fines on non-compliant economies. The transfer of monetary and exchange rate policy to an independent ECB, whose sole legally defined objective is to secure stable prices through the use of a single economic policy instrument, a common interest rate, is at complete variance to a Keynesian approach.

However, a key aspect of EU integration that has been embraced, albeit it naively, by large sections of the left is EMU, which is one of the most far-reaching economic developments of the current generation. Advocates claim that it would enhance competition, through price transparency and completing the SIM, thereby reducing prices for consumers and ensuring a superior allocation of resources as corporate restructuring facilitated a renewed global competitiveness. The economic infrastructure, moreover, has been established to focus upon the delivery of low inflation, and it is claimed that this will result in a superior economic performance.

In contrast, critics of participation in EMU point to the combination of substantial initial transfer costs and the danger of being trapped within a permanently fixed exchange rate system, magnified by the potentially deflationary impact of the monetarist-inspired institutional and policy framework within which the single currency has been introduced. Keynesian measures are further constrained by the SGP, which places firm limits upon budget deficits and thereby restricts the ability of counter-cyclical economic strategy. This is quite intentional, based upon monetarist assertions that Keynesian economics no longer works, if indeed it ever did. However, democratic socialists argue that the loss of national economic autonomy, combined with the multiple restrictions that EMU participation places upon the pursuit of macroeconomic policy, reduces the scope for achieving traditional democratic-socialist/social democratic objectives.

The progressive democratic-socialist case rests, therefore, largely upon Keynesian rather than monetarist/neo-classical assumptions, so that the market economy is perceived as experiencing significant cases of market failure and of cumulative causation. Consequently government intervention has the potential, if properly directed and accurately timed, of improving economic performance. This therefore rejects the new classical assumption of time inconsistency, which implies that all government intervention worsens those circumstances it is intended to improve, together with the monetarist belief in a long-term equilibrium rate of unemployment determined solely by labour market factors. Moreover, it rejects the viewpoint that globalization and the international free flow of capital has rendered national economic policy instruments impotent, so that it is difficult (if not impossible) to maintain a distinctive monetary policy and pursue exchange rate management. If this were true, tying economic policy within the monetarist EMU framework would make little difference, since government autonomy would have already been effectively eroded by the external economic environment.

This chapter highlights the incompatibility between the monetarist model, upon which EMU is constructed and the possibility of creating an AES grounded in Post-Keynesian tradition. Despite the inability of theorists to develop a universal Post-Keynesian theoretical model, due in large part to the complexity and dynamic nature of modern economies, it is nevertheless possible to identify a number of important themes that denote the essence of Post-Keynesian/traditional democratic-socialist thought.

Embracing the EU

The European left has been increasingly identified as one of the most fervent supporters of the 'European project'. Young (1998: 515) claims that European integration represents 'the given reality', whilst Favretto (2003: 136) states that New Labour views closer European integration as 'the only framework within which the European left can have a future'. Indeed, using rather apocalyptic language, Sassoon (1999: 35–6) claims that the potential failure of the European integration project would gravely undermine a sizeable proportion of contemporary social democratic strategy and, indeed

> would foreshadow the dissolution of the European left in any recognisable shape. It is unlikely, after all, that the left could reconstruct itself in any viable form out of the inevitable economic and political dislocation which would occur. With Europe sinking, once again, in regional rivalries, squabbling nationalisms, and narrow politicking, there would be no serious obstacle left to the world-wide hegemony of unfettered market forces.

This is in sharp contrast to the former preference for a national focus for social democratic organization and policy programmes. Indeed, for the British Labour movement, up until the late 1980s, the EU was distrusted due to a perceived bias in favour of 'big business' and against the interests of workers and the wider citizenry, together with a potential incompatibility with the 'Keynes plus' national macroeconomic policy strategy embodied within the AES (Hill, 2001; Daniels, 2003).

The shift towards the embracing of European integration, by a majority of the European left occurred for a number of inter-related reasons. In terms of electoral strategy, it was useful for the architects of the New Labour project to contrast a positive approach to the EU with the former strategy based upon the AES, which did not ultimately succeed in returning a Labour government (Whyman, 2006). Furthermore, one of the consequences of this electoral failure concerned the increased marginalization of the British trade union movement, as a combination of unfavourable Conservative industrial relations legislation, membership loss resulting in large part from the monetarist disaster masquerading as economic policy and being frozen out of political influence by a hostile government. It is not, therefore, surprising that the trade unions would embrace the vision of a Delorsian 'Social Europe', which embraced labour rights as core elements, and where trade unions would legitimize their role through social partnership at regional level (TUC, 1992; Baker *et al.*, 1999, 2002b).

The shift towards a more pro-European stance was not, however, simply a means of evading Thatcherism, an electoral tactic and nor a simplistic response that 'the enemy of your enemy is your friend', although this was undoubtedly one motivation. There were, additionally, more substantive factors involved in the recasting of the fundamental approach adopted by the majority of the European left at this time.

One of the most notable arguments proffered to explain social democratic-left support for European integration relates to the oft repeated claim that the globalization of the world economy has created a new environment within which progressive–social democratic actors need to adapt traditional programmes to remain relevant and arrest a perceived decline in the efficiency of their preferred policy instruments (Daniels, 2003; Whyman, 2003). A vision of globalization has been popularized where stateless corporations operate within a 'borderless world', relocating the location of production facilities with relative ease on the basis of calculations that optimize profits and productivity (Ohmae, 1990; Reich, 1992). Moreover, disconnected capital has experienced an exponential increase in importance, absolutely dwarfing the value of world trade (Eatwell, 2000; Watson, 2002). Accordingly, theorists have claimed that the very concept of a national economy is becoming meaningless, whilst globalization has been implicated in a 'decline' or 'crisis' of a 'hollowed out' nation-state (Ohmae, 1990, 1995; Strange, 1996, 2000). The implications arising from this perspective for progressive–social democratic strategy is catastrophic, since there remains no room for manoeuvre for discretionary Keynesian policy, and with governments having to revise policy programmes to conform to the dictates of international financial markets (Gray, 1998; Veseth, 1998; Perraton *et al.*, 2000; Baker *et al.*, 2002a). Indeed, chancellor of the exchequer, Gordon Brown argued that, in an economy characterized by 'deregulated, liberalized financial markets ... the Keynesian fine tuning of the past which worked in relatively sheltered, closed national economies and which tried to exploit a supposed long-term trade-off between inflation and unemployment, will simply not work' (Brown, 1998). Thus, 'luxuries' such as full employment, redistribution and the development of a universalistic welfare state may be no longer be afforded due to greater economic constraints (Hay, 1999).

The view amongst the left that European integration could provide a positive response to globalization is, however, problematic. For some, regionalization can represent a 'macro-nationalist', 'neo-protectionist' reaction against the dominance of global market forces (Scholte, 2000). Thus, the EU offers the possibility of resisting the worst ravages of the free operation of market forces through the adoption of a form of Euro-Keynesianism and thereby pursuit of full employment, development of European welfare states, the creation of an advanced common system of social protection and an inclusive form of industrial relations (Marquand, 1999; Baker *et al.*, 2002b). However, the political conditions have remained insufficient for this approach to be implemented at European level (Fouskas, 1998; Callaghan, 2000).

For others, however, the EU is viewed not as 'Fortress Europe', intended to *protect* a distinctive form of European capitalism from the full impact of market forces, but rather as a region where the power of the state should be used to adapt institutions and individual behaviour in ways that maximize their strength *within* the market (Giddens, 2001). Thus, regional integration can be viewed as a consequence of globalization and may represent an intermediate step upon the road towards full globalization (Tober, 1993; Hettne, 1994). Hence, the appropriate response should be to adapt to these changes rather than seek to minimize their impact, through deregulation, labour market flexibilization and the marketization of the public sector.

This perception of globalization is, however, a gross exaggeration. Specifically, nation-states retain considerable autonomy in national economic policy and hence choices available to the European left are nowhere near as limited as is often suggested (Garrett, 1995; Hirst and Thompson, 1996). Nevertheless, as so often in political debate, it is a fatalistic reaction to the *perception* of the impact arising from globalization, rather than its *reality*, that has shaped the left's response to changes in the external economic environment (Glyn, 1995; Hay, 1998; Whyman, 2006).

A second significant attraction for the left, relating to the evolution of the EU, concerns the development of what is often described as the ESM (Strange, 1997). Essentially, this refers to an idealized form of the post-war German *social market*, which combined a successful, competitive market economy with generous welfare provision and labour protection. Its central features include the encouragement of social institutions to mediate between state and market, whilst 'social partnership' is intended to facilitate 'voice' rather than 'exit', thereby facilitating productive investment (in physical and human capital), innovation and co-operation in adaptation to change (Glasman, 1997; Coates, 1999). A comprehensive system of welfare provision, combining quality public services with social transfers providing a high replacement ratio, a partial socialization of risk and decommodification of employees, should enable all citizens to participate fully within society.

It is not surprising that this Delorsian vision should prove attractive to the left after two decades of financial crises in the public sector and deregulation in the labour market. Nevertheless, it is the *vision* that proves attractive and not the *realization* of democratic-socialist aspirations. For example, the current form of social dimension being constructed across the EU, whilst it has had an impact in less regulated EU member states (such as the United Kingdom), remains a minimalist version of a fully-fledged system of social protection of the kind operated idealized in discussion of the ESM (Whyman, 2001). Indeed, Streeck (1992: 218–19) considers the 'retarded advancement of European-level political rights' and the 'almost complete absence of a European system of industrial citizenship' as indicating that there is little reason to anticipate these initiatives will prove particularly successful.

Moreover, underpinning these arguments is the assumption that a distinct, indefinable ESM exists. However, welfare states differ significantly from each other such that they can be classified into separate 'clusters' based on the concept of decommodification (Esping-Anderson, 1990). On this basis, four different kinds of welfare state have been identified within the EU; the social democratic (occurring in Scandinavia – 'the northern model'), the conservative-corporatist (located in France, Germany and the Benelux countries – 'the central model'), the Mediterranean (found in Greece, possibly Italy, Portugal and Spain – 'the southern model') and the uniquely hybrid UK system ('the offshore island model'). However, the ESM model, to which centre left EU advocates aspire, is the conservative-corporatist variant, implemented by the six original signatories to the Treaty of Rome. These countries are now a minority within the EU, but their long-standing and founder status gives them an influence far greater than their numbers would suggest (Burkitt, 2006).

A further reason for questioning the enthusiasm for European integration being predicated upon the creation of a 'Social Europe', concerns the existence of considerable pressure within the EU for a series of reforms intended to create a model more attuned to the neo-liberal precepts of the EU's economic framework (Bulmer, 2000; Whyman, 2001). It is within this context that Tony Blair has argued that 'we need to curb the European Social Model, not play around with it', suggesting that New Labour's approach can inform 'the foundation of a reformed European Social Model of which Britain can not only be part, but take a lead in helping to create', based upon the promotion of an enterprise agenda and improving competitiveness through increased flexibility and employability in labour markets, alongside a renewed commitment to equality of opportunity (Blair, 1998a, 1998b; Clift, 2001; Favretto, 2003). Likewise, the then prime minister-in-waiting, Gordon Brown, rejected the 'old European model, which stifled job creation with over-regulation and inflexibility' (cited in Callaghan, 2000: xi). Moreover, this approach has been reflected in the recent shift in approach by the EU Commission, as social policy is increasingly viewed as a means of promoting adaptability and flexibility across the European economy (Vaughan-Whitehead, 2003). Thus, the future direction of the EU remains a subject for political struggle and the attraction of a regional means of pursuing traditional social democratic objectives should be measured according to whether it has a superior probability to advance a progressive programme, as opposed to a national (or international) alternative.

Economic policy under EMU

Over the past decade the left has increasingly embraced European integration as a bulwark against globalization, but the belief that the EU provides the potential for realizing a progressive social and economic policy is problematic. As we have highlighted in previous chapters, much faith has been placed in the creation of a 'Social Europe' through the ESM, but this is patchy in both coverage and generosity. Moreover, the neo-liberal framework associated with EMU requires the separate formulation of monetary policy by the independent ECB from nationally determined fiscal policy, itself constrained by the SGP, leading to a lack of policy coordination prejudicial to the construction of a progressive economic framework. Hence, this approach is the antithesis to traditional democratic-socialist objectives. The recent neo-liberal drift in strategy espoused by the European Commission implies that, either the left has to redouble its efforts in a struggle within the EU to realize a fundamental reform of its institutions and policy framework, or else consider other, more nationally orientated alternatives. Such alternatives would embrace a competitive exchange rate, higher investment, a social contract to restrain inflationary pressures via planned redistribution, the reintroduction of exchange controls through a transactions tax on dealings unrelated to trade and the pursuit of an active industrial policy to increase the long-run competitiveness of domestic industry.

However, the conduct of economic policy within EMU is considerably different from that outside. Monetary policy (i.e. interest rates) is now set by the ECB, whilst national governments possess fiscal and supply-side policies. An additional problem for the eurozone countries is that at the present time there is no large federal fiscal system in place whereby a central government sets taxes and expenditure rules that apply in its constituent states or countries. A standard feature of monetary unions is their fiscal federal structures. When a state/country has a slump in growth, it pays less tax to the central government and gets more social security money without any decisions having to be taken. Hence, automatic stabilizers are at work courtesy of federal tax rates and federal rates of social security payments. Hence, fiscal policy is confined to backward-looking automatic stabilizers such that the only channel for a forward-looking policy is through interest rates. Thus, the fiscal framework in EMU increases the burden on monetary policy to react to shocks even before they have fed fully through into output and inflation.

Consequently, the conduct of economic policy within EMU is considerably different from that previously experienced by EU member states. Monetary policy (interest rates) is now set by the independent ECB, whilst national governments possess fiscal and supply-side policies. Hence, from an individual country's viewpoint, interest rates are now 'fixed' and will only move if the ECB decides that economic conditions are changing for the eurozone as a whole and not if an individual country, or group of countries, suffers an economic shock (McKinnon, 2003; von Hagen, 2003; Wyplosz, 2003). Thus, EMU-participating countries now have two choices. First, provided that it does not infringe the MCC/SGP it can use fiscal policy to counteract whatever shock has occurred (Gali and Perotti, 2003). Second, the country can wait for its labour market to alter wages and then prices and thus its overall degree of international competitiveness.

The IS-LM (investment–saving/liquidity preference–money supply) model was devised in 1937, one year after publication of Keynes' *General Theory*, to provide a determinate solution to the Keynesian system through being a model that can be used to show new equilibria for income/output (Y) and the rate of interest (r) after any of the exogenous variables or parameters of the system change. In more recent years it has gone out of fashion, being regarded as too simplistic given that its most basic form assumed that prices were fixed. Thus it was unable to explain and illustrate the high inflation rates of the 1970s, together with the increasing attention applied to the supply-side of the economy (the second policy option outlined above). However, the IS-LM model has regained its relevancy, first, given the more stable inflation environment across the EU, partially resulting from cheap labour in China and other emerging economies (*The Economist*, 2005); and second, in relation to the EMU policy debate in that it combines the real (fiscal policy) and financial (monetary policy) sides of the economy in the IS and LM schedules respectively. In any event, the IS-LM approach provides a relatively straightforward means of evaluating the impact of EMU upon economic policy determination and therefore for this reason at least is worthy of initial consideration.

Figure 8.1 illustrates the basic IS-LM model representation that an EMU country faces. The IS function retains its familiar downward-sloping nature, however, rather than thinking of it in terms of its traditional description of illustrating equilibrium in product markets, we can view it in terms of fiscal policy. This is the aspect of economic policy that national governments retain influence over, albeit within the stipulations of the SGP. In contrast the LM function does not possess its usual upward-sloping nature since national economies are effectively 'price takers' in relation to the rate of interest, which is determined by the independent ECB. Hence the LM or monetary policy is portrayed as being perfectly elastic (horizontal) since it is exogenously determined.

Through expansionary or contractionary fiscal policy national governments can manipulate the economy (FP_1) to achieve desired level of national income/output (FP_2), for example, seeking to attain the full employment level of income/output (Y_{FE}). However, as Figure 8.1 indicates the potential scenario facing EMU participants is that the SGP, if applied, could potentially impair the ability of governments to attain full employment through the sole use of fiscal policy (FP_3) with the economy achieving equilibrium at Y_2, thus resulting in a deflationary (unemployment) gap of Y_2–Y_{FE}. Hence, without the ability to adjust interest rates, via the national central bank, as a consequence of domestic economic conditions, EMU countries are only left with supply-side policies to attain full employment. Although most economists now accept the role of such policies, these are not an immediate remedy for the persistently high levels of unemployment that have been endemic across the Continent for the past decade.

Furthermore, many aspects of supply-side policies are inimical to the social model espoused by the majority of EU member states. Thus, in an attempt to extricate themselves from this self-inflicted deflationary position, the common reaction has been to blithely ignore the rules of the SGP and expand budget deficits (Germany, Greece and France) and debt-to-GDP ratios (Belgium, Germany, Greece, France, Italy, Austria, Portugal) beyond permitted limits (ECB, 2003).

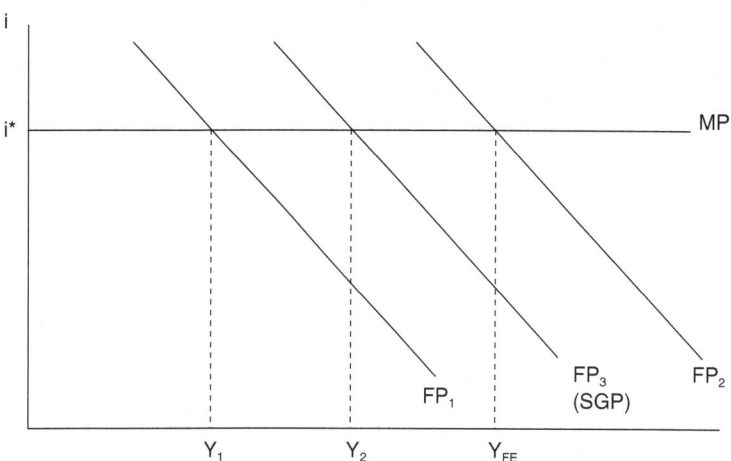

Figure 8.1 Monetary and fiscal policy under EMU.

This, however, is not without potential costs; first, in terms of stoking inflationary pressures and diminishing the external value of the euro, the consequence of which is that the ECB has been forced to maintain interest rates higher than is strictly necessary and hence initiating a vicious circle of exacerbating the high rates of unemployment that the breaking of SGP rules sought to address. Second, despite its resilience to immediate collapse due to the volume of political, and from 2010 financial, capital invested in it by the EU establishment, it remains a fundamentally flawed creation (Minford, 2002; Baimbridge and Whyman, 2008). In addition to the longstanding potential problems inherent with the creation of the eurozone, its design in terms of risks emanating from spill-over and free-rider effects resulting from a lack of fiscal discipline has been relentlessly exposed following the 2008 credit crunch induced recession (Baimbridge *et al.*, 2012).

Fiscal policy within EMU

EMU is based on a unique arrangement of public finance relations whereby fiscal policy remains decentralized to EU member states, but is subject to rules to combine discipline and flexibility (Buiter, 2003; Buti *et al.*, 2003). This is provided by the SGP, which complements and tightens the fiscal provisions laid down in the TEU. Specifically, the SGP consists of a Resolution adopted by the European Council in June of 1997, and two Council Regulations adopted in July of 1997. It clarifies the 'excessive deficits' procedure and penalties that were agreed in the TEU.[1] Buti and van den Noord (2003:4) argue that the SGP is 'unquestionably the most stringent supranational commitment technology ever adopted by sovereign governments on a voluntary basis in the attempt to establish and maintain sound public finances'. If fully applied it will have important implications for the behaviour of budgetary authorities in both the short-term (e.g. cyclical stabilization, policy co-ordination) and long-term (e.g. sustainability of public finances). It seeks to achieve a balance between constraining national fiscal policy to protect the ECB whilst it established credibility and permitting limited flexibility for counter-cyclical fiscal policy. This was deemed necessary since although ECB policy might be expected to create stable macroeconomic conditions for the eurozone as a whole it could not be expected to resolve regional cyclical imbalances.[2]

The SGP consists of several central elements (Buti *et al.*, 1998; EU Commission, 2000). First, a commitment to medium-term budgets that are 'close to balance or in surplus' which is interpreted by Canzoneri and Diba (2000) as an implied promise to balance structural (or cyclically adjusted) budgets. Second, submission of annual programmes specifying medium-term budgetary objectives thereby creating a track record when assessing compliance with the SGP, or convergence criteria in the case of member states that are not in the eurozone (EU Commission, 2000). Third, countries that run excessive deficits will be subject to financial penalties and public approbation. Deficits are defined as 'excessive' if they exceed 3 per cent of GDP, unless they occur under 'exceptional' circumstances which is defined as an annual decline in real output of more than 2 per cent of GDP, whilst a decline of 0.75 per cent of GDP might be deemed 'exceptional' if there is additional supporting evidence. The sanctions associated with such deficits are that the member state has to make an interest free deposit of 0.2 per cent of GDP, plus 0.1 per cent of the amount by which its deficit to GDP ratio exceeded 3 per cent. The maximum deposit would be capped at 0.5 per cent of GDP, which is forfeited after two years if the 'excessive deficit' persists. Canzoneri and Diba (2000) estimate that the foregone interest in the first year of sanctions would be in the range of €250 million to €500 million for one of the larger member states.

However, even after a decade of EMU little progress has been demonstrated towards lower public deficits and debts by participating nations in terms of budgetary consolidation, let alone in structural terms. Furthermore, following the omission of the automatic effects of growth on the budget, countries have relaxed their retrenchment efforts in the 1998–2002 period. In particular, the three largest countries of the euro area (Germany, France and Italy) as well as Portugal did not behave according to the SGP. Indeed, although the SGP appears rigid, it fails to address a typical failure of fiscal policy behaviour in Europe, namely the tendency to run expansionary pro-cyclical policies in good times (European Commission, 2000). Whilst an excess over the 3 per cent of GDP deficit ceiling is sanctioned, there is no apparent reward for appropriate budgetary behaviour during cyclical upswings, leading Buti and van den Noord (2003) to argue that the political temptation to 'spend the money when it comes in' may prove irresistible. Hence, the suggestion that the SGP is 'all sticks and no carrots' (Bean, 1998) and may result in a pro-cyclical bias in the conduct of budgetary policy since the only carrot is the opportunity for automatic stabilizers to operate during economic downturns. However, Buti and Martinot (2000) argue that if governments retain their historical budgetary culture they will tend to offset the working of the automatic stabilizers for sufficiently large, positive output gaps.

These questionable incentive structures may be further tested during electoral periods. In contrast to the advent of the euro, when the incentive to maintain the announced fiscal consolidation path were evident, the situation may be different once in EMU when adherence to the SGP's rules may be politically inefficient (Buti and Giudice, 2002). Resolving such political bias is likely to be problematic. Potential solutions range from the introduction of 'rainy-day' funds permitting countries to set aside revenue in good times (Buti et al., 2003) to the harmonization of electoral cycles in EMU, which would reduce politically induced distortions and be welfare-enhancing (Sapir and Sekkat, 1999). However, the most likely outcome is the increasing of budgetary surveillance focussing on structural balances and using peer pressure and 'early warnings' to curb fiscal misbehaviour (Viren, 2001; Korkman, 2001; EU Commission, 2002).

In addition to ensuring member states adhere to the rules of the SGP, a further series of difficulties have arisen regarding the convergence criteria reference values for both the deficit and the debt to GDP ratios, whilst none were defined for structural deficits. Subsequently, the SGP added a commitment to structural balance, but the 'excessive deficits' procedure is its only explicit enforcement mechanism. Thus, actual deficits are the focus of the SGP that appear to take primacy over both structural deficits and debt levels (Canzoneri and Diba, 2000). Consequently, it has been suggested that the SGP will become an impediment unless its focus is shifted from constraints on actual deficits and towards constraints on structural deficits, or better yet, constraints on debt levels (Canzoneri and Diba, 2000; Artis and Buti, 2001; Dalsgaard and de Serres, 2001; Rostangno *et al.*, 2001; Missale, 2001). Furthermore, various studies regarding the flexibility built into the 'excessive deficits' procedure suggest that once governments have further reduced structural deficits the 'excessive deficits' procedure should not constrain normal counter-cyclical efforts (EU Commission, 2000). However, at the present time, given the unlikely prospects for achieving structural balance, the current emphasis on the excessive deficits procedure seems misplaced (Balassone and Franco, 2001; Casella, 2001). Moreover, it is unclear how strictly the EU will interpret the provisions in the SGP with it possessing a history of exerting discretion in such decisions.

Whilst theoretically fiscal policy should be used as a countercyclical tool, governments may also use the policy for purely political reasons; however, if this is the case, fiscal policy may become challenging within a monetary union such as EMU through the occurrence of spill-over or free-rider effects (von Hagen and Wyplosz, 2008). The former may occur if EMU members run large budget deficits over a prolonged period of time leading to their fiscal stance being on an unsustainable path, which given its financing through the financial markets, results in ever higher interest rates on sovereign debt. Additionally, with such growing recourse to the financial market, the availability of finance may decrease and therefore further drive up interest rates. Thus, one member's debt issue spills over to others as financing sovereign debt becomes more expensive for all countries (Arezki *et al.*, 2011).

The potential hazard of free-rider effects materialises when a country cannot meet the repayment of its outstanding debt, with default on the horizon, it can either undertake surprise devaluation or inflation to reduce its debt's real value. However, for EMU members without sovereign monetary policy, these methods are no longer available, thereby increasing the possibility of outright default (McKinnon, 1996). Moreover, with the integration of financial markets, one country's bonds may be widely held by other EMU members. Thus, outright debt default harms not only domestic bond holders, but other government and private investors holding such bonds. Consequently, the pressure to bail out troubled fellow EMU members may increase, and, without restrictions on fiscal behaviour, a member country may allow its debt to increase continuously if they believe other governments will bail it out. Under a currency union, member countries lose not only their monetary independence, but also a central bank to back their sovereign debts. Thus eurozone governments become uniquely vulnerable to self-fulfilling panic over default.

Even in light of the issues discussed above, potentially the single largest problem for the eurozone is that at the present time there is no substantive federal fiscal system in place whereby a central government sets taxes and expenditure rules that apply in constituent states or countries (Italianer and Vanheukelen, 1993; Baimbridge and Whyman, 2004; Whyman, 2010). Hence, fiscal policy is confined to backward-looking automatic stabilizers confined by convergence criteria/SGP rules, such that the only channel for a forward-looking policy is through interest rates that are now controlled by the independent ECB.

Monetary policy under EMU

Whilst EMU in the shape of the MCC and SGP directly impacts upon national policymaking, the ECB is the sole body credited with determining the appropriate monetary and exchange rate policy for the entire eurozone and as such its ability to fulfil its stated objectives will be crucial to the eventual success or failure of EMU. Its architects sought to insulate it completely from political pressures permitting no clear accountability to neither national nor federal European institutions. The crucial operational features of the ECB are that its sole policy objective is the pursuit of price stability through defining and implementing the EU's monetary policy. This is founded upon both theoretical (Barro and Gordon, 1983; Alesina, 1989; Alesina and Grilli, 1991; Kydland and Prescott, 1997) and empirical (Bade and Parkin, 1988; Alesina, 1988, 1989; Cukierman, 1992; Alesina and Summers, 1993) studies whereby the transfer of monetary policy from governments to an independent central bank is likely to result in lower inflation.

However, the paucity of analysis regarding the ECB's ability to achieve low inflation, full employment, a sustainable balance of payments and good level of economic growth, should be of great concern for all interested in contesting the neoliberal path of European integration. First, in relation to its theoretical underpinnings where the belief that central banks should be independent has deep historical roots (Toniolo, 1988), primarily based on the view that arrangements raising the credibility of monetary policy will increase its effectiveness in pursuit of price stability (Cukierman, 1986; Blackburn and Christensen, 1989). However, this neo-liberal perspective can be challenged on several fronts. First, if central bank independence increases credibility it should be associated with greater rigidity in the setting of nominal prices and money wages, however, studies indicated that neither effect occurs (Posen, 1993, 1998). Indeed independence, not merely fails to reduce the cost of disinflation, but rather seems to increase it.

The theoretical case for independence is based on two analytical assumptions: the vertical long-term Phillips curve and the political business cycle. However, the vertical Phillips curve analysis rests upon the concept of a natural rate of unemployment, the frequently changing determinants of which economists remain largely ignorant (Davidson, 1998; Karanassou and Snower, 1998; Madsen, 1998; Nickell, 1998; Phelps and Zoega, 1998). Moreover, relatively little evidence exists for the occurrence of any systematic political business cycle (Kalecki, 1943; Breton, 1974; Nordhaus, 1975; MacRae, 1977; Wagner, 1977; Frey, 1978; Alesina, 1989).

However, the persuasive nature of monetarist ideas led to the widespread conviction that low inflation is an important condition for high and sustained growth. However, studies indicate that no significant relationship exists between low inflation and higher rates of growth, until double-digit rates of price increase occur (Thirlwall and Barton, 1971; Brown, 1985; Stanners, 1993). Moreover, if responsibility for price stability rests solely with an independent central bank, economic management potentially becomes more difficult due to the separation of monetary and fiscal policy (Rogoff, 1985a 1985b; Blake and Weale, 1998). Finally, when assessing the impact of central bank independence upon price stability, economists have mostly utilized imputed 'degrees of independence' to evaluate the heterogeneous character of central banks (Mangano, 1998). However, the value of such evidence is problematic, casting doubt upon the purported association between central bank independence and the attainment of price stability (Hansson, 1987; Alesina, 1988; Burdekin and Willett, 1990; Friedman and Schwartz, 1991; Muscatelli, 1998; Baimbridge and Whyman 2004).

In relation to the conduct of monetary policy by the ECB, initially the TEU left the role of the ECB uncertain, suggesting that it would mainly implement the policies determined by the national central banks by delegating the common monetary policy to the European System of Central Banks (ESCB) (von Hagen and Bruckner, 2002). In view of such institutional vagueness a key concern has been how ECB council members could reach an agreement on a common monetary policy, to what extent that policy would be affected by national circumstances and preferences and how it could be communicated effectively to a very heterogeneous European public (Cecchetti *et al.*, 1999). Initially the EMI preparatory work narrowed the choice of a monetary policy strategy down to monetary targeting versus inflation targeting (EMI, 1997). However, in October 1998, the Governing Council of the ECB announced a key aspect of monetary policy strategy in terms of a quantitative definition of price stability. Furthermore, in order to assess risks to price stability, the ECB would make use of two pillars. First, it attributes a prominent role to monetary indicators as signalled by the announcement of a quantitative reference value for the growth of a broad monetary aggregate and second, it undertakes a comprehensive analysis of a wide range of other economic and financial variables as indicators of price developments (ECB, 1998, 1999, 2001, 2002; Issing *et al.*, 2001).

However, for the new quantitative definition of price stability a precise definition was not initially established. In order to specify this objective more precisely, the Governing Council announced, in October 1998, the quantitative definition of price stability as 'a year-on-year increase in the Harmonized Index of Consumer Prices (HICP) for the euro area of below 2 per cent', which was 'to be maintained over the medium term' (ECB, 1998). Such an announcement is supposed to enhance the transparency of the overall monetary policy framework and provides a clear and measurable benchmark against which to hold the ECB accountable. Furthermore, it gives guidance to expectations of future price developments, thereby helping to stabilize the economy. Consequently, the ECB (2003) argued that this definition of price stability has been conducive to a firm anchoring of inflation expectations in the euro area at levels compatible with the definition, thereby helping to contain the inflationary effects of the substantial price shocks which have occurred. While the announcement of a quantitative numerical value for the price stability objective of the ECB was welcomed, there has been criticism regarding specific features of the definition.

First, regarding the choice of the price measure it has been argued that the ECB should put more emphasis on measures of 'core' or 'underlying' inflation, or even specify its objective in terms of a measure of core inflation (Gros *et al.*, 2001; Alesina *et al.*, 2001). Such measures could help to avoid the risk of monetary policy-makers focusing excessively on temporary price fluctuations. Second, that the ECB's quantitative definition may be too ambitious given a positive measurement bias in the HICP that could hamper the adjustment process at low levels of inflation, substantial divergences in inflation rates across countries that imply 'too low' a level of inflation, and possibly frequent deflationary situations and the presence of a zero boundary on nominal interest rates that could hamper the effectiveness of monetary policy in the face of large negative demand shocks and expose the euro area to the risks associated with deflation and deflationary spirals (de Grauwe, 1994; Fitoussi and Creel, 2002). Third, that the ECB's definition is imprecise and asymmetric as it specifies the upper boundary, but leaves the lower boundary undefined. This may result in it being less effective in anchoring inflation expectations and possibly hinder the clarity of explanations of policy moves. Consequently, it has been suggested that the ECB should make its objective more precise, for instance, by officially announcing a lower boundary in the definition or by specifying the objective in terms of a point inflation rate (IMF, 2002; Svensson, 2002, 2003). Finally, the choice of the specific quantitative objective requires a balance between the costs of inflation and rationales for small positive inflation rates. The costs primarily relate to the misallocation of resources, the inflation tax on real balances, the effects of inflation on income distribution and inflation uncertainty and associated risk premia, menu costs and those costs stemming from the interaction of inflation with the tax system. In contrast, the case for small positive inflation relates to measurement bias in the price index, downward nominal rigidities, sustained inflation differentials and the risk of protracted deflation or a deflationary spiral (Yates, 1998; Wynne and Rodriguez-Palenzuela, 2002; Coenen, 2003a, 2003b; Klaeffing and Lopez-Perez, 2003). Unfortunately, such a review of the costs and benefits of moderate inflation does not allow the optimal rate of inflation to be precisely defined; it indicates the need for an inflation objective embodying a sufficient safety margin against deflation. In response to this criticism the ECB (2003) suggested that inflation objectives above 1 per cent provide sufficient safety margins to ensure against these risks.[3]

In relation to the first pillar, its key characteristic is the announcement of a reference value for the annual growth of M3. Hence, the ECB seeks to communicate the medium-term focus of monetary policy to the public, as it relieves the central bank from responding to short-run fluctuations in financial and other variables (ECB, 2003). Furthermore, by signalling continuity of the Bundesbank's strategy, the ESCB hoped to quickly establish credibility (von Hagen and Bruckner, 2002). However, the role of money and monetary analysis has generated controversy regarding the robustness of the chosen leading indicator's properties with respect to price developments on the grounds that the correlation between money growth and inflation appears to have declined over time in parallel with restored conditions of price stability (Begg *et al.*, 2002). In this context, the necessity for announcing a reference value for money growth has also been queried, together with the usefulness per se of a separate 'money' pillar (Svensson, 2003).

In contrast, the second pillar consists of an assessment regarding future price developments (ECB, 1998). Initially, it represented the analysis of short-run price developments based on measures of real activity, wage cost, asset prices, fiscal policy indicators, together with indicators of business and consumer confidence (ECB, 1999). However, no framework was specified regarding how these variables would be used to assess price developments, nor their relative weights in such assessments. It is therefore an opaque part to the ESCB's strategy, being void of systematic analysis and fully discretionary (von Hagen and Bruckner, 2002). Furthermore, Gaspar *et al.* (2001) suggest that the analysis is now organized in the form of a macroeconomic projection, although the ECB does not provide confidence intervals for its projections (Gali, 2001).

According to the ECB (2003), the two pillars are used in parallel in monetary policy decision-making. However, there is no indication of what their relative weights are, resulting in an incomprehensible strategy, as Issing *et al.* (2001) partially acknowledge. Although there is nothing that would make the use and revelation of the relative weights of the two pillars impossible, the reason why the ECB has so far denied the public transparency of its strategy is more likely related to the internal decision-making processes (von Hagen and Bruckner, 2002).

Finally, from its ostensively monetarist pre-history the ECB argues that the majority of the eurozone's high unemployment originates from structural deficiencies on the supply side of its member states' economies. Consequently, it denies responsibility for increasing aggregate demand to lower unemployment, since no scope exists to reduce unemployment without accelerating inflation. However, if the sole objective of policy is to maintain a constant rate of inflation, wide variations in output and employment may be required. In so far as a potential conflict exists between steady inflation and full employment, the latter should enjoy priority, because the consequences of market failure in terms of high rates of employment are more serious than those associated with moderate levels of inflation.

The macroeconomic framework under EMU

EMU requires the ECB to possess the monopoly power to issue the euro, with existing national central banks becoming mere subsidiaries of this ultimate federal monetary authority. Thus the ECB is in sole charge of monetary policy for all participants in EMU through the establishment of a common interest rate, together with the management of the euro's external exchange rate.[4] To fulfil these responsibilities, the ECB is likely to set interest rates according to what the *median* member state requires, implying that there will always be some economies that require higher or lower interest rates, depending upon their individual circumstances.

The only realistic alternative to varying monetary policy according to the needs of the median participant is for the ECB to prioritize the self-interest of one section of the eurozone, perhaps by reflecting Germany's pre-occupation with low inflation at the expense of other priorities. Indeed, the TEU commits the ECB to pursue the goal of price stability at the expense of all other economic objectives, which, in any case, may be rendered impossible through an over-vigorous pursuit of squeezing the last vestiges of inflation out of the European economy. Such a strategy is supported by economic orthodoxy, which claims that there is no long-term trade-off between inflation and unemployment, so that tightening monetary policy to reduce inflation will not result in persistently high levels of unemployment. However, the fallacy of such an over-simplification of what is a much more complicated relationship was demonstrated by the restrictive monetary policy established by membership of the ERM, which caused most of Europe to suffer double-digit rates of unemployment over the last decade. It was only sterling's forced exit from the deflationary excesses of the ERM that established the competitive conditions for the United Kingdom's recent successful economic record.

The ECB faces another problem in framing monetary policy caused by differences in trade cycles and in the industrial and financial structures of participating countries, which imply that EMU is liable to suffer from asymmetric external shocks (Weber, 1991b; de Grauwe and Vanhaverbeke, 1993; Bayoumi and Eichengreen, 1993; Whyman, 1997a, 1997b). For example, an increase in oil prices will exert a beneficial impact upon the energy exporting sectors of the United Kingdom and the Netherlands, whilst having a detrimental impact upon all other EU member economies. If the ECB reacts to this variation in the external economic environment according to the needs of the majority, it will enact changes in monetary policy that are contrary to the needs of the United Kingdom and the Netherlands. Moreover, differential house-buying patterns between the United Kingdom and Ireland compared to continental member states, together with a greater preference for variable rate borrowing in the United Kingdom, mean that the rest of the EU is far less responsive to changes in monetary policy (Taylor, 1995; Bank for International Settlements, 1996; Burkitt *et al.*, 1996, 1997; Eltis, 1996). Indeed, simulations performed on the macroeconomic models used by various national central banks indicate that the impact of an interest rate change on UK domestic demand after two years is four times greater than the EU average (Bank for International Settlements, 1994; Pennant-Rea *et al.*, 1997). Consequently, the ECB is again placed in an impossible position since any changes in monetary policy will affect certain countries far more than others, resulting in either an over-tightening or over-loosening of monetary policy. The end result would be a dramatic increase in an economy's volatility as a direct result of the inefficiency of a 'one rate for all' monetary policy in the presence of systematic cyclical and structural differences between different economies, as the post-2010 eurozone crisis has illustrated (Baimbridge *et al.*, 2012).

Empirical studies confirm that supply and demand shocks will prove asymmetric for EMU participants, with 67 per cent of supply shocks and 82 per cent of demand shocks estimated to exert a divisive impact upon the EU economy, whilst the UK economy was found to react differently to those of other member states in no less than 87 out of 100 instances (Weber, 1991a; Bayoumi and Eichengreen, 1993). Comparisons between the United Kingdom and Germany produce a compatibility of only 54 per cent, suggesting that UK growth and inflation are moving in the opposite direction to that of Germany almost half of the time. Moreover, Ireland's growth record was related to Germany's on only 9 per cent of occasions, whilst Greek and Portuguese inflation had no statistical relationship with Germany (Bayoumi and Eichengreen, 1993). Advocates of EU integration dismiss these findings by arguing that the development of the SM will reduce the frequency and impact of asymmetric shocks as individual economies become increasingly inter-dependent and as large corporations straddle European borders (EC Commission, 1990; Goodhart, 1995). However, it is equally possible that industrial restructuring across Europe will concentrate certain industries in specific locations, such as car manufacture in Germany, thereby exacerbating existing differences (de Grauwe and Vanhaverbeke, 1993). In either case, EMU remains vulnerable to any sizeable asymmetric external shock which will highlight the inability of a single monetary authority to reconcile the different economic needs of individual participants by using only one policy instrument, the common interest rate, whose level is set in the interests of the majority of nations. Indeed, the loss of economic instruments for individual member states due to participation in EMU violates the Tinbergen (1952) rule, which states that if a number of independent policy targets are to be achieved with a number of effective policy instruments, the number of instruments will, in general, need to be at least as great as the number of targets. Consequently, the ability of individual member states to continue to pursue national rather than EU goals will be reduced by the loss of former economic instruments, against the recommendation of Tinbergen.

The extensive literature concerning nominal and real wage rigidity in Europe undermines faith in price flexibility as an equilibrating mechanism to restore full employment in the aftermath of an asymmetric shock.[5] With labour mobility far lower than experienced in mature monetary unions such as the United States (OECD, 1986; Ermisch, 1991; Eichengreen, 1992; Masson and Taylor, 1993), and capital mobility unlikely to generate sufficient short-term stabilization due to the time lags and transactions costs involved (von Hagen, 1993; Romer, 1994), fiscal policy is left as the primary stabilizing instrument (Kenen, 1969, 1995; Sala-i-Martin and Sachs, 1992; de Grauwe and Vanhaverbeke, 1993; Masson, 1996). However, national fiscal policy is constrained by participation in EMU, due to the requirements of the convergence criteria reinforced by the SGP.

Member states are committed by international treaty to prevent budget deficits exceeding 3 per cent of GDP and public debt to extend beyond 60 per cent of GDP, except in particularly deep recessions, defined as occurring when national income declines by more than 0.75 per cent in any given year. Failure to meet these criteria will result in fines being imposed upon the errant nation-state, up to 0.5 per cent of GDP, thereby worsening the problematic economic situation which led to rising budget deficits in the first place (EU Commission, 1992; Holland, 1995; Burkitt *et al.*, 1996, 1997; UNCTAD, 1996). Hence, governments such as Greece, Italy, Spain and Portugal are therefore faced with trying to cut public spending or to raise taxes in the middle of a slump, the inevitable result being to deepen the recession, just as pro-cyclical fiscal policy worsened conditions during the depression of the 1930s.

The alternative is for member states to run a budget surplus of perhaps 5–7 per cent of GDP during favourable economic periods, to avoid surpassing the 3 per cent deficit limit during a downturn.[6] A surplus of this magnitude has little economic justification. Moreover, the reduction in EU fiscal deficits from an average of 6.5 per cent of GNP in 1993 to 2.6 per cent in 1998 coincided with a period of mediocre economic growth rates for those EU nations determined to meet the conditions established for entry to the single currency (Ormerod 1999). Deficit reductions for certain countries, including Portugal, Italy, Spain and Sweden, were equivalent to between 4–6 per cent of GNP, thereby imposing a massive constraint upon the ability of the economy to maintain normal growth patterns during this period of fiscal retrenchment. The resulting mass unemployment across the continent, currently nearing 20 million people, is a damning testimony to the higher prioritization of EMU amongst EU governments than the alternative objectives of full employment and the promotion of economic growth. Nevertheless, to continue to meet the convergence criteria, fiscal restriction must be pursued further, as the average deficit levels are barely sufficient in favourable economic conditions, and must be improved by perhaps 7–9 per cent of national wealth in order to satisfy the SGP in the midst of an economic slow-down. However, further budget cuts or tax rises will only exacerbate the already existing problems of slow growth and rising unemployment. Thus, the annual growth rate of the EU's present membership averaged 4.8 per cent between 1961 and 1970, and slowed to 3.0 per cent between 1971 and 1980, to 2.4 per cent between 1981 and 1990, and to just 1.7 per cent between 1991 and 1998. The EU's growth since 1975 has been an average 0.4 per cent less than that of the United States each year.

A different option involves the expansion of fiscal policy at the federal level, which could act as an inter-regional public insurance scheme to redistribute income to 'adversely shocked' from 'favourably shocked' regions, thus preventing an 'unlucky' area bearing a disproportionate financial burden. However, the current EU budget, equivalent to only 1.24 per cent of EU GDP, is too small to exert a significant stabilizing effect upon EMU regions in the advent of an asymmetric external shock (Eichengreen, 1994; Bayoumi and Masson, 1995; EU Commission, 1996). Thus any shift towards fiscal federalism requires an increased flow of resources to a central fiscal authority.

Hence, EMU is an essentially political strategy based upon false economic assumptions of cyclical and structural convergence; in contrast, the national interest requires the implementation of a long-run opt-out from EMU, given that its participation is neither inevitable nor desirable. The central issue therefore becomes, what framework is needed for the formation of macroeconomic policy in a country outside the single currency on a permanent basis? One potential alternative to the monetarist bias institutionalized at the core of the EMU project is the theoretical predictions and policy prescriptions, which emerge from the broad Keynesian tradition (see Table 8.1 for a summary).

The policy imperatives imposed upon the state by cumulative causation and technology gaps (Myrdal, 1957; Hardin, 1982) are unlikely to be achieved over the whole of the EU's member states, which possess different trade cycles, economic structures, histories, languages and cultures. Advanced capitalist economies are inherently unstable; left to themselves, they cannot maintain full employment resources, whilst being marred by inequalities in the distribution of market power, income and wealth. Unfettered market forces via cumulative causation tend to exacerbate these instabilities and disparities. Hence, considerable scope exists for government involvement in initiating, pursuing and implementing economic policies; on the demand side insufficient aggregate demand and instability of investment are the key problems to resolve, whilst on the supply side, planning of prices and incomes, training plus active industrial measures to direct investment to resolve any balance of payments problems are central. However, in light of the current neo-liberal drift in EU strategy the prospect of an EU-wide strategy to achieve these objectives is remote, although supranational directives may prevent the implementation of effective, national policies.

In order to implement democratic-socialist economic policies, countries need to avoid the uniform monetary policy and the constraints upon budgetary measures imposed by the adoption of a single EU currency. Therefore, the crucial issue becomes, what framework is needed for the formation of macroeconomic policy? Broadly, a democratic-socialist economic strategy seeks to achieve both internal and external balance, where the former refers to more than the Maastricht target of price stability. Accordingly aggregate demand management could reduce unemployment, whilst a mixture of budgetary and monetary measures, a prices and incomes policy, the re-introduction of credit controls and coordinated national wage bargaining could restrain inflation. Although direct controls are unpopular with orthodox economists, who prefer the supposed allocative efficiency of free markets, the reality of sticky prices within oligopolistic markets creates the potential for governments to increase employment and growth, such options are discussed in Chapter 14.

Conclusion

This chapter has sought to outline the 'new' shape of economic policymaking within EMU. Although this has evolved from the initial blueprint, the direction

Table 8.1 A comparison between features of progressive alternative and EMU

	Democratic socialist viewpoint	Neo-liberal EMU
Macroeconomic assumptions		
Economy tends towards full employment	No, capitalism is inherently unstable	Yes
Demand side		
Aggregate demand level	Vital, but unstable	Important
Aggregate demand management	Essential prerequisite for full employed economy	Not important, no federal instrument to manage demand
Fiscal policy	Main instrument to manage AD	Unimportant, prerogative of nation state
Monetary policy	Supportive to fiscal policy; cheap money to stimulate investment and growth	Uniform interest rate – set to produce price stability
Counter-cyclical	Yes	Limited by MCC and SGP on budget deficits
Status of central bank	Democratically controlled – given multiple objectives	Independent – sole target is price stability
Supply side		
What causes unemployment?	Demand deficiency and supply-side problems	Structural/supply side factors
Model of unemployment	Hysteresis; tendency towards disequilibrium	Natural rate/NAIRU
Policies to reduce unemployment	Demand management, labour market policies, income policy (or wage bargaining co-ordination) industrial policy (including socialization investment)	Level and duration of benefits
External balance		
Exchange rate regime	Short term stability, long term flexibility	Single currency
How to defeat destabilizing speculation	Capital controls, financial regulation	Large single economy less prone to destabilization
Globalization	National autonomy remains possible	Integrated financial markets, no room for independent monetary policy

Source: Whyman *et al.* (2005).

is diametrically opposite to what would be beneficial to the United Kingdom. For example, the introduction of SGP to reinforce the budgetary aspects of the convergence criteria potentially leads to an unprecedented loss of national autonomy in terms of fiscal policy. However, there is little comfort to be gained from the marked failure of the SGP with numerous member states blithely flouting its provisions since this illustrates the fallacy of the entire Maastricht process in seeking to curtail national well-being for the greater good of the EU. Similarly, in 2003 the ECB undertook a major reassessment of its monetary policy stance given the destabilizing effect of the 'one size fit all' interest rate policy upon both domestic EMU economies and in terms of the euro external position upon global capital markets. However, once again the patchwork of remedial policies is far from those necessary to place monetary policy within the sphere of democratic accountability.

This leads us to the question of how economic policymaking could be improved within the eurozone. Two radical, but effective, reforms would be as follows. First, the Council of Ministers tells the commission that, from the next financial year, member states will finance only those parts of commission outlays that achieve a zero fraud rating from the European Court of Auditors, with all other EU expenditure reverting to national control. At a stroke, such a decision would eliminate about 95 per cent of commission activity. Gone would be the CAP, the CFP, plus the 'pork barrel' of regional and structural funds. In the last financial year, the auditors approved the accounts on only a derisory 5 per cent of the EU's €98 billion budget. The EU will never accept such a proposal that would compel the commission to put taxpayers' money to efficient and transparent use. However, national euro-realist governments could campaign for it and, when it is inevitably rejected, put it into practice unilaterally.

Second, control over economic policy should be repatriated from the ECB and the provisions of SGP to the nation-states. On 26 April 2004, the French finance minister complained that his job was to deliver economic growth, yet he was unable to do so, because authority over the levers of growth had been given away to the ECB. Given France's record in using the EU to gain advantage, the conclusion that the centralization of economic policy should be reversed is unavoidable.

9 Fiscal federalism

A missed opportunity or an emerging consensus?

Introduction

The pace of European integration accelerated considerably during the past decade, stimulated by the agreement to form the SM and enhanced by the process of forming an EMU amongst EU member states. However, whilst the nature of this community of nations significantly changed over this period, many aspects of the EU financial and administrative apparatus failed to evolve to meet these challenges. Whilst detailed consideration has been given to whether individual member states will meet the MCC for membership of EMU, the inadequacies of the EU's budgetary arrangements have received far less attention. Nevertheless, the advent of EMU would necessitate a fundamental review of fiscal policy within the EU. The present crisis talks, arising from the Greek fiscal crisis and destabilization of the eurozone, have meant tentative moves in this general direction, but as this chapter is written, a final consensus on these issues remains elusive and further work would appear necessary.

The MCC, combined with the proposed stability pact, would both reduce national fiscal flexibility whilst the operation of EMU promises to strengthen financial market integration and thereby reduce seigniorage revenues particularly for the Mediterranean member states. The combination of these factors will constrain the ability of participants to stabilize their own economies within an EMU which requires the transfer of monetary and exchange rate instruments to federal rather than national control. If perfect convergence had occurred and could be sustained in the long term, these changes would be of little importance. However, the likely persistence of asymmetric external shocks requires an alternative stabilizing mechanism to be developed to prevent monetary union being undermined by diverse economic and social forces to the extent that it could collapse, as have almost all other similar international monetary arrangements that have not been based upon a firm national identity.[1]

This chapter seeks to complement and extend the existing literature which discusses the evolution of fiscal policy within the context of EMU, and examines the potential for fiscal federalism to negate certain design flaws within EMU economic architecture, whilst providing a degree of stabilization for a diverse eurozone economy.

Fiscal policy architecture of EMU

The form of EMU adopted by the EU as previously discussed has a number of core features, namely the pooling of monetary policy under the auspices of the ECB, and the adoption of fiscal rules intended to prevent individual member states from running large budget deficits and public sector debts, which have been determined as incompatible with the long-term stability of the system (EC Commission, 1992). The fiscal rules formed two parts.

The first, pre-participation, involved the MCC, which set out five financial tests that potential members were supposed to meet prior to acceptance as full members of EMU. These rules were criticized as being too narrowly focused on financial rather than real economy effects, nevertheless, whether or not the convergence criteria were insufficiently developed, the failure to adequately police their implementation has cast its shadow over the contemporary problems with public debt in Greece, Italy and Spain. Post-participation, the SGP, derived from the 1997 Amsterdam Treaty, sought to make permanent and transparent the public finance obligations contained in the MCC. It has been suggested that fiscal 'discipline' is 'fundamental' for macroeconomic stability and hence laying the foundations for future economic growth (ECB, 2005:7). Thus, the fiscal architecture of EMU essentially lays a constraint upon the autonomy and flexibility of national fiscal policy amongst EMU participants.

This is based upon the assumption that the economy fluctuates around the economic concept of the NAIRU, whereby supply-side factors determine real economic variables such as unemployment and output. Hence, the resulting policy stance is to maintain a neutral fiscal policy and rely primarily upon monetary policy, through the medium of the interest rate policy instrument, to smooth demand shocks and thereby enable supply-side factors to determine development in the real economy. There is, therefore, no need for democratic control over fiscal or monetary policy, as these are supportive to the primary drivers of economic growth, and therefore these instruments can be subcontracted to technocratic specialists in the ECB and/or be constrained by the operation of the SGP.

It has been persuasively argued, however, that the design of the SGP is viewed as flawed in a number of respects, including; its rigidity, the one-size-fits-all nature of its operations (based upon no review of the evidence to indicate that fiscal policy should be run in the same way in different nations), its tightening of the MCC obligations (in terms of smaller budget deficit and public debt positions), lack of credibility as sanctions are rather onerous and imposed post-event, the fact that the SGP demands a pro-cyclical macroeconomic stance amidst economic downturns and, by focusing upon deficits and not surpluses, the pact is asymmetric in reinforcing national budgetary behaviour to the benefit of the monetary union as a whole (Monperrus-Veroni and Saraceno, 2006: 33–4).

Alternatives suggested include:

- Changing to a 'golden rule' concerned with structural deficits, potentially linked to output gaps – thereby increasing the degree of flexibility in the operation of the scheme, but retaining the constraint upon profligate fiscal behaviour imposed by a policy rule – theoretical estimates have claimed that this reform would improve the performance of the SGP (Eichengreen and Wyplotz, 1998).

- Introducing a European fiscal policy seeking to stabilize the EMU-zone – figures of around 2 per cent have been suggested as sufficient for purpose, provided that these amounts are well targeted (Goodhart and Smith, 1993; Currie, 1997), whereas other suggestions are for a figure closer to 5 per cent of GDP (Arestis and Sawyer, 2006: 67).

The fact that France and Germany preferred to avoid the strict interpretation of the SGP, when faced with determined opposition by organized labour, has led certain theorists to conclude that reform of the SGP is achievable, as long as trade unions and/or workers are prepared to collectively mobilize to achieve this objective (Bieler, 2006: 210; Mathers, 2007: 3).

Fiscal policy challenges of EMU

Participation in EMU involves national governments relinquishing exchange rate and monetary policy instruments to federal economic authorities. The significance of this reduction in policy tools available to manage individual economies depends upon the extent to which devaluation retains a real effect in the medium- to long-term and whether the financial markets within Europe are so closely integrated that independent monetary policy has been rendered impotent. However, should both of these conditions be satisfied, EMU would remain susceptible to destabilization to the extent that external shocks exert an asymmetric impact upon individual economies. Asymmetric shocks are minimized if monetary union occurs between countries with comparable industrial structures which are, simultaneously, highly diversified. The expectation is that diversification will cause industry-specific shocks to offset one another whilst broad similarities between economies imply that a given external shock will possess a similar impact and require a matching policy response, which could be satisfactorily accomplished by the ECB or another federal financial authority.

External shocks

The literature has indicated the persistence of significant differences between specific EU member states, which the pressures of the single currency magnify in importance. Thus, oil and gas production in the Netherlands and the United Kingdom, the manufacturing sector in Germany and the financial and media sectors in the United Kingdom, and the agricultural sector within many of the NMS, are each more developed than throughout the majority of EU nations. Similarly, the propensity for home ownership is different in Ireland and the United Kingdom than in continental Europe which, when combined with a higher proportion of variable rate mortgages, causes changes in monetary policy to have a faster and larger impact upon domestic consumption than in the rest of the EU. Moreover, differences in financial systems can have a significant impact upon the economic consequences of movements in a common EMU-wide interest rate for nations (such as the United Kingdom) with a much greater proportion of corporate and household debt paid at variable rates of interest (Burkitt *et al.*, 1997: 10–12).

The empirical analysis ascertaining whether EMU will predominantly experience symmetric or asymmetric shocks is therefore of fundamental importance to the design of the policy framework established to reinforce the union. Two such studies were undertaken by Weber (1991a) and Bayoumi and Eichengreen (1993). The former found that shocks to nominal variables, such as inflation rates, and supply-side shocks were largely and increasingly symmetric, whereas labour market and demand shocks were primarily asymmetric. Furthermore, Bayoumi and Eichengreen discovered that EU member states suffered from more inflationary shocks and a higher proportion of supply shocks than comparable US states. Moreover, EU countries experienced particularly pronounced asymmetric external shocks, with the average correlation of supply shocks measuring 0.33 amongst EU member states, compared to 0.46 amongst US regions, whilst average demand shocks measured a particularly asymmetric 0.18 compared to 0.37 in the United States. Thus, whereas 46 per cent of supply shocks and 37 per cent of demand shocks were found to be symmetric in the United States, the corresponding figures for the EU were only 33 per cent and 18 per cent respectively.

This problematic conclusion would be eased if EMU were to be limited to a 'core' group comprising Germany, France, Belgium, Denmark and the Netherlands, potentially extended to Austria and one or two NMS in due course, since external shocks had a profoundly more symmetric effect upon this group of countries than the remaining EU member states. Correlation coefficients for this core group of 0.58 and 0.31, for supply and demand shocks respectively, compares favourably with the values calculated for US regions. The correlation coefficients of 0.14 and 0.10 for the remaining EU member states demonstrates that their participation in EMU would severely strain the ability of the ECB to formulate a monetary and exchange rate policy which would be equally appropriate for all countries. Thus, current discussions about whether Greece should withdraw from the euro, potentially followed by one or more struggling economies (i.e. Ireland, Spain, Portugal, Italy), appear to be beneficial for both nations and the EMU zone as a whole. Whilst a two-speed Europe has never proven to be a politically appealing scenario for EU leaders, it does appear to conform more closely to the available economic evidence (Bayoumi and Eichengreen, 1993).

The high degree of external shock asymmetry amongst EU member states highlights the potential cost of EMU in the absence of countervailing forces or government policies. In the absence of devaluation, a nation experiencing a loss of competitiveness, for example due to slow productivity growth or a cost-push raw material price shock, would experience rising unemployment unless price flexibility or factor mobility were sufficient to maintain full employment.

However, the available evidence from academic studies suggests that neither of these mechanisms can provide more than marginal assistance. The consensus reached by most of the literature on nominal and real wage rigidity in Europe is that between 25 per cent and 75 per cent of price rises are passed onto wages depending upon the country in question, thereby weakening real wage flexibility as an equilibrating mechanism to restore full employment in the aftermath of an asymmetric shock (Bruno and Sachs, 1985; Sala-i-Martin and Sachs, 1992; Goodhart, 1995).

Labour mobility within European countries has been estimated to be three times lower than in the United States despite the existence of greater regional inequality and unemployment in Europe, implying that EU labour mobility is less responsive to employment and income incentives than the US labour market (OECD, 1986; Eichengreen, 1992). This is despite evidence that the dispersion of external shocks to labour markets were of a broadly similar frequency and magnitude for Britain, Italy and the United States (Eichengreen, 1993b: 155). Moreover, these estimates relate to labour mobility *within* individual countries, whereas mobility *between* countries is likely to be much lower due to language barriers, differences in culture and residual non-recognition of qualifications (Ermisch, 1991: 93–108; Goodhart and Smith, 1993: 422). Thus, it may require substantially higher unemployment and regional inequality to generate labour mobility on the scale required to resolve regional imbalances in the absence of devaluation and wage/price flexibility. This would be equally destabilizing for EMU cohesion due to the political implications of large-scale emigration, together with the tensions created by unemployment and relative poverty within a Europe made more transparent through the introduction of a single currency. Indeed, it is possible that, as in Germany after reunification, labour market rigidity will increase as pay differential transparency generates demands for pay equalization between employees performing equivalent work in different countries, irrespective of productivity equalization, with potentially damaging effects to competitiveness, output and employment (Doyle, 1989; Horn and Zwiener, 1992; Goodhart, 1995).

Capital mobility can, in principal, substitute for labour mobility in the long-run, as the relocation of productive processes to depressed, inexpensive areas may occur. However, given the time lags involved in the movement of physical, as opposed to financial capital, such movements are likely to reduce long-term regional disparities rather than offset short-term external shocks. The weakness of capital mobility to reduce long-term structural inequalities within existing nation-states, together with the insights provided by studies in cumulative causation and endogenous growth theory, caution against over optimistic assumptions of a rapid elimination of unemployment caused by shocks (Myrdal, 1957; Romer, 1994). Moreover, due to the transactions costs involved, factor movements are an inefficient means of reacting to transitory regional shocks (von Hagen, 1993: 278).

One argument which is frequently presented in the literature is that the further economic integration of Europe may reduce the probability of asymmetric shocks, so that existing policy instruments would be sufficient to moderate these disturbances (Emerson *et al.*, 1992: 136). However, the prevalence of regional asymmetric shocks within existing EU nation-states may equally indicate that the industrial concentration accompanying economic integration may magnify the frequency and importance of asymmetric shocks (de Grauwe and Vanhaverbeke, 1993: 112–25). Enlargement of the EU has magnified the diversity of the single economy, whilst the current financial crisis amidst the Southern European members of the eurozone would appear to point to additional tensions between the longer established EU member states. In view of the divergence of academic opinion on this point, it would be unwise for the architects of EMU to rely upon economic integration to provide a sufficient, permanent reduction in asymmetric shocks in the absence of the introduction of economic instruments designed to ensure the stability of the monetary union.

Fiscal policy assignment

The persistence of asymmetric shocks within an EMU, where monetary and exchange rate policy is determined at the federal level, and where price flexibility and labour mobility are insufficient to sustain full employment equilibrium, leaves fiscal policy as the primary stabilizing instrument (Kenen, 1969, 1995: 81; Masson, 1996: 1002). Critics of the stabilizing potential of fiscal policy argue that automatic stabilizers are counter-productive since they reduce the strength of price flexibility and labour mobility (Goodhart and Smith, 1993: 441; van der Ploeg, 1993: 144). A non-accommodative monetary and fiscal stance is claimed to reduce the time lag involved in adjusting to a new equilibrium position as individual economic actors internalize more of the costs of their actions, whilst the operation of EMU may reduce persistent rigidities (Majocchi and Rey, 1993). Furthermore, it is suggested that international policy co-ordination may undermine central bank credibility and cause an unanticipated increase in inflation by weakening the disciplining effects of excessive monetary growth upon the exchange rate (van der Ploeg, 1993: 156). Finally, von Hagen (1993: 265) rejects what he terms the 'parallel unification proposition', namely that currency unification requires fiscal policy unification, although without examining the merits of a policy framework being developed between the extremes of either full fiscal autonomy or complete centralization at the federal level. However, despite these criticisms, unless the discipline effect of EMU is powerful and immediate, the persistence of price and factor rigidities would appear to necessitate the use of fiscal policy as a stabilizing instrument to reduce the incentive for any country to leave the EMU and as an, albeit imperfect, substitute for exchange rate flexibility.

The conclusion that fiscal policy may become the principal instrument with which to counteract asymmetric external shocks, and therein prevent the destabilization of EMU, raises the issue of whether it should be deployed at national or federal level. The adoption of the decentralization theorem or 'layer-cake' concept, whereby functions are performed by the lowest efficient layer of government, accords with the EU's professed belief in subsidiarity and would indicate an initial preference for national fiscal autonomy within EMU (Oates, 1972: 35; Bayoumi and Masson, 1995: 268). However, the operation of the SGP, in restricting the pursuit of counter-cyclical fiscal policy, has significantly constrained the operation of national fiscal policy (Burkitt *et al.*, 1996, 1997: 3–6; EU Commission, 1997: 12).

Autonomous fiscal policy is further undermined by the operation of the SM and the loss of tax revenue for certain member states caused by EMU. The requirement for the abolition of exchange controls, contained within the SM legislation, not only contributed to the currency instability during 1992–1993, but was intended to enhance financial market integration within the EU. However, such integration reduces the ability of member states to borrow cheaply to enable debt-financed fiscal expansion (Courchene, 1993: 152).

The potential reduction in fiscal flexibility would be compounded for those member states which currently depend upon seigniorage for a significant proportion of their total tax revenue. This relates to the circumstances where the purchasing power of government securities is eroded by inflation, thus providing an inexpensive method to finance public expenditure by, in effect, borrowing at very low real rates of interest. A stable EMU would require a convergence in national inflation rates and, assuming that the ECB achieved the low inflation target established in its founding chapter, seigniorage would be limited to an estimated 0.4 per cent of GDP for all participants. This would particularly affect Portugal, as seigniorage revenues totalled 3.6 per cent of its GDP in 1990, whilst Greece (2.3 per cent), Spain (1.9 per cent) and Italy (1.3 per cent) would also lose a significant proportion of budget revenue (Dornbusch, 1988: 26; Eichengreen, 1993: 1335–6; Spahn, 1993: 577). Thus, the fiscal drain experienced by certain member states would cause fiscal retrenchment independently of the additional requirements imposed by the MCC (Masson, 1996).

The restrictions placed upon national fiscal policy during the transition to, and the subsequent operation of, EMU may, therefore, necessitate the enlargement of federal fiscal expenditure to ensure the stability of the European economy. This conclusion is reinforced by three further considerations. First, governments may not undertake an optimal level of counter-cyclical stabilization due to the existence of regional spillovers or externalities, whereby non-residents derive some benefit from the policy whilst residents must bear the full cost through higher debt or taxation. Factor mobility could also constrain governments from incurring high levels of debt since the risk of higher future taxes may encourage factor relocation to other regions, thus reducing the tax base and providing short-term stability at the price of long-term instability. To the extent that this prisoner's dilemma constrains government fiscal flexibility, the solution requires a co-ordinated stabilization strategy solution typical of non-co-operative game settings, necessitating either horizontal co-operation amongst member states or centralization under a federal authority (Rompuy *et al.*, 1993: 112–13).

Second, assuming that adverse shocks occur randomly, an inter-regional public insurance scheme can redistribute income from 'favourably shocked' to

'adversely shocked' regions to prevent an 'unlucky' area bearing a disproportionate financial burden. Moral hazard is minimized by ensuring that no incentives exist which encourage potential beneficiaries to manipulate the scheme to
their advantage and in so doing to discourage participation from other regions
(Wyplotz, 1993: 181; Courchene, 1993: 134–5).

Finally, the need to strengthen the cohesion of EMU through redistribution of
resources to weaker regions, which reinforces political and social solidarity
throughout all participating member states, may entail a significantly enhanced
role for federal financial authority. It does appear to be the case that all mature
monetary unions exhibit a significant degree of redistribution between wealthy
and poorer regions (Bayoumi and Masson, 1995).

Necessary level of stabilization

The experience of existing federations confirms the necessity for a federal
system of fiscal transfers between regions to promote stabilization and redistribution across the EMU zone. The path-breaking study conducted by Sala-i-
Martin and Sachs (1992) claimed that US federal fiscal policy offset
approximately 40 per cent of an initial $1 decline in average gross regional
product (GRP). However, this was challenged due to its failure to differentiate
between the cyclical and structural effects of fiscal policy. Von Hagen (1992)
argued that the stabilization effect of US federal fiscal policy was a mere 10
per cent, whilst Goodhart and Smith (1993) found 14 per cent of an initial
reduction in GRP offset by a combination of fiscal transfers and federal taxes.
These later studies were criticized, in turn, for underestimating the degree of
stabilization by narrowly focusing upon federal income taxes thereby neglect-
ing other federal taxes. The importance of this omission is clear from the simulation undertaken by Pisani-Ferry *et al.* (1993) where non-income federal
taxation generated a greater stabilizing influence than income taxation, leading
to a 17.1 per cent stabilization effect for the United States, whilst Bayoumi
and Masson (1995) found 30.2 per cent fiscal stabilization using a similar
methodology. The conflicting results produced by these studies impair the formation of a consensus concerning the scale of fiscal federalism necessary to
stabilize an EMU. However, the weight of evidence suggests that US fiscal
policy produces a stabilizing effect between 17 per cent and 30 per cent of an
initial external shock.

The generality of the conclusions reached by the literature require a comparison of the US results with those from additional federations. Accordingly, both
Goodhart and Smith (1993) and Bayoumi and Masson (1995) reproduced their
analysis using Canadian data and found a significantly larger stabilizing effect,
calculated at 24 per cent and 17.4 per cent respectively. Furthermore, Pisani-
Ferry *et al.* (1993) calculated that Germany achieved 42 per cent stabilization
through the interaction of taxation policy and fiscal transfers. These estimates
are largely consistent with the range of results from the United States, although
the apparently more pronounced counter-cyclical effectiveness of European

fiscal policy cannot be relied upon on the basis of only one study. Further research is therefore necessary to produce more reliable estimates on which a European Federal Transfer Scheme (EFTS) may rely, whilst additionally ascertaining whether predominantly North American evidence can legitimately be applied to the EU.

Fiscal federalism appears to perform a necessary stabilizing function through the counter-cyclical impact of taxation and fiscal transfers, moderating between 17 per cent and 30 per cent of an initial shock for North American federations. It is a reasonable hypothesis to assume that a European EMU federation might prefer a degree of stabilization at the higher end of this range, as a result of a historically more vigorous pursuit of social solidarity demonstrated through their higher welfare expenditure.

The current EU budget, equivalent to only 1.24 per cent of EU GDP, is too small to exert a significant stabilizing effect upon EMU regions in the advent of an asymmetric external shock, with structural funds accounting for a minority of this expenditure. Indeed, the present budget size limits the EU's ability to enhance member state stabilization to an estimated paltry 3 per cent, which is clearly inadequate in relation to the stabilization achieved by mature federations (Eichengreen, 1994: 186; Bayoumi and Masson, 1995: 266). Therefore, a plausible case exists for the enlargement of federal fiscal capability. The question concerns whether this occurs as part of the existing EU budget, thereby facilitating discretionary fiscal policy, or whether a system of automatic stabilizers should be established.

Discretionary or automatic stabilizers

Discretionary fiscal federalism was most notably advanced by the EU Commission's MacDougall Report. It suggested that asymmetric shocks could be countered by counter-cyclical grants made to regional or local governments, triggered by regional unemployment or GDP trend indicators, supplemented with an EU unemployment fund which would provide a direct fiscal injection into areas experiencing above average unemployment (MacDougall, 1977). The latter could be partly financed through individual contributions, although this would require unanimity across all member states concerning the absolute or proportionate payments made by taxpayers and companies to the fund, as well as the level of benefits received by individuals. German reunification experience suggests that such a scheme might increase demands for wage and benefit equalization throughout the EMU zone, as differentials become more visible irrespective of productivity differences, with resultant negative economic consequences. However, the transfer of certain social insurance programmes to the federal level receives wide support within the literature (Masson and Melitz, 1990; MacDougall, 1992). The MacDougall Report further advocated the expansion of redistributional transfers to reduce interregional differences in capital endowment and productivity. Thus, MacDougall's combination of policy measures required the gradual extension of the

EU budget from 2–2.5 per cent of GDP, in the transition period to EMU formation, to 5–7 per cent of EU GDP in the early years of EMU and ultimately expanding to 20–25 per cent of EU GDP in a mature EMU (MacDougall, 1992: 65; Majocchi and Rey, 1993: 473).

Discretionary fiscal policy is, however, criticized on two principal grounds. First, the New Classical approach perceives no justification for discretionary fiscal policy, and certainly not for its use as a counter-cyclical Keynesian mechanism, preferring to encourage economic authorities to develop a reputation for economic orthodoxy which would facilitate rule-based fiscal policy (Kydland and Prescott, 1977). A second criticism, however, concerns the imperfect availability of information which causes recognition and implementation time lags, thereby delaying the impact of discretionary policies by a sufficiently large margin that their effects may become *de-stabilizing* (Friedman, 1953; Baumol, 1961; Fisher and Cooper, 1973). Automatic stabilizers eliminate the implementation lag experienced in democratic countries, where major fiscal decisions are typically presented in an annual budget. Therefore, they reduce the probability of any destabilizing impact. Goodhart and Smith (1993: 432) further claim that the transparency of automatic stabilizers enables economic actors to internalize their effects when forming expectations.

An EFTS could ensure an equitable distribution of the gains and losses resulting from the impact of asymmetric shocks within EMU, whilst conforming to the subsidiarity principal because transfers are determined at the federal level but implemented locally (van der Ploeg, 1993: 144). Moreover, if borrowing is permitted to promote counter-cyclical stabilization, whilst ensuring that the budget is balanced over the economic cycle, the EFTS would avoid intertemporal debt redistribution (van der Ploeg, 1993: 144). Careful design can generate an EFTS which is a more efficient stabilizer than existing tax and transfer systems that developed to fulfil alternative objectives.

One proposal made by Italianer and Vanheukelen (1993) aims to achieve a similar degree of stabilization as the fiscal federalism of the United States for an average annual cost of ecu 11.2 billion, which is the equivalent of only 0.23 per cent of EU GDP (Italianer and Vanheukelen, 1993: 500). A more recent EFTS proposal places the average annual cost at between 0.17 per cent and 0.86 per cent of EU GDP for securing an 18 per cent stabilization of an initial shock within an EMU consisting of all current member states, whereas a more substantial 40 per cent stabilization target would cost between 0.38 and 1.9 per cent of EU GDP per annum, depending upon precise estimates of the elasticity of output loss associated with higher unemployment (Whyman, 1997). Thus, both studies conclude that a similar degree of stabilization may be achieved at a fraction of the central budget increases advocated by MacDougall, due to the greater efficiency of a stabilization system designed solely to perform that function. Moreover, it is possible that smaller, better targeted fiscal interventions can have a greater proportionate impact upon redistribution and income inequality than larger fiscal programmes (Costello, 1993: 274–7).

Distributional effects

Evaluation of discretionary and automatic federal fiscal policy measures depends upon their ability to stabilize EMU combined with their distributional impact upon the individual member states. Put simply, fiscal federalism works through the transfer of funds from economies out-performing the eurozone average to those under-performing, with the amounts determined by the size of the schemes involved and the scale of stabilization intended to achieve. Even assuming a particularly targeted initiative, the net transfers for individual member states can be quite substantial. One estimation suggests that the fiscal burden for the largest contributors to a fiscal federal scheme would have to be significant – comprising upwards of 3 per cent of GDP and figures exceeding 6 per cent of national budgetary expenditure – for any scheme to make an appreciable macroeconomic difference (Whyman, 1997b; Baimbridge and Whyman, 2008: 138–45). Amounts of this magnitude would require significant tax rises and/or expenditure reductions, or, alternatively, the transfer of substantial elements of current national spending to a federal level.

European financial stability facility

The type of conflict of interest, and resistance to fiscal federalism on behalf of national electorates, can be witnessed in the currently evolving sovereign debt crisis amongst certain EU member states; most notably Greece, Ireland, Spain, Italy and Portugal. The creation of the €440 billion European Financial Stability Facility (EFSF) is intended to provide medium-term security for the eurozone, by creating an instrument able to intervene on secondary financial markets to purchase the bonds of struggling debtor participant nations from the private sector investors who currently hold the assets.[2] The intention is to prevent fears over the insolvency of the debtor nations from causing a withdrawal of credit and substantially raising interest rates, thereby exacerbating their existing financial problems. Essentially, the EFSF would be nationalizing (or Europeanizing, I suppose would be more accurate) potentially bad debts, in the same way as many governments responded in their own markets during the recent 'credit crunch' financial crisis. Private investors would take a 'haircut' (receiving less than the full paper value of the assets) to prevent creating undue moral hazard, which would occur if investors didn't suffer any consequences for poor lending decisions.

The 15-point draft agreement on the creation of the EFSF is an interesting watershed moment for the eurozone. At one level, it demonstrates the practical and political problems inherent in the creation of fiscal federalism – i.e. that even at a time of considerable crisis, it has proven difficult to craft an innovation which all parties find acceptable. Indeed, this remains a framework agreement, and the detail of how this new fiscal policy instrument will operate and evolve in the future remains imprecise. Yet, the fact remains that this first, tentative step in the creation of some form of federal fiscal intervention has been taken, and the pressure of events will necessitate further developments during the following months and years, as the destabilization caused by the 'credit crunch' play out. This is comforting for those advocates of fiscal federalism being a necessary but not sufficient feature of a sustainable EMU.

A second aspect of the EFSF is less advantageous, however, since the financial support packages are intended to be reinforced by a stricter interpretation of the SGP. This is perhaps not a surprising condition to be placed upon debtor nations, as contributors to the schemes wish to limit their payments, under pressure from discontented taxpayers at home, and so they require a rapid fiscal consolidation on behalf of debtor nations, bringing deficits within the SGP limits during a very short two-year time period. Moreover, the 15-point proposal additionally includes proposals to strengthen the scrutiny of individual nations' fiscal plans and legal restraints to be placed upon national budgets.[3] Thus, the combination of the financial rescue schemes appears to provide sufficient short-term credit to debtor nations to enable them to deflate their economies in order to return to close to financial balance, without the ability to devalue (due to participation in the single currency) and at a time when most of the rest of the world is experiencing constrained economic growth prospects. This would appear to be too close to the UK preoccupation with the maintenance of the Gold Standard at an uncompetitive rate, combined with the disastrous response to budget deficits arising amidst the Great Depression – both squeezing growth prospects in order to try and balance the economy, and instead pushing the economy onto a downward spiral of negative growth and deteriorating budgetary position.[4]

Conclusion

The sustainability of EMU in the medium- and long-term will partly depend upon the implementation of a fiscal policy initiative, located at the federal rather than national level, which is sufficiently well resourced and targeted to stabilize member state economies in the face of asymmetric external shocks. Failure to do so leaves monetary union fatally exposed to asymmetric external shocks and divergent economic forces. In the absence of exchange rate or monetary autonomy, and with insufficient labour mobility and wage flexibility, individual regions may become characterized by persistent unemployment, low per capita income and ensuing social tension, coexisting in the EMU zone with neighbours enjoying full employment, high growth and greater prosperity. The cost, in terms of lost output and avoidable human misery, is compounded by the probability of countries withdrawing from EMU should such inequalities continue over a long period. The reluctance of many economists and policy-makers to address this problem is therefore of particular concern, given that EMU was instituted on 1 January 1999.

This chapter suggests that the development of a discretionary or semi-automatic stabilization mechanism is both feasible and essential for EMU to succeed. However, this will involve significant claims upon the productive resources of the majority of EU member states and generate difficult budgetary considerations for national governments. The EFSF demonstrates the difficulties in the creation of a fully functioning fiscal federalism across the eurozone, and yet it might itself develop into such a scheme, if it is allowed to evolve beyond a short-term solution to a specific problem into a permanent feature of EMU architecture. However, for this move to be successful, EU member states will have to confront the fact that the combination of the SGP and the constraints further strengthened by the EFSF might be viewed as positive in curbing excessive fiscal behaviour amongst participating economies, but this is simultaneously deflationary and growth-dampening, thereby exacerbating the existing tensions and diversity within the eurozone – indeed, the very things that a properly functioning stabilization scheme would be designed to counter. Thus, in attempting to solve an immediate problem, within constraints imposed by national electoral considerations, the question that remains unresolved is whether the current moves towards fiscal federalism within EMU constitute the type of long-term solution to asymmetries discussed in this chapter, or a missed opportunity. Only time will tell.

10 European social policy

Constructing a European Social Model and defending the European model of society?

Introduction

This chapter provides an overview of the development of European social policy during the CWO and NWO periods and, in so doing, it challenges the claim put forward by Ebbinghaus (1999), Hantrais (2007) and others that European social policy aimed to construct an ESM so as to defend the European model of society. The chapter advances four main arguments. First, that the European social policy agenda was consistently subjugated to the economic imperatives of competitiveness and economic liberalization and was not valued in its own right. Second, that the reification of market liberalism, the bias towards negative integration, the choice of social regulation and the EEC/EC/EU-level preferences for competition and economic liberalization conspired to preclude the creation of a common, Europe-wide social model and/or a unified EEC/EC/EU-level welfare state. Third, that during the CWO the EEC/EC influenced the nature and trajectory of Western Europe welfare states in a structural rather than direct sense. Fourth, that in the NWO the EC/EU aimed to influence the development of these entities in a direct as well as structural sense.

The chapter is divided into three main sections. The first section explores Europe's preference for soft rather than hard law in terms of European social policy development. The second section assesses the development of European social policy during the CWO. The third section evaluates the development of European social policy in the NWO.

European social policy: hard versus soft law

Europe's legal sources of authority included primary legislation, in the form of EEC/EC/EU treaties, and secondary legislation encompassing decisions, directives and regulations. These constituted hard law instruments in the sense that they were binding upon member states, which were obliged to implement them. By contrast, the soft law instruments of opinions, recommendations and Resolutions were advisory, while communications and memoranda were used to set out initial thoughts.

In terms of *hard law*, each of the EEC/EC/EU treaties contained a section on the social aspects of European integration which set out the main objectives of European social policy. These became increasingly complex and expansive over time as the treaties were revised and updated. Several directives were produced in the wake of the 1989 Social Charter, which set down the objectives for legislation but left member states to draft and implement the legislation. With the exception of those relating to the free movement of workers and the structural funds, very few regulations concerning social policy have been issued. In terms of *soft law*, 'recommendations have played an important role in developing a framework for concerted action and convergence of social policy' (Hantrais, 2007: 19). In short, there has been a clear preference at the European level for the soft law approach.

European social policy during the CWO

European social policy development during the CWO was shaped by the 1957 EEC Treaty, the 1961 Council of Europe social charter and the 1974 EC Social Action Programme.

The EEC Treaty

Of the 248 clauses in the EEC Treaty, ratified in March 1957, only 12 related to social policy. In Article 117, member states agreed to promote improved working conditions and an improved standard of living for workers. These would be delivered, it claimed, through the functioning of the Common Market, which purportedly favoured the harmonization of social systems, as a result of the procedures provided for in the EEC Treaty and from the approximation of provisions laid down by administrative action, law or regulation. The two-stage approximation process involved, first, the identification of administrative and legislative 'gaps' in member states' provision and, second, the issuance of guidance – and under Article 100, legally binding directives – to ensure compliance and to eliminate any differences among member states that might distort competition.

Article 118 stated that the European Commission should promote close co-operation between member states in matters relating to the right of association, collective bargaining, employment, labour law, the prevention of occupational accidents and diseases, occupational hygiene, social security, training and working conditions. It did not specify, however, how such co-operation should be achieved. Furthermore, it made clear that the European Commission was not compelled to produce legislation; instead, it suggested that the European Commission should liaise with member states to arrange consultations, deliver opinions and produce studies on the problems arising at the national and EEC level.

Article 119 established the principle of equal pay for equal work. Article 121 aimed to ensure common social security benefits for migrant workers, while Articles 123–8 set out the operational arrangements for the ESF which was created to ensure geographical and occupational mobility within Europe. Critically, however, the EEC Treaty neglected to address the differential entitlements and levels of welfare benefits amongst the Six; the EEC focus on removing barriers to competition meant that it did not see fit to 'interfere with redistributive benefits' which remained 'a matter for individual member states' (Collins, 1975: 9).

The limited nature of these articles led Hantrais (2007: 2, 3) to conclude that the EEC Treaty 'did not set the framework for a fully developed European social policy', and that the failure of the Six 'to agree about objectives and to set up mechanisms for achieving them led to ... a cautious, modest and narrowly focused social policy'. Collins (1975: 31) went further and argued that the EEC Treaty was 'broadly educational and promotional' in the sense that it left member states to 'define their own approaches to social policy'. In so doing, the EEC Treaty established the parameters and pattern for the subsequent development of European social policy: the prioritization of competition and economic liberalization and the subjugation of European social policy to these goals, the preoccupation with labour as a factor of production and the reluctance to directly intervene in national social systems.

The Council of Europe Social Charter

The intergovernmental Council of Europe issued its draft social charter in October 1961. The document was heralded as the economic and social counterpart to the European Convention on Human Rights, agreed in November 1950. The social charter established a set of policy objectives which aimed to guarantee the fundamental rights of citizens and workers. These included the rights to work, to decent, healthy and safe working conditions, to fair pay, to organize and collectively bargain, to protection for children and young people, to protection for working women, to vocational guidance and training, to health care, to social security and to welfare benefits, plus rights in several other areas. Although it did not have the same legally binding status of the convention, the social charter, which was ratified by all member states and came into effect in February 1965, served as a 'prototype' for the EEC according to Hantrais (2007).

The 1974 Social Action Programme

The Council of Ministers passed a Resolution in January 1974 which called for an EC Social Action Programme. Having declared that vigorous action in the social field was just as important as economic integration, the Council of Ministers sanctioned a set of concrete measures and agreed upon some ESF funding to bring about full and better employment, improved living and working conditions, greater involvement of managers and workers in economic and social decision-making, and the involvement of workers in their enterprises. Critically, however, the Resolution asserted that

The Council considers that the Community social policy has an individual role to play and should make an essential contribution to achieving the aforementioned objectives by means of Community measures or the definition by the Community of objectives for national social policies, without however seeking a standard solution to all social problems or attempting to transfer to Community level any responsibilities which are assumed more effectively at other levels.

(Council of Ministers, 1974: 2)

In short, and prefiguring the 1990s concept of subsidiarity, the Social Action Programme reaffirmed that the EEC Treaty did not require social policy action and it conceded that the EC possessed no instruments to directly intervene and so was reliant upon the 'political will' of member states. Nevertheless, during the 1970s there was some progress in terms of education, health and safety at work, poverty alleviation, training, women's rights and workers' rights.

European social policy in the NWO

European social policy development during the NWO was influenced by the 1985 social dialogue process, the 1986 SEA, the 1989 Social Charter, the 1991 Agreement on Social Policy, the 1993 and 1994 Green and White Papers, and the 1995–2000 Social Action Programmes. It was also shaped by the 1997 Amsterdam Treaty, the 2000 Charter of Fundamental Rights, the 2000 social policy agenda and the 2007 Lisbon Treaty.

The social dialogue process

The Delors presidency of the European Commission from January 1985 provided a new impetus to European social policy development. Delors' dream of creating a European social space with new regulatory frameworks was based upon the social dialogue process. Facilitating discussions between representatives of both employers and workers – more specifically the European Centre of Public Enterprises, the Union of Industrial and Employers' Confederations of Europe and the ETUC – at Val Duchesse in January and November 1985, Delors' hoped to

engage employers and unions in habits of discussion which, in time, might create mutual respect and trust and eventuate in more substantial 'contractual' conclusions. In addition, the process might help transform the actors themselves into agents with the power to deal.

(Ross, 1995: 45)

Furthermore, Delors exploited his social democratic credentials to help bring this about:

With labour, Delors could play on the studied ambiguities of his own position: '1992' was a liberal programme, but Delors himself was a social

democrat known for his strong advocacy of negotiation. Delors had inti-
mated, beginning with his speech to the European Parliament in January
1985, that completing the single market would necessitate 'flanking' programmes, including social programmes, and labour was attentive to this.
[Furthermore] labour leaders were hostage to Delors to the degree to which
they were aware that they were unlikely to get a better deal or a more sympathetic leadership than from him.

(Ibid.: 38)

Delors' expectation was that the 'social partners' would initiate social policy –
drawing up proposals containing general principles and objectives – on the
understanding that the European Commission would refrain from legislating and
that member states would transpose these principles and objectives into statute.
Although the Val Duchesse process initially achieved very little, as the employers refused to sign the negotiated texts unless the European Commission promised not to use the joint opinions as the basis for legislation, the social dialogue
process generated 21 joint opinions, seven high-level summits and two key
agreements between 1986 and 1995. The social dialogue process, with its
emphasis on consensus-building and voluntarism, exemplified Europe's preference for social regulation (Majone, 1996) over traditional (i.e. adversarial and
involuntary) social policy.

The SEA

The SEA, agreed in December 1985, revised EC social policy in five important
ways. First, in the preamble to the SEA, signatories agreed to work together to
promote the fundamental rights set down in the Council of Europe's European
Convention on Human Rights and its social charter. Second, the new Article
100a extended QMV to decision-making relating to the approximation of provisions for the establishment and functioning of the internal market. Fiscal provisions, the free movement of people and workers' rights were excluded however,
and these areas continued to be governed by the unanimity rule. Third, the new
Article 118a called for the harmonization of health and safety legislation. It
extended QMV to decision-making in this area and introduced a new co-
operation procedure which strengthened the role of the European Parliament in
the legislative process and imposed time limits. Fourth, the new Article 118b
officially recognized the social dialogue process at the EC level. Fifth, the new
treaty section, Title V, committed the EC to economic and social cohesion and
Articles 130a–e specified how the improved coordination of structural funds
could deliver such cohesion.

The Social Charter

Signed in December 1989 by all member states bar Britain, and heralded as the
social dimension of the SEA, the Community Charter of the Fundamental Social

Rights of Workers (i.e. the Social Charter) reaffirmed the EC objective of social policy harmonization. It suffered from two limitations however. First, like the Council of Europe social charter, it was not legally binding. Instead, it took the form of a 'solemn declaration' that left the implementation of measures to individual member states. Second, it focused upon the rights of workers rather than the broader rights of citizens.

Invited by the European Council to prepare a set of proposals, the European Commission responded by producing an Action Programme containing 47 supply-side-oriented proposals covering the freedom of movement of workers, collective bargaining, equality, health and safety, training, etc. The Action Programme had two main aims:

> To establish a sound base of minimum provisions, having regard on the one hand to the need to avoid any distortion of competition, and on the other to support moves to strengthen economic and social cohesion and contribute to the creation of jobs, which is the prime concern of completion of the internal market.
>
> (European Commission, 1989: 5)

The EC again demonstrated its reluctance to pursue social objectives for their own sake and to intervene to enforce standards.

The agreement on social policy

The expectation that the Social Charter would be integrated into the Maastricht Treaty, agreed in December 1991, evaporated when Britain insisted that it be removed from the treaty and appended as a separate protocol. The resulting Agreement on Social Policy, endorsed by the other 11 member states, replaced Article 117 of the EEC Treaty with Article 1 which pledged to pursue the promotion of employment, improved living and working conditions, proper social protection, dialogue between management and labour, the development of human resources with a view to lasting high employment and the combating of exclusion. Significantly, it also pledged to take account of the diverse forms of national practices, in particular in the field of contractual relations, and the need to maintain the competitiveness of Europe's economy. The EEC Treaty objective of social policy harmonization was thus abandoned.

Article 2 declared that the EU would work with member states in the areas of equality between men and women, health and safety at work, information and consultation of workers, the integration of people excluded from the labour market and working conditions. It also empowered the European Council to issue directives on the areas to member states, although small and medium-sized enterprises were to be exempted. The areas of conditions of employment for third-country nationals, financial assistance for job promotion, the protection of workers made redundant, representation and collective defence of employers and workers, and social security and social protection of workers were exempted, however, and were subject to unanimous voting by the 11 signatories. The areas of the right to association, the right to impose lock-outs, pay and the right to strike were excluded from the protocol altogether. Article 3 codified the social dialogue process by specifying that the European Commission had to consult the 'social partners' about the direction and content of proposals, and that the 'social partners' could forward an opinion or recommendation to the EU to initiate the agreement process.

The Green Paper and White Paper on European Social Policy

The European Commission issued a Green Paper on European Social Policy in November 1993, as part of a wide-ranging review of social policy across the EU, which invited contributions on the future objectives, measures and targets that member states and other social actors would find acceptable. It focused on the areas of equal opportunities, the labour market, social protection and exclusion, and training, and more than 500 submissions were deposited with the European Commission. The White Paper on European Social Policy, published in July 1994, stated that

> The objective in the coming period must be to preserve and develop the European Social Model as we move towards the 21st Century, to give the people of Europe the unique blend of economic well-being, social cohesiveness and high overall quality of life which was achieved in the post-war period.
>
> (European Commission, 1994: 1)

It asserted that the ESM was underpinned by a particular set of values – democracy and individual rights, free collective bargaining, the market economy, equality of opportunity for all, and social welfare and solidarity – and it argued that an 'innovative' and forward-looking' social policy was essential if Europe was to meet the challenges of globalization. Nevertheless, it made clear that Europe's main priority was to tackle unemployment and that to achieve this, improved competitiveness and labour market reforms by member states were crucial. Indeed, together with the 1993 'Growth Competitiveness, Employment' document, these White Papers explicitly committed European economic and social policy to the reform of Western Europe's welfare states. In contrast to the CWO, the EU in the NWO increasingly sought to influence both the nature and trajectory of these formations.

The 1995–2000 Social Action Programmes

Exploiting the momentum generated by the Green and White Papers, the European Commission launched its medium-term Social Action Programme in April 1995. The 1995–1997 Social Action Programme prioritized job creation and it stated that responsibility for this lay with member states. It declared, however, that the European Commission has a special role to play in promoting the changes needed to overcome the serious structural deficiencies [highlighted in the 1993 White Paper] and to strengthen their competitiveness. Overcoming such weaknesses requires the adaptation of overall employment systems, including the interplay of taxation and social policies, of lifelong education and training, and of industrial, environmental and regional policies.

(European Commission, 1995: 2)

Reaffirming the objectives of the 1989 Social Charter and 1991 Agreement on Social Policy, the programme extended European social policy into the new areas of disability, older people, poverty, public health, racism, anti-Semitism and xenophobia. Towards the end of this period, in March 1997, the European Commission published a review of the Social Action Programme which asserted that European social policy was a productive factor rather than a burden or obstacle to economic growth. It emphasized the growing importance of multi-level governance (i.e. civil society, member states, 'social partners', etc.) for European social policy development and implementation. It stressed the need to 'modernize' Europe's welfare states to meet the challenges of an aging population and workforce. It highlighted the changing nature of work, more specifically the rise in the number of part-time and temporary jobs, the increased number of working women and the need to coordinate social security schemes so as to support people moving within the EU. It also recommended the development of active employment policies, entailing the revision of social security and taxation systems, and the need to reform national health and pension systems (European Commission, 1997).

The European Commission launched another Social Action Programme in April 1998. Acknowledging that unemployment across Europe remained stubbornly high and that poverty and social exclusion existed alongside prosperity and wealth, the 1998–2000 Social Action Programme identified the challenges facing the EU: demographic changes, enlargement, globalization, the introduction of the single currency and the completion of the SM (European Commission, 1998). Towards the end of this period, in July 1999, the European Commission published a review of the Social Action Programme and concluded that the primary purpose of European social policy was to equip individuals for the changing world of work. This required concerted economic and social policy action to create sustainable health and pension systems, to promote social inclusion and to ensure that 'work pays' (European Commission, 1999).

The Amsterdam Treaty

Following the British opt-in, the Agreement on Social Policy was formally incorporated into the Amsterdam Treaty which was agreed in June 1997. No new social provisions were included. The treaty reemphasized that social policy was an area of shared competence and that the role of the EU was to support member states. The treaty also included an employment chapter which provided the foundations for the EES and EEP. These consolidated the integration of European economic and social policy and reaffirmed the supply-side agenda.

The Charter of Fundamental Rights

The Nice Treaty, agreed in February 2001, revised the decision-making procedures of the EU. Some of these had implications for European social policy development. More specifically, QMV and co-decision with the European Parliament were extended to anti-discrimination measures, aspects of economic and social cohesion, and labour mobility. The Nice Treaty also included the Charter of Fundamental Rights which expanded upon the worker-focused 1989 Social Charter, 1991 Agreement on Social Policy and 1997 Amsterdam Treaty social chapter by setting out 50 fundamental rights enjoyed by EU citizens. New areas, in terms of European social policy, included the rights to protection for children and older people, health care, housing and social assistance, religious belief and work–life balance. It also established the right to strike, which prompted the New Labour government in Britain to veto the charter. It was subsequently adopted as a 'solemn proclamation', which meant that it was not legally binding.

The social policy agenda

The European Commission launched its social policy agenda in June 2000. Covering the 2000–2005 period, the document stated that

> This Social Policy Agenda forms part of the integrated European approach towards achieving the economic and social renewal outlined at Lisbon. Specifically, it seeks to ensure the positive and dynamic interaction of economic, employment and social policy, and to forge a political agreement which mobilizes all key actors to work jointly towards the new strategic goal.
>
> (European Commission, 2000: 2)

Reiterating the argument put forward in the 1995–1997 Social Action Programme, that European social policy was a productive factor, and recycling the Lisbon Strategy themes, the agenda advocated the creation of more and better jobs, the 'modernization' of social protection, gender equality and the realization of fundamental rights – focusing in particular on discrimination. Reaffirming the approach adopted since 1991, the agenda stated unequivocally that the EU was not seeking social policy harmonization and that no new monies were required. Instead, it favoured the 'redirection of public expenditure to improve efficiency and investment in people' (ibid.: 7).

The Lisbon Treaty

The Lisbon Treaty, agreed in October 2007, preserved the status of social policy as a shared competence between member states and the EU but incorporated the

Charter of Fundamental Rights and thus granted it legal force. The treaty attributed new social objectives to the EU. These included full employment, equality, the combating of poverty and social exclusion, social justice and solidarity between the generations. The treaty established a 'social clause' which asserted that EU social objectives must be taken into account when defining and implementing all policies. The treaty also extended QMV to combating social exclusion and the modernization of social protection systems.

Conclusion

During the CWO, European social policy was relatively underdeveloped when compared to European economic policy. The pre-eminence of the market liberal model, manifest in the four freedoms of the EEC Treaty, hindered any attempt at positive integration. The prioritization of competition and economic liberalization, so as to create a common market and customs union, reinforced the negative integration bias of the EEC Treaty and resulted in a minimalist European social policy. Essentially, social policy was treated as a means to an end and not as an end in itself. The EEC objective of social policy harmonization, established by the EEC Treaty, was aspirational. Despite the 1974 Social Action Programme, there was no attempt to devise and enforce common standards, whether downwards or upwards harmonization, and, consequently, no Europe-wide social model and/or a unified EEC/EC-level welfare state developed. During this period, the EEC/EC did not attempt to directly determine the nature of Western Europe's welfare states – hence the persistence of welfare state diversity – but it did shape their trajectory in a structural sense.

In the NWO, some aspects of European social policy remained the same. The CWO limitations of European social policy – the subjugation of social policy to economic goals and the preoccupation with labour as a factor of production – persisted in the NWO. During the CWO, the EEC/EC ostensibly favoured social policy harmonization but lacked the political will and policy instruments to realize this. Consequently, no Europe-wide social model or EEC/EC-level welfare state developed. In the NWO, the objective of harmonization was abandoned in favour of respecting national differences in social systems but the effect was the same: no EU-level welfare state developed. Indeed, 'no proposals were put forward' by the EU institutions or the members states 'for a European social union' (Hantrais, 2007: 260).

Other aspects of European social policy changed significantly however. Three main differences can be identified. First, social policy was the preserve of member states during the CWO and EEC/EC action was voluntary. In the NWO, by contrast, the extension of EU competence to ever more areas of social life, whether that competence was exclusive or shared, meant that European social policy increasingly possessed legal force. Indeed, European social policy developed exponentially following the neo-liberal turn in 1985 such that 'few areas of social life remain untouched by official regulations, directives, decisions, recommendations, resolutions, communications or memoranda' (ibid.). Second,

European social policy during the CWO was formulated and deployed in the traditional sense (i.e. imposed by a central authority on other social actors). In the NWO, by contrast, the EU utilized social regulation (i.e. the social dialogue process) to augment the traditional social policy approach. Third, the EEC/EC was reluctant to intervene in national social systems during the CWO. In the NWO, by contrast, the EU developed a range of economic and social policy instruments, which were increasingly integrated, to 'reform' and 'modernize' Western Europe's welfare states. Over time, 'market forces and ECJ rulings had contributed to a gradual and irreversible erosion of national sovereignty and autonomy over welfare systems' (ibid.: 263).

The last point begs two important and interrelated questions: what was the aim of such intervention? Did the EEC/EC/EU aim to construct an ESM so as to defend the European model of society? The official European view, echoed by Ebbinghaus (1999), Adnett and Hardy (2005), Leibfried (2005) and Hantrais (2007), was that

> Rather than simply taking the form of a multi-tiered welfare system made up of the sum of its parts, the European Social Model was depicted as embodying core values, to which member states were committed and that they were prepared to nurture and protect. Whether national social protection systems were based on employment-related insurance of universal benefits funded primarily from taxation, and the extent to which they were controlled by, and dependent on, central government or the market were largely irrelevant. What mattered was that policies were being pursued with a common objective: 'to promote a decent quality of life and standard of living for all in an active, inclusive and healthy society that encourages access to employment, good working conditions, and equality of opportunity' [European Commission, 1998: 3].
>
> (Hantrais, 2007: 260–1)

Furthermore, whether or not this was achieved

> depended on the extent to which the Union's institutions could successfully weave together EU hard law, the social dialogue and active soft law into a hybrid system of regulation capable of accommodating diversity and of gaining the support of both governments and their electorates.
>
> (Ibid.: 263)

There are two fundamental problems with this position. First, as discussed in Chapter 3, there is no such thing as an ESM. Second, the evidence presented in Chapters 4, 5 and 14 suggests that Europe's social models are moving towards the market liberal model and away from the 'common objective' cited above.

11 Social partnership and labour market flexibility

Introduction

One of the central tenets of the ESM involves the creation of social partnership between employer and employee representatives in order to develop positive-sum solutions to issues pertaining to industrial relations. Social partnership between peak level actors is, additionally, intended to develop a wider legitimacy for the EU's decision-making process, and tailor directives to meet the requirements of those most closely affected by work-related relations. However, this model of inclusivity is contrasted against another stated aim advanced by the EU in the years since the production of the Lisbon Treaty, namely the promotion of a more flexible labour market. It is, therefore, this potential contradiction that this chapter examines.

The social partnership model

The maximal (strong) conception of the ESM has social partnership as a core proposition, whereby the promotion of interaction between social partners – employers and employees – is assumed to facilitate positive-sum solutions to mutual problems. This approach emphasizes the inclusion of workers and their unions in economic and business decision-making, and thereby facilitate 'voice' rather than 'exit' as a means of solving problems and promoting internal organizational efficiency. It is anticipated that social partnership, of this form, might enhance co-operation in adapting to change, lead to superior morale resulting in enhanced productivity and lower employee turnover, and finally contribute towards the prevention of low skill, low investment competitive alternatives stimulates productive investment and innovation (Streeck, 1992).

In this sense, the proposition is naive in that it assumes away the inevitable conflicts and differences of interest which exist in the work relationship, and indeed, in most forms of human interaction, when scarce resources come up against unlimited (or at least, less scarce) demands. This lies at the heart of the economic problem, discussed by students in the first few days of studying the subject. It also exists in a workplace where, to take the most obvious example, there is a diversification of interests in determining reward systems, when it is extremely difficult to decide upon what is fair and what rewards effort, whilst shareholders require payment for their risk capital and firms require resources to reinvest for future production. Differences of interest are, therefore, inevitable. However, that is not to say that there are not certain areas where mutual interest can be pursued, and where positive-sum (not zero-sum) solutions are possible. Thus, it is in the interests of all concerned that firms are competitive and profitable if achieved through new ideas and/or innovation, but not if the same achievements are gained through reducing wages and/or increasing work intensity.

There is also a further issue about the representation of the social partner groups. Thus, a key question might concern whether employee representatives should always be trade unions (typically the case), even where membership is rather low in a nation or workplace, or whether employer-facilitated employee forums could be recognized as appropriate substitutes. The latter would appear to conform to democratic principles, and yet such bodies would be more easily influenced by external factors (primarily employer interests) and therefore they might prove an ineffectual means of representing employee interests, in order to reach a mutually beneficial solution to a problem. However, more problematic is developing suitable partners with whom employee representatives can negotiate. This function is clear on a micro (firm-level) basis, and on a sectoral level in those member states where this remains the focus for national wage formation, nevertheless similar organizational forms at European level are fledgling at best, and indeed employers tend to demonstrate a distrust in providing their groupings with negotiating authority to prevent the kind of large-scale compromises inherent within a corporatist approach. Whether this is because employers wish to maintain their autonomy, or believe their interests are best served by decentralized bargaining situations, this absence of a suitable negotiating partner may ultimately frustrate or retard the potential of the initiative. Hence, the building up of the organizing capacity of supranational organizations, for both employers and employees, is identified as a key prerequisite for a Europeanization of industrial relations (Traxler, 1996: 289).

European wage bargaining

A strong form

Social partnership does not necessarily lead directly to a broadening of collective bargaining across member states, even though this is a key priority for the European trade union movement. Thus, rather than remaining a predominantly national preserve, so-called euro-bargaining reinforces social partnership as a component of wider integration objectives. In the same way as national (centralized) wage formation has the potential to manage macroeconomic outcomes arising from the labour market, euro-bargaining could conceivably perform a similar task at European (supra-national) level. Indeed, a large body of literature has indicated that co-ordinated wage formation produces a superior macroeconomic flexibility in real wages and hence industrial adjustment to external shocks to the economy (Bruno and Sachs, 1985; Calmfors and Driffill, 1988; Rowthorn and Glyn, 1990).

It is, moreover, suggested that the advent of EMU makes a form of euro-bargaining more useful, since labour market outcomes will become increasingly important as a means of maintaining competitiveness within a single currency, when devaluation and changes in monetary policy become the preserve of the single currency region as a whole and not individual nations. Thus, there might be additional pressure placed upon pay negotiators to ensure that, *in aggregate*, wages grow in line with productivity, which may be more easily achieved through a form of co-ordinated wage bargaining, occurring at central or industrial level, where all parties can internalize the inflationary implications of their decisions (Whyman, 2006: 126–8). The Netherlands, Germany and Ireland have sought to promote wage bargaining moderation through national or sector-level pay bargaining structures during the transition towards, and membership of, EMU (Teague, 1998: 119–20).

It would, moreover, be an obvious means to attempt to equalize working conditions and payment schemes across industries located within different member states (Peters, 1995: 321; Berthold and Fehn, 1998: 530). Thus, it would be difficult to achieve an equalization of conditions and rewards for a car worker in Italy and Germany without some form of European sectoral bargaining, whilst workers in the agricultural sectors of Poland and Lithuania might have very little in common with their equivalent figures in the United Kingdom or Sweden, in the absence of negotiations to establish common working conditions and/or a gradual equalization of pay rates. This would appear, to some, to be essential to turn a single European market into a benefit for all employees rather than just business interests.

The development does, however, have two distinct flaws. The first relates to the relative productivity and hence competitive differences between different European member states. If wages expand faster than productivity, encouraged by the transparency arising from payments made in a single currency, the result will be job losses in the less productive region, *ceteris paribus*. This is precisely the pattern observed in former East Germany, whereby the 1989 economic and political unification process ignored productivity differentials whilst political expressions of equal citizenship prompted currency fixing at parity.[1] Furthermore, trade unions were not dissuaded from demanding wage equalization; partly to discourage large-scale labour movement out of the former East Germany in search for improved living conditions. This was despite the East German economy being only about half as productive as their Western neighbours, although this efficiency gap was reduced by 20 per cent longer working hours and wages no higher than one-third the equivalent West German rates (Lumley, 1996: 26). Wage equalization reduced East German competitiveness, however, because wage rises in the East were not matched by increasing productivity. In 1991, gross wages in manufacturing in the East averaged 138 per cent of net value added. Predictably, manufacturing collapsed under the twin cost pressures of wage rises and exchange rate appreciation, with output falling by 67 per cent in the first year after unification and leading to 25 per cent of the entire labour market losing their jobs. A year after monetary union, only 44 per cent of the previous nine-million workforce of the DDR remained in the same employment relationship (Buechtemann and Schupp, 1992: 95–7, 102–4).

The combination of an over-valued currency being irrevocably fixed in value against its closest competitors and wage equalization stimulating inflationary pressure, have predictably negative macroeconomic consequences. Hence, the German unification case represented a stark warning of the dangers of mishandling a rapid move towards EMU (Doyle 1989; Horn and Zwiener 1992; Goodhart 1995). Wage equalization must not be allowed to proceed the narrowing of productivity differentials, unless the less efficient economy is to suffer unemployment and recession. Yet, this warning note conflicts with the desire to create a single European economy, where citizens have similar experiences of working life, and it conflicts with Keynes' observation that *relative* wages were at least as significant as real wages when formulating negotiating objectives.

The second problem with a strong (centralized) version of euro-bargaining is in the absence of unity of purpose amongst both trade union and employer interests. It is perhaps not surprising that European employer organizations remain hostile to this development, as previously stated. However, although advocated by the ETUC, the persistence of rivalries between unions, whether due to organizational competition, religious or ideological reasons, might equally impair coordinated bargaining across the entire European market (Turner, 1996: 330). The increased wage discipline which may arise due to the operation of EMU may exacerbate difficulties for the trade union movement in this regard (Melitz, 1997; Pissarides, 1997).

A weaker form

In the absence of the development of a fully functioning euro-bargaining framework, it has been suggested that TNCs, operating throughout Europe, might facilitate an embryo European system of industrial relations through the harmonization of pay and conditions for employees irrespective of the location of production. The EWC initiative is considered to further strengthen co-operation and the pooling of information between EU trade unions, potentially leading to euro-bargaining to establish universal minimum standards of training, anti-discrimination practice, promotion procedures and so forth (Waddington and Kerckhofs, 2003). Thus, a form of 'arm's-length' bargaining may evolve whereby management and unions do not negotiate directly with one another, but unions are able to have an additional form of input into the decision-making process. The intention was to enhance social partnership between different units of transnational organizations operating in different constituent parts of the EU. However, whilst an advance in certain respects, this does reinforce the tendency towards a firm-centred, rather than sectoral, national, or supra-national models of industrial relations (Traxler, 1996: 293–4). Thus, the result could be a type of European pattern bargaining, although TNCs are unlikely to concede such an arrangement whilst productivity differentials persist (Teague, 1991; Rhodes 1992: 45).

It is equally possible, however, that the creation of a European labour market may be limited to certain key groups of workers, possessing specific technical and managerial skills, and for particular categories of highly mobile labour, notably managers, construction workers, labourers and young people (Walsh *et al.*, 1995: 85). In this scenario, the higher incomes, which are commanded by key employees, may disrupt national labour markets by increasing income inequality or through low-wage countries losing skilled labour to higher-wage member states (Marsden, 1992: 593). Furthermore, while the advent of euro-bargaining could provide new opportunities for trade unions and their members, it could equally fragment unions along supranational company lines, and thereby undermine class solidarity. Accordingly, unions risk becoming 'partners ... of regional capital trying to survive in inter-regional free market competition' rather than 'agents of inter-regional redistribution' (Streeck and Schmitter, 1991: 55).

There is, additionally, a second group of factors, which may cause a general decentralization of industrial relations systems. The intensification of international competition has led many companies, particularly TNCs, to focus upon internal labour markets to establish multiple cost centres and implement initiatives to tailor working conditions to their specific business requirements in order to react flexibly to changing patterns of demand. Advances in information technology have facilitated a shift from administrative to performance-based control, with responsibility and accountability devolved to business units at lower levels of large organizations (Sisson and Marginson, 1995). These systems of 'managed autonomy', in which central management maintains control through an extensive web of formal and informal performance measures, place a premium on the bottom-line responsibility of individual business unit managers for labour as well as other costs. Multi-employer bargaining is ill suited to this process (Marginson and Sisson, 1996: 177–8). Furthermore, there is a claim that deregulatory pressures are the consequence of a 'paradigm shift' from Fordist to post-Fordist industrial organization, implying a duality of labour markets split between core and periphery workers (Atkinson, 1984). Thus, trade unions face being marginalized due to employers' preference for company-level 'productivity coalitions' rather than centralized concertation or sectoral bargaining (Lash and Urry, 1987; Windolf, 1989). According to this viewpoint, euro-bargaining is irrelevant to the needs of post-Fordist flexible production (Rhodes, 1992: 28).

The divergent tensions, threatening to further complicate European industrial relations, are likely to persist because current arrangements show no clear evidence of converging to a uniform pattern across the European economy. Demands for greater firm-centred flexibility fit very poorly with the macroeconomic imperative of maintaining wage moderation and thereby international competitiveness. Hence, the most likely prediction is for an uneven and spasmodic development of industrial relations, with the eventual emergence of an ad hoc, partly institutionalized system of pan-European labour relations (Rhodes, 1992: 43–4). Irrespective of the eventual evolution of industrial relations throughout Europe, trade unions face increasing challenges. One problem concerns the changing composition of the European labour market and lower unionization amongst groups being increasingly represented in the labour force and in the expanding sectors of the manufacturing and particularly service sectors. Another relates to the tension between union objectives of social solidarity and maintaining membership through delivery of real material benefits. The former may be better served by national or sectoral wage formation, where employers and government may participate to secure aggregate wage moderation, whilst the latter may be best achieved by decentralized bargaining for workers in the most profitable companies.

Neo-liberal critique of social partnership

Social partnership is not an uncontroversial concept. Indeed, there has been an increasingly vocal neo-liberal critique of welfare states, labour regulation and centralized wage bargaining as causes of 'Eurosclerosis' (Lawrence and Schultz, 1987; Minford, 1990). Generous welfare provision has been criticized by a number of economists as being responsible for a decline in economic performance (Feldstein, 1974, 1976; Lindbeck *et al.*, 1994; Agell, 1996). Increases in taxation to fund higher levels of government transfers are suggested to reduce work incentives, increase the rate of natural unemployment and depress economic dynamism, whilst social security reduces personal savings rates, thereby reducing the stock of capital and hence national income. Job security legislation is claimed to produce hysteresis, where an individuals' duration of unemployment is negatively related to their probability of getting a job (Lawrence and Schultz, 1987). However, the evidence is rather mixed, with welfare expenditure acting as an automatic stabilizer to prevent a drift into recession, whilst social insurance may enable workers to take greater risks in their working lives which may produce greater returns for society as a whole (Korpi, 1985, 1996; Barr, 1992). Moreover, when utilizing the appropriate mix of active labour market policies and co-ordinated wage formulation, corporatism tends to present an improved unemployment: inflation trade-off (Jackman *et al.*, 1990: 483; Rhodes, 1992: 29).

Nevertheless, the neo-liberal argument has been at least partially adopted by leading European figures, as demonstrated the ECB's senior economist, Otmar Issing, who blamed the poor performance of the euro on 'the adverse impact of minimum wage and employment protection legislation', which can only be overcome by a 'comprehensive programme of structural reform'.[2] In practice, this consists of creating what Cerny (1990) describes as a transition from welfare state to '*competition state*', in which policies are determined by the perceived demands of survival in the global economy. This requires the creation of flexible labour markets (on the microeconomic definition) and the promotion of industrial adjustment to global change. However, it is in direct conflict with the ESM approach, as universal welfare provision is replaced by education, training and mobility measures designed to enhance productivity and increase employment levels. Moreover, it would re-commodify individuals, albeit providing them with the opportunity to develop more skills and therefore be better placed in the labour market.

Labour market flexibility – a supply-side alternative?

In place of the concertation aspect of social partnership, an alternative discussion of labour market reforms has taken place throughout the EU, centring upon the desire to enhance labour market flexibility (Whyman, 2006: 112–28).

Most notably adopted as a priority within the Lisbon Agenda, labour market flexibility derives from the degree to which labour market outcomes are determined by the operation of market forces free from rigidities and/or restrictions imposed by powerful actors such as monopsony employers, trade unions and government. A perfectly flexible labour market would imply the absence of all hindrances to the free operation of market forces. This not only includes examples of labour market regulation, such as job protection legislation, and institutional arrangements, such as systems of sectoral wage bargaining, but also unorganized forms of market imperfection – for example, resulting from insider–outsider power imbalances and/or irrational employment practices arising from labour market segmentation or discrimination. Furthermore, there is a sizeable literature pointing to the existence of labour market inflexibility due to various factors, including implicit contracts, efficiency wages, transaction costs in the renegotiation of contracts and incentives provided due to the principle-agent problem (Bosworth *et al.*, 1996; Lindbeck and Snower, 1988). Clearly, certain types of labour market inflexibility are more easily subject to corrective government policy reforms, whilst others appear more intractable.

Labour market flexibility has been identified as one means of advancing a number of economic goals, including the achievement of superior financial performance and higher levels of productivity at firm level (Ichniowski *et al.*, 1996), together with favourable macroeconomic benefits including lower levels of unemployment and reducing inflationary bottlenecks in the labour market. Studies indicate that labour market flexibility might be able to shift a supply-determined long-run equilibrium rate of unemployment to the left, thereby reducing unemployment consistent with retaining a low rate of inflation (OECD, 1994a; Siebert, 1997; Nickell and Layard, 1999).

The attraction for the EU, and indeed other industrialized economies, is that it offers a means of pursuing higher productivity and growth at a time when government activism and Keynesian economic approaches (broadly defined) do not form the economic orthodoxy (Sassoon, 1999: 28). Thus, supply-side reforms are advanced as a means of enhancing economic performance without the need to coordinate national economic policies, or seek to gain sufficient support to introduce fiscal federalism and/or coordinated wage formation. Moreover, in the absence of an effective system of fiscal federalism, the labour market is likely to provide the focus for attempts to absorb asymmetric shocks persisting within EMU – whether through wage adjustment or by further increasing labour mobility between member states (Borghijs *et al.*, 2003: 29; Baimbridge and Whyman, 2008: 126–8). Nevertheless, the fact that the EU has itself accepted much of this prevailing wisdom does mark a significant shift in policy emphasis from the former quasi-Euro-Keynesianism of the Delors period (Black, 2002; Annesley, 2003).

Belief in the importance of supply-side (rather than aggregate demand management) measures to improve macroeconomic variables has led the ECB to called for an acceleration of reforms aimed at increasing labour market flexibility and thereby anticipating that this will result in a reduction in structural unemployment. These measures may include tax/benefit changes, a weakening of social policy decommodification, changes in wage bargaining and labour market deregulation, to facilitate enhanced flexibility (ECB, 2004: 7). However, this approach is not without criticism. Indeed, there is quite severe concern that the available evidence does not support the supply-side hypothesis.

For example, although supporters of the supply-side hypothesis advance a certain amount of evidence in favour of this approach, there are a large number of studies which have found little or no significant impact arising from labour market deregulation (OECD, 1999a: 88; Blanchard and Wolfers, 2000; Baker *et al.*, 2002b; Arestis and Sawyer, 2004: 93). Indeed, there would appear to be little evidence to identify more than a small proportion of the observable differences in unemployment between EU member states, and indeed temporally within specific national economies (OECD, 1999a; Baker *et al.*, 2002; Baccaro and Rei, 2006). By contrast, other studies tend to suggest that stimulatory macroeconomic policy is necessary to stimulate the creation of productive capacity and hence reduce unemployment rates (Arestis and Sawyer, 2006). One reason for this might derive from a tendency to downplay the importance of demand-side factors influencing unemployment, together with the fact that characteristics of labour market flexibility can themselves be influenced by the impact of aggregate demand upon investment, capacity utilization and indirect effects upon the viability of regulatory and institutional arrangements (Palley, 2001: 3; Schettkat, 2003; Stockhammer, 2004d). Moreover, it has been suggested that increased labour market flexibility may compound market failure in firms' provision of training (Appelbaum, 1989; Crouch, 1997).

Depending upon the means of pursuing flexibility, a further critique suggests that the erosion of traditional job demarcations, work intensification, downsizing, flattening hierarchies and giving employees greater responsibility, are all associated with heightened feelings of anxiety and stress, which, in turn, may result in demoralization and demotivation of concerned employees, thereby impairing productivity (Wichert, 2002). If the association and motivation of labour is intrinsically linked with employment security, then the high labour turnover associated with labour market flexibility could deprive firms of valuable skills and is likely to reduce firm-based investments in training (Gasteen *et al.*, 1999: 92). Similarly, the OCED acknowledged potential costs associated with an expansion in 'non-regular' forms of employment, including potential conflict between certain forms of greater flexibility of working hours and family life responsibilities (OECD, 2004: 12–13). Thus, the extraction of functional, numerical and labour-cost flexibility may be secured at the expense of attitudinal and/or behavioural inflexibility, thereby reducing the net value of potential gains (Mankelow, 2002: 137).

A final criticism of the labour market flexibility thesis concerns the theoretical limitations demonstrated by much of the existing literature relating to the assumption that employment is determined by supply-side factors in the labour market and is not therefore influenced by aggregate demand. This is an error, because it is well established that the level of demand impacts upon many of the other variables outlined in this chapter. For example, the literature indicates that the level of aggregate demand has a significant impact upon trade union membership, strike activity and wage bargaining power (Ashenfelter and Pencavel, 1969; Bain and Elsheikh, 1976; Booth, 1983; Carruth and Disney, 1988). Aggregate demand management may similarly impact upon the continued optimality of the wage bargaining institutions and patterns of bargaining (Calmfors and Driffill, 1988; Iversen, 1999). Aggregate demand is closely related to the degree of capacity pertaining in an economy at any given time, and this, in turn, is associated with encouraging industrial investment, enhancing productivity and acting as a significant determinant of the level of unemployment (Rowthorn, 1995; Arestis and Mariscal, 1997: 191, 2000: 487; Dow, 1998: 369; Arestis and Sawyer, 2003: 11; Baddeley, 2003). Therefore aggregate demand is a major factor influencing the supply curve of available labour, itself affecting numerical flexibility, whilst the buoyancy of the economy may influence the replacement ratio, degree of wage flexibility, willingness of employees to accept certain types of non-standard employment and so forth. Solow (1997: 3, 29), for example, argues that weakness in job creation is most likely the result of excessive and anti-competitive product-market regulation, restrictive macroeconomic policy, especially monetary policy, and inadequate discipline from the capital markets, and not the inflexibility of the labour market.

Social partnership and flexibility – which way forward?

In reviewing the proposals made to realize the ESM in the labour market, there seem to be a number of unambiguous contradictions. The social partnership approach would seem to be a clear manifestation of the ESM model, whether a maximalist (strong) version through euro-bargaining and concertation innovations, or a weaker variant comprising micro-level negotiations held between social partners relating to firm-level issues, which may or may not develop into something more akin to the former. In either case, the emphasis is upon organized interests discussing issues of mutual interest and seeking to utilize 'voice' to reach a positive-sum conclusion where this proves to be possible. By contrast, however, the newer emphasis upon flexibility and supply-side reforms in the labour market take quite a different approach, emphasizing 'exit' through the primacy of market mechanisms and the importance of reducing costs to maintain competitiveness, which is likely to prove to be less of a mutually beneficial solution for all concerned. These two approaches would appear to be contradictory.

This is not to suggest that labour market flexibility is necessarily inconsistent with social partnership, since it is perfectly plausible to negotiate a form of workplace flexibility which provides a benefit to both social partners. Many employees welcome temporal and functional forms of flexibility, which facilitate working patterns which may prove more suitable to fit in with childcare responsibilities, for example, whereas the opportunity to perform a wider range of tasks at work may be quite popular with many workers. So, it is not labour market flexibility per se that seemingly conflicts with the social partnership approach, but rather the emphasis of its use as a means of advancing a supply-side form of economics which views many of the tenets of the ESM as being detrimental to economic progress – itself best secured through market determination. Thus, it is the Lisbon Agenda, and the economic approach which lies behind it, which would appear to conflict with the achievement of a strong and comprehensive form of ESM.

This leaves advocates of the ESM with an awkward dilemma. Euro-bargaining would appear to be difficult to achieve, in the absence of employer agreement to engage in the process, and with continued diversity (particularly when considering NMS) providing arguments against the move towards rapid unification of wages and working conditions across the European economy. Similarly, micro-level partnership agreements would appear to be more feasible, but these drive potential wedges through solidarity based upon factors other than the employing organization, and may entrench differentials between European employees which the ESM was supposed to diminish. Simultaneously, a rising neo-liberalism within EU institutions, arising in large part as a reaction to the consequences deriving from the operation of EMU and its supportive architecture, place further pressure upon this element of the social model. The resolution of these different elements will be difficult, and hence Bieler's conception of a 'struggle' for an ESM would appear to be quite an accurate description of any resolution of this confused situation, as adherents to different political philosophies and economic stances seek to win the argument over the definition and implementation of the European social space.

Part IV

What future for a Social Europe?

12 Neoliberalization and enlargement
Incompatible goals?

Introduction

A significant transformation has taken place in Europe since the late 1980s when the EU was still emerging from its internal difficulties of Eurosclerosis and the 'iron curtain' was firmly in place across the continent. However, with the EU pursuing the single internal market programme and monetary union, the collapse of Communism triggered both an economic and political transformation that swept across CEECs and ultimately led to the clamour for EU membership. At the commencement of this process Redmond (1994) forwarded three reasons regarding the transformation of the EU into the leading economic and political force within Europe. First, the EU's position as the major player in Europe was firmly established following the resolution of the internal budgetary and agricultural disputes with non-EU countries having to re-evaluate their relationship to ensure market access such that the costs of non-membership were raised to unacceptable levels. Hence, the long-term option to resolve this dilemma became the seeking of EU membership as it appeared the only viable 'club' in Europe with the EFTA reduced to a rump of Iceland, Liechtenstein, Norway and Switzerland. Second, the momentous changes in the CEECs have transformed the economic and political landscape of the Continent with a range of new possibilities and scenarios opening up. In particular, the previously unimaginable prospect of EU membership became the goal of many countries that did not even exist as sovereign nations 20 years ago. Finally, the increasing globalization of world commerce has illustrated the importance of the EU as a regional trade bloc alongside those of NAFTA, Asia Pacific Economic Cooperation (APEC), Association of Southeast Asian Nations (ASEAN), Cairns Group and Mercosur to name but a few.

Its fifth enlargement increased the EU's membership to 25 on 1 May 2004 with ten of the 12 ACs being CEECs. A further enlargement in 2007incorporated Bulgaria and Romania, whilst in its second annual Stabilization and Association Process report, released in March 2003, the commission indicated that the enlargement process would extend to Albania, Bosnia and Herzegovina, Croatia, Macedonia and Serbia-Montenegro. However, although this enlargement process is unprecedented in terms of the number of countries, it is less so in terms of more important features such as population and economic status (Gross, 2002).

It is, however, informative to place this recent series of enlargements of the EU in the context of previous phases of accession. Table 12.1 summarises the history of EU enlargement dating back to the first addition in 1973 to the original Six. In particular it illustrates the variation in time countries have held candidate status which steadily declined through successive (and successful) enlargements to a period of only three years for Finland. In contrast, the latest EU expansion has witnessed time lags of 8–14 years reflecting both the economic and political legacy of the most recent ACs combined with the deepening process of integration undertaken by the EU since the early 1990s. As Table 12.2 indicates, this pattern appears likely to continue as Croatia is currently the only of the present CCs with a planned accession date, again some ten years following its application.

Consequently, together with the four PCCs shown in Table 12.3, EU membership is likely to extend towards 40 member states by the mid-2020s. Hence, the trajectory is clear in terms of the most recent and likely future enlargements encompassing countries with characteristics significantly more divergent than previous accessions as they are now extending beyond established western European mixed economies. Consequently, the key issue becomes whether this central tenet of European integration of 'widening' is compatible with that of 'deepening' in relation to EMU, which encapsulates the quintessence of EU neoliberalization. The initial part of this chapter reviews the major challenges raised by accession in terms of the main economic conditions of the Copenhagen and MCC criteria, followed by the route towards membership and macroeconomic policy reforms, which are necessary to meet the Copenhagen Criteria and to endorse the aim of EMU. Second, the chapter reviews the current position of the ACs that are outside the eurozone, together with the CCs and PACs, against the stipulated convergence criteria for EMU membership. Finally, the major part of the chapter examines the potential problems and prospects for the recent enlargement countries in achieving eurozone membership. These relate to the initially over-optimistic timetable envisaged, the necessity of addressing structural weaknesses, the frequently problematic definition of fiscal measures, conformity to ERM II, the interaction between inflation and exchange rates, together with adherence to the notions of OCA criteria. Hence this chapter seeks to explore whether enlargement possesses a heightened dilemma for the EU in terms of whether the push to broaden its membership is wholly compatible with its current neo-liberal philosophy.

The Copenhagen and Maastricht criteria

All CCs are expected to accept the EU accession criteria agreed at the June 1993 European Council meeting in Copenhagen which defined the economic and political conditions in order to accede to the EU (European Council, 1993). The Copenhagen Criteria were that the CC has achieved:

•   The existence of a functioning market economy as well as the capacity to cope with competitive pressure and market forces within the Union (*economic criteria*);

- Stability of institutions guaranteeing democracy, the rule of law, human rights and respect for and protection of minorities (*political criteria*);
- The ability to take on the obligations of membership including adherence to the aims of political, EMU (*acquis criteria*).

And has created:

- The conditions for its integration through the adjustment of its administrative structures, so that EC legislation transposed into national legislations implemented effectively through appropriate administrative and judicial structures.

Although they do not have to fulfil the MCC (price stability, low long-term interest rates, sound public finances and exchange rate stability) at the time of accession, in practice the ACs will not be in a position to opt-out of EMU which is considered to be a membership obligation (Lavrac, 1999). Hence, in contrast to the MCC, the Copenhagen Criteria define both economic and political standards. Consequently, the two sets of criteria constitute distinct benchmarks focusing upon nominal (MCC) and real/institutional/legal (Copenhagen) convergence (Backe, 1999). The Copenhagen Criteria first entails a comprehensive liberalization of the price, trade and foreign exchange regimes, a system of legal and commercial rules and the presence of institutions which

Table 12.1 Summary of EU accessions

Country	Application	Membership	Candidate status period
Ireland	July 1961	January 1973	12 years
United Kingdom	August 1961	January 1973	12 years
Denmark	August 1961	January 1973	12 years
Greece	June 1975	January 1981	6 years
Portugal	March 1977	January 1986	9 years
Spain	July 1977	January 1986	9 years
Austria	July 1989	January 1995	6 years
Sweden	July 1991	January 1995	4 years
Finland	March 1992	January 1995	3 years
Cyprus	July 1990	May 2004	14 years
Malta	July 1990	May 2004	14 years
Hungary	March 1994	May 2004	10 years
Poland	April 1994	May 2004	10 years
Slovakia	June 1995	May 2004	9 years
Latvia	October 1995	May 2004	9 years
Estonia	December 1995	May 2004	9 years
Lithuania	December 1995	May 2004	9 years
Czech Republic	January 1996	May 2004	8 years
Slovenia	June 1996	May 2004	8 years
Romania	June 1995	January 2007	12 years
Bulgaria	December 1995	January 2007	11 years

make possible decentralized intermediation through private economic agents. Second, it requires the development of some sectors which are essential for a modern and competitive market economy, in particular, public administration and the financial system. The former is needed not only to implement the requirements that EU members have to meet, but also to ensure high and sustained economic growth whilst the latter is a significant element in assessing a country's readiness for membership. Third, NMS will be expected to take on the *acquis communautaire* in full, which as the EU is more integrated and in a dynamic phase of integration, is a higher requirement compared with previous accessions.

Hence, given the magnitude of the task facing ACs seeking to join the EU, a major effort has been put in place for the progressive integration of the ACs into the EU's political and economic framework. This process started with the Europe Agreements and entered a new phase with the so-called pre-accession strategy adopted by the European Council at Essen in December 1994 which sought to create mutual confidence through a framework of regular contacts. In the economic domain, initiatives in the framework of the pre-accession strategy have entailed participation of ACs ministers of finance to ECOFIN, the organization of regular meetings for the discussion of major economic policy issues, the creation of various working groups, as well as collaboration at the technical level in areas like statistics or macroeconomic forecasting.

Table 12.2 EU CCs

Country	Application	Estimated membership	Estimated candidate status period
Turkey	April 1987		
Croatia	February 2003	July 2013	10 years
Macedonia	March 2004		
Montenegro	December 2008		
Iceland	July 2009		

Table 12.3 EU PCCs

Country	Application
Bosnia and Herzegovina[1]	June 2003
Kosovo[2]	April 2005
Albania	April 2009
Serbia	December 2009

Notes
1 Thessaloniki European Council confirms the Stabilisation and Association Process as the EU policy for the Western Balkans. However, no application for EU membership has yet been submitted.
2 The commission adopts the Communication to the Council and the European Parliament on 'A European Future for Kosovo'.

Following the economic and political criteria of the pre-accession phase, the next issue relates to the *acquis communautaire* in the area of EMU. For instance Ilzkovitz (1996) suggested that the major challenge for the ACs will not be to enter EMU, but to adopt the *acquis communautaire* in the area of EMU as initially non-participating countries. In this respect the NMS will participate fully regarding the procedures of co-ordination of economic policies, be required to follow the rules disciplining fiscal policy and shall have completed the liberalization of their capital movements.

Towards EMU membership?

As indicated, since 1993 under Article 109k of the TEU a condition of EU membership is that countries acceding after the commencement of Stage 3 of EMU accept monetary union in principle and are committed to its membership. The applied convergence criteria is expected to be the original TEU reference values for interest rates, price stability and debt in relation to concurrent macroeconomic performance of the EMU(14). Although derogation under Article 122 of the Copenhagen Treaty permits the ACs to accede without immediately joining EMU, they will be included in ERM II which represents an intermediate stage in the process towards their eventual membership of the euro (EC, 2002). However, as for all EU countries, economic policies become a matter of common concern and hence are subject to policy co-ordination and multilateral surveillance procedures. Hence, ACs are obliged to pursue a high degree of sustainable convergence required for the adoption of the euro, which will depend on the economic characteristics of each country and its success in applying the policies geared to sustainable convergence. The main instruments for co-ordination are the Broad Economic Policy Guidelines, the SGP and a number of processes which deal with specific policy areas.

Participation in EMU for the new ACs will be judged on the basis of the MCC whereby full participation means that the convergence criteria have to be fulfilled, not only when entering into Stage 3, but also on a permanent basis after a transition period. Therefore, the ability of the ACs to (a) adopt sound fiscal policies, (b) pursue disciplined and responsible monetary policies and (c) avoid large movements in nominal exchange rates and misalignments, have and will continue to be major factors in judging accessions. In relation to fiscal policy, the ACs have made progress reducing fiscal deficits to levels below those prevailing in many industrialized countries and most also possess low debt/GDP ratios. However, they are likely to face substantial revenue losses from customs duties following the reduction of tariffs combined with pressure on the expenditure side deriving from the continuous process of structural reforms (enterprise restructuring and consolidation of the financial system), non-performing bank loans, the accession process itself (approximation of legislation, strengthening of regulation, adoption of stricter environmental standards etc.) and social security (health care and pensions etc.). Furthermore, following accession the ACs will have set aside substantial budgetary resources to meet the co-financing

requirements for EU transfers from structural funds and devote transient budgetary compensation to mitigate any socially negative consequences of accession to
specific groups (Backe, 1999).

In terms of monetary policy the main question to be addressed is whether
reforms have gone far enough towards the establishment of an environment permitting the use of market based instruments, whilst the ACs capital markets continue to lack liquidity and deepness and continue to suffer from a number of
regulatory deficiencies (Rosati, 1995). Indeed, the considerable adjustments
which the ACs will need to face when joining EMU will have to be borne by
greater labour flexibility given that alternatives such as labour mobility or fiscal
transfers are only likely to play a minimal role (de Grauwe and Lavrac, 1999). In
relation to this Andreff's study (1999) found that since 1989 in the CEEC(10)
nominal convergence may take place in spite of real divergence. Whilst this is
reassuring in terms of the MCC, it highlights the potentially debilitating deflationary consequences upon real economic variables such as incomes and
employment. Finally, to this end it would seem expedient to improve their competitive positions with a view to smoothing the future incorporation into both the
internal market and EMU. This would relate to further developing and strengthening the financial sector, restructuring the enterprise sector, fostering competition and generally reforming all aspects of public administration (Backe, 1999).
Moreover, such is the potential time discrepancy between nominal and real convergence for the ACs with the EU(15) the extent to which their premature entry
into EMU could destabilize the operation of the eurozone becomes a key issue
(Read, 2002).

Table 12.4 illustrates the position of the 2004 and 2007 accession CEECs
with regard to the MCC as of the EU's most recent assessment of non-EMU
member states. Clearly areas for concern relate to price stability, interest rates,
fiscal deficit and public debt where they fail to adhere to the reference values 71
per cent of the time (17 out of 24). Moreover, whilst the Czech Republic does
meet these proscribed convergence criteria, it does not possess the required two-
year membership of the ERM II mechanism; although its currency has depreci-
ated the least amongst those CEECs with floating exchange rates. Consequently,
even allowing a degree of latitude for the continuing repercussions of the 2008
credit crunch recession impacting upon the ability of these EU member states to
attain the MCC, it would appear that they require further economic restructuring
to even contemplate eurozone membership whilst the lesson of Greece, Spain,
Portugal and Italy has demonstrated that joining the euro can be the least of a
country's problems (Baimbridge *et al.*, 2012). A similar picture emerges for the
CCs and PACs albeit for a limited series of MCC indicators, whereby only Mon-
tenegro fulfils that for price stability, whilst only Iceland fails that for the deficit/
debt criteria. However, there are significant definitional and measurement issues
with how these countries calculate public expenditure and national debt, which
call into question these apparently optimistic figures.

Initially EMU entry for the ACs following enlargement was suggested as
being possible in 2006 with this (now optimistic) forecast based on the notion of

a minimum delay between the commencement of EU membership and the required two-year period of purgatory within ERM II (Gross, 2003). Moreover, in contrast to the clear inability of the ACs to meet the MCC, Gross (2003) advanced a comparative analysis between them and the 'Club Med' countries of the EU(15) which suggests that the three major ACs (Poland, the Czech Republic and Hungary) were closer to achieving the MCC than the Club Med countries were at a comparable stage prior to the start of EMU. However, it should be remembered that speculative attacks upon the EMS in the early 1990s occurred at the time when most commentators similarly believed the convergence process nearing completion with the primary triggers being concerns over fiscal adjustment and overvalued currencies. Indeed, the former appears to be a growing difficulty for the ACs and there are indications that their currencies are overvalued (see Table 12.4) by devaluation against the euro, whilst they share some of the features (large current account deficits financed by FDI inflows and appreciating real exchange rates) of those EU member states most severely affected by speculative attacks. Consequently, Gross (2003) concludes by arguing that it would be dangerous for the ACs to tie their currencies to the euro within ERM II prior to having a clearer view of whether prevailing exchange rate parities are sustainable in the long-run.

Problems and prospects of monetary union

A traditional approach to determine a country's prospects when considering EU membership has been through cost–benefit analysis, although this rarely results in fully measurable outcomes given the sizable number of subjective features that need to be taken into consideration (e.g. policy autonomy over the exchange rate, national sovereignty and identity etc.). However, in contrast to many of the EU(15) member states, for the 2004 and 2007 enlargement countries this was potentially less finely balanced given that euro membership, for example, entails the loss of relatively weak currencies with ensuing benefits of enhanced monetary stability, certainty and investment, together with both reduced risk premia and interest rates (Read, 2002).

Consequently, economic studies have generally concluded that the benefits of enlargement outweigh the costs because the ACs started from a lower economic base. Indeed, the Directorate General for Economic and Financial Affairs (EC, 2001) estimated that enlargement could increase GDP growth of the acceding countries by 1.3–2.1 percentage points per annum and for existing members by 0.7 percentage points on a cumulative basis. An earlier study by Baldwin *et al.* (1997) estimated that accession of CEECs would, even in a conservative scenario, bring an economic gain for the EU(15) of €10 billion and for the new members of €23 billion. However, of this measurable benefit of 5.4–7.3 per cent of GDP, the majority of this (4.4–6 per cent) is a consequence of the single internal market rather than adopting the euro (Baldwin *et al.*, 1997; Gross, 2002). Whilst an analysis of business cycles argued that there are potentially significant economic and business gains of accession (ERT, 2001; Grabbe, 2001).

Table 12.4 Adherence to EMU convergence criteria

	Inflation (%)	Interest rates (%)	Fiscal deficit (% of GDP)	Public debt (% of GDP)	Entry into ERM II/change against the euro Two-years within ERM II	Currency regime
Reference value	1	6	3	60		
EU 2004 and 2007 accession countries						
Bulgaria	*1.7*	*6.9*	2.8	17.4	Stable	Currency board (EUR)
Czech Republic	0.3	4.7	5.7	39.8	Depreciated by 1.1 per cent	Floating
Estonia	−0.7	*na*	2.5	12.4	28 June 2004	
Hungary	4.8	*8.4*	4.1	78.9	Depreciated by 4.6 per cent	Floating
Latvia	0.1	*12.7*	8.6	48.5	2 May 2005	
Lithuania	*2.0*	*12.1*	8.4	38.6	28 June 2004	
Poland	*3.9*	*6.1*	7.3	53.9	Depreciated by 12 per cent	Floating
Romania	*5.0*	*9.4*	8.0	30.5	Depreciated by 12.9 per cent	Floating
EU CCs						
Croatia	*1.8*		2.2	40.8		
Iceland	*1.8*		−5.19	*103*		
Macedonia	*3.2*		0.6	39.5		
Montenegro	0.7			38		
Turkey	*5.1*		−1.3	38.8		
EU PCCs						
Albania	*3.3*		0.04	55.9		
Bosnia and Herzegovina	*1.5*		0.35	34		
Kosovo	*3.5*		0.65	7		
Serbia	*10.3*		0.48	37		

Source: EC (2010).

Notes
Figures in italics indicate non-compliance with convergence criteria.

Although the initial prospects for EMU participation seem promising in terms of their fiscal positions, the ACs lag behind the EU(15) in terms of price stability and convergence of interest rates (see Table 12.4). Such assessment nevertheless against the MCC requires careful consideration. First, ACs have frequently referred to the MCC to demonstrate their readiness for accession on the basis that if they outperform some EU countries in such an advanced matter as EMU it is logical to infer that they are more than ready for EU membership itself. However, the Copenhagen Criteria for admission are substantially different from this notion, whilst the MCC assume that Stages 1 and 2 of EMU have been successfully undertaken. Indeed, most ACs have yet to fully instigate all the single internal market requirements as precursors to Stage 3 of EMU, whilst it remains difficult to obtain reliable and compatible data on the MCC (Lavrac, 1999).

Second, embarking on a fast-track move towards full financial convergence and, in particular, towards complete monetary convergence as defined by the MCC could prove counterproductive. Such a policy stance could distract from the challenge of removing underlying structural weaknesses and/or lead to structural reform delays which would have negative effects on financial indicators in the short-term, but are important for long-term macroeconomic sustainability (Backe, 1999). Moreover, such a strategy could possibly lead to uneven policy mixes with the overburdening of monetary and exchange rate policy. Hence, the MCC should be viewed during the accession period as medium- and longer-term reference points and not immediate operational targets (Backe and Linder, 1996).

Third, some concepts such as long-term interest rates or fiscal deficits do not possess the same meaning as in established market economies, with data on long-term interest rates not fully comparable with those of the EU member states as long-term capital markets are still insufficiently developed in the ACs (Backe, 1999). The budget position is also difficult to assess given that it is calculated contrary to the basis of the TEU particularly in relation to the position of regional and local government budgets as well as of social security funds. Indeed, state enterprises continue to perform functions that in market economies are financed through the government budget, and which need to be properly accounted for in the budget; hence the potentially surprising figures shown in Table 12.4 with regard to the CCs and PACs who appear to be fiscally abstentious.

Fourth, until the ACs formally join the EU they cannot enter its mechanisms of monetary integration, in particular ERM II, which is only open to member states (Backe, 1999); although prior to this they have been able to prepare themselves for inclusion in ERM II through either shadowing, pegging or irrevocably fixing their exchange rate to the euro thereby committing themselves to a de facto monetary union albeit with an asymmetric cost burden. The arguments in favour of an early inclusion of ACs in ERM II range from the technical ability to fulfil the MCC, to giving ERM II meaning and importance and accustom them to the concepts of monetary and exchange rate discipline and co-operation (de Grauwe and Lavrac, 1999). Moreover, a relatively wide standard fluctuation band and interventions at the margins which will in principle be automatic and unlimited, combined with the timely adjustment of central rates should avoid significant misalignments (Lavrac, 1999).

A further potential complication for the ACs involves the interaction between inflation and exchange rates given the status of rapidly evolving economies. Although the ACs are expected to enjoy a process of productivity catch-up for the foreseeable future, real appreciation of their currencies is expected, which can be reconciled with nominally fixed exchange rates through inflation. This inflation is expected to result from the Balassa-Samuelson effect) whereby increased productivity will be larger in tradables than in non-tradables that are competing for the same labour (Halpern and Wyplosz, 1996; Égert, 2002). Therefore the faster productivity increases in tradables, the greater probability it will spill over in the form of higher inflation in domestic non-tradables and hence higher domestic inflation. However, this is in contradiction to the inflation criterion which will make compliance with the MCC potentially costly for ACs (Bratkowski and Rostowski, 1999; Kopits, 1999; Masson, 1999). Consequently, restraining domestic demand by fiscal and/or monetary policy with the risk of recession appears to be the only available anti-inflationary instruments. In this way nominal convergence in terms of the MCC will only be attained at the cost of real convergence, which should ultimately be the main priority. Hence, for commentators such as Schoors (2002), unilateral euroization immediately upon accession offers a feasible solution for the ACs until the convergence of the price levels of non-tradables slows down and they can enter EMU. Thus, in the absence of more reasonable criteria, unilateral euroization could negate difficulties prior to monetary union if the EU were not so vigorously opposed.

In addition to the general issues regarding exchange rates, fulfilment of the MCC criterion regarding this in terms of two-year membership of ERM II is potentially problematic. Given the current nature of international financial markets dominated by the dollar, euro and yen it is unclear whether the small currencies can pursue an independent monetary policy. Hence, the exchange rate may be a source of shocks, rather than acting as a shock-absorber. Consequently, for small countries the only sustainable exchange rate regimes are either a floating rate or an irreversibly fixed rate (Buiter, 2000; Larraín and Velasco, 2002). However, the official accession procedure indicates that ACs should maintain a stable exchange rate within ERM II for two years. Unfortunately, given the history of the original ERM this appears to be an example of an unsustainable exchange rate regime with potential for resulting havoc upon the small and volatile currencies. Moreover, one of the central pillars of ERM I, co-operation and co-financing in the defence of each other's parities, is now absent. A potential solution therefore is for countries to make their ERM-parity as credible and irreversible as possible. To this extent a number of commentators have discussed the concept of either euroization or dollarization, whereby ACs adopt and maintain euro currency boards during the two-year test period which precedes EMU-accession (Gulde *et al.*, 2000; Sulling, 2002; Bratkowski and Rostowski, 2002; Calvo, 2002; Coricelli, 2002; Nuti, 2002; Schoors and Gobbin, 2004).

Additionally, the principal requirements of the ACs successfully and sustainably entering an OCA are a degree of economic integration and labour market flexibility. The former is likely to evolve over time following EU accession, but fundamental differences in economic structures, patterns of productions and consumption suggest a continued susceptibility to asymmetric shocks in the short- to medium-term because of both the significant real economic divergence between them and also within the ACs themselves (Read, 2002). In terms of labour markets, the most likely immediate route towards greater flexibility is via wages rather than further shock-therapy retrenchment, together with inflows of capital from the EU(15). Although certain features such as labour market flexibility in the ACs may be at least similar to that within the EU(15), according to Dangerfield (2002) overall the ACs, whether as a whole or divided into sub-groups, are unlikely to satisfy the optimal currency criteria given the limited extent of trade and integration between themselves in spite of the Central European Free Trade Agreement and Baltic Free Trade Agreement. The emphasis therefore is that accession will encourage further trade and integration which in turn will result in increasing convergence between them and established EU member states (Gabrisch and Werner, 1999). Additionally, the speed and smoothness of economic integration will also be influenced by the future size and efficacy of regional policy under the auspices of EU Structural Funds (Gabrisch and Werner, 1999).

Moreover, a significant lowering of inflation will be difficult given the persistence of several elements of cost-push inflationary pressures, the entrenchment of inflationary expectations, the limited scope for further fiscal tightening and potential monetary management problems resulting from capital inflows. Significant cost-push factors relate to the still uncompleted liberalization of regulated prices or their full adjustment to cost-recovery levels and to nominal wage pressures if wages adjust to past inflation as a consequence of persistent inflationary expectations. Further, nominal exchange rate devaluations, imperfect competition and delays in enterprise and financial sector reform may also hamper disinflation. In the medium-term context of EU membership the ACs will experience a substantial upward adjustment towards EU price levels for agricultural goods and products, assuming full integration into the CAP, although this may be counterbalanced by falling prices for other goods and services. Finally, inflationary performance may be affected by cost-push effects resulting from the adoption of the EU's social and environmental standards.

However, progress in lowering inflation towards the EU-norm will be important for ACs' perspectives for moving towards low long-term interest rates and the subsequent ability to participate in ERM II. The attainment of the MCC interest rate criterion will require convergence to be perceived as sustainable by financial markets and a positive assessment of their ability to react to asymmetric shocks. However, it is likely that these features will take some time, thereby implying that interest rate convergence remains a distant prospect for the ACs. Consequently, they will need to maintain a degree of nominal exchange rate flexibility to develop substantial current account positions and negate capital flows following the liberalization of capital movements (Backe, 1999).

Following this series of studies reviewing specific aspects of the relationship between the ACs and EMU membership, a further branch of research has focussed on the issue of business cycle convergence which also refers the discussion back to the bedrock of OCA theory. The principle theme concerns the degree of synchronization between the recent ACs and the established eurozone countries which have been analysed through a variety of methodological approaches. Indeed, a meta-analysis of the literature examining the correlation of the business cycle between the eurozone and the ACs concluded that a number already possess high correlation with the eurozone business cycle even when discounting for the alternative methodological approaches adopted in the contributory studies (Fidrmuc and Korhonen 2006). Examining this in more detail, Ben Arfa (2009) finds that a number of the ACs possesses a high degree of correlation of demand shocks with the eurozone, but supply shocks are asymmetric whereby the association between the EMU members and the CEECs is negative. Consequently, even prior to the recent turmoil in the eurozone, it appears that the ACs need to undertake significant structural changes to their economies to successfully accommodate the single currency.

In addition to such overarching studies, specific groups of ACs, described by Johnson (2008) as 'pacesetters' (Estonia, Latvia, Lithuania, Slovenia and Slovakia) and 'laggards' (the Czech Republic, Hungary and Poland), have been the focus of several studies. For example, Broz (2010) found that the correlation, size and speed of adjustment in relation to demand and supply shocks were important if an AC is seeking to enter EMU since evidence of business cycle synchronization indicates willingness. The study concluded that Croatia was far from ready to adopt the euro, whilst Slovenia (who joined in 2007) and Latvia possessed the most synchronized convergence between their national business cycles and that of the EMU. However, these studies reveal inconsistent outcomes of the crucial level of synchronicity demonstrated by individual ACs and EMU members, which is potentially problematic. Inter alia Darvas and Szapary (2008) find that Hungary, Poland and Slovenia are highly synchronized for key economic indicators such as GDP, industry and exports, but not for consumption of services. In contrast the other recent ACs exhibit little or no association. However, when incorporating both contemporaneous linkages among the ACs and the eurozone and the business cycle itself, Aslanidis (2010) finds Hungary appearing relatively strongly synchronized, whilst synchronization is much weaker for the Czech Republic and Poland. Thus it would appear that until such studies unequivocally indicate that the ACs are synchronized in their business cycle with the existing EMU members, then proceeding with caution is perhaps the optimal strategy.

Conclusion

This chapter has sought to illustrate that reasons exist to suggest that EMU should not be an immediate target for the majority of the ACs. First, given the lateness of determining the appropriate timetable for accession it is conceivably more important that they should firmly cement their progress towards a functioning market economy, competitiveness and participation in the SM combined with sustainable macroeconomic stability. Second, it might indeed be difficult for most of them to implement the *acquis* in the area of EMU. Third, premature adoption of the convergence criteria could also be too constraining for them given the need in transition economies for public investment (Kok, 2003). Potential obstacles to implement the *acquis communautaire* in the area of EMU include their specificity as transition economies, whereby the ACs are likely to grow faster than Western Europe, catching-up in terms of productivity and standard of living. This process implies a real appreciation of their exchange rates which can result from either an appreciating nominal exchange rate or a higher inflation rate than in the EU. Further, the loss of the exchange rate instrument might also be too costly for some such that during the transition period, they might require some exchange rate flexibility to elevate capital inflows or inflationary pressures. Additionally, adopting too tight fiscal criteria should not be an immediate target for transition economies before restructuring is completed, whilst a high potential return on public investment should allow, to some extent, running budget and external deficits if money is being invested in transition. Finally, EU membership is likely to induce a further rise of capital inflows resulting in ACs potentially having increasing difficulties in preventing their economies from overheating and therefore achieving the objective of price and exchange rate stability (Daviddi and Ilzkovitz, 1997).

In view of these obstacles and challenges there has been much debate regarding the timeframe for ACs to meet the MCC and hence be in a position to join EMU, for example, Backe (1999) estimated a time horizon of 7–10 years. However, as this chapter has sought to demonstrate this would only be feasible under the assumption of appropriate economic and structural adjustment, together with sustainable compliance with the fiscal criteria. Hence, monetary convergence appears to be a more remote perspective and one which we would argue is far from being in the best interests of the ACs in venturing further down this neoliberalization path.

13 Social Europe and enlargement
Threat or opportunity?

Introduction

The enlargement process has created a larger and more diverse European SM, and this has potentially far-reaching consequences, not only for individual member states (both established and newer entrants), but also for the sustainable development of a Social Europe as a whole. For example, has enlargement effectively ended the conception of creating a single, homogenous European labour market, complete with identical labour regulation and social protection, or will the NMS rapidly converge towards this norm? If not, then are existing differences in social provision and labour protection an example of unacceptable 'social dumping', whereby states seek to gain a cost advantage within a SM by beggar-thy-neighbour competition for the lowest value placed on workers and citizens, or is it a natural reflection of states at different levels of economic development needing to maintain international competitiveness through a lower wage economy? These are fundamental questions which need to be satisfactorily answered before the future development of the ESM can be accurately predicted.

Embracing diversity

Post-enlargement, the labour markets and social provision provided by EU member states has become more heterogeneous in a number of respects (see Table 13.1).

Wages

Wage levels are significantly different between EU(15) and the NMS. Thus, the latest Eurostat figures for the eight former command economy NMS where data is available, annual wages averaged €5,371 compared to €34,683 for EU(14) nations – omitting Italy due to absence of data. This is particularly apparent when considering the former quasi-command economies, where lower wages were at least partly compensated by a wide range of services and benefits provided by employing organizations, including holidays, transport subsidies, free meals and so forth. However, lower wages are also a result of the policies

Table 13.1 Comparator statistics – European labour markets

	GDP per capita (EU-27 = 100)	Employment rate 2010	Unemployment rate 2011	NMW 2011 (Euro/month)	Gross average earnings, 2007 (euro/p.a.)
Bulgaria	44	60	11.4	122.71	2,626
Czech Republic	82	65	6.8	319.22	8,284
Estonia	65	61	13.8	278.02	n/a
Latvia	52	59	17.2	281.93	6,690
Lithuania	55	58	17.3	231.70	3,016 (1999)
Hungary	65	55	11.6	280.63	8,952
Poland	61	59	9.3	348.68	8,177
Romania	46	59	7.4	157.20	4,825
Slovenia	88	66	8.2	748.10	n/a
Slovakia	73	59	13.9	317.00	8,400
Cyprus	98	70	7.6	n/a	21,310
Malta	81	56	6.2	664.95	15,679
EU (27) av	100	64	9.4	n/a	n/a
EU (15) av	110	65	9.3	1,424.24 (EU-9)*	34,683 (EU-14)
Lowest EU(15) nation	Portugal 80	Italy 57	Spain 20.7	Portugal 565.83	Greece 16,739**

Source: Eurostat (2011).

Notes

* EU (9) average – not including Germany and the three Scandinavian EU member states.

** Greece data for 2003 (latest figures available).

pursued in this group of NMS, during the 17 years of transition to more fully-functioning market economies, where incomes policies caused wage earners to bear the brunt of the costs associated with the transition process (Vaughan-Whitehead, 1995; Clarke *et al.*, 2000). For example, during the first seven years of this transition, wages declined by approximately 65 per cent in Lithuania, 46 per cent in Latvia, 45 per cent in Estonia, 26 per cent in Hungary and by around one-fifth in Poland, the Slovak Republic and Slovenia. This situation subsequently improved. Nevertheless, real wages remain depressed in seven of the ten NMS (Vaughan-Whitehead, 2003: 47–8). The situation is slightly different for Cyprus and Malta, which have seen a large increase over the same period, and therefore, when comparing the average for all NMS, the differential diminishes by €2,600, but there still remains a substantial pay gap. Indeed, this has been a key factor behind the remarkable deceleration of unit labour cost growth (EU Commission, 2006: 56).

Wages are at least partially determined by productivity levels, and this is one explanation for relatively low remuneration rates paid within the NMS, where average labour productivity remains less than two-thirds of EU(15) levels (EU Commission, 2006: 56). Productivity differentials reflect lower levels of capital investment over the medium term, which reinforces comparative advantages for NMS within relatively low technology and labour intensive specialization, whereas EU(15) nations predominate in medium–high technology within a more innovative and capital-intensive industrial structure (EU Commission, 2006: 67). One would assume that, as FDI flows increase, and capital intensity increases, this productivity gap will decrease.

National minimum wages

Rates compare favourably with EU member states, in terms of the proportion of average wages covered by national minimum wage (NMW) rates, however, since average wages rates are substantially below EU(15) levels, the gross payment, in terms of euro-per-month, are correspondingly much lower.

Employment rates

One striking feature of those NMS undertaking a transition from command economies, relates to a substantial 15–20 per cent decline in employment rates since 1989, with the majority of this shift concentrated in the early transition period. Thus, whereas employment rates were higher in the NMS than in the other EU nations during the early 1990s, the reverse is now the case, with only Cyprus (70 per cent) and Slovenia (66 per cent) superseding the EU(15) average. Although this performance gap has narrowed since the middle of the last decade, the EU Commission (2006: 45) maintains that this is a reflection of weak employment growth, impacting disproportionately upon young, older and female workers.

Sectoral employment rates also differ markedly between established and newer member states, with employment in agriculture more than two-and-a-half times higher in NMS economies than in their more established EU neighbours, whilst industrial employment is around 50 per cent more significant in many of the NMS than for the remainder of the EU (EU Commission, 2006: 55, 101). The corollary of high agricultural and industrial employment is that the service sector in transition NMS is significantly less developed than in the more established member states, although Cyprus and Malta are once again exceptions to this general rule, as tourism is of key importance for their respective economies.

If the NMS are to continue to deliver economic growth rates above the EU average, and thereby close the development gap with their more established neighbours, it is likely that productivity in the agricultural sector will have to rise, leading to a substantial shedding of labour, thereby necessitating its absorption elsewhere within the individual economies, or trigger larger scale migration across the SIM. One effect of the structural change that the NMS have so far achieved during the past decade, through a combination of labour shedding and a shift from agricultural to industrial and service sector employment, has delivered substantial gains in labour productivity, albeit, as previously mentioned, that this still lags significantly behind rates achieved in the established EU nations.

Unemployment

The unemployment rate within the NMS, averaging 10.1 per cent (10.7 per cent for the former command economy NMS), is significantly higher than the 9.3 per cent average for the EU(15). These figures conceal a wide variation, with unemployment rates of 6.2 per cent in Cyprus and 6.8 per cent in the Czech Republic, whilst Latvia and Lithuania had rates exceeding 17 per cent. These differences reflect, to varying degrees, the historical residue of labour shedding resulting from restructuring, cyclical influences and structural rigidities; for example, UNICEF data suggests that transition NMS lost 26 million jobs during the transition period, with 14 million of these posts previously held by women (Lemke, 2001). Hence, the EU Commission (2006: 55) considers that, 'the persistence of high levels of unemployment and its concentration among certain groups and regions suggest that structural rigidities hamper the smooth functioning of the NMS labour markets'.

Casualization of work

Many of the NMS, and in particular the transition nations, have experienced a marked casualization in employment conditions, as a shift has occurred from life-long employment to less secure jobs and asymmetrical contracts. One means utilized by employers has been to shift risk onto employees through utilizing self-employment as a means to circumvent labour legislation, social contributions and tax liabilities. A second form, temporary employment, simply did not exist 17 years ago in the former communist economies, yet this has risen to significant levels in little over a decade, albeit still lower than the EU average, itself inflated by the marked use of such contracts in Spain (32.1 per cent of total employment) and Portugal (20.4 per cent). Nevertheless, it is important that this shift towards increased casualization is placed in its wider context. Thus, Table 13.2 indicates that, whilst hours worked and the proportion of the labour force designated as self-employed are notably higher in the NMS than the average for the rest of the EU, rates of temporary employment and part-time employment are substantially lower than amongst EU(15) nations. Hence, whilst casualization has certainly increased in importance within the transitional NMS economies, this takes a different form to patterns existing in EU(15) member states. This different pattern need not, by itself, imply an inferior set of working arrangements in the NMS. Yet, it would appear that the EU need extend their existing labour market regulations, protecting casual and part-time employees, to include the self-employed.

Industrial relations

The industrial relations climate within the NMS is, for the most part, markedly different from the experience within the more established EU member states. One notable feature relates to the weakness of the social partners within most NMS. This is particularly evident in terms of one of the distinctive features of the ESM, namely the inclusion of social partners in economic and social policy decision-making. For example, in the Czech Republic, social partners are excluded from most institutional arrangements established by government, whilst social partners in Hungary have been removed from their former involvement in the management of social security and pension funds. This is in contrast to the experience in Cyprus and Slovenia, where social partners have largely continued their former association with various social protection systems.

Collective employee representation is significantly less developed amongst most NMS. Trade union membership has fallen dramatically within all of the

Table 13.2 Casualization in selected NMS, 2000

	Average working hours	Self-employment as % total employed	Temporary employment as % total employment	Part-time employment as % total employment
Cyprus	40.8	21.4	10.4	8.3
Czech Republic	43.6	14.5	8.1	5.4
Estonia	40.5	8.1	2.3	6.7
Hungary	41.2	14.6	6.9	3.6
Latvia	42.1	10.7	6.7	10.8
Lithuania	38.8	15.9	3.8	8.6
Slovak Republic	42.6	7.8	4.0	1.9
Slovenia	41.6	11.2	12.9	6.1
EU(15) average	37.8	11.3	13.4	17.7

Source: Eurostat (2000).

NMS, with union density declining as low as 10 per cent in Estonia and 12 per cent in Lithuania, whilst in Hungary and Poland, membership rates have declined below one-fifth of the labour force (Vaughan-Whitehead, 2003: 254). It is only in the non-transition NMS, Cyprus (70 per cent) and Malta (56 per cent), where trade union membership remained the preserve of a majority of the working population. Causes of this decline include the effects of the economic dislocation following the transition from command to market economies in eight of the NMS, as unemployment and inequality rose, and trade unions seemed powerless to protect their members amidst such turbulent conditions. Moreover, privatization has further weakened trade union membership, whilst sectoral shifts in employment patterns have reinforced these changes. Trade union membership may, additionally, have lost part of its former legitimacy in the transition regimes, having been closely associated with the state apparatus. Thus, as economic reforms have increased the costs associated with the greater operation of free market forces, trade unions appear to have been unable to successfully counter these adverse trends for its potential membership.

The evidence for a decline in trade union membership does not, however, constitute a disproportionate problem for the creation of an ESM, because this decline has also been observed within a majority of EU(15) nations. Indeed, the very low levels of unionization experienced in the Baltic States are not enormously out of line with the experience of France. However, it is more problematic for the development of a comprehensive ESM when trade union activity is marginalized in terms of wage bargaining coverage and the dominant level where any such negotiations occur. In terms of the former, there is a markedly lower coverage of collective bargaining agreements amongst the NMS. Figures range from 100 per cent of the labour force in Slovenia, where state-sponsored national bargaining still pertains, and 68 per cent in Cyprus, to atypically low rates of coverage of 20 per cent in Latvia and 15 per cent in Lithuania. It is estimated that perhaps as few as one-quarter of employees, within the former Central and Eastern European NMS, have their terms and conditions at least partially determined by collective agreements. Amongst the EU(15) member states, these figures would be reversed, with around three quarters of employees being covered by collective agreements; although there is wide divergence between individual nations, with a handful having almost complete wage bargaining coverage whilst the United Kingdom has a rate worse than half of the NMS (see Table 13.3).

A second feature of wage bargaining relates to the importance of the different levels on which it takes place, namely whether this is predominantly determined at national, sectoral, company or workplace levels (see Table 13.3). The primary focus for wage bargaining throughout the EU(15) member states is at the sectoral level, albeit that three member states (Belgium, Finland and Ireland) have a greater degree of centralization of wage bargaining structures, whilst France relies upon a greater degree of state intervention and the United Kingdom is alone amongst more established member states in having company (or workplace) bargaining dominant. Amongst the NMS, wage setting primarily occurs at company and/or workplace level, with only Slovakia (sectoral) and Slovenia (inter-sectoral) deviating from this pattern (Vaughan-Whitehead, 2003: 244; EIRO, 2005).

The fact that wage bargaining is far more decentralized within the majority of NMS than their more established counterparts creates, therefore, a number of challenges for the development of the ESM and the further development of the new entrants. It weakens the case for the establishment of a comprehensive bargaining structure being established across the single European labour market, as promoted by the ETUC, because enlargement has resulted in a greater diversity of industrial relations structures than existed previously, thereby making agreement upon a single model far more difficult to achieve. Moreover, the combination of decentralized wage bargaining, and the low levels of trade union membership, implies that, in most NMS, the majority of workers will actually receive little or no opportunity to exercise their collective voice in meaningful wage negotiations.

There is a further problem for the expansion of meaningful social dialogue between social partners of equal worth, as envisioned by the ESM, namely the relative weakness of employer organizations capable of articulating the views and interests of a wide and representative body of organizations. This is

Table 13.3 Level and coverage of wage bargaining in EU member states, 2004

Coverage of collective bargaining (%)	Member states	Dominant level of wage bargaining
90+	Slovenia	Intersectoral
	Austria	Sectoral
	Sweden	Sectoral
	Belgium	Intersectoral
	Finland	Intersectoral
	Italy	Sectoral
	France	State intervention – no dominant sector
75–89	Netherlands	Sectoral
	Denmark	Sectoral
	Spain	Sectoral
50–74	Germany	Sectoral
	Greece	Sectoral
	Malta	Company/automatic wage indexing to prices
35–49	Ireland	Intersectoral
	Slovakia	Sectoral
	Hungary	Company
	Poland	Company
	United Kingdom	Company
20–34	Cyprus	Company
	Czech Republic	Company
	Estonia	Company
10–19	Latvia	Company
	Lithuania	Company

Source: EIRO (2005).

problematic amongst the former command economy NMS, as employer organizations did not really exist before the transition period, and therefore have not had the time nor opportunity to develop their authority within the business sector in these countries. Moreover, subsequent experience has witnessed a fragmentation of business interests amongst a wide range of employer organizations. Thus, even were trade unions to regain some of their former strength, and were processes within the ESM capable of facilitating opportunities for the establishment of social (and/or tripartite) partnership between representatives of labour and capital, it would appear difficult to achieve consensus due to the prevalence of multiple representative organizations, each with an interest to advance a partial interest agenda and possibly use its negotiation stance to compete for new members.

Distribution of income

The enlargement of the EU has had a number of effects upon the level of inequality, both within and between individual member states. The accession of the NMS has widened the existing income disparity within the larger EU, with the GDP per capita (measured in purchasing power standards) of individual member states ranging from 40 per cent of the EU(15) average in Latvia, to 210 per cent in Luxembourg (EU Commission, 2006: 2, 43). It is anticipated that this range of relative affluence will diminish over time due to the 'catch-up' process – although this depends upon a large number of factors, including the adoption of an appropriate economic policy framework, and is by no means as automatic as many commentators are apt to suggest (FitzGerald, 2006). Nevertheless, it remains the case that enlargement has increased inequality between nations.

In terms of the degree of inequality experienced within the NMS, the data suggests that this tends to be somewhat higher than for the average of other EU nations, albeit that the Gini coefficient calculation indicates that, with the exceptions of the Baltic States, this tends to be less pronounced than for one more established member state, namely the United Kingdom (see Table 13.4). However, it is interesting to note that the degree of inequality within Lithuania exceeds that of the United States, thereby presenting a definite challenge to one of the central motivations informing the ESM approach.

It is, furthermore, plausible that EU enlargement may itself cause further inegalitarian redistributive effects within individual nation-states. In EU(15) member states, it might be anticipated that increased migration from the NMS, together with the relocation of some production facilities in labour intensive industries to the new entrants, might depress wage rates for home nationals in direct competition for these types of jobs – i.e. typically, unskilled and semi-skilled workers. This might exacerbate income inequality within more established EU member states. For the NMS, those individuals with more transferable skills might be expected to benefit the most in the new SIM, although higher rates of economic growth should benefit the entire economy, albeit not necessarily at the same rate. Thus, inequality is likely to increase here also. Moreover, whilst studies employing economic modelling suggest that employees in both EU(15) and NMS may benefit after a long time lag – and then depending largely upon the anticipated boost to economic growth deriving from expanded trade in the larger SIM – capital owners tend to benefit rather rapidly via enhanced profits and equity values (Keuschnigg *et al.*, 1999). Consequently, this factor is likely to exacerbate income inequality, at least in the short run.

The expectation that enlargement is likely to exacerbate income inequality within EU member states, *ceteris paribus*, might reinforce arguments for a stronger and more unified ESM. However, a greater disparity of social inequality, both within and between member states, simultaneously presents a greater challenge to this model.

Social protection

Social protection provided by the former administrations in East and Central Europe used to be relatively comprehensive and uniform in nature, with benefits arising from an individual's employer (i.e. holidays, recreation facilities), together with the provision of free public services (i.e. education, health and certain aspects of public transportation), and with the prices of basic goods (i.e. bread, water, power, housing) subsidized by the state. This approach provided a broad coverage of social protection for most active citizens and it succeeded in curtailing the growth of poverty, albeit whilst allowing wages to be maintained at levels beneath those likely to have pertained under market determination. However, in the aftermath of the transition to more market-orientated economies, social policy objectives and provision has typically received a lower priority. Thus, rather than the development of comprehensive, European-style social welfare systems being utilized to lessen the social dislocation caused by the widespread introduction of market forces into all sectors of the economy, social expenditure has been squeezed. This is partly due to the adoption of a neo-liberal macroeconomic policy stance, which views generous social protection as inhibiting the efficiency of market mechanisms, and where social expenditure

Table 13.4 Distribution of income in selected NMS, 1998

Country	Gini coefficient
Czech Republic	25.9
Hungary	27.5
Latvia	33.6
Lithuania	34.5
Poland	30.0
Slovenia	30.7
EU average	25.9
United Kingdom	32.4
United States	34.4

Source: Vaughan-Whitehead (2003:53).

reductions are considered to moderate wage-cost inflation and cultivate the favour of international financial markets, thereby strengthening exchange rates and reducing the interest rate risk premium paid on external borrowing. Accordingly, social expenditure in Hungary, for example, has declined by around one-third during the first eight years following the transition towards a market economy, whilst equivalent figures for the Czech Republic and Poland indicate reductions of one-fifth and one-sixth of social expenditure respectively (Vaughan-Whitehead, 2003: 116).

As the calculation of social benefits is typically associated with the level of NMWs in the NMS, whilst the latter has an effect upon a wider set of wage rates (particularly at levels just above this legal minima), the maintenance of low levels of minimum wages has become a key government policy objective (Vaughan-Whitehead, 1995). Moreover, there has been a shift from the provision of universal benefits towards means testing (Eatwell *et al.*, 2000: 149).

Challenges

The greater diversity characterizing the enlarged EU labour market presents a number of challenges for policy makers. This chapter concludes by briefly examining four such dilemmas.

Convergence or divergence – will NMS adopt ESM when ready?

The fact that the NMS have acceded to EU membership with a relatively low level of GDP per capita, averaging only 50 per cent of the equivalent average for EU(15) nations,[1] has been taken to suggest that these nations will benefit disproportionately from the enlargement process, as membership facilitates inward investment, enhanced trading opportunities and guarantees net receipts from EU spending priorities, such as regional development and agricultural subsidies. Indeed, economic growth in the early period post-accession has typically risen

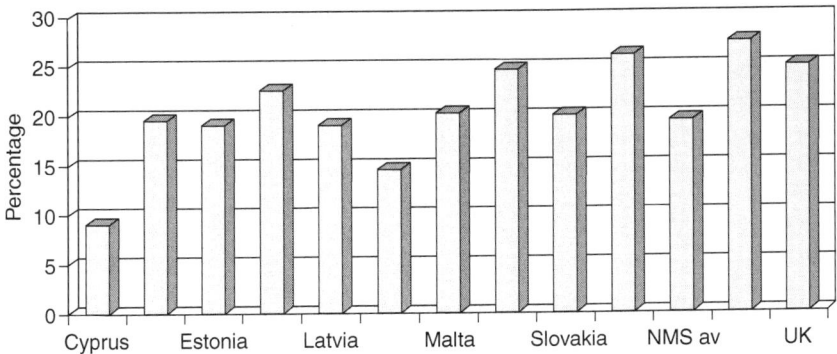

Figure 13.1 Social protection as percentage of GDP, 2000 (source: Vaughan-Whitehead, 2003: 117).

faster in the NMS (3.75 per cent p.a.) than in the more established EU members (2.5 per cent), with those countries having the lowest initial per-capita incomes tending to expand more rapidly (Kovács, 2004: 19; EU Commission, 2006: 5). Bearing in mind that eight of the NMS have undertaken a transition from quasi-command to fully-functioning market economies within two decades, the progress towards convergence amongst the NMS has been impressive. As a result, it has been suggested that the NMS will benefit from EU membership and continue to expand faster than EU(15) economies, thereby generating additional resources capable of being utilized to expand the scope and generosity of social programmes, amongst other government priorities.

The catching-up process, then, might ease the problems for the further development of the ESM caused by the consequences of the enlargement process. However, this is a problematic conclusion because it is not the case that less developed economies always grow faster than their more developed neighbours, as evidenced by many African and Latin American nations. Indeed, many of the NMS have themselves suffered a severe decline in national income during their transition process from command to market economy. Moreover, the consequences of the 'credit crunch' recession will have a persistent asymmetric (negative) impact for years to come, with the probability of a growing divergence between a small core and larger periphery of countries within the EU looking more probable as a result of the financial crisis afflicting the eurozone during 2011. Thus, national macroeconomic policy and the institutional underpinning of economic activity have a distinct impact upon the potential growth path of individual economies (Romer, 1986, 1990; Skott and Auerbach, 1995), suggesting that the 'catch-up' process is anything but certain.

Deriving evidence from previous enlargements of the EU, the evidence is mixed. Spanish GDP per capita in 1974, for example, approximately 80 per cent of the EU(15) average, whilst a quarter of a century later, after periods of policy shifts and oscillations in national fortunes, the relative per capita GDP figure stood at this same level. Portugal's GPD per capita rose from 45 per cent of the EU(15) average in 1960 to 60 per cent in 1974, then remained essentially unchanged until 1988, before rising again to 78 per cent by 2000. Irish GDP per capita stood at 65 per cent of the EU(15) average as recently as the mid-1980s, yet the previous pattern of slow growth accelerated significantly to the extent that its current income per capita, at 120 per cent of the EU(15) average, is second only to Luxembourg amongst EU member states. Greece actually declined in relative terms, during its first 15 years of EU membership, with GDP per capita falling from 80 per cent of the EU average in 1981 to 64 per cent in 1996, before relative catch-up commenced following the turn of the century. Possible reasons for these periods of stagnation and rapid relative expansion are almost certainly due to the interaction of national economic policies and the efficiency of institutional frameworks to facilitate or frustrate development given a common external economic environment (Boldrin, 2006: 381; EU Commission, 2006: 47).

Social dumping or competitive advantage?

A second issue for EU(15) member states concerns whether the 'social gap' could prove to be a form of 'social dumping'. Although this has never been properly defined by the EU, the essence of the issue relates to the reliance upon lower social and/or labour standards to gain a competitive advantage over another national economy. Social dumping may be illegal, if business practices breach national law and/or international obligations – such as the refusal to comply with bans on the use of child labour, failing to comply with health and safety rules and/or paying less than the NMW. However, the terminology tends to be used to describe a situation whereby national governments maintain lower levels of social protection to provide their firms with a cost advantage over producers based in other nations; a strategy that critics consider to be promoting 'unfair competition'. This creates pressure upon other member states to recover their competitive position by weakening their own provision. Consequently, reductions in social protection and/or labour market regulation may result in 'beggar-thy-neighbour' strategies employing the downgrading of social policy measures rather than employing options discouraged by EU membership, including devaluation and/or industrial subsidies, thus causing a 'race to the bottom'.

Certainly, it is the case that wages, non-wage costs, labour market regulation and social protection tend to be set at lower rates to the EU(15) average. However, there are large differences between the more established EU member states, and thus, to the extent that economic activity may be attracted to shift from high wage, regulated economies towards lower cost, weaker regulated neighbours, there was already ample scope for this type of shift to occur within the EU prior to the latest enlargement phase. The NMS do represent a greater degree of divergence from the poorer and/or less regulated EU(15) nations, nevertheless the issue is one of scale rather than opportunity.

There are two problems with the adoption of a pessimistic viewpoint on this issue. First, there is a significant amount of evidence to indicate that lower wages and/or employment protection rules are relatively weak attractors for FDI, at least compared to other factors such as the level of risk involved in the investment, the degree of skill and knowledge inherent within the labour force, the access to a high level of domestic demand, the quality of the infrastructure and accessibility to national-specific resources (Dunning, 1988; Cantwell, 1989; Boeri and Brucker, 2000). The establishment of networking, together with the 'embeddedness of companies in national institutions', provides information and a means of co-ordination between firms to secure common objectives, facilitates the development of a cluster of skilled labour and a technical supply chain specializing in the specific activity of the firm, thereby reducing the uncertainty arising from a dynamic business environment (Hirst and Thompson, 2000b: 306; Zysman, 2000: 120–3). Thus, a 'national system of innovation' can be extremely successful in developing international competitive advantage (Porter, 1990; Patel and Pavitt, 1991). Indeed, the fact that

81 per cent of global FDI stock is located in high wage, high tax OECD nations, indicates that cost reduction is not the overwhelming factor causing the globalization of production (Weiss, 1998: 186).

The second problem relates to the fact that at least part of the explanation for the NMS having relatively lower wage rates derives from differences in factor endowments, a reflection of poor productivity and the fact that most are labour-intensive economies. Productivity levels within the NMS are estimated to be only around 58 per cent of the EU(15) average, with Latvian productivity equating to only 38 per cent of the rate enjoyed by pre-enlargement economies (EU Commission, 2006: 56). One causal factor here relates to the greater reliance upon agricultural employment amongst many of the NMS, with its concomitant low rates of productivity growth – accounting for 19 per cent of the labour force in Poland, 16 per cent in Lithuania and 12.5 per cent in Latvia, compared to the 4 per cent EU(15) average rate (EU Commission, 2006: 7).

Examination of Total Factor Productivity data indicates that the combination of relatively low levels of labour force participation, together with high levels of unemployment, necessitate that growth rates in the NMS are reliant upon capital accumulation and technical progress. Thus, the ability of the NMS to 'catch-up' with more established EU member states is influenced by the inward flow of FDI (EU Commission, 2006: 45). Consequently, it is necessary to consider the appropriateness of the economic fundamentals in order to correctly assess whether a specific instance is an example of social dumping or the result of national economies at different stages of economic development. Were the NMS initially burdened with a comparable level of regulation and/or level of wages, without a compensatory increase in productive efficiency, this would provide a severe shock to these economies and impose a weighty burden upon their fledgling development profiles. This would have a similar effect to that experienced by the former East Germany in the aftermath of the German reunification process, when the revaluation of exchange rates and the steps taken towards the equalization of wages without equivalent rises in productivity rendered large swathes of former industrial activity uncompetitive (Buechtemann and Schupp, 1992; Whyman, 2001).

A more useful comparison for consideration of the social dumping debate relates to unit labour costs between EU(15) and NMS, which indicate far smaller differentials than when considering wage levels in isolation (Vaughan-Whitehead, 2003: 338). It is the relative (or unit) cost of labour that matters more than absolute cost levels, and since low wage economies tend to be low productivity economies. This explains why three-quarters of the FDI flows that have taken place over the past two decades have been concentrated amongst industrialized economies rather than moving from high-wage industrialized nations to low-wage developing nations (Dicken, 1992: 54; Hirst and Thompson, 1996: 67–8; Mishra, 1999: 22). Thus, whilst some evidence exists to indicate that social dumping is a real and potentially threatening phenomenon, it is thus far rather exaggerated (Adnett, 1995; Leibfried and Pierson, 1995b).

European wage formation

A third issue relates to the development of wage formation within the European economy, and the fact that it would appear that diverse systems will remain for the foreseeable future, and with the tendency for evolution being towards a decentralized firm- or sector-centred system, which runs quite contrary to the vision of the original advocates of the ESM. This issue is important because the literature suggests that internationalization (and by inference, European economic integration) disproportionately benefits capital at the expense of labour, due to the relaxation of financial regulation to facilitate capital movements and hence facilitates the (threat of) relocation of productive facilities within the SM, whilst enhanced international competition increases the sensitivity of wage developments (Driffill and van der Ploeg, 1993; Huizinga, 1993; Naylor, 1999). Wage co-ordination, in contrast, can reduce many of these effects and improve their bargaining position vis-à-vis employers (Borghijs *et al.*, 2003: 23). It enables trade unions to press for greater parity of pay across the single labour market, and thereby reduce the emphasis of restricting wage rates to maintain competitive position relative to other EU member states. Moreover, the ability of corporations to achieve wage concessions to prevent the relocation of production becomes less credible (Borghijs *et al.*, 2003: 29).

Macroeconomic effects are contested. One line of thought suggests that wage co-ordination may have the effect of encouraging higher wage demands compared to decentralized action (Borghijs *et al.*, 2003: 23). Moreover, centralized wage bargaining is associated with reduced wage differentials between regions, thereby raising the possibility that this may cause rising unemployment in those regions with lower labour productivity (Flanagan, 1999; Borghijs *et al.*, 2003: 30). However, monopoly union theory suggests that more highly co-ordinated wage setting may encourage the internalization of macroeconomic effects, thereby leading to greater consideration of international competitiveness than might occur under decentralized wage bargaining, where unions may engage in free riding by engaging in wage militancy and relying upon the maintenance of restraint elsewhere in the economy to prevent cost-push inflation undermining employment levels (Cameron, 1984; Rowthorn and Glyn, 1990; Whyman, 2003). Furthermore, it has been suggested that centralized wage bargaining within the context of an EMU may result in superior macroeconomic outcomes by solving co-ordination problems with the ECB (Hall and Franzese, 1998; Cukierman and Lippi, 1999).

Participation in EMU presents additional challenges for European labour markets, through the creation of pressure for increased flexibility (Burda, 2001). This is typically perceived in terms of micro-flexibility, such as enhancing numerate flexibility, through encouraging less standardized (and secure) employment contracts, facilitating labour mobility within and between nation-states, by creating incentives for individuals to undertake additional human capital development and securing a shift of benefit claimants into paid employment. However, these same effects can be achieved through macro-flexibility, via a form of wage co-ordination that can internalize the effects of wage pressure upon the international competitive position (Whyman, 2006: 112–28). The literature suggests a degree of support for this proposition by concluding that wage bargaining should occur at the level where shocks occur (Pissarides, 1997).

There are, however, plenty of obstacles to a greater co-ordination of European wage formation including significant differences in union density and coverage, the timing of wage bargaining, the role of unions in national policy determination, the bewildering variety of national labour market regulations, together with differing intensity of opposition from employer organizations reinforcing the perception of there existing 'substantial differences among EU countries with respect to trade union practices' (Borghijs *et al.*, 2003: 23–4).

EU enlargement has further complicated this picture by resulting in a greater diversity of industrial relations structures than existed previously, thereby making agreement upon a single model far more difficult to achieve. This is not to overlook the fact that trade union density rates varied considerably amongst EU(15) member states, with standard deviation measurements increasing from 17.8 to 25.8 between 1980 and 1994, largely due to distinctive developments amongst the Scandinavian economies (Borghijs *et al.*, 2003: 13). However the accession of the NMS has magnified previous differences. Moreover, the fact that wage bargaining is far more decentralized within the majority of NMS than their more established counterparts weakens the case for the establishment of a comprehensive bargaining structure being established across the single European labour market, as promoted by the ETUC (Borghijs *et al.*, 2003: 7). The combination of decentralized wage bargaining, and the low levels of trade union membership, implies that, in most NMS, the majority of workers will actually receive little or no opportunity to exercise their collective voice in meaningful wage negotiations.

There is a further problem for the expansion of meaningful social dialogue between social partners of equal worth, as envisioned by the ESM, namely the relative weakness of employer organizations capable of articulating the views and interests of a wide and representative body of organizations. This is particularly problematic amongst the former command economy NMS, as employer organizations did not really exist before the transition period, and therefore have not had the time or opportunity to develop their authority within the business sector in these countries. Moreover, subsequent experience has witnessed a fragmentation of business interests amongst a wide range of employer organizations. Thus, even were trade unions to regain some of their former strength, and were processes within the ESM capable of facilitating opportunities for the establishment of social (and/or tripartite) partnership between representatives of labour and capital, it would appear difficult to achieve consensus due to the prevalence of multiple representative organizations, each with a consciousness to advance a partial interest agenda and possibly use its negotiation stance to compete for new members.

To the extent that a degree of co-ordination of industrial relations is possible, it is equally likely that the creation of a European labour market may be limited to certain key groups of workers, possessing specific technical and managerial skills, and for particular categories of highly mobile labour, notably managers, construction workers, labourers and young people. In this scenario, the higher incomes, which are commanded by key employees, may disrupt national labour markets by increasing income inequality or through low-wage countries losing skilled labour to higher-wage member states. Furthermore, while the advent of euro-bargaining could provide new opportunities for trade unions and their members, it could equally fragment unions along supranational company lines, thereby undermining class solidarity. Accordingly, trade unions risk becoming 'partners ... of regional capital trying to survive in inter-regional free market competition' rather than 'agents of inter-regional redistribution' (Streeck and Schmitter, 1991: 55).

Initiatives such as the EWC Directive has the potential to mitigate such effects, by strengthening co-operation and the pooling of information between EU trade unions, and across national boundaries at the TNC level, potentially facilitating negotiation over the establishment of universal minimum standards of training, anti-discrimination practice and promotion procedures within the specific TNCs where each EWC is constituted (Rhodes, 1992: 45). It is, however, a matter of interpretation to decide whether initiatives of this type create the conditions favouring the future development of euro-bargaining, or whether they reinforce the fracturing of existing wage formation patterns.

The intensification of international competition may additionally cause companies to focus upon internal rather than national labour markets (Marginson and Sisson, 1996: 177–8). Trade unions therefore face marginalization due to employer preference for company-level 'productivity coalitions' rather than centralized concertation or sectoral bargaining. According to this viewpoint, euro-bargaining is irrelevant to the needs of post-Fordist flexible production. The divergent tensions, threatening to further complicate European industrial relations, are likely to persist into EMU because current arrangements show no clear evidence of converging to a uniform pattern across euro-land (Rhodes, 1992: 43–4).

Consequently, full wage co-ordination is unlikely, at least in the short term. It is possible that a 'softer' form of information exchange and benchmarking may spread from existing pockets of international co-operation; examples of this tendency include European Metalworkers' Federation attempts to adopt a common bargaining rule for its member unions, together with the Doorn agreement between unions in Belgium, Germany, Luxembourg and the Netherlands (Borghijs *et al.*, 2003: 25). Nevertheless, the evidence does not look promising for those advocating euro-bargaining as one potential aid towards strengthening macroeconomic flexibility whilst seeking to create a more unified labour market to complement more advanced efforts in the flows of goods, services and financial capital.

Labour mobility and migration

The final issue concerns the free movement of workers which has long formed a core feature of European integration and is enshrined in Article 48 of the 1957 Treaty of Rome. Hence, even with some member states introducing time limited restrictions to unlimited migration from the latest two entrants, Romania and Bulgaria, it was always anticipated that the addition of 12 NMS would increase net labour flows across the single European market. Indeed, this was welcomed, for its likely downward pressure on inflation (through lower wage increases), the greater labour mobility sought to mitigate external shocks that may be exacerbated by EMU, and due to the predicted demographic consequences of an aging population, with potential consequences for pension costs and a declining active population relative to the retired community. The EU Commission itself suggested that immigration rates need to be more than doubled, over the next decades, to stabilize labour markets and pension funds (EU, 2002).

A degree of concern was evident due to the fact that the recent enlargement involved considerably more people than in any previous phase. However, it was noted that, in 2000, only 0.1 per cent of the total EU(15) population moved their primary residence across EU member states (Vaughan-Whitehead, 2003: 433), whilst intra-EU migration accounted for only a small proportion of the stock of non-nationals in the working populations of those member states (Austria and Germany) with the highest overall penetration (EU Commission, 2006: 6). Moreover, it was suggested that any initial increase in labour flows from new to existing member states would prove temporary in nature, as past experience indicated a return to a steady-state after a few years, as new entrant economies benefited from 'catch-up' in GDP per capita prompted by membership.

These conclusions derive from the rather optimistic conclusions reached by the European Integration Consortium (2000) report, and, based upon rather optimistic assumptions made by the authors, misgivings proliferated concerning the possibility of the EU deliberately underestimating the likely of new entrant migration because of its political sensitivity (Fassmann and Münz, 2002; Vaughan-Whitehead, 2003: 432). For example, 'pull' effects for migration, such as differences in wage levels, were recognized by the EU but were predicted to be mitigated by the impact of historical and cultural ties (EU Commission, 2006: 79). Moreover, their analysis ignored the absence of experience of recent free migration amongst eight of the NMS, which might have suggested that enlargement would lead to a release of pent-up demand for international mobility. Instead, the EU's studies predicted a total effect equivalent to only 1.2 per cent of the projected working-age population of the former EU(15) in 2020, a total of three million people over a 15-year period, with a short run effect amounting to between 300,000 and 350,000 in the first few years following enlargement. If correct, this increase in immigration would be insufficient to affect the EU labour market in general (EU Commission, 2006: 79).

Experience over the first few years following enlargement has sharply contradicted these conclusions, with migration far exceeding the EUs own projections. In the United Kingdom alone, itself not the primary destination of choice for most new migrant workers, government figures suggest that 1.1 million migrant workers entered the labour market; a rate many times the EU estimate for the *entire* European economy. Moreover, initial UK government reports suggesting this level of immigration having only a negligible effect upon the employment and/or wage levels of existing residents is rather surprising, as *ceteris paribus* one might expect an increase in the supply of labour to have some noticeable effect upon one or other of these variables – unless these effects were overwhelmed by the impact of other forces, such as buoyant aggregate demand and/or stimulative effects arising from labour market policy (Dustmann *et al.*, 2003; Portes and French, 2005; Gilpin *et al.*, 2006; Riley and Weale, 2006). In fact, it would appear that a majority of the new jobs created in the United Kingdom over the past decade have gone to migrant workers,[2] preventing further reductions in unemployment and depressing wages below the levels which would have otherwise have resulted from tight labour markets. Indeed, the Bank of England has expressed its viewpoint that immigration has played a positive effect in restraining inflationary effects within the UK economy precisely because it has caused slower-than-anticipated wage growth (Blanchflower, 2007). The overall impact of this dramatic increase in immigration into the United Kingdom has been evaluated by a House of Lords inquiry, which found little evidence that this has led to significant per capita economic benefits, and with bottlenecks in housing and public services bearing part of the cost of transition (Wakeham, 2008).

The impact of such large-scale migration has also been experienced by the NMS, who have suffered an outflow of skilled labour, and with their economies therefore not gaining the full advantage of the investment in human capital undertaken to the benefit of these individuals. The fact that a proportion of this migration is only temporary will mitigate this loss, and indeed, partial data seems to suggest that the current economic slowdown (caused by the credit crunch) will exacerbate this trend. Nevertheless, migratory flows are likely to continue to present problems for both home and host nations, not least in terms of political tensions caused by the dislocation of communities and the redistribution of scarce resources.

Conclusion

Post enlargement, the EU labour market is more diverse, with wider variance in terms of labour market outcomes and institutional frameworks. This has created headaches for those desiring a more unified, harmonized European labour market, as differences in productivity, participation rates, industrial relations content and employment regulation, have diverged as a result of this process. Consequently, the most recent wave of enlargement gives cause for reflection concerning the desirability of future initiatives to be introduced with the intention of harmonizing individual labour market conditions, and raises the question of the impossibility of this endeavour.

Yet, a SM for goods, services and capital, without an equivalent SM for labour, would appear to be a rather one-sided model of integration. It is possible that a 'catch-up' process for the NMS might narrow these differences, but this is not a certainty and even if it occurs it is likely to take decades. Thus, for the foreseeable future, how the EU adapts to this diversity is likely to determine whether the dream of a harmonized, unified euro-land is realisable or whether the European project will remain a less consistent, more varied accommodation to existing reality.

14 National economic policy alternatives

Introduction

Participation in further EU integration will place an additional straightjacket upon sovereign macroeconomic policy and increase the difficulty of pursuing those policies optimal to its own national interest. For example, the model for EMU seeks to impose a particular institutional framework that restricts the flexibility of action of individual countries in order to enable economic policy to be determined, or at least co-ordinated, from the centre. Many economists (Jamieson, 1998; Ormerod, 1999a; Michie, 2000; Minford, 2000) argue that greater autonomy for individual nation-states, under the principle of subsidiarity, might provide a more stable economic environment in which to pursue further co-operation between countries. However, largely due to the political desire to tie members more closely together, the EU is seeking to progressively replace economic autonomy for a nation-state by the requirement to co-ordinate its economic strategy with the EU norm, or else be subject to sanctions levied by the EU Commission (Pennant-Rea *et al.*, 1997).

A decision to reject such developments would restore to national government those economic instruments essential to the management of its economy. Governments will be able to devise different economic programmes and, once endorsed by the electorate, will possess the means by which to pursue their chosen objectives. Democracy will, therefore, be restored, so that citizens can once again enjoy the opportunity to choose the economic strategy pursued by the government of the day. Moreover, governments will be able to pursue a more balanced economic programme, pursuing the multiple objectives of full employment, high economic growth and a sustainable balance of payments as well as low inflation. The opportunities are substantial.

To illustrate the broad range of different policies that could be enacted, this chapter outlines a number of broad alternative economic strategies that could be pursued once a nation is freed from the restrictive grip of the ECB and the requirements of the TEU, let alone any future developments. Additionally, it discusses the development of a complementary industrial strategy and exchange rate policy. The former can only prove effective if supplemented by fiscal and monetary policies that target growth and reject deflation. For example, inflation is not a disease in itself, but the symptom of an economy that cannot produce enough to satisfy domestic demand. The solution is to boost demand and channel it to domestic industry, improving profits, stimulating production and hence productivity, and providing the incentive to invest; thereby cutting unit costs and inflation through a considered policy of economic expansion. It can be achieved, free from EU constraints, through control of the exchange rate and the accompanying interest rate changes. Such a policy makes it profitable to produce domestically by utilizing the price mechanism to boost exports, encouraging import substitution and luring British industry back into sectors it has abandoned. A tax on imports would provide crucial support. An effective exchange rate policy is critical to the successful implementation of the outlined options for macroeconomic policy. The intention is to demonstrate, not only that national economic management is still feasible, but also that it is preferable to transferring the main levers of macroeconomic policy into the hands of the EU which is incapable of using them consistently in the best interests of all member states simultaneously.

Tight monetary policy – low interest rate strategy

The first potential economic strategy seeks to follow the framework established by Alan Greenspan and the US Federal Reserve Bank, whereby national monetary authorities (whether in the hands of an independent or democratically controlled central bank) seek a higher long-term growth rate by providing a favourable climate for industrial expansion through low inflation and hence reduced long-term interest rates. Fiscal policy is used to support the more dominant monetary policy by restraining inflationary pressures, thereby reinforcing the low interest rate objective. The globalization of financial markets prevents governments from 'persuading' financial institutions to finance public sector borrowing at less than the market rate. Consequently, the higher the level of public sector borrowing on the international money markets, the higher the price for that borrowing in terms of long-term interest rates. This approach assumes crowding-out in the financial markets due to limited resources for lending to prospective borrowers because, were banks to create money simply to meet the additional demand for funds so that the supply of loanable funds was relatively elastic, interest rates would be unaffected. However, the strategy seeks to reduce government expenditure in order to reduce borrowing and hence interest rates.

In 'hard' versions of this strategy, the government endeavours to maintain a high value for the currency in order to squeeze inflation further. The objective is comparatively easy to accomplish if the country enjoys a trade surplus, because the pressure on its exchange rate is upwards due to the country's competitive position, assuming the absence of speculative motives to counter this fundamental relationship. However, since many EU member states typically suffer from a current account trade deficit (particularly with Germany), a rise in short-term interest rates is needed to attract sufficient short-term capital investment into domestic securities to counterbalance trade-related downward pressures on the currency, thus maintaining a high value for sterling. However, these developments will impact long-term interest rates and thus conflict with the fundamental goal of the strategy. Nevertheless, there is no reason why a sovereign currency should not prove to be stronger than the euro, particularly due to the participation of high-inflation southern European member states and an ECB forced to balance economic policy between conflicting needs (Baimbridge *et al.*, 1999; Weber, 1991b). As witnessed over the past decade, the ECB has required time to establish its anti-inflation credibility and to demonstrate that it can ensure the long-term stability of EMU.[1] Moreover, unemployment remains the greatest economic problem for Europe to solve; thus it is probable that, sooner rather later, the ECB will come under pressure to loosen monetary policy.

A fiscal-based strategy

A second distinctive economic strategy involves the more active use of fiscal as well as monetary policy in order to pursue both internal and external balance for the economy. Internal balance refers to more than just low inflation, but also to low unemployment and to high rates of economic growth. Accordingly, a mixture of demand-side reflation and supply-side labour market policies, particularly measures encouraging re-training and labour mobility, could reduce unemployment. Thus, the net stimulative effect is targeted upon specific sectors of the economy that most require assistance, rather than raising aggregate demand per se and creating inflationary bottlenecks. Economic growth could be facilitated by the maintenance of a competitive exchange rate through managed floating, perhaps based upon a trade-weighted basket of currencies, together with tax incentives for firms that increase productive investment. A mixture of fiscal and monetary policy could restrain inflation; if this proved difficult to achieve, rather than abandon the other internal objectives, governments could enact additional measures to restrain inflationary pressures. These might include the temporary re-introduction of credit controls, an incomes policy (tax-based or otherwise) or co-ordinated national bargaining. Although currently unpopular amongst economists who prefer the allocative efficiency of free markets, the reality of sticky wages and prices, due to oligopolistic markets as much as the existence of trade unions, gives rise to the possibility of market failure resulting in persistently high unemployment and slower-than-trend output growth. In this case, government intervention is justified to achieve a superior outcome. It is a fact that the majority of the world's nations still retain exchange controls to assist them to manage their economies, whilst Ireland's remarkable recent growth rates have been facilitated by 'social contracts' with trade unions to prevent wage pressures undermining its competitive position. Finally, external balance can be achieved through the provision of a competitive exchange rate, although structural problems in export sectors may require supplementary supply-side measures to improve product quality and reliability and to encourage a shift of resources to provide goods and services in growing rather than stagnant markets.

The 'Keynesian' strategy is notably different from the first approach due to its positive role for government action in wider areas of economic activity. Accordingly, an approach of this nature would be facilitated by an industrial policy designed to enhance the long run competitiveness of a country's industry. For example, an analysis of trade flows indicates that Britain enjoys a comparative advantage in financial and media services, and those areas of manufacturing which rely upon a high degree of scientific innovation, such as telecommunications, pharmaceuticals, aerospace, energy exploration and generation, biochemicals and computer-related activity.[2] In contrast, Britain is less competitive in lower value added manufactures, most notably in engineering and metalworking sectors. Outside the EU, a country could strive to strengthen its competitive position by enhancing the productive potential of already strong sectors through *targeted* reductions in corporation tax, R&D tax credits, and greater spending upon education. Innovative research undertaken by universities and publicly funded research centres requires prioritization in terms of the allocation of government resources if higher growth is to be forthcoming. Labour market programmes designed to re-equip workers for the requirements of industries with a competitive advantage ensure that their maximum growth potential is not undermined by the lack of a skilled workforce, whilst facilitating the shift of resources to more productive uses. The promotion of domestic firms has the further advantage that it will substantially improve the balance of payments position in the long-run, whilst ensuring that the majority of the improvements in living standards and profitability are not repatriated abroad by TNCs. Moreover, the trend towards foreign-owned plants demanding ever-increasing 'sweeteners' to retain production raises the possibility that providing inexpensive finance or development grants might prove a cheaper alternative that generates an improved long-term growth reward.

An industrial strategy

An active industrial strategy must be based upon understanding of what promotes industrial competitiveness. Porter's (1990) exhaustive research demonstrated that economic success is achieved through the development of 'clusters' of mutually reinforcing internationally competitive industries. For example, Britain once enjoyed the benefits of clustering, as one sophisticated industry spawned and reinforced others; British goods pulled British services into overseas markets and vice versa, its multinationals served as loyal customers abroad, and the cluster of financial services and trade-related industries was highly self-reinforced. However, a gradual unwinding of industrial clusters occurred, with only pockets of competitive advantage remaining. British firms rely heavily on foreign inputs and machinery. As some UK industries became uncompetitive, they were increasingly poor buyers for other domestic products. The spiral continues downward, cushioned only by long tradition and the remnants of technological innovation. Thus many British manufacturing companies lag behind those of other industrial countries such as Germany, Japan and Sweden in process technology and in their willingness and ability to invest in new plant, undermining competitive advantage in industries producing manufacturing equipment such as machine tools, process controls and lift trucks. In the car industry, for instance, the United Kingdom lost competitive advantage in end products outside a small luxury sector and positions in a variety of automotive components eroded with it. The same process applied to an even greater extent in durable goods, such as appliances and consumer electronics.

The sectors where British firms sustain competitive advantage partly owe it to a cluster of related, supporting industries. In consumer goods and services, a vibrant retail industry creates pressures to innovate. Britain was among the first countries to permit television advertising, which created a fertile environment for companies to build skills in modern marketing. The City of London provides another sector where British strength relies upon the advantages of clustering. Britain's international position in financial services such as trading, investment management, insurance and merchant banking is concentrated in the City, along with supporting activities like information and telecommunications facilities, financial journalism, printing and publishing, legal services, financial advertising and public relations. The dynamism of this cluster attracts firms worldwide to locate in London.

However, national industry frequently lacks dynamism and the ability to upgrade its competitive position unaided, due to cumulative disadvantages which reinforce each other negatively in the spiral of relative decline. Problems in one industry hurt others. Falling competitiveness reduces relative living standards, making consumer demand less sophisticated. Downward pressure on government revenue leads to cutbacks in resource creation and social services, weakening still more industries, whereby remaining competitive advantages are insufficient to generate sufficient well-paid jobs for all its citizens. Therefore it is caught in the downward spiral of clustering and its relative living standards suffer accordingly. Loss of competitiveness creates its own momentum, which, once established, is hard to reverse without a major policy initiative. Indeed lingering market positions and customer loyalties allay any sense of urgency about the need for change.

A significant proportion of growth in skilled and value added UK employment has occurred from investment by foreign firms. Much of this, however, is attracted by relatively low production costs. Foreign investments are largely in assembly facilities, taking advantage of poorly paid, mostly unskilled labour, or in service industries such as hotels, golf courses and retail outlets. While overseas capital benefits British industry, an economy whose growth depends on assembly outposts of foreign companies will be constrained in terms of productivity increases. Certainly such investment alone cannot break the vicious circle between a weak balance of payments, slow growth and declining manufacturing.

Hence, for any economy needing to restart the upgrading process, a number of fundamental problems must be tackled by a coordinated industrial strategy if recovery is to occur:

i   It is difficult to regain innovation-driven competitiveness without a world-class educational and training system encompassing all socioeconomic and ability levels. The rate of investment in human skills must rise substantially, standards must be improved and technical expertise must be stressed. This is perhaps the most pressing issue facing Britain over the next decade, for the need to improve the quality and quantity of its labour force is great. Research conducted in France and Germany by the National Institute for Economic and Social Research (Prais and Wagner, 1988; Steedman, 1988; Jarvis and Prais, 1989) demonstrated that the level of technical qualifications of craft workers is far superior in those countries to that achieved in the United Kingdom. A further report (Prais and Jarvis, 1989) on training in the retail industry concluded that 'the United Kingdom was creating a certificated semi-literate underclass'. Moreover, training trends are deteriorating in the United Kingdom; in 1964 240,000 young people were in apprenticeships and 148,000 in industrial or mercantile training, but some 20 years later these figures had dropped to 55,700 and 36,700 respectively.

ii   Private sector companies, as well as the government, face a busy skills agenda. They need to realize that without a broader pool of trained human resources, their competitive advantage will be limited. This need embraces managerial staff, where British firms have traditionally employed far fewer university graduates than other industrial economies. Unless companies accept greater responsibility for internal training of all workers, they will make little progress relative to their competitors. The multi-skilling of the industrial workforce provides the route to productive flexibility, quality and innovation, while enhancing individuals' occupational status. The inability of individuals to contribute to their full potential is reflected in the stunted economic performance of many sectors. Narrow vocational training is a contradiction in an economy that seeks to place workers at the forefront of innovation. Consequently the emphasis must be on quality training to reflect new economic requirements.

iii Investment levels need to increase to match the improved labour force, primarily in manufacturing but also in the infrastructure of essential services. Machinery and plant in many sectors are currently antiquated, so that the development of advanced technologies as a basis for expanding into modern high value added production is held back. The future competitive advantage of firms can only be based on innovation in new products and new processes of production. Government aid to industry enabling the maintenance of high investment can play a crucial role in this process.

iv   The share of GDP allocated to R&D, whereby reallocation of both government and company resources towards commercial R&D is necessary for successfully reversing the spiral of relative decline, by stimulating both the generation and the diffusion of innovation. Supporting reform of the accounting treatment of R&D expenditure would also prove beneficial.

v   Without sophisticated buyers, innovation and dynamism will be stunted. Whilst Britain already enjoys demand-side advantages in luxury and leisure-related commodities, the challenge is to upgrade industrial demand to broaden the sphere over which British companies benefit from well-informed buyers. Improvement of managers' and workers' education contributes to this objective. The prosperous London and South East markets can be the cutting edge of new consumer demand conditions.

vi Some of the operations of national financial markets have become a barrier to competitive advantage. Institutional investors frequently possess little commitment to companies nor do they play an active role in corporate governance. A group of large British conglomerates has emerged, which buy and sell unrelated companies, but whose financial orientation does little in the long run to upgrade competitive advantage in domestic industry. The result of such trends is that US-style earnings pressures threaten to dominate management thinking. However, a long-run bias in industrial decision-making is in the interests of national prosperity.

vii Economic prosperity will never be complete without a faster rate of new business formation to make headway in reducing unemployment, because revitalization of established industries sometimes reduces the size of the workforce. However, new business formation depends on skills and ideas, on appropriate motivation and goals, on active competition, and access to capital. One of the urgent reasons for upgrading British education, especially in universities, is to seed new ventures. The United Kingdom cannot rely on foreign investment for job creation and prosperity (*The Economist*, 1991).

These measures should reduce the level of joblessness, leading to the long-term restoration of full employment. By reducing, and eventually eliminating, the long-run growth of imports and by stimulating an expansion in exports, the strategy aims to reconcile full employment with the simultaneous achievement of payments equilibrium.

However, such an industrial strategy cannot be reconciled with current EU regulations, let alone its future federal aspirations, thus a country's essential interests' may conflict directly with EU moves towards greater integration. However, with determination and imagination, there is no reason why it cannot acquire again the significant comparative advantages in the production of goods that once made it the workshop of the world. Services are a crucial complement to this process, but do not alone provide the growth momentum of manufacturing industry nor can they be relied upon to substitute for the deficits in overseas visible trade. The construction of such a competitive economy involves the complete unravelling and reconstruction of its relationship with the EU. It is to this relationship that we now return.

However, the policies required to revitalize a country's industry frequently run counter to current EU rules and would be frustrated by movement towards economic and political union. Major historical trends cannot be reversed quickly; a permanent increase in the national rate of productivity growth, for instance, requires sustained economic expansion, a difficult endeavour given the deflationary tendencies of EMU. Indeed, EU membership per se tends to frustrate the achievement of these objectives through three fundamental mechanisms. First, possessing a relatively weak competitive trade position with other EU nations prevents market forces from generating unaided the profits required for industrial regeneration. Experience demonstrates that market operations tend to accentuate strengths and deficiencies rather than eliminate them. Second, the Treaty of Rome severely limits aid to industry, whilst the public expenditure needed to complement the price mechanism in promoting industrial regeneration is circumscribed by the TEU convergence criteria and SGP. Third, the current functioning of EMU limits the scope for discretionary national economic policies. Therefore, both markets and governments are prevented from addressing basic problems by the very essence of EU operations and developments.

The scale of deindustrialization is uniquely intense in Britain, for example, requiring the implementation of a solution geared specifically to British problems rather than a blunter, less sensitive EU-wide programme. However, any strategy designed to confront the UK's deep-seated trading crisis within the EU will take many years to come to fruition. Therefore a danger arises that such a strategy could be jettisoned before it has had sufficient time to be effective, in the face of short-term pressures. This consideration suggests that government funds for industrial restructuring should be exempt from any immediate requirement for reducing public expenditure. Consequently a programme to stimulate industrial investment, boost jobs creation, and improve the quality of education and training must be rigorously maintained in the face of potential short-run problems. The benefits from such a programme would be reaped over a 5–10-year period if the constraints imposed by EU integration are prevented from undermining its potential. Survival in the interim requires the creation of a breathing space for the British economy until the programme becomes effective. The preservation of this essential space depends upon the UK government possessing an active exchange rate and trade policy, with discretionary control over movements in the external value of sterling and freedom to pursue independent fiscal and monetary policies.

Exchange rate policy

Export-led growth occurs because the firms that are competitive in world markets commence with the advantage of costs at least as low as their competitors, given that an economy is usually required to sell its output to the rest of the world at a competitive price. If it does so, it will embark on export-led growth, otherwise import-led stagnation is likely to follow. Moreover, once export-led growth is established a number of forces operate to keep fast growing economies moving ahead. Particularly significant is the impact of successive waves of investment, which tend to reduce the cost of goods in the internationally-traded goods sector so rendering export prices increasingly competitive. However, a key determinant of competitiveness is to establish and maintain a competitive exchange rate, i.e. one that achieves balance of payments equilibrium at full employment.

If a policy of expanding the economy through the export-led growth engendered by a competitive exchange rate is adopted, it is unlikely on the available evidence, to cause substantial inflation during its early stages. Indeed, it could lead to inflation falling. However, a further potential generator of price increases may be an overexpansion of domestic demand, so that the economy becomes overheated. Once demand exceeds the capacity to supply, prices begin to rise. Such a scenario must be avoided. However, these problems are not insurmountable; they can be contained through a variety of channels. First, the more resources that are deployed into sectors facing falling cost curves and engaged in foreign trade, the easier it is for self-sustaining growth to be achieved. Large returns on investment that can be obtained in these sectors can provide sufficient new profitability to finance additional new capital requirements. Second, for at least some shortages there is considerable scope for importing what cannot be obtained from domestic production. For many commodities there exists an elastic supply of foreign output to meet domestic shortages. Third, any attempt to reflate the economy in order to achieve full employment has got to include an undertaking of training, retraining and education, particularly covering engineering and technical work. A competitive exchange rate cannot in itself be a panacea for all a nation's economic problems. It will take some years to recreate full employment. When the pound's external value ensures competitive exports, it will still require price changes to produce substantial increases in output.

Hence, over a period the desired objectives of exchange rate policy are short-term stability and long-term flexibility. The dangers to avoid are long-term fixity and short-term volatility. The only way of achieving these goals is a system that permits long-run change whilst avoiding violent short-run fluctuations. Various policies are available to secure this end, but membership of the euro prevents them being implemented by establishing a permanent fixity which imposes deflation upon less competitive national economies. However, this does not reduce relative prices automatically; it does so by creating unemployment and stifling the future prospects for economic growth. That is what is meant by those who advocate EMU membership as a 'discipline' upon a member state's population.

The exchange rate between two currencies is a price like any other. Its movement enables the two economies to achieve trade and payments balance. If one country's exchange rate is over-valued its exports become more expensive in the foreign currency, while imports become cheaper in its own currency. Therefore export volumes tend to decline and import volumes to increase, so that eventually the trade balance moves into deficit and unemployment rises. Conversely, when a country lowers its exchange rate, exports became cheaper and expand, while imports are constricted. The trade balance usually improves[3] but at some contemporary sacrifice of real income due to higher internal prices.

The correct level for the exchange rate at any one time is that which enables an economy to combine full employment of productive resources simultaneously with approximate balance of payments equilibrium. A higher exchange rate generates overseas deficits and unemployment; a lower one leads to the build up of excessive foreign currency reserves and domestic inflation. However, it has been emphasized that this 'correct' exchange rate varies in value over time (Jay, 1990). The variety of influences affecting economic performance (trade balances, productivity, price movements, discoveries of natural resources, etc.) combines to ensure that the 'correct' value of the exchange rate alters with the years. Therefore a country needs to retain its ability to adjust the external value of its currency. To fix it irrecovably is as difficult as attempting to maintain in perpetuity the rate of income tax or the price of oil. The endeavour to do so generates economic inefficiency, usually in the form of accelerating inflation or a rise in unemployment.

Consequently the optimal strategy is to retain the national policy instruments required to increase its competitiveness in a socially acceptable manner. To achieve this it is essential that a country retains control over its interest rate, uses central bank intervention to smooth speculative fluctuations, encourages worldwide co-operation (e.g. through the G-20) between central banks and aims for the maximum long-term exchange rate flexibility combined with the maximum practical short-term stability. Under such a regime, the exchange rate fulfils its role as facilitator of greater growth, higher living standards and full employment, without becoming an end in itself.

There is always a rate of exchange that enables each country to employ its productive resources fully. In an ever-changing environment, the rate frequently alters to secure simultaneous full employment and trade balance. Therefore, when formulating economic policy outside the EU, any suggestion that the pound should 'shadow' the euro must be rebutted. Such targeting makes domestic objectives harder to achieve; in any case the pound moves more closely with the US dollar than with any European currency.

However, as the Chinese government has illustrated, it is possible for nations to choose where they want the exchange rate to be and, over the long-term, to hold it there within narrow margins. Of course there will be short-term fluctuations, but these are not important. It is the medium-term trend that counts. The question then becomes one of which policies can governments pursue to change the exchange rate, and then maintain it near the preferred level? A range of options is available which can be co-ordinated to generate a viable, nation-wide strategy.

First, is the monetary and interest rate stance that the government adopts. Strong evidence exists to suggest that tight monetary policies and the high interest rates, which accompany them, pull the exchange rate up, while more accommodating monetary policies and lower interest rates bring it down. Second, the actions of both the government and the central bank, when dealing with the foreign exchange market, exert a powerful influence in an area where expectations are crucial. If the government expresses a clear view that the exchange rate is too high or too low, the market will respond. Third, the government possesses a defined strategy to eliminate the foreign trade imbalance. Such a strategy requires a commitment to achieving a long-term competitive exchange rate, which achieves balance of payments equilibrium at full employment. This rate will, of course, alter over time. Fourth, tariff protection may be crucial in order to restrict the flows of imports to a level consistent with the targeted short-term exchange rate. Fifth, on the capital side of the balance of payments the government can control international financial flows to maintain a competitive exchange rate. Potential policies range from taxes to quantitative restrictions on speculative movements (Burkitt *et al.*, 1993).

However, if the value of the currency falls, there is a tendency for imports to stay initially at their previous volume, while the domestic revenue from exports falls because the exchange rate has gone down, the 'J curve' effect. A slow decline in the exchange rate generates a succession of 'J curve' effects flowing from each successive decrease, giving the impression that no improvement is in sight. Nonetheless the empirical evidence of exchange rate movements occurring in Britain and other countries, and of the availability of a battery of policy instruments to sustain a targeted external currency value, demonstrates that in the medium-term governments can determine exchange rates.

Historically, Britain's exchange rate policy has lurched from the ultra fixed systems such as the Gold Standard, through Bretton Woods and the ERM, to the freely floating days when monetarism and the rule of markets swept through governments across the industrialized world. Rarely has the decision to enter, or exit, one particular system been for any proven economic reasons. Instead the main driving force is whatever the current vogue of politicians and their advisers happens to be.

This is clearly an inefficient method of managing an economy, and of determining peoples' employment potential and standard of living. Rather within the context of this discussion concerning the development of an active exchange rate policy to facilitate national economic renewal, we argue that its over-riding function is to convert domestic prices of all factors of production, including, labour, energy, raw materials, into international prices at such a level as to encourage economic growth through the full use of resources and simultaneously to achieve trade balance. If the exchange rate cannot fulfil these functions over a sufficient period of time (to counter fluctuations), this offers conclusive evidence that the exchange rate is misaligned, so that the existing system must come under scrutiny. Whilst an exchange rate system to suit all economies for all seasons is an impossible reality, two systems, however, offer the greatest potential for combining an exchange rate that secures balance of payments equilibrium with full employment.

First, managed floating does not involve parities that the government is obliged to preserve. Instead the currency is free to float, but the authorities intervene to avoid what they regard to be undesirable consequences of excessive appreciation or depreciation. A weak currency may lead to excessive depreciation that the government may wish to avoid because of its repercussions on the domestic price of imports and the internal cost structure. Alternatively, countries with a strong currency may seek to avoid appreciation if they want to accumulate reserves and are indifferent to the effect on the money supply. Moreover, a country may even attempt to engineer the depreciation of its currency that would otherwise appreciate if the foreign exchange market were left to operate freely.

Second, multiple exchange rates offer a system whereby different exchange rates are enforced for different transactions either on the current or capital account. The IMF's official definition of a multiple exchange rate is 'an effective buying or selling rate which, as a result of official action, differs from parity by more than 1 per cent'. Multiple exchange rates can be viewed both as a form of exchange control (particularly over capital transactions) and as a rational response to the fact that different classes of goods have different price elasticities in world trade. Many countries, including Britain in the past with the 'dollar premium', charge a higher domestic price for foreign currency than the prevailing market rate for investment abroad in capital assets such as shares and property. Such a device acts in essence as a form of exchange control.

Misplaced criticism

Supporters of continued EU membership argue that the degree of economic autonomy for the nation-state outlined here is illusory, because globalization and the integration of financial markets will not allow differences in economic policy to persist. Therefore a country might as well join the single currency. Indeed, many left-of-centre supporters of economic and monetary integration profess the belief that only as part of a new euro-land can governments become sufficiently powerful to operate a form of Euro-Keynesianism without financial markets causing terminal destabilization via a currency crisis. However, both viewpoints are over-stated. For example, the experience of the UK economy between 1990 and 1992 demonstrated that being tied into a fixed exchange rate system at an uncompetitively high rate leads to a fall in output and a rise in unemployment.[4] However, departure from the ERM and the subsequent 20 per cent depreciation in sterling resulted in the resumption of economic growth, which facilitated a fall in unemployment to levels last experienced two-and-a-half decades earlier. Thus arguments that economic policy autonomy is impossible because of financial market integration are wrong, because both the UK's strategy and performance were significantly different from all other EU member states during this period; that is why it was so comparatively successful. Devaluation gave UK firms a much needed increase in competitiveness, which was not instantly lost due to inflation, as new classical theorists claim, but instead provided government with a freedom of manoeuvre that could have resulted in the adoption of either strategy outlined in this chapter or a multiplicity of alternatives.

A second argument for maintaining EU membership is the suggestion that the UK's European partners would engage in some form of trade protection, which would deny firms access to the single internal market and therefore cause considerable damage to its economy should a member state such as the United Kingdom remain outside the euro on a long-term basis. The argument is implausible. First, the United Kingdom has suffered a substantial trade deficit with the rest of the EU since accession in 1973; therefore, in the event of a trade war, our EU 'partners' would lose the most. Second, any such protectionist measures would fall foul of the Treaty of Rome, the SEA, the TEU and the WTO's regulations. All are international treaties, binding their signatories to respect reciprocity of trade.

Another argument favouring continued EU membership is that it will provide a country with additional political influence over the future development of the EU. Independence, according to the argument, equals powerlessness. However, the claim is spurious. Whilst the participants in the single currency may opt to discuss their common economic policy apart from other EU member states, there is no legal mechanism for any other decisions to be taken in this way. Thus the United Kingdom cannot be marginalized simply due to its non-participation in the single currency. Moreover, its position would be strengthened further by consultation and co-operation with other EU member states who have exercised their opt-out (Denmark and Sweden) or been deemed too divergent for immediate membership (Greece). Further enlargement of the EU will increase the number of member countries incapable or unwilling to sacrifice other policy objectives for conformity to EMU's 'one-size-fits-all' policies. When such uniform monetary measures create areas of high structural unemployment, as they inevitably will, it is essential for opt-out nations to possess a collectively pre-agreed strategy of vetoing any plan to provide EU-wide aid to those areas. Problems created by the euro's operations should not be the responsibility of non-participants, but should be wholly financed by those embracing the single currency. Additionally, because *all* historical monetary unions not based upon political union have collapsed amidst substantial economic difficulties, these non-members would be wise to encourage the EU to formulate a contingency plan for the re-establishment of individual currencies if (or when) the demise of the euro occurs.

In reality, EU member states enjoy an effective long-run choice concerning its future strategy; it can embrace an essentially European identity or, if it decides to opt-out of the euro, it can pursue a global strategy. Moreover, the advantages of free trade within the EU and the imposition of a common external tariff on outside imports have become progressively smaller since 1973, as restrictions on trade have been steadily diminished world-wide. Under the auspices of GATT and its successor, the WTO, the average tariff on industrial goods between developed countries has been reduced to just 3.8 per cent. Consequently, the industrialized nations are closer to the free trade ideal than they have ever been. In this gradually emerging new world economy, access to the EU single internal market for UK business is assured.

A country need not fear that a long-term disengagement with movements towards further EU integration will lead to a powerless isolation. For example, Britain is a member of the G8 industrial nations; its economy ranks as one of the largest in the world and the third largest in the EU; it is a member of the World Bank and the IMF; it possesses a seat on the United Nations Security Council and remains the head of the Commonwealth, whose potential for expanded trade has recently been grossly neglected (West, 1995; Burkitt *et al.*, 1996; Cameron, 2010; Howell, 2010; Baimbridge *et al.*, 2010). Moreover, Britain enjoys a substantial portfolio of overseas assets and investments, and attracts the highest level of inward investment in the EU. It is the world's second largest financial centre and global investor. It has more companies in the world's top 500 than any other EU country. The United Kingdom is well placed to be one of the most dynamic and innovative global economies (Taylor, 1995).

The widely held view that countries have 'no alternative' but to participate in European integration is at odds with the facts; instead a range of possible alternatives exists. A member state could remain within the EU and secure, under WTO rules, free trading arrangements with the EMU-zone through a series of mutually beneficial, bilateral agreements. It could explore the possibility of a closer relationship with the North American Free Trade Association, as recently suggested by Canadian opposition leaders. Above all, it should intensify its trading and investment links with the nations of the Pacific Rim. In these ways a country would be able to pursue its true contemporary role of global trader and investor, while at the same time retaining its scope for a largely autonomous economic and social policy, such as the two possible strategies detailed above. Furthermore, outside the single currency, the choice between and among such strategies would be taken through the democratic process.

Conclusion

The design of a macroeconomic framework for a complex advanced economy depends upon a multiplicity of diverse factors, including recognition of its unique industrial structure, monetary and fiscal policy transmission mechanisms, the practice of wage formation, propensity for owner-occupation, national savings rates and technological progress. A combination of differences in consumer tastes, political choices, natural resources and centres of competitive excellence, together with the actions of institutions established to implement economic and social policy, necessitates differences in economic policy between nations. For example, the labour market operates very differently in the United States, where non-collective bargaining is the rule, than in Sweden where trade union representation is close to saturation at 90 per cent density, irrespective of whether their fiscal or monetary authorities followed a similar strategy. Moreover, exchange rate regimes tend to have a greater impact upon smaller, export-orientated nations than upon their larger neighbours, where only a relatively small proportion of GDP is traded. Consequently, it is extremely difficult for one international economic authority to replace national macroeconomic management by one common interest or exchange rate. It is simply that many economies of EU member states are too divergent cyclically and structurally from their neighbours for any claim of prior convergence to be convincing and, without such evidence, a common economic strategy is unlikely to be simultaneously in their individual interests.

In view of such fundamental weakness at the heart of the EU project, the decision to reject participation retains for national government the economic instruments vital to successful macroeconomic management. Exchange rates can fulfil their function of equalizing the demand and supply for a currency by the variation of its price, thereby preventing a basic uncompetitive imbalance from causing mass unemployment and falling standards of living. Fiscal policy, freed from the twin restrictions of the TEU convergence criteria and the SGP, can smooth cyclical fluctuations, avoiding periodic unemployment that wastes productive resources and generates associated human misery. The purpose of monetary policy is, then, to prevent unstable boom and slump conditions in housing and financial markets, whilst seeking to ensure a low interest rate for investors in productive capital. Supply-side policies, including selective labour market programmes and investment in the economy's physical and IT superstructure, do not require a rejection of the single currency to be applied, although the benefit of a macroeconomic structure tailored to the needs of the economy would provide a more fertile environment for their implementation. Thus, rather than being weakened by the refusal to be dominated by an EU agenda, which will often conflict with the interests of its economy, the United Kingdom would be both stronger and possess a superior ability to adapt to changing international market conditions. In the process, democratic choice would be enhanced and encourage the United Kingdom to end its undue preoccupation with events in a small corner of the European continent at the expense of a vigorous attempt to meet the growing demands of emergent markets across the globe.

In view of the overwhelming evidence supporting the maintenance of national self-determination of economic policy, two factors remain to provide the momentum towards further integrationalist economic participation. The first relates to the determination of a small political elite, together with the representatives of multinational corporations, to complete the European integration project; the former perhaps seek the increased influence a 'United States of Europe' would play in world events, whereas the latter desire to evade national regulatory regimes and thereby enhance profits. However, these small elites are increasingly neither representative of the wider European electorate, nor even of the majority of business. In a democracy, governments should act in the interests of all the people, which requires the rejection of abandoning national economic policy.

The second factor undermining the vigorous assertion of national independence is the fear of failure. For example, the notion of the United Kingdom as a declining nation has long sapped its resolve to follow its own interests and has caused many to prefer safety in 'Fortress Europe', with economic policy dictated by outside 'experts'. Yet, as illustrated in this chapter, there is no reason for such defeatism. The question remains whether national advantage can be better realized within an EU model of deeper economic and political integration, a looser relationship with the EU, or through a more independent arrangement, possibly involving withdrawal as a first step towards this reorientation of priorities. This is a question for considered evaluation of all the evidence and not to be closed off due to political prejudice or an ill-thought-through agenda that conflicts with contemporary debate. This is an important question since it goes to the very heart of what a sovereign country will make of itself and whether it places artificial limitations upon its ability to deliver the priorities espoused by its citizens.

15 From rescue and stimulus to the age of austerity

The European response to the great recession and the prospects for Social Europe

Introduction

This chapter reviews the responses of the EU and its member states to the 2008 economic crisis and, in light of these, evaluates the contemporary prospects for Social Europe. The chapter advances four main arguments. First, that the response of the EU and its member states during the first phase of the economic crisis – the coordinated and Keynesian rescue and stimulus packages – was a temporary one to rescue capitalism; it did not signal a fundamental shift in the nature and trajectory of the EU or its member states. Second, that the response during the second phase of the economic crisis – the adoption of austerity measures – consolidated the neo-liberal nature and trajectory of the EU and accelerated the transformation of Europe's social models towards the market liberal form. Third, that the medium-term plans devised by the EU in the wake of the economic crisis – to expand its power over member states' economic policy-making – amounted to a power grab. Fourth, and following from the second and third arguments, that the prospects for Social Europe in the so-called age of austerity are grim. While progressive social forces such as the far left and the greens favour the construction of radical alternatives to the EU, and while social democratic parties favour the reform of the EU, the balance of power lies with the international financial nexus, and capital more generally, which demand the dismantling of social protection systems.

The chapter is divided into four main sections. The first section summarizes the response of the EU and its member states during the first phase of the economic crisis. The second section considers the response during the second phase. The third section exposes the medium-term plans developed by the EU during this period. The fourth section discusses the contemporary struggle between the forces of capital and progressive social forces and, in light of this, assesses the prospects for a Social Europe.

The Keynesian interregnum

The so-called credit crunch, originating in the United States in 2007 and spreading throughout the global financial sector in 2008, plus the worldwide Great

Recession that followed, strained the notion of solidarity and the network of relationships that underpinned the European project. Indeed, the governments of Belgium, Cyprus, the Czech Republic, Hungary, Ireland, Latvia, Portugal and Spain all collapsed as a direct or indirect result of the economic crisis. The first phase of the economic crisis – the private debt crisis – which lasted from autumn 2008 until the end of 2009 when most of the major economies emerged from recession, predominantly affected the private sector and was tackled in a concerted and Keynesian way by governments across the world in the form of fiscal stimuli, state-backed guarantees, interest rate reductions, liquidity provision, nationalizations, quantitative easing, scrappage schemes, etc. (Jackson, 2009; Nanto, 2009; Edmonds and Marshall, 2010; United Nations, 2010). The IMF estimated in July 2009 that, globally, governments had spent over $10 trillion on these efforts to contain the economic crisis, while the International Labour Organization (2009) estimated that the fiscal stimulus measures in 2009 amounted to 1.7 per cent of global GDP.

Such global Keynesianism ensured that the 2008–2009 Great Recession was not as long or as deep as the Great Depression. Most of these measures benefited capital much more than labour however. In Britain, for example, the Bank of England quantitative easing programme saw the creation of £200 billion of new money which was mostly spent on government bonds. The programme boosted the prices of many assets, including commodities and shares, and, consequently, corporate profits increased by £11 billion during the recession. Real wages, on the other hand, fell by £4 billion. For BCA Research, 'the evidence suggests that quantitative easing cash ends up overwhelmingly in profits, thereby exacerbating already extreme income inequality' (cited in Stewart, 2011b). Furthermore, studies of the programme indicated that much of this money flowed overseas and did not directly benefit Britain (O'Grady, 2009).

The economic crisis, which coincided with the tenth anniversary of the euro, highlighted the persistent fissures in the EU, both within and between eurozone and non-eurozone countries, in terms of differential economic performance and policy preferences. Furthermore, there were tensions between member states over how to deal with the economic crisis; France, for example, initially favoured expansionary policies and industrial activism, while Germany defended fiscal conservatism and monetary stability. At the emergency eurozone summit and European Council in October 2008, however, the EU and its member states approved a Keynesian response to the economic crisis, with five main components. First, member states agreed to coordinate national and EU rescue and stimulus packages worth €2 trillion in an attempt to boost Europe's economies (see Table 15.1).

Second, they agreed to temporarily relax the SGP regime to allow member states to maintain, if not enlarge, their budget deficits and public debt levels during the recession. Third, they agreed to waive state aid rules to enable member states to temporarily support ailing sectors of their economies. Fourth, they agreed that the ECB should abandon its preoccupation with inflation and focus instead upon restoring financial market confidence, drastically cutting its interest rate as part of a globally coordinated series of reductions. Fifth, they agreed that the ECB should adopt a more interventionist stance by directly providing credit, and thus liquidity, to banks and the wider financial sector.

These measures were augmented by the European Economic Recovery Plan, published by the European Commission in November 2008, which set out two objectives: in the short-term, to inject purchasing power into the economy so as to boost demand and confidence; and, in the longer term, to boost Europe's competitiveness via 'smart investment' in green technologies and infrastructure. For the first time since July 1978, when the European Council (1978: 1) endorsed 'stimulating demand' to overcome recession, the EU explicitly adopted a Keynesian approach: 'The Commission is proposing that, as a matter of urgency, member states and the EU agree to an immediate budgetary impulse amounting to €200 billion (1.5 per cent of GDP) to boost demand' (European Commission, 2008b: 2). Importantly, however, it recommended that member states' responses should be 'timely, targeted and temporary' and that member states 'should commit to reverse the budgetary deterioration and return to the aims set out in the medium-term objectives' (ibid.: 7) as governed by the SGP. In other words, the European Commission remained committed to neo-liberal, supply-side reforms and was *not* advocating a new Keynesian direction for the EU. The Keynesian solution was also endorsed by the G-20 London Summit in April 2009 which pledged $1.1 trillion to tackle the economic crisis.

Table 15.1 European rescue and stimulus packages in 2008 (by size and value)

Country	Percentage share (GDP)	Billions ($)
Austria	4.5	18.8
Belgium	1.0	4.9
Czech Republic	1.8	3.9
Denmark	2.5	8.7
Finland	3.5	9.5
France	1.3	36.2
Germany	2.2	80.5
Hungary	10.9	17.0
Italy	0.7	16.8
Lithuania	1.9	0.9
Luxembourg	3.6	2.0
Netherlands	1.0	8.4
Norway*	0.6	2.9
Poland	2.0	10.6
Portugal	1.2	3.0
Slovenia	1.0	0.5
Spain	0.9	15.3
Sweden	2.8	13.4
Switzerland*	0.5	2.5
United Kingdom	1.4	38.0

Source: United Nations (2010: 20).

Note
* = Non-EU countries.

The European Commission estimated in March 2009 that the total fiscal effort by member states – including the automatic stabilizers and discretionary spending – amounted to more than €400 billion or 3.3 per cent of EU GDP which, it claimed, would 'generate new investment, support workers and their families and boost demand' (European Commission, 2009a: 2). The following month, the European Commission reported that spending in the EU to combat the economic crisis totalled approximately €3 trillion:

> The total maximum volume of crisis measures so far approved by the European Commission, national schemes and ad hoc measures taken together, entails amounts of around €3,000 billion. This corresponds to around 24 per cent of the EU GDP. This figure represents the overall maximum amount of guarantee umbrellas, rescue and restructuring packages and other measures set up by member states.
>
> (European Commission, 2009b: 15)

Furthermore, the maximum value of the guarantee schemes reviewed by the European Commission was estimated at €2.3 trillion (ibid.).

In the wake of the economic crisis, the European Commission sponsored the creation of a high-level group on financial supervision in the EU, chaired by Jacques de Larosière, which published its report in February 2009. The European Commission also supervised a series of 'stress tests' of European banks and financial institutions to ascertain how they would cope with a range of adverse scenarios. The results of the tests were published in July 2010 and July 2011 and, of the 90 institutions tested, seven failed the 2010 test and eight failed the 2011 test.

The de Larosière (2009) report, with its 29 recommendations, informed the agenda of the European Council in March 2009 which called for greater regulation of credit derivatives, hedge funds, private equity and credit rating agencies, plus action against 'non-transparent jurisdictions' (i.e. tax havens). The European Council specifically endorsed the call to establish colleges of supervisors for all major cross-border financial institutions. It instructed the European Commission to prepare proposals on strengthening financial institutions' capital requirements, on executive remuneration, and on the regulation of hedge funds and private equity. It also stated that 'the rapid increase in unemployment is a cause of great concern' and stressed that 'it is important to prevent and limit job losses and negative social impacts' (European Council, 2009: 7). No concrete measures were considered however.

The first phase of the economic crisis boosted the fortunes of the euro. The weakness of the British and US economies, exposed by the credit crunch and the subsequent recession, reversed the situation that existed in autumn 2000 and served to strengthen the euro against the US dollar and the pound sterling. At its launch in January 1999, €1 was worth $1.17 and £0.71. The euro reached an all-time low against the pound in May 2000 (£0.57) and against the dollar in October 2000 ($0.83). By contrast, it hit an all-time high against the dollar in April 2008 ($1.60) and against the pound in December 2008 (£0.98). Meanwhile, the role of the euro as a reserve currency was bolstered by such movements: official reserves held in euros increased from 18 per cent of the world total in 1998 to 27 per cent in 2008 (Atkins, 2008b). The perception of the eurozone as a safe haven was also reflected in a *Financial Times*/Harris poll conducted in December 2008 which found that majorities in all four of the biggest eurozone economies – France, Germany, Italy and Spain – were opposed, in the midst of the economic crisis, to any return to their national currencies (Atkins, 2008a). Hungary and Poland announced in spring 2009 that, in an attempt to deter currency speculation and market volatility, they were bringing forward their plans to join the eurozone. Likewise, Denmark and Sweden contemplated holding further referendums on euro entry, while Iceland – following the demise of its banking system, currency and government – signalled its intention to press for EU and euro entry.

The sovereign debt crisis

As a result of the credit crunch and the Great Recession, the non-eurozone countries of Hungary, Latvia, Poland and Romania applied for conditional IMF loans in 2008 and 2009 and were subsequently instructed to implement austerity measures. For most of Europe, however, the austerity drive began in 2010. Indeed, with the exception of Sweden, which implemented austerity measures in the 1990s, the age of austerity became the new consensus across the EU. The second phase of the economic crisis – the sovereign debt crisis – began in spring 2010 and centred upon the increased budget deficits and higher public debt levels of nation-states (see Table 15.2).

Critically, such indebtedness was due, in large part, to the government bailouts of the financial sector during the first phase of the crisis. In other words, the transfer of liabilities, losses and risk from the private sector to the state was followed by the state coming under sustained attack from the very private sector that the state had rescued. In contrast to the first phase, the sovereign debt crisis posed a serious threat to the euro project if not the EU itself – manifest in the falling value of the euro vis-à-vis other currencies (de Grauwe, 2010; ING, 2010). The return to orthodoxy (i.e. permanent austerity), following the brief Keynesian interregnum, was precipitated by internal and external forces.

Internally, the rescue and stimulus packages implemented by member states and the EU provided only a temporary reprieve because the more fundamental problems facing the eurozone – differential economic performance and structural imbalances – were not addressed. As Marsh (2009) observed, 'fixing exchange rates among countries with disparate patterns of prices and productivity' led to 'changes in relative competitiveness' which were not easily remedied within a single currency area. Indeed, the concerns of the financial markets about the design flaws of the euro project – the inability of eurozone members to devalue to restore competitiveness, the absence of adequate mechanisms to deal with intra-EU imbalances and the growing indebtedness of several member states – were reflected in the growing 'gap in bond yields between the (benchmark) German bonds and the sovereign debt of Greece, Ireland, Italy, Portugal

Table 15.2 Budget deficits and public debt levels across Europe

Country	Budget deficit as % of GDP (2009)	Public debt as % of GDP (2009)	Projected budget deficit as % of GDP	Unemployment rate as % of labour force (December 2010)
Austria	3.5	66.5	3.0 (2011)	5.0
Belgium	6.0	96.7	n/a	8.1
Bulgaria	4.7	14.8	2.5 (2011)	10.1
Cyprus	6.0	56.2	n/a	7.3
Czech Republic	5.8	35.3	4.6 (2011)	7.7
			3.5 (2012)	
			2.9 (2013)	
Denmark	2.7	41.6	n/a	8.2
Estonia	1.7	7.2	n/a	16.1
Finland	2.5	44.0	n/a	8.1
France	7.5	77.6	6.0 (2011)	
			3.0 (2013)	
			2.0 (2014)	
Germany	3.0	73.2	n/a	6.6
Greece	13.6	115.1	7.8 (2010)	12.9
			7.0 (2011)	
Hungary	4.4	78.3	3.8 (2011)	11.7
Ireland	14.4	64.0	3.0 (2014)	13.8
			2.9 (2015)	

Italy	5.3	115.8	2.7 (2012)	8.6
Latvia	10.2	36.1	6.0 (2011)	18.3
Lithuania	9.2	29.3	n/a	18.3
Luxembourg	0.7	14.5	n/a	4.9
Malta	3.8	69.1	n/a	6.2
Netherlands	5.4	60.9	n/a	4.3
Poland	7.2	51.0	7.3 (2010)	10.0
Portugal	9.3	76.8	4.6 (2011)	10.9
Romania	8.6	23.7	n/a	7.3
Slovakia	7.9	35.7	4.9 (2011) 3.0 (2013)	14.5
Slovenia	5.8	35.9	n/a	7.8
Spain	11.1	53.2	6.0 (2011)	20.2
Sweden	0.9	43.2	n/a	7.8
United Kingdom	11.4	68.1	1.0 (2015)	7.8

Sources: Eurostat and European Commission.

Note
n/a = not available.

and Spain' (Oakley and Mallet, 2009). Predictably, the credit rating agencies downgraded the government bonds of Greece, Portugal and Spain in January 2009. That same month, Ireland passed a raft of emergency measures in an attempt to reduce its budget deficit. These were deemed insufficient by the credit rating agencies, however, and Ireland's bonds were downgraded in March. In a forlorn attempt to mask the design flaws of the euro project, the European Council in March 2009 reaffirmed its commitment to the national and EU rescue and stimulus packages but insisted that member states should return to 'positions consistent with sustainable public finances as soon as possible' (European Council, 2009: 4). One month later, the European Commission, as the guardian of the SGP, urged member states to reduce their budget deficits.

Externally, the Organization for Economic Co-operation and Development (OECD) (2009) and the IMF (2010) supported fiscal consolidation and the implementation of structural reforms across the EU, regardless of the economic and social consequences. Meanwhile, at the G-20 Summit in Toronto in June 2010, the advanced economies declared that they would halve their deficits by 2013 and would stabilize or reduce their debt-to-GDP ratios by 2016.

Unsurprisingly, during the course of 2010 and in response to the concerns expressed by the EU, the financial markets, the G-20, the IMF and the OECD, governments across Europe, bar Sweden, announced that they would implement austerity programmes in an attempt to reduce their budget deficits and public debt levels (see Table 15.3). Such retrenchment encountered significant opposition and precipitated widespread social unrest.

The specific fear of Greece defaulting on its sovereign debt, and the more general concern about the sustainability of the eurozone, precipitated a special economic summit which was held in Brussels in February 2010. In a bid to calm the financial markets, the summit issued a statement endorsing the Greek government's austerity measures and promising that, if necessary, the eurozone would take coordinated and determined action to safeguard financial stability in the eurozone as a whole.

The summit statement was tested in May 2010 when the EU and the IMF agreed a bailout package, worth €110 billion, to enable Greece to finance its debt without recourse to the financial markets. Rather than tackle tax evasion by corporations and wealthy individuals – the Greek state lost around $20 billion a year according to Associated Press (2010), while €8–10 billion left the country in late 2009 in anticipation of the austerity measures (Smith, 2010) – and thus spare the 20 per cent of the population that lived below the poverty line, the conditional EU–IMF loan demanded public spending cuts and tax rises worth €30 billion in an attempt to reduce the budget deficit from 13.6 per cent of GDP in 2010 to 3 per cent by 2014. In addition, the medium-term fiscal strategy for 2012–2015, announced by the Greek government in April 2011, stated that Greece needed to further reduce public spending by €23 billion and that it would privatize €50 billion worth of state assets – including stakes in airports and ports, banks, defence companies, energy companies, government-owned buildings and land, government-run services, Olympic venues, railway companies, etc. – in an attempt to comply with the SGP.

Following the threat of the then French president, Nicolas Sarkozy, to quit the euro unless further action was taken to defend it, the Greek bailout package was augmented by a €750 billion bundle of emergency measures to defend the single currency. The centrepiece of this package, agreed in May 2010, was the creation of the EFSF which could issue bonds, guaranteed by eurozone member states, and provide loans of up to €440 billion to countries in financial difficulty. The EFSF was augmented by IMF loans of up to €250 billion, an EU balance of payments facility worth €60 billion, and ECB pledges to intervene in private and public debt markets and to boost eurozone bank liquidity.

The announcement of this package served to halt the slide of the euro, which had fallen to a 14-month low against the US dollar, but Germany exacted a high price for its support; Merkel (2010) rejected 'the vision of a union for transfer payments as a model for the financial future of the EU' and demanded instead 'a new culture of stability with balanced budgets, rigorous measures to regulate financial markets, and the ruthless identification and remedying of all structural weaknesses'. Furthermore, Merkel insisted that there would be no automatic entitlement to loans, strict IMF surveillance of loan recipients and no departure from the sole ECB objective of price stability. Merkel also backed the imposition of penalties on member states that failed to tackle their budget deficits, called for a renewed focus on economic union and not just monetary union, recommended additional economic policy-making power for the EU and favoured allowing member states to restructure their debts in an orderly way.

The summit statement was tested for a second time in November 2010 when the EU and the IMF agreed a bailout package, worth €90 billion, to enable Ireland to finance its debt without recourse to the financial markets. The conditional loan, augmented by additional assistance from individual countries such as Britain, demanded €10 billion in public spending cuts and €5 billion in tax rises over three years in an attempt to reduce the budget deficit from 14.3 per cent of GDP in 2010 to 3 per cent by 2014. It also demanded the fundamental downsizing and reorganization of Ireland's banking sector.

The summit statement was tested for a third time in April 2011 when the EU and the IMF agreed a bailout package, worth €78 billion, to enable Portugal to finance its debt without recourse to the financial markets. The conditional loan demanded public spending cuts and tax rises equivalent to 10 per cent of GDP in an attempt to reduce the budget deficit from 9.1 per cent in 2010 to 3 per cent by 2013.

These bailout packages failed to assuage the financial markets however; when the EU statistics agency, Eurostat, announced in April 2011 that Greece and Portugal were more indebted than had previously been estimated (Inman, 2011), speculation mounted that both countries would end up defaulting and restructuring their debts (Hope, 2011). Indeed, this option was discussed at a secret meeting of finance ministers from Finland, France, Germany and the Netherlands (i.e. EU creditor nations). Rumours that the meeting had also discussed the possibility of Greece withdrawing from the eurozone, however, were denied by the German and Greek governments (Stewart, 2011a).

Table 15.3 Austerity across Europe from 2010

Country	Austerity measures

Austria
Announced in October 2010
	Public expenditure cuts (€1.6 billion):
	    Child benefits
	    Family benefits
	    Social care benefits
	    Ministries to cut expenditure by 3.6 per cent
	Tax increases (€1.17 billion):
	    Bank levy
	    Aviation tax
	    Petrol and tobacco duties

Belgium	No government at time of writing but the political elite wants to save €22 billion by 2015 to eliminate the budget deficit

Bulgaria
Announced in March 2010
	Public expenditure cuts (of 20 per cent):
	    Administration
	    Education
	    Healthcare
	    Pensions (via increased contributions and increase in the retirement age)
	    Public sector jobs cut by 10 per cent
	    Civil servants' pay cut by 10 per cent
	    Wage freeze for three years
	    Infrastructure expenditure cuts
	Other measures:
	    Privatization of state-owned minority stakes in 55 companies

Cyprus
Announced in April 2010

Public expenditure cuts:
   Reduction in the number of public sector jobs by 1,000 per year
   Wage freeze
   Reduction in the state's operating costs
   More targeted welfare benefits
Tax increases:
   Corporation tax
   Petrol duty
   Property tax
   VAT
Other measures:
   Efforts to combat tax avoidance and evasion

Czech Republic
Announced in June 2010

Public expenditure cuts (€1.4 billion):
   Public sector wages cut by 10 per cent
   Benefit cuts to birth allowance, carers' allowance, child benefit, sick pay and unemployment benefit
   Transfers to the regions cut by 20 per cent
   Cuts in subsidies for housing construction
   Health and pension reforms
   Wage freeze
Tax increases:
   Excise duties
   VAT

Denmark
Announced in May 2010

Public expenditure cuts (€4 billion):
   Reduction in the number of public sector jobs by 20,000
   Child benefit cut by 5 per cent
   Unemployment benefit eligibility reduced from four to two years
   University budget cut
   Ministerial salaries cut by 5 per cent
   Pension levels frozen from 2012
   Overseas aid budget cut
   Municipal expenditure freeze

continued

Table 15.3 Continued

Country	Austerity measures

Estonia
Announced in January 2009
	Public expenditure cuts (€432 million):
	  Reduction in the number of civil servants
	  Health care cuts
	  Pension cuts
	  Infrastructure cuts
	  'Internal devaluation' of prices and wages
	Tax increases:
	  VAT

Finland
Announced in January 2009
	Public expenditure cuts:
	  Reduction in the number of public sector jobs by 14,000 (via non-replacement of retirees)
	  'People's Pension' tax (on employers) abolished
	Tax increases:
	  Energy tax
	  Excise duties on soft drinks and sweets
	  VAT
	Other changes:
	  Employers withdrew from centralized pay bargaining

France
Announced in June 2010
	Public expenditure cuts (€42 billion):
	  Reduction in the number of public sector jobs by 31,000 in 2011
	  Three-year freeze on public expenditure
	  Non-indexation of civil servants' wages
	  State's operating costs reduced by 10 per cent
	  Increased retirement age
	  Social security benefits increase by 1.2 per cent (in effect a cut given the rate of inflation)
	  Health expenditure cut by €1.5 billion
	  Unemployment benefit cut by €1 billion
	  Transfers to local authorities cut by €3 billion

Tax increases:
    Corporation tax
    Income tax
    Pension contributions
    Social contributions (individuals and companies)
    (Possible) bank levy
Other measures:
    Closing tax loopholes

Germany
Announced in June 2010

Public expenditure cuts (€80 billion):
    Reduction in the number of public sector jobs by 15,000
    Welfare benefits cut by €30 billion over four years
    Increased retirement age
    Wage cuts for civil servants
    Reduction in subsidies to individuals and companies
    Reduction in the number of armed forces personnel by 40,000
    Transfers to local authorities cut by €15 billion
Tax increases:
    Aviation tax
    Nuclear power tax
    (Possible) bank levy

continued

Table 15.3 Continued

Country	Austerity measures
Greece Announced in March 2010 Augmented by conditional EU/IMF-sponsored bailout package, announced in May 2010, and a second EU/IMF-sponsored bailout package, announced in June 2011	Public expenditure cuts (€30 billion): Public sector wages cut by 25 per cent Public sector pay and pension level freeze until 2014 Increase in the retirement age, eligibility requirement (i.e. number of years worked) increased and final salary schemes axed Cuts in unemployment benefit Education cuts Health cuts Tax increases: Alcohol, tobacco and fuel duties increased by 10 per cent VAT Other measures: Privatization of state assets Measures to reduce corruption within the tax service Measures to reduce tax avoidance and evasion Reduction in the minimum wage for young people Collective bargaining mechanism weakened Redundancy limits on employers relaxed
Hungary Conditional IMF loan of $10 billion announced in October 2008 Austerity plan announced in June 2010	Public expenditure cuts: Public sector expenditure cut by 15 per cent Wage cuts Sickness benefit cut by 10 per cent Public sector pension levels frozen Increase in the retirement age Housing subsidies cut Political parties' subsidies cut Bonuses for politicians and civil servants cut Reduction in the number of seats in the national and local assemblies

Tax increases:
Bank levy in 2010 and 2011 (€735 million per year)
VAT
Other measures:
€430 million from efficiency savings

Ireland
Austerity budgets announced in December 2007, October 2008 and April 2009

Augmented by conditional EU/IMF bailout package, announced in November 2010

Public expenditure cuts(€6 billion):
Reduction in the number of public sector jobs by 25,000 (10 per cent of total) and recruitment freeze
Wage cuts in public sector of 5-15 per cent
Public sector pensions above €12,000 per year cut by 4 per cent
Child benefit cut by €10 per child per month
Unemployment benefit cut by 4 per cent
Working age welfare benefit cut by €8 per week
Maternity entitlement cut by €8 a week
Jobseekers' Allowance and Supplementary Welfare Allowance for young people cut by €6 a week
Minimum wage cut by 11 per cent
Increase in the retirement age
Childcare and health budget cut by €746 million
Education cuts
Transfers to local authorities cut
Infrastructure cuts
Tax increases:
Tax-free earning threshold lowered
VAT
Capital gains tax
Carbon tax
Petrol duty
Residential property transaction tax
Water tax
Abolition of some tax relief schemes

continued

Table 15.3 Continued

Country	Austerity measures

Italy
Announced in May 2010
	May 2010 austerity package
	Public expenditure cuts (€25 billion)
	  Wage freeze for public sector workers and wage cuts for high earning civil servants
	  Wage cuts for ministers and parliamentarians
	  Recruitment freeze in the public sector at rate of 20 per cent by 2013 and 50 per cent by 2014
	  Trade unions' institutes, which administer social security benefits for workers and pensioners, cut by €30 million between 2011 and 2013
	  Family policy budget cut by 70 per cent
	  Youth policy budget cut by 66 per cent
	  Health budget cuts
	  Regional social policy fund abolished
	  Political parties' subsidies cut
	  Increase in retirement age
	  Ministries to cut expenditure by 10 per cent in 2011
	  Transfers to regional government cut by €9 billion
	Tax increases:
	  Bonuses and stock options tax
	  Road tolls
	Other measures:
	  Efforts to combat tax evasion (estimated to cost €120 billion per year)

Augmented by a second austerity package, announced in August 2011, as a condition of ECB assistance	August 2011 austerity package
	Public expenditure cuts
	  €20 billion of cuts in 2012
	  €25 billion of cuts in 2013
	  Reduction in number of public sector jobs by 50,000
	  Transfers to regional government cut

Tax increases:
  New 'solidarity tax' of 10 per cent on high earners
  Tax on divided and earned interest of 7.5 per cent

Latvia
Conditional EU/IMF bailout package
announced in December 2008

Public expenditure cuts ($1.5 billion):
  Public sector wages cut by 25 per cent
Tax increases:
  Real estate tax
  VAT

Lithuania
Announced in January 2009

Public expenditure cuts:
  Public sector expenditure cut by 30 per cent
  Wage freeze
  Public sector pensions cut by 11 per cent
  Parental leave benefits cut
Tax increases:
  Alcohol and pharmaceutical duties
  Corporation tax
  VAT

Luxembourg
Announced in April 2010

Public expenditure cuts (€777 million):
  Education
  Social benefits cut
  Transport
  Pension levels frozen until 2014
  End to inflation-indexing of wages
Tax increases:
  Emergency crisis tax (0.8 per cent and temporary)
  Solidarity tax (employment fund) paid by individuals and private companies
Other measures:
  Private companies' subsidies cut by 10 per cent

continued

Table 15.3 Continued

Country	Austerity measures

Malta
Announced in October 2010
	Public sector cuts:
	  Public sector jobs reduced by 50 per cent over time (via non-replacement policy)
	  Increase in the retirement age

Netherlands
Announced in September 2010
	Public expenditure cuts:
	  €1.8 billion cut in 2011
	  €3.2 billion cut, from 2010 level, by 2015
	  Child benefits
	  Health benefits
	  Immigrant integration benefits
	  Reduction in the number of public sector jobs by 4,000
	  Wage freeze for civil servants

Poland
Conditional IMF loan of $20.5 billion announced in May 2009
 	
Austerity plan announced in October 2010
	Public expenditure cuts (€14.4 billion):
	  Reduction in the number of public sector jobs by 10 per cent in 2011 and maintain a 'reduced workforce level' until 2013
	  Public expenditure increases capped (at inflation + 1 per cent)
	  Military expenditure cuts
	  Pension reform
	Tax increases:
	  VAT
	Other measures:
	  Tripartite body, which set the guidelines for negotiating wage levels, was abolished

Portugal
Announced in March 2010

Augmented by conditional EU/IMF-sponsored bailout package, announced in May 2011

Public expenditure cuts:
  Wage cuts in the public sector of between 3.5 and 10 per cent
  Wage freeze
  Education
  Military expenditure cut by 40 per cent by 2013
  Poverty reduction budget
  University budget
  Social benefits cuts (including children's allowance, health, social security and unemployment benefit)
  Higher retirement age and pension level freeze
Tax increases:
  Corporation tax
  Income tax
  VAT
Other measures:
  17 enterprises will be privatized
  Promotion of flexible working

Romania
Conditional IMF loan of $27 billion announced in March 2009

Austerity plan announced in May 2010

Public sector cuts:
  Reduction in the number of public sector jobs by 115,000 by 2011 (eventual toll estimated at 250,000)
  Public sector wage cuts of 25 per cent
  Social benefits cut by 15 per cent
  Pension cut of 15 per cent and increase in retirement age
Tax increases:
  VAT
Other measures:
  Workers' rights downgraded and industrial relations system restructured

continued

Table 15.3 Continued

Country	Austerity measures
Slovakia Announced in September 2010	Public expenditure cuts (€1.75 billion): Ministerial salaries cut by 10 per cent Tax increases: Alcohol and tobacco duties VAT
Slovenia Announced in November 2010	Public expenditure cuts (€600 million): Public sector wages cut Health care cuts Infrastructure cuts Increase in retirement age Tax increases: Excise duty on energy Tobacco duty
Spain Announced in May 2010 (austerity package carried by one vote)	Public expenditure cuts (€15 billion): Reduction in the number of public sector jobs by 13,000 Public sector wages cut by 5 per cent Social benefits cut (including birth allowance, older people's allowance, housing benefit and unemployment benefit) Pension levels frozen Ministries' budgets cut by 15.6 per cent Research and development cut by 7 per cent Overseas aid budget cut by 20 per cent Infrastructure expenditure cut by €6 billion Transfers to the regions cut by €1.2 billion Wind power subsidies cut by 35 per cent

Tax increases:
  Income tax
  VAT
  Tobacco duty
Other measures:
  Equality ministry abolished
  Housing ministry abolished
  Part-privatization of state assets
  Workers' rights downgraded (easier to sack workers and severance pay reduced)
  Sector wage agreements weakened and limits placed on collective wage increases

United Kingdom
Announced in June and October 2010

Public expenditure cuts (£81 billion):
  Reduction in the number of public sector jobs by 490,000
  Public sector wage freeze
  Social security and welfare benefits cut by £18 billion (including child benefit, housing benefit and unemployment benefit)
  Benefit and tax credits to increase in line with (lower) Consumer Prices Index rather than Retail Prices Index
  Departmental cuts of 19 per cent (average)
  Further and higher education budget cuts
  Increase in retirement age and higher contributions
  Infrastructure expenditure cuts
  Transfers to local authorities cut by 30 per cent
Tax increases:
  Bank levy
  Capital gains tax
  Income tax
  VAT

Sources: European Institute; European Trade Union Confederation; media reports

Following these bailout packages, the European Council agreed in December 2010 to amend the Lisbon Treaty to enable the formalization of future financial assistance to member states. The permanent procedure, the European Stability Mechanism, would succeed the EFSF and would be underpinned by a strict surveillance and supervisory regime administered by the European Commission. It was expected to become operational in June 2013.

Financial markets' anxiety about Greece – more specifically the concerns about the rising level of debt, the further contraction of the economy and the lack of progress in terms of implementing the austerity measures and privatization programme – led to rising borrowing costs which hit 'danger' levels in summer 2011. Having been downgraded to 'junk' status, the spread between two-year Greek bonds and German bonds increased to 23.8 per cent in June 2011, while the costs of insuring against a Greek default also set new records. The German government was initially resistant to further assistance for Greece unless private creditors holding Greek debt accepted significant losses. Pressure from the United States, exercised through the IMF (Traynor, 2011), plus opposition from the ECB, France and other member states, however, precipitated a partial German U-turn and a second bailout package, worth €109 billion, was agreed at an emergency EU summit in July 2011. The EU hoped that the package would enable Greece to reduce its debt-to-GDP ratio to a more 'sustainable' level.

The second Greek bailout package was activated after the Greek parliament passed additional public expenditure cuts and tax rises worth €28.4 billion. The package, the implementation of which was closely monitored by the supervisory 'troika' of the ECB, European Commission and IMF, extended the repayment period on Greek loans from 7.5 years to 15–30 years and allowed Greece to pay a lower interest rate on its bailout loans. The package also involved some debt restructuring; banks and other private sector investors contributed €37 billion by taking a 'haircut' (i.e. a loss) worth 21 per cent of the market value of their debts. The relatively 'short haircut' aside, Hau (2011) characterized the package as a

> €200 billion subsidy to sovereign creditors [and] a gigantic wealth transfer from the taxpayer to essentially the richest 5 per cent in the world. In the US, the richest 5 per cent of households control roughly 70 per cent of all financial wealth and this percentage is not much different in the rest of the world. Ultimate ownership of bank capital and sovereign debt is so concentrated among high-wealth individuals that we should characterize the bailout subsidy as a … wealth tax supporting the rich.

Nevertheless, the rating agency, Fitch, subsequently declared that the 'haircut' constituted a 'restricted default' event.

The summit agreed to develop 'a comprehensive strategy for growth and investment' and it welcomed the European Commission's decision to establish a Task Force to work with the Greek government to target EU Structural Funds 'on competitiveness and growth, job creation and training'. Having promised that 'we will mobilize EU funds and institutions such as the EIB towards this goal and relaunch the Greek economy', the summit made clear that there would be no new monies. Instead, it declared that 'member states and the European Commission will immediately mobilize all resources necessary in order to provide exceptional technical assistance to help Greece implement its reforms' (quoted in Wearden, 2011) – in other words, greater external surveillance over Greece. Indeed, in an attempt to ensure that the Greek government delivered on its privatization programme, the troika insisted that an independent agency, headquartered in Brussels, should supervise the scheme and the key ministries involved. This aspect of the package was arguably the most alarming. While participation in the European integration process entailed a loss of sovereignty for the countries involved, the European project had hitherto developed through a series of steps – each of which member states had consented to, whether in an informed way or not, via a parliamentary process or a referendum. In this case, the EU exploited the crisis and imposed its will on Greece *without* the explicit consent of the Greek parliament or the public. Nonetheless, with an estimated €300 billion of state-owned property, the Greek government subsequently encouraged foreign investors and sovereign wealth funds to spend their money in Greece. Germany also indicated that it was interested in buying assets in the energy and tourism sectors (Smith, 2011).

The summit extended the repayment periods for Ireland and Portugal's bailout loans and reduced their interest rate payments. It did not seek to revise Ireland's 12.5 per cent corporate tax rate, as Ireland feared it would, and there was no attempt to levy a €50 billion EU-wide bank tax as promoted by France.

The summit also agreed to extend the power of the EFSF, which would be allowed to act in a precautionary way by providing loans to countries not in receipt of bailout funds and to intervene in secondary markets where there were risks of contagion and financial instability. The reform of the EFSF required the parliamentary approval of all eurozone member states, however, and the ratification process, which was expected to be fraught and to take months to complete, encouraged further speculation against Italy and Spain by the financial markets. Indeed, yields on ten-year Italian and Spanish bonds rose above 6 per cent in August 2011 – perilously close to the 7 per cent level that precipitated the Irish and Portuguese bailouts.

Higher borrowing costs for Italy and Spain prompted six responses by the EU and its member states. First, in an attempt to calm the financial markets, the Italian government announced a new austerity package in August 2011 which pledged to eliminate the budget deficit by 2013. The austerity package included public expenditure cuts of €20 billion in 2012 and €25 billion in 2013, a 10 per cent solidarity tax surcharge on high earners and an increase in capital gains tax. These measures were enacted immediately by decree and were only later subject to parliamentary approval.

Second, having spent €75 billion on purchasing Greek, Irish and Portuguese government bonds in 2010 and 2011, including €16.5 billion in May 2010 alone, the ECB agreed to buy Italian and Spanish bonds in August 2011. This support was not unconditional however; the ECB sent a letter to the Italian government, which was leaked to the media, which set out what the ECB expected in return:

> The ECB demands almost amounted to a new government programme.... There are the measures to be taken and there is the timetable according to which they must be implemented. Not even the legislative instruments the ECB asks the government to use have been left out. These measures included liberalization,... privatization, including those of companies owned by local authorities ... and sweeping reform of the labour market to abolish the rigid distinction between cosseted 'insiders' in permanent employment and 'outsiders' on short-term contracts with few rights and scant entitlements.
>
> (Hooper and Willsher, 2011)

The leader of the opposition later complained that 'it is incredible and unacceptable that the opposition had ... not had any account of the conditions being imposed upon us by the European and international communities' (ibid.). Furthermore, the then president of the ECB, Jean-Claude Trichet, revealed that 'the same thing has been asked of the Spanish Government' (Hooper, 2011). For the second time, the EU exploited the crisis and imposed its will, this time on Italy and Spain, *without* the explicit consent of their parliaments or publics.

The former European commissioner, Monti, complained that ' "in effect decisions were already being taken by a market-driven ... supranational, technical government" – its offices spread between Brussels, Frankfurt, Berlin, London and New York' (quoted in Dinmore, 2011). The ECB spent €22 billion on Italian and Spanish bonds (Atkins and Milne, 2011) and the intervention, in the short-term, was judged a success; bond yields on Italian and Spanish debt decreased to 5.4 per cent and 5.2 per cent respectively in the days that followed (Hawkes, 2011). Given that the combined size of Italy and Spain's bond markets was €2,100 billion and that their joint borrowing requirements until the end of 2012 were estimated at €660 billion, however, speculation began to mount that, in the long-term, the ECB interventions would not be sufficient. Likewise, questions were asked about whether the IMF could afford to intervene. The IMF estimated that a bailout for Spain might cost between €200–300 billion, while 'Italy is too big for the IMF to make a serious contribution. In any case ... if Italy faces a funding crisis the problem would have become a continent-wide conflagration' (Beattie, 2011).

Third, in an attempt to contain the speculative activity against Italy, Spain and the wider eurozone, Belgium, France, Italy and Spain introduced a temporary ban on the short selling of financial instruments in August 2011. The ban affected the convertibles, equities and equity derivatives, but not credit default swaps, of more than 60 financial institutions – including major banks and insurance companies. The move encouraged Germany to renew its call for EU-wide restrictions on so-called shorting in order to curb 'destructive speculation'.

Britain, Italy, the Netherlands and Sweden opposed such a policy however. Although the ban was temporary, it nevertheless demonstrated that nation-states are not powerless vis-à-vis the international financial nexus if they possess the necessary political will.

Fourth, Britain abandoned its long-standing opposition to the development of a two-speed EU. In an interview with the *Financial Times* in August 2011, Chancellor George Osborne, stated that

> The crisis in the eurozone has turned conventional British thinking on European integration on its head. For years British foreign policy orthodoxy has been to resist greater union between members of the single currency, fearing that Britain would be relegated to second division status, with all the big decisions taken elsewhere. But … the 'remorseless logic of monetary union takes the single currency members in the direction of greater fiscal union … I think we have to accept that greater eurozone integration is necessary to make the single currency work and that is very much in our national interest. … We should be prepared to let that happen'.
>
> (Quoted in Parker and Giles, 2011)

As part of such a move, Osborne also supported the introduction of EU bonds. Meanwhile, the House of Commons European Scrutiny Committee announced that it would conduct an inquiry into the effects that a eurozone fiscal union would have on Britain's economic independence (Helm and Stewart, 2011), while the People's Pledge Campaign called for a referendum on Britain's continued membership, if such a union came into being, on the basis that

> if the eurozone moves towards a single tax system … then the EU will become a fundamentally different organization to the one that Britain joined in 1973. Many … fear that Britain will come under intense pressure to adapt its tax and regulatory policies to conform more closely with the eurozone once fiscal union is under way, even if Britain remains out of the single currency.
>
> (Ibid.)

Fifth, Osborne's intervention reignited the long-standing debate about whether or not to introduce an EU bond. The then prime minister of Luxembourg, Jean-Claude Juncker, and the then Italian finance minister, Giulio Tremonti, published an article in the *Financial Times* in December 2010 which advocated the creation of a European debt agency which would replace the EFSF and which would issue 'e-bonds' (Juncker and Tremonti, 2010). Likewise, the former prime ministers of Italy, France, Portugal and Belgium – Giuliano Amato, Michel Rocard, Mario Soares and Guy Verhofstadt respectively – plus Monti and Holland, published articles and letters in the *Financial Times* in July and August 2011 making the case for EU bonds (Amato and Verhofstadt, 2011; Monti, 2011; Holland, 2011). On the eve of a Franco-German summit in

August 2011, however, Merkel and Sarkozy rejected EU bonds as a solution to the eurozone crisis. The German finance minister, Wolfgang Schäuble, ruled out EU bonds 'for as long as member states conduct their own financial policies, and we need different rates of interest in order that there are possible incentives and sanctions to enforce fiscal solidity'. Similarly, French officials stated that 'eurobonds would require a much more determined integration of budgetary policy. ... It could be a long-term project, but you cannot have Eurobonds and at the same time national economic and budgetary policies' (quoted in Hollinger *et al.*, 2011a).

Sixth, France and Germany pledged to create a 'real economic government for the eurozone' (Peel and Hollinger, 2011) in August 2011. This would involve at least two summits per year of eurozone member states, chaired by the European Council president, the coordination of budget planning and economic forecasting, and the development of a common corporate tax base. Merkel and Sarkozy called for the eurozone-17 to adopt binding clauses on balanced budgets into their constitutions by mid-2012 and announced that France and Germany would implement a joint financial transactions tax. On EU bonds, however, Sarkozy insisted that these may be introduced 'at the end of the process of integration of the eurozone but not at the beginning' (quoted in Hollinger *et al.*, 2011b).

The European Commission issued a proposal to relax the co-financing rules for EU Structural Funds and other EU funding sources in August 2011. The previous regime required that, in order for EU monies to be released, member states had to finance at least 15 per cent of project costs. Under the proposed new system, a contribution of only 5 per cent was needed and this was expected to reduce the costs for Greece, Hungary, Ireland, Latvia, Portugal and Romania by about €3 billion in 2011–2012 and 'have a much bigger impact by unlocking tens of billions of euros in EU funds, which many of those governments are entitled to but have struggled to claim' (Chaffin, 2011).

In the wake of the downgrade of US sovereign debt by the Standard and Poor's rating agency in August 2011, following the stand-off between democrats and republicans in the US Congress over raising the debt ceiling, France was the next target of the international financial nexus. 'France has come under the spotlight as markets hunt for the next downgrade candidate' (Hollinger and Milne, 2011). One banker explained that

> we expect that France, with its high public debt and deficit, and popular resistance to cutbacks in its, even by euro area standards, extremely large welfare state, is now likely to be the G-7 country at the highest risk of losing its AAA rating.
>
> (Quoted in Neate *et al.*, 2011)

Responding to such pressure, manifest in the falling share prices of several French banks, Sarkozy instructed his ministers to find €20 billion worth of savings to ensure that France reduced its budget deficit to 3 per cent by 2013

(Hollinger, 2011). Meanwhile, Islam (2011) reported that US hedge funds were shorting against eurozone members via the unregulated credit default swaps market – which was part of the 'shadow banking system' – and that speculators were sometimes making profits of 800–1,000 per cent. The cases of France, Greece, Ireland, Italy, Portugal, Spain, the United States and several other countries suggested that the financial markets had, in effect, declared a generalized war against all governments that *they* considered to be 'profligate' and they were making substantial profits in the process.

The EU power grab

The eurozone crisis prompted Trichet to lament that 'Europe is undoubtedly in the worst situation since the second world war' (quoted in Kollowe, 2010). Others, however, viewed the crisis as an opportunity. The then European Commission president, José Manuel Barroso, proclaimed that 'in the end, we cannot have a monetary union without an economic union', while the then European Council president, Herman van Rompuy, went even further and declared that 'we can't have a monetary union without some form of economic and ... political union' (quoted in Garton Ash, 2010). Likewise, Merkel warned that

> If the euro fails ... Europe fails too, and the idea of European unification. We have a common currency, but no common economic and political union. And this is exactly what we must change ... therein lies the opportunity of this crisis. This test is existential – it must be passed.
>
> (Quoted in Goncalves, 2010)

Furthermore, Trichet recommended the further reform of the EU and the creation of 'a confederation of sovereign states of an entirely new type' and he questioned whether

> in this new union of tomorrow, or of the day after tomorrow, would it be too bold, in the economic field, with a single market, a single currency and a single central bank, to envisage a ministry of finance of the union?
>
> (Quoted in Peel, 2011b)

Such a ministry, he suggested, should be responsible for the surveillance of competitiveness policy and fiscal policy and should have a veto right over specific spending decisions by member states. Such a situation had already come about, of course, as a result of the ECB interventions in Greece, Italy and Spain in May and August 2011.

A further manifestation of the return to orthodoxy, in addition to member states' austerity packages, were the medium-term plans developed by the EU. These included the Europe 2020 Strategy, the European Commission economic governance proposals, the Barroso–van Rompuy economic plan, the Euro Plus Pact and the Single Market Act.

The Europe 2020 Strategy

The Europe 2020 Strategy was produced by the European Commission and was adopted by the European Council in March 2010. The successor to the Lisbon Strategy, the Europe 2020 Strategy prioritized 'smart', sustainable and inclusive growth and it set forth a number of specific objectives: first, to raise the employment rate to 75 per cent; second, to increase the average proportion of GDP spent on R&D to 3 per cent; third, to meet the '20/20/20' climate change and energy security targets;[1] fourth, to improve educational attainment; and fifth, to reduce the number of Europeans living below the national poverty lines by 25 per cent. In the short-term, the Europe 2020 Strategy called for a credible exit strategy from the national and EU rescue and stimulus packages introduced in October 2008, the reform of the financial system, budgetary consolidation in line with the SGP and greater coordination in terms of EMU. It also proposed a number of longer term initiatives which would help the EU to deliver on these objectives. These included the provision of finance for innovation and research, the expansion of high-speed Internet coverage, energy conservation measures, an industrial policy underpinned by public–private partnerships, labour market modernization via flexicurity and greater intra-EU labour mobility, and efforts to tackle poverty and social exclusion. The implementation of these objectives entailed both country-specific and thematic surveillance by, and reporting to, the European Commission and European Council. Moreover, the whole process was integrated with the SGP procedure. Furthermore, Europe 2020 Guidelines replaced the Integrated Guidelines, introduced in March 2005, and these enabled the European Commission to issue both policy recommendations and warnings for non-compliance.

European economic governance

In the wake of the Europe 2020 Strategy, a debate was launched about how the EU could improve its economic governance. The European Commission issued a discussion paper in May 2010, entitled 'Reinforcing Economic Policy Coordination', which stated that Europe's high levels of public debt were unsustainable, that 'hard choices' had to be made and that the European Commission wished to make full use of the surveillance instruments provided for in the Lisbon Treaty. Indeed, it declared that 'existing instruments should be modified and complemented', that 'compliance with the SGP' should be reinforced and that 'surveillance of macroeconomic imbalances' should be extended (European Commission, 2010a: 3). More specifically, it recommended that member states should integrate the EU objective of 'sound' public finances into national law and it suggested that EU obligations on budgetary discipline i.e. the SGP could be specified through legally binding instruments. A second discussion paper issued in June, entitled 'Enhancing Economic Policy Coordination for Stability, Growth and Jobs: Tools for Stronger EU Economic Governance', further developed these ideas. Similar themes figured in the Task Force to the European

Council Report, entitled 'Strengthening Economic Governance in the EU', which was published in October 2010.

The European Council in June 2010 observed that 'several member states have recently strengthened and frontloaded budgetary consolidation' and it asserted that 'all member states are ready, if necessary, to take additional measures to accelerate fiscal consolidation' (European Council, 2010: 2). The European Council also discussed the European Commission economic governance proposals. First, in terms of budgetary surveillance, the European Commission advocated increased EU supervision over the budgets of member states. Importantly, it believed that national budgets should be presented to the European Commission and the European Council *before* being discussed by the elected assemblies in the member states.

Second, in terms of fiscal surveillance, the European Commission suggested that all member states should have accredited accounting standards, independent national statistical offices and credible forecasting systems – preferably based on its forecast benchmarks. It also suggested that member states should switch to a multi-annual budgetary planning system, should devise national fiscal rules that are consistent with EU treaty obligations and the SGP in terms of budget deficits and public debt levels, and should ensure that national fiscal plans are comprehensive – covering all areas of spending at all levels of government.

Third, in terms of macroeconomic surveillance, the European Commission favoured the creation of a *preventive arm* with an alert mechanism and a *corrective arm* with a set of remedies to prevent macroeconomic imbalances – understood as 'unsustainable levels of consumption, housing bubbles, and the accumulation of external and internal debt' (European Commission, 2010a: 3). It advised that the *preventive arm* should take the form of a scoreboard of indicators and that any member state at risk of macroeconomic imbalances should be issued with country-specific policy recommendations by the European Council and early warnings from the European Commission. Importantly, it stated that these policy recommendations should be broad in their scope:

> Policy recommendations could address *both the revenue and expenditure side of fiscal policy* (in the context of the Stability and Growth Pact) as the crisis has shown that the evolution of *the composition of government revenues* is also an important lead-indicator of potential imbalances. In this context, recommendations could address the functioning of labour, product and services markets in line with the broad economic policy and employment guidelines. They should also cover macro-prudential aspects to prevent or curb excessive credit growth or exuberant asset price developments.
>
> (Ibid.: 7, emphasis added)

Furthermore, in particularly serious cases the European Commission should place a member state in an 'excessive imbalances position', which it would determine and which should trigger the *corrective arm* of the system. The enforcement mechanism, the excessive imbalances procedure, should involve stricter surveillance by the EU and, for serial offenders that were jeopardizing EMU, the imposition of additional, though unspecified, measures.

Fourth, in terms of the thematic surveillance of the implementation of the structural reforms underpinning the Europe 2020 Strategy, the European Commission proposed that it should assess each member state's progress towards the five key objectives of the strategy and that it should evaluate whether implementation was 'consistent with the macro-fiscal constraints' (ibid.: 6). Furthermore, it should: identify any 'bottlenecks' which impeded or delayed the attainment of these objectives; evaluate member state performance against the main trading partners of the EU; and be granted the right to issue policy recommendations and warnings.

Fifth, in terms of the enhanced SGP surveillance, the European Commission declared that there should be an increased focus upon public debt levels and fiscal sustainability. Regarding the *preventive arm*, it stated that there should be a 'faster pace of progress towards a general government balance' (ibid.: 7). Regarding the *corrective arm*, it proposed that

> the debt criterion of the excessive deficit procedure [should] be implemented effectively through a clear and simple numerical benchmark for defining a satisfactory pace of debt reduction: member states with debt ratios in excess of 60 per cent of GDP could become subject to the excessive deficit procedure if the decline of debt in a given preceding period falls short of this benchmark (fraction of the gap between the debt level and the 60 per cent of GDP threshold). In the same vein, bringing the deficit below 3 per cent of GDP may not be sufficient for the abrogation of the excessive deficit procedure if the debt has not been put on a sustainable declining path.
>
> (Ibid.: 8)

Sixth, in terms of enforcement incentives and sanctions, the European Commission argued that, given past non-compliance of member states with the SGP and other EU treaty obligations,

> there is clearly a need to strengthen the credibility of the EU fiscal surveillance framework through a more rule-based application of sanctions. To increase their effectiveness in the future, a wider range of sanctions and incentives should be used more preventively and kick in at an earlier stage. The deterrent effect of financial sanctions should constitute a real incentive for compliance with the rules.
>
> (Ibid.: 8–9)

It specifically called for the development of a sanction toolbox comprised of deposits, fines, conditionality on the disbursement of EU monies, etc.

Seventh, in terms of coordinating this activity, the European Commission felt that there should be a coordination cycle, termed the European Semester, which should be underpinned by an *ex ante* approach. Following the preparation of an

Annual Growth Survey by the European Commission in January, the European Council should agree to provide policy guidance to member states by February which should be integrated into their Stability and Convergence Programmes and National Reform Programmes, submitted in April. The European Council should produce country-specific policy guidance in early July and member states should finalize their budgets in the autumn. In the Annual Growth Survey of the following year, the European Commission should then assess how member states took the EU guidance into account. The process was presented diagrammatically by Rehn (2011) (see Figure 15.1).

These radical proposals prompted Barroso (2011) to declare that

> What is going on is a silent revolution – a silent revolution in terms of stronger economic governance by small steps. The member states have accepted – and I hope they understood it exactly – but they have accepted very important powers of the European institutions regarding surveillance, and a much stricter control of the public finances.

In the first Annual Growth Survey, published in January 2011, the European Commission recommended that, to tackle high budget deficit and public debt levels, member states should frontload their deficit reduction efforts in 2011, broaden their tax bases rather than increase tax levels, and if tax rises were necessary, introduce indirect (i.e. regressive) rather than direct (i.e. progressive) taxes. Furthermore, to address the lack of competitiveness, member states should apply strict and sustained wage moderation, revise wage indexation systems, liberalize their service sectors, restructure their banking sectors and gradually reduce any public support, reduce taxes on labour, increase the retirement age, develop complementary private saving arrangements to bolster state pensions,

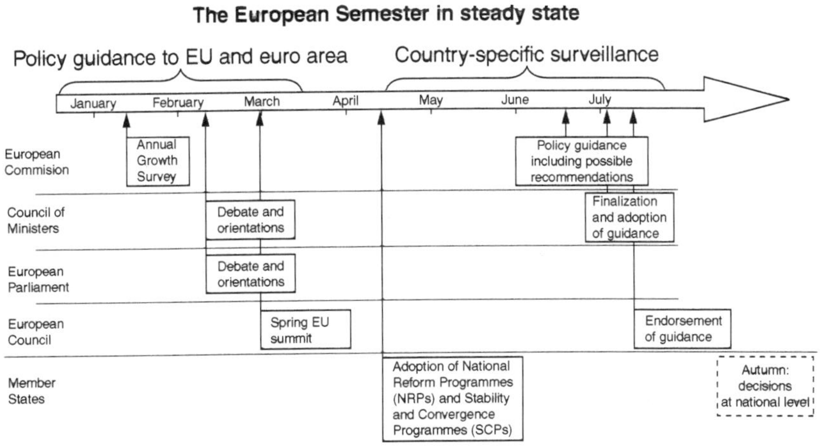

Figure 15.1 The European Semester in action (source: presentation by Commissioner Olli Rehn, 12 January 2011).

impose greater conditionality on the receipt of welfare benefits and reduce the 'over-protection' of workers on permanent contracts (European Commission, 2011a).

In addition to the European Commission and Task Force proposals, individual member states contributed to the economic governance debate. Germany advocated a more intergovernmental approach to future European integration. Merkel, in a speech in Bruges in November 2010, critiqued the perceived failings of the Community method, particularly the slow pace of structural reform across Europe, and suggested instead that the EU should proceed by means of the so-called Union method:

> If all the major stakeholders – the Union institutions, the member states and their parliaments – complement each other by acting in a coordinated manner in the areas for which they are responsible, the immense challenges facing Europe can be tackled successfully. [As a result of the Lisbon Treaty] ... the Heads of State and Government of the 27 member states and the President of the European Commission lay down jointly with the President of the European Council guidelines on how the Union should develop. Given this new division of competences, I believe we must put old rivalries behind us, we must agree common goals and we must adopt common strategies. Perhaps we can agree on the following description of this approach: coordinated action in a spirit of solidarity – each of us in the area for which we are responsible but all working towards the same goal. That for me is the new 'Union method'.
>
> (Merkel, 2010: 7–8)

The response of the European Commission was robust. Barroso told the European Parliament that he intended to ensure that member states were 'fully respecting the role of European institutions' (quoted in Peel, 2011a). Barroso argued that 'the EU treaty provides the right framework and instruments to achieve economic coordination' and he warned that 'we would not further our case if parallel structures were to work in an ultimately incoherent manner' (ibid.).

A concrete example of the proposed Union method was the Franco-German competitiveness pact put forward in February 2011. The pact recommended that to ensure greater economic convergence and increased competitiveness within the EU, member states should improve price competitiveness, achieve sustainable public debt levels and deliver minimum rates of investment in education, infrastructure, and R&D. It called for member states to agree quantifiable indicators relating to these objectives, for the European Commission to assess progress and issue reports, and for the European Council to consider devising a sanctions regime for non-compliance. France and Germany also called for six steps to be taken within 12 months to improve competitiveness within the EU: the abolition of automatic indexation of wages to prices, the mutual recognition of professional qualifications, a common corporate tax base, pension reform that included increases in the retirement age, the incorporation of debt alert mechanisms into national constitutions, and the creation of national crisis management regimes for banking systems.

The Barroso–van Rompuy economic plan

In an attempt to regain the initiative and to assuage the concerns of smaller member states that Germany was, once again, attempting to dominate the EU, Barroso and van Rompuy issued their own economic plan in February 2011. With the exception of the debt alert mechanism, however, their proposals mirrored those in the Franco-German competitiveness pact (Barroso and van Rompuy, 2011).

The Euro Plus Pact

The European Commission economic governance proposals and its first Annual Growth Survey, the Franco-German competitiveness pact and the Barroso–van Rompuy economic plan formed the basis of the Euro Plus Pact which was agreed by the European Council in March 2011. Endorsed by the eurozone heads of state and government, plus the non-eurozone countries of Bulgaria, Denmark, Latvia, Lithuania, Poland and Romania, signatories pledged to promote competitiveness, increase employment levels, achieve sustainable public finances, support financial stability and consider tax policy coordination. To promote competitiveness, signatories would focus upon productivity and wage costs and would use the measure of unit labour costs to quantify these. Productivity would be raised via the deregulation of sheltered sectors of the economy and investment in education, infrastructure and R&D, while wages would be lowered by decentralizing wage bargaining systems, reforming indexing mechanisms and reducing pay settlements in the public sector. To increase employment levels, signatories would pursue labour market reforms (i.e. flexicurity), utilize lifelong learning schemes, reduce taxes on labour and increase the participation of second earners in the workforce. To achieve sustainable public finances, signatories would reform their health, pension and social security systems to take account of demographic changes and reduce government liabilities, and would translate the fiscal rules of the SGP into national legislation via a balanced budget law, debt brake or expenditure rule. Importantly, the latter should apply at the national *and* sub-national levels and the preferred system would need to be endorsed by the European Commission to ensure that it is compliant with EU treaty obligations. To support financial stability, signatories would monitor the levels of private debt held by banks, households and non-financial companies and would conduct regular bank stress tests. In terms of tax policy coordination, signatories were asked to consider common action against fraud and tax evasion and to note the European Commission proposal for a common consolidated corporate tax base. To achieve these goals, signatories were invited to specify a set of concrete actions to be implemented within 12 months and to incorporate these into their

Stability and Convergence Programme and National Reform Programme which would be evaluated by the European Commission and European Council as part of the European Semester.

The Single Market Act

The Single Market Act was adopted by the European Commission in April 2011. During the Keynesian interregnum, Barroso tasked the then commissioner for the internal market, Mario Monti, with preparing a report on the re-launch of the SM so as to counter the 'strong temptation, particularly when times are hard, to roll back the SM and to seek refuge [in] economic nationalism' (Monti in House of Lords Select Committee on the European Union, 2010: 2–3). The resulting Monti Report, published in May 2010, set out a number of recommendations and many of these were incorporated into the Single Market Act. The 12-point action plan, to be implemented by the end of 2012 – the twentieth anniversary of the SM project – called for easier access to credit for small- and medium-sized businesses, the further development of digital technologies, investment in pan-European energy and transport infrastructure, the creation of a European patent regime, the liberalization of public procurement and greater worker mobility, amongst other objectives.

Social forces and Social Europe

In the contemporary struggle over the future of Europe, the forces of capital are seeking to further enmesh the EU and its member states in the neo-liberal project. The age of austerity consolidates the gains made by capital during the three-stage neo-liberal counter revolution, which began in the 1970s, but it also provides new opportunities. Capital's objectives in the current period are four-fold. First, to construct a hegemonic austerity agenda, in both a discursive and policy sense, that will bind social forces into the neo-liberal project. Second, to transfer liabilities, losses and risk from the private sector to the public sector so as to restore profitability and, more fundamentally, temporarily save capitalism from its contradictions and excesses. Third, to extend liberalization and privatization into previously 'closed' (i.e. state-run) sections of the economy and so create new markets and profit-making opportunities. Fourth, to dismantle and/or neuter the remnants of social democracy, and counter any new forces of opposition, so as to sustain the neo-liberal project.

At the global level, the assault by capital is being waged by the international financial nexus and the financial markets – manifest in the speculative attacks against individual member states, and the eurozone as a whole, to enforce austerity. These efforts are augmented by the actions and pronouncements of international organizations such as the IMF and OECD.

At the EU level, Business-Europe[2] (2010a, 2010b) and the ERT (2010) support the austerity drive across the continent and their agenda is shared by the ECB, the European Commission and the European Council which have exploited the economic crisis to impose EU/IMF-sponsored bailouts (i.e. SAPs) on individual member states. EU institutions have also devised medium-term plans (i.e. the economic governance agenda) to lock-in such austerity among all member states.

At the national level, and taking Britain as an example, the British Chambers of Commerce (BCC), the CBI, the Federation of Small Businesses (FSB) and the IoD – representing different fractions of capital – all support the public spending cuts imposed by the Conservative–Liberal Democratic coalition government elected in May 2010. In its Emergency Budget in June and Comprehensive Spending Review in October (BCC, 2010; Cave, 2010; CBI, 2010; IoD, 2010; Patel, 2010; Jaffa and Cave, 2011), the coalition government set out to eliminate the budget deficit within four years, with 80 per cent of the reduction coming from public expenditure cuts and 20 per cent from tax increases.

A survey of small businesses by the FSB in May 2010 found that 93 per cent of respondents supported deficit reduction (FSB, 2010), an IoD survey in June 2010 found that 90 per cent of directors supported the emergency budget (cited in Groom, 2010), while an Ipsos-MORI survey in January 2011 found that 89 per cent of business leaders supported the coalition government's economic policy (Ipsos-MORI, 2011). Importantly, however, while some sections of the private sector expected to profit from the outsourcing of goods and services previously provided by the state (Booth *et al.*, 2010), not all businesses stood to gain; analysis by the TUC suggested that those companies which were dependent on public sector contracts would be negatively hit by the austerity drive (TUC, 2010), while Oxford Economics suggested that at least 2.3 million private sector jobs were at risk as a result of the spending cuts (cited in Local Futures, 2010). These changes to the amount of public subsidy for private profit granted to different fractions of capital highlight the paradox that is capitalism.

Governments of all types – conservative, green, liberal, social democratic and socialist – are, regardless of professed ideology, helping capital to achieve its objectives by imposing austerity on their publics. Indeed, the most austere packages – those adopted in Greece, Portugal and Spain – were implemented by governing parties that were ostensibly socialist. Albo and Evans (2010) highlighted the collusion of sections of the left in Britain, Greece and Ireland with the austerity agenda. New Labour in Britain, for example, during the 2010 general election campaign pledged to halve the budget deficit over the term of the next parliament with 70 per cent of the reduction coming from public expenditure cuts and 30 per cent from tax increases (i.e. not that dissimilar to the coalition government's 80/20 split).

Arrayed against the forces of capital is an ensemble of counter-hegemonic forces that are seeking to create a Social Europe as an alternative to the neoliberal EU. Some of these progressive social forces, sections of Europe's social democratic parties for example, seek to reform the EU from within, while others – many of Europe's far left and green parties – favour the construction of a new formation.

Europe's social democrats and Social Europe

Following the electoral defeat of several social democratic and socialist governments in the aftermath of the 2008 economic crisis, and in the wake of the disastrous results for the Party of European Socialists in the 2009 European elections,
the Fabian Society and the Foundation for European Progressive Studies established the 'New Left' research programme. Its report, entitled *Europe's Left in the
Crisis* (Katwala and Stetter, 2011), was published in January 2011 and it began:

> In this age of European austerity, Europe's left finds itself on the sidelines,
> not in the driving seat. The political right commands the political and eco-
> nomic agenda. A global recession, caused by the bursting of a financial
> bubble, has been reframed as a crisis of excessive public spending. A failure
> to regulate has ended up being about the over-reach of government. If the
> multilateral response to the immediate crisis in the autumn of 2008 and
> spring of 2009 succeeded in preventing systemic collapse and a 1929-style
> global slump, hopes of a coordinated plan for economic recovery have given
> way to governments embarking on separate deep national deficit reduction
> programmes, each hoping to cut its way to generating the conditions for
> future growth. This ascendancy of the right both reflects and represents the
> political failure of Europe's left.
>
> (Ibid.: 1)

The report identified three crises confronting the European left. First, the crisis
of political support, manifest in the electoral defeat of social democratic parties,
reflected the left's inability to construct and maintain cross-class electoral coalitions. Second, the crisis of political economy meant that social democracy struggled to create the sustainable capitalism it needed to resource its ambitions.
Third, the crisis of multilateral legitimacy, more specifically the disconnection
between Europe's citizens and the EU, was making it difficult to construct a
viable European project to replace the redundant 'social democracy in one
country' strategy. The report also identified how social democracy could renew
itself and thus overcome the 'triple crises'. First, social democrats should re-
emphasize their ideological values and principles and should organize themselves in an open and more pluralistic way. Second, while social democracy has
long promoted economic prosperity, environmental sustainability and social
justice, 'the scale of the insecurities created by contemporary capitalism'
(ibid.: 9) meant that social democrats needed to re-energize the 'fairness contract'. Third, social democrats should embrace the localization agenda and re-
engage with the communities they seek to serve via community organization and
the social media. Many of these themes were taken up in the speech on the European left delivered by the former New Labour foreign secretary and Labour leadership contender, David Miliband, in March 2011.

For all that the report called for 'new thinking' and for a 'new generation' to
form the 'next left, it was distinctly backward looking at times. It claimed as

common knowledge that 'globalization made it impossible for one state alone to determine all its policies' (ibid.: ii), that 'rising costs ... will become an unsupportable drag on future welfare state sustainability' (ibid.: 18) and that 'it is no use blaming the populism of the media for ordinary people's narrow-mindedness' (ibid.: 26). It asserted that 'high public sector deficits are justifiable temporarily on legitimate Keynesian anti-recessionary grounds' but that if social democrats 'imply that they are permanently not a problem it would be a recipe for economic irrelevance and political impotence' (ibid.: 27). It also stated that wage competition from Central and Eastern Europe is inevitable and legitimate' (ibid.: 28). In short, much of the report's analysis and many of its prescriptions were redolent of the revisionism of Crosland (1956) if not the structural constraints thesis developed by Przeworski (1985).

In terms of Europe, the report accurately diagnosed many of the problems afflicting the European project in the current period.

> The medium term position in Europe looks bad. The Southern Mediterranean member states and Ireland are locked in what looks like a long-lasting triple vice of austerity. For them there is no alternative to sustained deficit reduction – despite the negative consequences for growth. Appeasing bond market fears of debt sustainability has to come first. And the pain of gradual disinflation to restore their competitiveness within the eurozone – through an 'internal devaluation' of relative cuts in the real value of wages and social benefits – could go on for years. A decade of high unemployment and social tension is in prospect.... The private sector banks' reduced appetite for risk will mean less finance for new and growing business or big risky projects. At the same time the requirements of fiscal consolidation will contain social ambitions ... and the overhang of deficit reduction will cast a long shadow, as Europe this decade has also to come to terms with public finance consequences of its aging demography.
>
> (Ibid.: 26–7)

The report set forth a number of ideas to solve these problems. First, it suggested that social democrats should pursue a new 'grand bargain' which would accept binding rules on budget deficits in exchange for obligations on surplus-creating member states to boost demand. This would necessitate wage coordination between member states, plus minimum wages, new forms of profit sharing, regional transfers and action on social dumping.

Second, social democrats should aim for the decarbonization of the economy through the modernization and reconfiguration of Europe's energy and transport infrastructure. A European low carbon investment bank should be established, as part of the EIB, and new EU bonds should be issued to fund low carbon infrastructure. 'This would be "borrowing to invest" for clear and specific infrastructure purposes; not bailouts for member states with unsustainable debt and deficits' (ibid.: 29).

Third, social democrats should strive to stimulate 'private sector-led commercial innovation at the high-technology knowledge frontier' (ibid.) to maintain Europe's competitiveness vis-à-vis the United States and other advanced economies. This would require additional investment in education, R&D, etc.

Fourth, social democrats should prioritize the completion of the SM in order to drive a new wave of innovation. To ensure that the benefits are shared and to promote long-term social partnership and stakeholder accountability over short-term shareholder value, however, corporate governance laws should be reinforced and state aid rules revised to permit active government.

Fifth social democrats should work towards a Social Europe. This would need an enlarged EU budget, EU fiscal coordination and new EU-wide taxes on carbon emissions and financial transactions, the adoption of flexicurity and welfare state modernization. The EU should focus its attention on childcare provision, early intervention for disadvantaged children, educational attainment, access to higher education and social mobility.

The report also contained some polling by YouGov which suggested that there was an appetite in Britain for many of these ideas. While 45 per cent of those surveyed felt that Britain's membership of the EU was a 'bad thing', 21 per cent believed that member states should co-operate more to deal with major international issues. These included tackling climate change (55 per cent in favour), regulating banks (53 per cent) and recovering from the recession (45 per cent). Furthermore, the poll found that 55 per cent agreed that the EU should establish minimum levels of workers' rights, 47 per cent supported minimum levels of tax on large businesses and 42 per cent favoured a Europe-wide financial transactions tax – if it was part of a global agreement.

Not only were the report's recommendations extremely modest and not that dissimilar to the Party of European Socialists' 2009 manifesto – which delivered only 25 per cent of the popular vote in the 2009 European elections – but they were woefully inadequate given the scale of the problems. The report accepted the existing EU institutional and treaty arrangements, with their negative integration and neo-liberal bias, and it failed to set out a strategy for reforming the EU towards a Social Europe. In short the report failed to address the quadruple lock that faces any progressive European strategy: how to build a coalition of support for such measures, how to ensure the simultaneous election of such coalitions, how to deliver the unanimity needed to revise the EU treaties and how to withstand the hostility of the international financial nexus to such a programme.

Europe's far left and greens and Social Europe

The Party of the European Left, which fought the 2009 European elections on the basis of the 'Together for Change in Europe' manifesto, rejected the neoliberal EU in favour of a Social Europe. The manifesto supported CAP reform, the provision of affordable credit for productive sectors of the economy, the democratization of the ECB and lower interest rates, improved environmental protection and action on global warming. It favoured the nationalization of financial systems, minimum wage and minimum income guarantees, an expanded public sector, a Europe-wide financial transactions tax, action against tax havens, EU tax harmonization, a 35-hour working week and workers' control. It backed the replacement of the SGP with a solidarity pact, which would prioritize economic growth, environmental protection and full employment, and it called for the dissolution of NATO and the creation of a European welfare state.

The European Greens, who fought the 2009 European elections on the basis of the 'Green New Deal for Europe' manifesto, warned of a resource crunch and a climate crisis in addition to the credit crunch and financial crisis. The manifesto called for CAP reform, greater energy efficiency and a non-nuclear renewable energy policy, environmental sustainability, drastically reduced greenhouse gas emissions, improved pollution controls and sustainable transport policies. Economically and socially, it favoured the full implementation of the Charter of Fundamental Rights, extending affordable credit to European enterprises, investment in education, research and science, fair trade, the regulation of financial markets, a Europe-wide financial transactions tax and action against tax havens, minimum wage and minimum income guarantees, and an expansion of workers' rights.

Laudable as many of these ideas are, and although there are millions of people in Europe who doubtless support such objectives – as the mass campaigns, demonstrations and strikes demonstrate – Europe's far left and green parties have also failed to explain how an alternative to the neo-liberal EU could be constructed. In common with Europe's social democrats, they have neglected to engage with the quadruple lock. Furthermore, Europe's far left and green parties secured only 7.5 per cent and 4.8 per cent respectively of the popular vote in the 2009 European elections – compared to the 36 per cent polled by conservatives. Put simply, progressive social forces do not, at present, have the necessary power resources to construct a Social Europe within or without the existing EU.

Conclusion

If the disintegration of the Soviet bloc in 1989–1991 constituted a crisis which was exploited by capital in the United States, the EU and elsewhere to impose neo-liberalism across Eastern Europe and Russia, so the 2010 sovereign debt crisis in Western Europe arguably provided an opportunity for a renewed assault on progressive social forces and the consolidation of neo-liberalism within the EU. The shift from the era of rescue and stimulus to the age of austerity was significant in several respects. First, the coordinated and Keynesian rescue and stimulus packages that were introduced from October 2008 were temporary. Their purpose was to rescue capitalism and to prevent a global slump as long and as deep as the Great Depression. Pronouncements at the time concerning the demise of neo-liberalism and the rehabilitation of the state proved to be premature. Although Europe's far left, greens and social democrats made the case for the fundamental reform of the capitalist system and the creation of a Social Europe, they failed to press their advantage or to assemble the necessary power resources. The 'window of opportunity' was lost.

Second, the debate about whether Western Europe's welfare states were resilient or retrenching was resolved; the austerity drive from 2010 clearly indicated that Western Europe's social models were retrenching towards the market liberal model. Despite significant variations in the budget deficit, public debt and unemployment levels across the EU, austerity measures were adopted in a uniform manner. That is to say, although the balance between public expenditure cuts and tax increases varied from member state to member state, the burden generally fell more heavily on the former. This contrasted with the MCC-induced austerity drive during the 1990s; an OECD investigation of 15 cases of fiscal consolidation in 11 countries found that, in all but one case – that of Ireland between 1986 and 1989 – increased revenue, rather than expenditure cuts, accounted for the majority of fiscal consolidation (OECD, 1996b). In the age of austerity, by contrast, nearly all of the member states that adopted austerity measures targeted public expenditure and welfare benefits and nearly all increased the rate of value added tax which is a regressive form of taxation. Consequently, such cuts and tax increases had a disproportionate impact on the poorest. As the report by Oxford Analytica (2010) concluded:

> In order to reduce their deficit and public debt levels, most European countries are in the process of transforming their welfare states, driven by an austerity imperative that is yielding deep and far-reaching cuts to public spending. As aspects of the welfare state previously considered sacrosanct are targeted – including pensions, healthcare, unemployment and incapacity benefits, and child allowances – and some taxes are raised, European citizens are paying more to receive less.

Likewise, the reports by the European Anti-Poverty Network (2009, 2010, 2011), Janssen (2010), Coates (2011), Degryse and Natali (2011), the European Trade Union Institute (2011) and Heise and Lierse (2011) highlighted the regressive nature of the austerity measures and the negative consequences for the European Stability Mechanism. Meanwhile, although a number of member states introduced bank levies, pledged to combat tax avoidance and evasion, and expressed support for some form of financial transactions tax, there was no concerted effort by any member state to target the wealthy individuals, financial institutions or TNCs that had caused the economic crisis. Put simply, a wealth tax as an alternative to austerity was firmly *off* the agenda. Such a measure enjoyed public support however. In a YouGov poll in Britain, conducted in June 2010, 74 per cent of those surveyed supported a wealth tax on the richest 10 per cent of people. A tax of 20 per cent on this £4,000 billion of personal wealth would generate £800 billion – enough to close the deficit and pay off much of Britain's debt (Philo, 2010).

Third, having backed the national and EU rescue and stimulus packages in 2008, plus the bailout packages for the euro and for Greece, Ireland and Portugal in 2010 and 2011, the financial markets and institutions such as employers' organizations, the European Commission and European Council, the IMF, the OECD and rating agencies welcomed, if not demanded, some form of austerity. Indeed, the European Commission launched an investigation in April 2011 into 16 of the world's largest financial institutions, 'many of which had been rescued by their host governments from collapse', over 'suspicions they colluded and abused their positions in providing the financial derivatives many blame for exacerbating the eurozone sovereign debt crisis' (Goodley, 2011). In short, the impetus for public spending cuts came from both internal (e.g. employers' organizations) and external (e.g. the EU, IMF and OECD) sources.

Fourth, there was no call by any member state or the EU – whether the European Commission or the European Council – to defend the ESM during the economic crisis. The European Commission (2008: 7) made it plain that the 2008 rescue and stimulus packages should be 'timely, targeted and temporary' and that member states should comply with the SGP as soon as practicable. Importantly, the European Council agreed. Indeed, the European Commission and the European Council exploited the age of austerity to further lock in neo-liberalism: their responses to the sovereign debt crisis included the Europe 2020 Strategy, the Barroso–van Rompuy economic plan, the Euro Plus Pact and the Single Market Act with their supply-side reform objectives which enhanced EU economic policy-making power at member states' expense. Responding to these initiatives, the ETUC (2010) declared that

> Economic governance, as currently proposed by the Commission, is about nothing else than cuts, cuts, cuts; cutting wages, cutting jobs, cutting protection against easy firing, cutting social benefits and cutting public services. Workers are being presented with all of the huge costs of the crisis.

Likewise, the Corporate Europe Observatory (2011) feared that

> A European version of the 'shock doctrine' is about to be applied in the European Union. In the wake of the euro crisis, new EU powers to intervene in labour markets and in member states' budgets – including social spending – will effectively impose a neo-liberal straightjacket on national economies.

A Social Europe is an impossible dream.

Notes

1 The European Social Model

1 Although Layard et al. (1991: 9) seek to avoid the conflation of NAIRU with the earlier NRU version of an equilibrium rate of unemployment, they nevertheless, describe the former as 'the state to which the system will return after a disturbance'. Moreover, in the long run, unemployment is described as being 'entirely determined by long-run supply factors and equals the NAIRU' (Layard et al., 1991: 16).
2 A Keynesian alternative theoretical model, emphasizing the importance of corporate retained earnings and the creation of bank credit, would not operate in this way, because the crowding out hypothesis rests upon the assumption of exogenous money and a resultant given level of savings, whereas post-Keynesian theory holds that an expansion of effective demand will stimulate investment which, in turn, will generate additional income and thereby boost rather than reduce savings (Palley, 1998: 141).
3 First coined by Ohlin in a paper in the *Economic Journal* in 1937, the 'Stockholm School' included Dag Hammarskjöld, Alf Johansson, Erik Lindahl, Erik Lundberg, Gunnar Myrdal, and Bertil Ohlin (Hansson, 1991: 168–213). Their analysis was developed in parallel to Keynesianism but with greater emphasis upon disequilibrium analysis, derived from assumptions of irrational factors influencing economic actors and uncertainty of expectations in a dynamic economy, inferring that static theory is an inaccurate approximation of dynamic reality (Myrdal, 1927; Winch, 1966: 170). They argued that market economies contain a large element of cyclical instability and therefore governments *should* control the business cycle via fiscal policy.

2 Liberal Europe during the Cold War Order (1947–1982): from the European Recovery Program to the socialist challenge

1 The process of 'spill-over' envisaged that integration in one sector of the economy would lead to integration in other sectors and that political integration would follow economic integration.
2 The United States' federal budget was 30 times the size of the EU budget in 1996.
3 A series of landmark legal decisions in the 1960s and 1970s heralded a new era of judicial activism. The ECJ ruled that individual citizens could sue their national governments for the non-enforcement of treaty obligations – the direct effect principle; that European law had primacy over national law – the supremacy and pre-emption principles; and that the ECJ could determine the constitutionality of executive and legislative acts of government and could define their respective powers and rights – the judicial review principle (Starr-Deelan and Deelan, 1986).

4 The present formulation of subsidiarity is contained in Article 5(3) of the TEU:

> Under the principle of subsidiarity, in areas which do not fall within its exclusive competence, the Union shall act only if and in so far as the objectives of the proposed action cannot be sufficiently achieved by the Member States, either at central level or at regional and local level, but can rather, by reason of the scale or effects of the proposed action, be better achieved at Union level.

3 The political economy of Western Europe's social models in the Cold War Order: inevitable and convergent welfare states?

1 For CPE conceptual–theoretical studies of the CWO, see van der Pijl (1984, 1998), Cox (1987, 1996), Rupert (1995) and Robinson (1996). For CPE critiques and conceptual–theoretical studies of European integration, see van Apeldoorn (1998, 2000, 2001, 2002), Bieler and Morton (2001), van Apeldoorn *et al.* (2003), Gill (2003) and Nousios *et al.* (2011). For CPE conceptual–theoretical studies of particular social models, see Overbeek (1990) on Britain; Holman (1993a, 1993b, 1996, 1998) on the Czech Republic, Hungary, Poland and Spain; Mommen (1993) on Belgium; Ryner (2002) on Sweden; Becker (2003, 2005) and van Apeldoorn (2009) on the Netherlands; Clift (2003) on France; and van der Wurff (1993) and Ryner (2003) on Germany. For CPE conceptual–theoretical studies of welfare regimes more generally, see Jessop (2003) and Ryner (2009).
2 Correspondence with Noam Chomsky (Professor, Massachusetts Institute of Technology), 18 December 2002.

4 Neo-liberal Europe in the New World Order (1985–2007): from the single market to the European Constitution

1 The NWO, as enunciated by the United States president, George Bush, actually began in 1991 following the end of the Cold War. The ideas and policies which characterized the NWO, i.e. neo-liberalism, however, were launched at the EC level in 1985 – in the form of the SM project; the title of NWO is therefore used in a political rather than (strictly accurate) temporal sense.
2 One of Jacques Delors' associates explained why his strategy was like a 'Russian doll': 'You take the first doll apart and then, inside it is another one, which leads you to another and so on ... until it is too late to turn back' (cited in Ross,1995: 39).
3 The present formulation of subsidiarity is contained in Article 5(3) of the TEU:

> Under the principle of subsidiarity, in areas which do not fall within its exclusive competence, the Union shall act only if and in so far as the objectives of the proposed action cannot be sufficiently achieved by the Member States, either at central level or at regional and local level, but can rather, by reason of the scale or effects of the proposed action, be better achieved at Union level.

4 The so-called MCC stipulated that, in order to achieve economic convergence amongst potential participants, countries aspiring to join EMU must meet five criteria. First, each country's rate of inflation must be no more than 1.5 per cent above the average of the three lowest inflation rates in the EMS. Second, each country's long-term interest rate must be within 2 per cent of the aforementioned three countries. Third, each country must have been a member of the ERM for at least two years without any currency realignment. Fourth, each country's budget deficit must not be regarded as 'excessive' by the European Council, defined as a deficit greater than 3 per cent of GDP for reasons other than of a 'temporary' or 'exceptional' nature. Fifth, each country's national debt must not be 'excessive', defined as 60 per cent of gross domestic product.
5 The *acquis communautaire* refers to the accumulated legal judgments and treaties of the EU.

6 The SGP reaffirmed the MCC of budget deficits not exceeding 3 per cent of gross domestic product. If this limit was ignored, and the country was not in recession, then fines of between 0.2 and 0.5 per cent of GDP would be levied by the ECB. The SGP also agreed that, in the long term, budget deficits should be limited to 1 per cent of GDP.

7 The 'golden rules', adopted by the Treasury in July 1997, pledged that, over the economic cycle, the government would borrow only to invest and would not borrow to fund current expenditure, while public debt as a proportion of national income would be held over the economic cycle at a stable and prudent level.

5 The political economy of Western Europe's social models in the New World Order: retrenching welfare states and the emergence of Social Europe?

1 For CPE conceptual–theoretical studies of the NWO, see van der Pijl (1998) and Cox (1996). For CPE critiques and conceptual–theoretical studies of European integration, see van Apeldoorn (1998, 2000, 2001, 2002), Bieler and Morton (2001), van Apeldoorn *et al.* (2003), Gill (2003) and Nousios *et al.* (2011). For CPE conceptual–theoretical studies of particular social models, see Overbeek (1990) on Britain; Holman (1993a, 1993b, 1996, 1998) on the Czech Republic, Hungary, Poland and Spain; Mommen (1993) on Belgium; Ryner (2002) on Sweden; Becker (2003, 2005) and van Apeldoorn (2009) on the Netherlands; Clift (2003) on France; and van der Wurff (1993) and Ryner (2003) on Germany. For CPE conceptual–theoretical studies of welfare regimes more generally, see Jessop (2003) and Ryner (2009).

2 The concept of flexicurity was defined by the European Commission in June 2007. Underpinned by four components – flexible employment arrangements, lifelong learning, active labour market policies and modern social security systems – it aimed to deliver more and better jobs through flexibility and security (European Commission, 2007; also see Burroni and Keune, 2011).

3 The Trilateral Commission was established in 1972 as an elite planning organization composed of hundreds of academic, corporate and political leaders from Europe, Japan and North America (see Shoup and Minter, 1977; Sklar, 1980).

4 These figures do not include non-equity arrangements, such as franchising, licensing, subcontracting, and strategic alliances which TNCs utilize to further consolidate their control of assets and markets.

5 Correspondence with Noam Chomsky (Professor, Massachusetts Institute of Technology), 18 December 2002.

6 Progressive social forces and the transformation of the World Order: radical national alternatives

1 'Bounce', according to Donoughue (1987: 66), is used to partially conceal or underplay what is being described: an unelected group of civil servants trying to impose their views on the government.

2 Interview with Tony Benn, 25 April 2002.

3 The *Centre d'Études de Recherche et d'Éducation Socialiste* operated as a left-wing pressure group and think tank within the PS. Established in 1964, its aim was to encourage the party to adopt and implement a radical programme (Bell and Shaw, 1983).

7 Progressive social forces and the transformation of the World Order: Euro-Keynesian and radical European alternatives

1 The 'Tobin Tax' refers to the 1972 idea of the economist, James Tobin, that, to curb volatile currency speculation, a transaction tax of say 0.5 per cent should be levied to help dissuade short-termism. It has since been adopted by the anti-globalization movement and many sections of the left.

8 Operation of economic policy

1 Stark (2001) discusses the rationale for the original German proposal regarding the SGP. For a description of its basic features see Buti *et al.* (1998) and Cabral (2001), whilst EU Commission (2000) and Fischer and Giudice (2001) discuss the implementation and operation of the SGP.

2 See Brunila *et al.* (2001) for an overview of the institutional, legal, theoretical and empirical aspects of the SGP.

3 This is also in line with the practice followed by all of the central banks of the major developed countries that have specified numerical values for their objectives; all have a midpoint above 1 per cent. For example: the Bank of England: 2.5 per cent (RPIX index, approximately 1.75 on average in HICP terms); Sveriges Riksbank: 2±1 per cent (CPI); Norges Bank: 2.5±1 per cent (CPI); Bank of Canada: 1–3 per cent (CPI); Bank of Australia: 1–3 per cent (CPI); Reserve Bank of New Zealand: 1–3 per cent (CPI). The Federal Reserve System and the Bank of Japan have not specified a quantitative definition of their price stability objectives. The Swiss National Bank has adopted a definition of price stability that is equivalent to that of the ECB.

4 EU Commission (1992) lists its founding regulations, whilst Baimbridge *et al.* (1999) provides a comprehensive critique of the ECB.

5 The literature includes: Bruno and Sachs (1985), Carlin and Soskice (1990), Dréze and Bean (1990), Eichengreen (1990), Layard *et al.* (1991), Bini-Smaghi and Vori (1992), Blanchard and Katz (1992), Sala-i-Martin and Sachs (1992), Eichengreen (1993), Goodhart and Smith (1993), Pisani-Ferry *et al.* (1993), Kenen (1995) and Goodhart (1995).

6 Compliance with the convergence criteria is a long-term commitment to be fulfilled in cyclical troughs as well as peaks. To avoid budget deficits exceeding 3 per cent of GDP in recessions, the surplus during boom years must exceed the total variation in budget balance over the cycle. For example, UK government finances varied from a 5.3 per cent deficit at the depth of the 1980–1981 recession to a 3 per cent surplus at the height of the 1988–1989 boom. The following deficit exceeded 8 per cent during 1993–1994, whilst the chancellor's current predictions estimate a 2 per cent surplus by early next century. The cyclical variation, 8.3 per cent of GDP during the 1980s rising to 9–10 per cent presently, indicates that, for deficits to remain above 3 per cent at the low point of the business cycle, the UK budget must be in surplus by a minimum of 6–7.5 per cent of GDP, necessitating tax increases or reductions in public expenditure to the extent of £23.3 to £46.1 billion at current prices.

9 Fiscal federalism: a missed opportunity or an emerging consensus?

1 Examples include the Latin Monetary Union, Scandinavian Currency Union, Gold Standard, Modified Gold Standard and Bretton Woods. The monetary union between Belgium and Luxembourg has not collapsed, although this is perhaps more an example of a small country tying its currency to that of a large, important trading partner, than a model for successful EMU between equal partners.

2 EFSF website, online, available at: www.efsf.europa.eu/about/index.htm.

3 Council of the European Union press release, online, available at: www.consilium. europa.eu/uedocs/cms_data/docs/pressdata/en/ecofin/122072.pdf.

4 *New York Times*, online, available at: www.nytimes.com/2011/01/16/magazine/16Europe-t.html?pagewanted=all.

11 Social partnership and labour market flexibility

1 The decision to adopt parity conversion of Ostmark to DM occurred despite official debts being valued at an exchange rate of 24:1 and the unofficial exchange rate was between 6:1 and 10:1 (Incomes Data Services European Report, 1990c).

2 Blair (2000).

13 Social Europe and enlargement: threat or opportunity?

1 This feature has been exaggerated by the accession of Bulgaria and Romania, as their GDP per capita represents only 27 per cent and 26 per cent of the EU(25) average, respectively (Liargovas, 2006: 135).
2 Cited in the *Guardian*, 11 December 2007: 4.

14 National economic policy alternatives

1 Kydland and Prescott (1977) argue that rules or pre-commitment are more relevant when the monetary and fiscal authorities enjoy a reputation for discipline and consistency over time, whereas discretionary policy is more appropriate when such credibility is lacking.
2 It is worth noting that the international price structures of many of these key products are denominated in US dollars. Moreover, the euro is likely to have a more volatile medium-term relationship with the US dollar than sterling has experienced since the UK's withdrawal from the ERM in September 1992.
3 The converse occasionally occurs, if import and export volumes do not change sufficiently to offset the price movements; the Marshal–Lerner condition states that the trade balance will improve when the sum of the elasticities of demand for exports and imports exceeds unity.
4 One estimate, made by Burkitt *et al.* (1996), concluded that the UK's two-year membership of the ERM cost an estimated £68.2 billion in 1992 prices (equivalent to 11.5 per cent of UK GDP), in terms of lost output and one-and-a-quarter million more unemployed.

15 From rescue and stimulus to the age of austerity: the European response to the great recession and the prospects for Social Europe

1 The 20/20/20 targets, agreed in December 2008, committed the EU to reducing greenhouse gas emissions by 20 per cent, improving energy efficiency by 20 per cent and increasing renewable energy production by 20 per cent.
2 Business-Europe, representing 40 employers' federations across the continent, was formerly known as the Union of Industrial and Employers' Confederations of Europe and was officially renamed in 2007.

Bibliography

Aaronovitch, S. (1981) *The Road from Thatcherism: The Alternative Economic Strategy*, London: Lawrence and Wishart.

Abrahamson, P. (1991) 'Welfare and Poverty in the Europe of the 1990s: Social Progress or Social Dumping?' *International Journal of Health Services*, vol. 21, no. 2, pp. 237–64.

Abrahamson, P. (1992) 'Welfare Pluralism: Towards a New Consensus for a European Social Policy?' in L. Hantrais, S. Mangen and M. O'Brien (eds) *Mixed Economy of Welfare*, Cross-national Research Paper no. 6, Loughborough: Loughborough University.

ActionAid (2004) *Trade Traps: Why EU-ACP Economic Partnership Agreements Pose a Threat to Africa's Development*, London: ActionAid.

Adelantado, J. and Calderón Cuevas, E. (2006) 'Globalization and the Welfare State: The Same Strategies for Similar Problems?' *Journal of European Social Policy*, vol. 16, no. 4, pp. 374–86.

Adnett, N. (1995) 'Social Dumping and European Economic Integration', *Journal of European Social Policy*, vol. 5, no. 1, pp. 394–415.

Adnett, N. (2001) 'Modernizing the European Social Model: Developing the Guidelines', *Journal of Common Market Studies*, vol. 39, no. 2, pp. 353–64.

Adnett, N. and Hardy, S. (2005) *The European Social Model: Modernization or Evolution*, Cheltenham: Edward Elgar.

Agee, P. and Wolf, L. (1978) *Dirty Work: The CIA in Western Europe*, New York: Lyle Stuart.

Agee, P. and Wolf, L. (1979) *Dirty Work 2: The CIA in Africa*, New York: Lyle Stuart.

Agell, J. (1996) 'Why Sweden's Welfare State Needed Reform', *Economic Journal*, vol. 106, no. 439, pp. 1760–71.

Aglietta, M. (1976) *A Theory of Capitalist Regulation: The US Experience*, London: Verso.

Aiginger, K. (2008) 'New Challenges for the European Model and the How to Cope with It' in W. Bienkowski, J. Brada and M. Radlo (eds) *Growth versus Security: Old and New EU Members' Quest for a New Economic and Social Model*, Basingstoke: Palgrave Macmillan.

Alber, J. (2006) 'The European Social Model and the United States', *European Union Politics*, vol. 7, no. 3, pp. 393–419.

Alber, J. (2010) 'What the European and American Welfare States have in Common and where they Differ: Facts and Fiction in Comparison of the European Social Model and the United States', *Journal of European Social Policy*, vol. 20, no. 2, pp. 102–25.

Alber, J. and Standing, G. (2000) 'Social Dumping, Catch-up or Convergence? Europe in a Comparative Global Context', *Journal of European Social Policy*, vol. 10, no. 2, pp. 99–119.

Albert, M. (1993) *Capitalism against Capitalism*, London: Whurr.

Albo, G. (1994) 'Competitive Austerity' and the Impasse of Capitalist Employment Policy' in R. Miliband and L. Panitch (eds) *Socialist Register 1994: Between Globalism and Nationalism*, London: Merlin Press.

Albo, G. and Evans, B. (2010) 'From Rescue Strategies to Exit Strategies: The Struggle over Public Sector Austerity' in L. Panitch, G. Albo and V. Chibber (eds) *Socialist Register 2011: The Crisis this Time*, London: Merlin Press.

Aldrich, R. (2001) *The Hidden Hand: Britain, America and Cold War Secret Intelligence*, London: John Murray.

Alesina, A. (1988) *Macroeconomics and Politics: NBER Macroeconomic Annual*, Cambridge, MA: NBER.

Alesina, A. (1989) 'Politics and Business Cycles in Industrial Democracies', *Economic Policy*, no. 8, pp. 58–98.

Alesina, A. and Grilli, V. (1991) 'The European Central Bank: Reshaping Monetary Policies in Europe', Discussion paper 563 (CEPR).

Alesina, A. and Summers, L.H. (1993) Central Bank Independence and Macroeconomic Performance: Some Comparative Evidence, *Journal of Money, Credit and Banking*, vol. 25, no. 2, pp. 151–62.

Alesina, A., Blanchard, O., Galì, J., Giavazzi, F. and Ulhig, H. (2001) *Defining a Macroeconomic Framework for the Euro Area*, Monitoring the European Central Bank 3, CEPR, London.

Alexiou, C. and Pitelis, C. (2003) 'On Capital Shortages and European Unemployment: A Panel Data Investigation', *Journal of Post Keynesian Economics*, vol. 25, no. 4, pp. 613–31.

Allen, J. and Scruggs, L. (2004) 'Political Partisanship and Welfare State Reform in Advanced Industrial Societies', *American Journal of Political Science*, vol. 48, no. 3, pp. 496–512.

Alsasua, J., Bilbao-Ubillos, J. and Olaskoaga, J. (2007) 'The EU Integration Process and the Convergence of Social Protection Benefits at National Level', *International Journal of Social Welfare*, vol. 16, no. 4, pp. 297–315.

Alter-EU (2008) *Secrecy and Corporate Dominance: A Study on the Composition and Transparency of European Commission Expert Groups*, Brussels: Alter-EU.

Alter-EU (2010) *Bursting the Brussels Bubble: The Battle to Expose Corporate Lobbying at the Heart of the EU*, Brussels: Alter-EU.

Althusser, L. (1969) *For Marx*, London: Allen Lane.

Althusser, L. (1970) 'Marxism is Not Historicism' in L. Althusser and E. Balibar (eds) *Reading Capital*, London: Verso.

Amato, G. and Verhofstadt, G. (2011) 'A Plan to Save the Euro and Curb Speculators', *Financial Times*, 4 July.

Andor, L. and Summers, M. (1998) *Market Failure: Eastern Europe's 'Economic Miracle'*, London: Pluto.

Andreff, W. (1999) Nominal and Real Convergence – At What Speed?; in J.M. van Brabant (ed.) *Remaking Europe: the European Union and the Transition Economies*, London: Rowman and Littlefield.

Andrews, E. (1999a) 'German Finance Aide Quits: European Markets Jubilant', *New York Times*, 12 March.

Andrews, E. (1999b) 'German Stock Market Soars as Leftist Fiscal Chief Quits', *New York Times*, 13 March.

Annesley, C. (2003) 'Americanised and Europeanised: UK Social Policy Since 1997', *British Journal of Politics and International Relations*, vol. 5, no. 2, pp. 143–65.

Annesley, C. (2007) 'Lisbon and Social Europe: Towards a European "Adult Worker Model" Welfare System', *Journal of European Social Policy*, vol. 17, no. 3, pp. 195–205.

Apeldoorn, B. van (1998) 'Transnationalization and the Restructuring of Europe's Socio-Economic Order', *International Journal of Political Economy*, vol. 28, no. 1, pp. 12–53.

Apeldoorn, B. van (2000) 'Transnational Class Agency and European Governance: The Case of the European Round Table of Industrialists', *New Political Economy*, vol. 5, no. 2, pp. 157–81.

Apeldoorn, B. van (2001) 'The Struggle Over European Order: Transnational Class Agency in the Making of 'Embedded Neo-liberalism' in A. Bieler and A. Morton (eds) *Social Forces in the Making of New Europe: The Restructuring of European Social Relations in the Global Political Economy*, Basingstoke: Palgrave.

Apeldoorn, B. van (2002) *Transnational Capitalism and the Struggle over European Integration*, Abingdon: Routledge.

Apeldoorn, B. van (2009) 'A National Case-Study of Embedded Neo-liberalism and its Limits: The Dutch Political Economy and the "No" to the European Constitution' in B. van Apeldoorn, J. Drahokoupil and L. Horn (eds) *Contradictions and Limits of Neo-liberal European Governance: From Lisbon to Lisbon*, Basingstoke: Palgrave Macmillan.

Apeldoorn, B. van, Overbeek, H. and Ryner, M. (2003) 'Theories of European Integration: A Critique' in A. Cafruny and M. Ryner (eds) *A Ruined Fortress? Neo-liberal Hegemony and Transformation in Europe*, Oxford: Rowman and Littlefield.

Apeldoorn, B. van, Drahokoupil, J. and Horn, L. (eds) (2009) *Contradictions and Limits of Neo-liberal European Governance: From Lisbon to Lisbon*, Basingstoke: Palgrave Macmillan.

Appelbaum, E.(1989) 'The Growth in the US Contingent Labour Force', in R. Drago and R. Perlman (eds) *Microeconomic Issues in Labour Economics: New Approaches*, New York, Harvester Wheatsheaf.

Arestis, P. and Mariscal, I. (1997) 'Conflict, Effort and Capital Stock in UK Wage Determination', *Empirica*, vol. 24, no. 3, pp. 179–93.

Arestis, P. and Mariscal, I. (1998) 'Capital Shortages and Asymmetries in UK Unemployment', *Structural Change and Economic Dynamics*, vol. 9, no. 2, pp. 189–204.

Arestis, P. and Mariscal, I. (2000) 'Capital Stock, Unemployment and Wages in the UK and Germany', *Scottish Journal of Political Economy*, vol. 47, no. 5, pp. 487–503.

Arestis, P. and Sawyer, M. (2001) 'The Economics of the Third Way: Introduction', in P. Arestis and M. Sawyer (eds) *The Economics of the Third Way: Experiences from Around the World*, Cheltenham: Edward Elgar, pp. 1–10.

Arestis, P. and Sawyer, M. (2003) 'Aggregate Demand, Conflict and Capacity in the Inflationary Process', *Levy Economics Institute Working Paper* no. 391, Levy Economics Institute, Bard College, Annandale-on-Hudson, New York.

Arestis, P. and Sawyer, M. (2004) *Re-examining Monetary and Fiscal Policy for the 21st Century*, Cheltenham :Edward Elgar.

Arestis, P. and Sawyer, M. (2006) 'Alternatives for the Policy Framework of the Euro', in W. Mitchell, J. Muysken and T. Van Veen (eds) *Growth and Cohesion in the European Union: The Impact of Macroeconomic Policy*, Cheltenham: Edward Elgar, pp. 57–73.

Arezki, R., Candelon, B. and Sy, A.N.R. (2011) *Sovereign Rating News and Financial Markets Spillovers: Evidence from the European Debt Crisis*, IMF Working Paper 11/68, Washington, DC: International Monetary Fund.

Armingeon, K. and Bonoli, G. (eds) (2006) *The Politics of Post-Industrial Welfare States: Adapting Post-war Social Policies to New Social Risks*, Abingdon: Routledge.

Arnaud, J. (1997) 'A Reappraisal of Europe's Social Model', Seminar no. 3, Brussels: *Notre Europe.*

Arnaud, J. (1998) '15 Countries in a Boat: Economic and Social Cohesion – The Cornerstone of European Integration', Seminar Report, Brussels: *Notre Europe.*

Arnaud, J. (2001) 'The Reform of the Council of Ministers', Seminar Report, Brussels: *Notre Europe.*

Artis, M.J. and Buti, M. (2001) Setting Medium-term Fiscal Targets in EMU; in A. Brunila, M. Buti and D. Franco (eds) *The Stability and Growth Pact: The Architecture of Fiscal Policy in EMU*, Palgrave Macmillan, London.

Artis, M.J. and Cobham, D. (eds) (1991) *Labour's Economic Policies, 1974–1979*, Manchester: Manchester University Press.

Ashenfelter, O. and Pencavel, J.H. (1969) 'American Trade Union Growth: 1900–1960', *Quarterly Journal of Economics*, vol. 83, pp. 434–48.

Aslanidis, N. (2010) Business Cycle Synchronization between the CEEC and the Euro-area: Evidence from Threshold Seemingly Unrelated Regressions, *Manchester School*, vol. 78, no. 6, pp. 538–55.

Associated Press (2010) 'Greeks and the State – An Uncomfortable Couple', Associated Press, 3 May.

Atkins, R. (1999) 'Clash of Thunder Gods Leads to Opportunity to Start Afresh', *Financial Times*, 13 March.

Atkins, R. (2008a) 'Europeans Laud Euro but give ECB Bad Marks over Inflation', *Financial Times*, 29 December.

Atkins, R. (2008b) 'Onwards and Upwards: 10 Years of the Euro', *Financial Times*, 31 December.

Atkins, R. and Milne, R. (2011) 'ECB Reveals €22bn Cost of Crisis Move', *Financial Times*, 16 August.

Atkinson, J. (1984) 'Manpower Strategies for Flexible Organisations', *Personnel Management*, August, pp. 28–31.

Baccaro, L. and Rei, D. (2006) 'Institutions and Unemployment in OECD Countries: A Panel Data Analysis', in W. Mitchell, J. Muysken and T. Van Veen (eds) *Growth and Cohesion in the European Union: The Impact of Macroeconomic Policy*, Cheltenham: Edward Elgar, pp. 130–56.

Backe, P. (1999) 'Integrating Central and Eastern Europe into the European Union: The Monetary Dimension', in P. de Grauwe and V. Lavrac (eds) *Inclusion of Central European Countries in the European Monetary Union*, Kluwer: London.

Backe, P. and Linder, I. (1996) 'European Monetary Union: Prospects for EU Member States and Selected Candidate Countries from Central and Eastern Europe', *Focus on Transition*, vol. 1, no. 2.

Bacon, R. and Eltis, W. (1976) *Britain's Economic Problem: Too Few Producers*, London: Macmillan.

Baddeley, M.C. (2003) *Investment: Theories and Analysis*, Basingstoke: Palgrave.

Bade, R. and Parkin, M. (1988) 'Central Bank Laws and Monetary Policy', working paper (University of Western Ontario).

Bagdikian, B. (2004) *The New Media Monopoly*, Boston: Beacon Press.

Baimbridge, M. (ed.) (2007) *The 1975 Referendum on Europe – Volume 1: Reflections of the Participants*, Exeter: Imprint Academic.

Baimbridge, M. and Whyman, P.B. (2004) *Fiscal Federalism and European Economic Integration*, Routledge, London.

Baimbridge, M. and Whyman, P.B. (2008) *Britain, the Euro and Beyond*, Aldershot: Ashgate.

Baimbridge, M., Burkitt, B. and Whyman, P. (1999) *The Bank that Rules Europe? The ECB and Central Bank Independence*, London: Bruges Group.

Baimbridge, M., Whyman, P. and Mullen, A. (2006) *The 1975 Referendum on Europe – Volume 2: Current Analysis and Lessons for the Future*, Exeter: Imprint Academic.

Baimbridge, M., Whyman, P.B. and Burkitt, B. (2010) *Britain in a Global World: Options for a New Beginning*, Exeter: Imprint Academic.

Baimbridge, M., Burkitt, B. and Whyman, P. (2012) 'The Eurozone as a Flawed Currency Area', *Political Quarterly*, vol. 83.

Bain, G. and Elsheikh, F. (1976) *Union Growth and the Business Cycle: An Econometric Analysis*, Oxford: Blackwell.

Bainbridge, T. (2002) *The Penguin Companion to European Union*, second edition, London: Penguin.

Baker, D. (2000) 'Something New in the 1990s: Looking for Evidence of an Economic Transformation', in J. Marick (ed.) *Unconventional Wisdom: Alternative Perspectives on the New Economy*, New York: Century Foundation Press, pp. 207–37.

Baker, D., Gamble, A., Ludlam, S. and Seawright, D. with Bull, K. (1999) 'MPs and Europe: Enthusiasm, Circumspection or Outright Scepticism', in J. Fisher, P. Cowley, D. Denver and A. Russell (eds) *British Elections and Parties Review*, vol. ix, London: Frank Cass, pp. 171–85.

Baker, D., Gamble, A. and Seawright, D. (2002a) 'Sovereign Nations and Global Markets: Modern British Conservatism and Hyper Globalism', *British Journal of Politics and International Relations*, vol. 4, no. 3, pp. 399–428.

Baker, D., Glyn, A., Howell, D. and Schmitt, D. (2002b) 'Labour Market Institutions and Unemployment: A Critical Assessment of Cross-Country Evidence', *CEPA Working Paper* 17, New School University, New York.

Baker, R. (2005) *Capitalism's Achilles Heel: Dirty Money and How to Renew the Free Market System*, New Jersey: John Wiley.

Balanyá, B., Doherty, A., Hoedeman, O., Ma'anit, A. and Wesselius, E. (2000) *Europe Inc. Regional and Global Restructuring and the Rise of Corporate Power*, London: Pluto.

Balassone, F. and Franco, D. (2001) 'Public Investment, the Stability Pact and the Golden Rule', in A. Brunila, M. Buti and D. Franco (eds) *The Stability and Growth Pact: The Architecture of Fiscal Policy in EMU*, London: Palgrave Macmillan.

Baldwin, P. (1991) *The Politics of Social Solidarity*, Oxford: Oxford University Press.

Baldwin, P. (1992) 'Measurable Dynamic Gains from Trade', *Journal of Political Economy*, vol. 100, no. 1, pp. 162–74.

Baldwin, R.E., Francois, J.F., Portes, R., Rodrik, D. and Szekely, I.P. (1997) 'The Costs and Benefits of Eastern Enlargement: The Impact on the EU and Central Europe', *Economic Policy*, 24: 125–76.

Ball, L. (1994) 'Disinflation and the NAIRU', in C. Romer and D. Romer (eds) *Reducing Inflation: Motivation and Strategy*, Chicago: University of Chicago Press.

Ball, L. (1999) 'Aggregate Demand and Long-Run Unemployment', *Brookings Papers on Economic Activity*, no. 2, pp. 189–236.

Bank for International Settlements (1994) *Financial Structure and the Monetary Transmission Mechanism*, Basel: Bank for International Settlements.

Bank for International Settlements (1996) *Central Bank Survey of Foreign Exchange and Derivatives Market Activity*, Basel: Bank for International Settlements.

Barber, T. and Guerrera, F. (2002) 'Eurozone Consumers Feel Cheated', *Financial Times*, 1 March.

Barnard, C. (2000) 'Social Dumping and the Race to the Bottom: Some Lessons for the European Union from Delaware', *European Law Review*, vol. 25, February, pp. 57–78.

Barnes, T. (1981) 'The Secret Cold War: The CIA and American Foreign Policy in Europe, 1946–1956, Part 1', *Historical Journal*, vol. 24, no. 2, pp. 399–415.

Barnes, T. (1982) 'The Secret Cold War: The CIA and American Foreign Policy in Europe, 1946–1956, Part 2', *Historical Journal*, vol. 25, no. 3, pp. 649–70.

Barnier, J. (2008) 'Social Europe and the Limits of Soft Law: The Example of Flexicurity' in R. Rogowski (ed.) *The European Social Model and Transitional Labour Markets*, Farnham: Ashgate.

Barr, N. (1992) 'Economic Theory and the Welfare State: A Survey and Interpretation', *Journal of Economic Literature*, vol. 30, pp. 741–803.

Barratt Brown, M. (2001) 'The Captive Party: How Labour was Taken Over by Capital', *Socialist Renewal*, Second Series, no. 2, Nottingham: Spokesman.

Barro, R. and Gordon, R. (1983) 'Rules, Discretion and Reputation in a Model of Monetary Policy', *Journal of Monetary Economics*, vol. 12, no. 1, pp. 101–21.

Barroso, J. (2011) 'The European Union and Multilateral Global Governance', Speech at the European University Institute Conference, Florence, 18 June.

Barroso, J. and van Rompuy, H. (2011) 'Enhanced Economic Policy Coordination in the Euro Area: Main Features and Concepts', Luxembourg: Office for Official Publications of the European Communities.

Baumol, W.J. (1961) 'Pitfalls in Counter-Cyclical Policies: Some Tools and Results', *Review of Economics and Statistics*, vol. 43, no. 1, pp. 21–6.

Bayoumi, T. and Eichengreen, B. (1993) 'Shocking Aspects of European Monetary Integration', in F. Torres and F. Giavazzi (eds) *Adjustment and Growth in the European Monetary Union*, Cambridge: Cambridge University Press.

Bayoumi, T. and Masson, P.R. (1995) 'Fiscal Flows in the United States and Canada: Lessons for Monetary Union in Europe', *European Economic Review*, vol. 39, pp. 253–74.

Bean, C. (1989) 'Capital Shortages and Persistent Unemployment', *Economic Policy*, no. 8, pp. 11–53.

Bean, C. (1994) 'European Unemployment: A Retrospective', *European Economic Review*, vol. 38, nos. 3–4, pp. 523–34.

Bean, C., Bentolila, S., Bertola, G. and Dolado, J. (1998) *Social Europe: One For All?*, London: Centre for Economic Policy Research.

Bean, C.R. (1998) 'Discussion', *Economic Policy*, vol. 26, pp. 104–7.

Beattie, A. (2011) 'Debt Crisis Tests Scope of IMF's Role', *Financial Times*, 5 August.

Becht, M. and da Silva, L. (2007) 'External Financial Markets Policy: Europe as Global Regulator?' in A. Sapir (ed.) *Fragmented Power: Europe and the Global Economy*, Brussels: Bruegel.

Becker, U. (2003) 'Competitive Corporatism? National and Transnational Elements in the Dutch Employment "Miracle"' in H. Overbeek (ed.) *The Political Economy of European Employment: European Integration and the Transnationalization of the (Un)employment Question*, Abingdon: Routledge.

Becker, U. (2005) 'An Example of Competitive Corporatism? The Dutch Political Economy 1983–2004 in Critical Examination', *Journal of European Public Policy*, vol. 12, no. 6, pp. 1078–102.

Beder, S. (2006a) *Suiting Themselves: How Corporations Drive the Global Agenda*, London: Earthscan.

Beder, S. (2006b) *Free Market Missionaries: The Corporate Manipulation of Community Values*, London: Earthscan.

Begg, D., Canova, F., Grauwe, P. de, Fatás, A. and Lane, P. (2002) *Surviving the Slowdown*, Monitoring Europe, 3rd Report of the CEPS Macroeconomic Policy Group, London.

Begg, I., Draxler, J. and Mortensen, J. (2007) *Is Social Europe Fit for Globalization? A Study on the Social Impact of Globalization in the European Union*, Brussels: Centre for European Policy Studies/European Commission.

Bell, D. and Shaw, E. (1983) *The Left in France: Towards the Socialist Republic*, Nottingham: Spokesman Books.

Ben Arfa, N. (2009) 'Analysis of shocks affecting Europe: EMU and some Central and Eastern Acceding Countries', *Panoeconomicus*, vol. 56, no. 1, pp. 21–38.

Benn, T. (1981) *Arguments for Democracy*, Harmondsworth: Penguin.

Benn, T. (1989) *Office without Power: Diaries 1968–1972*, London: Arrow Books.

Benn, T. (1990) *Against the Tide: Diaries, 1973–1976*, London: Arrow Books.

Bercusson, B. (2007) 'The Trade Union Movement and the European Union: Judgment Day', *European Law Journal*, vol. 13, no. 3, pp. 279–308.

Bergsten, F. (1973) 'The Threat from the Third World', *Foreign Policy*, vol. 11, Summer, pp. 102–24.

Berthold, N. and Fehn, R. (1998) 'Does EMU Promote Labour-market Reforms?', *Kyklos*, vol. 51, no. 4, pp. 509–36.

Bieler, A. (2000) *Globalization and Enlargement of the EU: Austrian and Swedish Social Forces in the Struggle over Membership*, Abingdon: Routledge.

Bieler, A. (2003) 'What Future Union? The Struggle for a Social Europe', Queen's Papers on Europeanization, no. 1, Belfast: Queen's University.

Bieler, A. (2005) 'European Integration and the Transnational Restructuring of Social Relations: The Emergence of Labour as a Regional Actor?' *Journal of Common Market Studies*, vol. 43, pp. 461–84.

Bieler, A. (2006) *The Struggle for a Social Europe: Trade Unions and EMU in Times of Global Restructuring*, Manchester: Manchester University Press.

Bieler, A. (2009) 'Globalization and Regional Integration: The Possibilities and Problems for Trade Unions to Resist Neo-liberal Restructuring in Europe' in B. van Apeldoorn, J. Drahokoupil and L. Horn (eds) *Contradictions and Limits of Neo-liberal European Governance: From Lisbon to Lisbon*, Basingstoke: Palgrave Macmillan.

Bieler, A. and Morton, A. (eds) (2001) *Social Forces in the Making of New Europe: The Restructuring of European Social Relations in the Global Political Economy*, Basingstoke: Palgrave.

Bieler, A. and Torjenson, S. (2001) 'Strength through Unity? A Comparative Analysis of Splits in the Austrian, Norwegian and Swedish Labour Movements over EU Membership' in A. Bieler and A. Morton (eds) *Social Forces in the Making of New Europe: The Restructuring of European Social Relations in the Global Political Economy*, Basingstoke: Palgrave.

Bieling, H. (2003) 'Social Forces in the Making of the New European Economy: The Case of Financial Market Integration', *New Political Economy*, vol. 8, no. 2, pp. 203–24.

Bieling, H. (2006) 'EMU, Financial Integration and Global Economic Governance', *Review of International Political Economy*, vol. 13, no. 3, pp. 420–48.

Bieling, H. and Jäger, J. (2009) 'Global Finance and the European Economy: The Struggle over Banking Regulation' in B. van Apeldoorn, J. Drahokoupil and L. Horn (eds) *Contradictions and Limits of Neo-liberal European Governance: From Lisbon to Lisbon*, Basingstoke: Palgrave Macmillan.

Bilderberg (1956) Minutes of Steering Group Meeting, 13 May, (Hugh Gaitskell Papers, G211, University College London).

Bini-Smaghi, L. and Vori, S. (1992) 'Rating the EC as an Optimum Currency Area: Is it Worse than the US?', in R. O'Brien (ed.) *Finance and the International Economy*, Oxford: Oxford University Press.

Bish, G. (1979) 'Drafting the Manifesto' in K. Coates (ed.) *What Went Wrong?* Nottingham: Spokesman Books.

Bislev, S. (1992) 'European Welfare States and the EC: Social Dimension and Societal Diversity' in P. Beije (ed.) *Transnational Business in Europe: Economic and Social Perspectives*, Tilburg: Tilburg University.

Black, I. (2002). 'Blair Allied with European Right in Summit Labour Talks: EU Talks in Barcelona Pit Prime Minister's Vision against Concerns of British Unions and Continental Leaders', *Guardian*, 16 March.

Blackburn, K. and Christensen, M. (1989) 'Monetary Policy and Policy Credibility', *Journal of Economic Literature*, vol. 27, no. 1, pp. 1–45.

Blair, A. (2000) *Managing Change: A National and International Agenda of Reform?*, Speech given at the World Economic Forum, Davos, Switzerland, 28 January

Blair, T. (1998a) Speech to the New York Stock Exchange, 28 September.

Blair, T. (1998b) Speech at The Hague, 20 January.

Blair, T. and Schröder, G. (1999) *Europe: The Third Way*, London: Fabian Society.

Blake, A.P. and Weale, M. (1998) 'Costs of Separating Budgetary Policy from Control of Inflation: A Neglected Aspect of Central Bank Independence', *Oxford Economic Chapters*, vol. 50, no. 3, pp. 449–67.

Blanchard, G. (1995) 'The Single Market Revisited', Economist Intelligence Unit, Briefing Paper 95/3, London: *The Economist.*

Blanchard, O. and Katz, L. (1992) Regional Evolutions, *Brookings Papers on Economic Activity*, vol. 1, pp. 1–61.

Blanchard, O. and Muet, P.-A. (1993) 'Competitiveness through Disinflation: An Assessment of the French Macroeconomic Strategy, *Economic Policy*, no. 16, pp. 12–50.

Blanchard, O. and Summers, L. (1988) 'Beyond the Natural Rate Hypothesis', *American Economic Review*, vol. 78, no. 2, pp. 182–87.

Blanchard, O. and Wolfers, J. (2000) 'The Role of Shocks and Institutions in the Rise of European Unemployment: The Aggregate Evidence', *Economic Journal*, vol. 110, pp. 1–33.

Blanchard, O., Dornbusch, R. and Layard, R. (eds) (1986) *Restoring Europe's Prosperity: Macroeconomic Papers from the Centre for European Policy Studies*, London: MIT Press.

Blanchard, O.J. (1984) 'Current and Anticipated Deficits, Interest Rates and Economic Activity, *European Economic Review*, vol. 25, pp. 5–27.

Blanpain, R. and Dickens, L. (2008) *Challenges in European Employment Relations: Employment Regulation, Trade Union Organization, Equality, Flexicurity, Training and New Approaches to Pay*, London: Kluwer Law International.

Blanpain, R., Colucci, M. and Sica, S. (eds) (2006) *The European Social Model*, Oxford: Intersentia.

Bloch, F. and Fitzgerald, P. (1983) *British Intelligence and Covert Action*, Dingle: Brandon.

Blum, W. (2000) *Rogue State: A Guide to the World's Only Superpower*, London: Zed Books.

Blum, W. (2003) *Killing Hope: US Military and CIA Interventions since World War II*, London: Zed.

Boeri, T. and Brucker, H. (2000) *The Impact of Eastern Enlargement on Employment and Labour Markets in the EU Member States*, Berlin and Lilan: European Integration Consortium.

Boldrin, M. (2006) 'Regional Policies after the EU Enlargement', in M. Artis, A. Banerjee and M. Marcellino (eds) *The Central and Eastern European Countries and the European Union*, Cambridge: Cambridge University Press, pp. 365–86.

Bomba, T. (2006) 'The European Social Model(s): Which Directions and Responsibilities for the EU? Presentation and Summary of the Workshop Contributions', Brussels: *Notre Europe.*

Bonefeld, W. (1992) 'Social Constitution and the Form of the Capitalist State' in W. Bonefeld, R. Gunn, J. Holloway and K. Pychopedis (eds) *Open Marxism – Volume 1: Dialectics and History*, London: Pluto.

Bonefeld, W. (1995) 'Capital and Subject and the Existence of Labour' in W. Bonefeld, R. Gunn, J. Holloway and K. Pychopedis (eds) *Open Marxism – Volume 3: Emancipating Marx*, London: Pluto.

Bonoli, G. (2001) 'Political Institutions, Veto Points and the Process of Welfare State Adaptation' in P. Pierson (ed.) *The New Politics of the Welfare State*, Oxford: Oxford University Press.

Bonoli, G. and Palier, B. (1998) 'Changing the Politics of Social Programmes: Innovative Change in British and French Welfare Reforms', *Journal of European Social Policy*, vol. 8, no. 4, pp. 317–30.

Bonoli, G., George, V. and Taylor-Gooby, P. (2000) *European Welfare Futures: Towards a Theory of Retrenchment*, Cambridge: Polity.

Booker, C. and North, R. (2003) *The Great Deception: The Secret History of the European Union*, London: Continuum.

Booth, A. (1983) 'A Reconsideration of Trade Union Growth in the United Kingdom', *British Journal of Industrial Relations*, vol. 21, pp. 377–91.

Booth, R., Wachman, R. and Vasagar, J. (2010) 'Austerity Drive will Hand Billions to Private Sector', *Guardian*, 16 July.

Borger, S. (2007) 'Moscow Signals Place in New World Order', *Guardian*, 11 April.

Borghijs, A., Ederveen, S. and de Mooij, R. (2003) 'European Wage Coordination: Nightmare or Dream to Come True? An Economic Analysis of Wage Bargaining Institutions in the EU', *CPB Discussion Paper* 17, The Hague.

Bosch, G. (2009) 'Low Wage Work in Five European Countries and the US', *International Labour Review*, vol. 148, no. 4, pp. 337–56.

Bosworth, D., Dawkins, P. and Stromback, T. (1996) *The Economics of the Labour Market*, Harlow: Addison Wesley Longman.

Bouget, D. (1998) 'Social Policy in the EMU Area: Between a Dream and a Nightmare', *Transfer*, vol. 4, no. 1, pp. 67–87.

Bouget, D. (2003) 'Convergence in the Social Welfare Systems in Europe: From Goal to Reality', *Social Policy and Administration*, vol. 37, no. 6, pp. 674–93.

Boyer, R. (1989) *The Regulation School: A Critical Introduction*, New York: Columbia University Press.

Brady, D. (2005) 'The Welfare State and Relative Poverty in Rich Western Democracies, 1967–1997', *Social Forces*, vol. 83, no. 4, pp. 1329–64.

Brandt Commission (1980) *North–South: A Programme for Survival – Report of the Independent Commission on International Development*, London: Pan Books.

Brandt Commission (1983) *Common Crisis North–South: Cooperation for World Recovery*, London: Pan Books.

Bratkowski, A. and Rostowski, J. (1999) 'Unilateral Adoption of the Euro by EU Applicant Countries: The Macroeconomic Aspects', *CASE-CEU*, Working Paper 26.

Bratkowski, A. and Rostowski, J. (2002) 'The EU Attitude to Unilateral Euroization: Misunderstandings, Real Concerns and Sub-optimal Admission Criteria', *Economics of Transition*, vol. 10, no. 2, pp. 445–68.

Brenner, R. (1998) 'The Economics of Global Turbulence: A Special Report on the World Economy, 1950–1998', *New Left Review*, no. 229.

Breton, A. (1974) *The Economic Theory of Representative Government*, London: Macmillan.

Bricmont, J. (2007) *Humanitarian Imperialism: Using Human Rights to Sell War*, New York: Monthly Review Press.

British Chambers of Commerce (2010) *Delivering for Britain: A Business Blueprint for Opportunity, Jobs and Growth*, London: British Chambers of Commerce.

Brooks, C. and Manza, J. (2007) *Why Welfare States Persist: The Importance of Public Opinion in Democracies*, London: University of Chicago Press.

Brown, A.J. (1985) *World Inflation since 1950*, Cambridge: Cambridge University Press.

Brown, B. (ed.) (1979) *Euro-communism and Euro-socialism: The Left Confronts Modernity*, London: Cyrco Press.

Brown, G. (1998) 'Strengthening International Financial Systems: Chancellor's Statement', *HM Treasury's New Release* no. 179/98, 30 October.

Brown, G. (2010) *Beyond the Crash: Overcoming the First Crisis of Globalization*, London: Simon and Schuster.

Broz, T. (2010) Introduction of the Euro in CEE Countries – is it Economically Justifiable? The Croatian Case, *Post-Communist Studies*, vol. 22, no. 4, pp. 427–47.

Brunila, A., Buti, M. and Franco, D. (2001) *The Stability and Growth Pact: The Architecture of Fiscal Policy in EMU*, London: Palgrave Macmillan.

Bruno, M. and Sachs, J.D. (1985) *Economics of World-wide Stagflation*, Oxford: Blackwell.

Buechtemann, C.F. and Schupp, J. (1992) 'Repercussions of Reunification: Patterns and Trends in the Socio-economic Transformation of East Germany', *Industrial Relations Journal*, vol. 23, no. 2, pp. 90–106.

Buiter, W.H. (2000) Exchange Rate Regimes for Accession Countries, *EBRD Annual Meeting*, Riga, Latvia.

Buiter, W.H. (2003) 'Ten Commandments for a Fiscal Rule in E(M)U', *Oxford Review of Economic Policy*, vol. 19, no. 1, pp. 84–99.

Bulmer, S. (2000) 'European Policy: Fresh Start or False Dawn?'; in D. Coates and P. Lawler (eds) *New Labour in Power*, Manchester: Manchester University Press pp. 240–54.

Burchill, S. (2005) *The National Interest in International Relations Theory*, Basingstoke: Palgrave.

Burchill, S. (ed.) (2009) *Theories of International Relations*, Basingstoke: Palgrave.

Burdekin, R.C.K. and Willett, T.D. (1990) *Central Bank Reform: The Federal Reserve in International Perspective*, paper prepared for the special issue of Public Budgeting and Financial Management.

Burgoon, B. (2001) 'Globalization and Welfare Compensation: Disentangling the Ties that Bind', *International Organization*, vol. 55, no. 3, pp. 509–51.

Burk, K. and Cairncross, A. (1992) *'Goodbye Great Britain': The 1976 IMF Crisis*, New Haven, CT: Yale University Press.

Burkitt, B. (2006) 'The European Social Model', in P. Whyman, M. Baimbridge and B. Burkitt (eds) *Implications of the Euro: A Critical Perspective from the Left*, London: Routledge.

Burkitt, B., Baimbridge, M. and Mills, J. (1993) *What Price the Pound? The Exchange Rate and Full Employment*, Discussion Paper no. 2, Full Employment Forum, London.

Burkitt, B., Baimbridge, M. and Whyman, P. (1996) *There is an Alternative: Britain and its Relationship with the EU*, Oxford: Nelson and Pollard.

Burkitt, B., Baimbridge, M. and Whyman, P. (1997) *A Price not Worth Paying: The Economic Cost of EMU*, Oxford: Nelson and Pollard.

Burnham, P. (1994) 'Open Marxism and Vulgar International Political Economy', *Review of International Political Economy*, vol. 1, no. 2, pp. 221–31.

Burnham, P. (1995) 'State and Market in International Political Economy: Towards a Marxist Alternative', *Studies in Marxism*, no. 2, pp. 135–59.

Burroni, L. and Keune, M. (2011) 'Flexicurity: A Conceptual Critique', *European Journal of Industrial Relations*, vol. 17, no. 1, pp. 75–91

Business-Europe (2010a) *Go for Growth – An Agenda for the EU 2010–2014*, Brussels: Business-Europe.

Business-Europe (2010b) *Combining Fiscal Sustainability and Growth: A European Action Plan*, Brussels: Business-Europe.

Buti, M. and Giudice, G. (2002) 'Maastricht Fiscal Rules at Ten: An Assessment', *Journal of Common Market Studies*, vol. 40, no. 5, pp. 823–47.

Buti, M. and Martinot, B. (2000) 'Open Issues in the Implementation of the Stability and Growth Pact', *National Institute Economic Review*, vol. 174, pp. 92–104.

Buti, M. and Noord, P. van den (2003) *Discretionary Fiscal Policy and Elections: The Experience of the Early Years of EMU*, OECD Economics Department Working Paper no. 351.

Buti, M., Franco, D. and Ongena, H. (1998) 'Fiscal Discipline and Flexibility in EMU: the Implementation of the Stability and Growth Pact', *Oxford Review of Economic Policy*, vol. 14, pp. 81–97.

Butler, D. and Kavanagh, D. (1974) *The British General Election of February 1974*, London: Macmillan.

Butler, D. and Kavanagh, D. (1975) *The British General Election of October 1974*, London: Macmillan.

Butler, D. and Kavanagh, D. (1980) *The British General Election of 1979*, London: Macmillan.

Butler, D. and Kavanagh, D. (1984) *The British General Election of 1983*, London: Macmillan.

Butler, D. and Kitzinger, U. (1996) *The 1975 Referendum*, second edition, Basingstoke: Macmillan.

Cabinet Office (1941) Minutes of the Meeting between Anthony Eden and Joseph Stalin, 16 December, London: National Archives CAB 66/220.

Cabral, A.J. (2001) 'Main Aspects of the Working of the Stability and Growth Pact', in A. Brunila, M. Buti and D. Franco (eds) *The Stability and Growth Pact: The Architecture of Fiscal Policy in EMU*, London: Palgrave Macmillan.

Cafruny, A. (2003) 'The Geopolitics of US Hegemony in Europe: From the Breakup of Yugoslavia to the War in Iraq' in A. Cafruny and M. Ryner (eds) *A Ruined Fortress? Neo-liberal Hegemony and Transformation in Europe*, Lanham, MD: Rowman and Littlefield.

Cafruny, A. (2009) 'Geopolitics and Neo-liberalism: US Power and the Limits of European Autonomy' in B. van Apeldoorn, J. Drahokoupil and L. Horn (eds) *Contradictions and Limits of Neo-liberal European Governance: From Lisbon to Lisbon*, Basingstoke: Palgrave Macmillan.

Cafruny, A. and Ryner, M. (eds) (2003) *A Ruined Fortress? Neo-liberal Hegemony and Transformation in Europe*, Lanham, MD: Rowman and Littlefield.

Cairncross, A., Giersch, H., Lamfalussy, A, Petrilli, G. and Uri, P. (1974) *Economic Policy for the European Community: The Way Forward*, New York: Colombia University Press.

Callaghan, J. (2000) 'Rise and Fall of the Alternative Economic Strategy: From Internationalization of Capital to "Globalization"', *Contemporary British History*, vol. 14, no. 3, pp. 105–130.

Callaghan, J. (2000) *The Retreat of Social Democracy*, Manchester: Manchester University Press.

Callaghan, J., Fielding, S. and Ludlam, S. (eds) (2003) *Interpreting the Labour Party: Approaches to Labour Politics and History*, Manchester: Manchester University Press.

Calmfors, L. and Driffill, J. (1988) 'Bargaining Structure, Corporatism and Macroeconomic Performance', *Economic Policy*, no. 6, pp. 13–62.

Calvo, G.A. (2002) 'On Dollarization', *Economics of Transition*, vol. 10, no. 2, pp. 393–403.

Cameron, B. (2010) 'Building the Transatlantic Bridge: The Potential for Canada–UK Trade', in M. Baimbridge, P.B. Whyman and B. Burkitt (eds) *Britain in a Global World: Options for a New Beginning*, Exeter: Imprint Academic.

Cameron, D. (1978) 'The Expansion of the Public Economy: A Comparative Analysis', *American Political Science Review*, vol. 72, no. 4, pp. 1243–61.

Cameron, D.R. (1984) 'Social Democracy, Corporatism, Labour Quiescence and the Representation of Economic Interest in Advanced Capitalist Society', in J.H. Goldthorpe (ed.) *Order and Conflict in Contemporary Capitalism*, Oxford: Clarendon Press, pp. 143–78.

Caminada, K., Goudswaard, K. and Van Vliet, O. (2010) 'Patterns of Welfare State Indicators in the EU: Is there Convergence?' *Journal of Common Market Studies*, vol. 48, no. 3, pp. 529–56.

Camps, M. (1974) *The Management of Interdependence: A Preliminary View*, New York: Council on Foreign Relations.

Cantwell, J. (1989) *Technical Innovations in Multinational Corporations*, London: Blackwell.

Canzoneri, M.B. and Diba, B.T. (2000) *The Stability and Growth Pact Revisited: A Delicate Balance or an Albatross?* Mimeo.

Carchedi, G. (2001) *For another Europe: A Class Analysis of European Economic Integration*, London: Verso.

Cardoso, H. (1971) *Dependency and Development in Latin America*, Berkeley, CA: University of California Press.

Carew, A. (1987) *Labour under the Marshall Plan: The Politics of Productivity and the Marketing of Management Science*, Manchester: Manchester University Press.

Carey, A. (1995) *Taking the Risk Out of Democracy*, Sydney: University of New South Wales Press.

Carlin, W. and Soskice, D. (1990) *Macroeconomics and the Wage Bargain*, Oxford: Oxford University Press.

Carroll, W. (2007) 'Tracking the Transnational Capitalist Class: The View from On High', Paper presented at the International Sunbelt Social Network Conference, 1–6 May, Corfu (Greece).

Carroll, W. (2010) *The Making of a Transnational Capitalist Class: Corporate Power in the 21st Century*, London: Zed.

Carroll, W. and Carson, C. (2003) 'Forging a New Hegemony? The Role of Transnational Policy Groups in the Network and Discourses of Global Corporate Governance', *Journal of World-Systems Research*, vol. 9, no. 1, pp. 67–102.

Carroll, W. and Fennema, M. (2002) 'Is There a Transnational Business Community?' *International Sociology*, no. 17, pp. 393–419.

Carroll, W. and Sapinski, J. (2010) 'The Global Corporate Elite and the Transnational Policy Planning Network, 1996–2006', *International Sociology*, vol. 25, no. 4, pp. 501–38.

Carruth, A.A. and Disney, R. (1988) 'Where Have Two Million Trade Union Members Gone?', *Economica*, vol. 55, pp. 1–20.

Casella, A. (2001) 'Achieving Fiscal Discipline through Tradable Deficit Permits', in A. Brunila, M. Buti and D. Franco (eds) *The Stability and Growth Pact: The Architecture of Fiscal Policy in EMU*, London: Palgrave Macmillan.

Castellina, L. (1988) 'The European Community: Opportunity or Negative Conditioning? The Impact of the Integration Process on the Left', *Socialism in the World*, no. 66, pp. 26–33.

Castles, F.G. (ed.) (1982) *The Impact of Parties: Politics and Policies in Democratic Capitalist States*, London: Sage.

Castles, F.G. (1998) 'When Politics Matters: Public Expenditures Development in a Era of Economic and Institutional Constraints', Paper presented at the European Forum, Centre for Advanced Studies, European University Institute, 26 November.

Castles, F.G. (2004) *The Future of the Welfare State: Crisis Myths and Crisis Realities*, Oxford: Oxford University Press.

Castles, F.G. and Mitchell, D. (1993) 'Worlds of Welfare and Families of Nations' in F. Castles (ed.) *Families of Nations: Patterns of Public Policy in Western Democracies*, Aldershot: Dartmouth.

Cave, A. (2010) *Small Business, Big Vote: The Route to Recovery, FSB 2010 Manifesto*, London: Federation of Small Businesses.

Cave, W. and Himmelstrup, P. (eds) (1995) *The Welfare Society in Transition: Problems and Prospects for the Welfare Model*, Copenhagen: Danish Cultural Institute.

Cecchetti, S., McConnell, M.M. and Perez-Quiros, G. (1999) *Policy Makers Revealed Preferences and the Output-Inflation Variability Trade-off: Implications for the European System of Central Banks*. Mimeo.

Cecchini, P., Catinat, M., Jacquerin, A. and Robinson, J. (1988) *1992 – The European Challenge: The Benefits of a Single Market*, Aldershot: Wildwood House.

Cerny, P. (1990) *The Changing Architecture of Politics: Structure, Agency and the Future of the State*, London: Sage.

Chaffin, J. (2011) 'EU Seeks to Speed Funds to Weak Economies', *Financial Times*, 31 July.

Challen, C. (1998) *The Price of Power: The Secret Funding of the Tory Party*, London: Vision.

Chang, L. and Kornbluh, P. (eds) (1998) *The Cuban Missile Crisis, 1962: A National Security Archive Documents Reader*, Second Edition, New York: New Press.

Chantrey Vellacott (2001) 'Economic Convergence Index', *Spring Quarterly Bulletin*, London: Chantrey Vellacott.

Chaulia, S. (2005) 'Democratization, Colour Revolutions and the Role of NGOs: Catalysts or Saboteurs?'. Online, available at: www.globalresearch.ca (accessed 20 October 2006).

Cheshire, P. (1999) 'Cities in Competition: Articulating the Gains from Integration', *Urban Studies*, vol. 36, no. 5–6, pp. 843–64.

Chomsky, N. (1985) *Turning the Tide: US Intervention in Central America and the Struggle for Peace*, London: Pluto.

Chomsky, N. (1992) *Deterring Democracy*, London: Vintage.

Chomsky, N. (1994) *World Orders, Old and New*, London: Pluto.

Chomsky, N. (1997) 'Market Democracy in a Neo-liberal Order: Doctrines and Reality', *Z Magazine*, November.

Chomsky, N. (1999) *The New Military Humanism: Lessons from Kosovo*, London: Pluto.

Chomsky, N. and Herman, E. (1979) *The Washington Connection and Third World Fascism – The Political Economy of Human Rights: Volume 1*, Boston, MA: South End Press.

Chomsky, N. and Zinn, H. (eds) (1972) *The Pentagon Papers: Critical Essays – vol. v*, Senator Gravel Edition, Boston, MA: Beacon Press.

Chossudovsky, M. (1997) *The Globalization of Poverty: Impacts of IMF and World Bank Reforms*, London: Zed.

Clarke, L., de Gijsel, P. and Janssen, J. (eds) (2000) *The Dynamics of Wage Relations in the New Europe*, London: Kluwer Academic Publishers.

Clayton, R. and Pontusson, J. (1998) 'Welfare State Retrenchment Revisited: Entitlement Cuts, Public Sector Restructuring and In-egalitarian Trends in Advanced Capitalist Societies', *World Politics*, vol. 50, no. 4, pp. 67–98.

Clift, B. (2001) 'New Labour's Third Way and European Social Democracy', in S. Ludlam and M.J. Smith (eds) *New Labour in Government*, London: Macmillan, pp. 55–73.

Clift, B. (2003) 'The Changing Political Economy of France: Dirigisme under Duress' in A. Cafruny and M. Ryner (eds) *A Ruined Fortress? Neo-liberal Hegemony and Transformation in Europe*, Oxford: Rowman and Littlefield.

Clift, B. (2005) *French Socialism in a Global Era: The Political Economy of the New Social Democracy in France*, London: Continuum.

Coase, R. (1937) 'The Nature of the Firm', *Economica*, vol. 4, no. 16, pp. 386–405.

Coates, D. (1999) 'Models of Capitalism in the New World Order', *Political Studies*, no. 47, pp. 643–60.

Coates, D. (ed.) (2011) *Exiting from the Crisis: Towards a Model of More Equitable and Sustainable Growth*, Brussels: European Trade Union Institute.

Coates, K. (ed.) (1979) *What Went Wrong?* Nottingham: Spokesman Books.

Coates, K. (ed.) (1986) *Joint Action for Jobs: A New Internationalism*, Nottingham: Spokesman Books.

Coates, K. and Barratt Brown, M. (eds) (1993) *A European Recovery Programme*, Nottingham: Spokesman Books.

Coates, K. and Holland, S. (1995) *Full Employment for Europe*, Nottingham: Spokesman Books.

Coates, K., Van Lancker, A., Vinci, L. and Otto Wolf, F. (eds) (1998) 'Full Employment: A European Appeal', *Spokesman*, no.64, pp.1–163.

Cockett, R. (1995) *Thinking the Unthinkable: Think Tanks and the Economic Counter-revolution, 1931–1983*, London: HarperCollins.

Coenen G. (2003a) *Downward Nominal Wage Rigidity and the Long-run Phillips Curve: Simulation-based Evidence for the Euro Area*, Background Study for ECB Governing Council, ECB, Frankfurt.

Coenen G., (2003b) *Zero Lower Bound: Is it a Problem in the Euro Area?*, Background Study for ECB Governing Council, ECB, Frankfurt.

Coldrick, P. (1998) 'The ETUCs Role in the EU's New Economic and Monetary Architecture', *Transfer*, vol. 4, no. 1, pp. 21–35.

Coleman, P. (1989) *The Liberal Conspiracy: The Congress for Cultural Freedom and the Struggle for the Mind of Post-war Europe*, London: Collier.

Collier, J. (1994) 'Regional Disparities, the Single Market and European Monetary Union' in J. Michie and J. Grieve Smith (eds) *Unemployment in Europe*, London: Academic Press.

Collignon, S. (2005) 'The Lisbon Strategy and the Open Method of Coordination: 12 Recommendations for an Effective Multi-level Strategy', Policy Paper no. 12, Brussels: *Notre Europe*.

Collins, D. (1975) *The European Communities: The Social Policy of the First Phase – Volume 2 The European Economic Community, 1958–1972*, London: Martin Robertson.

Collins, H. (2008) *The European Civil Code: The Way Forward*, Cambridge: Cambridge University Press.

Comparative Social Research (2007) vol. 16, Special Issue.

Confederation of British Industry (2000) 'Delivering a More Competitive Europe: The CBI View of the Convention on the Future of Europe', London: Confederation of British Industry.

Confederation of British Industry (2010) *Time for Action: Reforming Public Services and Balancing the Budget*, London: Confederation of British Industry.

Coricelli, F. (2002) 'Exchange Rate Policy during Transition to the European Monetary Union: The Option of Euroization', *Economics of Transition*, vol. 10, no. 2, pp. 405–17.

Cornelisse, P. and Goudswaard, K. (2002) 'On the Convergence of Social Protection Systems in the European Union', *International Social Security Review*, vol. 55, no. 3, pp. 3–17.

Corporate Europe Observatory (2005) *Lobby Planet Guide: Brussels – The EU Quarter*, Third Edition, Brussels: Corporate Europe Observatory.

Corporate Europe Observatory (2011) *Corporate EUtopia: How New Economic Governance Measures Threaten Democracy*, Brussels: CEO.

Costello, D. (1993) 'The Redistributive Effects of Inter-Regional Transfers: A Comparison of the European Community and Germany', in 'The Economics of Community Public Finance', *European Economy*, Reports and Studies, no. 5, pp. 271–8.

Coughlin, R. (1980) *Ideology, Public Opinion and Welfare Policy: Attitudes toward Taxes and Spending in Industrialized Societies*, Berkeley: Institute of International Studies, University of California.

Council of Ministers (1974) 'Council Resolution of 21 January 1974 Concerning a Social Action Programme', *Official Journal of the European Communities*, C13/1, 12 February.

Council on Foreign Relations (1941) Memorandum P-B23, 10 July, *War-Peace Studies*, Evanston, IL: Northwestern University Library.

Council on Foreign Relations (1942a) Memorandum T-A25, 20 May, *War-Peace Studies*, Stanford, CA: Hoover Library on War, Revolution and Peace.

Council on Foreign Relations (1942b) *An Interest in the Economic Unification of Europe with Respect to Trade Barriers*, New York: CFR.

Courchene, T.J. (1993) 'Reflections on Canadian Federalism: Are There Implications for European Economic and Monetary Union?', in 'The Economics of Community Public Finance', *European Economy*, Reports and Studies, no. 5, pp. 127–66.

Cox, A. (1988) 'The Failure of Corporatist State Forms and Policies in Post-war Britain' in A. Cox and N. O'Sullivan (eds) *The Corporate State: Corporatism and the State Tradition in Western Europe*, Aldershot: Edward Elgar.

Cox, R. (1987) *Production, Power and World Order: Social Forces in the Making of History*, New York: Columbia University Press.

Cox, R. (1996) *Approaches to World Order*, Cambridge: Cambridge University Press.

Cox, R.H. (2001) 'The Social Construction of an Imperative: Why Welfare Reform Happened in Denmark and the Netherlands but not in Germany', *World Politics*, vol. 53, no. 3, pp. 463–98.

Crepaz, M. and Birchfield, V. (2000) 'Global Economics, Local Politics: Lijphart's Theory of Consensus Democracy and the Politics of Inclusion' in M. Crepaz, T. Koelble and D. Wilsford (eds) *Democracy and Institutions: The Life Work of Arend Lijphart*, Ann Arbor: University of Michigan Press.

Cripps, F. and Ward, T. (1993) *Europe Can Afford to Work*, Nottingham: Spokesman Books.

Crosland, A. (1956) *The Future of Socialism*, London: Jonathan Cape.

Crouch, C. (1997) 'Skills-based Full Employment: The Latest Philosopher's Stone', *British Journal of Industrial Relations*, vol. 35, no. 3, pp. 367–91.

Crouch, C. (2002) 'The Euro and Labour Market and Wage Policies', in K. Dyson (ed.) *European States and the Euro: Europeanisation, Variation and Convergence*, Oxford: Oxford University Press, pp. 278–304.

Crozier, M., Huntington, S. and Watanuki, J. (1973) *The Crisis of Democracy: Report on the Governability of Democracies to the Trilateral Commission*, New York: New York University.

Cukierman, A. (1986) 'Central Bank Behaviour and Credibility: Some Recent Theoretical Developments', *Federal Reserve Bank of St Louis Review*, vol. 68, no. 5, pp. 5–17.

Cukierman, A. (1992) *Central Bank Strategy, Credibility and Independence*, Cambridge, MA: MIT Press.

Cukierman, A. and Lippi, F. (1999) 'Central Bank Independence, Centralisation of Wage Bargaining, Inflation and Unemployment: Theory and Some Evidence', *European Economic Review*, no. 43, pp. 1395–434.

Culpeper, R. (2002) 'Approaches to Globalization and Inequality within the International System', Programme Paper 6, Geneva: United Nations Research Institute for Development.

Cumings, B. (1988) *Korea: The Unknown War*, New York: Random House.

Cumings, B. (2010) *The Korean War: A History*, New York: Modern Library.

Currie, D. (1997) *The Pros and Cons of EMU*, London: HM Treasury,.

Curtis, M. (1995) *The Ambiguities of Power: British Foreign Policy since 1945*, London: Zed.

Curtis, M. (2010) 'The EU's Ugly Resource Grab', *Guardian*, 14 November.

Dahrendorf, R. (1981) 'A Little Silver Lining on a Dark Horizon' in R. Dahrendorf (ed.) *Europe's Economy in Crisis*, London: Weidenfeld and Nicholson.

Dalsgaard, T. and de Serres, A. (2001) 'Estimating Prudent Budgetary Margins for EU Countries: A Simulated SVAR Model Approach', in A. Brunila, M. Buti and D. Franco (eds) *The Stability and Growth Pact: The Architecture of Fiscal Policy in EMU*, Palgrave Macmillan, London.

Dangerfield, M. (2002) 'Integrating the "New Europe": What Role (if any) does CEFTA have?', in H. Ingham and M. Ingham (eds) *EU Expansion to the East: Prospects and Problems*, Cheltenham: Edward Elgar.

Daniels, P. (2003) 'From Hostility to "Constructive Engagement": The Europeanisation of the Labour Party', in A. Chadwick and R. Heffernan (eds) *The New Labour Reader*, Cambridge: Polity Press, pp. 223–30.

Darvas, Z. and Szapary, G. (2008) 'Business Cycle Synchronization in the Enlarged EU', *Open Economies Review*, vol. 19, no. 1, pp. 1–19.

Daviddi, R. and Ilzkovitz, F. (1997) 'The Eastern Enlargement of the European Union: Major Challenges for Macro-economic Policies and Institutions of Central and East European Countries', *European Economic Review*, vol. 41, no. 3–5, pp. 671–80.

Davidson, P. (1983) 'The Marginal Product of Labor is not the Demand Curve for Labor and Lucas's Labor Supply Function is not the Supply Curve for Labor in the Real World', *Journal of Post Keynesian Economics*, vol. 6, no. 3, pp. 105–17.

Davidson, P. (1998) 'Post Keynesian Employment Analysis and the Macroeconomics of OECD Unemployment', *Economic Journal*, vol. 108, no. 2, pp. 817–31.

Davies, A. (2008) 'One Step Forward, Two Steps Back? The *Viking* and *Laval* Cases in the ECJ', *Industrial Law Journal*, vol. 37, no. 2, pp. 126–48.

Davis, A. (2002) *Public Relations Democracy: Public Relations, Politics and the Mass Media in Britain*, Manchester: Manchester University Press.

Deacon, B. (2000) 'Eastern European Welfare States: The Impact of the Politics of Globalization', *Journal of European Social Policy*, vol. 10, no. 2, pp. 146–61.

Degryse, C. and Natali, D. (eds) (2011) *Social Developments in the European Union*, Brussels: European Trade Union Institute.

Delors, J. (1992) *Our Europe*, London: Verso.

Delsen, L. (2002) *Exit Polder Model? Socioeconomic Changes in the Netherlands*, London: Praeger.

Desai, R. (1994) 'Second-hand Dealers in Ideas: Think Tanks and Thatcherite Hegemony', *New Left Review*, vol. 203, pp. 27–64.

Desai, S. (2009) 'G-20 will become Main Economic Council: UK's Brown', *Reuters*, 24 September.

Deutsch, K. (1957) *Political Community and the North Atlantic Area*, Princeton, NJ: Princeton University Press.

Dicken, P. (1992) *Global Shift*, London: Paul Chapman Publishing.

Dierx, A. and Ilzkovitz, F. (2006) 'Economic Growth in Europe: Pursuing the Lisbon Strategy', in S. Mundschenk, M.H. Stierle, U. Stierle-von Schutz and I. Traistaru (eds) *Competitiveness and Growth in Europe: Lessons and Policy Implications for the Lisbon Treaty*, Cheltenham: Edward Elgar, pp. 15–46.

Dimitrakopoulos, D. (2010) *Social Democracy and European Integration*, London: Routledge.

Dinan, W. and Miller, D. (eds) (2007) *Thinker, Faker, Spinner, Spy: Corporate PR and the Assault on Democracy*, London: Pluto.

Dinmore, G. (2011) 'Italians await Pay-off from Budget Vows', *Financial Times*, 8 August.

Dixon, K. and Perraud, D. (1982) 'The French Experiment', *Marxism Today*, May.

Dombey, D. (2002) 'Euro is Widely Blamed for Price Increases', *Financial Times*, 1 June.

Donais, T. (2002) 'The Politics of Privatization in Post-Dayton Bosnia', *Southeast European Politics*, vol. 3, no. 1, pp. 3–19.

Donoughue, B. (1987) *Prime Minister: The Conduct of Policy under Harold Wilson and James Callaghan*, London: Jonathan Cape.

Dorey, P. (ed.) (2006) *The Labour Governments, 1964–1970*, London: Routledge.

Dornbusch, R. (1988) 'The European Monetary System, the Dollar and the Yen', in F. Giovazzi, S. Micossi and M. Miller (eds) *The European Monetary System*, Cambridge: Cambridge University Press, pp. 23–35.

Dow, G. (1992) 'The Economic Consequences of Economists.' *Australian Journal of Political Science*, vol. 27, no. 2, pp. 258–81.

Dow, J.C.R. (1998) *Major Recessions: Britain and the World, 1920-1995*, Oxford: Oxford University Press.

Dower, J. (1972) 'The Super-domino in Post-war Asia: Japan In and Out of the Pentagon Papers' in N. Chomsky and H. Zinn (eds) *The Pentagon Papers: Critical Essays – vol. V*, Senator Gravel Edition, Boston, MA: Beacon Press.

Doyle, M.F. (1989) 'Regional Policy and European Integration', in Committee for the Study of Economic and Monetary Union, *Report on Economic and Monetary Union in the European Community* – collection of papers, Office for the Official Publications of the European Communities, Luxembourg, pp. 69–80.

Draxler, J. and Van Vliet, O. (2010) 'European Social Model: No Convergence from the East', *European Integration*, vol. 32, no. 1, pp. 115–35.

Dreger, C. (2006) 'The Impact of Institutions on the Employment Threshold in European Labour Markets, 1979–2001', in S. Mundschenk, M.H. Stierle, U. Stierle-von Schutz and I. Traistaru (eds) *Competitiveness and Growth in Europe: Lessons and Policy Implications for the Lisbon Treaty*, Cheltenham: Edward Elgar, pp. 158–73.

Dréze, J. and Bean, C.R. (1990) 'European Unemployment: Lessons from a Multicountry Econometric Study', *Scandinavian Journal of Economics*, vol. 92, no. 2, pp. 135–65.

Driffill, J. and van der Ploeg, F. (1993) 'Monopoly Unions and the Liberalisation of International Trade', *Economic Journal*, vol. 103, no. 417, pp. 379-85.

DuBoff, R. (1989) *Accumulation and Power: An Economic History of the United States*, Armonk, NY: M.E. Sharpe.

Dunning, J.H. (1988) *Multinationals, Technology and Competitiveness*, Boston, MA: Unwin Hyman.

Dunphy, R. (2004) *Contesting Capitalism? Left Parties and European Integration*, Manchester: Manchester University Press.

Dustmann, C., Fabbri, F., Preston, I. and Wadsworth, J. (2003) 'Labour Market Performance of Immigrants in the UK Labour Market', Home Office Online report 05/03, online, available at: http://eprints.ucl.ac.uk/16488/1/16488.pdf.

Dyson, K. (1999) 'Benign or Malevolent Leviathan? Social Democratic Governments in a Neo-liberal Euro Area', *Political Quarterly*, vol. 70, no. 2, pp. 195–209.

Eatwell, J. (1989) *Whatever Happened to Britain? The Economics of Decline*, Oxford: Oxford University Press.

Eatwell, J. (1993) 'The Global Money Trap', *American Prospect*, Winter.

Eatwell, J. (2000) 'Unemployment: National policies in a Global Economy', *International Journal of Manpower*, vol. 21, no. 5, pp. 343–73.

Ebbinghaus, B. (1999) 'Does a European Social Model Exist and Can It Survive?' in G. Huemer and F. Traxler (eds) *The Role of Employer Associations and Labour Unions in the EU*, Aldershot: Ashgate.

EC (2010) Convergence Report 2010, *European Economy 3*, Luxembourg: Publications Office of the European Union.

ECB (European Central Bank) (1998) *A Stability Oriented Monetary Policy Strategy for the ESCB*. ECB, Frankfurt.

ECB (European Central Bank) (1999) *Monthly Bulletin*, Frankfurt: ECB.

ECB (European Central Bank) (2001) *Monthly Bulletin*, Frankfurt: ECB.

ECB (European Central Bank) (2002) *Evaluation of the 2002 Cash Changeover*, Frankfurt: ECB.

ECB (European Central Bank) (2003) *Overview of the Background Studies for the Reflections on the ECBs Monetary Policy Strategy*, Frankfurt: ECB.

ECB (European Central Bank) (2004) *Monthly Bulletin*, October, Frankfurt: ECB.

ECB (European Central Bank) (2005) *Monthly Bulletin*, March, Frankfurt: ECB.

EC Commission (1957) Treaty establishing the European Economic Community, Luxembourg: Office for Official Publications of the European Communities.

EC Commission (1992) *Treaty on European Union*, Luxembourg: Office for the Official Publications of the European Communities.

Edmonds, J. (2000) 'The Single Currency and the European Social Model', in M. Baimbridge, B. Burkitt and P. Whyman (eds) *The Impact of the Euro: Debating Britain's Future*, London: Macmillan, pp. 191–9.

Edmonds, T. and Marshall, J. (2010) 'European Responses to the Financial Crisis', House of Commons Library, Standard Note SN/BT/5099, London: House of Commons.

Edwards, D. and Cromwell, D. (2006) *Guardians of Power: The Myth of the Liberal Media*, London: Pluto.

Edwards, D. and Cromwell, D. (2009) *Newspeak in the 21st Century*, London: Pluto.

Égert, B. (2002) 'Investigating the Balassa-Samuelson Hypothesis in the Transition: Do we Understand what we See? A Panel Study', *Economics of Transition*, vol. 10, no. 2, pp. 273–309.

Eichengreen, B. (1990) 'One Money for Europe? Lessons from the US Currency Union', *Economic Policy*, vol. 10, pp. 118–87.

Eichengreen, B. (1992) 'Is Europe an Optimum Currency Area?', in S. Borner and H. Grubel (eds) *The European Community After 1992: Perspectives from the Outside*, London: Macmillan, pp. 138–61.

Eichengreen, B. (1993a) 'European Monetary Unification', *Journal of Economic Literature*, vol. 31, September, pp. 1321–57.

Eichengreen, B. (1993b) 'Labour Markets and European Monetary Unification', in P.R. Masson and M.P. Taylor (eds) *Policy Issues in the Operation of Currency Unions*, Cambridge: Cambridge University Press, pp. 130–2.

Eichengreen, B. (1994) 'Fiscal Policy and EMU', in B. Eichengreen and J. Frieden (eds) *The Political Economy of European Monetary Integration*, Oxford: Westview Press, pp. 167–90.

Eichengreen, B. (2007) *The European Economy since 1945: Co-ordinated Capitalism and Beyond*, Oxford: Princeton University Press.

Eichengreen, B. and Iversen, T. (1999) 'Institutions and Economic Performance: Evidence from the Labour Market', *Oxford Review of Economic Policy*, vol. 15, no. 4, pp. 121–38.

Eichengreen, B. and Wyplotz, C. (1998) 'The Stability Pact: More than a Minor Nuisance?', *Economic Policy: A European Forum*, vol. 26, pp. 65–104.

EIRO (European Industrial Relations Observatory) (2005) *Changes in National Collective Bargaining Systems since 1990*, Dublin: EIRO.

Eisenberg, C. (1983) 'Working Class Politics and the Cold War: American Intervention in the German Labour Movement, 1945–1949', *Diplomatic History*, vol. 7, no. 4, pp. 283–306.

Eisenberg, C. (1998) *Drawing the Line: The American Decision to Divide Germany, 1944–1949*, Cambridge: Cambridge University Press.

Eller, J.W. and Gordon, R.J. (2002) 'Inflation and Unemployment in the New Economy: Is the Trade-Off Dead or Alive?', paper presented at the Workshop on the Phillips Curve: New Theory and Evidence, Trade Union Institute for Economic Research, Stockholm, 25/26 May.

Elliott, W. (1955) *The Political Economy of American Foreign Policy: Its Concepts, Strategy and Limits*, New York: Holt, Rinehart and Winston.

Elmendorf, D.W., Liebman, J.B. and Wilcox, D.W. (2002) 'Fiscal Policy and Social Security Policy During the 1990s', in J.A. Frankel and P.R. Orszag (eds) *American Economic Policy in the 1990s*, Cambridge, MA: MIT Press, pp. 61–119.

Eltis, W. (1996) 'If EMU Happens should Britain Join?', *International Currency Review*, vol. 23, no. 3, pp. 61–6.

Emerson, M. (1989) *The Economics of 1992*, Oxford: Oxford University Press.

Emerson, M., Gros, D., Italianer, A., Pisani-Ferry, J. and Reichenbach, H. (1992) 'One Market, One Money', Commission of the European Economies, *European Economy*, October 1990, no. 44, special edition.

Erickson, C. and Kuruvilla, S. (1994) 'Labour Costs and the Social Dumping Debate in the European Union', *Industrial and Labor Relations Review*, vol. 48, no. 1, pp. 28–47.

Eringer, R. (1980) *The Global Manipulators: The Bilderberg Group and the Trilateral Commission – Covert Power Groups of the West*, London: Pentacle.

Ermisch, J. (1991) 'European Integration and External Constraints on Social Policy: Is a Social Charter Necessary?', *National Institute Economic Review*, no. 136, May, pp. 93–108.

Ernst and Young (2010) 'Eurozone Forecast, Spring 2010', London: Ernst and Young.

Esping-Andersen, G. (1985) *Politics against Markets*, Princeton, NJ: Princeton University Press.

Esping-Andersen, G. (1990) *The Three Worlds of Welfare Capitalism*, Cambridge: Polity.

Esping-Andersen, G. (1999) *Social Foundations of Post-industrial Economies*, Oxford: Oxford University Press.

Esping-Andersen, G. (ed.) (1996) 'Conclusion: Positive-sum Solutions in a World of Trade-offs?', in G. Esping-Andersen (ed.) *Welfare States in Transition: National Adaptations in Global Economies*, London: Sage.

Estulin, D. (2009) *The True Story of the Bilderberg Group*, second edition, Walterville, OR: Trine Day.

EU (2000) 'European Social Agenda', in *Presidency Conclusions: Nice European Council Meeting*, 7–9 December, EN SN 400/00, ADD1 (Annex 1).

EU Commission (1992) *Treaty on European Union*, Luxembourg: Office for the Official Publications of the European Communities.

EU Commission (1996) *The Community Budget – 1996 Edition*, Luxembourg: Office for the Official Publications of the European Communities.

EU Commission (1997) 'The Stability and Growth Pact', *InfEuro*, Luxembourg: Office for the Official Publications of the European Communities.

EU Commission (2000) *Public Finances in EMU – 2000*, Brussels: Report of the Directorate General for Economic and Financial Affairs.

EU Commission (2006) 'Enlargement, Two Years After: An Economic Evaluation', *European Economy – Occasional Papers no. 24*, Brussels: EU Commission.

European Anti-Poverty Network (2009) *Social Cohesion at Stake: The Social Impact of the Crisis and of the Recovery Package*, Brussels: European Anti-Poverty Network.

European Anti-Poverty Network (2010) *Is the European Project Moving Backwards? The Social Impact of the Crisis and of the Recovery Policies in 2010*, Brussels: European Anti-Poverty Network.

European Anti-Poverty Network (2011) *Wealth, Inequality and Social Polarization in the EU*, Brussels: European Anti-Poverty Network.

European Commission (1970a) 'The Establishment by Stages of Economic and Monetary Union in the Community', Luxembourg: Office for Official Publications of the European Communities.

European Commission (1970b) 'Attainment of the Economic and Monetary Union', *Bulletin of the European Communities*, Supplement 7/73, Luxembourg: Office for Official Publications of the European Communities.

European Commission (1977) 'Report of the Study Group on the Role of Public Finance in European Integration', Luxembourg: Office for Official Publications of the European Communities.

European Commission (1989) 'Action Programme Relating to the Implementation of the Community Charter of Basic Social Rights for Workers', COM (89) 568 Final, Luxembourg: Office for Official Publications of the European Communities.

European Commission (1990) 'Industrial Policy in an Open and Competitive Environment', COM (90) 556 Final, Luxembourg: Office for Official Publications of the European Communities.

European Commission (1992) Treaty on European Union, Luxembourg: Office for the Official Publications of the European Communities.

European Commission (1993) 'Growth, Competitiveness, Employment: The Challenges and Ways Forward in the 21st Century', Com (93) 700 Final, Luxembourg: Office for Official Publications of the European Communities.

European Commission (1994) 'European Social Policy – A Way Forward for the Union', Com (94) 333 Final, Luxembourg: Office for Official Publications of the European Communities.

European Commission (1995) 'Medium-term Social Action Programme 1995–1997', COM (95) 134 Final, Luxembourg: Office for Official Publications of the European Communities.

European Commission (1996) Single Market Review Series. Online, available at: http://ec.europa.eu/internal_market/economic-reports/studies_en.htm (accessed 16 June 2011).

European Commission (1997) 'Modernizing and Improving Social Protection in the European Union', COM (97) 102 Final, Luxembourg: Office for Official Publications of the European Communities.

European Commission (1998) 'Social Action Programme 1998–2000', COM (98) 259 Final, Luxembourg: Office for Official Publications of the European Communities.

European Commission (1999) 'A Concerted Strategy for Modernizing Social Protection', COM (99) 347 Final, Luxembourg: Office for Official Publications of the European Communities.

European Commission (2000) 'Social Policy Agenda 2000–2005', COM (2000) 379 Final, Luxembourg: Office for Official Publications of the European Communities.

European Commission (2001) 'The Economic Impact of Enlargement', Brussels: Directorate General for Economic and Financial Affairs.

European Commission (2002) *Towards the Enlarged Union: Strategy Paper and Report of the European Commission on the Progress Towards Accession by each of the Candidate Countries*, Brussels: Directorate General for Economic and Financial Affairs.

European Commission (2007) 'Towards Common Principles of Flexicurity: More and Better Jobs through Flexibility and Security', COM 2007 359 Final, Luxembourg: Office for Official Publications of the European Communities.

European Commission (2008a) 'The Raw Materials Initiative – Meeting Our Critical Needs for Growth and Jobs in Europe', COM 2008 699 Final, Luxembourg: Office for Official Publications of the European Communities.

European Commission (2008b) 'A European Economic Recovery Programme', COM 2008 800 Final, Luxembourg: Office for Official Publications of the European Communities.

European Commission (2009a) 'Driving European Recovery', COM (2009) 114 Final, Luxembourg: Office for Official Publications of the European Communities.

European Commission (2009b) 'State Aid Scoreboard – Spring 2009 Update – Special Edition on State Aid Intervention in the Current Financial and Economic Crisis', COM (2009) 164 Final, Luxembourg: Office for Official Publications of the European Communities.

European Commission (2010a) 'Reinforcing Economic Policy Coordination', COM 2010 250 Final, Luxembourg: Office for Official Publications of the European Communities.

European Commission (2010b) 'Enhancing Economic Policy Coordination for Stability, Growth and Jobs: Tools for Stronger EU Economic Governance', COM 2010 367/2 Final, Luxembourg: Office for Official Publications of the European Communities.

European Commission (2010c) 'Report Lists 14 Critical Mineral Raw Materials', MEMO/10/263, Luxembourg: Office for Official Publications of the European Communities.

European Commission (2010d) 'Bilateral Relations: United States'. Online, available at: http://ec.europa.eu/trade/creating-opportunities/bilateral-relations/countries/united-states/ (accessed 4 June 2011).

European Commission (2011a) 'Annual Growth Survey: Advancing the EU's Comprehensive Response to the Crisis', COM 2011 11 Final, Luxembourg: Office for Official Publications of the European Communities.

European Commission (2011b) 'Tackling the Challenges in Commodity Markets and on Raw Materials', COM 2011 25 Final, Luxembourg: Office for Official Publications of the European Communities.

European Council (1978) *Conclusions of the Presidency of the European Council – 6–7 July, Bremen*, Luxembourg: Office for Official Publications of the European Communities.

European Council (1993) *Presidency Conclusions: Copenhagen European Council – 21–22 June 1993*, Luxembourg: Office for Official Publications of the European Communities.

European Council (1994) *Presidency Conclusions: Essen European Council – 9–10 December 1994*, Luxembourg: Office for Official Publications of the European Communities.

European Council (2000) *Presidency Conclusions: Lisbon European Council – 23–24 March 2000*, Luxembourg: Office for Official Publications of the European Communities.

European Council (2003) *European Security Strategy: A Secure Europe in a Better World*, Luxembourg: Office for Official Publications of the European Communities.

European Council (2007) *Declaration on the Occasion of the Fiftieth Anniversary of the Signature of the Treaties of Rome*, Luxembourg: Office for Official Publications of the European Communities.

European Council (2009) *Presidency Conclusions: Brussels European Council – 19–20 March 2009*, Luxembourg: Office for Official Publications of the European Communities.

European Council (2010) *Presidency Conclusions: Brussels European Council – 25–26 March 2010*, Luxembourg: Office for Official Publications of the European Communities.

European Integration Consortium (2000) *The Impact of Eastern Enlargement on Employment and Labour Markets in the EU Member States*, Report for the Employment and Social Affairs Directorate General of the European Commission, Berlin/Milan.

European Monetary Institute (1997) *The Single Monetary Policy in Stage Three*, Frankfurt: EMI.

European Parliament (1992) Resolution on the Results of the Intergovernmental Conferences, 7 April, A3–0123/92, Strasbourg: European Parliament.

European Round Table of Industrialists (2001) *Opening up the Business Opportunities of EU Enlargement*, May, Brussels: European Round Table of Industrialists.

European Round Table of Industrialists (2010) *ERT Vision for a Competitive Europe in 2025*, Brussels: European Round Table of Industrialists.

European Trade Union Confederation (2010) 'European Governance needs to Promote Stimulus and Fair Wages, Not Austerity and Wage Cuts', ETUC Statement on European Governance, 28 October, Brussels: European Trade Union Confederation.

European Trade Union Institute (2011) *Benchmarking Working Europe 2011*, Brussels: European Trade Union Institute.

Evangelista, M. (1982) 'Stalin's Post-war Army Reappraised', *International Security*, vol. 7, no. 3, pp. 110–38.

Ewing, K. (2007) *The Cost of Democracy: Party Funding in Modern British Politics*, London: Hart Publishing.

Fajertag, G. and Pochet, P. (eds) (1997) *Social Pacts in Europe*, Brussels: European Trade Union Institute/Observatoire Social Européen.

Falkner, G., Trieb, O., Hartlapp, M. and Leiber, S. (2005) *Complying with Europe: EU Harmonization and Soft Law in the Member States*, Cambridge: Cambridge University Press.

Fassmann, H. and Münz, R. (2002) 'EU Enlargement and Future East–West Migration in Europe', in International Organisation for Migration, *Migrations Challenges in Central and Eastern Europe*, Geneva: International Centre for Migration Policy and Development.

Favretto, I. (2003) *The Long Search for a Third Way: The British Labour Party and the Italian Left Since 1945*, London: Palgrave.

Fay, S. and Young, H. (1978) *The Day the £ Nearly Died*, London: Pan.

Federation of Small Businesses (2010) 'Budget must Deliver Plans on Deficit Reduction, Say FSB Members', FSB News Release, PR 2010 24, 17 May. Online, available at: www.fsb.org.uk/news.aspx?loc=pressroom&rec=6296 (accessed 24 May 2011).

Feffer, J. (1999) *Shock Waves: Eastern Europe after the Revolutions*, Boston, MA: South End Press.

Feldstein, M.S. (1974) 'Social Security, Induced Retirement and Aggregate Capital Accumulation', *Journal of Political Economy*, vol. 82, pp. 905–26.

Feldstein, M.S. (1976) 'Temporary Layoffs in the Theory of Unemployment', *Journal of Political Economy*, vol. 84, pp. 937–57.

Fennema, M. (1982) *International Networks of Banks and Industry*, The Hague: Martinus Nijhoff Publishers.

Ferguson, T. (1995) *Golden Rule: The Investment Theory of Party Competition and the Logic of Money-Driven Political Systems*, London: University of Chicago Press.

Ferrera, M. (2003) 'Reforming the European Social Model: Dilemmas and Perspectives', *European Legacy*, vol. 8, no. 5, pp. 587–98.

Ferrera, M. (2005) *The Boundaries of Welfare: European Integration and the New Spatial Politics of Social Protection*, Oxford: Oxford University Press.

Ferrera, M. (2008) 'The European Welfare State: Golden Achievements, Silver Prospects', *West European Politics*, vol. 31, no. 1, pp. 82–107.

Ferrera, M. and Rhodes, M. (eds) (2000) *Recasting European Welfare States*, London: Frank Cass.

Ferrera, M., Hemerijck, A. and Rhodes, M. (2000a) *The Future of Social Europe*, Lisbon: Celta Editora.

Ferrera, M., Hemerijck, A. and Rhodes, M. (2000b) 'Recasting European Welfare States for the 21st Century', *European Review*, vol. 8, no. 3, pp. 427–46.

Ferrera, M., Hemerijck, A. and Rhodes, M. (2001) 'The Future of the Europe "Social Model" in the Global Economy', *Journal of Comparative Analysis: Research and Practice*, vol. 3, no. 2, pp. 163–90.

Fidrmuc, J. and Korhonen, I. (2006) 'Meta-analysis of the Business Cycle Correlation between the Euro Area and the CEECs', *Journal of Comparative Economics*, vol. 34, no. 3, pp. 518–37.

Financial Times (1999) 'A Farewell to Oskar', Editorial, *Financial Times*, 13 March.

Fischer, J. and Giudice, G. (2001) 'Fiscal Surveillance under the Pact: The Stability and Convergence Programmes', in A. Brunila, M. Buti and D. Franco (eds) *The Stability and Growth Pact: The Architecture of Fiscal Policy in EMU*, London: Palgrave Macmillan.

Fisher, S. and Cooper, J.P. (1973) 'Stabilisation Policy and Lags', *Journal of Political Economy*, vol. 81, no. 4.

Fitoussi, J.-P. and Creel, J. (2002) *How to Reform the European Central Bank*, London: Centre for European Reform.

Fitoussi, J.-P., Atkinson, A., Blanchard, O., Flemming, J., Malinvaud, E., Phelps, E. and Solow, R. (1993) *Competitive Disinflation*, Oxford: Oxford University Press.

FitzGerald, J. (2006) 'Lessons from 20 Years of Cohesion', in S. Mundschenk, M.H. Stierle, U. Stierle-von Schultz and I. Traistaru (eds) *Competitiveness and Growth in Europe: Lessons and Policy Implications for the Lisbon Strategy*, Cheltenham: Edward Elgar, pp. 66–100.

Flanagan, R. (1999) 'Macroeconomic Performance and Collective Bargaining: An International Perspective', *Journal of Economic Literature*, vol. 37, no. 3, pp. 1150–75.

Flora, P. (ed.) (1986) *Growth to Limits: The Western European Welfare States since World War II*, New York: De Gruyter.

Flora, P. and Alber, J. (1981) 'Modernization, Democratization and the Development of Welfare States in Western Europe' in P. Flora and A. Heidenheimer (eds) *The Development of Welfare States in Europe and America*, London: Transaction Books.

Flora, P. and Heidenheimer, A. (eds) (1981) *The Development of Welfare States in Europe and America*, London: Transaction Books.

Follesdal, A., Giorgi, L. and Heuberger, R. (2007) 'Envisioning European Solidarity between Welfare Ideologies and the European Social Agenda', *Innovation*, vol. 20, no. 1, pp. 75–92.

Fones-Wolf, E. (1994) *Selling Free Enterprise: The Business Assault on Labor and Liberalism, 1945–1960*, Chicago: University of Illinois Press.

Foot, P. (1989) *Who Framed Colin Wallace?*, London: Macmillan.

Forsyth, D. and Notermans, T. (1997) *Regime Changes: Macroeconomic Policy and Financial Regulation in Europe from the 1930s to the 1990s*, Oxford: Berghahn Books.

Foster, D. and Scott, P. (eds) (2003) *Trade Unions in Europe: Meeting the Challenge*, Oxford: PIE-Peter Lang.

Foukas, V.K. (1998) *Italy, Europe, the Left; the Transformation of Italian Communism and the European Imperative*, Aldershot: Ashgate.

Frangakis, M., Hermann, C., Huffschmid, J. and Lóránt, K. (eds) (2009) *Privatization against the European Social Model: A Critique of European Policies and Proposals for Alternatives*, Basingstoke: Palgrave Macmillan.

Franklin, B. (1994) *Packaging Politics: Political Communications in Britain's Media Democracy*, second edition, London: Arnold.

Freedman, D. (2003) *Television Policies of the Labour Party, 1951–2000*, London: Frank Cass.

Frey, B.S. (1978) *Modern Political Economy*, Oxford: Martin Robertson.

Friedman, M. (1953) 'The Lags of a Full Employment Policy on Economic Stability: A Formal Analysis', in M. Friedman, *Essays in Positive Economics*, Chicago: University of Chicago Press.

Friedman, M. (1962) *Capitalism and Freedom*, Chicago: University of Chicago Press.

Friedman, M. (1968) 'The Role of Monetary Policy', *American Economic Review*, vol. 58, pp. 1–17.

Friedman, M. and Schwartz, A.J. (1991) 'Alternative Approaches to Analysing Economic Data', *American Economic Review*, vol. 81, no. 1, pp. 39–49.

Fukuyama, F. (1989) 'The End of History?' *National Interest*, Summer.

Gabrisch, H. and Werner, H. (1999) 'Structural Convergence – through Industrial Policy', in J.M. van Brabant (ed.) *Remaking Europe: the European Union and the Transition Economies*, London: Rowman and Littlefield.

Gaddis, J.L. (1982) *Strategies of Containment: A Critical Appraisal of the American National Security Policy during the Cold War*, Oxford: Oxford University Press.

Galbraith, J.K. (1997) 'Time to Ditch the NAIRU', *Journal of Economic Perspectives*, vol. 11, no. 1, pp. 93–108.

Galgóczi, B., Keune, M. and Watt, A. (2007) 'Relocation: Challenges for European Trade Unions', Working Paper WP2007.03, Brussels: European Trade Union Institute.

Gali, J. (2001) *Monetary Policy in the Early Years of EMU*, Paper presented at the European Commission Workshop on The Functioning of EMU: Challenges of the Early Years.

Gali, J. and Perotti, R. (2003) 'Fiscal Policy and Monetary Integration in Europe', *Economic Policy*, vol. 37, pp. 533–72.

Gamble, A. (1994) *Britain in Decline: Economic Policy, Political Strategy and the British State*, Basingstoke: Palgrave Macmillan.

Ganser, D. (2005) *NATO's Secret Armies: Operation Gladio and Terrorism in Western Europe*, London: Frank Cass.

Gardner, J. (1991) *Effective Lobbying in the European Community*, Deventer: Kluwer.

Garrett, G. (1995) 'Capital Mobility, Trade and the Domestic Politics of Economic Policy', *International Organisation*, vol. 49, pp. 657–87.

Garrett, G. (1998) *Partisan Politics in the Global Economy*, Cambridge: Cambridge University Press.

Garrett, G. (2000) 'Shrinking States? Globalization and National Autonomy' in N. Woods (ed.) *The Political Economy of Globalization*, London: Palgrave.

Garrett, G. and Mitchell, D. (2001) 'Globalization, Government Spending and Taxation in the OECD', *European Journal of Political Research*, vol. 39, no. 2, pp. 145–77.

Garton Ash, T. (2010) 'Britain and Europe are Living Separate Crises. Underneath, it's the Same One', *Guardian*, 12 May.

Gaspar, V., Masuch, K. and Pill, H. (2001) *The ECB's Monetary Policy Strategy: Responding to the Challenges of the Early Years*, Mimeo.

Gasteen, A., Houston, J. and Asenova, D. (1999) 'Labour Market Flexibility and the Public Finances', in L. Funk (ed.) *The Economics and the Politics of the Third Way: Essays in Honour of Eric Owen Smith*, London: Lit Verlag, pp. 88–99.

Gelissen, J. (2000) 'Public Support for Institutionalized Solidarity: A Comparison between European Welfare States', *International Journal of Social Welfare*, vol. 9, no. 4, pp. 285–300.

Gellman, B. (1992) 'Keeping the US First: Pentagon would Preclude a Rival Super-power', *Washington Post*, 11 March.

George, A. (ed.) (1991) *Western State Terrorism*, London: Polity.

George, V. and Taylor-Gooby, P. (1996) *European Welfare Policy: Squaring the Welfare Circle*, Basingstoke: Macmillan.

Gervasi, S. (1992) 'Germany, US and the Yugoslav Crisis', *Covert Action Quarterly*, no. 43, Winter, pp. 41–5.

Geyer, R. (1993) 'Socialism and the EC after Maastricht: From Classic to New-Model European Social Democracy' in A. Cafruny and G. Rosenthal (eds) *The State of the European Community – vol. 2: The Maastricht Debates and Beyond*, Harlow: Longman.

Geyer, R. (1998) 'Globalization and the (Non-) Defence of the Welfare State', *West European Politics*, vol. 21, no. 3, pp. 77–102.

Giddens, A. (1998) *The Third Way: The Renewal of Social Democracy*, Cambridge: Polity Press.

Giddens, A. (1999) 'Risk and Responsibility', *Modern Law Review*, vol. 62, no. 1, pp. 1–10.

Giddens, A. (2001) 'Introduction', in A. Giddens (ed.) *The Global Third Way Debate* Cambridge: Polity, pp. 1–23.

Giddens, A. (2007) *Europe in the Global Age*, Cambridge: Polity.

Giddens, A., Diamond, P. and Liddle, R. (2006) *Global Europe, Social Europe*, Cambridge: Polity.

Giger, N. (2011) *The Risk of Social Policy? The Electoral Consequences of Welfare State Retrenchment and Social Policy Performance in OECD Countries*, Abingdon: Routledge.

Gilbert, N. (2002) *Transformation of the Welfare State: The Silent Surrender of Public Responsibility*, New York: Oxford University Press.

Gill, S. (1998) 'European Governance and New Constitutionalism: Economic and Monetary Union and Alternatives to Disciplinary Neo-liberalism in Europe', *New Political Economy*, vol. 3, no. 1, pp. 5–26.

Gill, S. (2001) 'Constitutionalizing Capital: EMU and Disciplinary Neo-liberalism' in A. Bieler and A. Morton (eds) *Social Forces in the Making of New Europe: The Restructuring of European Social Relations in the Global Political Economy*, Basingstoke: Palgrave.

Gill, S. (2003) 'A Neo-Gramscian Approach to European Integration' in A. Cafruny and M. Ryner (eds) *A Ruined Fortress? Neo-liberal Hegemony and Transformation in Europe*, Oxford: Rowman and Littlefield.

Gill, S. and Law, D. (1988) *The Global Political Economy: Perspectives, Problems and Policies*, Baltimore, MD: Johns Hopkins University Press.

Gillingham, J. (2003) *European Integration, 1950–2003*, Cambridge: Cambridge University Press.

Gilpin, N., Henty, M., Lemos, S., Portes, J. and Bullen, C. (2006) 'The Impact of Free Movement of Workers from Central and Eastern Europe on the UK Labour Market', *Working Paper 29*, London: Department of Work and Pensions.

Ginsberg, N. (1979) *Class, Capital and Social Policy*, London: Macmillan.

Ginsburg, N. (1992) *Divisions of Welfare*, London: Sage.

Glasgow University Media Group (1976) *Bad News*, London: Routledge and Kegan Paul.

Glasgow University Media Group (1980) *More Bad News*, London: Routledge and Kegan Paul.

Glasgow University Media Group (1982) *Really Bad News*, London: Writers and Readers Publishing Cooperative Society.

Glasman, M. (1997) 'The siege of the German social market', *New Left Review*, no. 225, pp. 134–9.

Global Social Policy (2003) vol. 3, no. 2, Special Issue.

Glyn, A. (1992) 'Real Wages and Reconstruction Applied Economics', Discussion Paper no. 147, Oxford: Institute of Economics and Statistics.

Glyn, A. (1995) 'Social Democracy and Full Employment', *New Left Review*, vol. 211, May/June, pp. 31–55.

GoForex (2007) 'Forex Market Snapshot'. Online, available at: www.goforex.net (accessed 12 January 2008).

Golinger, E. (2006) *The Chavez Code: Cracking US Intervention in Venezuela*, London: Pluto.

Goncalves, S. (2010) 'Markets Calm amid New Austerity for Portugal', Reuters, 14 May.

Goodhart, C.A.E. (1995) 'The Political Economy of Monetary Union', in Kenen, P.B. (ed.) *Understanding Independence: The Macroeconomics of the Open Economy*, Princeton: Princeton University Press.

Goodhart, C.A.E. and Smith, S. (1993) 'Stabilisation', in 'The Economics of Community Public Finance', *European Economy*, Reports and Studies, no. 5, pp. 419–55.

Goodin, R. and LeGrand, J. (1987) 'Not Only the Poor' in R. Goodin and J. LeGrand (eds) *Not Only the Poor: The Middle Classes and the Welfare State*, London: Allen and Unwin.

Goodley, S. (2011) 'EU Inquiry into Bank Collusion Claims', *Guardian*, 30 April.

Gorzelak, G., Jalowiecki, B., Kuklinski, A. and Zienkowski, L. (1994) *Eastern and Central Europe 2000*, Brussels: European Commission.

Gough, I. (1979) *The Political Economy of the Welfare State*, London: Macmillan.

Gough, I. (1999) 'Social Welfare and Competitiveness', *New Political Economy*, vol. 1, no. 2, pp. 209–32.

Gowan, P. (1999a) *The Global Gamble: Washington's Faustian Bid for World Domination*, London: Verso.

Gowan, P. (1999b) 'The Twisted Road to Kosovo', *Labour Focus on Eastern Europe*, Special Issue, vol. 62, Spring.

Gowan, P. (1999c) 'The NATO Powers and the Balkan Tragedy', *New Left Review*, no. 234, pp. 83–105.

Gowan, P. (2000) 'The Euro-Atlantic Origins of NATO's Attack on Yugoslavia' in T. Ali (ed.) *Masters of the Universe: NATO's Balkan Crusade*, London: Verso.

Grabbe, H. (2001) *Profiting from EU Enlargement*, London: Centre for European Reform, June.

Grahl, J. and Teague, P. (1989) 'The Cost of Neo-liberal Europe', *New Left Review*, no. 174, pp. 33–50.

Grahl, J. and Teague, P. (1997) 'Is the European Social Model Fragmenting?' *New Political Economy*, vol. 2, no. 3, pp. 405–26.

Grant, C. (1994) *Delors: Inside the House that Jacques Built*, London: Nicholas Brealey Publishing.

Grant, W. (ed.) (1993) *Business and Politics in Britain*, second edition, Basingstoke: Palgrave.

Grant, W. (2002) *Economic Policy in Britain*, Basingstoke: Palgrave Macmillan.

Grauwe, P. de (1994) *The Economics of Monetary Integration*, Oxford: Oxford University Press.

Grauwe, P. de (2010) 'The Financial Crisis and the Future of the Eurozone', Bruges European Economic Policy Briefing no. 21, Bruges: College of Europe.

Grauwe, P. de and Lavrac, V. (1999) Challenges of European Monetary Union for Central European Countries; in P. de Grauwe and V. Lavrac (eds) *Inclusion of Central European Countries in the European Monetary Union*, London: Kluwer.

Grauwe, P. de, and Vanhaverbeke, W. (1993) 'Is Europe an Optimum Currency Area?', in P.R. Masson and M.P. Taylor (eds) *Policy Issues in the Operation of Currency Unions*, Cambridge: Cambridge University Press, pp. 111–29.

Gray, A. (2004) *Unsocial Europe*, London: Pluto Press.

Gray, J. (1998) *False Dawn: The Delusions of Global Capitalism*, London: Granta.

Green Cowles, M. (1995) 'Setting the Agenda for a New Europe: The ERT and EC 1992', *Journal of Common Market Studies*, vol. 33, no. 4, pp. 501–26.

Green, D. (1971) *The Containment of Latin America: A History of the Myths and Realities of the Good Neighbor Policy*, Chicago: Quadrangle.

Green, E. (1992) 'The Influence of the City over British Economic Policy' in Y. Cassin (ed.) *Finance and Financiers in European History*, Cambridge: Cambridge University Press.

Green-Pedersen, C. (2002) *The Politics of Justification: Party Competition and Welfare State Retrenchment in Denmark and the Netherlands from 1982 to 1998*, Amsterdam: Amsterdam University Press.

Green-Pedersen, C. and Haverland, M. (2002) 'The New Politics and Scholarship of the Welfare State', *Journal of European Social Policy*, vol. 12, no. 1, pp. 43–51.

Greve, B. (1996) 'Indications of Social Policy Convergence in Europe', *Social Policy and Administration*, vol. 30, no. 4, pp. 348–67.

Grieder, W. (1997) *One World Ready or Not: The Manic Logic of Global Capitalism*, New York: Simon and Schuster.

Groom, B. (2010) 'IoD Poll shows 'Emphatic' Support for Budget', *Financial Times*, 23 June.

Groot, H. de, Nahuis, R. and Tang, P. (2006) 'The Institutional Determinants of Labour Market Performance: Comparing the Anglo-Saxon Model and a European-Style Alternative', in W. Mitchell, J. Muysken and T. Van Veen (eds) *Growth and Cohesion in the European Union: The Impact of Macroeconomic Policy*, Cheltenham: Edward Elgar, pp. 157–79.

Gros, D., Jimeno, J., Monticelli, C., Tabellini, G. and Thygesen, N. (2001) *Testing the Speed Limit for the European Central Bank*, 4, London: CEPR.

Gross, D. (2002) 'Health not Wealth: Enlarging the EMU', in P. Mair and J. Zielonka, (eds) *The Enlarged European Union: Diversity and Adaptation*, Frank Cass: London.

Gross, D. (2003) 'Central Europe on the Way to EMU', in S. Manzocchi (ed.) *The Economics of Enlargement*, London: Palgrave Macmillan.

Guillén, A. and Matsaganis, M. (2000) 'Testing the "Social Dumping" Hypothesis in Southern Europe: Welfare Policies in Greece and Spain in the Last 20 Years', *Journal of European Social Policy*, vol. 10, no. 2, pp. 120–45.

Gulde, A.-M., Kähkönen, J. and Keller, P. (2000) 'Pros and Cons of Currency Board Arrangements in the Lead-up to EU Accession and Participation in the Euro Zone', *IMF Discussion Paper*, PDP/00/1.

Gunder Frank, A. (1967) *Capitalism and Under-development in Latin America*, London: Modern Reader.

Haas, E. (1958) *The Uniting of Europe: Political, Social and Economic Forces, 1950–1957*, Stanford, CA: Stanford University Press.

Habermas, J. and Derrida, J. (2003) 'February 15, or What Binds Europeans Together: a Plea for a Common Foreign Policy, Beginning in a Core of Europe', *Constellations*, vol. 10, no. 3, pp. 291–7.

Hagen, J. von (1992) 'Fiscal Arrangements in a Monetary Union: Evidence from the US', in D. Fair and C. de Boissieux (eds) *Fiscal Policy, Taxes and the Financial System in an Increasingly Integrated Europe*, Deventer: Kluwer.

Hagen, J. von (1993) 'Monetary Union and Fiscal Union: A Perspective from Fiscal Federalism', in P.R. Masson and M.P. Taylor (eds) *Policy Issues in the Operation of Currency Unions*, Cambridge: Cambridge University Press, pp. 264–96.

Hagen, J. von (2003) 'EMU: Monetary Policy Issues and Challenges', in M. Baimbridge and P. Whyman (eds) *Economic and Monetary Union in Europe: Theory, Evidence and Practice*, Cheltenham: Edward Elgar.

Hagen, J. von and Brückner, M. (2002) 'Monetary Policy in Unknown Territory: The European Central Bank in the Early Years', *ZEI Working Paper*, B18.

Hagen, J. von and Wyplosz, C. (2008) 'EMU's Decentralized System of Fiscal Policy', *European Economy – Economic Papers*, no. 306, pp. 1–19.

Hahnel, R. (2005) *Economic Justice and Democracy: From Competition to Cooperation*, London: Routledge.

Haines, J. (1977) *The Politics of Power*, London: Jonathan Cape Ltd

Hale, S., Leggett, W. and Martell, L. (eds) (2004) *The Third Way and Beyond: Criticisms, Futures, Alternatives*, Manchester: Manchester University Press.

Halimi, S., Michie, J. and Milne, S. (1994) 'The Mitterrand Experience' in J. Michie and J. Grieve Smith (eds) *Unemployment in Europe*, London: Academic.

Hall, D., Cronin, B. and Catchpole, L. (2007) *Outsourcing and Offshoring: Implications for Organizational Capability*, London: Work Foundation.

Hall, P. (1986) *Governing the Economy*, Cambridge: Polity Press.

Hall, P. (1987) 'The Evolution of Economic Policy under Mitterrand' in G. Ross, S. Hoffmann and S. Malzacher (eds) *The Mitterrand Experiment: Continuity and Change in Modern France*, Cambridge: Polity Press.

Hall, P. and Franzese, R. (1998) 'Mixed Signals: Central Bank Independence, Coordinated Wage Bargaining and European Monetary Union', *International Organisation*, vol. 52, no. 3, pp. 505–35.

Hall, P. and Soskice, D. (eds) (2001) *Varieties of Capitalism: The Institutional Foundations of Comparative Advantage*, Oxford: Oxford University Press.

Halliday, F. (1983) *The Making of the Second World War*, London: Verso.

Halpern, L. and Wyplosz, C. (1996) 'Equilibrium Exchange Rates in Transition Economies', IMF Working Paper, 125.

Hammond, P. and Herman, E. (eds) (2000) *Degraded Capability: The Media and the Kosovo Crisis*, London: Pluto.

Hancké, B. (ed.) (2008) *Beyond Varieties of Capitalism: Conflict, Contradictions and Complementarities*, Oxford: Oxford University Press.

Hansson, A. (1987) *Politics, Institutions and Cross-country Inflation Differentials*, unpublished.

Hansson, B. (1991) 'The Stockholm School and the Development of the Dynamic Method', in B. Sandelin (ed.) *The History of Swedish Economic Thought*, London: Routledge, pp. 168–213.

Hantrais, L. (2007) *Social Policy in the European Union*, third edition, Basingstoke: Palgrave Macmillan.

Hardin, R. (1982) *Collective Action*, Baltimore, MD: Johns Hopkins Press.

Harmon, M. (1997) *The British Labour Government and the 1976 IMF Crisis*, Basingstoke: Macmillan.

Harrington, M. (1986) *The Next Left: The History of a Future*, New York: Henry Holt and Co.

Harrington, M. (1989) *Socialism: Past and Future*, New York: Little, Brown and Co.

Harvey, D. (2007) *A Brief History of Neo-liberalism*, Oxford: Oxford University Press.

Haseler, S. (2004) *Super-state: The New Europe and its Challenge to America*, London: IB Tauris

Hatfield, M. (1978) *The House the Left Built: Inside Labour Policy-making, 1970–1975*, London: Victor Gollancz.

Hau, H. (2011) 'Europe's €200 Billion Reverse Wealth Tax Explained', 28 July. Online, available at: www.social-europe.eu/2011/07/europes-e200-billion-reverse-wealth-tax-explained/ (accessed 1 August 2011).

Hawkes, A. (2011) 'ECB Intervention brings Short-term Relief in Volatile Day for Markets', *Guardian*, 8 August.

Hay, C. (1998) 'Globalisation, Welfare Retrenchment and the "Logic of No Alternative": Why Second Best won't do', *Journal of Social Policy*, vol. 27, no. 4, pp. 525–32.

Hay, C. (1999) *The Political Economy of New Labour: Labouring Under False Pretences?* Manchester: Manchester University Press.

Hay, C. (2010) 'Chronicles of a Death Foretold: The Winter of Discontent and Construction of the Crisis of British Keynesianism', *Parliamentary Affairs*, vol. 63, no. 3, pp. 446–70.

Hay, C. and Rosamond, B. (2002) 'Globalization, European Integration and the Discursive Construction of Economic Imperatives', *Journal of European Public Policy*, vol. 9, no. 2, pp. 147–67.

Hay, C., Watson, M. and Wincott, D. (1999) *Globalization, European Integration and the Persistence of European Social Models*, POLSIS Working Paper 3/99, Birmingham: University of Birmingham.

Hayek, F. von (1944) *The Road to Serfdom*, Abingdon: Routledge.

Hayek, F. von (1948) 'The Economic Conditions of Interstate Federalism' in F. von Hayek (ed.) *Individualism and Economic Order*, Chicago: University of Chicago Press.

Healey, D. (1990) *The Time of My Life*, London: Penguin Books.

Heidenreich, M. and Zeitlin, J. (2009) *Changing European Employment and Welfare Regimes: The Influence of the Open Method of Coordination on National Reforms*, Abingdon: Routledge.

Heise, A. and Lierse, H. (2011) *Budget Consolidation and the European Social Model: The Effects of European Austerity Programmes on Social Security Systems*, Berlin: Friedrich-Ebert-Stiftung.

Helleiner, E. (1994) *States and the Re-emergence of Global Finance: From Bretton Woods to the 1990s*, Ithaca, NY: Cornell University Press.

Helm, T. and Stewart, H. (2011) 'Calls for Referendum on EU Membership after David Cameron's U-turn on Tax', *Observer*, 14 August.

Hemerijck, A. (2002) 'The Self-transformation of the European Social Model(s)', *International Politics and Society*, vol. 4, pp. 1–24.

Hemming, R., Kell, M. and Mahfouz, S. (2002a) 'The Effectiveness of Fiscal Policy in Stimulating Economic Activity: A Review of the Literature', *IMF Working Paper no. 02/208*, Washington, DC: International Monetary Fund.

Henderson, D. (1998) *The Changing Fortunes of Economic Liberalism, Yesterday, Today and Tomorrow*, London: Institute of Economic Affairs.

Hendrickx, F. (ed.) (2008) *Flexicurity and the Lisbon Agenda: A Cross-Disciplinary Reflection*, Mortsel: Intersentia.

Herman, E. and Chomsky, N. (1988) *Manufacturing Consent: The Political Economy of the Mass Media*, New York: Pantheon.

Herman, E. and McChesney, R. (1997) *The Global Media: The New Missionaries of Corporate Capitalism*, London: Cassell.

Herman, E. and Peterson, D. (2007) 'The Dismantling of Yugoslavia: A Study in In-Humanitarian Intervention and a Western Liberal-Left Intellectual and Moral Collapse', *Monthly Review*, vol. 59, no. 5, pp. 1–64.

Hermann, C. and Hofbauer, I. (2007) 'The European Social Model: Between Competitive Modernization and Neo-liberal Resistance', *Capital and Class*, Special Issue 'The Left and Europe', no. 93, pp. 125–39.

Hettne, B. (1994) 'The Regional Factor in the Formation of a New World Order', in Y. Sakamoto (ed.) *Global Transformation: Challenges to the State System*, Tokyo: United Nations University, pp. 134–66.

Hettne, B. (ed.) (1995) *International Political Economy: Understanding Global Disorder*, London: Zed.

Hicks, A. (1999) *Social Democracy and Welfare Capitalism: A Century of Income Security Politics*, Ithaca, NY: Cornell University Press.

Hickson, K. (2005) *The IMF Crisis of 1976 and British Politics*, London: I.B. Tauris.

Hill, R. (2001) *The Labour Party and Economic Strategy 1979–1997: The Long Road Back*, London: Palgrave.

Hill, S. (2010) *Europe's Promise: Why the European Way is the Best Hope in an Insecure Age*, London: University of California Press.

Hirst, P. and Thompson, G. (1996) *Globalisation in Question: The International Economy and the Possibilities of Governance*, Cambridge: Polity Press.

Hirst, P. and Thompson, G. (2000a) *Globalization in Question: The International Economy and the Possibilities of Governance*, second edition, London: Polity Press.

Hirst, P. and Thompson, G. (2000b) 'Globalisation and the Future of the Nation State', in Higgott, R. and Payne, A. (eds) *The New Political Economy of Globalisation*, volume one, Cheltenham: Edward Elgar.

Hoffman, S. (1966) 'Obstinate or Obsolete? The Fate of the Nation State and the Case of Western Europe', *Daedalus*, vol. 95, no. 3, pp. 862–915.

Hogan, M. (1987) *The Marshall Plan: America, Britain and the Reconstruction of Western Europe, 1947–1952*, Cambridge: Cambridge University Press.

Hogan, M. (1998) *A Cross of Iron: Harry S. Truman and the Origins of the National Security State, 1945–1954*, Cambridge: Cambridge University Press.

Holland, S. (ed.) (1978) *Beyond Capitalist Planning*, Oxford: Basil Blackwell.

Holland, S. (ed.) (1983) *Out of Crisis: A Project for European Recovery*, Nottingham: Spokesman Books.

Holland, S. (1985) 'An Alternative European Strategy', *END Papers*, no. 11, Winter.

Holland, S. (1993) *The European Imperative: Economic and Social Cohesion in the 1990s*, Nottingham: Spokesman Books.

Holland, S. (1995) 'Squaring the Circle: the Maastricht Convergence Criteria, Cohesion and Employment', in K. Coates and S. Holland (eds) *Full Employment for Europe*, Spokesman, Nottingham.

Holland, S. (1997) 'Britain and Europe since 1945' Institute of Contemporary British History Lecture, 26 March (Stuart Holland Private Papers).

Holland, S. (2004) 'The Industrial Strategy' in A. Seldon and K. Hickson (eds) *New Labour, Old Labour: The Wilson and Callaghan Governments, 1974–1979*, London: Routledge.

Holland, S. (2011) 'Solid Reasons why Eurobonds can be Made to Work', Letter, *Financial Times*, 16 August.

Hollinger, P. (2011) 'Sarkozy Prepares for Cuts after Stall in Growth', *Financial Times*, 13 August.

Hollinger, P. and Milne, R. (2011) 'France Feels Pressure on Debt Targets', *Financial Times*, 10 August.

Hollinger, P., Bryant, C. and Peel, Q. (2011a) 'Berlin and Paris Rule Out Eurobond to Fix Crisis', *Financial Times*, 15 August.

Hollinger, P., Peel, Q. and Atkins, R. (2011b) 'Paris and Berlin Vow to Defend Euro', *Financial Times*, 17 August.

Hollingsworth, M. (1986) *The Press and Political Dissent: A Question of Censorship*, London: Pluto.

Holloway, J. (1995) 'Global Capital and the Nation State' in W. Bonefeld and J. Holloway (eds) *Global Capital, National State and the Politics of Money*, London: Macmillan.

Holloway, J. and Picciotto, S. (1978) *State and Capital: A Marxist Debate*, London: Edward Arnold.

Holloway, J. and Picciotto, S. (1980) 'Capital, the State and European Integration', *Research in Political Economy*, no. 3, pp. 123–54.

Holman, O. (1992) 'Transnational Class Strategy and the New Europe', *International Journal of Political Economy*, vol. 22, no. 1, pp. 3–22.

Holman, O. (1993a) 'Transnationalism in Spain: The Paradoxes of Socialist Rule in the 1980s' in H. Overbeek (ed.) *Restructuring Hegemony in the Global Political Economy: The Rise of Transnational Neo-liberalism in the 1980s*, Abingdon: Routledge.

Holman, O. (1993b) 'Internationalization and Democratization: Southern Europe, Latin America and the World Economic Crisis' in S. Gill (ed.) *Gramsci, Historical Materialism and International Relations*, Cambridge: Cambridge University Press.

Holman, O. (1996) *Integrating Southern Europe: EC Expansion and the Transnationalization of Spain*, Abingdon: Routledge.

Holman, O. (1998) 'Integrating Eastern Europe: EU Expansion and the Double Transformation in Poland, the Czech Republic and Hungary', *International Journal of Political Economy*, vol. 28, no. 2, pp. 12–43.

Holman, O. (2004) 'Asymmetrical Regulation and Multidimensional Governance in the EU', *Review of International Political Economy*, vol. 11, no. 4, pp. 714–35.

Hooper, J. (2011) 'Trichet Defends Spain and Italian Bond Purchases', *Guardian*, 10 August.

Hooper, J. and Willsher, K. (2011) 'European Central Bank Mounts Rescue for Italy and Spain – But Sets its Price', *Guardian*, 9 August.

Hope, K. (2011) 'Greek PM Urges Greater Effort on Fiscal Reform', *Financial Times*, 29 April.

Hopkin, J. and Wincott, D. (2006) 'New Labour, Economic Reform and the European Social Model', *British Journal of Politics and International Relations*, vol. 8, no. 1, pp. 50–68.

Hopkins, T. and Wallerstein, I. (eds) (1996) *The Age of Transition: Trajectory of the World-System, 1945–2025*, London: Zed Books.

Horn, G.A. and Zwiener, R. (1992) 'Wage Regimes in a United Europe', in R. Barell and J. Whitley (eds) *Macroeconomic Policy Co-ordination in Europe*, London: Sage, pp. 83–101.

House of Lords European Union Select Committee (2000) *How is the Euro Working? 18th Report*, London: Stationery Office.

House of Lords European Union Select Committee (2007) *Modernizing European Union Labour Law: Has the UK Anything to Gain?* 22nd Report, London: Stationery Office.

House of Lords European Union Select Committee (2010) Inquiry into Re-Launching the Single Market: Oral and Associated Written Evidence. Online, available at: www.parliament.uk/documents/lords-committees/eu-sub-com-b/singlemarketinquiry/singlemarketwo.pdf (accessed 20 March 2012)

Howell, D. (2010) 'Time for New Partners', in M. Baimbridge, P.B. Whyman and B. Burkitt (eds) *Britain in a Global World: Options for a New Beginning*, Exeter: Imprint Academic.

Huber, E. and Stephens, J. (2001) *Development and Crisis of the Welfare State: Parties and Politics in Global Markets*, London: University of Chicago Press.

Huffschimd, J. (2005) *Economic Policy for a Social Europe: A Critique of Neo-liberalism and Proposals for Alternatives*, Basingstoke: Palgrave Macmillan.

Hughes, M. (1994) *Spies at Work*, Bradford: 1 in 12 Publications. Online, available at: www.1in12events.co.uk/archive/publications/library/spies/spies.htm (accessed 21 September 2010).

Huizinga, H. (1993) 'International Market Integration and Union Wage Bargaining', *Scandinavian Journal of Economics*, vol. 95, no. 2, pp. 249–55.

Hutton, W. (1994) *The State We're In*, London: Cape.

Hyman, R. (2005) 'Trade Unions and the Politics of the European Social Model', *Economic and Industrial Democracy*, vol. 26, no. 1, pp. 9–40.

Ichniowski, C., Kochan, T.A. Levine, D., Olson, C. and Struss, G. (1996) 'What Works at Work: Overview and Assessment', *Industrial Relations*, vol. 35, pp. 299–333.

Ilzkovitz, F. (1996) *Challenges for the Monetary and Exchange Rate Policies of CECs: A European Perspective*, Proceedings of the Conference Central and Eastern Europe: Directing Monetary Policy Towards European Union Integration, Organised by the Gsterreichische Nationalbank and the Vienna Institute for Comparative Economic Studies.

ING (2010) 'EMU Break-up: Quantifying the Unthinkable', Global Economics Research Paper, 7 July, London: ING.

Ingham, G. (1984) *Capitalism Divided? The City and Industry in British Social Development*, Basingstoke: Macmillan.

Ingham, M. and Ingham, H. (eds) (2002) *EU Expansion to the East: Prospects and Problems*, Cheltenham: Edward Elgar.

Inman, P. (2011) 'Greece and Portugal Debts Worse than Expected', *Guardian*, 26 April.

Institute of Contemporary British History (1989) 'Symposium: The 1976 IMF Crisis', *Contemporary Record*, vol. 3, no. 2, pp. 39–45.

Institute of Directors (2010) *Don't Go Wobbly, George!* London: Institute of Directors.

International Journal of Political Economy (1998a) vol. 28, no. 1, Special Issue.

International Journal of Political Economy (1998b) vol. 28, no. 2, Special Issue.

International Labour Organization (1995a) *From Protection to Destitution*, Geneva: International Labour Organization.

International Labour Organization (1995b) 'Perspectives: Experience of Social Pacts in Western Europe', *International Labour Review*, vol. 134, no. 3, pp. 407–8.

International Labour Organization (2009) *The Financial and Economic Crisis: A Decent Work Response*, Geneva: International Labour Organization.

International Monetary Fund (1997) *World Economic Outlook*, Washington, DC: International Monetary Fund.

International Monetary Fund (2002) *Concluding Statement of the IMF Mission on the Economic Policies of the Euro Area – in the Context of the 2002 Article IV Consultation Discussions with the Euro Area Countries*, Washington, DC: International Monetary Fund.

International Monetary Fund (2007) *World Economic Outlook*, Washington, DC: International Monetary Fund.

International Monetary Fund (2010) *World Economic Outlook*, Washington, DC: International Monetary Fund.

Ipsos-MORI (2011) 'Business Leaders Show Overwhelming Support for the Coalition and Cuts', Press Release, 5 January. Online, available at: www.ipsos-mori.com/news-events/latestnews/621/Business-leaders-show-overwhelming-support-for-the-Coalition-and-cuts.aspx (accessed 24 May 2011).

Islam, F. (2011) 'The New Big Short – against the Euro, which Suggests France is Riskier than Panama', 15 August. Online, available at: http://blogs.channel4.com/faisal-islam-on-economics/the-new-big-short-against-the-euro-that-suggests-france-is-riskier-than-panama/14630 (accessed 16 August 2011).

Islam, F. and Keegan, W. (2002) 'Switch to Euro Cost Citizens €3bn', *Observer*, 3 February.

Issing, O., Gaspar, V., Angeloni, I. and Tristani, O. (2001) *Monetary Policy in the Euro Area: Strategy and Decision Making at the European Central Bank*, Cambridge: Cambridge University Press.

Italianer, A. and Vanheukelen, M. (1993) 'Proposals for Community Stabilisation Mechanisms: Some Historical Applications', in 'The Economics of Community Public Finance', *European Economy*, Reports and Studies, no. 5, pp. 495–510.

Iversen, T. (1999) *Contested Economic Institutions: The Politics of Macroeconomics and Wage Bargaining in Advanced Democracies*, Cambridge: Cambridge University Press.

Iversen, T. and Cusack, T. (2000) 'The Causes of Welfare State Expansion: Deindustrialization or Globalization?' *World Politics*, vol. 52, no. 3, pp. 313–49.

Jackman, R., Pissarides, C. and Savouri, S. (1990) 'Labour Market Policies and Unemployment in the OECD', *Economic Policy*, vol. 5, no. 2, pp. 449–90.

Jackson, J. (2009) 'The Financial Crisis: Impact on and Response by the European Union', Research Paper, 24 June, Washington, DC: Congressional Research Service.

Jacquemin, A. and Sapir, A. (1991) 'Europe Post-1992: Internal and External Liberalization', *American Economic Review*, vol. 81, no. 2, pp. 166–70.

Jacquemin, A. and Wright, D. (1993) 'Corporate Strategies and European Challenges Post-1992', *Journal of Common Market Studies*, vol. 31, no. 4, pp. 525–37.

Jaffa, M. and Cave, A. (2011) *An Agenda for Stability and Growth*, London: Federation of Small Businesses.

Jamieson, B. (1998) *Britain: Free to Choose*, London: Global Britain.

Janssen, R. (2010) 'Cuts, Austerity and Fiscal Pain: The Way into Prolonged Stagnation', Economic Discussion Note 2010/11, Brussels: European Trade Union Confederation.

Jarvis, V. and Prais, S.J. (1989) 'Two Nations of Shopkeepers', *National Institute Economic Review*, 128, May, 58–74.

Jay, D. (1990) *The European Monetary System: The ERM Illusion*, London: Labour Common Market Safeguards Committee.

Jeffers, P. (2009) *The Bilderberg Conspiracy: Inside the World's Most Powerful Secret Society*, New York: Citadel.

Jepsen, M. and Serrano Pascual, A. (eds) (2006) *Unwrapping the European Social Model*, Bristol: Policy Press.

Jespen, M. and Serrano Pascual, A. (2005) 'The European Social Model: An Exercise in Deconstruction', *Journal of European Social Policy*, vol. 15, no. 3, pp. 231–45.

Jessop, B. (1990) *State Theory: Putting the Capitalist State in its Place*, Cambridge: Polity Press.

Jessop, B. (2003) 'Changes in Welfare Regimes and the Search for Flexibility and Employability' in H. Overbeek (ed.) *The Political Economy of European Employment: European Integration and the Transnationalization of the (Un)employment Question*, Abingdon: Routledge.

Johnson, J. (2008) The Remains of Conditionality: The Faltering Enlargement of the Euro Zone, *Journal of European Public Policy*, vol. 15, no. 8, pp. 826–41.

Johnstone, D. (2002) *Fools' Crusade: Yugoslavia, NATO and Western Delusions*, London: Pluto.

Jorgensen, H. and Madsen, P. (eds) (2007) *Flexicurity and Beyond: Finding a New Agenda for the European Social Model*, Copenhagen: DJOF Publishing.

Jospin, L. (2002) *My Vision of Europe and Globalization*, Cambridge: Polity Press.

Jouen, M. (2001) 'How to Enhance Economic and Social Cohesion in Europe after 2006', Seminar Report, Brussels: *Notre Europe.*

Jouen, M. and Palpant, C. (2005a) 'Social Europe in the Throes of Enlargement', Policy Paper no. 15, Brussels: *Notre Europe.*

Jouen, M. and Palpant, C. (2005b) 'For a New European Social Contract', Studies and Research no. 43, Brussels: *Notre Europe.*

Judt, T. (2005) 'Europe versus America', *New York Review of Books*, 10 February.

Juncker, J.-C. and Tremonti, G. (2010) 'E-bonds would end the crisis', *Financial Times*, 5 December.

Kalecki, M. (1943) 'The Political Aspects of Full Employment', *Political Quarterly*, vol. 4, no. 14, pp. 322–31.

Kananen, J., Taylor-Gooby, P. and Larsen, T. (2006) 'Public Attitudes and New Social Risk Reform' in K. Armingeon and G. Bonoli (eds) *The Politics of Post-Industrial Welfare States: Adapting Post-war Social Policies to New Social Risks*, Abingdon: Routledge.

Kapstein, E. (1994) *Governing the Global Economy: International Finance and the State*, Cambridge, MA: Harvard University Press.

Karanassou, M. and Snower D. (1998) 'How Labour Market Flexibility affects Unemployment: Long-term Implications of the Chain Reaction Theory', *Economic Journal*, vol. 108, no. 448, pp. 832–49.

Katwala, S. and Stetter, E. (eds) (2011) *Europe's Left in the Crisis: How the Next Left can Respond*, London; Fabian Society/Foundation for European Progressive Studies.

Katzenstein, P. (1985) *Small States in World Markets: Industrial Policy in Europe*, Ithaca, NY: Cornell University Press.

Keane, J. (1987) 'Introduction' in C. Offe *Contradictions of the Welfare State*, third edition, Cambridge, MA: MIT Press.

Keller, B. and Sorries, B. (1997) 'The New Social Dialogue: Procedural Structuring, First Results and Perspectives', *Industrial Relations Journal* (European Annual Review), pp. 77–98.

Keman, H. (2003) 'Explaining Miracles: Third Ways and Work and Welfare', *West European Politics*, vol. 26, no. 2, pp. 115–35.

Kenen, P.B. (1969) 'The Theory of Optimum Currency Areas: An Eclectic View', in R. Mundell and A. Swoboda (eds) *Monetary Problems of the International Economy*, Chicago: University of Chicago Press.

Kenen, P.B. (1995) *Economic and Monetary Union in Europe: Moving Beyond Maastricht*, Cambridge: Cambridge University Press.

Kenen, P.B. (1995) 'What Have We Learned from the EMS Crises?', *Journal of Policy Modelling*, vol. 17, no. 5, pp. 449–61.

Kenner, J. (2000) 'The Paradox of the Social Dimension', in P. Lynch, N. Neuwahl and W. Rees (eds) *Reforming the European Union: From Maastricht to Amsterdam*, Harlow@ Pearson, pp. 108–29.

Kersbergen, K. van (2000) 'The Declining Resistance of Welfare States to Change' in S. Kuhnle (ed.) (2000) *Survival of the European Welfare State*, Abingdon: Routledge.

Keuschnigg, C., Keuschnigg, M. and Kohler, W. (1999) *Eastern Enlargement to the EU: Economic Costs and Benefits for the EU Present Member States?*, Luxembourg: EU Commission Study XIX/B1/9801.

Keynes, J.M. (1936) *The General Theory of Employment, Interest and Money*, London: Macmillan.

Kidron, M. (1970) *Western Capitalism since the War*, Harmondsworth: Pelican.

Kinnock, N. (1984) 'A New Deal for Europe', *New Socialist*, March.

Kirkegaard, J. (2005) 'Outsourcing and Offshoring: Pushing the European Model over the Hill Rather than Off the Cliff', Working Paper WP05–1, Washington, DC: Institute for International Economics.

Kitschelt, H. (2001) 'Partisan Competition and Welfare State Retrenchment – When Do Politicians Choose Unpopular Policies?', in P. Pierson (ed.) *The New Politics of the Welfare State*, Oxford: Oxford University Press.

Kittel, B. and Obinger, H. (2003) 'Political Parties, Institutions and Welfare State Dynamics in Times of Austerity', *Journal of European Public Policy*, vol. 10, no. 1, pp. 20–45.

Klaeffling M. and Lopez-Perez, V. (2003) *Inflation Targets and the Liquidity Trap*. Background Study for ECB Governing Council, Frankfurt: ECB.

Klare, M. and Kornbluh, P. (eds) (1988) *Low Intensity Warfare: Counter-insurgency, Pro-insurgency and Anti-terrorism in the Eighties*, New York: Pantheon.

Klein, L. and Pomer, M. (2001) *The New Russia: Transition Gone Awry*, Stanford, CA: Stanford University Press.

Klein, N. (2008) *The Shock Doctrine: The Rise of Disaster Capitalism*, London: Penguin.

Kleinman, M. (2002) *A European Welfare State? European Union Social Policy in Context*, Basingstoke: Palgrave.

Knottnerus, R. and Esteban, A. (2007) *From Washington Consensus to Vienna Consensus? The EU's Free Trade Agenda for Latin America and the Caribbean*, Amsterdam: Transnational Institute.

Kok, W. (2003) *Enlarging the European Union: Achievements and Challenges*, Report to the European Commission, Florence: European University Institute.

Kolko, G. (1988) *Confronting the Third World: United States Foreign Policy, 1945–1980*, New York: Pantheon.

Kollowe, J. (2010) 'Central Bank Chief: Euro Crisis is Worst since the War', *Observer*, 16 May.

Kopits, G. (1999) 'Implications of EMU for Exchange Rate Policy in Central and Eastern Europe', *IMF Working Paper*, WP/99/9.

Korkman, S. (2001) 'Should Fiscal Policy Co-ordination go beyond the SGP?', in A. Brunila, M. Buti and D. Franco (eds) *The Stability and Growth Pact: The Architecture of Fiscal Policy in EMU*, London: Palgrave Macmillan.

Korpi, W. (1983) *The Democratic Class Struggle*, Abingdon: Routledge and Kegan Paul.

Korpi, W. (1985) 'Economic Growth and the Welfare System: Leaky Bucket or Irrigation System?', *European Sociological Review*, vol. 1, pp. 97–118.

Korpi, W. (1996) 'Eurosclerosis and the Sclerosis of Objectivity: On the Role of Values among Economic Policy Experts', *Economic Journal*, vol. 106, no. 439, pp. 1727–46.

Korpi, W. (2003) 'Welfare State Regress in Western Europe: Politics, Institutions, Globalization and Europeanization', *Annual Review of Sociology*, vol. 29, pp. 589–609.

Korpi, W. and Palme, J. (2003) 'New Politics and Class Politics in the Context of Austerity and Globalization: Welfare State Regress in 18 Countries, 1975–1995', *American Political Science Review*, vol. 97, no. 3, pp. 425–46.

Kovács, M. (2004) 'Disentangling the Balassa-Samuelson Effect in CEC5 Countries in the Prospect of EMU Enlargement', in G. Szapáry and J. von Hagen (eds) *Monetary Strategies for Joining the Euro*, Cheltenham: Edward Elgar, pp. 79–105.

Kregel, J., Matzner, E. and Grabher, G. (1992) *Market Shock: An Agenda for Economic and Social Reconstruction of Central and Eastern Europe*, Ann Arbor: University of Michigan Press.

Kröger, S. (2009) 'The Open Method of Coordination: Under-conceptualization, Over-determination, De-politicization and Beyond' in S. Kröger (ed.) 'What We Have Learnt: Advances, Pitfalls and Remaining Questions in OMC Research', *European Integration Online Papers*, Special Issue 1, vol. 13, Article 5.

Kuhnle, S. (1999) 'Survival of the European Welfare State', Working Paper 99/19, Oslo: University of Oslo ARENA Centre for European Studies.

Kuhnle, S. (ed.) (2000) *Survival of the European Welfare State*, Abingdon: Routledge.

Kupchan, C. (2002) 'The End of the West' *Atlantic Monthly*, vol. 290, no. 4, pp. 42–4.

Kvist, J. and Saari, J. (eds) (2007) *The Europeanization of Social Protection*, Bristol: Policy Press.

Kydland, F.E. and Prescott, E.C. (1977) 'Rules rather than Discretion: The Time Inconsistency of Optimal Plans', *Journal of Political Economy*, vol. 85, pp. 473–99.

Labour Party (1973) *Labour's Programme for Britain*, London: Labour Party.

Labour Party (1976) *Annual Conference Report*, London: Labour Party.

Labour Party (1979) *General Election Manifesto*, London: Labour Party.

Ladrech, R. (1998) 'Towards a Social Europe? Policy Issues and the French Socialist Government', Paper Presented at the Political Studies Association Annual Conference, Keele, 7 April.

LaFaber, W. (1984) *Inevitable Revolutions: The United States in Central America*, New York: W.W. Norton and Co.

Lafontaine, O. (2000) *The Heart Beats on the Left*, Cambridge: Polity Press.

Larosière, J. de (2009) 'High-level Group on Financial Supervision in the EU', Brussels: European Commission.

Larraín, F. and Velasco, A. (2002) 'How Should Emerging Economies Float their Currencies?', *The Economics of Transition*, vol. 10, no. 2, pp. 365–92.

Lash, S. and Urry, J. (1987) *The End of Organised Capitalism*, Oxford: Polity Press.

Lashmar, P. and Oliver, J. (1998) *Britain's Secret Propaganda War, 1948–1977*, Stroud: Sutton.

Latham, P. (2001) 'The Captive Local State: Local Democracy under Siege', *Socialist Renewal*, Second Series, no. 6, Nottingham: Spokesman.

Lauk, K. (2009) 'The European Social Model: In Urgent Need of Redefinition', *European View*, vol. 8, pp. 53–63.

Lavrac, V. (1999) 'Inclusion of Central European Countries in the European Monetary Integration Process', in P. de Grauwe, and V. Lavrac (eds) *Inclusion of Central European Countries in the European Monetary Union*, London: Kluwer.

Lawrence, R. and Schultz, C. (1987) (eds) *Barriers to European Growth: A Transatlantic View*, Washington, DC: Brookings Institution.

Layard, R., Nickell, S. and Jackman, R. (1991) *Unemployment: Macroeconomic Performance and the Labour Market*, Oxford: Oxford University Press.

Leach, G. (2000) 'EU Membership – What's the Bottom Line?' Policy Paper, London: Institute of Directors.

Le Cacheux, J. (2005) 'The European Budget', Studies and Research no. 41, Brussels: *Notre Europe.*

Le Cacheux, J. (2007) 'Funding the EU Budget with a Genuine Own Resource: The Case for a European Tax', Studies and Research no. 57, Brussels: *Notre Europe.*

Leffler, M. (1992) *A Preponderance of Power: National Security, the Truman Administration and the Cold War*, Stanford: Stanford University Press.

Leibfried, S. (1993) 'Towards a European Welfare State?' in C. Jones (ed.) *New Perspectives on the Welfare State*, Abingdon: Routledge.

Leibfried, S. (2005) 'Social Policy: Left to Courts and Markets?' in H. Wallace, W. Wallace and M. Pollack (eds) *Policy-making in the European Union*, fifth edition, Oxford: Oxford University Press.

Leibfried, S. and Pierson, P. (1995a) 'The Dynamics of Social Policy Integration', in S. Leibfried and P. Pierson (eds) *Fragmented Social Policy: the European Community's Social Dimension in Comparative Perspective*, Washington, DC: Brookings Institution.

Leibfried, S. and Pierson, P. (eds) (1995b) *European Social Policy: Between Fragmentation and Integration*, Washington, DC: Brookings Institution.

Leigh, D. (1988) *The Wilson Plot*, New York: Pantheon.

Lemke, C. (2001) 'Social Citizenship and Institution Building: EU-Enlargement and the Restructuring of Welfare States in East Central Europe', *Centre for European Studies Working Paper Series*, 01.2.

Leonard, M. (2005) *Why Europe will Run the 21st Century*, London: Fourth Estate.

Levy, J. (1999) 'Vice onto Virtue? Progressive Politics and Welfare Reform in Continental Europe', *Politics and Society*, vol. 27, no. 2, pp. 239–73.

Lewis, W. (1971) *Rome or Brussels? An Economist's Comparative Analysis of the Development of the European Community and the Aims of the Treaty of Rome*, London: Institute of Economic Affairs.

Lightfoot, W. (2010) *Sorry, We Have No Money: Britain's Economic Problem*, London: Searching Finance.

Lindbeck, A. (1995) 'Hazardous Welfare State Dynamics', *American Economic Review*, vol. 85, no. 2, pp. 9–15.

Lindbeck, A. and Snower, D.J. (1988) *The Insider–Outsider Theory of Employment and Unemployment*, Cambridge MA: MIT Press.

Lindbeck, A., Molander, P., Persson, T., Petersson, O., Sandmo, A., Swedenborg, B. and Thygesen, N. (1994) *Turning Sweden Around*, London: MIT Press.

Lindberg, L. (1963) *The Political Dynamics of European Economic Integration*, Stanford: Stanford University Press.

Lindert, P. (2004a) *Growing Public Volume 1: Social Spending and Economic Growth since the Eighteenth Century*, Cambridge: Cambridge University Press.

Lindert, P. (2004b) *Growing Public Volume 2: Social Spending and Economic Growth since the Eighteenth Century*, Cambridge: Cambridge University Press.

Lipietz, A. (1987) *Mirages and Miracles: Crisis in Global Fordism*, London: Verso.

Lipietz, A. (1992) *Towards a New Economic Order: Post-Fordism, Ecology and Democracy*, Oxford: Oxford University Press.

Liptak, A. (2010) 'Justices, 5–4, Reject Corporate Spending Limit', *New York Times*, 21 January.

Lloyd, J. (1994) 'How to Make a Market', *London Review of Books*, vol. 16, no. 21, 10 November.

Local Futures (2010) 'Barometer: The Geography of Public Sector Cuts', July. Online, available at: www.localfutures.com/Assets/3949/public%20sector%20employment%20 barometer.pdf (accessed 4 October 2010).

Lombard, M. (1995) 'A Re-examination of the Reasons for the Failure of the Keynesian Expansionary Policies in France 1981–1983', *Cambridge Journal of Economics*, vol. 19, no. 2, pp. 359–72.

London Conference of Socialist Economists (1979) 'Crisis, the Labour Movement and the Alternative Economic Strategy', *Capital and Class*, no. 8, pp. 68–92.

London Conference of Socialist Economists (1980) *The Alternative Economic Strategy: A Labour Movement Response to the Economic Crisis*, London: CSE Books.

Lordon, F. (1998) 'The Logic and Limits of *Désinflation Competitive*', *Oxford Review of Economic Policy*, vol. 14, no. 1, pp. 96–113.

Lowenthal, A. (1991) *Exporting Democracy: The United States and Latin America – Themes and Issues*, Baltimore: Johns Hopkins University Press.

Lucas, R. (1976) 'Econometric Policy Evaluation: A Critique', in K. Brunner and A. Meltzer (eds) *Carnegie-Rochester Series in Public Policy*, Amsterdam: North-Holland.

Lucas, C. and Hines, C. (2000) *From Seattle to Nice: Challenging the Free Trade Agenda at the Heart of Enlargement*, Brussels: Green Party/European Free Alliance.

Ludlam, S. (1992) 'The Gnomes of Washington: Four Myths of the 1976 IMF Crisis', *Political Studies*, vol. 40, no. 4, pp. 713–27.

Lumley, R. (1996) 'Labour Markets and Employment Relations in Transition: The Case of German Unification', *Employee Relations*, vol. 17, no. 1, pp. 24–37.

Lundestad, G. (1998) *'Empire by Integration': The United States and European Integration, 1945–1997*, Oxford: Oxford University Press.

Macartney, H. (2011) *Variegated Neo-liberalism: EU Varieties of Capitalism and International Political Economy*, London: Routledge.

McChesney, R. (1999) *Rich Media, Poor Democracy: Communication Politics in Dubious Times*, Chicago: University of Illinois Press.

McChesney, R., Meiksins Wood, E. and Bellamy Foster, J. (eds) (1998) *Capitalism and the Information Age: The Political Economy of the Global Communication Revolution*, New York: Monthly Review Press.

McClintock, M. (1992) *Instruments of Statecraft: US Guerrilla Warfare, Counter-insurgency and Counter-terrorism, 1940–1990*, New York: Pantheon Books.

McCormick, J. (2007) *The European Superpower*, Basingstoke: Palgrave Macmillan.

McCormick, J. (2010) *Europeanism*, Oxford: Oxford University Press.

MacDougall, D. (1977) *The Role of Public Finance in the European Communities*, Luxembourg: Office for the Official Publications of the European Communities.

MacDougall, D. (1992) 'Economic and Monetary Union and the European Community Budget', *National Institute Economic Review*, May, pp. 64–8.

Machin, H. and Wright, V. (1985) (eds) *Economic Policy and Policy-making under the Mitterrand Presidency, 1981–1984*, London: Frances Pinter.

McKenzie, R. (1955) *British Political Parties: The Distribution of Power with the Conservative and Labour Parties*, London: Heinemann.

McKinnon, R. (1996) *Default Risk in Monetary Union*, Background report for the Swedish government commission on EMU, Stockholm.

McKinnon, R. (2003) 'Monetary Regimes, Collective Fiscal Retrenchment and the Political Economy of EMU', in M. Baimbridge and P. Whyman (eds) *Economic and Monetary Union in Europe: Theory, Evidence and Practice*, Cheltenham: Edward Elgar.

McNeill, W. (1982) *The Pursuit of Power: Technology, Armed Force and Society since AD1000*, Chicago: University of Chicago Press.

MacRae, C.D. (1977) 'A Political Model of the Business Cycle', *Journal of Political Economy*, vol. 85, pp. 239–63.

McRae, S. (2005) *Hidden Voices: The CBI, Corporate Lobbying and Sustainability*, London: Friends of the Earth.

Madsen, J. (1998) 'General Equilibrium Macroeconomic Models of Unemployment: Can They Explain the Unemployment Path in the OECD?', *Economic Journal*, vol. 108, pp. 850–67.

Madsen, P. (2008) 'Flexicurity in Denmark: A Model for Labour Market Reforms in the EU?', in W. Bienkowski, J. Brada and M. Radlo (eds) *Growth Versus Security: Old and New EU Members' Quest for a New Economic and Social Model*, Basingstoke: Palgrave Macmillan.

Mahnkopf, B. (2008) 'EU Multi-level Trade Policy: Neither Coherent nor Development-Friendly', Global Labour University Working Paper no. 2, Kassal: University of Kassal.

Maier, C. (1987) *In Search of Stability: Explorations in Historical Political Economy*, Cambridge: Cambridge University Press.

Majocchi, A. and Rey, (1993) 'A Special Financial Support Scheme in Economic and Monetary Union: Need and Nature', in 'The Economics of Community Public Finance', *European Economy*, Reports and Studies, no. 5, pp. 459–80.

Majone, G. (1993) 'The European Community between Social Policy and Social Regulation', *Journal of Common Market Studies*, vol. 31, no. 2, pp. 153–70.

Majone, G. (1996) *Regulating Europe*, London: Routledge.

Major, J. (1999) *John Major: The Autobiography*, London: HarperCollins.

Mallet, V. and Dinmore, G. (2011) 'Negative Effects', *Financial Times*, 9 June.

Mangano, G. (1998) 'Measuring Central Bank Independence: A Tale of Subjectivity and of its Consequences', *Oxford Economic Papers*, vol. 50, no. 3, pp. 468–92.

Mankelow, R. (2002) 'The Organisational Costs of Job Insecurity and Work Intensification', in B. Burchell, D. Ladipo and F. Wilkinson (eds) *Job Insecurity and Work Intensification*, London: Routledge, pp. 137–53.

Mann, M. (1996) 'Ruling Class Strategies and Citizenship' in M. Bulmer and A. Rees (eds) *Citizenship Today: The Contemporary Relevance of T.H. Marshall*, London: UCL Press.

Manning, N. (2004) 'Diversity and Change in Pre-accession Central and Eastern Europe since 1989', *Journal of European Social Policy*, vol. 14, no. 3, pp. 211–32.

Marginson, P. and Sisson, K. (1996) 'Multinational Companies and the Future of Collective Bargaining: A Review of the Research Issues', *European Journal of Industrial Relations*, vol. 2, no. 2, pp. 173–97.

Marginson, P. and Sisson, K. (2002) 'European Integration and Industrial Relations: A Case of Convergence *and* Divergence?' *Journal of Common Market Studies*, vol. 40, no. 4, pp. 671–92.

Marquand, D. (1999) 'Premature Obsequies: Social Democracy comes in from the Cold', in A. Gamble and T. Wright (eds) *The New Social Democracy*, Oxford: Blackwell.

Marsden, D. (1992) 'Incomes Policy for Europe? Or Will Pay Bargaining Destroy the Single European Market?', *British Journal of Industrial Relations*, vol. 30, no. 4, pp. 587–604.

Marsh, D. (2009) 'France, Germany and Fissures in the Eurozone', *Financial Times*, 12 January.

Marshall, T. (1950) *Citizenship and Social Class and Other Essays*, Cambridge: Cambridge University Press.

Martin, A. and Ross, G. (2004) *Euros and Europeans: Monetary Integration and the European Model of Society*, Cambridge: Cambridge University Press.

Martin, C. (2004) 'Reinventing Welfare Regimes: Employers and the Implementation of Active Social Policy', *World Politics*, vol. 57, no. 1, pp. 39–69.

Martin, H. and Schumann, H. (1997) *The Global Trap: Globalization and the Assault on Democracy and Prosperity*, London: Zed.

Marx, K. (1977 [1859]) *A Contribution to the Critique of Political Economy*, Moscow: Progress Publishers.

Masson, P.R. (1996) 'Fiscal Dimensions of EMU', *Economic Journal*, vol. 106, no. 437, pp. 996–1004.

Masson, P.R. (1999) Monetary and Exchange Rate Policy of Transition Economies of Central and Eastern Europe after the Launch of EMU, *IMF Policy Discussion Paper*, PDP/99/5.

Masson, P.R. and Melitz, J. (1990) 'Fiscal Policy Independence in a European Monetary Union', *Open Economies Review*, vol. 2.

Masson, P.R. and Taylor, M.P. (1993) 'Common Currency Areas and Currency Unions: An Analysis of the Issues, Parts I and II', *Journal of International and Comparative Economics*, vol. 1, no. 3–4, pp. 231–94.

Mathers, A. (2007) *Struggling for a Social Europe: Neo-Liberal Globalisation and the Birth of a European Social Movement*, Aldershot: Ashgate.

Mattera, P. (1992) *World Class Business: A Guide to the 100 Most Powerful Global Corporations*, New York: Henry Holt and Co.

Mau, V. (1994) 'Russia', in J. Williamson (ed.) *The Political Economy of Policy Reform*, Washington, DC: Institute for International Economics.

Mayhew, A. (1998) *Recreating Europe: European Union's Policy towards Central and Eastern Europe*, Cambridge: Cambridge University Press.

Meidner, R. (1993) 'Why did the Swedish Model Fail?' *Socialist Register*, pp. 211–18.

Melitz, J. (1997) 'The Evidence about the Costs and Benefits of EMU', *Swedish Economic Policy Review*, vol. 4, pp. 359–410.

Melman, S. (1970) *Pentagon Capitalism: The Political Economy of War*, New York: McGraw-Hill.

Merkel, A. (2010) 'Protecting the Euro to Preserve the European Vision', German Government Statement, 19 May. Online, available at: www.bundeskanzlerin.de (accessed 16 June 2010).

Miaouli, N. (2001) 'Employment and Capital Accumulation in Unionised Labour Markets', *International Review of Applied Economics*, vol. 15, no. 1, pp. 5–30.

Michie, J. (2000) 'The Economic Consequences of EMU for Britain', in Baimbridge, M., Burkitt, B. and Whyman, P. (eds) *The Impact of the Euro: Debating Britain's Future*, London: Macmillan.

Michie, J. and Grieve Smith, J. (eds) (1994) *Unemployment in Europe*, London: Academic Press.

Micklewright, J. and Stewart, K. (1999) 'Is the Well-being of Children Converging in the European Union?' *Economic Journal*, no. 109, pp. 692–714.

Middlemas, K. (1979) *Politics in Industrial Society: The Experience of the British System since 1911*, London: André Deutsch.

Middlemas, K. (1986) *Power, Competition and the State – Volume 1: Britain in Search of Balance*, Basingstoke: Palgrave.

Middleton, R. (1996) *Government versus the Market: The Growth of the Public Sector, Economic Management and British Economic Performance, c.1890–1979*, Cheltenham: Edward Elgar.

Mill, J.S. (2005 [1859]) *On Liberty*, London: Penguin.

Miller, D. and Dinan, W. (2008) *A Century of Spin: How Public Relations Became the Cutting Edge of Corporate Power*, London: Pluto.

Miller, H. (2001) 'Hard Sell for the Euro', *Observer*, 24 June.

Mills, J. (1998) *Europe's Economic Dilemma*, Basingstoke: Macmillan.

Milward, A. (1984) *The Reconstruction of Western Europe, 1945–1951*, Berkeley: University of California Press.

Milward, A. (1994) *The European Rescue of the Nation-state*, Abingdon: Routledge.

Minford, P. (1990) 'Rational Expectations and Monetary Policy', in T. Bandyopadhyay and S. Ghatak (eds) *Current Issues in Monetary Economics*, London: Harvester Wheatsheaf, pp. 233–52.

Minford, P. (2000) 'The Single Currency – Will it Work and Should we Join?',; in M. Baimbridge, B. Burkitt and P. Whyman (eds) *The Impact of the Euro: Debating Britain's Future*, London: Macmillan.

Minford, P. (2002) *Should Britain Join The Euro?*, London: Institute of Economic Affairs.

Minkin, L. (1980) *The Labour Party Conference: A Case Study in Intra-party Democracy*, Manchester: Manchester University Press.

Minsky, H. (1985) 'The Financial Instability Hypothesis: A Restatement', in P. Arestis and T. Skouras (eds) *Post Keynesian Economic Theory: A Challenge to Neo-Classical Economics*, Sussex: Wheatsheaf.

Mishel, L., Bernstein, J. and Schmitt, J. (1999) *The State of Working America*, Ithaca, NY: Cornell University Press.

Mishra, R. (1977) *Society and Social Policy: Theoretical Perspectives on Welfare*, Basingstoke: Macmillan.

Mishra, R. (1990) *The Welfare State in Capitalist Society*, Hemel Hempstead: Harvester Wheatsheaf.

Mishra, R. (1998) 'Beyond the Nation-state: Social Policy in an Age of Globalization', *Social Policy and Administration*, vol. 32, no. 5, pp. 481–500.

Mishra, R. (1999) *Globalisation and the Welfare State*, Cheltenham: Edward Elgar.

Missale, A. (2001) 'How Should the Debt be Managed? Supporting the Stability Pact', in A. Brunila, M. Buti and D. Franco (eds) *The Stability and Growth Pact: The Architecture of Fiscal Policy in EMU*, Palgrave Macmillan, London.

Mitchell, W. and Muysken, J. (2006) 'The Brussels–Frankfurt Consensus: An Answer to the Wrong Question', in W. Mitchell, J. Muysken and T. Van Veen (eds) *Growth and Cohesion in the European Union: The Impact of Macroeconomic Policy*, Cheltenham: Edward Elgar, pp. 3–31.

Mitchell, W.F. (1998) 'Macroeconomic Policy in Australia 1983–1996', *Centre for Full Employment and Equity Working Paper no. 98–03*, New South Wales: University of Newcastle.

Moller, S., Bradley, D., Huber, E., Nielsen, F. and Stephens, J.D. (2003) 'Determinants of Relative Poverty in Advanced Capitalist Democracies', *American Sociological Review*, vol. 68, pp. 22–51.

Mommen, A. (1993) 'The Neo-liberal Experiment and the Decline of the Belgian Bourgeoisie' in H. Overbeek (ed.) *Restructuring Hegemony in the Global Political Economy: The Rise of Transnational Neo-liberalism in the 1980s*, Abingdon: Routledge.

Monbiot, G. (2000) *Captive State: The Corporate Takeover of Britain*, Basingstoke: Macmillan.

Monnet, J. (1978) *Memoirs*, London: Collins.

Monperrus-Veroni, P. and Saraceno, F. (2006) 'Whither Stability Pact? An Assessment of Reform Proposals', in W. Mitchell, J. Muysken and T. Van Veen (eds) *Growth and Cohesion in the European Union: The Impact of Macroeconomic Policy*, Cheltenham: Edward Elgar, pp. 32–56.

Montanari, I. (2001) 'Modernization, Globalization and the Welfare State: A Comparative Analysis of Old and New Convergence of Social Insurance since 1930', *British Journal of Sociology*, vol. 52, no. 3, pp. 469–94.

Montanari, I., Nelson, K. and Palme, J. (2008) 'Towards a European Social Model? Trends in Social Insurance among EU Countries, 1980–2000', *European Societies*, vol. 10, no. 5, pp. 787–810.

Monti, M. (2011) 'Eurobonds are the Only Answer', *Financial Times*, 21 July.

Moore, B. (1966) *Social Origins of Dictatorship and Democracy: Lord and Peasant in the Making of Modern World*, Boston, MA: Beacon Press.

Moran, M. (1981) 'Finance Capital and Pressure Group Politics in Britain', *British Journal of Political Science*, vol. 11, no. 4, pp. 381–404.

Moravcsik, A. (1993) 'Preferences and Power in the European Community: A Liberal Intergovernmentalist Approach', *Journal of Common Market Studies*, vol. 31, no. 4, pp. 473–524.

Moravcsik, A. (1997) 'Taking Preferences Seriously: A Liberal Theory of International Politics', *International Organization*, vol. 54, no. 1, pp. 513–53.

Moravcsik, A. (1998) *The Choice for Europe: Social Purpose and State Power from Messina to Maastricht*, Ithaca, NY: Cornell University Press.

Morgan, K. (1985) *Labour in Power, 1945–1951*, Oxford: Oxford University Press.

Morrell, F. (1985) 'AES: The Alternative European Strategy', *New Socialist*, October.

Morrell, F. (1988) 'Beyond One-nation Socialism: An Agenda for the European Left', *Political Quarterly*, vol. 59, no. 3, pp. 300–10.

Muet, P.-A. (1997) 'Lack of Economic Growth and Unemployment: The Costs of Non-cooperation', Studies and European Issues no. 1, Brussels: *Notre Europe.*

Mulaj, I. (2005) 'Delayed Privatization in Kosovo: Causes, Consequences and Implications' in S. Kusic (ed.) *Path-dependent Development in the Western Balkans: The Impact of Privatization*, Frankfurt: Peter Lang.

Mullally, L. and O'Brien, N. (eds) (2006) *Beyond the European Social Model*, London: Open Europe.

Mullen, A. (2007) *The British Left's 'Great Debate' on Europe*, London: Continuum.

Mullen, A. (forthcoming) *Anti- and Pro-European Propaganda in Britain*, London: Continuum.

Mundschenk, S., Stierle, M.H., Stierle-von Schutz, U. and Traistaru, I. (2006) 'Competitiveness and Growth in Europe: An Overview', in S. Mundschenk, M.H. Stierle, U. Stierle-von Schutz and I. Traistaru (eds) *Competitiveness and Growth in Europe: Lessons and Policy Implications for the Lisbon Treaty*, Cheltenham: Edward Elgar, pp. 3–12.

Muscatelli, V.A. (1998) 'Political consensus, uncertain preferences, and central bank independence', *Oxford Economic Papers*, vol. 50, no. 3, pp. 412–30.

Myrdal, G. (1927) *Prisbildningsproblemet och föränderligheten* [The Price Determination Problem and Variability], Uppsala and Stockholm: Almqvist and Wiksell.

Myrdal, G. (1957) *Economic Theory and Underdeveloped Regions*, London: Duckworth.

Nanto, D. (2009) 'The Global Financial Crisis: Analysis and Policy Implications', Washington, DC: Congressional Research Service.

National Security Council (1948a) NSC1/3, 'Position of the United States with Respect to Italy', 8 March, *Foreign Relations of the United States*, vol. III, p. 775.

National Security Council (1948b) NSC-20/4, 'US Objectives with Respect to the USSR to Counter Soviets Threats to US Security', 23 November, *Foreign Relations, 1948*, vol. I, p. 546.

National Security Council (1950) 'United States Objectives and Programs for National Security', NSC-68, 7 April. Online, available at: www.fas.org (accessed 1 June 2010).

National Security Council (1954) NSC-5432, 'US Policy towards Latin America', *Foreign Relations, 1952–1954*, vol. IV, p. 83.

Navarro, V, Schmitt, J. and Astudillo, J. (2004) 'Is Globalization Undermining the Welfare State?' *Cambridge Journal of Economics*, vol. 28, no. 1, pp. 133–52.

Naylor, R. (1999) 'Union Wage Strategies and International Trade', *Economic Journal*, vol. 109, pp. 102–25.

Neate, R., Willsher, K. and Garside, J. (2011) 'French Bank Shares Slump as Rumours Swirl around SocGen', *Guardian*, 11 August.

Neergaard, U., Nielsen, R. and Roseberry, L. (eds) (2008) *The Services Directive: Consequences for the Welfare State and the European Social Model*, Copenhagen: DJOF Publishing.

Nelson, K. (2008) 'Is There a Convergence on Social Policy in the European Union? Minimum Income Protection and European Integration: Trends and Levels of Minimum Benefits in Comparative Perspective, 1990–2005', *International Journal of Health Services*, vol. 38, no. 1, pp. 103–24.

Neubourg, C. de, and Castonguay, J. (2006) 'Enhancing Productivity: Social Protection as Investment Policy', in Mitchell, W., Muysken, J. and Van Veen, T. (eds) *Growth and Cohesion in the European Union: The Impact of Macroeconomic Policy*, Cheltenham: Edward Elgar, pp. 180–205.

Neville, J.W. (2000) 'Can Keynesian Policies Stimulate Growth in Output and Employment?', in S. Bell (ed.) *The Unemployment Crisis in Australia: Which Way Out?*, Cambridge: Cambridge University Press, pp. 149–75.

Newton, S. (1984) 'The Sterling Crisis of 1947 and the British Response to the Marshall Plan', *Economic History Review*, vol. 37, no. 1, pp. 391–408.

Newton, S. and Porter, D. (1988) *Modernization Frustrated: The Politics of Industrial Decline in Britain since 1900*, London: Unwin Hyman.

Nickell, S. (1998) 'Unemployment: Questions and Some Answers', *Economic Journal*, vol. 108, no. 448, pp. 802–16.

Nickell, S. and Layard, R. (1999) 'Labour Market Institutions and Economic Performance', in O. Ashenfelter and D. Card (eds) *Handbook of Labour Economics – vol. 3*, Amsterdam: North Holland.

No Campaign (2002) *No Campaign Bulletin*, 10–18 October, London: No Campaign.

Nollert, M. and Fielder, N. (2000) 'Lobbying for a Europe of Big Business: the European Roundtable of Industrialists' in V. Bornschier (ed.) *State-building in Europe: The Revitalization of Western European Integration*, Cambridge: Cambridge University Press.

Nordhaus, W.D. (1975) 'The Political Business Cycle', *Review of Economic Studies*, no. 42, pp. 169–90.

Norris, J. (2005) *Collision Course: NATO, Russia and Kosovo*, New York: Praeger.

North, D. (1990) *Institutions, Institutional Change and Economic Performance*, Cambridge: Cambridge University Press.

Norton-Taylor, R. (1990) 'The Gladio file', *Guardian*, 5 December.

Notermans, T. (2000) 'Europeanisation and the Crisis of Scandinavian Social Democracy', in R. Geyer, C. Ingebritsen and J.W. Moses (eds) *Globalisation, Europeanisation and the End of Social Democracy?*, London: Macmillan, pp. 23–44.

Nousios, P., Overbeek, H. and Tsolakis, A. (eds) (2011) *Globalization and European Integration: Critical Approaches to Regional Order and International Relations*, Abingdon: Routledge.

Nuti, D.M. (2002) 'Costs and Benefits of Unilateral Euroization in Central Eastern Europe', *Economics of Transition*, vol. 10, no. 2, pp. 419–44.

Nye, J. (1990) *Bound to Lead: The Changing Nature of American Power*, New York: Basic Books.

Nye, J. (2004) *Soft Power: The Means to Success in World Politics*, Cambridge, MA: Perseus.

Oakley, D. and Mallet, V. (2009) 'Spain Hit by Public Finance Warning', *Financial Times*, 12 January.

Oakley, D. and Wise, P. (2009) 'Portugal's Credit Rating is Lowered', *Financial Times*, 22 January.

Oates, W.E. (1972) *Fiscal Federalism*, New York: Harcourt-Brace and Jovanovich.

Obinger, H., Leibfried, S. and Castles, F. (2005) *Federalism and the Welfare State: New World and European Experiences*, Cambridge: Cambridge University Press.

O'Brien, K. (1995) 'Interfering with Civil Society: CIA and KGB Covert Political Action during the Cold War', *International Journal of Intelligence and Counter-intelligence*, vol. 8, no. 4, pp. 431–56.

O'Connor, J. (1973) *The Fiscal Crisis of the State*, New York: St Martin's Press.

O'Connor, J. (1988) 'Convergence or Divergence? Change in Welfare Effort in OECD Countries 1960–80', *European Journal of Political Research*, vol. 16, pp. 277–99.

O'Connor, J. (2005) 'Policy Coordination, Social Indicators and the Social Policy Agenda in the European Union', *Journal of European Social Policy*, vol. 15, no. 4, pp. 345–61.

OECD (1986) *Flexibility in the Labour Market*, Paris: OECD.

OECD (1988) *The Future of Social Protection*, Paris: OECD.

OECD (1994a) *The OECD Jobs Study: Facts, Analysis, Strategies*, Paris: OECD.

OECD (1996a) *Boosting Jobs and Incomes: Policy Lessons from the Review of the 1994 Jobs Study*, Paris: OECD.

OECD (1996b) 'The Experience with Fiscal Consolidation in OECD Countries', *OECD Economic Outlook*, vol. 59 (June), pp. 33–41.

OECD (1999a) *OECD Employment Outlook*, June, Paris: OECD.

OECD (1999b) 'Employment Protection and Labour Market Performance', *OECD Economic Outlook*, Paris: OECD.

OECD (2006) *OECD Employment Outlook*, Paris: OECD.

OECD (2009) *Government at a Glance*, Paris: OECD.

OECD (2011) *Divided We Stand: Why Inequality Keeps Rising*, Paris: OECD.

Offe, C. (1984) *Contradictions of the Welfare State*, Cambridge, MA: MIT Press.

O'Grady, S. (2009) 'Bailout Money is Flowing Abroad', *Independent*, 14 March.

O'Hagan, E. (2002) *Employee Relations in the Periphery of Europe: The Unfolding Story of the European Social Model*, Basingstoke: Palgrave Macmillan.

O'Hara, G. and Parr, H. (2006) *The Wilson Governments 1964–1970 Reconsidered*, London: Routledge.

Ohmae, K. (1990) *The Borderless World: Power and Strategy in the Interlinked Economy*, London: Collins.

Ohmae, K. (1995) *The End of the Nation-State: The Rise of Regional Economies*, London: Harper Collins.

Open Europe (2007) *A Guide to the Constitutional Treaty*, London: Open Europe.

Open Europe (2008) *Open Europe Bulletin*, 18 September, London: Open Europe.

Open Eye (1991) 'Gladio and the European Secret Armies', *Open Eye*, no. 1, pp. 31–6.

Ormerod, P. (1999a) 'A Currency for Jobs?', *European Journal*, July, 7–8.

Ormerod, P. (1999b) 'The Euro-attack on Jobs', in J. Bush (ed.) *Everything you Always Wanted to Know about the Euro*, London: New Europe.

Our Europe (1996) '*Notre Europe's* Charter: A Project for the European Union', Brussels: Notre Europe.

Overbeek, H. (ed.) (1993) *Restructuring Hegemony in the Global Political Economy: The Rise of Transnational Liberalism in the 1980s*, Abingdon: Routledge.

Overbeek, H. (2000) 'Transnational Historical Materialism' in R. Palan (ed.) *Global Political Economy: Contemporary Theories*, Abingdon: Routledge.

Overbeek, H. (ed.) (2003) *The Political Economy of European Employment: European Integration and the Transnationalization of the (Un)employment Question*, Abingdon: Routledge.

Overbeek, O. (1990) *Global Capitalism and National Decline: The Thatcher Decade in Perspective*, London: Unwin Hyman.

Oxfam (2008) *Partnership or Power Play? How Europe Should Bring Development into its Trade Deals with African, Caribbean and Pacific Countries*, Briefing Paper, Oxford: Oxfam.

Oxford Analytica (2010) 'Europe: Welfare State Model Shrinks Under Austerity', Daily Brief Service, 13 December, Oxford: Oxford Analytica.

Ozenda, M. and Strauss-Kahn, D. (1985) 'French Planning: Decline or Renewal?', in H. Machin and V. Wright (eds) *Economic Policy and Policy-making under the Mitterrand Presidency, 1981–1984*, London: Frances Pinter.

Palier, B. (2000) '"Defrosting" the French Welfare State', *West European Politics*, vol. 23, no. 2, pp. 113–36.

Palier, B. (2002) 'Beyond Retrenchment: Four Problems in Current Welfare State Research and One Suggestion How to Overcome Them' in J. Clasen (ed.) *What Future for Social Security?* Bristol: Policy Press.

Palier, B. and Sykes, R. (2001) 'Challenges and Change: Issues and Perspectives in the Analysis of Globalization and the European Welfare States' in R. Sykes, B. Palier and P. Prior (eds) *Globalization and European Welfare States: Challenges and Change*, Basingstoke: Palgrave.

Palley, T. (1998) *Plenty of Nothing: The Downsizing of the American Dream and the Case for Structural Keynesianism*, Princeton: Princeton University Press.

Palley, T. (2001) 'The Role of Institutions and Policies in Creating High European Unemployment: The Evidence', *The Levy Economics Institute Working Paper no. 336*, New York: Annandale-on-Hudson.

Palme, J. (2001) 'Will Social Europe Work?' in M. Kohli and M. Novak (eds) *Will Europe Work?*, London: Routledge.

Palpant, C. (2006) 'European Employment Strategy: An Instrument of Convergence for the New Member States?', Policy Briefing no. 18, Brussels: *Notre Europe.*

Panić, M. (2007) 'Does Europe Need Neo-liberal Reforms?' *Cambridge Journal of Economics*, vol. 31, pp. 145–69.

Panitch, L. and Gindin, S. (2005) 'Superintending Global Capital', *New Left Review*, vol. 35, pp. 101–23.

Parker, C. and Giles, C. (2011) 'Steering Clear of the "Greek Mangle"', *Financial Times*, 21 July.

Parker, R. (1994) 'Clintonomics for the East', *Foreign Policy*, no. 94, pp. 53–68.

Parti Socialiste (1980) *Projet Socialiste pour la France des années 80*, Paris: *Club Socialiste du Livre.*

Parti Socialiste (1992) *Le Poing et le Rose*, no. 135, January.

Parti Socialiste (1993) *Vendredi*, no. 212, 17 December.

Patel, P. (2010) *Submission to the Comprehensive Spending Review 2010*, London: Federation of Small Businesses.

Patel, P. and Pavitt, K. (1991) 'Large Firms in the Production of the World's Technology: An Important Case of Non-Globalisation', *Journal of International Business Studies*, vol. 22, no. 1, pp. 1–21.

Peel, Q. (2011a) 'Merkel Shifts on Economic Governance', *Financial Times*, 3 February.

Peel, Q. (2011b) 'Trichet Calls for Common EU Finance Ministry', *Financial Times*, 3 June.

Peel, Q. and Hollinger, P. (2011) 'Merkel and Sarkozy Back Euro', *Financial Times*, 17 August.

Pelkmans, J. (1980) 'Economic Theories of Integration Revisited', *Journal of Common Market Studies*, vol. 28, no. 4, pp. 333–56.

Pelkmans, J. (2006) 'European Industrial Policy', Bruges European Economic Policy Briefing no. 15, Bruges: College of Europe.

Pennant-Rea, R., Bean, C.R., Begg, D., Hardie, J., Lankester, T., Miles, D.K., Portes, R., Robinson, A., Seabright, P. and Wolf, M. (1997) *The Ostrich and the EMU – Policy Choices Facing the UK*, London: Centre for Economic Policy Research.

Pentagon Papers: The Defense Department History of United States Decision-making on Vietnam: The Senator Gravel Edition – Vol. I. (1971) Boston, MA: Beacon Press.

Perraton, J., Goldblatt, D., Held, D. and McGrew, A. (2000) 'The Globalisation of Economic Activity', in R. Higgott and A. Payne (eds) *The New Political Economy of Globalisation*, Volume I, Cheltenham: Edward Elgar.

Pestieau, P. (2006) *The Welfare State in the European Union: Economic and Social Perspectives*, Oxford: Oxford University Press.

Peters, M. (1996) 'Bilderberg and the Origins of the EU', *Lobster*, no. 32, pp. 2–9.

Peters, T. (1995) 'European Monetary Union and Labour Markets: What to Expect', *International Labour Review*, vol. 134, no. 3, pp. 315–32.

Petras, J. and Vieux, S. (1996) 'Bosnia and the Revival of US Hegemony', *New Left Review*, no. 218, pp. 3–25.

Phelps, E.S. (1968) 'Money–Wage Dynamics and Labor Market Equilibrium', *Journal of Political Economy*, vol. 78, pp. 678–711.

Phelps, E.S. and G. Zoega (1998) 'Natural-rate Theory and OECD Unemployment', *Economic Journal*, vol. 108, no. 448, pp. 782–801.

Philine ter Haar, B. and Copeland, P. (2010) 'What are the Future Prospects for the European Social Model? An Analysis of EU Equal Opportunities and Employment Policy', *European Law Journal*, vol. 16, no. 3, pp. 273–91.

Philo, G. (2010) 'Deficit Crisis: Let's be really in it Together', *Guardian*, 15 August.

Pierson, C. (1991) *Beyond the Welfare State*, Cambridge: Polity Press.

Pierson, P. (1994a) *Dismantling the Welfare State? Reagan, Thatcher and the Politics of Retrenchment*, Cambridge: Cambridge University Press.

Pierson, P. (1994b) 'The Path to European Integration: A Historical Institutionalist Perspective', Working Paper no. 5.2, Cambridge, MA: Harvard University Minda de Gunzberg Center for European Studies.

Pierson, P. (1996) 'The New Politics of the Welfare State', *World Politics*, vol. 48, no. 2, pp. 143–79.

Pierson, P. (1998) 'Irresistible Forces, Immovable Objects: Post-industrial Welfare States Confront Permanent Austerity', *Journal of European Public Policy*, vol. 5, no. 4, pp. 539–60.

Pierson, P. (ed.) (2001) *The New Politics of the Welfare State*, Oxford: Oxford University Press.

Pijl, K. van der (1984) *The Making of an Atlantic Ruling Class*, London: Verso.

Pijl, K. van der (1998) *Transnational Classes and International Relations*, Abingdon: Routledge.

Pijl, K. van der (2006) *Global Rivalries: From the Cold War to Iraq*, London: Pluto.

Pilger, J. (2003) *The New Rulers of the World*, London: Verso.

Pilling, G. (1987) *The Crisis of Keynesian Economics: A Marxist View*, Beckenham: Croom Held.

Pisani, S. (1992) *The CIA and the Marshall Plan*, Edinburgh: University of Edinburgh Press.

Pisani-Ferry, J., Italianer, A. and Lescure, R. (1993) 'Stabilisation Properties of Budgetary Systems: A Simulation Analysis', in 'The Economics of Community Public Finance', *European Economy*, Reports and Studies, no. 5, pp. 513–38.

Pissarides, C. (1997) 'The Need for Labour Market Flexibility in European Economic and Monetary Union', *Swedish Economic Policy Review*, vol. 4, no. 2, pp. 513–46.

Pistor, M. (1995) 'Agency, Structure and European Integration: Critical Political Economy and the New Regionalism in Europe' in E. Jones and A. Verdun (eds) *The Political Economy of European Integration: Theory and Analysis*, Abingdon: Routledge.

Plant, R., Beech, M. and Hickson, K. (eds) (2004) *The Struggle for Labour's Soul: Understanding Labour's Political Thought since 1945*, London: Routledge.

Ploeg, F. van der (1993) 'Macroeconomic Policy Co-ordination Issues during the Various Phases of Economic and Monetary Integration in Europe', in 'The Economics of EMU', *European Economy*, Special Edition 1, pp. 136–64.

Polanyi, K. (1957) *The Great Transformation: The Political and Economic Origins of Our Time*, Boston: Beacon Press.

Pollock, A. (2004) *NHS Plc: The Privatization of Our Health Care*, London: Verso.

Pontusson J. (2005) *Inequality and Prosperity: Social Europe vs. Liberal America*, Ithaca, NY: Cornell University Press.

Porte, C. de la and Pochet, P. (eds) (2002) *Building Social Europe through the Open Method of Co-ordination*, Brussels: Peter Lang.

Porter, M.E. (1990) *The Competitive Advantage of Nations*, London: Macmillan.

Portes, J. and French, S. (2005) 'The Impact of Free Movement of Workers from Central and Eastern Europe on the UK Labour Market: Early Evidence'. *DWP Working Paper*, 18.

Posen, A. (1993) 'Why Central Bank Independence does Not Cause Low Inflation: There is no Institutional Fix for Politics', in R. O'Brien (ed.) *Finance and the* International Economy, vol. 7, Oxford: Oxford University Press.

Posen, A. (1998) 'Central Bank Independence and Disinflationary Credibility: A Missing Link', *Oxford Economic Papers*, vol. 50, no. 3, pp. 335–59.

Poulantzas, N. (1973) *Political Power and Social Classes*, London: New Left Books.

Poulantzas, N. (1975) *Classes in Contemporary Capitalism*, London: New Left Books.

Poulantzas, N. (1978) *State, Power, Socialism*, London: Verso.

Prais, S.J. and Wagner, K. (1988) 'Productivity and Management: The Training in Foremen in Britain and Germany', *National Institute Economic Review*, vol. 123, February, pp. 34–47.

Preece, D. (2009) *Dismantling Social Europe: The Political Economy of Social Policy in the European Union*, London: First Forum Press.

Price, L. (2010) *Where Power Lies: Prime Ministers versus the Media*, London: Simon and Schuster.

Project on Government Oversight (2004) *The Politics of Contracting*. Online, available at: www.pogo.org/pogo-files/reports/government-corruption/the-politics-of-contracting/gc-rd-20040629.html (accessed 6 June 2011).

Pryor, F. (1969) *Public Expenditures in Communist and Capitalist Nations*, London: Allen and Unwin.

Przeworski, A. (1985) *Capitalism and Social Democracy*, Cambridge: Cambridge University Press.

Ramsay, R. (1986) 'Wilson, MI5 and the Rose of Thatcher: Covert Operations in British Politics, 1974–1978', *Lobster*, no. 11.

Ramsay, R. (1996) *The Clandestine Caucus: Anti-socialist Campaigns and Operations in the British Labour Movement since the War*, Hull: Lobster.

Ramsay, R. (1998) *Prawn Cocktail Party: The Hidden Power Behind New Labour*, London: Vision.

Ramsay, R. and Dorril, S. (1986) *Smear! Wilson and the Secret State*, London: Grafton.

Raveaud, G. (2007) 'The European Employment Strategy: Towards More and Better Jobs?', *Journal of Common Market Studies*, vol. 45, no. 2, pp. 411–34.

Read, R. (2002) 'Monetary Union and Eastward Expansion of the EU', in H. Ingham and M. Ingham (eds) *EU Expansion to the East: Prospects and Problems*, Cheltenham: Edward Elgar.

Reddaway, P. and Glinski, D. (2001) *The Tragedy of Russia's Reforms: Market Bolshevism against Democracy*, Washington, DC: United States Institute for Peace Press.

Redmond, J. (ed.) (1994) *Prospective Europeans: New Members for the European Union*, London: Harvester Wheatsheaf.

Rehn, O. (2011) 'Annual Growth Survey 2011: Advancing the EU's Comprehensive Response to the Crisis', Presentation at the 'Towards Integrated Economic Governance in the EU: The European Semester' Conference, Brussels, 12 January. Online, available at: http://ec.europa.eu/economy_finance/events/2011/1201_the_european_semester/pdf/presentation_olli_rehn_en.pdf (accessed 1 March 2011).

Reich, R. (1992) *The Work of Nations*, New York: Vintage.

Reich, R. (2011) 'The Great Switch by the Super Rich', 18 May. Online, available at: www.social-europe.eu/2011/05/the-great-switch-by-the-super-rich/ (accessed 10 June 2011).

Reid, T. (2004) *The United States of Europe: The New Superpower and the End of American Supremacy*, London: Penguin.

Rhinard, M. (2010) *Framing Europe: The Policy Shaping Strategies of the European Commission*, Dordrecht: Republic of Letters Publishing.

Rhodes, M. (1992) 'The Future of the Social Dimension: Labour Market Regulation in Post-1992 Europe', *Journal of Common Market Studies*, vol. 30, no. 1, pp. 23–51.

Rhodes, M. (1996) 'Globalization and West European States: A Critical Review of Recent Debates', *Journal of European Social Policy*, vol. 6, no. 4, pp. 305–27.

Rhodes, M. (1997) *Globalization, Labour Markets and Welfare States: A Future of Competitive Corporatism?* European University Institute Working Paper RSC 97/36, Florence: European University Institute.

Rhodes, M. (1998) 'Globalization, Labour Markets and Welfare States: A Future of "Competitive Corporatism"?' in M. Rhodes and Y. Mény (eds) *The Future of European Welfare: A New Social Contract?* Basingstoke: Macmillan.

Rhodes, M. (2002) 'Why EMU is – or May Be – Good for European Welfare States' in K. Dyson (ed.) *European States and the Euro*, Oxford: Oxford University Press.

Rhodes, M. (2005) '"Varieties of Capitalism" and the Political Economy of European Welfare States', *New Political Economy*, vol. 10, no. 3, pp. 363–70.

Richardson, I., Kakabadse, A. and Kakabadse, N. (2011) *Bilderberg People: Inside the Exclusive Global Elite*, Abingdon: Routledge.

Riley, R. and Weale, M. (2006) 'Commentary: Immigration and its Effects', *National Institute Economic Review*, vol. 198 (October), pp. 4–9.

Robinson, W. (1996) *Promoting Polyarchy: Globalization, US Intervention and Hegemony*, Cambridge: Cambridge University Press.

Robinson, W. and Harris, J. (2000) 'Towards a Global Ruling Class? Globalization and the Transnational Capitalist Class', *Science and Society*, vol. 64, no. 1, pp. 11–54.

Rodrik, D. (1997) *Has Globalization Gone Too Far?* Washington, DC: Institute for International Economics.

Rodrik, D. (1998) 'Why Do More Open Economies Have Bigger Governments?' *Journal of Political Economy*, vol. 106, no. 5, pp. 997–1032.

Rogoff, K. (1985a) 'The Optimal Degree of Commitment to an Intermediate Monetary Target', *Quarterly Journal of Economics*, vol. 100, pp. 1169–90.

Rogoff, K. (1985b) 'Can International Monetary Policy Coordination be Counterproductive?', *Journal of International Economics*, vol. 18, pp. 199–217.

Rogow, A. and Shore, P. (1955) *The Labour Government and British Industry, 1945–1951*, Oxford: Basil Blackwell.

Rogowski, R. (ed.) (2008) *The European Social Model and Transitional Labour Markets*, Farnham: Ashgate.

Romer, P.M. (1986) 'Increasing Returns and Long-Run Growth'. *Journal of Political Economy*, vol. 94, pp. 1102–37.

Romer, P.M. (1990) 'Endogenous Technical Change', *Journal of Political Economy*, vol. 98, pp. S71-S102.

Romer, P.M. (1994) 'The Origins of Endogenous Growth', *Journal of Economic Perspectives*, vol. 8, no. 1, pp. 3–22.

Rompuy, P.V., Abraham, F. and Heremans, D. (1993) 'Economic Federalism and the EMU', in 'The Economics of EMU – Background Studies', *European Economy*, no. 44, pp. 109–35.

Rosati, D., (1995) *Exchange Rate Policies during Transition from Plan to Market*, Paper presented at the XXI Century Foundation/CEPR Conference: Convertibility and Exchange Rate Policy, Sofia, 22/23 September.

Ross, F. (2000a) ' "Beyond Left and Right": The New Partisan Politics of Welfare', *Governance: An International Journal of Policy and Administration*, vol. 13, no. 2, pp. 155–83.

Ross, F. (2000b) 'Framing Welfare Reform in Affluent Societies: Rendering Restructuring More Palatable?' *Journal of Public Policy*, vol. 20, no. 2, pp. 169–93.

Ross, G. (1995) *Jacques Delors and European Integration*, Cambridge: Polity.

Rostagno, M., Hiebert, P. and Pérez-Garcia, J. (2001) 'Optimal Debt under a Deficit Constraint', in A. Brunila, M. Buti and D. Franco (eds) *The Stability and Growth Pact: The Architecture of Fiscal Policy in EMU*, London: Palgrave Macmillan.

Rothstein, B. (2000) *The Future of the Universal Welfare State: An Institutional Approach*, London; Routledge.

Rowthorn, B. and Glyn, A. (1990) 'The Diversity of Unemployment Experience Since 1973', in S.A. Marglin and J.B. Schor (eds) *The Golden Age of Capitalism: Reinterpreting the Post-war Experience*, Cambridge: Clarendon Press, pp. 187–217.

Rowthorn, R.E. (1995) 'Capital Formation and Unemployment', *Oxford Review of Economic Policy*, vol. 11, no. 1, pp. 26–39.

Rowthorn, R.E. (1999) 'Unemployment, Wage Bargaining and Capital-labour Substitution', *Cambridge Journal of Economics*, vol. 23, no. 3, pp. 413–25.

Rubio, E. (2009) 'Social Europe and the Crisis: Defining a New Agenda', Policy Paper no. 36, Brussels: *Notre Europe.*

Rueda, D. (2005) 'Insider–Outsider Politics in Industrialized Democracies: The Challenge to Social Democratic Parties', *American Political Science Review*, vol. 99, no. 1, pp. 61–74.

Rüdiger, K. (2007) 'Offshoring: A Threat for the UK's Knowledge Jobs? Globalization and the Extent and Impact of Offshore Outsourcing', Working Paper, London: Work Foundation.

Ruggie, J. (1982) 'International Regimes, Transactions and Change: Embedded Liberalism in the Post-war Economic Order', *International Organization*, vol. 36, no. 2, pp. 379–415.

Rupert, M. (1995) *Producing Hegemony*, Cambridge: Cambridge University Press.

Ryner, M. (2002) *Capitalist Restructuring, Globalization and the Third Way: Lessons from the Swedish Model*, Abingdon: Routledge.

Ryner, M. (2003) 'Disciplinary Neo-liberalism, Regionalization and the Social Market in German Restructuring' in A. Cafruny and M. Ryner (eds) *A Ruined Fortress? Neoliberal Hegemony and Transformation in Europe*, Oxford: Rowman and Littlefield.

Ryner, M. (2007) 'US Power and the Crisis of Social Democracy in Europe's Second Project of Integration', *Capital and Class*, Special Issue 'The Left and Europe', no. 93, pp. 7–26.

Ryner, M. (2009) 'Neo-liberal European Governance and the Politics of Welfare State Retrenchment: A Critique of the Neo-Malthusians' in B. van Apeldoorn, J. Drahokoupil and L. Horn (eds) *Contradictions and Limits of Neo-liberal European Governance: From Lisbon to Lisbon*, Basingstoke: Palgrave Macmillan.

Ryner, M. and Schulten, T. (2003) 'The Political Economy of Labour-Market Restructuring and Trade Union Responses in the Social-Democratic Heartland' in H. Overbeek (ed.) *The Political Economy of European Employment: European Integration and the Transnationalization of the (Un)employment Question*, Abingdon: Routledge.

Sakellaropoulos, T. and Berghman, J. (eds) (2004) *Connecting Welfare Diversity within the European Social Model*, Oxford: Hart Publishing.

Sala-i-Martin, X. and Sachs, J. (1992) 'Fiscal Federalism and Optimum Currency Areas: Evidence for Europe from the United States', in M.B. Canzoneri, V. Grilli and P.R. Masson (eds) *Establishing a Central Bank: Issues in Europe and Lessons from the US*, Cambridge: Cambridge University Press, pp. 195–219.

Sanders, J. (1983) *Peddlers of Crisis: The Committee on the Present Danger and the Politics of Containment*, Boston, MA: South End Press.

Sapir, A. (2005) *Globalization and the Reform of European Social Models*, Background Document for the Presentation at ECOFIN Informal Meeting, Manchester, 9 September, Brussels: Bruegel.

Sapir, A. and Sekkat, K. (1999) 'Optimum Electoral Areas: Should Europe Adopt a Single Election Day?', *European Economic Review*, vol. 43, pp. 1595–619.

Sapir, A., Aghion, P., Bertola, G., Hellwig, M., Pisani-Ferry, J., Rosati, D., Vinals, J. and Wallace, H. (2004) *An Agenda for a Growing Europe: The Sapir Report*, Oxford: Oxford University Press.

Sassoon, D. (1996) *One Hundred Years of Socialism: The West European Left in the Twentieth Century*, London: IB Tauris.

Sassoon, D. (1999) 'European Social Democracy and New Labour: Unity in Diversity?', in A. Gamble and T. Wright (eds) *The New Social Democracy*, Oxford: Blackwell, pp. 19–37.

Sawyer, M. (2003) 'The NAIRU, Labour Market "Flexibility" and Full Employment', in J. Stanford and L. Vosko (eds) *Challenging the Market: The Struggle to Regulate Work and Income*, Belfast: McGill-Queen's University Press.

Sayer, A. (1992) *Methods in Social Science: A Realist Approach*, Second Edition, Abingdon: Routledge.

Sbragia, A. (2000) 'The European Union as Coxswain: Governance by Steering' in J. Pierre (ed.) *Debating Governance: Authority, Steering and Democracy*, Oxford: Oxford University Press.

Scarbrough, E. (2000) 'West European Welfare States: The Old Politics of Retrenchment', *European Journal of Political Research*, vol. 38, pp. 225–59.

Scharpf, F. (1997) 'Economic Integration, Democracy and Welfare States', *Journal of European Public Policy*, vol. 4, no. 1, pp. 18–36.

Scharpf, F. (1999) *Governing in Europe: Effective and Democratic?* Oxford: Oxford University Press.

Scharpf, F. (2000) 'The Viability of Advanced Welfare States in the International Economy: Vulnerabilities and Options', *Journal of European Public Policy*, vol. 7, no. 2, pp. 190–228.

Scharpf, F. (2002) 'The European Social Model: Coping with the Challenges of Diversity', *Journal of Common Market Studies*, vol. 40, no. 4, pp. 645–70.

Schettkat, R. (2003) 'Are Institutional Rigidities at the Root of European Unemployment?', *Cambridge Journal of Economics*, vol. 27, no. 6, pp. 771–87.

Schmid, A. and Berends, E. (1985) *Soviet Military Intervention since 1945*, New Jersey: Transaction Books.

Schmid, C. (2010) 'A European Civil Code as a Building Block for a European Social Model?' *European Law Review*, vol. 35, no. 1, pp. 103–11.

Schmidt, I. (2009) 'New Institutions, Old Ideas: The Passing Moment of the European Social Model', *Studies in Political Economy*, vol. 84, pp. 7–28.

Schmidt, V. (2000) 'The Role of Values and Discourse in Welfare State Reform: The Politics of Successful Adjustment' in F. Scharpf (ed.) *Welfare and Work in the Open Economy: Volume 1 – From Vulnerability to Competitiveness*, Oxford: Oxford University Press.

Schmidt, V. (2002) 'Does Discourse Matter in the Politics of Welfare State Adjustment? *Comparative Political Studies*, vol. 35, no. 2, pp. 168–93.

Schmidt, V. (2005) 'The Role of Public Discourse in European Social Democratic Reform Projects', *European Integration Online Papers*, vol. 9. Online, available at: http://eiop.or.at/eiop/texte/2005–008a.htm (accessed 10 February 2011).

Scholte, J.A. (2000) *Globalisation: A Critical Introduction*, London: Macmillan.

Schoors, K. (2002) 'Should the Central and Eastern European Accession Countries Adopt the Euro before or after Accession?', *Economics of Planning*, vol. 35, no. 1, pp. 42–77.

Schoors, K. and Gobbin, N. (2004) 'Enlargement', in M.P. van der Hoek (ed.) *Handbook of Public Administration and Policy in the European Union*, New York: Dekker.

Schröter, E. (2004) 'How Many Third Ways? Comparing the British, French and German Left in Government', Working Paper no. 7, Berkeley: University of California Institute of European Studies.

Sciarra, S. (ed.) (2001) *Labour Law in the Courts*, Oxford: Hart Publishing.

Sciarra, S. (2002) 'Market Freedom and Fundamental Social Rights' in B. Hepple (ed.) *Social and Labour Rights in a Global Context: International and Comparative Perspectives*, Cambridge: Cambridge University Press.

Seillière, A. (2007) 'Perspectives of the Social Dialogue in Europe', Speech to European Trade Union Confederation Congress, 21 May, Sevilla.

Seldon, A. and Hickson, K. (eds) (2004) *New Labour, Old Labour: The Wilson and Callaghan Governments, 1974–1979*, London: Routledge.

Setterfield, M., Gordon, D.V. and Osberg, L. (1992) 'Searching for a Will O' Wisp: An Empirical Study of the NAIRU in Canada', *European Economic Review*, vol. 36, no. 1, pp. 119–36.

Seyd, P. (1987) *The Rise and Fall of the Labour Left*, Basingstoke: Macmillan.

Shalev, M. (1983) 'The Social Democratic Model and Beyond: Two 'Generations' of Comparative Research on the Welfare State', *Comparative Social Research*, vol. 6, pp. 315–51.

Shaxson, N. (2011) *Treasure Islands: Tax Havens and the Men who Stole the World*, London: Bodley Head.

Shleifer, A. and Summers, L. (1990) 'The Noise Trader Approach to Finance', *Journal of Economic Perspectives*, vol. 4, no. 2, pp. 19–34.

Shoup, L. and Minter, W. (1977) *Imperial Brain Trust: The Council on Foreign Relations and United States Foreign Policy*, London: Monthly Review Press.

Shoup, L. and Minter, W. (1980) 'Shaping a New World Order: The Council on Foreign Relations' Blueprint for World Hegemony, 1939–1945' in H. Sklar, (ed.) *Trilateralism: The Trilateral Commission and Elite Planning for World Management*, Boston, MA: South End Press.

Sidjanski, D. (2001) 'The Federal Approach to the European Union or the Quest for an Unprecedented European Federalism', Policy Paper no. 14, Brussels: *Notre Europe.*

Siebert, H. (1997) 'Labor Market Rigidities: At the Root of Unemployment in Europe', *Journal of Economic Perspectives*, vol. 11, pp. 37–54.

SIMFA (2007) *Securities Industry and Financial Markets – Global Addendum 2007*, SIMFA Research Report, November.

Simpson, C. (1994) *Science of Coercion: Communication Research and Psychological Warfare, 1945–1960*, Oxford: Oxford University Press.

Sinn, H. (2002) 'EU Enlargement and the Future of the Welfare State', *Scottish Journal of Political Economy*, vol. 49, no. 1, pp. 104–15.

Sisson, K. and Marginson, P. (1995) 'Management: Systems, Structures and Strategy', In Edwards, P. (ed.) *Industrial Relations: Theory and Practice in Britain*, Oxford: Blackwell, pp. 89–122.

Sivard, R. (1981) *World Military and Social Expenditures 1981*, Washington, DC: World Priorities Inc.

Skelton, C. (9/6/2010) 'Bilderberg 2010: Don't call it a Pow-wow!'. Weblog online, available at: www.guardian.co.uk/world/blog/2010/jun/09/bilderberg-charlie-skelton-2010 (accessed: 20 June 2010).

Skidelsky, R. (2009) *Keynes: The Return of the Master*, London: Allen Lane.

Sklair, L. (2000) *The Transnational Capitalist Class*, Oxford: Wiley-Blackwell.

Skocpol, T. and Amenta, E. (1986) 'States and Social Policies', *Annual Review of Sociology*, vol. 12, pp. 131–57.

Skott, P. (1995) 'Financial Innovation, Deregulation and Minsky Cycles', in G. Epstein and H. Gintis (eds) *Macroeconomic Policy After the Conservative Era*, Cambridge: Cambridge University Press.

Skott, P. and Auerbach, P. (1995) 'Cumulative Causation and the "New" Theories of Economic Growth', *Journal of Post Keynesian Economics*, vol. 17, no. 3, pp. 381–402.

Slijper, F. (2005) *The Emerging EU Military-Industrial Complex: Arms Industry Lobbying in Brussels*, Briefing Paper no. 1, Amsterdam: Transnational Institute.

Slothuus, R. (2007) 'Framing Deservingness to Win Support for Welfare State Retrenchment', Scandinavian Political Studies, vol. 30, no. 3, pp. 323–44.

Smith, D. and Wanke, J. (1993) '1992: Who Wins? Who Loses?', in A. Cafruny and G. Rosenthal (eds) *The State of the European Community – vol. 2: The Maastricht Debates and Beyond*, Harlow: Longman.

Smith, H. (2010) 'Super-wealthy Investors Move Billions Out of Greece', *Observer*, 7 February.

Smith, H. (2011) 'Greece Begins €50 Billion Privatization Drive', *Guardian*, 1 August.

Sneddon, N. (1999) 'Interest Groups and Policy-making: The Welfare State, 1942–1964', Unpublished PhD Thesis, University of Glasgow.

Socialist International Committee on Economic Policy (1985) *Global Challenge – From Crisis to Cooperation: Breaking the North–South Stalemate*, London: Pan Books.

Solow, R. (1997) 'What is Labor Market Flexibility? What is it Good For?', 1997 Keynes Lecture to the British Academy, 30 October, London.

South Commission (1990) *The Challenge to the South*, Oxford: Oxford University Press.

Spahn, B. (1993) 'The Consequences of Economic and Monetary Union for Fiscal Relations in the Community and the Financing of the Community Budget', in 'The Economics of Community Public Finance', *European Economy*, Reports and Studies, no. 5, pp. 543–84.

Special Ad hoc Committee (of the State-War-Navy Coordinating Committee) (1947) Report of Committee Meeting, 21 April, *Foreign Relations of the United States*, vol. III, pp. 164–5.

Staiger, D., Stock, J.H. and Watson, M.W. (1997) 'How Precise are Estimates of the Natural Rate of Unemployment', in C.D. Romer and D.H. Romer (eds) *Reducing Inflation: Motivation and Strategy*, Chicago: University of Chicago Press.

Stanners, W. (1993) 'Is Low Inflation an Important Condition for High Growth?', *Cambridge Journal of Economics*, vol. 17, no. 1, pp. 79–107.

Stark, J. (2001) 'Genesis of a Pact', in A. Brunila, M. Buti and D. Franco (eds) *The Stability and Growth Pact: the architecture of fiscal policy in EMU*, London: Palgrave Macmillan.

Starke, P. (2006) 'The Politics of Welfare State Retrenchment: A Literature Review', *Social Policy and Administration*, vol. 40, no. 1, pp. 104–20.

Starke, P. (2008) *Radical Welfare State Retrenchment: A Comparative Analysis*, Basingstoke; Palgrave Macmillan.

Starke, P., Obinger, H. and Castles, F. (2008) 'Convergence Towards Where? In What Ways, if any, are Welfare States becoming more Similar?', *Journal of European Public Policy*, vol. 15, no. 7, pp. 975–1000.

Starr-Deelan, D. and Deelan, B. (1986) 'The European Court of Justice as a Federator', *Publius*, Fall, pp. 81–97.

State Department (1947) 'Memorandum from George Kennan to Dean Acheson, 23 May', *Foreign Relations of the United States*, vol. III, p. 229.

State Department (1948) Executive Committee on Economic Foreign Policy, 'Statement of United States credit and investment policy', 11 August, *Foreign Relations of the United States*, vol. I, part 2, p. 947.

State Department (1949) Memorandum to the Secretary of State, 8 February, *Foreign Relations of the United States*, vol. I, p. 632.

State Department (1951) Policy Planning Staff Paper, 26 June, *Foreign Relations of the United States*, vol. I, pp. 99–100.

State Department (1966) Memorandum from George Ball to Lyndon Johnson, 22 July, *Foreign Relations of the United States*, vol. 12, p. 150.

Steedman, H. (1988) 'Vocational Training in France and Britain', *National Institute Economic Review*, vol. 126, November, pp. 57–70.

Steele, J. (1997) 'Invest in the United Fates of Europe', *Observer*, 1 June.

Stephens, J. (1979) *The Transition from Capitalism to Socialism*, London: Macmillan.

Stephens, J., Huber, E. and Ray, L. (1999) 'The Welfare State in Hard Times' in H. Kitschelt, G. Marks and P. Lange (eds) *Continuity and Change in Contemporary Capitalism*, Cambridge: Cambridge University Press.

Stewart, H. (2011a) 'Eurozone Fights to Contain Crisis Amid New Bid to Rescue Greece', *Observer*, 8 May.

Stewart, H. (2011b) 'Quantitative Easing "Contributes to Social Unrest"', *Observer*, 14 August.

Stockhammer, E. (2004a) 'Explaining European Unemployment: Testing the NAIRU Theory and a Keynesian Approach', *International Review of Applied Economics*, vol. 18, no. 1, pp. 3–23.

Stockhammer, E. (2004b) 'The Rise of European Unemployment: A Synopsis', *Political Economy Research Institute Working Paper no. 76*, Amherst: University of Massachusetts.

Stockhammer, E. (2004c) 'Financialisation and the Slowdown of Accumulation', *Cambridge Journal of Economics*, vol. 28, no. 5, pp. 719–41.

Stockhammer, E. (2004d) *The Rise of Unemployment in Europe*, Cheltenham: Edward Elgar.

Stoner Saunders, F. (2000) *Who Paid the Piper? The CIA and the Cultural Cold War*, London: Granta.

Strange, G. (1997) 'The British Labour Movement and Economic and Monetary Union in Europe', *Capital and Class*, vol. 63, pp. 13–24.

Strange, G. (2006) 'The Left against Europe? A Critical Engagement with New Constitu-tionalism and Structural Dependence Theory', *Government and Opposition*, vol. 41, no. 2, pp. 197–229.

Strange, G. and Worth, O. (eds) (2007) 'The Left and Europe' Special Issue, *Capital and Class*, no. 93.

Strange, S. (1970) 'International Economics and International Relations: A Case of Mutual Neglect', *International Affairs*, vol. 46, no. 2, pp. 304–15.

Strange, S. (1988) *States and Markets*, London: Pinter.

Strange, S. (1996) *The Retreat of the State: The Diffusion of Power in the World Economy*, Cambridge: Cambridge University Press.

Strange, S. (2000) 'The Defective State', in R. Higgott and A. Payne (eds) (2000) *The New Political Economy of Globalisation*, Volume I, Cheltenham: Edward Elgar.

Stråth, B. (2007) 'Social Models? A Critical View on a Concept from a Historical and European Perspective', *European Review*, vol. 15, no. 3, pp. 335–52.

Streeck, W. (1992) *Social Institutions and Economic Performance: Studies of Industrial Relations in Advanced Capitalist Economies*, London: Sage.

Streeck, W. (2001) 'International Competition, Supranational Integration, National Soli-darity: The Emerging Constitution of "Social Europe"', in M. Kohli and M. Novak (eds) *Will Europe Work? Integration, Employment and the Social Order*, Abingdon: Routledge.

Streeck, W. and Schmitter, P.C. (1991) 'From National Corporatism to Transnational Plu-ralism: Organised Interests in the Single European Market', *Politics and Society*, vol. 2.

Sulling, A. (2002) 'Should Estonia Euroize?', *Economics of Transition*, vol. 10, no. 2, pp. 469–90.

Sussman, G. (2005) *Global Electioneering: Campaign Consulting, Communications and Corporate Financing*, Oxford: Rowman and Littlefield.

Svallfors, S. (1997) 'Worlds of Welfare and Attitudes to Redistribution: A Comparison of Eight Western Nations', *European Sociological Review*, vol. 13, no. 3, pp. 283–304.

Svallfors, S. and Taylor-Gooby, P. (1999) *The End of the Welfare State? Responses to State Retrenchment*, Abingdon: Routledge.

Svensson, L.E.O. (2002) *A Reform of the Eurosystems Monetary Policy Strategy is Increasingly Urgent*, Briefing Paper, Committee on Economic and Monetary Affairs, European Parliament.

Svensson, L.E.O. (2003) *How should the Eurosystem Reform its Monetary Strategy?*, Briefing Paper, Committee on Economic and Monetary Affairs, European Parliament.

Swain, G. and Swain, N. (2009) *Eastern Europe since 1945*, fourth edition, Basingstoke: Palgrave Macmillan.

Swank, D. (2001) 'Political Institutions and Welfare State Restructuring: The Impact of Institutions on Social Policy Change in Developed Democracies' in P. Pierson (ed.) *The New Politics of the Welfare State*, Oxford: Oxford University Press.

Swank, D. (2002) *Global Capital, Political Institutions and Policy Change in Developed Welfare States*, Cambridge: Cambridge University Press.

Swedenborg, B. (2008) 'Lessons from Sweden's Welfare State: An American–Swedish Perspective' in W. Bienkowski, J. Brada and M. Radlo (eds) *Growth Versus Security: Old and New EU Members' Quest for a New Economic and Social Model*, Basing-stoke: Palgrave Macmillan.

Sykes, R., Palier, B. and Prior, P. (2001) *Globalization and European Welfare States: Challenges and Change*, Basingstoke: Palgrave.

Tanzi, V. and Schuknecht, L. (2000) *Public Spending in the 20th Century: A Global Perspective*, Cambridge: Cambridge University Press.

Tax Justice Network (2005) 'The Price of Offshore', Briefing Paper, London: Tax Justice Network.

Taylor, M. (1995) *A Single Currency – Implications for the UK Economy*, London: Institute of Directors.

Taylor, P. (2007) *The End of European Integration: Anti-Europeanism Examined*, London: Routledge.

Taylor-Gooby, P. (1988) 'The Future of the British Welfare State: Public Attitudes, Citizenship and Social Policy under the Conservative Governments of the 1980s', *European Sociological Review*, vol. 4, no. 1, pp. 1–19.

Taylor-Gooby, P. (1999) *The End of the Welfare State? Responses to State Retrenchment*, Abingdon: Routledge.

Taylor-Gooby, P. (2001) *Welfare States Under Pressure*, London: Sage.

Taylor-Gooby, P. (2004) *New Risks, New Welfare: The Transformation of the European Welfare State*, Oxford: Oxford University Press.

Teague, P. (1991) 'Introduction' to the Cross-National Research Seminar on "Workers' Rights in Europe"', London School of Economics and Political Science, 13 April.

Teague, P. (1994) 'Between New Keynesianism and Deregulation: Employment Policy in the European Union' *Journal of European Public Policy*, vol. 1, no. 3, pp. 316–45.

Teague, P. (1997) 'Lean Production and the German Model', *German Politics*, vol. 6, no. 2, pp. 76–94.

Teague, P. (1998) 'Monetary Union and Social Europe', *Journal of European Social Policy*, vol. 8, no. 2, pp. 117–39.

The Economist (1991) 'Japanese Spoken Here', 14 September.

The Economist (2005) 'A Working Model', 13 August.

Therborn, G. (1987) 'Welfare States and Capitalist Markets', *Acta Sociologica*, vol. 30, pp. 237–24.

Therborn, G. and Roebroek, J. (1986) 'The Irreversible Welfare State: Its Recent Maturation, its Encounter with the Economic Crisis and its Future Prospects', *International Journal of Health Services*, vol. 16, no. 3, pp. 319–38.

Thirlwall, A.P. and Barton, C.A. (1971) Inflation and Growth: The International Evidence, *Banca Nazionale del Lavoro – Quarterly Review*, vol. 98, pp. 682–95.

Thomas, J. (2005) *Popular Newspapers, the Labour Party and British Politics*, London: Routledge.

Thompson, P. (1980) 'Bilderberg and the West' in H. Sklar (ed.) *Trilateralism: The Trilateral Commission and Elite Planning for World Management*, Boston, MA: South End Press.

Tinbergen, J. (1952) *On the Theory of Economic Policy*, Amsterdam: North-Holland.

Tinbergen, J. (1954) *International Economic Integration*, Amsterdam: North-Holland.

Tindemans, L. (1976) 'European Union (Tindemans Report): Report by Mr. Tindemans to the European Council', *Bulletin of the European Communities*, EC 1/76, Brussels: EU Commission.

Titmuss, R. (1974) *Social Policy: An Introduction*, London: George Allen and Unwin.

Tober, D. (1993) 'One World, One Vision for Business', in S. Bushrui, I. Ayman and E. Laszlo (eds) *Transition to a Global Society*, Oxford: Oneworld, pp. 98–107.

Tocqueville, A. de (2003 [1851]) *Democracy in America*, London: Penguin.

Tomka, B. (2003) 'Western European Welfare States in the 20th Century: Convergences and Divergences in a Long-run Perspective', *International Journal of Social Welfare*, vol. 12, pp. 249–60.

Tomlinson, J. (2009) *The Labour Governments 1964–1970 – Volume 3: Economy Policy*, Manchester: Manchester University Press.

Toniolo, G. (1988) *Central Banks Independence in Historical Perspective*, Berlin: Walter de Gruyter.

Torfing, J. (1999) 'Towards a Schumpeterian Workfare Post-national Regime: Path-shaping and Path-dependency in Danish Welfare State Reforms', *Economy and Society*, vol. 28, no. 3, pp. 369–402.

Trade Union Advisory Committee to the OECD (2004) 'Trade, Offshoring of Jobs and Structural Adjustment: The Need for a Policy Response', Discussion Paper, 23 November, Paris: TUAC.

Trades Union Congress (2010) 'Cuts will Hit the £4,000 per Head that the Government Spends in Private Sector', Press Release, 7 September. Online, available at: www.tuc.org.uk/economy/tuc-18425-f0.cfm (accessed 24 May 2011).

Trades Union Congress (1992) *Europe 1992: Maximising the Benefits, Minimising the Costs*, Trades Union Congress.

Trampusch, C. (2006) 'Industrial Relations and Welfare States: The Different Dynamics of Retrenchment in Germany and the Netherlands', *Journal of European Public Policy*, vol. 16, no. 2, pp. 121–33.

Tranholm-Mikkelsen, J. (1991) 'Neo-functionalism: Obstinate or Obsolete? A Reappraisal in the Light of the New Dynamism of the EC', *Millennium*, vol. 20, no. 1, pp. 1–22.

Travis, A. (2001) 'Europe Loses Faith in the Euro', *Guardian*, 15 January.

Traxler, F. (1996) 'European Trade Union Policy and Collective Bargaining: Mechanisms and Levels of Labour Market Regulation in Comparison', *Transfer*, vol. 2, no. 2, pp. 287–97.

Traynor, I. (2007) 'Merkel to Push for Constitution in Bid to Save Europe's Soul', *Guardian*, 18 January.

Traynor, I. (2011) 'Hardline IMF Forced Germany to Guarantee Greek Bailout', *Guardian*, 17 June.

Traynor, I. and Pilkington, E. (2001) 'Russians begin Long Trek to EU', *Guardian*, 26 May.

Traynor, I. and Walker, D. (1998) 'Pretty in Pink', *Guardian*, 15 September.

Trilateral Commission (1974) 'A Turning Point in North–South Economic Relations', *Triangle Paper no. 5*, New York: Trilateral Commission.

Truman, E. (2007) 'Sovereign Wealth Funds: The Need for Greater Transparency and Accountability', Policy brief PB07–6, Washington, DC: Peterson Institute for International Economics.

Tufte, E. (1978) *Political Control of the Economy*, New Jersey: Princeton University Press.

Tunney, S. (2007) *Labour and the Press: From New Left to New Labour*, Brighton: Sussex Academic Press.

Turgeon, L. (1996) *Bastard Keynesianism: The Evolution of Economic Thinking and Policy-making since World War II*, London: Praeger.

Turner, J. (1984) 'The Politics of Business' in J. Turner (ed.) *Businessmen and Politics: Studies of Business Activities in British Politics, 1900–1945*, London: Heinemann.

Turner, L. (1996) 'The Europeanisation of Labour: Structure before Action', *European Journal of Industrial Relations*, vol. 2, no. 3, pp. 325–44.

Tyler, P. (1992) 'Pentagon's Document Outlines Ways to Thwart Challenges to Primacy of America', *New York Post*, 7 March.

UNCTAD (1992) *World Investment Report 1992: Transnational Corporations as Engines of Growth*, Geneva: United Nations.

UNCTAD (1996) *Trade and Development Annual Report*, New York: UNCTAD.

UNCTAD (1998) *World Investment Report 1998: Trends and Determinants*, Geneva: United Nations.

UNCTAD (2000) *World Investment Report 2000: Cross-border Mergers and Acquisitions and Development*, Geneva: United Nations.

UNCTAD (2001) *World Investment Report 2001: Promoting Linkages*, Geneva: United Nations.

UNCTAD (2002) *World Investment Report 2002: Transnational Corporations and Export Competitiveness*, Geneva: United Nations.

UNCTAD (2005) *World Investment Report 2005: Transnational Corporations and the Internationalization of R&D*, Geneva: United Nations.

UNCTAD (2007) *World Investment Report 2007: Transnational Corporations, Extractive Industries and Development*, Geneva: United Nations.

UNICEF (1993) *Public Policy and Social Conditions: Central and Eastern Europe in Transition*, Florence: United Nations.

United Nations (2010) *World Economic Situation and Prospects*, Geneva: United Nations.

United Nations Conference on Trade and Development (1994) *World Investment Report 1994*, New York: United Nations.

Useem, M. (1984) *The Inner Circle: Large Corporations and the Rise of Political Activity in the US and UK*, Oxford: Oxford University Press.

Van Vliet, O. (2010) 'Divergence within Convergence: Europeanization of Social and Labour Market Policies', *Journal of European Integration*, vol. 32, no. 3, pp. 269–90.

Vaughan-Whitehead, D.C. (1995) *Workers' Financial Participation: East–West Experiences*, Geneva: OLO.

Vaughan-Whitehead, D.C. (2003) *EU Enlargement versus Social Europe? The Uncertain Future of the European Social Model*, Cheltenham: Edward Elgar.

Veseth, M. (1998) *Selling Globalisation: The Myth of the Global Economy*, Boulder, CA: Lynne Rienner.

Viren, M. (2001) 'Fiscal Policy, Automatic Stabilisers and Policy Co-ordination in EMU', in A. Brunila, M. Buti and D. Franco (eds) *The Stability and Growth Pact: The Architecture of Fiscal Policy in EMU*, London: Palgrave Macmillan.

Visser, J. and Hemerijck, A. (1997) *A Dutch Miracle: Job Growth, Welfare Reform and Corporatism in the Netherlands*, Amsterdam: University of Amsterdam Press.

Vobruba, G. (2001) 'Coping with Drastic Social Change: Europe and the US in Comparison' in W. Beck, F. van der Maesen, F. Thomèse and A. Walker (eds) *Social Quality: A Vision for Europe*, London: Kluwer Law International.

Waddington, D. and Kerckhofs, P. (2003) 'European Works Councils: What is the Current State of Play?', *Transfer*, vol. 9, no. 2, pp. 322–40.

Wagner, R.E. (1977) 'Economic Manipulation for Political Profit: Macroeconomic Consequences and Constitutional Implications', *Kyklos*, vol. 30, pp. 395–410.

Wakeham, Lord (2008) *Economic Impact of Immigration*, London: House of Lords Economic Affairs Committee.

Walker, M. (1999) 'West Tries to Lure Russia back into Partnership', *Guardian*, 17 May.

Wallace, W. (1973) 'The Administrative Implications of Economic and Monetary Union within the European Community: Report of a Federal Trust Study Group', *Journal of Common Market Studies*, vol. 12, no. 4, pp. 414–20.

Wallerstein, I. (1979) *The Capitalist World Economy*, Cambridge: Cambridge University Press.

Walsh, J., Zappala, G. and Brown, W. (1995) 'European Integration and the Pay Policies of British Multinational', *Industrial Relations Journal*, vol. 26, no. 2, pp. 84–96.

Walters, W. and Henrik Haahr, J. (2005) *Governing Europe: Discourse, Governmentality and European Integration*, London: Routledge.

Warburg, J. (1953) *Germany: Key to Peace*, Cambridge, MA: Harvard University Press.

Watson, M. (2002) 'Sand in the Wheels, or Oiling the Wheels of International Finance? New Labour's Appeal to a "New Bretton Woods"', *British Journal of Politics and International Relations*, vol. 4, no. 2, pp. 193–221.

Watson, M. (2006) 'The European Social Model: Between a Rock and a Hard Place?', in P.B. Whyman, M. Baimbridge and B. Burkitt (eds) *Implications of the Euro: A Critical Perspective from the Left*, London: Routledge, pp. 145–54.

Wearden, G. (2011) 'European Debt Crisis Meeting', *Guardian*, 21 July.

Weber, A.A. (1991a) 'Reputation and Credibility in the European Monetary System', *European Economy*, vol. 12, pp. 57–102.

Weber, A.A. (1991b) 'EMU and Asymmetries and Adjustment Problems in the EMS', in 'The Economics of EMU', *European Economy*, Special Edition 1.

Weiner, A. and Diez, T. (eds) (2009) *European Integration Theory*, second edition, Oxford: Oxford University Press.

Weiss, L. (1998) *The Myth of the Powerless State: Governing the Economy in a Global Era*, Cambridge: Polity Press.

Weissman, R. and Donahue, J. (2009) *Sold Out: How Wall Street and Washington Betrayed America*, Washington, DC: Essential Information/Consumer Education Foundation.

West, K. (1995) *Economic Opportunities for Britain and the Commonwealth*, London: Royal Institute for International Affairs.

West European Politics (2002) vol. 25, no. 2, Special Issue.

White House (1990) *The National Security Strategy of the United States*, Washington, DC: White House.

White House (1995) *A National Security Strategy of Engagement and Enlargement*, Washington, DC: White House.

Whitfield, D. (2001) *Public Services or Corporate Welfare: Remaking the Nation-state in the Global Economy*, London: Pluto.

Whitfield, D. (2010) *Global Auction of Public Assets: Public Sector Alternatives to the Infrastructure Market and Public Private Partnerships*, Nottingham: Spokesman Books.

Whyman, P. (1997a) 'Fiscal Policy Consequences of Economic and Monetary Union in Europe', *Working Paper* no. 97:1, Department of Social and Economic Studies, Bradford: University of Bradford.

Whyman, P. (1997b) *Fiscal Federalism and EMU: A Proposal for a European Federal Transfer Scheme*, Working Paper no. 97.10.5, Department of Social and Economic Studies, Bradford: University of Bradford.

Whyman, P., Burkitt, B. and Baimbridge, M. (2005) 'Post-Keynesianism and a Neo-liberal EMU: The Case for Economic Independence', *Contemporary Politics*, vol. 11, no. 4, pp. 259–70.

Whyman, P.B. (2001) 'Can Opposites Attract? Monetary Union and the Social Market', *Contemporary Politics*, vol. 7, no. 2, pp. 113–28.

Whyman, P.B. (2002) 'British Trade Unions and EMU', *Industrial Relations*, vol. 41, no. 3, pp. 467–76.

Whyman, P.B. (2003) *Sweden and the 'Third Way': A Macroeconomic Evaluation*, Aldershot: Ashgate.

Whyman, P.B. (2006) *Third Way Economics*, Basingstoke: Palgrave.

Whyman, P.B. (2007) 'The European Social Model and EMU', in Baimbridge, M. and Whyman, P., *Britain, the Euro and Beyond*, Aldershot: Ashgate, pp. 147–60.

Whyman, P.B. (2008) 'British Trade Unions, the 1975 European Referendum and its Legacy', *Labor History*, vol. 49, no. 1, pp. 23-46.

Whyman, P.B. (2010) 'Stabilising Economic and Monetary Union in Europe: The Potential for a Semi-automatic Stabilisation Mechanism', in A. Tavidze (ed.) *Progress in Economics Research, Volume 18*, Hauppauge, NY: Nova Science Publishers.

Whyman, P.B. and Baimbridge, M. (2008) *Britain the Euro and Beyond*, Basingstoke: Ashgate.

Wickham-Jones, M. (1996) *Economic Strategy and the Labour Party: Politics and Policy-making, 1970–1983*, Basingstoke: Macmillan.

Wichert, I. (2002) 'Job Insecurity and Work Intensification: The Effects on Health and Well-being'; in B. Burchell, D. Ladipo and F. Wilkinson (eds) *Job Insecurity and Work Intensification*, London: Routledge, pp. 92–111.

Wilensky, H. (1975) *The Welfare State and Equality: Structural and Ideological Roots of Public Expenditures*, Los Angeles: University of California Press.

Wilensky, H. (2002) *Rich Democracies: Political Economy, Public Policy and Performance*, London: University of California Press.

Wilford, H. (2002) 'American Labour Diplomacy and Cold War Britain', *Journal of Contemporary History*, vol. 37, no. 1, pp. 45–65.

Wilford, H. (2003) *The CIA, the British Left and the Cold War: Calling the Tune?* London: Frank Cass.

Wilkinson, R. and Pickett, K. (2009) *The Spirit Level: Why More Equal Societies Almost Always Do Better*, London: Allen Lane.

William Engdhal, F. (2009) *Full Spectrum Dominance: Totalitarian Democracy in the New World Order*, Chippenham: Third Millennium Press.

Winch, D. (1966) 'The Keynesian Revolution in Sweden', *Journal of Political Economy*, no. 74, pp. 168–78.

Windolf, P. (1989) 'Productivity Coalitions and the Future of European Corporatism', *Industrial Relations*, vol. 28, no. 1, pp. 1–20.

Wolf, M. (2009) *Fixing Global Finance: How to Curb Financial Crisis in the 21st Century*, London: Yale University Press.

Woodward, S. (1995) *Balkan Tragedy: Chaos and Dissolution after the Cold War*, Washington, DC: Brookings Institute.

World Bank (1994) *Growth, Employment and Living Standards in Pre-Accession Poland*, Washington, DC: World Bank.

World Bank (2001) *Finance for Growth: Policy Choices in a Volatile World*, Washington, DC: World Bank.

Wring, D. (2005) *The Politics of Marketing the Labour Party*, Basingstoke: Palgrave Macmillan.

Wurff, R. van der (1993) 'Neo-liberalism in Germany? The "Wende" in Perspective' in H. Overbeek (ed.) *Restructuring Hegemony in the Global Political Economy: The Rise of Transnational Neo-liberalism in the 1980s*, Abingdon: Routledge.

Wynne, M. and Rodriguez-Palenzuela, D. (2002) 'Measurement Bias in the HICP: What do we Know and What do we Need to Know?', *ECB Working Paper*, 131, Frankfurt: ECB.

Wyplosz, C. (1993) 'Monetary Union and Fiscal Policy Discipline', in 'The Economics of EMU – Background Studies', *European Economy*, no. 44, pp. 165–84.

Wyplosz, C. (2003) 'Policy Challenges under EMU'; in M. Baimbridge and P. Whyman (eds) *Economic and Monetary Union in Europe: Theory, Evidence and Practice*, Cheltenham: Edward Elgar.

Yates T. (1998) 'Downward Nominal Rigidity and Monetary Policy', *Bank of England Working Paper*, 82, London: Bank of England.

Yi-Chong, X. and Bahgat, G. (eds) (2011) *The Political Economy of Sovereign Wealth Funds*, Basingstoke: Palgrave Macmillan.

Young, H. (1998) *This Blessed Plot: Britain and Europe from Churchill to Blair*, London: Macmillan.

Ziltener, P. (2000) 'EC Social Policy: The Defeat of the Delorist Project' in V. Bornschier (ed.) *State-building in Europe: The Revitalization of Western European Integration*, Cambridge: Cambridge University Press.

Zonnewind (2010) 'Bilderbergers Decide the Policy for the Coming Year, Former Secretary-General of NATO Admits', Radio Interview Transcript. Online, available at: www.zonnewind.be/bilderberg/2010/media-schade-beperken-2-interview-transcript. shtml&rur (accessed 20 June 2010).

Zysman, J. (1996) 'The Myth of a "Global" Economy: Enduring National Foundations and Emerging Regional Realities', *New Political Economy*, vol. 1, no. 2, pp. 157–84.

Zysman, J. (2000) 'The Myth of a "Global" Economy: Enduring National Foundations and Emerging Regional Realities', in R. Higgott and A. Payne (eds) *The New Political Economy of Globalisation*, Cheltenham: Edward Elgar.

Index

Page numbers in *italics* denote tables, those in **bold** denote figures.

Index 393

France: imports 134–5; *Programme Commun du Gouvernement* (PCG) 131–8; risk of downgrade 306–7
Franco-German competitiveness pact 312–13
Franks, Oliver 29
free movement of workers 263–5
free-rider effects 187
free trade agreement, with Mercosur 71
Friedman, Milton 109
Fukuyama, F. 102
full employment 4, 153

G20, response to economic crisis 288
General Agreement on Tariffs and Trade (GATT) 32
general reflation 151
German rearmament 29
German reunification 67, 206, 224–5
Germany, partition 53
Gill, S. 56, 111
Gillingham, J. 31, 63, 64
Gini coefficient 255
global level social forces 45–7
globalization: of financial markets 267; and instability 14; and national power 101–2; perceptions of 179–81; of production 4–5
globalization and EU enlargement debate 85–8
Goodhart, C.A.E. 205
Gorbachev, Mikhail 108–9
governance, multilevel 218
government bonds 100, 282, 288, 303–4
government intervention, and economic performance 178
Gowan, P. 109
Grand Area plan 45–6, 47–50, 53, 57, 59, 98, 113, 131, 138
grand theory, retreat from 43–4
Great Recession *see* economic crisis, 2008
Greece 20, 55, 288–9, 302–3
Green Paper on European Social Policy 217
Greenland 36
Greenspan, Alan 267
gross domestic product (GDP) 258
'Growth, Competitiveness, Employment' White Paper 161–2
growth rates: average growth rates in the pre-Keynesian and Keynesian periods 96; and inflation 189; Keynesian and neo-liberal periods compared 96

Hagen, J. von 203, 205
Hague Summit 34–5
Hahnel, R. 133, 140, 141, 142
Haines, J. 127
Halimi, S. 134, 136–8, 141
Hantrais, L. 67, 213, 221
hard law, vs. soft law 211–12
'hard' power 81
Harmonized Index of Consumer Prices (HICP) 189–90
Harrington, M. 56, 133, 135, 141
Hau, H. 302
Healey, Dennis 126, 128, 129
hegemony, United States 103–4
Hemerijck, A. 90
Hermann, C. 95
High Authority 29–30

high-level group on financial supervision 284
Hofbauer, I. 95
Hoffman, Paul 49
Holland, Stuart 31, 34, 36, 124, 163
Hooper, J. 304
house buying 192
House of Commons European Scrutiny Committee 305
human skills, investment in 271
Hyman, R. 95
hyper-liberalism 107
hysteresis hypothesis 14–15

import and price controls 123
imports, France 134–5
inclusion, of workers 5–6
income distribution 255–6; new member states 257
industrial policy 158–60
'Industrial Policy in an Open and Competitive Environment' 158–9
industrial relations 216–17, 223–7, 252–5, 262–3
industrial strategy 269–73
industrialization, state-led 52–3
industry 269–72
inequality 255
inevitability debate 42–3
inflation: and exchange rates 244; and growth rates 189; and stability 204
information technology 226
Institutional Affairs Committee 65
institutional framework 22
institutional investors 272
insurance sector: public ownership 153–4; UK 123
Integrated Guidelines for Growth and Jobs 75
integration: positive and negative 31–3; through trade 1–2
intelligence agencies, destabilization campaign (UK) 126
inter-regional public insurance 204–5
interest rate convergence 244
interest rates 73; ECB and notional 'appropriate rate' in member states 73; setting 192
Intergovernmental Conferences 70, 160
internal balance 268
international competition 263
international institutions 45
International Monetary Fund (IMF): crisis 127–9; Out of Crisis Project recommendations 154; pressure on governments 127–9; response to economic crisis 288
International Ruhr Authority 29
internationalization 111
Intra-Western European foreign trade 51
investment: in human skills 271; in industry 271; institutional 272; inward 278
Ireland 288, 289, 303
IS-LM (investment–saving/liquidity preference–money supply) model 183–5, 184
isolation 278
Issing, Otmar 227
Italianer, A. 207
Italy 303–4

'J curve' effect 276
Jacquemin, A. 65
Jepsen, M. 92
Jessop, B. 39–40, 53, 56, 108